Guide to
English
Language
Teaching

2006

Guide to
English
Language
Teaching

2006

MODERN
ENGLISH
PUBLISHING

Guide to English Language Teaching 2006

This Third Edition
Published 2005 by: Modern English Publishing Ltd
 PO Box 50121, 32-34 Great Peter Street, London SW1P 2XD, UK
Tel: +44 (0)20 7222 1155
Fax: +44 (0)20 7222 1551
Web: www.CareersInELT.com
Email: guide@modernenglishpublishing.com

Fourth edition 2006

© Modern English Publishing, 2006

Editor Simon Collin
Editorial Director Peter Collin

Design Modern English Publishing

Section Acknowledgments:
Training: Mary Ellen Butler-Pascoe, Susan Matson.
Working Overseas: The British Council, James Beetham, Roger Chrisman, Guillaume Gazembetti,
 Chung Han, Michael Howard, Alistair Kennedy, Dianne James, Ian McNamara,
 Martha Oral, Edward Prados, Mark Sigrist, Yuri Tambovtsev, Celia Thompson,
 Mark Warschauer, Colin Underwood, Paul Vreeland, Joe Ziegler,
 Brian Garity, Tony Donovan.
Career Development: Tina Carver, Lin Lougheed, Andy Martin, Mark Peterson, Mona Scheraga,
 Barbara Stipek.

British Library Cataloguing-in-Publication Data

A catalogue record for this book is available from the British Library

ISBN 1-904549-14-4

Printed by LRL, Didcot, UK

NOTE: Every effort has been made to ensure that the information contained in this book is accurate and up-to-date at the time of going to press. However, details are bound to change, especially with regard to information that refers to visa requirements, state certification, exchange rates and working conditions. The publisher is not responsible for any problems or disappointments encountered during your training, qualifications or travels.

If your school is mentioned in this guide and you would like to update your information for the next edition of the guide, please visit our website **www.CareersInELT.com** where you can update your information using the forms online or use the form at the back of this book.

Contents

Foreword

Being an English language teacher can be whatever you want it to be: a passport to world travel; a stable and fulfilling career; a way of helping others or the first step to owning your own business. This guide will help you choose how best to get qualified, find a job, develop professionally and travel the world. World demographics will result in sustained demand for teachers of English for at least the next twenty years – that's about as secure a job market as you will find these days.

Like it or not, English has become the world's language and it is growing in importance every day. Globalization and developments in communications are fuelling demand for the language around the world. About 85% of the Internet's web-pages are in English and everyone has acknowledged that English is essential for efficient use of the web – recently the governments of Japan and Korea announced policies to encourage all of their working populations to acquire a basic level of English.

If you are looking for a way to travel and work overseas, then teaching English is an obvious path. There are teachers from the UK, USA, Canada, Australia and New Zealand working as English teachers in almost every country in the world. Hundreds of thousands of young people have used teaching English as a means to see the world and understand other cultures.

By the year 2050 it is estimated that half the world's population will be competent users of English. This learning frenzy will not take place because of some love for the language, but due to the realization that people will be left behind in work and social situations unless they can communicate with the rest of the world.

And even in native-English-speaking countries, the demand for learning English is high: for example, in the UK, there are hundreds of ELT schools that gain most of their student intake from overseas visitors combining lessons with travel – from young learners visiting with a school for a week to professionals learning business English for their job development. And in the USA, teaching people to speak English accounts for almost half of all adult education!

This book will show you how you can work in English language teaching: if you are looking for a stable, long term career; to give something back to your community or to the rest of the world through voluntary work; or a good way to pay for your round-the-world adventure, this guide will explain how to do it through teaching English.

Using This Guide

This *Guide* is designed for use by people thinking of becoming teachers as well as those who have started training and experienced teachers. Although you can read the *Guide* from cover to cover, you may find it easier to start with the section that is most suited to your own particular needs.

One: Training to Teach (p.12) – is aimed at readers who are thinking of becoming teachers of English as a second or foreign language and who are interested in getting qualified to teach. We provide an overview of the different training courses on offer – short term introductory and certificate courses – and details of training courses held around the world.

Two: Finding a job (p.68) – explains how best to find a job as a newly qualified teacher. This covers job agencies, applying directly to schools and using the Internet. Country-specific information and a directory of schools to approach for a job are listed in section 4.

Three: Preparation – before you go (p.78) – covers the topics that you need to address before you set off and travel the world! This includes insurance, tax issues and how to handle problems when you reach your school.

Four: Working Around the World (p.86) – is written for readers who want to explore the exciting prospects of combining teaching with travel. The section provides detailed profiles of over 100 countries, together with their work prospects, regulations (including tax and visas), contact details of the local embassy and British Council office and, most importantly, a directory of the main job prospects: the schools in the country together with their contact details.

Five: Career Development (p.238) – is the section intended for language teachers with experience who want to develop their skills and professional lives. We include directories of Diploma courses, universities that provide Master's courses and doctorates. We also cover specialist English subjects, including young learners and business English. Lastly, we cover school management and how to get published.

Appendix (p.291) contains a list of useful websites, addresses for teacher-associations, schools, publishers, suppliers, travel-related sites, British Council offices and US embassies around the world.

Acronyms

For many new teachers, the first lesson is to learn the acronyms that are used in the profession. Here are some of the more common acronyms.

Basic

CALL: Computer Assisted Language Learning.

DOS: Director of Studies

EAP: English for Academic Purposes–The study or teaching of English with specific reference to an academic (usually a university- or college-based) course.

ECIS: European Council of International Schools

EFL: English as a Foreign Language–English language programmes in countries where English is not the common or official language. It is used in American university programmes where international students study English although the use of the word "foreign" is now avoided in some schools because of its xenophobic connotations.

ELICOS: English Language Intensive Courses for Overseas Students. Acronym used in Australia to refer to EFL.

ELL: English Language Learner–a term that has become popular in California designed to replace the acronym "LEP" (see below) which many teachers felt to be pejorative.

ELT: English Language Teaching or Training– a term coined in the UK and designed to replace EFL. It is in use around the world but has yet to catch on in the USA.

EOP: English for Occupational Purposes

ESL: English as a Second Language–English language programmes in countries where English is the dominant or official language. In the U.S. programmes designed for non-English-speaking students in the U.S. are ESL programmes; in the UK, this term is not used - ESOL is used instead.

ESOL: English to Speakers of Other Languages – in the U.S. this acronym is often used to describe elementary and secondary English language programmes; in the UK it refers to a specific type of English language teaching for newcomers to the country who might have complex requirements (perhaps asylum seekers or refugees) and learn English to integrate and take further education. It is sometimes used to distinguish ESL classes within adult basic education programmes.

ESP: English for Specific Purposes–a term that refers to teaching or studying English for a particular career (like law or medicine) or for business in general.

IEP: Intensive English Program–refers to an intensive course designed to help non-English-speaking students prepare for academic study at a university or college.

L1: First language (**L2:** Second language)

LEP: Limited English Proficient–a term used for many years to designate children in the school systems for whom English was not their first language. Now replaced by terms like ELL.

Teacher Training

ACE: Access Certificate in Education. An entry-level training certificate being piloted by Pitmans/City and Guilds in the UK.

CELTA: Certificate in English Language Teaching to Adults. Widely-recognised certificate course developed in the UK by University of Cambridge ESOL (UCLES) and RSA. DELTA is the advanced Diploma course.

CELTYL: Certificate in English Language Teaching to Young Learners. A certificate course developed in the UK by University of Cambridge ESOL (UCLES); normally taken as an add-on option with CELTA.

Cert.TEB: Certificate in Teaching English for Business. A certificate course developed by LCCI for teachers specialising in business English (see LCCIEB, below)

Cert.TESOL: Certificate in TESOL. Widely-recognised certificate course developed in the UK by Trinity College London. The advanced version for experienced teachers is the Lic.Dip.TESOL.

Cert.TEYL: Certificate in Teaching English to Young Learners. A certificate course extension developed by Trinity College London; normally taken as an add-on option with Cert.TESOL.

COTE: Certificate for Overseas Teachers of English. A certificate-level course developed by University of Cambridge ESOL (UCLES) - now replaced by ICELT

DELTA: Diploma in English Language Teaching to Adults. The advanced (post-experience) qualification from University of Cambridge ESOL (UCLES)

FTBE: (Further Certificate for Teachers of Business English) - awarded by LCCIEB

ICELT: In-Service Certificate in English Language Teaching - certificate for teachers awarded by CambridgeESOL, designed to replace COTE, and used to help improve a working teacher's skills

LTCL.Dip.TESOL: Licentiate Diploma in TESOL. The advanced (post-experience) qualification from Trinity College London

TEFL: Teaching English as a Foreign Language – a term that refers to teacher training programmes in EFL.

TESL: Teaching English as a Second Language–a term that refers to teacher training programmes in ESL.

TESOL: Teaching English to Speakers of Other Languages–a term that is used to distinguish English language teaching as a professional activity that requires specialized training. Also refers to the teacher examinations developed by Trinity College London (Cert.TESOL and LTCL.Dip.TESOL)

TKT: Teaching Knowledge Test -new award developed by Cambridge ESOL to provide and test the basic teaching requirements of any teacher.

Associations

AAIEP: American Association of Intensive English Programmes is a group of university and college-based intensive English programmes

ACELS: Advisory Council for English Language Schools in Ireland

ARELS: Association of Recognised English Language Schools in the UK

BASELT: British Association of State English Language Teaching schools in the UK

CRELS: Combined Registered English Language Schools of New Zealand

ELTAs: English Language Teacher Associations groups for teachers in Germany and Austria

IATEFL: International Association of Teachers of English as a Foreign Language is based in the UK with members around the world.

JALT: Japanese Association for Language Teaching

JET: Japanese Exchange and Teaching Programme

NABE: National Association for Bilingual Education is an association that represents the interests of bilingual teachers in the USA.

NEAS: National ELT Accreditation Scheme, for course providers in Australia

RELSA: Recognised English Language Schools Association. The organisation of independent language schools in Ireland

TESL: Teaching English as a Second Language, Canada – national federation of teachers and providers in Canada

TESOL: US-based international association of teachers of English as a second or foreign language. There are regional affiliates and many countries have their own affiliated associations.

Exams/Exam Boards

Assessment and Qualifications Alliance (AQA) (formerly AEB & NEAB) Certificate in English Language Skills (ESOL), JET SET, range of graded exams for ESOL. www.aqa.org.uk

Cambridge *see* University of Cambridge

Chauncey Group (part of ETS, below) US-based group that administers the TOEIC student examination. www.toeic.com

ESB (English-Speaking Board International) Oral assessments in (spoken) English www.esbuk.demon.co.uk

ETS (Educational Testing Service) Based in Princeton, NJ, the world's biggest examination board, administrators of the TOEFL student examination. www.ets.com

City & Guilds Based in the UK, offers a wide range of student exams and the ACE certificate for teachers.

Institute of Linguists Diploma in English for International Communication. www.iol.org.uk

International English Language Testing System (IELTS) Managed by UCLES, the British Council and IDP Australia for academic and vocational English. www.ielts.org

London Chamber of Commerce and Industry Exam Board (LCCIEB) Range of business and specialist English examinations. www.lccieb.com

London Examinations – Edexcel International London Tests of English range of exams graded from basic to proficient. www.edexcel.org.uk

Pitman Qualifications Range of general ESOL exams, including spoken English and business English. www.pitmanqualifications.com

RSA Royal Society of Arts is a body that works with UCLES (*see below*).

Trinity College London Responsible for the Certificate in TESOL and the Licentiate Diploma in TESOL examinations. www.trinitycollege.co.uk

UCLES (University of Cambridge Local Examinations Syndicate) Syndicate of local examination centres around the world that administer the University of Cambridge ESOL examinations. www.ucles.org.uk

University of Cambridge ESOL (administered locally by UCLES) is a British-based organization responsible for developing a number of important English language exams (including PET, FCE, CAE) and teacher training programmes including the CELTA, CELTYL, and DELTA examinations. www.cambridgeESOL.org

Training To Teach

This chapter offers a comprehensive guide to achieving one of the teaching credentials that will be essential for your working career. Although the profession is not governed by a single body or a single qualifying entrance exam, there are many ways to become a qualified teacher – the following sections explain how.

Whether you plan to teach in your own country or travel overseas, you will need to consider the type of training you will require in order to be employed; opinions within the teaching field are varied on this question.

Some teachers argue that you don't need a TEFL Certificate to teach English around the world. Others argue that a Master's degree is an unnecessary waste of time and money and that it is easy to get a job at a school or college without one. Teachers of this mindset are convinced that the teacher training industry is some sort of vast conspiracy set up in order to fleece unsuspecting students of their money by conning them into taking courses for qualifications which are almost useless. The reality is that you can get a job teaching English without a formal qualification, though it is increasingly difficult. It is true that not every single ESL lecturer has a Master's degree in TESL, TEFL or TESOL but most do, especially in the UK, Australia, New Zealand, USA and Canada.

And another consideration: Do you really want to start teaching with no idea of what you are doing? Is this fair on you? Is it fair on your students? There are gifted teachers born with a natural ability, but even these teachers need guidance and feedback from peers and mentors.

This section of the *Guide* is designed to give you an idea of the courses and programmes on offer and which qualification suits your needs best when training to be a teacher. For post-experience courses (i.e. once you have taught for several years and want to develop your career), see page 238.

The English language teaching profession is not governed by a single body. Instead of a single qualifying entrance exam, there are multiple routes to qualification as an English language teacher. You can start with a simple introductory course – often designed to help you decide if this is the career for you – then move on to a basic certificate course. You can then teach around the world, before perhaps working on a diploma, Master's degree or postgraduate qualification.

Training and Qualifications

There are several ways to become a qualified English language teacher and your choice of qualification route mainly depends on where and who you want to teach. The time you have to train and the cost of training are also important considerations.

Can anyone be an English language teacher?

It is still possible to get a job teaching EFL/ESL without any formal qualification, but this is becoming increasingly rare. There is a global shortage of teachers, but unqualified teachers are only recruited locally and the pay is usually poor. In major cities and tourist centres only qualified teachers will be taken on.

Is there a standard TEFL qualification?

No. There are many routes to qualification as a TEFL teacher ranging from intensive four-week Certificate courses to two-year Master's Degrees. In the USA and some of the Far East, a good first degree is adequate; whereas in Europe, the Commonwealth and South America teachers are preferred to have taken a TEFL course. Of these TEFL courses, the two best-known practical teaching certificates are CELTA and Certificate in TESOL, validated by University of Cambridge ESOL (administered around the world by UCLES) and Trinity College London respectively. Once you have experience as a teacher, you can move on to a post-experience course such as the Diploma in ELT (from Cambridge) or the Licentiate Diploma in TESOL (from Trinity College London) – see page 238 for details of these courses, MAs and doctorates in ELT.

Am I too old to teach ?

Many middle-aged people faced with redundancy or early retirement decide to embark on a career in English language teaching. Although age can be a barrier in some parts of the world, most schools welcome the added depth of life experience that a more mature teacher can bring to the classroom.

I'm not sure if I want to commit to long course. What should I do?

There are a number of introductory courses in teaching EFL/ESL offered by various institutions if you think that you might not want to commit yourself to a career in teaching, but many employers may not consider you qualified unless you have at least a Certificate (see below).

Choosing a Course

How do you choose a Certificate course? There are hundreds of schools, several accredited courses and various levels and ways to study. However, they will all cost you money and take a couple of months (or longer) of study to complete.

Those teachers who want to grow, personally and professionally, are turning to TEFL Certificate courses. But not every course will be right for you – and you can only find a suitable course by asking the right questions. Here are some essential questions to ensure you choose the best school for you:

What are the qualifications of your trainers?

A Diploma or Master's degree (MATESOL) for all or most trainers is a good sign. If those who will be your role models only have a TEFL Cert. themselves, look deeper into the curriculum offered and ask about their years of experience.

While a Master's is not a guarantee of good training, it does suggest deeper understanding about the theory behind the methods and a clear commitment to the field.

Have any complaints ever been filed against your school?

If you are studying in the USA, any complaints must, by State licensing agencies, be reported – justified or not. The nature of the complaint will tell you what the programme may not publicly advertise.

Is your certificate recognized?

Although many excellent certificate programmes are not affiliated with an exam board such as Cambridge or Trinity London, many employers (particularly in Europe and Australia/Asia) favour teachers with a recognised CELTA or Cert.TESOL qualification (from Cambridge and Trinity College London, respectively).

What about the duration of your programme and practicum?

Ask about both classroom time and practicum hours. Intensive programmes can run 120 to 150 hours. The more practicum hours, closely supervised, the better. It is very difficult for a teacher to learn from his or her mistakes if given only three or four opportunities to teach. The ideal programme will allow you chances to work with beginning, intermediate, and advanced speakers of English. Note: part-time programmes lack the immediacy of feedback seen in intensive, full-time programmes.

What is your hire/placement track record?

Proprietary programmes are required to keep close records on how many graduates get jobs. The vast majority, over 80%, should be getting jobs within two months of hire, given the intense market for EFL/ESL teachers.

Tell me about your job network

At minimum, a school should have an extensive list of employers throughout the world and access to Internet postings. Some programmes also offer job counselling, CV advice, and a means of providing feedback from graduates who are now teaching overseas.

In the USA, are you licensed by any state agency?

If you are studying in the USA, this is an important point: licensure for proprietary schools does not mean that you will qualify for a public school job, but rather that the school meets stringent state standards. For example, in California, these include standards for qualifications of trainers and administrators, strict record keeping, and a refund procedure.

How are trainees tested?

If you do poorly at written tests, you won't perform well in a TEFL programme that requires passing a test for graduation. All programmes should have highly specific criteria for evaluating you, particularly in the area of practicum teaching. These should be in written form, to help

prevent any bias on the part of an observer. And if you do find there is a chance of failing, you'll want to know it early on, while there is still a chance to get a refund or improve your performance.

What kind of coursework and topics do you have?

A comprehensive programme will at least introduce you to the basics of classroom management, lesson planning, student evaluation, and techniques for teaching grammar, reading, writing, listening, speaking, and pronunciation.

What is your trainee/trainer ratio?

The programme should allow for easy exchanges in class work and for closer counselling as needed. Classes of more than 15 trainees may make it more difficult to get the best from your teacher. Your practical classes should be observed by more than one trainer, as opinions on your strengths and weaknesses will vary.

How do you get your students for the practicals?

The ideal is students who really do not know the material you will be teaching, so that their responses will be genuine. Make sure you will have a guaranteed number of students for your practical sessions in order to do pair and group work.

How are refunds handled?

Many unanticipated events may force a drop-out – family crisis, illness, or a mismatch of trainee and programme goals. The best programmes allow you to leave within the first few days with few, if any, financial penalty. Others will pro-rata the amount coming back to you depending on the time spent in the programme.

What will I receive on completion?

Trainee teachers disperse quickly after a course ends. An efficient programme will make sure that on graduation day, they receive a certificate, a letter of recommendation, and, perhaps, a transcript of courses taken and the results.

How much will it all cost?

Of course you will want to know about course tuition, but don't forget to add in extras such as books and day trips, and accommodation.

Training: Types of Course

Before you start to teach, you should take an initial teacher training course; when applying for a job, some school do not require any qualifications of their teachers, but with a qualification you will find it easier to get a job, easier to manage classes and organise lessons and essential if you want to offer good training for you and your prospective students.

Introductory Courses

Introductory courses are designed for prospective teachers who want to experience teaching before making the decision to train formally and obtain qualifications. The courses usually last from a week up to four weeks. These are not certificate courses and you will not be regarded as a qualified teacher after completion of your Introductory course. You will, however, be able to say that you have had some experience of English language teaching. Some schools require trainee teachers to take an introductory course before starting a Certificate course.

Certificate courses

The majority of trainee teachers who would like to teach take a certificate course in teaching EFL/ESL. A certificate course provides basic grounding in teaching, lesson development, managing students and, in particular, the different stages of teaching English. Certificate courses are great for trainee teachers who have no experience of teaching – perhaps have a degree or experience in a totally different field – and want to ensure that they are well prepared for their first 'real' class (as a trainee teacher, part of your certificate course will be to experience practical teaching in a classroom). Most certificate courses are intensive and run over a four or six week period. You can take distance-study courses or take a certificate course on a part-time basis over several months.

Once you have a certificate in teaching English, you can start to apply for jobs at school around the world (see the main section on page 86). Although there is no single qualification, there are two main certificate courses: University of Cambridge CELTA and Trinity College London Cert.TESOL. Either one is well recognised around the world.

Aside from these two main certificate qualifications, many school, colleges and universities have their own certificate course developed in-house. Make sure that you ask the course provider about their qualification and if they will provide assistance finding a job once you have completed your course.

As well as the basic certificate course, you can also study for additional modules that will gain you experience and qualifications in specialist subjects (see also the section on ESP, page 273); for example, teaching young learners or teaching business English.

Certificate Qualification Providers

When you look at the different courses on offer you will find they provide a range of different certificate courses. There are a number of certificates awarded by different organisations - they have different names, provide emphasis on different types of teaching but all have the same goal to ensure that you are able to manage your first class teaching English. The main organisations offering certificate awards are:

University of Cambridge ESOL

TKT

The TKT (Teaching Knowledge Test) is a new award from Cambridge. Its focus is on the core teaching skills and requirements needed by teachers of English and provides a foundation for new or prospective teachers who could then progress on to CELTA or ICELT awards.

CELTA

The Cambridge CELTA (Certificate in English Language Teaching to Adults) is the longest established qualification for English language teachers and has over 8,000 student-teacher enrolments per year. It was developed by the University of Cambridge ESOL and managed around the world by the University of Cambridge Local Examination Syndicate (UCLES).

The CELTA is a pre-experience course, usually run on a four-week intensive basis, though some schools do run part-time courses. CELTA is run in over 40 countries around the world and is externally validated by University of Cambridge ESOL; a course normally costs between £700-1000 ($1300-1800).

A CELTA course is normally a 4-week intensive programme, with an examination at the end (the fee for the examination is normally included as part of the course fee). There are a few part-time CELTA courses, but these are very much the exception.

CELTA courses are, like the Trinity College London Certificate course (see next page), based on practical teaching – with observed teaching practice integral to any course. Pass rates are generally high, since applicants are carefully selected: when applying, you will be interviewed and might have to take a language awareness test. Candidates are assessed over the duration of the course (with moderation by external examiners), and there is no final examination. Successful candidates are awarded a Pass, a Pass B or a Pass A.

Many candidates are recent university graduates, but the course attracts a wide range of applicants, including mature professionals looking for a change of career or even an alternative

to retirement. Although certain levels of previous academic achievement are recommended by the administrators, there are no specific entry requirements, and admission is at the discretion of the course provider. Most centres will accept non-native speakers who can demonstrate an acceptable level of written and spoken English.

The course is available throughout the year in more than 50 countries, and is taken by more than 10,000 candidates annually. It consists of a minimum of 114 hours, and includes an element of teaching practice to genuine ESOL students.

CELTYL

Cambridge CELTYL (Certificate in English Language Teaching to Young Learners) is administered by the University of Cambridge Local Examination Syndicate (UCLES). This course provides a course in teaching age groups of 5–10, 8–13 or 11–16. Some candidates are new to TESOL, others are practising teachers who wish to develop their skills. Most of the details given above about the CELTA also apply to CELTYL. As an alternative to the full CELTYL course, successful CELTA candidates can take a Young Learners extension course (CELTYL Ext).

COTE

Cambridge COTE (Certificate for Overseas Teachers of English) is a pre-experience course that is taken as an alternative to CELTA by non-native-speakers who already have teaching experience in their own language. You will probably still see this in brochures and advertisments, but it has now been replaced by the similar ICELT examination (below).

ICELT (In-service Certificate in English Language Teaching)

An in-service award for practising teachers who want to improve their skills in the context in which they are currently working. Candidates taking ICELT courses are normally assessed teaching their own classes. A modular option enables courses to focus on language for teaching purposes only or for the full award to be gained in two phases. ICELT replaced the broadly similar COTE (Certificate for Overseas Teachers of English) from the start of 2004.

University of Cambridge
ESOL Examinations
1 Hills Road
Cambridge, CB1 2EU, UK
Tel: + 44 (0)1223 553355
Fax: +44 (0)1223 460278
Email: esolhelpdesk@ucles.org.uk
Website: www.cambridgeESOL.org

Trinity College London

Certificate in TESOL

The Certificate in TESOL (Teaching English to Speakers of Other Languages) – often referred to as *certTESOL* is administered by Trinity College London. It has over 4,000 student-teachers enrolments per year and is, like the CELTA (above) a well-recognised Certificate in practical ELT teaching. Trainees are expected to take courses in a foreign language, to understand the difficulties in teaching a foreign language. No two courses are the same, as course designers can introduce their own ideas and elements, so you will need to verify the details of the specific course. Cert.TESOL courses are usually full-time intensive and last between four to six weeks, although part-time courses are available at a few centres. The costs are very similar to a CELTA, £700-1000 ($1300-1800).

Certificate in TEYL

The Certificate in Teaching English to Young Learners is administered by Trinity College London. This is a pre-experience course that is normally taken as an add-on module to a Cert.TESOL course and is designed for teachers who would like to specialise in teaching to young learners of English (which is a strong market that is growing rapidly, especially in Italy, Korea, Japan, and Greece).

Trinity-ARELS One-to-One Certificate

A one-week/25-hour course for teachers of individual students on a one-to-one basis. Most candidates have an initial certificate (for example CertTESOL), but relevant experience is in some cases acceptable as an alternative. Availability is limited at present, but may increase.

Trinity College London
89 Albert Embankment
London , SE1 7TP, UK
Tel: +44 (0)20 7820 6100
Fax: +44 (0)20 7820 6161
Email: info@trinitycollege.co.uk
Website: www.trinitycollege.co.uk

Pitman / City & Guilds

ACE

The Access Certificate in English language teaching (ACE) is a Pitman/City & Guilds qualification developed with Manchester University in the UK. It offers a initial-level certificate for people who have never taught before or for teachers with some experience who want a formal qualification or for teachers experienced in teaching another subject who want to switch to teaching English. The training is in two parts covering theory and practical teaching activities.

City & Guilds
1 Giltspur StreetLondon, EC1A 9DD, UK
Tel: 020 7294 2800
Fax: 020 7294 2400
Email: enquiry@city-and-guilds.co.uk
Website: www.city-and-guilds.co.uk

School for International Training (SIT)

SIT TESOL Certificate

SIT is a US-based international organisation offering two qualifications for teachers of English (TESOL). The SIT Certificate in Teaching English to Speakers of Other Languages is available from a few dozen test centres around the world; the course of study is normally offered as an intensive four-week course. SIT also offer an advanced diploma (the IDLTM - International Diploma in Language Teaching Management) as a graduate-level diploma.

SIT
Kipling Road, P.O. Box 676,
Brattleboro, Vermont 05302-0676, USA
Tel: (802) 257-7751
Fax: (802) 258-3248
Website: www.sit.edu

Private Language School Certificates

Some chains of private language schools offer their own 'in-house' training courses and certificates. As a general rule, if these are free and likely to lead to employment or promotion within the organisation, they may be well worth considering. If, however, fees are payable, it is not really advisable to accept any, often vague, assurances that the certificate is internationally-known or respected or that it is equivalent to a CELTA or Cert.TESOL.

Ask to see a list of employers who accept the qualification and contact them to ask if they really do consider this to be a full equivalent of an independent, mainstream certificate.

The best private language school TESOL courses leading to in-house certificates tend to be offered as a supplement to mainstream qualifications (for example, a refresher course) rather than as an alternative.

University Certificate Courses

University Certificate courses are usually short courses running from one to six months and are an alternative to the Cambridge or Trinity certificates (above). These are the most common pre-experience courses available, with almost every university and college in the UK offering some form of English language teaching course. There are also 'in-service' certificate courses

available for those teachers who have classroom experience but no formal qualifications.

Distance Learning Courses

Some training courses in English language teaching are offered on a distance basis, though these are not generally popular with employers unless they include an observed period of teaching practice and are externally validated. But if you are already teaching English abroad, they can be a viable option. For listings of distance learning courses, see page 58.

Certificates for Teaching English for Business

There are a number of different examinations for teachers who would like to train to teach English for business: Chauncey group, LCCIEB, Pitman and University of Cambridge ESOL all offer specialist qualifications. These are covered in detail on page 238 in the section on Professional Development.

Do I need a degree?

In some countries such as Japan and Korea a university degree is a legal requirement (the requirement is for a degree in any subject rather than in TESOL/TEFL). In Spain some schools look for teachers to have a degree because government contracts demand it. We cover degrees, diplomas and post-graduate qualifications in chapter 5, page 238.

Certificate Training Courses

This section lists the main institutions around the world that offer teacher-training courses that lead to pre-experience certification in teaching ESL/EFL (that you would then use to get a job as a teacher). See the previous chapter for a description of the different types of course available. In this section, we list the institutes that offer certificate courses (including the popular CELTA, Cert.TESOL, CELTYL and ICELT courses).

For specialist certificates (such as business English), and post-experience diplomas and MAs, see the chapter on Career development, page 238.

Key
CELTA, CELTYL, ICELT, TKT - CambridgeESOL
Cert.TESOL, Cert.TEYL - Trinity College London

ARGENTINA (+54)

Academia Arguello
Av. Rafael Nunez 5675, Arguello, Cordoba 5147
Tel: 3543 443030
Fax: 35 43 443 030
Email: Uclescba@Ciudad.Com.Ar
Courses Offered: TKT

Asociacion Argentina De Cultura Inglesa
Suipacha 1333, Buenos Aires 1011
Tel: 11 4393 2004
Fax: 11 4326 3015
Email: Cambridge@Aaci.Org.Ar
Website: www.aaci.org.ar
Courses Offered: TKT

Asociacion Argentina De Cultura Inglesa, Parana Entre Rios
Alem 140, Parana, Entre Rios 3100
Tel: 343 4316 384
Email: Lacultural@Arnet.Com.Ar
Courses Offered: TKT

Asociacion Bahiense De Cultura Inglesa
Zelarrayan 245, Bahia Blanca 8000
Tel: 291 4521493
Fax: 291 4556127
Email: Director@Abci.Com.Ar
Website: www.abci.com.ar
Courses Offered: TKT

Asociacion De Cultura Saint Johns
Avda. Cordoba 238 (Este), San Juan 5400
Tel: 264-4220580
Fax: 264 4225 108
Email: Culturasaintjohns@Infovia.Com.Ar
Courses Offered: TKT

Asociacion Rosarina De Cultura Inglesa
Buenos Aires 1174, Rosario 2000
Tel: 00-54-341-449-4993 /8892
Fax: 00-341-440-0859
Email: Direccioncultura@Ciudad.Com.Ar
Courses Offered: TKT

Buenos Aires Open Centre 1
"Azcuenaga 1077 1 ""D", Capital Federal
Buenos Aires 1115
Tel: 11 4826 1299
Fax: 11 4823 2912

Email: Bsasopencentre@Sion.Com
Courses Offered: TKT

Casa de Inglés
Entre Rios 362, Resistencia, 3500
Email: casadeingles@infovia.com.ar
Tel: 03722 443443
Fax: 03722 443443
Courses Offered: Cert.TESOL

CENTUM Servicios de Idiomas
Bartolomé Mitre 811, 4°piso, Capital Federal, C 1036 AA
Email: centum@datamarkets.com.ar
Tel: 4328 2385/8572/5150
Courses Offered: Cert.TESOL

Cultural Inglesa De Neuquen
Carlos H. Rodriguez 439, Neuquen 8300
Tel: 299 4423691
Fax: 299 4423691
Email: Cin.Direccion@Speedy.Com.Ar
Courses Offered: TKT

Colegio Britanico Rio Gallegos
Mariano Moreno 116, Rio Gallegos 9400
Tel: 2966 422184
Fax: 2966 421347
Email: Colegiobritanico@Infovia.Com.Ar
Courses Offered: TKT

Essarp
Esmeralda 672, Piso 7, C1007abf Buenos Aires
Tel: 11 4322 2480
Fax: 11 4322 9203
Email: Denright@Essarp.Org.Ar
Website: www.essarp.org.ar
Courses Offered: TKT

Instituto Chaqueno De Cultura Inglesa
Don Bosco 256, Resistencia 3500
Tel: 3722 425571
Fax: 3722 425571
Email: Culturarcia@Gigared.Com
Courses Offered: TKT

Instituto Cult Argent De Lenguas Vivas
Lenguas Vivas, 25 De Mayo 347, San Miguel De Tucuman 4000
Tel: 381 4229 151
Fax: 381 4215 293
Email: Icalvtuc@Arnet.Com.Ar
Courses Offered: TKT

Itesl
Domingo F Sarmiento 1975, 1602 Florida, Buenos Aires
Tel: 114 797 2775
Fax: 114 797 2775
Email: Info@Itesl.Com
Website: www.itesl.com
Courses Offered: ICELT

Santa Monica School Of Languages
Hipólito Yrigoyen 4605, A 1824 ABC Lanús Oeste, Buenos Aires
Tel: 4241 2667
Fax: 4241 2667
Email: santa_monica@ciudad.com.ar
Courses offered: ICELT

AUSTRALIA (+61)

Attc Brisbane (Venue)
Level 1, 295 Ann Street, Brisbane Qld 4000
Tel: 7 3229 0350
Fax: 2 9389 6880
Courses offered: TKT

Attc Cairns (Venue)
Level 2, Village Lane, 20 - 32 Lake Street, Cairns Qld 4870
Tel: 2 9389 7822
Fax: 2 9389 6880
Courses offered: TKT

Attc Perth (Venue)
Johnston House, 259 Adelaide, Perth, Wa 6000
Tel: 8 9325 7822
Fax: 2 9389 6880
Courses offered:: TKT

Australian College of English
Level 1, 295 Ann Street, Brisbane, Queensland 4000
Tel: 73 229 0350
Fax: 73 229 0850
Email: em@ace.edu.au
Website: www.ace.edu.au
Courses offered: CELTA

Australian International College Of Language
Stradbroke Plaza, 66 Marine Parade, Southport, Queensland
Tel: 7 5531 1990
Fax: 7 5591 4510
Courses offered: ICELT

Australian TESOL Training Centre,
PO Box 82, Bondi Junction, NSW 2022
Tel: 2 93890249.
Fax: 2 93896880.
Email: lynnev@ace.edu.au
Website: attc.nsw.edu.au
Courses offered: CELTA, TKT

Buckingham College of English
21 Hindmarsh Square, Adelaide, South Australia 5000
Tel: 8 8359 3535.
Fax: 8 8359 3550.
Courses Offered: CELTA.
Course Length: 4 weeks FT or 12 weeks PT.
Email: enquiries@bce.sa.edu.au
Website: www.bce.sa.edu.au

Cambridge Exams Centre Adelaide
97 Beattie Street, Balmain, Sydney, Nsw 2041
Tel: 2 9555 9752
Fax: 2 9555 9760
Email: Cambridge@Cambexams.Com.Au
Courses offered:: TKT

Cambridge Exams Centre Brisbane
97 Beattie Street, Balmain, Sydney, Nsw 2041
Tel: 2 9555 9752
Fax: 2 9555 9760
Email: Cambridge@Cambexams.Com.Au
Courses offered: TKT

Curtin University
School of Languages and Intercultural Education
GPO Box U1987, Perth, Western Australia 6845
Tel: 89266 4224
Fax: 89266 3186
Email: p.mercia@curtin.edu.au
Website: www.celta.curtin.edu.au
Courses offered: CELTA

Edith Cowan University
International English Centre, Goldsworthy Road,
Claremont, Western Australia 6010
Tel: 89 442 1412
Fax: 89 442 1452
Email: s.crivelli@ecu.edu.au
Website: www.ecu.edu.au
Courses offered: CELTA

Holmesglen Language Centre
PO Box 42, Chadstone, Victoria 3148
Tel: 3 9564 1820
Fax: 3 9564 1712
Emaik: larryf@holmesglon.vic.edu.au

Website: www.holmesglon.vic.edu.au
Courses Offered: CELTA, Graduate Cert in TESOL.

Holmes Institute Teacher Training Centre
185 Spring Street, Melbourne 3000
Tel: 39662 2055
Fax: 39662 2083
Email: celta@holmescolleges.com
Website: www.holmescolleges.com
Courses offered: CELTA

Insearch (University Of Technology, Sydney)
Level 3, 10 Quay Street, Sydney, NSW 2000
Tel: 2 9218 8646
Fax: 2 9211 4334
Email: david.noble@insearch.edu.au
Website: www.insearch.edu.au
Courses Offered: CELTA

Institute of Continuing TESOL Education
University of Queensland, St Lucia, Queensland 4072.
Tel: 7 3365 6720.
Fax: 7 3365 6599.
Email: tesol.enrol@mailbox.uq.edu.au
Website: www.icte.uq.edu.au
Courses Offered: CELTA, TKT

International House, Brisbane, Queensland
PO Box 2229, Brisbane, Queensland 4001
Tel: 7 3220 1011
Fax: 7 4031 3464
Email simon@ihqld.com
Website: www.ihqld.com
Courses offered: CELTA

International House, Cairns, Queensland
130 McLeod St, Cairns, Queensland 4870
Tel: 74031 3466
Fax: 74031 3464
Email: clive@ihqld.com
Website: www.ihqld.com
Courses offered: CELTA

International House, Sydney
Level 3, 89 York Street, Sydney, New South Wales 2000
Tel: 29279 0733
Fax: 29279 4544
Email:teachertraining@ihsydney.com
Website: www.training.ihsydney.com
Courses offered: CELTA, TKT

La Trobe University Language Centre,
Bundoora, Melbourne, Victoria 3083

Tel: 3 9479 1772
Fax: 3 9479 3676
Email: celta@latrobe.edu.au
Website: www.latrobe.edu.au/language
Courses Offered: CELTA.

Monash University English Language Centre
Monash International, PO Box 73, Clayton, Victoria 3800
Tel: 39905 5261
Fax: 39905 5274
Email: Adrian.Rice@monint.monash.edu.au
Website: www.monash.edu.au
Courses offered: CELTA

Milner International College Of English
375 Hay Street, Perth, Western Australia 6000
Tel: 8 9325 5444.
Fax: 8 9221 2392.
Email: milner@wantree.com.au
Website: www.milner.wa.edu.au
Courses offered: CELTA

Phoenix English Language Academy,
223 Vincent Street, Perth, Western Australia 6006
Tel: 8 9227 5538.
Fax: 8 9227 5540.
Email: pjones@phoenixela.com.au
Website: www.phoenixela.com.au
Courses offered: CELTA

RMIT English Worldwide
Level 6, 393 Swanston Street, Melbourne, 3000
Tel: 39657 5800
Fax: 39663 8504
Email: english.worldwide@rmit.edu.au
Website: www.rmitenglishworld.com
Courses offered: CELTA

St Mark's International College
PO Box 8480, Stirling Street, Perth 6489
Tel: 89227 9888
Fax: 89227 9880
Email: cathy@geosperth.com.au
Website: www.stmarksperth.com.au
Courses offered: CELTA

South Australian College of English (SACE)
254 North Terrace, Adelaide, South Australia 5000
Tel: 8 8238 0335
Fax: 8 8223 7206
Email: registrar@sacecoll.sa.edu.au
Website: www.sacecoll.sa.edu.au
Courses offered: CELTA

University of Tasmania
PO Box 252-14, Hobart, Tasmania 7001
Tel: 3622 62 579
Fax: 3622 62 525
Email: Kate.McPherson@utas.edu.au
Website: www.international.utas.edu.au
Courses offered: CELTA

AUSTRIA (+43)

Berufsförderungsinstitut Wien (bfi Wien)
Schönbrunnerstraße 213/3, A-1090 Vienna
Tel: 1 81178 365
Fax: 1 81178 105
Email: sprachen2.bat@bfi-wien.or.at
Website: www.bfi-wien.or.at
Courses offered: CELTA

BAHRAIN (+973)

British Council
PO Box 452, 146 Shaikh Salman Highway, Manama 356
Tel: 973 261 555
Fax: 973 258 689
Email: Esther.Hay@britishcouncil.org.bh
Website: www.britcoun.org/bahrain/
Courses offered: CELTA

BANGLADESH (+880)

British Council
754b Satmasjid Road, Dhanmondi, Dhaka 1205
Tel: 880 2 911 6171 / 911 6545
Fax: 880 2 811 6554
Email: martha.gibson@bd.britishcouncil.org
Website: www.britishcouncil.org/bangladesh
Courses offered: CELTA

BRAZIL (+55)

Britannia International English
Rua General Rabelo Gávea, Rio de Janeiro, CEP 22541-010
Tel: 21 2511 0143
Fax: 21 2512 4707
Email: mavisradley@hotmail.com
Website: www.britannia.com.br
Courses offered: CELTA, ICELT

Britannia Porto Alegre
Rua Dr Timoteo 752, Porto Alegre Rs, 90570-040
Tel: 51 3222 9663
Fax: 51 3346 1109
Email: Britpoa@Uol.Com.Br;
Moinhos@Britannia.Com.Br
Website: www.britannia.com.br
Courses Offered: TKT

CEL-LEP
Centro de Ensino de Linguas, Avenida dos Tajurás
212, São Paulo - SP, CEP 05670-000
Tel: 11 814 2822 / 55 11 212 6183
Fax: 11 210 0698 / 55 11 210 0698
Email: training@cel-lep.com.br
Website: www.cellep.com
Courses offered: ICELT

Centro De Cultura Britanica, Vitoria
Rua Eugenio Neto 223, Praia Do Canto, Vitoria Es,
29055-270
Tel: 27 3345 9271
Fax: 27 3345 8523
Email: Cicambridge@Gmail.Com
Courses Offered: TKT

Cultura Inglesa Centro de Estudo Britanicos
Av Bras de Aguiar 478, Nazare - Belem, PA
67035-000
Tel: 91 223 6284
Fax: 91 222 1919
Email: cultura@culturainglesa-pa.com.br
Courses offered: ICELT

Cultura Inglesa - Belo Horizonte
Rua Jornalista Djalma, Andrade, 46-4° Andar,
30320-570, Belo Horizonte
Tel: 31 3264 2555
Fax: 31 3264 2500
Email: Exames@Culturabh.Com.Br
Website: www.culturabh.com.br
Courses Offered: Icelt, TKT

Cultura Inglesa, Mato Grosso
Rua 12 De Outubro 227, Centro, Cuiaba, Mato Grosso
78005 - 510
Tel: 65 6242079
Fax: 65 6235009
Email: Terrymatfield@Culturainglesamt.Com.Br
Courses Offered: TKT

Cultura Inglesa De Duque De Caxias
Rua Conde De Porto Alegre 59, Centro, Duque De
Caxias 25070-150

Tel: 21 26714346
Fax: 21 26714346
Email: Pinhosilva@Uol.Com.Br
Courses Offered: TKT

Cultura Inglesa Florianopolis
Rua Marechal Floriano Peixoto 303, Centro,
89010-500 Blumenau
Tel: 48 3224 2696
Fax: 48 3224 2696
Email: Info@Culturainglesa-Sc.Com.Br
Website: www.culturainglesa-sc.com.br
Courses Offered: TKT

Cultura Inglesa Goiania
Ave Republica Do Libano 2525, Galeria Um, Piso Um,
Setor Oeste, 74115-050 Goiania -Go
Tel: 62 231 4400
Fax: 62 214 4401
Email: Cult.Ing.Sul@Persogo.Com.Br
Courses Offered: TKT

Cultura Inglesa, Joao Pessoa
Av. Epitacio Pessoa 2953, Tambauzinho, Joao Pessoa
Pb, Cep 58038-000
Tel: 83 3244 9900
Fax: 83 3224 9479
Email: Diretoria@Culturainglesapb.Com.Br
Website: www.culturainglesapb.com.br
Courses Offered: TKT

Cultura Inglesa Juiz De Fora
Av Dos Andradas 536, Juiz De Fora, Minas Gerais 360
36000
Tel: 32 3215 5169
Fax: 32 3215 9659
Email: Sbcijf@Terra.Com.Br
Courses Offered: TKT

Cultura Inglesa, Maringa
Rua Arthur Thomas 770, Maringa, 87013-250
Tel: 44 3226 7570
Fax: 44 3226 0070
Email: Director@Culturainglesamaringa.Com.Br
Courses Offered: TKT

Cultura Inglesa Porto Alegre
Rua Quintino Bocaiuva 1447, Bairro Rio Branco,
Porto Alegre, Rs 90440-051
Tel: 51 3333 4033
Fax: 51 3321 1069
Email: Secretaria.Porto.Alegre@Culturainglesa.Net
Website: www.culturainglesa.net
Courses Offered: TKT

Cultura Inglesa Sao Carlos
Rua 15 De Novembro, 1630, Sao Carlos 13560-240
Tel: + 55-16-3372-2276
Fax: + 55-16-3372-9875
Email: Irmtrud@Culturainglesascl.Com.Br
Courses Offered: TKT

Cultura Inglesa Da Bahia
Rua Mato Grosso, 481, Pituba, Salvador - Bahia, Cep
41830 151
Tel: 71 2480255
Fax: 71 2481117
Email: Leocadio@Svn.Com.Br
Website: www.svn.com.br
Courses Offered: Icelt

Cultura Inglesa Sao Joao Del Rei
Rua Dr. Balbino Du Cunha 181, Centro, Sao Joao Del
Rei 36307 350
Tel: 32 3371 7035
Fax: 32 3371 7035
Email: Romulo@Culturainglesasjdr.Com.Br
Website: www.culturainglesasjdr.com.br
Courses Offered: TKT

Cultura Inglesa - Sao Paulo
Rua Ferreira De Araujo, 741 - 3o. Andar, Sao Paulo
05428-002
Tel: 11 3039 0543
Fax: 11 3039 0562
Email: Exames@Culturainglesasp.Com.Br
Website: www.culturainglesasp.com.br
Courses Offered: TKT

Instituto Da Lingua Inglesa
Avenida Do C P A 15, 78008-000 Cuiaba Mt
Tel: 00 55 65 624 1197
Fax: 00 55 65 624 1197
Email: Zenaideb@ili.Com.Br; Instituto@Ili.Com.Br
Website: www.ili.com.br
Courses Offered: TKT

Lemec - Lassance Modern English Course
Rua Lopes Trovao 181, Icarai, Niteroi, Rio de Janeiro,
24 220 - 070
Tel: 21 610 3528/ 714 7954
Fax: 21 610 8852
Email: lamec@urbi.com.br
Courses offered: ICELT

S B C I Fortaleza
Rua Ana Bilhar 171, Meireles, Fortaleza, Ceara
60160-110
Tel: 85 3224 3784

Fax: 85 3242 9971
Email: Evandro@Veloxmail.Com.Br
Courses Offered: TKT

S B C I Manaus
Rua Natal 553, Adrianapolis, Manaus, Amazonas,
69057-090
Tel: 92 611 1635
Fax: 92 611 1635
Email: Zaira@Vivax.Com.Br
Courses Offered: TKT

S B C I - Franca
Rua Ouvidor Freire 2380, Centro, Franca 14400-630
Tel: 16 3722 0011
Fax: 16 3722 0011
Email: Culturainglesa@Culturainglesafranca.Com.Br
Courses Offered: TKT

S B C I Ribeirao Preto
Rua Visconde De Inhauma 1022, Centro, Ribeirao
Preto, Sp Sao Paulo 14010-100
Tel: 16 610 6616
Fax: 16 627 6616
Email: Amiranda@Culturainglesaribeirao.Com.Br
Website: www.culturainglesaribeirao.com.br
Courses Offered: TKT

S B C I Uberaba
Av Guilherme Ferreira 650-2° Andar, Caixa Postal
162, Uberaba-Mg 338022-200
Tel: 34 33120159
Fax: 34 33120159
Email: Cultura@Mednet.Com.Br
Courses Offered: TKT

SBCI Belo Horizonte
Rua Fernandes Tourinho, 457 - Savassi, Belo
Horizonte, Minas Gerais, CEP 30122 000
Tel: 31 284 1284
Fax: 31 284 1280
Email: celeste@culturainglesabh.com.br
Website: www.culturainglesabh.com.br
Courses offered: ICELT

SBCI, Curitibá
Alameda Julia da Costa 1500, Bigorrilho, Curitibá -
Paraná, CEP 80730-070
Tel: 41 222 7339
Fax: 41 224 1024
Email: cinglesa@onda.com.br
Courses offered: ICELT

SBCI Da Bahia
Rua Mato Grosso, 481, Pituba, Salvador - Bahia, CEP
41830 151
Tel: 71 248 0255
Fax: 71 248 1117
Email: leocadio@svn.com.br
Website: www.culturainglesa-ba.com.br
Courses offered: ICELT

SBCI Recife
Av. Visc Albuqueoque 205, Madalena, Recife - PE
50.610-090
Tel: +55 81 3228 6649
Fax: +55 81 3445 8434
Email: roddy@nlink.com.br
Website: www.culturainglesa.com/pe
Courses offered: CELTA

SBCI Rio De Janeiro
Rua São Clemente, 258-3 e 4 andares, Botafogo, Rio
de Janeiro, CEP 22260 000
Tel: 21 537 2700
Fax: 21 535 4141
Email: sbcirio@embratel.net.br
Courses offered: ICELT

SBCI Sao Paulo
Rua Ferreira de Araujo 741, 3° andar - Pinheiros, São
Paulo - SP, CEP 05428-002
Tel: 11 3039 0551
Fax: 11 3039 0562
Email: crisraja@culturainglesasp.com.br
Website: www.culturainglesasp.com.br
Courses offered: ICELT

Seven English Español
Rua Antonio Carlos 319, São Paulo - SP, CEP 01309
011
Tel: 11 258 9131
Fax: 11 258 9131
Email: seven@sevenidiomas.com.br
Website: www.sevenidiomas.com.br
Courses offered: ICELT

Up Language Consultants
Avenida Eng. Luiz Carlos Berrini 1461 - 10 andar, São
Paulo - SP, CEP 04571-903
Tel: 11 5505 0200
Fax: 11 5505 0200
Email: maynard@uplanguage.com.br
Website: www.uplanguage.com.br
Courses offered: CELTA

Vitoria Point Language School
Rua Nicolau Von Schilgen 04, Mata Da Praia, Vitoria,
29065-130
Tel: 27 3 200 3021
Fax: 27 3 200 3021
Email: Point@Pointls.Com.Br
Website: www.pointls.com.br
Courses Offered: TKT

BULGARIA (+359)

AV0-3 School Of English
2a Krakra Street, 1504 Sofia
Tel: 2 944 3 032
Fax: 2 943 3 943
Email: binnie@avo-3.com
Website: www.avo-3.com
Courses offered: CELTA

CANADA (+1)

Canadian Institute of English
P.O. Box 23028, Brantford, Ontario N3T 6K4
Tel: (877) 264-5CIE, (519) 757-1966
Fax: (519) 757-1158
Email: tesolinfo@cie.ca
Courses Offered: TESOL Certificate.

Centre for Second Language
(Extension Division), University of Saskatchewan, 238
R.J.D. Williams Building, 221 Cumberland Ave. N.,
Saskatoon, Saskatchewan S7N 1M3
Tel: (306) 966-4351
Fax: (306) 966-4356
Courses Offered: C E RTESL.

Columbia College
500-555 Seymour Street, Vancouver, British Columbia
V6B 6J9
Tel: (604) 683 8360
Fax: 604 682 7191
Email: mmorgan@columbiacollege.ca
Website: www.columbiacollege.bc.ca
Courses offered: CELTA

Coventry House International
Suite 300, 27 Prince Arthur Avenue, Toronto, M5R 1B2
Tel: 001 416 929 0227
Fax: 001 416 929 9464
Website: www.study-at-coventry.com
Email: info@study-at-coventry.com
Courses Offered: Cert.TESOL

Global Village Toronto

180 Bloor Street West - Suite 202, Toronto M5s 2v6
Tel: +1 416 9681405
Fax: +1 416 968 3996
Email: Ddaly@Sgvenglish.Com
Courses Offered: TKT

Global Village Vancouver Teacher Training & Services Inc

888 Cambie Street, Suite 101, Vancouver, Bc; V6b 2p6
Tel: 00 1604 684 1010
Fax: 00 1604 648 2124
Email: Cambridge@Gvteachertraining.Com
Courses Offered: CELTA, CELTYL Ext

Global Village English Centre, Calgary

200, 515- 1 Street SE, Calgary, Alberta, T2G 2G6
Tel: 403 543 7300
Fax: 403 543 7309
Email: info@sgvenglish.com
Website: www.gvenglish.com
Courses offered: CELTA

International Language Schools of Canada

1134 St Catherine Street West, Suite 310, Montreal, H3B 1H4
Tel: 514 876 4572
Fax: 514 876 4053
Email: nbaladi@ilsc.ca
Website: www.ilsc.ca
Courses offered: CELTA

International Language Institute

7071 Bayers Road, Halifax, Nova Scotia B3L 2C2
Tel: (902) 429 3636
Fax: (902) 429 2900
Email: registrar@englishcanada.org
Website: www.englishcanada.org
Courses Offered: CELTA

Kwantlen University College

8771 Lansdowne Road, Richmond, Vancouver, British Columbia V6X 3V8
Tel: (604) 599-2693
Fax: (604) 599-2716
Email: celta@kwantlen.bc.ca
Courses Offered: CELTA.

Language Studies Canada (LSC)

124 Eglinton Avenue West, Suite 400, Toronto, Ontario M4R 2G8
Tel: 416 488 2200

Fax: 416 488 2225
Email: tmcdonald@lsc-canada.com
Website: www.lsc-canada.com
Courses offered: CELTA, TKT

Languages International

330 Bay Street, Suite 910, Toronto, Ontario M5H 2S8
Tel: (416) 361 2411
Fax: (416) 361 2403
Courses Offered: TESL Certificate.
Course Length: 8 weeks.
Start dates: January, April, July, October.

Language Studies International (LSI)

1055 Yonge Street, Suite 1152, Toronto, Ontario, M4W - 2L2
Tel: 416 928 6888
Fax: 416 928 3388
Email: CELTA@lsi.edu
Website: www.lsi.edu
Courses offered: CELTA

Pan Pacific International

707 Johnson Street, Victoria, British Columbia V8W 1M8
Tel: (250) 380 9030
Fax: (250) 380 9033
Courses Offered: TESL Certificate.
Course Length: 12 weeks FT / 20weeks PT.
Start dates: January, April, July, September.

Shane Global Village English Centre

Westcoast English Language Centre Ltd, 888 Cambie Street, Vancouver BC, V6B 2P6
Tel: 604 684 2112
Fax: 604 648 2124
Email: teachertraining_van@sgvenglish.com
Website: www.sgvenglish.com
Courses offered: CELTA, CELTYL

Study Abroad Canada

51 University Avenue, Charlottetown, Prince Edward Island C1A 7N9
Tel: (902) 628 2379
Fax: (902) 892 1198
Courses Offered: TESL / TEFL Cert.

Vancouver English Centre

840 Howe Street, Suite 200, Vancouver, British Columbia V6Z 2L2
Tel: (604) 687 1600
Fax: (604) 687 1660
Email: info@vec.bc.ca

Courses Offered: TEFL Certificate.
Course Length: 4 weeks.

Winfield College
788 Beatty Street, Vancouver, British Columbia V6B 2M1
Tel: (604) 608-0538
Email: study@winfieldcollege.com
Courses Offered: TEFL Certificate

YMCA International College
955 Burrard Street, Vancouver, BC, V6Z 1Y2
Tel: (604) 633 3586
Fax: (604) 899 4162
Email: mona.mah@vanymca.org
Website: www.ymcacollege.org
Courses offered: CELTA

CHILE (+56)

British School
Casilla 379, Waldo Seguel 454, Punta Arenas
Tel: 61 223 381
Fax: 61 223 381
Email: Vicerector@Britishschool.Cl
Website: www.britishschool.com
Courses Offered: TKT

British Institute Santiago
Casilla, Santa Lucia 124, Santiago 3900
Tel: 2 4132000
Fax: 2 6326637
Email: Mcbrieba@Britanico.Cl
Website: www.britanico.cl
Courses Offered: TKT

Inst Chileno-Britanico De Cultura De Concepcion
San Martin 531, Concepcion 2607
Tel: 41 243 505
Fax: 41 234 044
Email: Cambridge@Ibritanico.Com
Website: www.ibritanico.com
Courses Offered: TKT

Inst.Chileno Británico De Cul
3 Norte 824, P.O Box 929, Vina Del Mar
Tel: 32 971061
Fax: 32 686656
Email: Info@Icbc.Cl
Courses Offered: TKT

CHINA (+86)

Language-Link: Sub-Centre Beijing
In UK: 181 Earls Court Road, London, SW5 9RB, UK
In Beijing: China Trade Center, 3rd Fl, Guanghua Zhi Jiao Hotel, 36 Dong San Huan Bei Road, 100004 Beijing, China
Tel: +86 10 6581 0426
Fax: +86 10 6581 8104
Email: celta@languagelink.com.cn
Website: www.languagelink.com.cn
Courses offered: CELTA

Sydney Institute of Language and Commerce
Shanghai University Shanghai, PRC, 149 Yan Chang Lu, Shanghai University, Shanghai, 200072
Tel: 56333082 Yan Chang Campus
Tel: 69980016 Jia Ding Campus
Email: hans_klar@sina.com
Courses offered: CELTA

COLOMBIA (+57)

The British Council, Bogotá
Calle 87 No. 12-79, Apartado Aereo 089231, Bogotá
Tel: 1 618 0118
Fax: 1 621 4989
Email: seamus.harkin@britishcouncil.org.co
Website: www.britishcouncil.org.co
Courses offered: CELTA, ICELT, TKT

COSTA RICA (+506)

Instituto Britanico Costa Rica
Apartado Postal 8184, San José 1000
Tel: +506 225 0256
Fax: +506 253 1894
Email: ehunt@institutobritanico.co.cr
Website: www.institutobritanico.co.cr
Courses offered: CELTA, TKT

CYPRUS (+357)

Forum Language Centre
PO Box 25567, Nicosia 1310
Tel: +357 2 2446 344
Fax: +357 2 2446 345
Email: peterlucantoni@forum.ac.cy
Website: www.forum.ac.cy
Courses offered: CELTA, CELTYL

CZECH REPUBLIC (+42)

Akcent International House
Bítovská 5, Praha 4, 1400 00
Tel: +420 261 109 249
Fax: +420 261 109 254
Email: dana@akcent.cz
Website: www.akcent.cz
Courses offered: CELTA, ICELT, TKT

European Language Centres
Stepanska 24, Praha 1, 110 00
Tel: 0 2222 32932
Fax:0 2222 30518
Email: info@eurotefl.com
Website: www.eurotefl.com
Courses Offered: Cert.TESOL

ITC International
Spanielova 1292, 163 00 Prague 6.
Tel: 0 2 301 9784
Courses Offered: International TEFL Certificate.
Course Length: 4 weeks.
Start dates: All year round.

Masaryk University
Dept. of English and American Studies, Faculty of Arts,
Masaryk University, Arna Novaka 1, 660 88 Brno
Tel: +420 549 498 403
Fax: +420 549 491 522
Email: tesolte@rect.muni.cz
Website: www.rect.muni.cz/tesol
Courses offered: CELTA

Oxford TEFL
Konvitska 291/24, Prague 1
Tel: 0 224 233572
Fax: 0 224 234507
Email: info@oxfordtefl.cz
Courses Offered: Cert.TESOL

Prague Schools
Na Sekyrce 1392/2 , Dejvice, Praha 6, 160 000
Tel: 0 604 271 159
Fax: 0 233 223 779
Email: gareth.davies@pragueschools.co.uk
Courses Offered: Cert.TESOL

ECUADOR (+593)

Centro de Estudios Interamericanos,
Gran Colombia 11-02 & General Torres. Casilla 597
Cuenca

Tel: 7 839003
Fax: 7 833593
Email: english@cedei.org
Courses Offered: TEFL Certificate

Colegio Cruz Del Sur
Colina De Los Ceibos, Junto Al Campus Politecnico
Guayaquil
Tel: 4 850020
Fax: 4 2850020
Email: Johngwarren@Yahoo.Co.Uk
Courses Offered: TKT

Key Language Services Quito
Po Box 17-07-9770, Quito
Tel: 2 220956 Or 902241
Fax: 2 220956
Email: Kls@Hoy.Net
Courses Offered: TKT

FRANCE (+33)

A.E.C.A.L.E., St Germain En Laye
Bp 8218, Saint Germain En Laye 78108
Tel: +33 1 3973 5348
Fax: +33 1 3973 6432
Email: Aecale@Free.Fr
Courses Offered: TKT

American University of Paris
102 rue Saint-Dominique, 75007 Paris.
Tel: 1406207 20
Fax: 140 6207 17
Courses Offered: TESOL Certificate.
Course Length: 3 months

British Council Paris
9/11 Rue De Constantine, 75340 Paris
Tel: +33 1 4955 7342
Fax: +33 1 4705 7702
Email: Francoise.Vella@Britishcouncil.Fr
Courses Offered: TKT

International Language Centre (France) S.A.
13 Passage Dauphine, 75006 Paris
Tel: 1 4441 8020
Fax: 1 4441 8021
Email: bror@ilcfrance.com
Website: www.ilcfrance.com
Courses offered: CELTA

Greta Des Ardennes
27 Rue Du Petit Bois, Charleville-Mezieres, 08000

Tel: +33 3 2433 7415
Fax: +33 3 2433 7401
Email: Espace.Langues@Ardennes.Greta.Fr
Courses Offered: TKT

Greta Touraine

6 Avenue De Sevigne, Bp 411, 37204 Tours Cedex 3
Tel: +33 2 47 48 77 20
Fax: +33 2 47 48 77 19
Email: M.Sheath@Greta-Touraine.Com
Courses Offered: TKT

Greta Du Golfe, Vannes

6 Av. Du Marechal De Lattre De Tassigny, Bp 565,
Vannes 56017
Tel: +33 2 9746 6666
Fax: +33 2 9763 2566
Email: Greta.Du.Golfe@Wanadoo.Fr
Courses Offered: TKT

Icl Clarife

Universite Catholique De Lille, 83 Boulevard Vauban,
Bat A, Lille 59800
Tel: +33 3 2057 9219
Fax: +33 3 2015 2930
Email: Clarife@Icl-Lille.Fr
Courses Offered: TKT

International Language Centre (France) S.A.

13 Passage Dauphine, 75006 Paris
Tel: + 33 1 4441 8020
Fax: + 33 1 4441 8021
Email: CELTAtrainers@Ilcfrance.Com
Courses Offered: CELTA

Institut Catholique De Toulouse

Faculte Libre Des Lettres 31, Rue De La Fonderie - Bp
7012, Toulouse 31000
Tel: 00 33 5 61 36 81 30
Fax: 00 33 5 61 36 81 37
Email: Iulcf@Ict-Toulouse.Asso.Fr
Courses Offered: TKT

Transfer

20 Rue Godot De Mauroy, 75009 Paris
Tel: + 33 1 42 66 14 11
Fax: + 33 1 56 69 22 35
Email: Teachertraining@Transfer.Fr
Website: www.transfer.fr
Courses Offered: CELTA

TRANSFER

15 Rue de Berri, 75008 Paris
Tel: 1 5669 22 30

Fax: 1 5669 22 35
Email: teachertraining@transfer.fr
Web: www.transfer.fr/celta
Courses offered: CELTA

University Of London Institute In Paris

11 Rue De Constantine, Paris Cedex 07, 75340
Tel: +33 1 4411 7373
Fax: +33 1 4550 3155
Email: Exam@Ulip.Lon.ac.uk;
Courses Offered: TKT

GERMANY (+49)

Berlin School of English

Dorotheenstrasse 90, 10117 Berlin
Tel: 30-2290456
Fax: 30-2290471
Email: info@berlin.school-of-english.de
Website: www.berlin.school-of-english.de
Courses offered: CELTA

Hamburg School of English

Eppendorfer Landstrasse 93, 20249 Hamburg
Tel: 40 480 2119
Fax: 40 46 06 90 76
Email: aholloway@hamburg.school-of-english.de
Website: www.hamburg.school-of-english.de
Courses offered: CELTA

Hessischer Volkshochschulverband

Winterbachstrasse 38, 60320 Frankfurt Am Main
Tel: +49 69 5600 0833
Fax: +49 69 5600 0810
Email: Meden@Vhs-In-Hessen.De
Courses Offered: TKT

Landesverband Der Volkshochschulen Schleswig-Holsteins E.V.

Holstenbrücke 7, 24103 Kiel
Tel: +49 431 979840
Fax: +49 431 96685
Email: S@Vhs-Sh.De
Courses Offered: TKT

Münchner Volkshochschule

Postfach 80 11 64, 81611 München
Tel: 89 4800 6165
Fax: 89 4800 6253
Website: www.munichcelta.co.uk
Courses offered: CELTA

St Mary's College
Netteweg 17, 41844 Wegberg, Monchengladbach
Tel: 02434 25766
Courses Offered: Cert.TESOL

Volkshochschulverband Baden-Wuerttemberg E.V.
Raiffeisenstrasse 14, 70771 Leinfelden-Echterdingen
Tel: +49 711 7590027
Fax: +49 711 7590041
Email: Schill@Vhs-Bw.De
Courses Offered: TKT

GREECE (+30)

City College Manchester
IEK IBS Institute, 25 Chrisostomou Street, 71 306 Heraklion
Tel: 81 342700
Fax: 81 24221
Courses Offered: Cert.TESOL

City College Manchester
Eleni Soubli School of Languages, 1 Aristomenous Street, Kalamata
Tel: 27210 21477
Email: lsoubli@hotmail.com
Courses Offered: Cert.TESOL

Celt Athens
77 Academias Street, 106 78, Athens
Tel: 00 301 3302406, 00 301 3301455
Fax: 00 301 3301202
Email: CELTAth@Otenet.Gr;Info@Celt.Edu.Gr
Courses Offered: CELTA

Eurognosi S.A.
54 Lambraki Street, 166 74, Athens
Tel: 00 302 10 963 6100
Fax: 00 301 20 962 0313
Email: Academic.Director@Eurognosi.Com
Courses Offered: CELTA

Profile
Frantzi 4 and Kallirois Street, 117 45 Athens
Tel: 210 922 3752
Fax: 210 924 1543
Email: info@profiletraining.gr
Website: www.profiletraining.gr
Courses offered: ICELT

Study Space
Tsimiski 86, Thessaloniki 54622
Tel: 231 0269 697
Fax: 231 0269 697
Email: studyspa@otenet.gr
Website: www.studyspace.gr
Courses offered: CELTA, CELTYL

HONG KONG (+852)

British Council, Hong Kong
3 Supreme Court Road, Admiralty
Tel: 2913 5100
Fax: 2913 5588
Email: info@britishcouncil.org.hk
Website: www.britishcouncil.org.hk
Courses offered: CELTA, CELTYL, CELTYL Ext

English for Asia
Unit 301-303 Workingbond Commercial Centre, 162 Prince Edward Road West, Kowloon
Tel: 2366 3792
Fax: 2392 2424
Website: www.englishforasia.com
Email: info@englishforasia.com
Courses Offered: Cert.TESOL

HUNGARY (+36)

British Council, Budapest
Benczur utca 26, Budapest, H-1068
Tel: 1 478 4700
Fax: 1 342 5728
Courses Offered: Cert.TESOL

ILI Godollo (City College Manchester)
International Languages Institute (ILI), Korosfoi utca 2, 2100 Godollo
Tel: 28 511 366
Fax: 28 411 266
Website: www.ili.hu
Courses Offered: Cert.TESOL

International House, Budapest
1022 Budapest, Bimbo Ut 7
Tel: 1345 7046
Fax: 1 316 2491
Email: ttraining@ih.hu
Website: www.ih.hu
Courses offered: CELTA, TKT

International Education & Testing Centre
4a Budaorsi Str. 1118 Budapest
Tel: +36 1 361 0248

Fax: +36 1 209 6229
Email: Interex@Hu.Inter.Net
Courses Offered: ICELT

INDIA (+91)

British Council, Kolkata
British Deputy High Commission, L&T Chambers, 16
Camac Street, Calcutta 700 017
Tel: +91 33 22825370
Fax: +91 33 22824804
Email: Suchitra.Mukherjee@In.Britishcouncil.Org
Courses Offered: TKT

British Council, Mumbai
Mittal Tower "C" Wing 2nd Floor, Nariman Point,
Mumbai - 400 021
Tel: 222 282 3560
Fax: 222 285 2024
Email: Havovi.kolsawalla@in.britishcouncil.org
Website: www.britishcouncil.org.in
Courses offered: CELTA, TKT

British Council, New Delhi
17 Kasturba Gandhi Marg, New Delhi 110 001
Tel: 11 2371 1401 ext 245
Fax: 11 2371 0717
Email: delhi.askaquestion@in.britishcouncil.org
Website: www.britishcouncil.org.in
Courses offered: CELTA, TKT

INDONESIA (+62)

The British Institute
Plaza Setiabudi 2, Jalan Rasuna Said, Jakarta 12920
Tel: 21 525 6750
Fax: 21 520 7574
Email: rob@tbi.co.id
Website: www.tbi.co.id
Courses offered: CELTA, CELTYL Ext

Indonesia Australia Language Foundation
Jalan Kapten Agung 17, Denpasar, 80238
Tel: 361 221782
Fax: 361 263509
Website: www.ialfbali.co.id
Email: EHunt@ialfbali.co.id
Courses Offered: Cert.TESOL

Planet English Assessments
Komplek Harmoni Plaza B48-50, Jalan Suryopranoto
2, Jakarta Pusat 10130
Tel: 62-21-70756643

Fax: 62 21 7075 6643
Email: Planetedupro@Centrin.Net.Id
Courses Offered: TKT

IRELAND (+353)

Atlantic S.E.A.L.
Cooradarrigan, Schull, Eire
Tel: 28 28943
Fax: 28 28946
Email: atlanticseal@esatclear.ie
Courses Offered: Cert.TESOL

Language Centre of Ireland
45 Kildare Street, Dublin 2
Tel: 1 671 6266
Fax: 1 671 6430
Email: info@lci.ie
Website: www.lci.ie
Courses offered: CELTA

University College Cork
The Language Centre, College Road, Cork
Tel: 2 1 490 2962 / 2043
Fax: 2 1 490 3223
Email: rmasterson@langcent.ucc.ie
Website: www.ucc.ie
Courses offered: CELTA

ITALY (+39)

Accademia Britannica Latina
Via Bruxelles 55, 04100 Latina
Tel: +39 0773 624917
Fax: +39 0773 608450
Email: Conchita.Ricchi@Ablatina.Com
Courses Offered: TKT

British Centre S.A.S, Mondovi
Via Torino 20, Mondovi 12084
Tel: + 39 0174 43052
Fax: +39 0174 555385
Email: Info@Britishmondovi.It
Courses Offered: TKT

The British Council, Milan
Via Manzoni 38, 20121Milan
Tel: +39 02 7722 2213
Fax: +39 02 781 119
Email: Margaret.Fowler@Britishcouncil.It
Courses Offered: CELTA, Delta, TKT, Celtyl Ext

The British Council, Naples
Via R. Morghen 31, 80129 Naples
Tel: + 39 081 578 8247
Fax: + 39 081 556 2585
Email: Donatella.Dellecese@Britishcouncil.It
Courses Offered: CELTA, Celtyl Ext

The British School, Bari
Via Celentano 27, Bari 70121
Tel: +39 080 5247335
Fax: +39 080 5247396
Email: Bari1@Britishschool.Com
Courses Offered: TKT

British Council, Milan
Via Manzoni 38, 20121 Milano
Tel: 02 772221
Fax: 02 781119
Email: enquiries.milan@britishcouncil.it
Website: www.britishcouncil.it/milan
Courses offered: CELTA

British Council, Naples
Via Morghen 31, 80129 Napoli
Tel: 081 558 5817
Fax: 081 556 2585
Email: enquiries.naples@britishcouncil.it
Website: www.britishcouncil.it
Courses offered: CELTA

British Council, Rome
Via delle Quattro Fontane 20, 00184 Rome
Tel: 06 478 141
Website: www.britishcouncil.it
Email: enquiries.rome@britishcouncil.it
Courses Offered: Cert.TESOL

The British School Pisa
Via Rigattieri 37, 56100 Pisa
Tel: +39 050 573434
Fax: +39 050 573434
Email: Britpi@Tin.It ; S.Ellis@Virgilio.It
Courses Offered: TKT

British Council Rome
Via Quattro Fontane 20, Rome 00186
Tel: +39 06 4781 4212
Fax: +39 06 4871070
Email: Gaby.Forgione@Britishcouncil.It
Courses Offered: TKT

The British School Of Udine
Vicolo Pulesi 4, Angolo Via Mercato Vecchio, Udine
33100

Tel: +39 043 2507171
Fax: +39 043 2507546
Email: Udine@British-Fvg.Net
Courses Offered: TKT

Cambridge School of English
Via Rosmini 6, 37123 Verona
Tel: 045 800 3154
Fax: 045 801 4900
Email: info@cambridgeschool.it
Website: www.cambridgeschool.it
Courses offered: CELTA

Cambridge School, Salerno
Via Mercanti 36, Salerno 84121
Tel: +39 089 228942
Fax: +39 089 252523
Email: Peterzobel@Hotmail.Com
Courses Offered: TKT

Cambridge Esol Examinations Centre, Turin
Via Susa 3, Turin 10138
Tel: +39 011 4346195
Fax: +39 011 4346195
Email: Gundan@Astranet.It
Courses Offered: TKT

English Language Centre, Varese
Viale Milano 20, Varese 21100
Tel: +39 332 282732
Fax: +39 33 2236385
Email: Elc@Elcro.It
Courses Offered: TKT

Gruppo L2 S.A.S.
Via Di Porta S. Angelo 27
05100 Terni
Tel: 0744 598 04
Fax: 0744 409537
Email: Linguad@Tin.It
Courses Offered: TKT

International House Milan
Mr Morgan Cox, Via Alfonsine 40, 20097 San Donato
Milan
Tel: 2 5279 124
Fax: 2 5560 0324
Email: info@teachertraining.it
Website: www.teachertraining.it
Courses offered: CELTA

International House
Viale Manzoni 22, 00185 Rome.
Tel: 06 7049 7894.

Fax: 06 7049 7842.
Email: info@ihromamz.it
Website: www.ihromamz.it
Courses Offered: CELTA, CELTYL

International House
Via Quintino Sella 70, 90139 Palermo
Tel: 091 584954
Fax: 091 323965
Email: ihpalermo@ihpalermo.it
Website: www.ihpalermo.it
Courses offered: CELTA

International House, Palermo
Via Quintino Sella 70, 90139 Palermo, Sicilia
Tel: +39 091 58 49 54
Fax: +39 091 32 39 65
Email: Ihpa1@Ihpalermo.It
Courses Offered: CELTA

International House - Accademia Britannica
Viale Manzoni, 22, Rome 00185
Tel: +39 06 7047 6894 / 6802
Fax: +39 06 7049 7842
Email: T.Training@Ihromamz.It
Courses Offered: CELTA, Delta, TKT, Celtyl Ext

Lingua Centre Srl, Jesi
Viale Don Minzoni 3, Jesi 60035
Tel: +39 731 213146
Fax: +39 731 208788
Email: Info@Linguacenter.Com
Courses Offered: TKT

Regent Italia
27 Via Filzi Fabio, Milano
Tel: 00 393 288 873 365
Email: Info@Teachertraining.It
Courses Offered: CELTA

San Donato Milan
Via Alfonsine 40, 20097 San Donato Milanese (Mi)
Tel: + 39 02 867 903
Fax: + 39 02 5560 0324
Email: Exams@Ihmilano.It
Courses Offered: CELTA, TKT

Wsi Education Srl
Via Xx Settembre 68, Crema 26013
Tel: +39 0373 82333
Fax: +39 0373 250019
Email: Crema1@Wallstreet.It
Courses Offered: TKT

JAPAN (+81)

The British Council, Tokyo
2 Kagurazaka 1-Chome, Shinjuku-ku, Tokyo 162-0825
Tel: 3 3235 8011
Fax: 3 3235 0049
Email: sheena.palmer@britishcouncil.or.jp
Website: www.uknow.or.jp
Courses offered: CELTA

Language Resources
Taiyo Building, 6F 1-2 Kitanagasa-dori, 5-chome,
Chuo-Ku, Kobe 650-0012
Tel: 78 382 0394
Fax: 78 371 2681
Courses Offered: CELTA

J. B. Academic Centre
16-118b Shinyashiki Cho, Kagoshima City, 892-0838
Tel: 00 81 99 216 8800
Fax: 00 81 99 216 8801
Email: Academic@Jellybeansed.Com
Courses Offered: TKT

KASAKHSTAN (+7)

Reach
Koktem 3, Dom 20 KB 76, Almata, 480068
Tel: 3272 479117
Fax: 3272 479117
Email: hjlewis@pactec.net
Courses Offered: Cert.TESOL

KOREA (+82)

British Council, Seoul
Joongwhoo Building, 61-21 Taepyungro 1 Ka,
Choong-Ku, Seoul 100-101
Tel: 2 3702 0600
Fax: 2 3702 0660
Email: info@britishcouncil.or.kr
Website: www.britishcouncil.or.kr
Courses offered: CELTA, ICELT, TKT, CELTYL

LEBANON (+961)

American Lebanese Language Center
Confidence Center, PO Box 55463, Sin El Fin, Beirut
Tel: 1 500 978
Fax: 1 510 485
Email: allcs@inco.com.lb

Website: www.allcs.edu.lb/main.htm
Courses offered: CELTA, CELTYL

British Council Beirut
Fawzi Azar Bldg, Sadat/Sidani Str. Ras, Beirut
Tel: +961 1 740123
Fax: +961 1 739461
Email: Faten.Itani@Lb.Britishcouncil.Org
Courses Offered: TKT

MALTA (+356)

inlingua School of Languages
9, Guze Fava Street, Off Bisazza St, Sliema SLM 15
Tel: 6 313158
Fax: 6 318903
Courses Offered: TEFL Induction Course.

Institute of English Language Studies
15 Matthew Pulis Street, Sliema SLM 15
Tel: 6 320381/2/3
Fax: 6 343332
Courses Offered: TEFL Induction Course.
Course Length: 6 weeks.
Start dates: February, March, October.

NSTS English Language Institute
220 St Paul Street, Valletta VLT 07
Tel: 255 88 500
Fax: 21 341 392
Email: lgrech@nsts.org
Website: ww.nsts.org
Courses offered: CELTA

MALAYSIA (+60)

British Council Language Centre
Ground Floor, West Block, Wisma Selangor Dredging,
142C Jalan Ampang, 50450 Kuala Lumpur
Tel: 3 2723 7900
Fax: 3 2713 6599
Email: kualalumpur@britishcouncil.org.my
Website: www.britcoun.org/malaysia
Courses Offered: CELTA, ICELT, TKT, CELTYL

Erican Language Centres
Megan Avenue Ii, C-19-4 No 12, Jalan Yap Kwan
Seng, Kuala Lumpur 50450
Tel: 00 603 21 64 9999
Fax: 00 603 21 64 0900
Email: Lynnemc@Erican.Edu.My
Courses Offered: TKT

P.O.D. Education Sdn Bhd
3rd Floor Bangunan Yee Seng, 15 Jalan Raja Chulan,
Kuala Lumpur 50200
Tel: 00 603 2031 2282
Fax: 00 603 2031 2298
Email: Pod_Edu@Streamyx.Com
Courses Offered: TKT

MEXICO (+52)

Anglia Training Centre
Miguel Angel de Quevedo No. 8-106, Chimalistac
01050 Mexico D.F.
Tel: 56 623 517
Fax: 56 623 517
Email: ceciliabarea@hotmail.com
Courses offered: ICELT

British Centre, Monterrey
Bolivia 2, Col. Vista Hermosa, Monterrey, NL, CP
64620
Tel: 83 48 8834 / 333 4102
Fax: 83 48 8834 / 333 4402
Email: stephen@britishcentre.com.mx
Website: www.britishcentre.com.mx
Courses offered: ICELT

British Council, Mexico
Lope de Vega 316, Col. Chapultepec Morales
(Polanco), 11570 Mexico D.F.
Tel: 55 5263 1965
Fax: 55 5263 1960
Email: bcmexico@britishcouncil.org.mx
Website: www.britishcouncil.org.mx
Courses offered: ICELT, TKT

Instituto Anglo Mexicano de Cultura A.C.
Anglocentro Coyoacán, Paris No. 36, Col. del Carmen
04100 Mexico D.F
Tel: 5 55 75 81 81
Fax: 5 54 79 56/67
Email: rosymonte@hotmail.com
Courses offered: ICELT

Instituto Anglo Mexicano de Cultura A.C.
Antonio Caso 127, Col. San Rafael, CP 06470
Tel: 55 3000 1819
Fax: 55 5592 1847
Email: egonzalez@theanglo.org.mx
Website: www.theanglo.com.mx
Courses offered: ICELT, TKT

Instituto Anglo Mexicano de Cultura A.C.
Circuito Puericultores 1-B, Cd. Satélite, C.P. 53100
Tel: 55 56 23 392
Fax: 55 37 4 0 461
Courses offered: ICELT

International House Riviera Maya
Lote 8, Calle Catorce Norte, No 171, Playa del Carmen
Quintana Roo, CP 77710
Tel: 98 48 03 33 88
Fax: 98 48 03 43 06
Email: training@bcn.ihes.com
Website: www.ihrivieramaya.com/celta/tesol.html
Courses offered: CELTA

NETHERLANDS (+31)

British Language Training Centre
Oxford House, N.Z. Voorburgwal 328 E, 1012 RW
Amsterdam
Tel: 20 622 3634
Fax: 20 626 4962
Email: bltc@bltc.nl
Website: www.bltc.nl
Courses offered: ·CELTA, CELTYL

NEW ZEALAND (+64)

Alpha Educational Institute
8 Bishopdale, PO Box 20-211, Christchurch 8005
Tel: 3 359 1525
Fax: 3 359 1535
Email: office@alpha.school.nz
Website: www.alpha.school.nz
Courses Offered: Cert.TESOL

Aspect ILA, Christchurch
PO Box 25 - 170, Christchurch 8001
Tel: 3 353 7672
Fax: 3 379 5373
Email: training@ila.co.nz
Website: www.ila.co.nz
Courses offered: CELTA

Auckland Language Centre
PO Box 105 035, Auckland
Tel: 9 303 1962
Fax: 9 307 9219
Email: jeanette@akldlang.co.nz
Website: www.geosalc.co.nz
Courses offered: CELTA

Campbell Institute
PO Box 24-300, Level 2, 104-108 Dixon Street,
Wellington
Tel: 04 803 3434
Fax: 04 803 3435
Email: warwick.isaacs@campbell.ac.nz
Courses Offered: Cert.TESOL

Capital Language Academy
PO Box 1100, Wellington
Tel: 4 385 0600
Fax: 4 385 6655
Courses Offered: CELTA

Christchurch College of English Ltd
PO Box 31-212, Christchurch
Tel: 3 343 3790
Fax: 3 343 3791
Email: study@ccel.co.nz
Website: www.ccel.co.nz
Courses: CELTA

Christchurch Polytechnic Institute of Tech.
PO Box 540, Christchurch
Tel: 3 940 8296
Fax: 3 379 1435
Email: hornbym@cpit.ac.nz
Website: www.cpit.ac.nz
Courses offered: CELTA

EDENZ College
PO Box 10-222 Dominion Road, Mt Eden, Auckland,
1030
Tel: 9 522 1211
Fax: 9 522 1511
Email: rosetesol@hotmail.com
Courses Offered: Cert.TESOL

English Language Academy
University of Auckland, Private Bag 92019, Auckland,
92019
Tel: 9 921 7689
Fax: 9 919 7899
Email: chadfield@ela.auckland.ac.nz
Courses Offered: Cert.TESOL

International Pacific College
Private Bag 11 021, Palmerston North
Tel: 6 354 0922
Fax: 6 354 0935
Email: dbeatson@ipc.ac.nz
Website: www.ipc.ac.nz
Courses Offered: Cert.TESOL

Languages International
PO Box 5293, Auckland 1036
Tel: 9 309 0615
Fax: 9 377 2806
Courses Offered: CELTA

Oceania International College
Private Bag 93-239, Parnell, Auckland
Tel: 9 307 2127
Fax: 9 307 2128
Email: office@oceania.co.nz
Courses offered: YL Extension

Rotorua English Language Academy Rela
PO Box 2079, Rotorua
Tel: 7 349 0473
Fax: 7 349 0753
Email: english@rela.co.nz
Website: www.rela.co.nz
Courses offered: CELTA

Saxoncourt Teacher Training
Level 2, 138 Queens Street, PO Box 105347, Auckland
Tel: 9 309 2201
Email: teachertraining@shane-english.co.nz
Website: www.shane-english.co.nz
Courses Offered: Cert.TESOL

Seafield School of English
99 Seaview Road, New Brighton, PO Box 18516,
Christchurch
Tel: 3 388 3850
Email: succeed@seafield.co.nz
Website: www.seafield.co.nz
Courses Offered: Cert.TESOL

TotalEnglish Language Institute
PO Box 6899, Wellington
Tel: 4 472 6800
Fax: 4 472 6802
Email: Enquiries@totalenglish.info
Website: www.totalenglish.co.nz
Courses offered: CELTA

Unitec School of Languages and Applied Linguistics
SEAL UNITEC, Carrington Road, Mt Albert, Private
Bag 92025, Auckland
Tel: 9 815 4321
Fax: 9 815 2901
Website: www.unitec.ac.nz/eal
Courses offered: CELTA

University of Waikato Language Institute
PO Box 1317, Waikato Mail Centre, Hamilton
Tel: 7 858 5698
Fax: 7 838 4689
Email: info@waikato.ac.nz
Website: www.waikato.ac.nz
Courses offered: CELTA

Victoria University at Welington
School of LALS, P.O. Box 600, Wellington
Tel : 4 463 5600
Fax : 4 463 5604
Email: lals@vuw.ac.nz
Website: www.vuw.ac.nz
Courses Offered: Cert.TESOL

Waiariki Institute of Technology
Private Bag 3028, Mokoia Drive, Rotorua
Tel: 7 347 2400 / 346 8999
Fax: 7 346 8721
Email: info@waiariki.ac.nz
Website: www.waiariki.ac.nz
Courses offered: CELTA

OMAN (+968)

British Council, Muscat
P.O. Box 73, Postal Code 115, Madinat al Sultan
Qaboos, Muscat, Sultanate of Oman
Tel: 542 737
Fax: 542 296
Website: www.britcoun.org/oman
Courses offered: CELTA, TKT

SEEB
Caledonian College of Engineering, P.O. Box 2382
CPO, Seeb - 111
Tel: 536 165
Fax: 535 675
Email: t.goodliffe@caledonian.edu.om
Website: www.caledonianoman.org
Courses offered: CELTA

PAKISTAN (+92)

SPELT
SPELT House, 206 New Kauser Square, Frere Town
Clifton, Karachi 75530
Tel: 21 567 6307
Fax: 21 514 531
Email: spelt@spelt.org
Courses offered: ICELT

PARAGUAY (+595)

Asociación Cultural Paraguayo-Británica
Centro Anglo-Paraguayo, Av. Artigas 356, Asunción
Tel: 021 225 525
Fax: 021 203 871
Email: admin@anglo.edu.py
Website: www.anglo.edu.py
Courses offered: CELTYL

Stael Ruffinelli de Ortiz English
Avda General Santos No 606, C/ Juan de Salazar, Asuncion
Tel: 21 202 630
Fax: 21 226 062
Email: staelins@mmail.com.py
Courses Offered: Cert.TESOL

PERU (+51)

Asociación Cultural Peruano Británica
Av Arequipa 3495, Lima 27
Tel: 14 218 407
Fax: 14 216 004
Email: pferreyr@acpb.edu.pe
Website: www.britanico.edu.pe
Courses offered: ICELT

POLAND (+48)

ELS - Bell Gdansk
ul. Matejki 6, 80-238 Gdansk
Tel: 58 344 7312
Fax: 58 344 0784
Email: ziolkowska@elsbell.pl
Website: www.bellschools.pl
Courses offered: CELTA

ELS - Bell (Warsaw)
ul. Nowy Swiat 2, 00-497 Warszawa
Tel: 58 344 7312
Fax: 58 344 0784
Email: ziolkowska@elsbell.com
Website: www.bellschools.pl
Courses offered: CELTA

English School of Communication Skills
ul. Kosciuszki 1, 34-400, Nowy Targ
Tel: 18 266 6879
Fax: 18 266 6879
Email: escsnt@polbox.com
Courses Offered: TEFLA

International House, Kraków
ul. Pitsudskiego 6, 31-109 Kraków
Tel: 12 422 6482
Fax: 12 430 1000
Email: admin@ih.pl
Website: www.ih.pl
Courses offered: CELTA

International House, Wroclaw
ul. Leszczynskiego 3, 50-078 Wroclaw
Tel: 71 781 7290
Fax: 71 781 7290
Email: ttcentre@ih.com.pl
Website: www.ih.com.pl
Courses offered: CELTA, CETYL, Cert.TEBusiness

Lektor International House, Poznan
ul. Sw Marcin 66/72, 61-807 Poznan
Tel: 61 851 6171
Fax: 61 851 6171
Email: TeacherTraining.IH.Poznan@poczta.fm
Website: www.lektor-ih.pl
Courses offered: CELTA

UEC Bell School Of English
Plac Trzech Krzyzy 4/6, 00-499 Warsaw
Tel: 22 625 4792
Fax: 22 629 5865
Courses Offered: CELTA

PORTUGAL (+35)

International House, Lisbon
Rua Marquês Sá Da Bandeira, 16, 1050-148 Lisboa
Tel: 1 21 315 1493
Fax: 1 21 353 0081
Email: ttraining@ihlisbon.com
Website: www.ihlisbon.com
Courses offered: CELTA, CELTYL

QATAR (+974)

The British Council, Qatar
PO Box 2992, Doha
Tel: 442 6193
Fax: 442 3315
Email: general.enquiries@qa.britishcouncil.org
Courses offered: CELTA

RUSSIA (+7)

Language Link
Novoslobodskaya ul. 5/2, 103030 Moscow
Tel: 095 238 0225
Fax: 095 234 0703
Courses Offered: CELTA

BKC - International House, Moscow
ul. Tverskaya 9a, Building 4, 103009 Moscow
Tel: 095 234 0314
Fax: 095 234 0316
Email: t-training@bkc.ru
Website: www.bkc.ru
Courses offered: CELTA

SERBIA (+381)

Embassy CES / Rainbow School of English
Kolo Srpskih Sestara 8, 21000 Novi Sad
Tel: 21 363
Email: infouk@embassyces.com
Courses offered: CELTA

SINGAPORE (+65)

The British Council, Singapore
362 Holland Road, Singapore 278696
Tel: 6469 4263
Fax: 6472 1010
Email: britcoun@britishcouncil.org.sg
Website: www.britishcouncil.org/singapore
Courses offered: CELTA, Mode 'C'

SOUTH AFRICA (+27)

Good Hope Studies
Po Box 24065, Claremont, 7735 Capetown
Tel: 21 686 0060
Fax: 21 686 0061
Email: celta@ghs.co.za
Website: www.ghs.co.za
Courses offered: CELTA

International House Durban
PO Box 50800, Musgrave, Durban 4062
Tel: 31 261 9445
Fax: 31 261 9474
Email: info@ihdurban.co.za
Website: www.ihdurban.co.za
Courses offered: CELTA

International House Language Lab, Johannesburg
4th Floor, Aspern House, 54 De Korte Street,
Braamfontein 2001, Johannesburg
Tel: 11 339 1051
Fax: 11 403 1759
Email: laurencek@ihjohannesburg.co.za
Website: www.ihjohannesburg.co.za
Courses offered: CELTA

Shane English Schools, Cape Town
PO Box 52199, V & A Waterfront, 8002 Cape Town
Tel: 21 419 8524
Fax: 21 419 8527
Email: gpardenwatcher@shaneglobal.com
Website: www.shaneglobal.com
Courses offered: CELTA

SPAIN (+34)

British Council, Madrid
English Language Projects, Pº Gral. Martínez Campos
31, 28010 Madrid
Tel: 91 337 3593
Fax: 91 337 3600
Email: Madrid.jovenes@britishcouncil.es
Website: www.britishcouncil.es
Courses offered: ICELT

British Language Centre
Calle Bravo Murillo 377, 2º, 28020 Madrid
Tel: 91 733 0739
Fax: 91 314 5009
Email: ted@british-blc.com
Website: www.british-blc.com
Courses offered: CELTA

Cambridge School
Placa Manel Montanya 4, 08400 Granollers
Tel: 93 870 2001
Fax: 93 879 5111
Email: teachertraining@cambridgeschool.com
Courses offered: CELTA

Campbell College
Calle Pascual y Genís, 14 pta 4, 46002 Valencia
Tel: 96 352 4217
Fax: 96 351 5402
Email: campbell@cpsl.com
Website: www.cpsl.com/campbell
Courses offered: CELTA

Chester School of English
Jorge Juan 125, Madrid 28004
Tel: 91 402 5879
Fax: 91 431 5054
Email: chester@bitmailer.net
Courses Offered: Cert.TESOL

City College Manchester
Marlowe Centre Idiomas, Edif. Puerta Nueva 2. Bajo
B, Plaza Puerta Nueva 3, Murcia, 30008
Tel: 968 23 22 57
Fax: 968 20 12 05
Courses Offered: Cert.TESOL

English Academy
Paseo Rey Don Jaime 1, num. 3 - estresuelo, Oliva,
Valencia 46780
Tel: 96 285 6382
Email: olleeket@oliva.infoville.net
Courses Offered: Cert.TESOL

European Language Centres
C/Garcia de Vinuesa, 29., Seville, 41001
Tel: 954 293 278
Fax: 954 293 278
Email: info@eurotefl.com
Website: www.eurotefl.com
Courses Offered: Cert.TESOL

Hyland Language Centre
Calle Serrano 19, 2, 28001 Madrid
Tel: 91 431 9757
Fax: 91 575 7292
Email: training@hylandmadrid.com
Website: www.hylandmadrid.com
Courses offered: CELTA

Instituto de Idiomas
 Avenida de Castelao S/N, 15705 Santiago de
Compostela, a Coruña
Tel: 981 566 743
Fax: 981 547 062
Email: redpath@wandadoo.es
Website: www.usc.es/idiomas/celta
Courses offered: CELTA

International House, Barcelona
Trafalgar 14, 08010 Barcelona
Tel: 93 268 4511
Fax: 93 268 0239
Email: training@bcn.ihes.com
Website: www.ihes.com/bcn
Courses offered: CELTA, CELTYL

International House, Madrid
Calle Zurbano 8, 28010 Madrid
Tel: 91 319 7224
Fax: 00 3491 308 5321
Email: ttraining@ihmadrid.es
Website: www.ihmadrid.es
Courses offered: CELTA

International House, Palma
Calle Bonaire 9, Esc. 2, 1°, 07012 Palma de Mallorca
Illes Balears
Tel: 97 172 6408
Fax: 97 172 6045
Email: ihpalma@pal.ihes.com
Website: www.ihes.com/pal
Courses offered: CELTA

International House, Seville
Teacher Training Centre, Calle Menez Nunez 7, 41001
Seville
Tel: 954 50 03 16
Fax: 954 50 08 36
Email: training@clic.es
Website: www.clic.es
Courses offered: CELTA, IHCYL

Langside College
The Language Centre, Calle Clavel No.8, La Estrella,
La Garita, Telde, 35200
Courses Offered: Cert.TESOL

Language Institute
Calle Oliva 11, 2°, 36001Pontevedra
Tel: 986 862 461
Fax: 986 871 978
Website: www.tlispain.com
Email: enquiries@tlispain.com
Courses Offered: Cert.TESOL

Lewis School of Languages, S.L.
Gran Vía Carlos III, 97 Bajos K, 08028 Barcelona
Tel: 93 280 66 97
Fax: 93 411 13 33
Email: info@lewis-school.com
Website: www.lewis-school.com
Courses offered: CELTA

Marlowe Centre Idiomas
Edif. Puerta Nueva 2. bajo B, Plaza Puerta Nueva 3,
Murcia, 30008
Tel: 968 238 257
Fax: 968 201205
Email: marloweidiomas@ono.com
Courses Offered: Cert.TESOL

Universal Language Training
Centro de Idiomas, Colegio Universitario, San
Torcuato, 43, Zamora, 49014
Tel: 980 53 1561
Fax: 980 50 9088
Courses Offered: Cert.TESOL

The Windsor Institute of Languages
Gran Via de Les Corts Catalanes, 575, 1o, 1a,
Barcelona, 8011
Tel: 93452 5340
Fax: 93452 5341
Email: claire@windsorinstitute.com
Website: www.windsorinstitute.com
Courses Offered: Cert.TESOL

SRI LANKA (+94)

The British Council, Colombo
49 Alfred House Gardens, Colombo 3
Tel: 1 58 11 71
Fax: 1 58 70 79
Email: enquiries@britishcouncil.lk
Website: www.britishcouncil.lk
Courses offered: CELTA

SWITZERLAND (+41)

Bell Language School
12 Chemin des Colombettes, 1202 Geneva
Tel: 22 740 2022
Fax: 22 740 2044
Email: info@bell-school.ch
Website: www.bell-school.ch
Courses offered: CELTYL, CELTA

Bell Language School
Genferstrasse 23, 8002 Zürich.
Tel: 1 281 0781.
Fax: 1 281 0787.
Courses Offered: CELTA

Inlingua
Badener Str 15, CH-8004, Zürich
Website: www.inlingua.com
Courses Offered: Cert.TESOL

International House Geneva
72 rue de Lausanne, GENEVA 1202
Tel: 22 731 8520
Fax: 22 738 2158
Email: admin@asc-ih.ch

Website: www.asc-ih.ch
Courses offered: CELTA

Klubschule Migros
Bahnhofplatz 2, 9001 St. Gallen
Tel: 71 228 1609
Fax: 71 228 1601
Email: lee.walker@ksmos.ch
Website: www.klubschule.ch
Courses offered: ICELT

University of Bern
CELTA Centre, Dept. of Applied Linguistics,
Unitobler, 3000 Bern 9
Tel: 31 631 83 91.
Fax: 31 631 36 03.
Courses Offered: CELTA.
Course Length: 1 month (FT) and 6 months (PT).
Start dates: January (6-month); July (1-month).

Volkshochschule Bern
Graben Promenade 7, 3000 Bern 3
Tel: 33 345 5117
Fax: 33 345 8117
Email: jackiegottschalk@gmx.ch
Website: www.aal.unibe.ch/englisch/CELTA.html
Courses offered: CELTA

Volkshochschule Zürich
Volkshochschule des Kantons Zürich, Splügenstrasse
10, 8002 Zürich
Tel: 1 205 8494
Fax: 1 205 8485
Email: margrit.stark@vkszh.ch
Website: www.vhszh.ch
Courses offered: CELTA

Zürich Flying Teachers GMBH
Volkshochschule des Kantons Zürich
Universitätstrasse 86, 8006 Zürich
Tel: 1 350 33 44
Fax: 1 350 33 45
Email: office@flying teachers.ch
Website: www.flyingteachers.ch
Courses offered: CELTA

THAILAND (+66)

ECC (Thailand)
430/17-24 Chula Soi 64, Siam Square, Patumwan,
Bangkok 10330
Tel: 02 252 8570
Fax: 02 254 2243

Email: steve@ecc.ac.th
Website: www.eccthai.com
Courses offered: CELTA

Elite Training Institute
2nd Floor, Kongboonma Building, 699 Silom Road,
Bangrak, Bangkok 10500
Tel: 02 635 3356
Fax: 02 237 1997
Email: elitecelta@hotmail.com
Website: www.eliteinstitute.com
Courses offered: CELTA

TUNISIA (+216)

The British Council, Tunisia
47 Avenue Habib Bourguiba, Tunis 1001
Tel: 71 353 568 / 354 346
Fax: 71 353 985
Email: info@britishcouncil.org
Website: www.britishcouncil.org/tunisia
Courses offered: CELTA

TURKEY (+90)

Bilkent University
School of English Language, 06533 Bilkent, Ankara
Tel: 312 290 5190
Fax: 312 266 4320
Email: elif@bilkent.edu.tr
Website: www.bilkent.edu.tr/~busel
Courses offered: ICELT

The British Council, Izmir
1374 Sokak No. 18, Selvili Is Merkezi Kat.3, 35210
Çankaya, Izmir
Tel: 238 446 0131 ext 17
Fax: 238 446 0130
Email: bc.izmir@britishcouncil.org.tr
Website: www.britishcouncil.org.tr
Courses offered: CELTA

The British Council, Istanbul
Barbaros Bulvari Akdogan, 43 Kat 2-7, 81690 Besitas,
Istanbul
Tel: 212 327 2700 ext 1511
Fax: 212 327 2719
Email: bc.istanbul@britishcouncil.org.tr
Website: www.britishcouncil.org.tr
Courses offered: CELTA

Eastern Mediterranean University
School of Foreign Languages, Magosa, PO Box 95,
Mersin 10
Tel: 392 630 2163
Fax: 392 365 0785
Email: stephen.pike@emu.edu.tr
Website: www.emu.edu.tr
Courses offered: CELTA, ICELT

International Training Institute (I.T.I)
Kallavi Sok 7-9 Kat: 4, Istiklal Cad, Galatasaray,
Istanbul
Tel: 212 243 28 88
Email: iti_ist@yahoo.com
Website: www.itistanbul.org
Courses offered: CELTA, ICELT

UKRAINE (+380)

International House Kyiv
7 V. Vasilevskoy St., PO Box 6411, KYIV 03055
Tel: 44 238 9870 / 9796
Email: school@ih.kiev.ua
Website: www.ih.kiev.ua
Courses offered: CELTA

The London School of English
Central Post Office, PO Box 158 "B", Kiev
Tel: 044 241 86 54
Fax: 044 241 86 54
Email: admin@lse.kiev.ua
Website: www.lse.com
Courses offered: CELTA

UNITED ARAB EMIRATES (+971)

British Council, Abu Dhabi
PO Box 46523, Abu Dhabi
Tel: 2 665 9300 ext 28
Fax: 2 666 4340
Email: information@britishcouncil.org
Website: www.britishcouncil.org/uae
Courses offered: CELTA

Dubai Women's College
PO Box 16062, Dubai
Tel: 4 208 9474
Fax: 4 267 3939
Email: aleya.james@hct.ac.ae
Website: www.hct.ac.ae
Courses offered: CELTA

Email: fran.linley@barnet.ac.uk
Website: www.barnet.ac.uk
Courses offered: CELTA

Basil Paterson Edinburgh
22-23 Abercromby Place, Edinburgh EH3 6QE
Tel: 0131 556 7695
Fax: 0131 557 8503
Email: celta@basilpaterson.co.uk
Website: www.basilpaterson.co.uk
Courses offered: CELTA

Basingstoke College of Technology
Languages Department, Worting Road, Basingstoke, RG21 8TN
Tel: 01256 306350
Fax: 01256 306444
Email: maurice.gower@bcot.ac.uk
Website: www.bcot.ac.uk
Courses Offered: Cert.TESOL

Bath Spa University College
SIS, 19 Somerset Place, Room 18 G.4, Bath BA1 5HA
Tel: 01225 875667 / 875667
Fax: 01225 87315328
Email: h.walker@bathspa.ac.uk
Website: www.citybathcoll.ac.uk
Courses offered: CELTA

Bedford College,
Enterprise House, Old Ford End Road, Bedford MK40 4PF
Tel: 01234 271 492
Fax: 01234 364 272
Email: hweaver@bedford.ac.uk
Website: www.bedford.ac.uk
Courses offered: CELTA

Belfast Institute of Further Education and Higher Education
Brunswick Street, Belfast, BT2 7GX, Northern Ireland
Tel: 02890 265 142/5184
Fax: 02890 265 101
Email: adasilva@belfastinstitute.ac.uk
Website: www.belfastinstitute.ac.uk
Courses offered: CELTA

Bell Language School
1 Red Cross Lane, Cambridge CB2 2QX
Tel: 01223 278804
Fax: 01223 412410
Email: info@bell-centres.com
Website: www.bell-centres.com
Courses offered: CELTA

Bell Language School
Bowthorpe Hall, Norwich NR5 9AA
Tel: 01603 745615
Fax: 01603 747669
Email: info.norwich@bell-centres.com
Website: www.bell-centres.com
Courses offered: CELTA

Blackburn College,
Feilden Street, Blackburn BB2 1 LH.
Tel: 01254 292258
Start dates: September.
Email: m.osmaston@blackburn.ac.uk
Website: www.blackburn.ac.uk/courses
Courses offered: CELTA

Blackpool and the Fylde College
Ashfield Road, Bispham, Blackpool FY2 0HB
Tel: 01253 352352
Fax: 01253 356127
Website: www.blackpool.ac.uk
Email: TBRA@blackpool.ac.uk
Courses Offered: Cert.TESOL

Bolton Community College
ESOL Staffroom, Manchester Road, Bolton BL2 1ER
Tel: 01204 531411
Fax: 01204 380774
Email: celta@bolton-community-college.ac.uk
Website: www.bolton-community-college.ac.uk
Courses Offered: Cert.TESOL

Bournemouth and Poole College of FE
Lansdowne Centre, Christchurch Road, Bournemouth BH1 3JJ
Tel: 01202 205738
Fax: 01202 205739
Email: Lwedge@bpc.ac.uk
Courses offered: CELTA

Bournville College of Further Education
Bristol Road South, Northfield, Birmingham B31 2AJ
Tel: 0121 483 1000
Fax: 0121 411 2231
Email: info@bcfe.ac.uk
Courses offered: CELTA, Cert.TESOL

Bracknell & Wokingham College
Montague House, Broad St, Wokingham RG40 1AU
Tel: 0118 9029156
Fax: 0118 9029160
Website: www.bracknell.ac.uk
Email: colette.galloway@bracknell.ac.uk
Courses Offered: Cert.TESOL

Bradford College
English Language Centre, Great Horton Road,
Bradford BD17 5PX
Tel: 01274 753034
Fax: 01274 741553
Website: www.bilk.ac.uk
Email: elc@bilk.ac.uk
Courses Offered: Cert.TESOL

Brasshouse Language Centre
50 Sheepcote Street, Birmingham B16 8AJ
Tel: 0121 303 0114
Fax: 0121 303 4782
Email: jo_johnson@birmingham.gov.uk
Website: www.birmingham.gov.uk/brasshouse
Courses offered: CELTA

Bromley College of Further and Higher Education
Faculty 2 - Rookery Lane, Bromley BR2 8HE
Tel: 0208 295 7000 ext 7108
Fax: 0208 295 7057
Email: Sian.Pearce@bromley.ac.uk
Website: www.bromley.ac.uk
Courses offered: CELTA

Brooklands College
Adult Education in the Community, Heath Road,
Weybridge KT13 8TT
Tel: 01932 847029
Fax: 01932 797800
Website: www.brooklands.ac.uk
Courses Offered: Cert.TESOL, CELTA

Bury College
Peel Centre, Parliament Street, Bury BL9 0TE
Tel: 0161 280 8432
Website: www.burycollege.ac.uk
Email: claire.flynn@burycollege.ac.uk
Courses Offered: Cert.TESOL

Canterbury Christ Church University College
North Holmes Road, Canterbury CT1 1QU
Tel: 01227 782585
Email: p.j.aboshiha@cant.ac.uk
Website: arts-humanities.cant.ac.uk/Language-Studies
Courses offered: CELTA

Cheltenham International Language Centre
University of Gloucestershire, Cornerways,
Cheltenham, Gloucestershire, GL50 2QF
Tel: 01242 532925
Fax: 01242 532926
Email: cilc@glos.ac.uk

Website: www.glos.ac.uk/cilc
Courses offered: CELTA

Chichester College of Arts, Science and Technology
Westgate Fields, Chichester PO19 1SB
Tel: 01243 536294
Fax: 01243 775783
Email: intunit@chichester.ac.uk
Website: www.chichester.ac.uk
Courses offered: CELTA

CILC (Cheltenham Intl. Language Centre)
University of Gloucestershire, Dunholme Villa, PO
Box 220, The Park, Cheltenham GL50 2QF
Tel: 01242 532925
Fax: 01242 532926
Email: mmharrison@glos.ac.uk
Website: www.glos.ac.uk/cilc
Courses offered: CELTA

City and Islington College
Dame Alice Owen Centre, 311-312 Goswell Road
London EC1V 7DD
Tel: 0207 520 0615
Fax: 0207 520 7481
Email: jallema@candi.ac.uk
Website: www.talent.ac.uk
Courses offered: CELTA

City College Brighton and Hove
Pelham Street, Brighton BN1 4FA
Tel: 01273 667788
Fax: 01273 667703
Website: www.ccb.ac.uk
Email: gp@ccb.ac.uk
Courses Offered: Cert.TESOL

City College Coventry
School of Languages and Teacher Training, Butts
Centre, Butts, Coventry CV1 3GD
Tel: 024 7652 6700
Fax: 024 7652 6789
Website: www.covcollege.ac.uk
Email: c.fry@staff.covcollege.ac.uk
Courses Offered: Cert.TESOL

City College Handsworth
Soho Road, Handsworth, Birmingham B21 9DP
Tel: 0121 256 1099
Fax: 0121 523 4447
Email: brigidbird@hotmail.com
Courses offered: CELTA

City College Manchester

Fielden Centre, 141 Barlow Moor Road, West
Didsbury, Manchester M20 2PQ
Tel: 0161 957 1660
Fax: 0161 434 0443
Website: www.ccm.ac.uk
Email: aspencer@ccm.ac.uk
Courses Offered: Cert.TESOL

City of Bath College

Avon Street, Bath BA1 1UP
Tel: 01225 312191
Fax: 01225 444213
Email: bulld@citybathcoll.ac.uk
Website: www.citybathcoll.ac.uk
Courses offered: CELTA

City of Bristol College

Department of Languages, Cabot House, Brunel Centre
Ashley Down, Bristol BS7 9BU
Tel: 0117 904 5163
Fax: 0117 904 5180
Email: emma.kieran@cityofbristol.ac.uk
Website: www.cityofbristol.ac.uk
Courses offered: CELTA

Colchester Institute

EFL/TEFL Dept., Sheepen Road, Colchester CO3 3LL
Tel: 01206 518713
Fax: 01206 518186
Website: www.colch-inst.ac.uk
Courses Offered: Cert.TESOL

College of North West London

Kilburn Centre, Priory Park Road, London NW6 7UJ
Tel: 0208 208 5230
Fax: 0208 208 5225
Email: krystyna.vargas@cnwl.ac.uk
Courses offered: CELTA

Concorde International Study Centre

Arnett House, Hawks Lane, Canterbury CT1 2NU
Tel: 01227 451 035
Fax: 01227 762 760
Email: info@concorde.ltd.uk
Website: www.concorde.ltd.uk
Courses offered: CELTA

Continuing Education and Training Service

Faculty of English, Maths and Languages, South
Norwood Centre, Sandown Road, London SE25 4XE
Tel: 0208 656 6620
Fax: 0208 662 1828
Email: janet_ott@croydon.gov.uk

Website: www.cets.co.uk
Courses offered: CELTA

Crest Schools of English

192b Station Road, Edgware, HA8 7AR
Tel: 0208 952 8040
Fax: 0208 952 4980
Email: info@crestschools.com
Website: www.crestschools.com
Courses offered: CELTA

Crawley College

College Road, Crawley, West Sussex, RH10 1NR
Tel: 01293 442295
Fax: 01293 442399
Courses Offered: Cert.TESOL

Darlington College of Technology

School of Humanities, Cleveland Avenue, Darlington
DL3 7BB
Tel: 01325 503050
Fax: 01325 503000
Website: www.darlington.ac.uk
Email: kwilson@darlington.ac.uk
Courses Offered: Cert.TESOL

Dundee College

ESOL, Melrose Campus, Melrose Terrace, Dundee,
DD3 7QX
Tel: 01382 834834
Fax: 01382 458153
Email: e.turner@dundeecoll.ac.uk
Website: www.dundeecoll.ac.uk
Courses offered: CELTA

Ealing, Hammersmith and West London College

Gliddon Road, London, W14 9BL
Freephone: (in UK only): 0800 980 2175
Fax: 0208 563 8247
Email: michael.abraham@wlc.ac.uk
Website: www.hwlc.ac.uk
Courses offered: CELTA

East Berkshire College, Langley Centre

Faculty of Arts and Humanities, Station Road,
Langley, Slough SL3 8BY
Website: www.eastberk.ac.uk
Email: chris.hammonds@eastberk.ac.uk
Tel: 01753 793000
Fax: 01753 793316
Courses Offered: Cert.TESOL

Eastleigh College of Further Education
Chestnut Avenue, Eastleigh SO50 5HT
Tel: 023 8091 1071
Fax: 023 8032 2131
Email: lwoodland@eastleigh.ac.uk
Website: www.eastleigh.ac.uk
Courses offered: CELTA

EF English First
36 - 38 St Aubyns, Hove, BN3 2TD
Tel: 01273 201433
Fax: 01273 746742
Email: Sharon.reed@englishfirst.com
Website: www.englishfirst.com
Courses Offered: Cert.TESOL

EF English First
5th Floor, Arthur House, Chorlton Street, Manchester, M1 3FH
Tel: 0161 236 7494
Email: david.bish@englishfirst.com
Courses Offered: Cert.TESOL

Elite College
45 Wimbledon Hill Road, Wimbledon, London, SW19 7NA
Tel: 0208 946 7888
Fax: 0208 946 7999
Email: shanel@elitecollege.com
Courses offered: CELTA

Embassy CES
8 Grange Road, Cambridge CB3 9DU
Tel: 01223 311344
Fax: 01223 461411
Email: stevelaslett@hotmail.com
Website: www.embassyCES.com
Courses offered: CELTA

Embassy CES
Palace Court, White Rock, Hastings TN34 1JY
Tel: 01424 720100
Fax: 01424 720323
Email: training@embassyces.com
Website: www.embassyces.com
Courses offered: CELTA

English Language Centre
6B Church Street, Reading RG1 2SB
Tel: 0118 9391 833
Fax: 0118 9391 833
Email: katepepper@ntlworld.com
Courses offered: CELTA

English Language Centre
5 New Street, York YO1 8RA
Tel: 01904 423594
Fax: 01904 672200
Email: english@btinternet.com
Website: www.elcyork.com
Courses offered: CELTA

English Language House
Church of Christ the Cornerstone, 300 Saxon Gate West, Milton Keynes MK9 2ES
Tel: 01908 694 357
Email: info@englishlanguagehouse.co.uk
Website: www.englishlanguagehouse.co.uk
Courses offered: CELTA

Farnborough College
Boundary Road, Farnborough GU14 6SB
Tel: 01252 407030
Fax: 01252 407007
Website: www.farn-ct.ac.uk
Courses offered: CELTA

Filton College
Filton Avenue, Bristol BS34 7AT
Tel: 0117 909 2279
Fax: 0117 931 2233
Email: international@filton-college.ac.uk
Website: www.filton-college.ac.uk
Courses offered: CELTA

Frances King Teacher Training
5 Grosvenor Gardens, London SW1W 0BB
Tel: 020 7630 8055
Fax: 020 7630 8077
Courses Offered: CELTA
Course Length: 4 weeks
Start dates: Throughout the year

Gateshead College
Durham Road, Gateshead NE9 5BN
Website: www.gateshead.ac.uk
Email: jill.oliver@post.gateshead.ac.uk
Tel: 0191 490 0300
Fax: 0191 490 2313
Courses Offered: Cert.TESOL

Geos English Academy
55-61 Portland Road, Hove BN3 5DQ
Tel: 01273 735975
Fax: 01273 732884
Email: info@geos-brighton.com
Website: www.geos-brighton.com
Courses offered: CELTA

Gloscat
Princess Elizabeth Way, Cheltenham
GL51 7SJ
Tel: 01242 532144
Fax: 01242 532023
Email: wiltoa@gloscat.ac.uk
Courses offered: CELTA

Golders Green College
Golders Green Teacher Training Centre, 11 Golders
Green Road, London NW11 8DY
Tel: 020 8731 0963
Fax: 020 8455 6528
Email: teachertraining@ggcol.fsnet.co.uk
Courses Offered: Cert.TESOL

Greenwich Community College
94 Plumstead Rd, London SE18 7DQ
Tel: 020 8488 4800
Fax: 020 8488 4899
Email: info@gcc.ac.uk
Website: www.woolwich.ac.uk
Courses offered: CELTA

Guildford College of Further & Higher Ed.
Stoke Park, Guildford GU1 1EZ
Tel: 01483 448500
Fax: 01483 448600
Website: www.guildford.ac.uk
Email: mmayne@guilford.ac.uk
Courses Offered: Cert.TESOL

Hackney Community College
Shoreditch Campus, Falkirk Street, London N1 6HQ
Tel: 0207 613 9341
Fax: 0207 613 9089
Email: xliao@comm-coll-hackney.ac.uk
Courses offered: CELTA

Hammersmith and West London College
Gliddon Road, London W14 9BL
Tel: 0800 980 2175
Fax: 020 8563 8247
Email: cic@hwlc.ac.uk
Website: www.hwlc.ac.uk
Courses offered: CELTA

Harrow College
Lowlands Road, Harrow HA1 3AQ
Tel: 0208 909 6594
Fax: 0208 909 6061
Email: lkoten@harrow.ac.uk
Website: www.harrow.ac.uk
Courses offered: CELTA

Harrow House International College
Harrow Drive, Swanage, Dorset BH19 1PE
Tel: 01929 424421
Fax: 01929 427175
Email: emma.barnes@Harrowhouse.co.uk
Website: www.harrowhouse.com
Courses offered: CELTA

Hastings College of Arts and Technology
Archery Road, St. Leonard's-on-Sea TN38 0HX
Website: www.hastings.co.uk
Email: academic@hastings.co.uk
Courses Offered: Cert.TESOL

Hopwood Hall College
Rochdale Campus, St Mary's Gate, Rochdale OL12
6RY
Tel: 01706 345346
Fax: 01706 641 426
Website: www.hopwood.ad.uk
Email: enquiries@hopwood.ac.uk
Courses Offered: Cert.TESOL

Hounslow West Thames College
Heath House, London Road, Isleworth TW7 4HS
Tel: 020 8326 2000
Fax: 020 8569 7787
Email: info@west-thames.ac.uk
Website: www.west-thames.ac.uk
Courses offered: CELTA

Hull College
Humanities and Languages, Park Street Centre, Park
Street, Hull HU2 8RR
Tel: 01482 598949
Fax: 01482 598989
Courses Offered: Cert.TESOL

ICELS - Oxford Brookes University
International Centre for English Language Studies
Harcourthill, Oxford, OX2 9AT
Tel: 01865 488 609
Fax: 01865 484 377
Email: mljones@brookes.ac.uk
Website: www.brookes.ac.uk/icels
Courses offered: CELTA

Inlingua School of Languages
Rodney Lodge, Rodney Road, Cheltenham, GL50
1HX
Tel: 01242 253171
Fax: 01242 253181
Website: www.inlingua.com
Courses Offered: Cert.TESOL

Intensive School of English
34 Duke Street, Brighton BN1 1BS
Tel: 01273 384800
Email: info@ise.uk.com
Website: www.ise.uk.com
Courses offered: CELTA

International House
106 Piccadilly, London W1J 7NL
Tel: 020 7518 6928
Fax: 020 7518 6921
Email: fernando.nonohay@ihlondon.co.uk
Website: www.ihlondon.com
Courses offered: CELTA

International House
14-18 Stowell Street, Newcastle upon Tyne NE1 4XQ
Tel: 0191 238 9551
Fax: 0191 238 1126
Email: info@ihnewcastle.com
Website: www.ihnewcastle.com
Courses offered: CELTA

International School
1-3 Mount Radford Crescent, Exeter Ex2 4EW
Website: www.internationalschool.co.uk
Email: kim@internationalschool.co.uk
Tel: 01392 254102
Fax: 01392 434432
Courses Offered: Cert.TESOL

International Training Network
Exchange Buildings, Upper Hinton Road,
Bournemouth BH1 2HH
Tel: 01202 789089
Fax: 01202 789089
Website: www.international-training-network.org.uk
Email: office@international-training-network.org.uk
Courses Offered: Cert.TESOL

ISIS Greenwich
259 Greenwich High Road, Greenwich, SE10 8NB
Tel: 020 8293 1444
Fax: 020 8293 1199
Email: mark@isisgroup.co.uk
Website: www.isisgroup.co.uk
Courses Offered: Cert.TESOL

ITTC United Kingdom
Nortoft Road, Charminster, Bournemouth BH8 8PY
Tel: 01202 397 721
Email: tefl@ittc.co.uk
Website: www.ittc.co.uk
Courses offered: CELTA

Joseph Priestley College
Alec Beevers Centre, Burton Avenue, Leeds LS11 5ER
Website: www.joseph-priestly.ac.uk
Email: hhartmann@joseph-priestley.ac.uk
Tel: 0113 3076002
Fax: 0113 271 3546
Courses Offered: Cert.TESOL

Keele University
English Language Unit, Department of Academic Affairs, Keele, Staffordshire ST5 5BG
Tel: 01782 584293
Fax: 01782 584237
Courses Offered: Cert.TESOL

Kensington and Chelsea College
Hortensia Centre, Hortensia Road, London SW10 0QS
Tel: 0207 573 5234
Fax: 0207 351 0956
Email: j.delaney@kcc.ac.uk
Website: www.kcc.ac.uk
Courses offered: CELTA

Kent School of English
3 Granville Road, Broadstairs CT10 1QD
Tel: 01843 874870
Fax: 01843 860418
Website: www.kentschool.co.uk
Email: enquiries@kentschool.co.uk
Courses Offered: Cert.TESOL

Kingston Adult Education
North Kingston Centre, Richmond Road, Kingston KT2 5PE
Tel: 0208 547 6724
Fax: 0208 547 6776
Email: jenny.arokiasamy@rbk.kingston.gov.uk
Courses offered: CELTA

Kingston College
Kingston Hall Road, Kingston-upon-Thames KT1 2AQ
Tel: 020 8546 2151
Fax: 020 8268 2900
Website: www.kingston-college.ac.uk
Email: kise@kingston-college.ac.uk
Courses Offered: Cert.TESOL

Langside College
50 Prospecthill Road, Glasgow G42 9LB
Website: www.langside.ac.uk
Email: tfoster@langside.ac.uk
Tel: 0141 649 4991

Fax: 0141 632 5252
Courses Offered: Cert.TESOL

Language Link
21 Harrington Road, London SW7 3EU
Tel: 020 7225 1065
Fax: 020 7370 1123
Email: info@languagelink.co.uk
Website: www.languagelink.co.uk
Courses offered: CELTA

Language Project
27 Oakfield Road, Clifton, Bristol BS8 2AT
Tel: 0117 9090911
Fax: 0117 907 7181
Website: www.languageproject.co.uk
Email: info@languageproject.co.uk
Courses Offered: Cert.TESOL

Languages Training and Development
187 Corn Street, Witney OX8 7DP
Tel: 01993 894710
Fax: 01993 706066
Website: www.ltdoxford.com
Email: info@ltdoxford.com
Courses Offered: Cert.TESOL

Leeds Metropolitan University
Centre for Language Study, Beckett Park Campus,
Leeds LS6 3QS
Tel: 0113 283 7440
Fax: 0113 274 5966
Website: www.lmu.ac.uk
Email: cls@lmu.ac.uk
Courses Offered: Cert.TESOL, CELTA

Lewisham College
Tressillian Building, Lewisham Way, London SE4
1UT
Tel: 0208 694 3295
Fax: 0208 694 3349
Email: sjo@staff.lewisham.ac.uk
Website: www.lewisham.ac.uk
Courses offered: CELTA

Liverpool Community College
ESOL Department, Colquitt Street, Liverpool L1 4DB
Tel: 0151 252 4577
Fax: 0151 252 4574
Email: christina.griffiths@liv-coll.ac.uk
Website: www.liv-coll.ac.uk
Courses offered: CELTA

Liverpool Hope University College
International Studies Dept
The Centre for English Language Studies
Room 009 Warrington Building, Liverpool Hope
University College, Hope Park, Liverpool, L16 9JD
Tel: 0151 291 3105
Fax: 0151 291 3836
Email: mccabel@hope.ac.uk
Courses offered: CELTA

Loughborough University
English Language Study Unit, Ashby Road,
Loughborough LE11 3TU
Tel: 01509 222058
Fax: 01509 223919
Website: www.lboro.ac.uk
Email: j.e.ellis@lboro.ac.uk
Courses Offered: Cert.TESOL

Making Training Work
26 Links Yard, Spelman Street, London E1 5LX
Tel: 0207 247 2944
Fax: 0207 247 3811
Email: makingtraining.work@virgin.net
Courses offered: CELTA

Manchester Academy of English
St Margaret's Chambers, 5 Newton Street, Manchester
M1 1HL
Tel: 0161 237 5619
Fax: 0161 237 9016
Website: www.manacad.co.uk
Email: english@manacad.co.uk
Courses Offered: Cert.TESOL

Manchester College of Arts and Technology
Dept. of Language Studies, City Centre Campus,
Lower Hardman Street, Manchester M3 3ER
Tel: 0161 953 2266
Fax: 0161 953 2259
Website: www.mancat.ac.uk
Email: efl-unit@mancat.ac.uk
Courses Offered: Cert.TESOL

Medway Adult and Community Learning
Rochester Centre, Eastgate, Rochester ME1 1EW
Tel: 01634 845359
Fax: 01634 405673
Website: www.medway.gov.uk
Email: delia.halsey@medway.gov.uk
Courses Offered: Cert.TESOL

Middlesbrough College

Kirby Campus, Roman Road, Middlesbrough TS5 5PJ
Tel: 01642 333 333
Fax: 01642 333 310/333320
Website: www.middlesbro.ac.uk
Email: r.smith@middlesbro.ac.uk
Courses Offered: Cert.TESOL

Mid Kent College of Higher and FE

Language Services, Oakwood Park, Tonbridge Road,
Maidstone ME16 8AQ
Tel: 01622 691555 ext 329
Fax: 01622 695049
Email: abracey@midkent.ac.uk
Website: www.midkent.ac.uk
Courses offered: CELTA

Multi Lingua

Abbot House, Sydenham Road, Guildford, Surrey GU1
3RL
Tel: 01483 535 118
Fax: 01483 534 777
Email: mhibberd@surrey-college.co.uk
Website: www.multi-lingua.co.uk
Courses offered: CELTA

New College Durham

West House, Potters Bank, Neville's Cross, Durham
DH1 3RR
Email: joannafayram@hotmail.com
Tel: 0191 375 4383
Fax: 0191 375 4216
Courses Offered: Cert.TESOL

New College Nottingham

Languages Dept. (Room E170), Clarendon City
College, The Adams Building, Stoney Street,
Nottingham NG1 1NG
Tel: 0115 910 4677
Fax: 0115 910 4622
Email: rose.underwood@ncn.ac.uk
Website: www.clarendon.ac.uk
Courses offered: CELTA

Newcastle College

ESOL Section, BSELS, Rye Hill Campus, Scotswood
Road, Newcastle upon Tyne NE4 7SA
Tel: 0191 200 4467
Fax: 0191 273 3155
Email: s.johnson@ncl-coll.ac.uk
Website: www.ncl-coll.ac.uk
Courses offered: CELTA

Newham College of Further Education

East Ham Campus, High Street South, London E6 6ER
Tel: 0208 257 4246
Fax: 0208 257 4300
Email: andreamcmahon@newham.ac.uk
Courses offered: CELTA

Northampton College

Military Road Centre, Northampton NN1 3ET
Tel: 01604 734 170/2
Fax: 01604 734183
Courses Offered: Cert.TESOL

Northbrook College

Modern Languages Centre, Littlehampton Road,
Goring-by-Sea, Worthing BN12 6NU
Tel: 01903 606243
Fax: 01903 606207
Website: www.nbcol.ac.uk
Email: s.scowen@nbcol.ac.uk
Courses Offered: Cert.TESOL

North Hertfordshire College

Cambridge Road, Hitchin, G4 OJD
Tel: 01462 424242
Fax: 01462 443054
Email: lmachin@nhc.ac.uk
Courses Offered: Cert.TESOL

Nottingham Trent University

Nottingham Language Centre, Newton Building,
Room 519, Burton Street, Nottingham NG1 4BU
Tel: 0115 941 8418 / 923 1466
Email: linda.taylor@ntu.ac.uk
Website: www.nlc.ntu.ac.uk
Courses offered: CELTA

Oaklands College

St Albans City Campus, St Peter's Road, St Albans
AL1 3RX
Tel: 01727 737000
Fax: 01727 737273
Website: www.oaklands.ac.uk
Email: helen.day@oaklands.ac.uk
Courses Offered: Cert.TESOL

Oxford Brookes University

International Centre for English Language Studies,
Headington Campus, Gipsy Lane, Oxford OX3 0BP
Tel: 01865 483 874
Fax: 01865 484 377
Email: icels@brookes.ac.uk
Website: www.brookes.ac.uk/icels
Courses offered: CELTA

Oxford Cherwell College
Oxpens Road, Oxford, OX1 1SA
Tel: +44 1865 269268
Fax: +44 1865 269412
Email: Steven_Haysham@oxfordcollege.ac.uk
Website: www.oxfordcollege.ac.uk
Courses offered: CELTA

Oxford College of Further Education
1 Oxpens Road, Oxford OX1 1SA
Tel: 01865 269268
Fax: 01865 269412
Email: Steven_Haysham@oxfordcollege.ac.uk
Website: www.oxfordcollege.ac.uk
Courses offered: CELTA

Oxford House College
28 Market Place, Oxford Circus, London W1W 8AW
Tel: 020 7580 9785
Fax: 020 7323 4582
Email: teachertraining@oxfordhouse.co.uk
Website: www.oxfordhousecollege.co.uk
Courses offered: CELTA

Park Lane College
Park Lane, Leeds LS3 1AA
Tel: 0113 216 2000
Fax: 0113 216 2020
Website: www.parklanecoll.ac.uk
Email: j.barraclough@parklanecoll.ac.uk
Courses Offered: Cert.TESOL

Peterborough Regional College
Park Crescent, Peterborough, PE1 4DZ
Tel: 01733 767366
Fax: 01733 767986
Email: info@peterborough.ac.uk
Courses Offered: Cert.TESOL

Pilgrims
Orchard Street, Canterbury, Kent CT2 8BF.
Tel: 01227 762111
Fax: 01227 45902
Email: sarah.br@pilgrims.co.uk
Website: www.pilgrims.co.uk
Course Length: 4 weeks
Courses Offered: CELTA

Plymouth College of Further Education
Department of Arts and Humanities, Kings Road,
Devonport, Plymouth PL1 5QG
Tel: 01752 305282
Fax: 01752 305098
Website: www.pcfe.ac.uk

Email: ggodfrey@pcfe.ac.uk
Courses Offered: Cert.TESOL

Polyglot Language Centre
214 Trinity Road, London SW17 7HP
Tel: 0208 767 9113
Fax: 0208 767 9104
Email: info@polyglot.co.uk
Website: www.polyglot.co.uk
Courses offered: CELTA

Randolph School of English
63 Frederick Street, Edinburgh EH2 1LH
Tel: 0131 226 5004
Fax: 0131 226 5003
Email: randolphse@aol.com
Website: www.members.aol.com/randolphse
Courses offered: CELTA

Reading College and School of Arts & Design
Crescent Road, Reading RG1 5RQ
Tel: 0118 967 5411
Fax: 0118 967 5441
Email: baberm@reading-college.ac.uk
Website: www.reading-college.ac.uk
Courses offered: CELTA

Regency School of English
Royal Crescent, Ramsgate CT11 9PE
Email: regency.school@btinternet.com
Tel: 01843 591212
Fax: 01843 850035
Courses Offered: Cert.TESOL

Regent Edinburgh
29 Chester Street, Edinburgh EH3 7EN
Website: www.regent.org.uk
Email: edinburgh@regent.org.uk
Tel: 0131 225 9888
Fax: 0131 225 2133
Courses Offered: Cert.TESOL, CELTA

Regent Language Training
12 Buckingham Street, London WC2N 6DF
Tel: 0207 872 6620
Fax: 0207 872 6630
Email: london@regent.org.uk
Website: www.regent.org.uk
Courses offered: Cert.TESOL, CELTA

Regent Oxford Teacher Training
Godmer House, 90 Banbury Road, Oxford OX2 6JT
Tel: 01865 515566
Fax: 01865 512538

Email: oxford@regent.org.uk
Website: www.regent.org.uk
Courses offered: CELTA, Cert.TESOL

St Brelade's College
Mont Les Vaux, St Brelade, Jersey JE3 8AF
Email: sbc@itl.net
Tel: 01534 741305
Fax: 01534 41159
Courses Offered: Cert.TESOL

St George International
Teacher Training Department, 76 Mortimer Street,
London W1N 7DE
Tel: 020 7299 1700
Fax: 020 7299 1711
Website: www.stgeorges.co.uk
Email: teflenq@stgeorges.co.uk
Courses Offered: Cert.TESOL

St Giles College, Brighton
3 Marlborough Place, Brighton, East Sussex BN1 1UB
Tel: 01273 682747
Fax: 01273 689808
Email: stgiles@pavilion.co.uk
Courses offered: CELTA

St Giles College, London
154 Southampton Row, London WC1B 5JX
Tel: 020 7837 0404
Fax: 020 7837 4099
Website: www.stgiles.co.uk
Email: londoncentral@stgiles.co.uk
Courses Offered: Cert.TESOL

St Giles College, London
51 Shepherds Hill, London N6 5QP
Tel: 0208 340 0828
Fax: 0208 348 9389
Email: edtrust@stgiles.co.uk
Website: www.tefl-stgiles.com
Courses offered: CELTA

St Mary's College
Waldegrave Road, Strawberry Hill, Twickenham TW1 4SX
Website: www.smuc.ac.uk
Tel: 020 8240 4346
Fax: 020 8240 4365
Courses Offered: Cert.TESOL

Sandwell College
Smethwick Campus, Crocketts Lane, Smethwick B66 3BU
Tel: 0121 253 6238
Fax: 0121 253 6322
Website: www.sandwell.ac.uk
Email: gill.clarke@sandwell.ac.uk
Courses Offered: Cert.TESOL

Saxoncourt Teacher Training
59 South Molton Street, London W1Y 1HH.
Tel: 020 7499 8533.
Fax: 020 7499 9374.
Website: www.sgvenglish.com
Courses Offered: CELTA, CELTYL

Saxoncourt Teacher Training
5 Cambridge Terrace, St Aldates, Oxford OX1 1UP
Tel: 01865 246620
Fax: 01865 246857
Email: jo@british-study.com
Website: www.british-study.com
Courses offered: CELTA

Saxoncourt Teacher Training
Nightingale House, 56-70 Queensway, Petts Wood
Bromley BR5 1DH
Tel: 01689 873 355
Fax: 01689 872 100
Email: abn.whitehead@saxoncourt.com
Website: www.sgvenglish.com
Courses offered: CELTA, YL Extension

School of Oriental and African Studies
Thornhaugh Street, Russell Square, London WC1H
OXG
Tel: 0207 074 5052
Courses offered: CELTA

Sheffield College
Castle Centre, Granville Road, Sheffield S2 2RL
Tel: 0114 260 2600
Fax: 0114 260 2101
Courses Offered: Cert.TESOL

Sheffield Hallam University, TESOL Centre
36 Collegiate Campus, Sheffield S10 2BP
Tel: 0114 225 2240
Fax: 0114 225 2280
Website: www.shu.ac.uk
Email: tesol@shu.ac.uk
Courses Offered: Cert.TESOL

Sidmouth International School
May Cottage, Sidmouth EX10 8EN
Website: www.sidmouth-int.co.uk
Email: efl@sidmouth-int.co.uk
Tel: 01395 516754

Fax: 01395 579270
Courses Offered: Cert.TESOL

Skola Teacher Training

27 Delancey Street, Camden Town, London
NW1 7RX
Tel: 0207 388 6644
Fax: 0207 387 6363
Email: london@skola.co.uk
Website: www.skola.co.uk
Courses offered: CELTA

Solihull College

The Language Exchange, Blossomfield Road, Solihull,
Birmingham B91 1SB
Tel: 0121 678 7173
Fax: 0121 678 7276
Email: pat.morris@Solihull.ac.uk
Website: www.solihull.ac.uk
Courses offered: CELTA

Somerset College of Arts & Technology

Wellington Road, Taunton TA1 5AX
Website: www.somerset.ac.uk
Email: dsp@somerset.ac.uk
Tel: 01823 366366
Fax: 01823 366418
Courses Offered: Cert.TESOL

South Devon College

EFL/School of International Languages, Newton Road
Torquay TQ2 5BY
Tel: 01803 406488 / 406338
Fax: 01803 406333
Email: veblack@hotmail.com
Website: www.southdevon.ac.uk
Courses offered: CELTA

South East Essex College

Carnarvon Road, Southend-on-Sea SS2 6LS
Tel: 01702 220400
Fax: 01702 432380
Website: www.se-essex-college.ac.uk
Email: learning@se-essex-college.ac.uk
Courses Offered: Cert.TESOL

Southgate College

School of EFL/ESOL, High Street, London N14 6BS
Tel: 020 8886 6521
Fax: 020 8982 5051
Email: english@southgate.ac.uk
Website: www.southgate.ac.uk
Courses offered: CELTA

South Leicestershire College

Language Centre, Station Road, Wigston Magna LE18
2DW
Tel: 0116 288 5051
Fax: 0116 288 0823
Email: jane@wigston-college.ac.uk
Website: www.wigston-college
Courses offered: CELTA

South Thames College

50-52 Putney Hill, London SW15 6QX
Tel: 0208 918 7305
Fax: 0208 918 7347
Email: eis@south-thames.ac.uk
Website: www.south-thames.ac.uk
Courses offered: CELTA

Southwark College

Waterloo Centre, The Cut, London SE1 8LE
Tel: 020 7815 1682
Fax: 020 7261 1301
Website: www.southwark.ac.uk
Email: philj@southwark.ac.uk
Courses Offered: Cert.TESOL

Stanton Teacher Training Courses Ltd

Stanton House, 167 Queensway, London W2 4SB
Tel: 0207 221 7259
Fax: 0207 792 9047
Email: study@stanton-school.co.uk
Website: www.stanton-school.co.uk
Courses offered: CELTA

Stevenson College,

ELT Section, Bankhead Avenue, Edinburgh EH11
4DE, Scotland.
Tel: 0131 535 4600.
Fax: 0131 535 4666.
Website: www.stevenson.ac.uk
Email: info@stevenson.ac.uk
Courses Offered: CELTA.

Stockport College of Further & Higher Ed.

EFL Dept, Wellington Road South, Stockport SK1
3UQ
Tel: 0161 958 3100
Fax: 0161 480 6636
Website: www.stockport.ac.uk
Email: elaine.henry@stockport.ac.uk
Courses Offered: Cert.TESOL

Stoke-on-Trent College

EFL Section, Language Department, Cauldon Campus
Stoke Road, Stoke-on-Trent ST4 2DG

Tel: 01782 208208 ext 3269
Fax: 01782 603646
Email: skinslsc@stokecoll.ac.uk
Website: www.stokecoll.ac.uk/
Courses offered: CELTA

Students International Ltd
158 Dalby Road, Melton Mowbray LE13 0BJ
Tel: 01664 481997
Fax: 01664 563332
Email: studentsint@cs.com
Courses Offered: Cert.TESOL

Studio School of English
6 Salisbury Villas, Station Road, Cambridge CB1 2JF
Tel: 01223 369701
Fax: 01223 314944
Email: info@studiocambridge.co.uk
Website: www.studiocambridge.co.uk
Courses offered: CELTA

Sutton College of Liberal Arts
St Nicholas Way, Sutton SM1 1EA
Tel: 0208 770 6902
Fax: 0208 770 6933
Website: www.scola.ac.uk
Email: info@scola.ac.uk
Courses Offered: Cert.TESOL

Sussex Downs College
International Student Centre, Grove House, Cross Levels Way, Eastbourne BN21 2UF
Tel: 01323 637240
Fax: 01323 637228
Email: info@sussexdowns.ac.uk
Website: www.ecat.ac.uk
Courses offered: CELTA, Cert.TESOL

Swindon College
Regent Circus, Swindon, SN1 1PT
Tel: 01793 491591
Fax: 01793 641794
Email: RussHawton@swindon-college.ac.uk
Website: www.swindon-college.ac.uk
Courses offered: CELTA

TEFL Centre
The Queen's University Of Belfast, College Park, Belfast BT7 1NN, Northern Ireland.
Tel: 01238 335374.
Fax: 01238 335379.
Courses Offered: CELTA

Thanet College
EFL Section, Thanet College , Ramsgate Road Broadstairs, CT10 1PN
Tel: 01843 605040 x 5568
Fax: 01843 605013
Email: efl@thanet.ac.uk
Website: www.thanet.ac.uk
Courses Offered: Cert.TESOL

Torbay Language Centre
Conway Road, Paignton TQ4 5LH
Tel: 01803 550930
Fax: 01803 559606
Website: www.LALschool.org/torbay
Courses offered: CELTA

Tower Hamlets College
Poplar Centre, Poplar High Street, London E14 0AF
Tel: 0207 510 7660
Fax: 0207 538 9153
Website: www.tower.ac.uk
Courses offered: CELTA

Universal Language Services
43 - 45 Cambridge Gardens, Hastings TN34 1EN
Tel: 01424 438025
Fax: 01424 438050
Website: www.unversallanguageservices.com
Email: enquiries@universallanguageservices.com
Courses Offered: Cert.TESOL

Universal Language Training
Woking College, Rydens Way, Woking GU22 9DL
Tel: 01483 770911
Fax: 01483 770848
Website: www.universal-language.co.uk
Email: enquiry@universal-language.co.uk
Courses Offered: Cert.TESOL

University of Bath
English Language Centre, Claverton Down, Bath BA2 7AY
Tel: 01225 323139
Fax: 01225 323135
Email: mlssfw@bath.ac.uk
Website: www.bath.ac.uk/elc/delta.htm
Courses offered: CELTA

University of Bristol
Language Centre, 30/32 Tyndall's Park Road, Bristol BS8 1PY
Tel: 0117 974 1311
Fax: 0117 974 1377
Email: V.Fernandes@bris.ac.uk

Website: www.bris.ac.uk/Depts/LangCent
Courses offered: CELTA

University College Chichester
Centre for International Education, The Dome, Upper Bognor Road, Bognor Regis PO21 1HR
Website: www.ucc.ac.uk
Email: r.kiely@ucc.ac.uk
Tel: 01243 816271
Fax: 01243 816272
Courses Offered: Cert.TESOL

University of Durham
The Language Centre, Elvet Riverside, New Elvet Durham DH1 3JT
Tel: 0191 374 3716
Fax: 0191 374 7790
Email: CELTA.training@durham.ac.uk
Website: www.durham.ac.uk/language.centre
Courses offered: CELTA

University of East Anglia (UEA)
Centre for English Language & British Studies University of East Anglia, Norwich NR4 7TJ
Tel: 01603 592976
Fax: 01603 250200
Email: s.burge@uea.ac.uk
Courses offered: CELTA

University of Glasgow
EFL Unit, 52 Hillhead Street, Glasgow G12 8QB
Tel: 0141 330 4220
Fax: 0141 330 3381
Email: C.Irvine@efl.arts.gla.ac.uk
Website: www.efl.arts.gla.ac.uk
Courses offered: CELTA

University Of Liverpool
Department of English Modern Languages Building Chatham Street, Liverpool, L69 7ZR
Tel: +44 151 794 6737
Fax: +44 151 794 2739
Email: cnewton@liverpool.ac.uk
Website: www.liv.ac.uk/english/elu.html
Courses offered: CELTA

University of Paisley
Languages Division, Business School, University of Paisley, High Street, Paisley PA1 2BE
Tel: 0141 848 3381
Fax: 0141 848 3618
Email: annemarie.bradley@paisley.ac.uk
Courses offered: CELTA

University of Portsmouth
School of Languages and Area Studies, Park Building, King Henry 1 Street, Portsmouth, PO1 2DZ
Tel: 023 9284 8484
Fax: 023 9284 6040
Website: www.port.ac.uk
Courses Offered: Cert.TESOL

University of St Andrews
English Language Teaching Centre, Butts Wynd, St Andrews KY16 9AL
Tel: 01334 462255
Fax: 01334 462270
Website: www.st-andrews.ac.uk
Courses Offered: Cert.TESOL

University of Sussex Language Institute
Falmer, Brighton BN1 9QN
Tel: 01273 678006 X 2051
Fax: 01273 678476
Website: www.sussex.ac.uk
Email: a.loske@sussex.ac.uk
Courses Offered: Cert.TESOL

University of Wales, Aberystwyth
Language and Learning Centre, Llandinam Building, Penglais Campus, Aberystwyth SY23 3DB
Tel: 01970 622545
Fax: 01970 622546
Website: www.aber.ac.uk
Email: jge@aber.ac.uk
Courses Offered: Cert.TESOL

University of Wales College
Allt-yr-yn Campus. PO Box 180, Newport NP20 5XR, Wales
Tel: 01633 432379
Fax: 01633 432443
Courses Offered: CELTA
Course Length: 4 weeks

University of Westminster
School of Languages, 309 Regent Street, London W1B 2UB
Tel: 0207 911 5000
Fax: 0207 911 5106
Email: efl@wmin.ac.uk
Website: www.wmin.ac.uk
Courses offered: CELTA

University of the West of England
Faculty of Languages & European Study, Frenchay Campus Coldharbour Lane, Bristol BS16 1QY
Tel: 0117 965 6261

Fax: 0117 344 2820
Website: www.uwe.ac.uk
Email: george.mann@uwe.ac.uk
Courses Offered: Cert.TESOL

University of Wolverhampton
School of Humanities, Languages & Social Sciences,
Stafford Street, Wolverhampton WV1 1SB
Tel: 01902 322552
Fax: 01902 322739
Website: www.wlv.ac.uk
Email: efl@wlv.ac.uk
Courses Offered: Cert.TESOL

Uxbridge College
Park Road, Uxbridge UB8 1NQ
Tel: 01895 853414
Fax: 01895 853377
Email: pmccann@uxbridge.ac.uk
Website: www.uxbridge.ac.uk
Courses offered: CELTA

Waltham Forest College
Forest Road, London E17 4JB
Tel: 0208 501 8178
Fax: 0208 501 8001
Email: lawlor@waltham.ac.uk
Website: www.waltham.ac.uk
Courses offered: CELTA

Warwickshire College
Thornbank Centre, Warwick New Road, Leamington
Spa CV32 5JE
Tel: 01926 318 165
Fax: 01926 427 317
Email: bbuxton@warkscol.ac.uk
Website: www.warkscol.ac.uk
Courses offered: CELTA

West Cheshire College
International Study Centre, Eaton Road, Handbridge
Chester CH4 7ER
Tel: 01244 670568
Fax: 01244 670611
Email: c.weaver@west-cheshire.ac.uk
Website: www.west-cheshire.ac.uk
Courses offered: CELTA

West Kent College
Brook Street, Tonbridge, Kent TN9 2PW
Tel: 01732 358101
Fax: 01732 771415
Email: judy@herbert40.freeserve.co.uk
Courses offered: CELTA

Westminster Kingsway College
Castle Lane, London SW1E 6DR
Tel: 0207 963 8515
Fax: 0207 233 8509
Email: annecandan@westking.ac.uk
Courses offered: CELTA

Wigan and Leigh College
PO Box 53, Parsons Walk, Wigan WN1 1RS
Tel: 01942 761563
Fax: 01942 761572
Website: www.wigan-leigh.ac.uk
Courses offered: CELTA

Windsor Schools TEFL
21 Osborne Road, Windsor SL4 1RU
Website: www.windsorschools.co.uk
Email: info@windsorschools.co.uk
Tel: 01753 858995
Fax: 01753 831726
Courses Offered: Cert.TESOL

Wirral Metropolitan College
Conway Park Campus, Europa Boulevard, Birkenhead,
CH41 4NT
Tel: 0151 551 7088
Fax: 0151 551 7001
Email: elu@wmc.ac.uk
Courses Offered: Cert.TESOL

York College
Tadcaster Road, York YO24 1UA
Tel: 01904 770 343
Fax: 01904 770 363
Email: dknowles@yorkcollege.ac.uk
Website: www.yorkcollege.com
Courses offered: CELTA

UNITED STATES OF AMERICA (+1)

American Language and Teaching Academy
English Dept., Columbia Union College, 7600 Flower
Avenue, Takoma Park, MD 20912
Tel: 301 891 4059
Fax: 301 891 4060
Email: gocelta@aol.com
Courses offered: CELTA

American University
Department of Language and Foreign Studies, 4400
Massachusetts Avenue NW, Washington DC
20016-8045.
Tel: (202) 885 2582.

Fax: (202) 885 1076.
Email: tesol@american.edu
Courses Offered: TESOL Certificate.
Start dates: Year round including summer institute.

Approach Intl. Students center
196 Harvard Ave., Suite 6, Boston, MA 02134.
Tel: (617) 787 5401
Fax: (617) 787 4926
Courses Offered: ESL Teaching Certificate Program
Course Length: 250 hours Short Program; 125 Long Program

Boston Language Institute
648 Beacon Street, Boston, MA 02215
Tel: (877) 998 3500
Fax: (617) 262 3595
Website: www.teflcertificate.com
Email: info@teflcertificate.com
Courses Offered: TEFL Certificate
Course Length: FT 4 weeks; PT 12 weeks.
Start dates: FT Monthly throughout the year; PT January, April, July, September

California State University
800 N. State College Blvd., Fullerton, CA 92831
Tel: (714) 278 2300
Fax: (714) 278 7549
Courses Offered: TESOL Certificate

College of Lake County
19351 W Washington Street, Greyslake, Illinois 60030
Tel: 847 543 2565
Fax: 847 543 3565
Email: jacath@clcillinois.edu
Website: http://clconline.clcillinois.edu/celta/
Courses offered: CELTA

College of Notre Dame
1500 Ralston Avenue, Belmont, CA 94002-1997
Tel: (650) 508 3593
Fax: (650) 508 3736
Email: mgiusti@cnd.edu
Courses Offered: TESL / TEFL
Course Length: 90 days.
Start dates: May, September.

Colorado School of English
1325 S. Colorado Blvd., Suite 101, Denver, CO 80222
Tel: (303) 758 3123
Fax: (303) 758 3002
Courses Offered: TESL/TEFL Certificate
Course Length: FT 12 weeks; PT 36 weeks.
Start dates: June.

Columbia University
American Language Program, 504 Lewisohn Hall, M.C. 4113, 2970, Broadway, New York, NY 10027-6902
Tel: (212) 854 3584
Fax: (212) 932-7651
Courses Offered: Postbaccalaureate TESOL Certificate.
Course Length: 8 weeks.
Admission requirements: BA or equivalent.

Cy-Fair College
9191 Barker Cypress Road, Cypress, Texas 77433
Tel: 832 422 1005
Fax: 281 290 5283
Email: Jeffrey.D.Mohamed@nhmccd.edu
Website: www.cy-faircollege.com
Courses offered: CELTA

Denver Bridge Linguatec Ltd
915 S Colorado Boulevard, Denver, Colorado
Tel: 1800 724 4210
Fax: 303 777 7246
Email: tefl@bridgelinguatec.com
Website: www.bridgelinguatec.com
Courses offered: CELTA

Eastern Michigan University
Ypsilanti, MI 48197
Tel: (734) 487-4081
Fax: (313) 487-0338
Courses Offered: (1) Graduate Certificate in TESL; (2) K-12 ESL Certificate/Endorsement.
Admission requirements: First degree + at least one year's college study of a foreign language.

Embassy CES
6th Floor, 330 Seventh Avenue (at 29th Street) New York, NY 10001
Tel: 212 629 7300
Fax: 212 736 7950
Email: lpainter@studygroupintl.com
Website: www.embassyces.com
Courses offered: CELTA

Embassy CES
301 East Las Olas Boulevard, Fort Lauderdale, FL 33301
Tel: (954) 522 8810
Fax: (954) 522 6955
Website: www.embassyces.com
Courses Offered: CELTA

Hamline University
Graduate School of Education, 1526 Hewitt Avenue, St. Paul, MN 55104
Tel: (800) 888 2182 / (651) 523 2900
Fax: (651) 523 2489
Email: gradprog@gw.hamline.edu
Courses Offered: TEFL Certificate

Intercultural Communications College
1601 Kapiolani Blvd. Suite 1000, Honolulu HI 96814
Tel: 808 946 2445
Fax: 808 946 2231
Email: jweaver@icchawaii.edu
Website: www.icchawaii.edu
Courses offered: CELTA

International House
2725 Congress Street, Suite 2M, San Diego, CA 92110
Tel: 619 299 2339
Fax: 619 299 0235
Email: info@ih-sandiego.com
Website: www.ih-usa.com
Courses offered: CELTA

International House Portland
200 SW Market Street, Suite 111, Portland, OR 97201
Tel: 503 224 1960
Fax: 503 224 2041
Email: teachertraining@ih-portland.com
Website: www.ih-usa.com
Courses offered: CELTA

International House
49 Powell Street, Suite 200, 2nd Floor, San Francisco, CA 94102
Tel: 415 989 4473
Fax: 415 989 4440
Email: cheyns@ih-sanfrancisco.com
Website: www.ih-usa.com
Courses offered: CELTA

International House
1148 4th Street, Santa Monica, CA 90401
Tel: 310 394 8618
Email: ihsminfo@aol.com
Website: www.ih-usa.com
Courses offered: CELTA

Lado International College
2233 Wisconsin Avenue NW, Washington DC 20007
Tel: (202) 333 4222
Fax: (202) 337 1118
Courses Offered: Lado Teaching Certificate.

Language Exchange International
Teacher Training Department, 2715 East Oakland Park Blvd., 3rd floor, Fort Lauderdale, FL 33306
Tel: (954) 568 7998
Fax: (954) 568 9496
Website: www.tefltraining.com
Email: tefltraining@hotmail.com
Courses Offered: CELTA

Midwest Teacher Training Program
19 N. Pinckney Street, Madison, WI 53703
Tel: (608) 257 4300
Fax: (608) 257 4346
Email: information@wesli.com
Courses Offered: TEFL Certificate

Mississippi State University
Department of English, P.O. Box 5325. Mississippi State, MS 39762
Tel: (662) 325 2383
Courses Offered: TESOL Certificate.
Course Length: PT 2 years.

New World Teachers
605 Market Street, Suite 800, San Francisco, CA 94105
Tel: (800) 644 5424
Fax: (415) 546 4196
Courses Offered: TEFL Certificate.
Course Length: 4 weeks.

North Harris College, Texas
2700 W.W. Thorne Drive, Houston, Texas 77073
Tel: 281 618 5604
Fax: 281 618 5633
Email: albarea@nhmccd.edu
Website: esl.nhmccd.edu
Courses offered: CELTA

St. Giles Language Teaching Center
One Hallidie Plaza (Suite 350), San Francisco, CA 94102
Tel: 415 788 3552
Fax: 415 788 1923
Email: info@stgiles-usa.com
Website: www.stgiles-usa.com
Courses offered: CELTA
Course Length: 4 weeks.

St. Michael's School of Int. Studies
One Winooski Park, Colchester, VT 05439
Tel: (802) 654 2300
Fax: (802) 654 2595
Website: www.smcvt.edu/sis/

Email: sis@smcvt.edu
Courses Offered: Summer Diploma programme in TESL / TEFL.

School for International Training
Kipling Road, P.O. Box 676, Brattleboro, VT 05302-0676
Tel: (802) 258 3350
Fax: (802) 258 3316
Email: tesolcert@sit.edu
Website: www.sit.ed/tesolcert
Courses Offered: TESOL Certificate.
Course Length: 3 weeks.

School of Teaching ESL
2601 NW 56th Street, Seattle, WA 98107
Tel: (206) 781-8607
Fax: (206) 781-8922
Website: www.seattleu.edu/soe/stesl
Courses Offered: (1) Initial; (2) Advanced - Certificate in Teaching English as a Second or Foreign Language.
Course Length: (1) 4 weeks; (2) 3 weeks.
Admission requirements: BA although waivers are possible.

Transworld Schools
701 Sutter Street, 2nd Floor, San Francisco, CA 94109
Tel: (415) 928 2835
Fax: (415) 928 0261
Website: www.transworldschools.com
Courses Offered: Certificate in Teaching English as a Foreign Language (CTEFL).
Start dates: Courses are held throughout the year.

University of California, Berkeley
1995 University Avenue, Berkeley, CA 94720
Tel: (510) 642-1173
Fax: (510) 643-8683
Email: tefl@unx.berkeley.edu
Course Offered: (1) TESOL Certificate (Evening Program); (2) TEFL Certificate.
Admission requirements: BA. or equiv.

University of California, Irvine
PO Box 6050, Irvine, CA 92716-6050
Tel: (949) 824-7945
Fax: (949) 824-2090
Website: www.unex.uci.edu/certificates/tesl.html
Email: unex-educate@uci.edu
Courses Offered: (1), (2) TEFL Certificate; (3) TESL Certificate.
Course Length: (1) 4 weeks; (2) 16 weeks; (3) 5 months.

University of California, LA
10995 Le Conte Avenue, Los Angeles, CA 90024-2883
Tel: (310) 206-9734
Fax: (310) 206-5123
Courses Offered: (1) TEFL Certificate; (2) TESOL Certificate.

University of California, Riverside
1200 University Avenue, Riverside, CA 92507
Tel: (909) 787 4346
Fax: (909) 787 5796
Courses Offered: (1) TEFL Certificate; (2) TESOL Certificate.

West Chester University
516 Main Hall, West Chester, PA 19383
Tel: (610) 436-2916
Email: cmicheau@wcupa.edu
Courses Offered: Certificate of Preparation in ESL Teaching. Course

Worldwide Teachers
Worldwide Teachers Development Institute, 264 Beacon Street, Boston, MA 02116
Tel: (617) 262 5722
Fax: (617) 262 0308
Website: www.bostontefl.com
Email: admissions@bostontefl
Courses Offered: Certificate in Teaching English as a Foreign Language (CTEFL).

URUGUAY (+598)

Dickens Institute
21 De Setiembre 2744, Montevideo, 11300
Website: www.dickens.edu.uy
Email: dickens@dickens.edu.uy
Tel: 2 711 2103
Fax: 2 711 3487
Courses Offered: Cert.TESOL

Queen Victoria Institute
Libertad 2791, Montevideo, CP 11300
Tel: 2 708 2577
Fax: 2 708 0943
Email: qvi@adinet.com.uy
Website: www.queenvictoria.com.uy
Courses offered CELTYL

VIETNAM (+84)

Language Link Vietnam
Third Floor, 36 Cat Linh Street, Hanoi
Tel: 4 733 8402
Fax: 4 733 8429
Email: celta@dtt.languagelink.edu.vn
Website: www.languagelink.edu.vn
Courses offered: CELTA

RMIT International University Vietnam
21 Pham Ngoc Thach, District 3, Ho Chi Minh City
Tel: 8 822 4992
Fax: 8 822 5039
Email: peter-bainbridge@rmit.edu.vn
Website: www.rmit.edu.vn
Courses offered: CELTA

Certificates by Distance Learning

Distance learning is an alternative option for trainee teachers and uses the Internet, post and telephone. These institutions offer a range of courses to gain a certificate before you start teaching (pre-experience). See also p238 for post-experience Diplomas.

When selecting a distance-learning course, ask if the school provides live teacher sessions (either using the net or in a 'real' location) where you can meet to discuss topics with the teacher. Note: all School telephone/fax numbers show the full international dialling code.

Canada

Worldport ESL
480 University Avenue, West Windsor, Ontario N9A 5P8
Tel: +1 (519) 977 7100
Fax: +1 (519) 977 7677
Email: teachesl@worldportesl.com
Course Length: 12 weeks.
Courses Offered: TESL Certificate.

Ireland

Bluefeather School of Languages
35 Montpelier Parade, Monkstown, Dublin, Ireland
Tel: +353 1 280 6288
Email: info@bluefeather.ie
Website: www.bluefeather.ie
Courses Offered: TEFL Certificate.

Japan

The Distance Learning Center
1-4-3-202 Maruyamadai Wako-shi, Saitama 351-01
Tel: +82 48 4633077
Email: info@distance-learning.org
Courses Offered: TEFL Certificate.
Course Length: 3 months' maximum.

UK

Aston University
Aston Triangle, Birmingham B4 7ET
Tel: 0121 359 3611
Fax: 0121 359 6350
Courses Offered: Advanced Certificate in TESOL

The English Centre
Standbrook House, Suite 3C, 2-5 Old Bond Street, London W1X 3TB, United Kingdom
Tel: +44 1925 470903
Email: info@englishlanguagecentre.com
Courses Offered: Certificate in TEFL / TESL

English Teaching College
PO Box 7426, Glasgow G42 9WB
Tel: +44 (0)141 583 9514
Email: admin@englishteachingcollege.com
Website: www.englishteachingcollege.com
Courses offered: range of courses

English Training Centre
Box 104, The University of Birmingham, Edgbaston Park Road , Birmingham B15 2TU
Fax: +44 (0) 121 449 2221
Email: info@englishtc.co.uk
Website: www.englishtc.co.uk
Courses Offered: Certificate in TEFL

Eurolink Teacher Training
3, Abbeydale Road South, Millhouse, Sheffield S7 2QL
Tel: +44 (0)114 262 1522
Email: info@eurolinkcourses.co.uk
Website: www.eurolinkcourses.co.uk
Courses offered: range of certificates and programmes

Global English
71 Parkway, Exeter, Devon EX2 9NB
Tel: +44 (0)1392 664378
Email: info@global-english.com
Website: www.global-english.com
Courses offered: TEFL certificate and optional business English course

INTESOL
19 Lower Oakfield, Pitlochry PH16 5DS, Scotland UK
Tel/Fax: +44 (0)1796 474199
Email: Lynda@INTESOL.freeserve.co.uk
Website: www.intesoltraining.com
Courses Offered: Certificate in TESOL.

i-to-i
9 Blenheim Terrace, Leeds
Tel: +44 (0)870 333 2332
Email: info@i-to-i.com
Website: www.i-to-i.com
Courses Offered: TEFL course

Language 2 Associates
25 Woodway Crescent, Harrow, Middx HA1 2NH
Tel: +44 (0)20 8907 2618
Email: langtwo@beeb.net
Courses offered: range of TEFL courses

London Teacher Training
140 Ashley Crescent, London SW11 5QZ
Tel: +44 (0)1323 488357
Fax: +44 (0)1323 483809
Email: lttc@teachenglish.co.uk
Website: www.teachenglish.co.uk
Courses Offered: range of awards

London TEFL Bureau
Suite 401, 302 Regent Street, London W1R 6HH
Tel: +44 (0)20 7580 4242
Courses offered: TEFL certificate, also English for young learners and business English

Languages Training & Development
116 Corn Street, Witney, Oxfordshire OX28 6BU
Tel: +44 (0)1993 894710
Fax: +44 (0)1993 706066

Email: info@ltdoxford.com
Website: www.ltdoxford.com
Courses offered: certificate in teaching business English

National Extension College
The Michael Young Centre, Purbeck Road, Cambridge CB2 2HN
Tel: +44 (0)1223 400200
Fax: +44 (0)1223 400325
Email: info@nec.ac.uk
Courses Offered: introductory course

Net Learn
28 Appledore Ave, Ruislip, Middx HA4 0UU
Tel: +44 (0)20 8845 5555
Email: info@colte.com
Website: www.netlearnlanguages.com
Courses offered: certificate in TEFL

Open Learning International
72 Pentyla Baglan Road, Port Talbot SA12 8AD, Wales, United Kingdom
Email. Train@olionline.com
Courses Offered: OCR (Oxford, Cambridge, RSA) Certificate in Teaching Foreign Languages to Adults

Robaco
8 Nesburn Road, Barnes, Wearside SR4 7LR
Tel: +44 (0)7712 579775
Email: admin@robaco.net
Website: www.robaco.net
Courses offered: TEFL certificate

Sheffield Hallam University
Collegiate Crescent Campus, Sheffield S1 1WB
Tel: 0114 225 2240
Website: www.shu.ac.uk/tesol
Courses offered: MA / Certificate TESOL

USA

ICAL
Website: www.teacher-training.net
Email: admin@teacher-training.net
Courses Offered: TEFL Certificate.

New York School of English Language Studies
68 Fifth Avenue, New York, NY 10011
Tel: +1 (212) 229-5372
Email: kimbrouv@newschool.edu
Courses Offered: ELT Certificate.

University Degree Courses

Although qualifications in TEFL/TESL and TESOL are usually offered at the postgraduate level, there are a few programmes which enable undergraduate students to study for a Bachelor's degree in this area. Contact individual universities for information regarding admission requirements. For Diploma and post-experience university courses, see the chapter on career development, p238.

NEW ZEALAND (+64)

Victoria University, Wellington
PO Box 600, Wellington 6001, New Zealand
Tel: 4 472 1000
Fax: 4 499 4601
Courses Offered: B.A. Linguistics.

UK (+44)

Coventry University
Priory Street, Coventry CV1 5FB
Tel: 024 7688 7688
Website: www.coventry.ac.u
Courses Offered: English and TEFL BA (Hons)

De Montfort University
The Gateway, Leicester, LE1 9BH
Tel: (0116) 255 1551
Website: www.dmu.ac.uk
Courses Offered: Education Studies and TEFL

Northumbria University
Ellison Place, Newcastle upon Tyne, NE1 8ST
Tel: 0191 238 6002
Website: www.northumbria.ac.uk
Courses Offered: TESOL BA

Nottingham Trent University
Burton Street, Nottingham NG1 4BU
Tel: 0115 941 8418
Website: www.ntu.ac.uk
Courses offered: English and TESOL BA (Hons)

University of Wales Swansea
Singleton Park, Swansea, SA2 8PP
Tel: 01792 205678
Website: www.swan.ac.uk
Courses Offered: English and TEFL BA

University of Sunderland
Edinburgh Building, City Campus, Chester Road, Sunderland SR1 3SD.
Tel: 0191 515 3154
Website: www.sunderland.ac.uk
Courses Offered: English and TESOL BA

University of Middlesex
North London Business Park, Oakleigh Road South, London N11 1QS
Tel: 020 8411 5000
Website: www.mdx.ac.uk
Courses Offered: English and TEFL BA

University of Manchester
Department of Linguistics, Oxford Road, Manchester M13 9PL, UK

Tel: 0161 275 3187
Courses Offered: B.A. Linguistics; B.A. English Language.

University of Sterling
centre for English Language Teaching, Stirling FK9 4LA, Scotland UK
Courses Offered: B.A. ELT; B.A. EFL (both for non-native speakers).

University of Sussex
Falmer, Brighton BN1 9QH, UK
Tel: 01273 678195
Fax: 01273 671320.
Courses Offered: B.A. Linguistics.

Wolverhampton University
Wulfruna St., Wolverhampton WV1 1SB, UK
Tel: 01902 322222
Course Length: 3 years.
Courses Offered: B.A. TESOL.

USA & CANADA (+1)

Brigham Young University, UT
Dept. of Linguistics, 2129 JKHB, Provo, UT 84602-6278
Tel: (801) 378-4789
Course Length: 4/5 semesters.
Start Dates: Fall, Winter.
Courses Offered: B.A. Linguistics.

Brigham Young University, HI
Hawaii Campus, P.O. Box 1940, Laie, HI 96762.
Tel: (808) 293 3614
Fax: (808) 293 3448
Courses Offered: B.A. TESOL.

Cal. State, Northridge
Linguistics Program, 18111 Nordhoff St., Northridge, CA 91330-8306
Course Length: 8 semesters.
Start Dates: Any semester.
Courses Offered: B.A. Linguistics.

Caroll College
161 N. Benton Ave., Helena, MT 59625
Courses Offered: BA TESOL.
Course Length: 8 semesters.
Start Dates: Any semester.

Central Washington University
400 E. 8th Ave., Ellensburg, WA 98926-7562.

Course Length: 4/5 quarters.
Start Dates: Any quarter.
Courses Offered: B.Ed. TESOL.

Eastern Kentucky University
Case Annex 270-1340, Richmond, KY 40475
Course Length: 8 semesters.
Start Dates: Any semester.
Course Offered: B.A. English with TESL Endorsement.

Eastern Mennonite University
1200 Park Road, Harrisonburg, VA 22802–2462
Tel: (540) 432 4000
Fax: (540) 432 4444
Start Dates: Any semester.
Courses Offered: Minor in TESL.

Iowa State University
300 Pearson Hall, Ames, IA 50011.
Tel: (515) 294 4555
Fax: (515) 294 9914
Courses Offered: Interdisciplinary Linguistics Program; K-12 ESL Teaching Endorsement.

US International University
10455 Pomerado Road, San Diego, CA 92131
Tel: (858) 635 4772
Fax: (858) 635 4739
Courses Offered: B.A. TESOL.

University of Florida
Gainesville, FL 32611
Tel: (352) 392 3261
Courses Offered: B.A. in Linguistics with Minor in TESOL.

University of Rochester
Dept. of Linguistics, 503 Lattimore Hall, P.O. Box 270096, Rochester, NY 14627-0096.
Tel: (716) 275 8053
Courses Offered: B.A. Linguistics.

University of Texas, Austin
Dept. of Linguistics, Austin TX 78712-1196.
Tel: (512) 471 1701
Courses Offered: B.A. Linguistics.

University of Calgary
2500 University Drive NW, Calgary, Alberta, T2N 1N4, Canada.
Tel: (403) 220 5110
Courses Offered: B.A. Linguistics.

Finding a Job

This chapter gives you leads and ideas on how best to find a job as an English language teacher. The main employers are ELT/ESL schools around the world, but there are also jobs in large international companies, and other specialist organisations. You can find jobs on our website, apply directly to a school or through a recruitment agency, use one of the hundreds of websites, or look for adverts in the trade newspapers and journals.

One of the great advantages of being an English language teacher is that you can travel the world and still get a job; almost every country has a requirement for English language teachers – some need teachers specialising in a particular accent (British or American), others have a focus on a particular age-range. However, once you have either a recognised qualification (see previous chapter) or basic experience, you can travel and find work around the world. This means that any ELT job section must cover travel and working practice around the world (see the next chapter) as well as covering agencies that can get you a job in a particular country. Over the next few pages, you will see how to find a job, how to get through an interview, how to get a job in a different country and how to prepare for the culture shock of travelling and teaching in a new environment.

How Do I Find A Job?

Probably the easiest way to find a job is to use the resources we provide! Either contact the schools and teacher recruitment agencies listed in this book or visit our sister magazine websites (www.eslmag.com for American English teachers and www.etprofessional.com for international English language teachers) and view 100s of job vacancies online.

To apply directly to a school, use the information listed in the country sections of this guide – you'll find this starting on page 86. If you want to teach English abroad as a volunteer, turn to p75 for more information. When it comes to preparing your CV, be sure to stress any practical teaching you may have as well as any qualifications you have earned.

What Should I Do When I Receive A Job Offer?

Ask your prospective employer if you can contact teachers who are working at the school for references. If the school is reputable, the owner or principal should have no problems with this

request. If no other native-speaking teachers are currently employed at the school ask to speak to former employees. If this request does cause a problem, then you should be wary about accepting a job offer from this school. Another point to remember is that some teachers do criticize schools they have worked for even if the problems were mostly of their own making. Lazy and bad teachers do exist – even if they speak the same language as you do! Use common sense in a situation where you are confronted with conflicting stories from schools and teachers. After all, you're going to have to rely on your own judgement when you are living and working in a new environment.

What If A Dispute Arises?

No single aspect of teaching EFL overseas causes more heartache, grief, and anguish than disputes between teachers and employers arising from contractual problems. Historically, certain countries, such as South Korea, were notorious for such disputes although there have been moves to stop these unpleasant episodes from arising. A few words of advice: don't be surprised if you find yourself caught in a dispute over a matter like wages, hours or accommodation. It has happened to thousands of EFL teachers before you and you won't be the last. Try to make sure you have a written contract and insist that it is translated into English. In many countries, the English language contract will not be valid so try to find a third party who knows both the language of your employer and English who can check that both contracts say the same thing.

If a dispute arises, try to be civil and courteous with your employer. Again, if you can find a third party to mediate the dispute this may help diffuse the situation. Some experienced teachers have reported that yelling at an employer has brought about the desired results but this is not advisable unless you are confident you can find a job if you get fired! If you find that your employer is consistently underpaying you or is increasing your hours without giving you money then start looking for another job. Unless you are in a remote region, there will probably be other language schools that will welcome your experience.

Recruitment Agencies and International School Groups

There are plenty of commercial recruitment agencies specialising in the English language market – working for a school to help find teachers or helping a teacher find a job. The agencies are normally paid by the employer (the school), though make sure that you check before you sign up! Agencies normally cover a particular area or country – and will help you put together a good CV, send you new job opportunities and even advice on relocating, accommodation and visas.

Almost all the jobs for ELT or ESL teachers are with English language schools. The majority of all schools are run on an individual basis, with the director of studies also the person who interviews and appoints new teachers. But there are some major chains of schools who have their own internal recruitment agencies who can help you find a job within the schools in their group. Once you have a job in the group, the internal job-agency often works to help find a job in another school within the group or in a different country.

The biggest ELT employer in the world is the British Council, which has its own recruitment service – see page 65 for more details on the British Council.

As a good starting point, try these commercial agencies and major international school groups:

Anglo Pacific
Suite 32, Nevilles Court, Dollis Hill Lane, London
NW2 6HG
Tel: +44 (0)20 8452 7836
Agency that specializes in recruitment in SE Asia

Avalon House
8 Denmark Street, London WC2H 8LS
Tel: +44 (0)20 7279 1998
Email: info@avalonschool.co.uk
Web: www.avalonschool.co.uk
Recruitment for its schools in China, France, Spain,
Poland, UK

Bell Educational Trust
Overseas Department, Hillscross, Red Cross Lane,
Cambridge, CB2 2QX
Tel: +44 (0)1223 246644
Fax: +44 (0)1223 414080
Email: info.overseas@bell-schools.ac.uk
Web: www.bell-schools.ac.uk
Major group that has schools around the world; most
schools recruit locally, but this office can provide
contact information

Benedict Schools
3 Place Chauderon, PO Box 270, 1000 Lausanne 9,
Switzerland
Tel: +21 323 6655
Fax: +21 323 6777
Email: info@benedict-schools.com
Web: www.benedict-schools.com
Major group with over 80 schools (in Europe, Africa
and America); most schools recruit locally, but this
office can provide contact information

Berlitz
Lincoln House, 296-302 High Holborn, London
WC1V 7JH
Tel: +44 (0)20 7915 0909
Fax: +44 (0)20 7915 0222
Web: www.berlitz.com
Major group that has over 400 centres around the
world; teachers are trained in the Berlitz way of
teaching

Billington Recruitment
1 Mariners Close, St James Court, Victoria Dock,
Kingston upon Hull, HU9 1QE
Email: bill1312@hotmail.com
Agency that covers Europe

British Council
Education and Training Group, 10 Spring Gardens,
London SW1A 2BN
Tel: +44 (0)20 7389 4596
Fax: +44 (0)20 7389 4594
Email: assistants@britishcouncil.org
Web: www.languageassistant.co.uk
Provides language assistants to schools around the
world. (See section on British Council on next page)

CG Associates
83 Clarence Mews, London
Tel: +44 (0)7802 211542
Email: info@christopherg.co.uk
Agency offering worldwide coverage.

CIEE
52 Poland Street, London W1F 7AB
Tel: +44 (0)20 7478 2020
Fax: +44 (0)20 7734 7322
Web: www.councilexchanges.org.uk
Looks after the JET (Japan Exchange Teaching)
programme as well as Teach in China and Teach in
Thailand programmes

EF - English First
Teacher Recruitment, 36-38 St Aubyns, Hove, East
Sussex, BN3 2TD
Tel: +44 (0)1273 201431
Fax: +44 (0)1273 746742
Email: recruitment.uk@englishfirst.com
Web: www.englishfirst.com
Major group that has schools around the world

ELS Language Centers
400 Alexander Park, Princeton, NJ 08540
Tel: +1 609 750 3512
Fax: +1 609 750 3596
Email: info@els.com
Web: www.els.com
Major group that works with Berlitz for its language
centers – however its 40-plus schools still recruit
through this central address

ERC Recruitment
New Tyning, Stone Allerton, Axbridge, BS26 2NJ
Tel: +44 (0)1934 713892
Email: info@erc-recruitment.co.uk
Web: www.erc-recruitment.co.uk
Agency offering worldwide coverage

GEOS English Academy
Compton Park, Compton Park Road, Eastbourne,
BN21 1EH
Email: info@geos.com
Web: www.geos.com
Major group that has over 500 schools around the
world

GTCE
52 Loampit Hill, Lewisham, London SE13 7SW
Tel: +44 (0)20 8691 6569
Email: info@gtce.co.uk
Web: www.gtce.co.uk
Agency that concentrates on China

International House
106 Piccadilly, London W1V 7NL
Tel: +44 (0)20 7518 6970
Fax: +44 (0)20 7518 6971
Email: hr@ihlondon.co.uk
Web: www.ihworld.com
Major group that has over 120 schools around the
world

Linguarama
Personnel Department, 89 High Street, Alton,
Hampshire, GU34, 1LG
Tel: +44 (0)1420 80899
Fax: +44 (0)1420 80856
Email: personnel@linguarama.com
Web: www.linguarama.com
Major group that has schools around the world

Protocol Professional
Tel: +44 (0)115 911 1177
Email: recruitment@protocol-professional.co.uk
Web: www.protocol-professional.co.uk
Agency that specializes on the UK

Saxoncourt
124 New Bond Street, London W1S 1DX
Tel: +44 (0)20 7491 1911
Fax: +44 (0)20 7493 3657
Email: recruit@saxoncourt.com
Web: www.saxoncourt.com
Major group of schools and recruitment centre that
places over 500 teachers per year around the world

Sterling Recruitment
49 Sudbury Ave, Wembley, Middx, HA0 3AN
Tel: +44 (0)20 8903 4424
Fax: +44 (0)20 8903 3566
Recruitment Agency for jobs in London

Wall Street Institute
Paca de Catalunya 9, 4th Floor, 08002 Barcelona,
Spain
Tel: +93 306 33 00
Fax: +93 302 08 29
Web: www.wallstreetinstitute.com
Major chain of over 400 schools around the world.

The British Council

The British Council has over 60 language teaching centres, offices in over 100 countries and is the by far the biggest ELT employer in the world, with over 7500 staff (most of whom are involved in teaching). The Council is funded by the British Government, but works in a non-political way promoting British English and culture around the world.

For job-hunters, the British Council can help in two ways:

1. Each local office is a mine of information about local schools, job opportunities and conditions of work. Many offices have pre-printed information for prospective job-hunters and sometimes provide contacts to known schools in the country. For a list of local offices, see our directory on page 302 or visit www.britishcouncil.org

2. The British Council has over 60 teaching centres and it recruits around 300 teachers per year. For more information, contact Educational Enterprises, British Council, 10 Spring Gardens, London SW1A 2BN, Tel: +44 (0)20 7389 4931, Fax: +44 (0)20 7389 4140, Email: teacher.vacancies@britishcouncil.org

The British Council also publishes a wide range of leaflets and information packs about training to be an English language teacher and opportunities within the organisation. Either visit the information-packed website (www.britishcouncil.org) or contact its information centre: Bridgewater House, 58 Whitworth Street, Manchester M1 6BB, Tel: +44 (0)161 957 7755, Fax: +44 (0)161 957 7762

UK Summer Schools

The UK has a very strong summer-school industry (with several hundred schools working the season) that always has a need for qualified teachers. The summer schools cater for students who want to learn English over a summer holiday; these students can be either young learners or young adults – but, even with the current downturn in international travel, the summer schools are still very busy – as is their requirement for teachers.

The rates of pay for work in summer schools is often higher than usual. In the past, some summer schools have not offered very good quality teaching, but with the work of industry associations, particularly English UK (www.EnglishUK.com) - the newly-merged organisation previously known as ARELS (Association of Recognised English Language Schools) and BASELT (British Association of State English Language Teaching) - and the British Council (www.britishcouncil.org), the schools are being accredited and standards are now high.

With so many schools on their lists, it's impossible to fit all these into this book: the best way to search for a suitable school to approach for a job is to use a site such as English in Britain (www.EnglishInBritain.com) or the English UK (www.EnglishUK.com) websites – both have search features.

Jobs in the USA

In the USA, each state has its own requirements for teacher qualifications (read the requirements in the directory on p 224). The schools within a state must also be registered with their state education body – and each state, again, has its own requirements for schools operating in their area. To find a list of schools, the simplest route is to use the Internet. The next few pages include ESL job sites in the US. Alternatively, use the website directory for the individual states to search for schools in the state.

Jobs on the Internet

There are hundreds of websites specialising in the ELT/ESL job sector. Some simply provide advice, others offer help with interviews, others provide lists of jobs available in a particular region or country.

Starting Points

Try these sites for a varied flavour of what the Internet offers job-hunters – these are some of the main sites from each of the following sections.

British Council Vacancies
www.britishcouncil.org/vacancies/indexmain.html

English Teaching Professional
www.etprofessional.com

ESL Magazine
www.eslmag.com

International House Recruitment Services
www.ihworld.com/recruitment/index.asp

Peace Corps
www.peacecorps.gov

Saxoncourt
www.saxoncourt.com

The Times Educational Supplement
www.tesjobs.co.uk/homepage.asp

VSO (Voluntary Service Overseas)
www.vso.org.uk/volunteering/education_tefl.htm

Career Advice

Starting a Career in TESOL (tesol.org)
www.tesol.org/careers/counsel/

Teaching English Abroad
www.cal.org/ericcll/digest/snow0001.html

Best Bets for Teaching Abroad
www.uci.edu/~cie/iop/teaching.html

Creating a CV
www.onestopenglish.com/Jobs/

200 FREE Cover Letters For Job Hunters
www.careerlab.com/letters/

Finding a Job – all-in-one sites

BestPeople
www.bestpeople.co.uk

CareerCentral
www.careercentral.com

CareerMosaic UK
www.careermosaic-uk.co.uk

Gradunet-Virtual Careers Office
www.gradunet.co.uk

JobHunter
www.jobhunter.co.uk

Jobs Unlimited
www.jobsunlimited.co.uk

JobSearch
www.jobsearch.co.uk

JobSite UK
www.jobsite.co.uk

Monster
www.monster.co.uk

Reed Online
www.reed.co.uk

ELT-specific Jobs

All English Job
www.allenglishjob.com

Canadian Institute for Teaching Overseas (CITO)
www.nsis.com/~cito/CITO.html

Dave's ESL Café: Job centre
www.eslcafe.com/jobs/

Easter School Agency
www.easterschool.com

Edufind ELT Job Centre
www.jobs.edufind.com

EFLTeachingJobs.com
www.eflteachingjobs.com

English Club ESL Jobs Centre
http://jobs.englishclub.com

English Job Maze
www.englishjobmaze.com

English Teacher Recruitment: Greece
www.teach.english.freeservers.com

English Worldwide – Recruitment & Training
www.englishworldwide.com

English-International.com
www.english-international.com

Erudite Café Job centre
www.eruditecafe.net/job_centre1.php

ESL Career.com
www.eslcareer.com

ESLclassifieds.com
www.eslclassifieds.com/esljobsoffered.html

ESL Employment
www.eslemployment.com

ESL Job Search
www.esljobsearch.com

ESL Magazine
www.eslmag.com

ESL Resume Database
my.globalesl.net/

ESL Teachers Club
www.eslteachersclub.com

ESL WideWord Teach English
www.eslwideworld.com

ESLworldwide.com
www.ESLworldwide.com

ETNI – Advertising Teaching Positions in Israel
www.etni.org.il/anntchadver.htm

Foreignteacher.com
www.foreignteacher.com/currentjobs.htm

Global ESL Network
www.globalesl.net

Jobs Offered
www.englishclub.net/cgi-bin/jobs/jobs_o.pl

Russian School Placement
www.sv-agency.udm.ru/svfiles/school.htm

Saxoncourt & English Worldwide
www.saxoncourt.com

TeachAbroad.com
www.teachabroad.com

Teaching Abroad
www.teaching-abroad.co.uk

Teaching Abroad .net
www.teachingabroad.net

Teaching ESL at Kuwait University
www.iteslj.org/Articles/Martin-Kuwait

TEFL Jobs
www.tefljobs.net

TEFLnet
www.tefl.net/jobs/

TEFL Professional Network
www.tefl.com

University EFL/ESL Positions
www.ultimateenglish.com

Work Abroad ESL.com
www.workabroadesl.com

ELT Jobs in Asia

Collection of Teaching Positions in Taiwan
http://esltaiwan.20M.com

Ding Ding Dang Recruiting
www.dingdingdang.com

EFL in Asia
www.geocities.com/Tokyo/Flats/7947/eflasia.htm

English Teaching programme in Thailand
www.taiteach.com

EnglishWork.com
www.englishwork.com

ESL City
www.eslcityjobs.com

ESL House: China
www.eslhouseonline.com

HBS Consulting: Korea
www.hbscompany.com

International Avenue Consulting
www.iacc.com.tw

Japanese Jobs
www.japanesejobs.com/textonly/index.html

Jobs in Japan
www.eltnews.com/jobsinjapan.shtml

KOAM Academy: Korea
www.koam.org

O-Hayo Sensei: Japan
www.ohayosensei.com

Reena Recruiting Co. Ltd.
www.reena-recruit.com

Russell Recruiting
www.asiangateway.net

Taiwan Teacher
www.geocities.com/Athens/Delphi/1979/

Teach English in South Korea
www.teachenglish.co.uk/jobs.htm

teacheslabroad.com: Korea
www.teacheslabroad.com

Teaching English and Educating in Korea
www.keepro.com

Teaching English in China
www.EnglishTeachersExpress.com

teach-in-thailand.com
www.teach-in-thailand.com

TeachinginJapan
www.teachinginjapan.com

teachkorea.com
www.teachkorea.com/mb.htm

Volunteer Programmes

In some countries the demand for adult English language teachers outstrips the supply; as state-funded programmes struggle to provide needed services with shrinking funds, the role of volunteers in teaching English becomes crucial. And this happens in developing countries as well as western countries such as the USA.

The following organisations arrange for volunteer teachers to travel and teach in volunteer programmes around the world, particularly into China and Africa. There are also volunteer groups providing support and teachers into local communities, for example, into regions of the USA where there is a great need for volunteer teachers. The volunteer groups should help arrange your travel, training, accommodation and any visas.

AmeriCorps
www.americorps.org
AmeriCorps is a United States-based organization. The domestic Peace Corps has more than 40,000 Americans in intensive, results-driven service each year. AmeriCorps has built its foundation on teaching children to read, attempting to make neighborhoods safer, building affordable homes, and responding to natural disasters. AmeriCorps serves with projects such as Habitat for Humanity, the American Red Cross, and Boys and Girls Clubs. After a term of service, AmeriCorps members receive education awards to help finance college tuition or pay back student loans.

AmeriSpan Unlimited
www.amerispan.com
AmeriSpan has become a major force for anyone wanting to study language abroad in Latin America. AmeriSpan's network offers language programmes in nearly every Spanish-speaking country in the Americas.

Amity Institute
www.amity.org
Amity Institute was founded in 1962. It is a non-profit educational exchange programme that gives young people around the world the opportunity to represent their countries, by sharing their languages and cultures in language classrooms of all levels. Amity tries to encourage and enhance international understanding and friendship through the study of world languages and cultures.

Christians Abroad
www.cabroad.org.uk
Provides advice and information for volunteers of any faith who are considering working abroad as a volunteer. It provides job vacancies through a monthly listing newsletter – the majority of its postings are to Asia and Africa. Also visit www.wse.org.uk for online information packs.

Colorado China Council
www.asiacouncil.org
The primary focus of CCC is to send people to teach English in China, as well as other academic subjects, at universities and secondary schools throughout the country. The Council has placed over 200 teachers, making it one of the U.S.'s largest non-religious providers of teachers to China.

Cross-Cultural Solutions
www.crossculturalsolutions.org
Cross-Cultural Solutions offers short-term and long-term programmes that give volunteers from all over the world the opportunity to come face to face with global issues and become part of productive

solutions. CCS has close partnerships with social service pioneers in our host countries. The focus of CCS's work is health care, education and social development

Friends of World Teaching
www.fowt.com
Friends of World Teaching helps teachers find jobs around the world. Friends of World Teaching works with English-speaking schools and colleges throughout the world that offer employment opportunities to American and Canadian teachers. There are some student teaching programmes as well.

Global Routes
www.globalroutes.org
Global Routes is a tax-exempt non-profit, is a non-governmental, non-sectarian organization whose aim is to strengthen the global community. It has designed community-service/cross-cultural-exchange programmes that bring people with different world-views together.

i-to-i
www.i-to-i.com
School and agency that provides TEFL training and manages extensive volunteer placements around the world (specialising in South and Central America and Asia). The agency provides accommodation, travel and support in-country. If you have never taught, it also offers courses for trainee-teachers.

India Literacy Project
www.ilpnet.org
India Literacy Project is a US-based non-profit, volunteer organization that focuses on literacy in India. Its aim is to empower every individual we serve with functional literacy and an understanding of their basic rights and responsibilities. India Literacy Project's goal is 100% literacy in India.

Intl. Foundation for Ed. & Self-help
www.ifesh.org
The International Foundation for Education and Self-Help (IFESH) was established as a non-governmental, nonprofit, charitable organization. IFESH aims to reduce hunger and poverty, empower people through literacy, train and place the unskilled and unemployed in jobs, provide preventive and basic health care to individuals in need, deal with population and environment problems, develop employment through economic development activities, foster cultural, social, and economic relations between Africans and Americans, particularly African Americans, and others.

International Rescue Committee
www.intrescom.org
International Rescue Committee was founded in 1933. The IRC is a nonsectarian, voluntary organization that provides relief, protection and resettlement services for refugees and victims of oppression or violent conflict throughout the world.

Intl. Schools Internship programme
www.tieonline.com
A TIE subscription gives you immediate access to the most prominent schools looking for staff: from 90 to 150 schools are always on the Job Ads web page. And the TIE Resume Bank means over 200 headmasters of International schools can access your file; and from there they can contact you through email, phone, your website, etc. Schools can, and often do, change their vacancies weekly at so you can be the first to know when a vacancy in the country you want opens up!

Laubach Literacy
www.laubach.org/home.html
Laubach Literacy Action (LLA), the U.S. programme Division of Laubach Literacy, is the largest volunteer-based literacy organization in the United States. We provide a full range of literacy services to more than 175,000 students annually through more than 1,000 local member programmes, 45 state organizations. Instruction is provided by a national network of more than 80,000 volunteer trainers and tutors .

Literacy Volunteers
www.literacyvolunteers.org
Literacy Volunteers of America, Inc. has served adults at the lowest levels of literacy and their families since 1962, and has assisted more than half a million people to acquire literacy skills. LVA offers a professionally designed and field-tested workshop that enables volunteers to tutor adults in English for speakers of other languages. After being matched with an adult learner or a small group of learners, tutors receive regular support and opportunities for additional training through the local LVA affiliate.

National Adult Literacy Database
www.nald.ca
The National Adult Literacy Database Inc. (NALD) is a federally incorporated, non-profit service organization which fills the crucial need for a single-source, comprehensive, up-to-date and easily

accessible database of adult literacy programmes, resources, services and activities across Canada. It also links with other services and databases in North America and overseas.

PeaceCorps

www.peacecorps.org

As an English teaching volunteer, you will help expand the horizons and opportunities of students and teachers alike in Peace Corps' largest programme. There is no other experience like helping a middle school, secondary school, or university. More than 7,000 Peace Corps volunteers are serving in 76 countries. They are working to bring clean water to communities, teach children, help start new small businesses, and stop the spread of AIDS. Since 1961, more than 161,000 Americans have joined the Peace Corps, serving in 134 nations.

VolunteerMatch

www.volunteermatch.org

VolunteerMatch, ImpactOnline's main service, uses the power of the Internet to help individuals find volunteer opportunities posted by local non-profit and public sector organizations.

Volunteers in Asia

www.volasia.org

VIA is a private, non-profit, non-sectarian organization whose aim it is to increase understanding between the United States and Asia. Its Volunteer Programs in Asia have provided young Americans with an opportunity to work and live within an Asian culture while meeting the needs of Asian host institutions, since 1962.

VSO (Voluntary Service Overseas)

www.vso.org.uk

The VSO is one of the biggest and best-known of the volunteer agencies. It works in over 70 countries around the world, with a current majority of postings to China and Africa. The VSO offers volunteers a complete package, including basic training (volunteers are expected to have a degree or be experienced TEFL teachers), airfares and, importantly, in-country support centres.

VSO Canada

www.vsocan.com

People are what VSO Canada is all about– and you just might be one of them. VSO's people share their skills in developing countries.

WorldTeach

www.worldteach.org

WorldTeach is a non-profit, non-governmental organization based at the centre for International Development at Harvard University which provides opportunities for individuals to make a meaningful contribution to international education by living and working as volunteer teachers in developing countries.

Gap year travel (huge in the UK, unknown in the USA) is a way for students to take a year out and travel before settling down to their studies at university, often working as a volunteer (and teaching English is a popular option). The needs and expectations of both sides (agency and volunteer) are very different for gap year compared to a qualified teacher taking a career break or travelling, so there are agencies that specialise in this work. For information about working in your gap year, visit these websites:

The gap year company www.gapyear.com

GAP Activity projects www.gap.org.uk

Gap Challenge www. world-challenge.co.uk

Preparation: Before you go

This section covers the preparation you need to consider before you head off on your travels around the world: in particular, income tax on earnings and insurance.

Before you go

If you are thinking of teaching English in another country, you should have a lot of questions on your mind. Here are some of the most frequent questions asked by prospective teachers and the answers.

When Should I Plan To Go?

This depends on where you want to teach. In many countries, everything shuts down during certain months of the year, usually in the summer. Our country profiles, later in this book, provide general information about the best time to apply for jobs. You can apply for jobs from home or you can turn up on spec. Both approaches have their own merits and drawbacks depending on the country you want to teach in. The country guides offer more detailed answers to this question.

What Should I Take With Me?

Essentials – like obtaining health insurance valid for your stay overseas – are dealt with later in this chapter. Do remember to check if your passport will be valid for the period of time you plan to be away – it's amazing the number of teachers who forget to do this!

Make sure you take clothes appropriate for the climate you will be living in. Remember that a country that is hot and sunny in the summer can be freezing cold in the winter. Clothing

may be expensive in your new country so take a good supply of things you like to wear. Check with the school to see if you will be required to dress formally when you teach. If you will be going out to look for a teaching job on spec it would not hurt to take clothes that you would wear to an interview. Appearance really does count when you are job hunting, almost as much your CV in some cases! You might want to invest in some ESL/ EFL teaching books as these may be hard to obtain in your destination country – they may be in short supply. A good dictionary and a grammar guidebook will always come in handy when you are faced with any awkward questions about word definitions or the nature of past participles. Also, make sure you have a few good novels for your leisure time. If you are learning the language of your destination country (it's a good idea), then take along some tapes, books and a Walkman.

Will I Need A Teaching Qualification?

Not necessarily. But, as we have stressed throughout this book (see the "Training" section at the start of this book), it's a good idea to get some training before you go or why not take a teaching course while you are on your travels? Whether you train in your home country or while you are away is your decision, but if you plan to train in another country make sure that there are appropriate courses on offer.

Insurance

When planning to travel abroad you should you have adequate health insurance. With so many different types of coverage available it can be very confusing deciding which plan is right for you. Here's what to look for.

Don't leave home without it

All European Union citizens are entitled to the same level of medical care in any other country of the EU as they would receive at home. To secure this coverage as a UK citizen, you must obtain form E111 from the Department of Health and Social Security before you leave the UK.

If you plan to stay for more than a few months, you should check what your local social security contributions entitle you to and decide whether you need to take out a private health care scheme. A private scheme gives you more flexibility about where you are treated, but you should check carefully exactly what your coverage is. It is also possible to obtain coverage for repatriation in a real emergency.

Home Country Coverage: your existing health plan cover

This section will be of particular importance to citizens of the US (and other countries that do not have a good, free, state-funded health service) who typically have their own private health and medical insurance polices.

For US citizens, if you already have strong benefits at home, it is wise to double-check what exactly is covered while you are out of the country. Most health plans limit coverage to a maximum of 30 or 60 days outside the States, and HMOs and PPOs will likely impose severe – out of network – penalties for all but the most basic emergency care. More importantly, you will

want to insure you have 24 hour access to emergency evacuation if you are sick or hurt in an area where quality care is not available. For those over 65, Medicare will not cover treatment outside the U.S. If you do not have any domestic coverage, travel insurance is a must. Once you have answered these questions, you will need to know what benefits and policy provisions to look for in a travel medical plan.

Short Trips (two weeks or less)

Assuming you have solid coverage at home you may only need a small supplemental plan, with features like emergency evacuation and 24 hour worldwide assistance, along with a limited benefit for medical expenses (£10,000 to £50,000 is typical). These plans are readily available through your travel agent and may include lost luggage and trip cancellation protection too. Be wary of plans that require you settle all bills yourself and then seek reimbursement when you return home.

Intermediate Trips (two weeks to six months)

The longer you are away the less likely it is your own plan will cover you and therefore the more importance you should place on the medical benefits of the plan. In addition to a higher emergency evacuation benefit, your plan should cover between £100,000 to £1 million in medical expenses. Other features to look for include coverage for a family member to come to your assistance if you are taken to hospital in a foreign country and an option to include "hazardous activities" such as scuba diving, skiing and bungee jumping.

Longer Trips (six months+)

The travel insurance you purchase will most likely be your primary or only health insurance. Be sure that your plan includes all of the above, with higher maximum benefits (£1 million or more) as well as some provision for coverage when you return home. If you spend a year abroad but return home for a vacation, make sure you are still covered.

Multiyear or Open Ended Trips

Standard medical plans are usually limited to one year, with the option to renew for another. If you anticipate being abroad for a longer period of time, look into a permanent international major medical plan. This type of coverage contains all the benefits of a travel medical plan, but once you are accepted you can maintain coverage year after year simply by paying the premium. Most importantly, you are covered for medical treatment anywhere in the world, including back at home. Note that these plans are medically underwritten, and people with prior health problems may have trouble obtaining coverage.

All of the plan types discussed share some common features; you will normally have a deductible and co-insurance payment or premium to meet, and pre-existing conditions are usually excluded. Worldwide assistance is sometimes done by the plan administrator, or through an independent assistance company. The market for these plans is growing rapidly and new companies enter the market all the time. Be sure the company you are dealing with has at least five to ten years' experience in the international market.

Doing a little research before you go can mean security and peace of mind while you are away, and allows you to concentrate on the exciting and fulfilling adventure that international travel and work can be!

Brian Garity, founder of International Health Insurance.com, has specialized in international health insurance for over ten years.

Tax

If you are planning to work abroad, it is important that you know your financial position, especially what your liability for tax will be. In the directory of countries, page 87, we note any special requirements of local tax authorities – often, you will have to register with the local tax office before starting work. However, there are plenty of potential problems when declaring your earned income in your home country. Regulations differ for citizens of different countries. Here are some guidelines for teachers from some Commonwealth countries and from the USA.

Australian nationals

If you are an Australian national, you have to fill in your own tax return. If you work abroad for less than a full tax year, when you return you will need to declare your earnings and tax, and will either receive a tax credit for the excess tax you have paid or be taxed for the shortfall. If you are abroad for longer periods, there will be a break in your tax requirements in Australia for the period you are away. But check your social security arrangement as payments made overseas will not be credited.

Canadian nationals

If you are a Canadian national, you will need to consider what your residency status is while you are working abroad. If you work abroad for a short term but keep your ties with Canada, you are considered a factual resident and will be liable to pay federal taxes, etc. If you work abroad for a longer period, you can be considered a non-resident. In this case your tax position in Canada will change. You will need to check with the authorities or consult a financial advisor to see what your position is.

UK nationals

It is most important to check whether or not the country you are going to has a reciprocal tax agreement with your home country.

If you are a UK national, you will get tax relief (even up to 100%) if you are out of the country for at least 365 days and do not stay in the UK for more than 62 consecutive days in the tax period. There is a difference between non-resident status and exemption from tax in the UK. If you are classed as a non-resident, you are not liable for tax on unearned income from abroad but you are still considered to be domiciled in the UK. To qualify as a non-resident you must work overseas for more than a full tax year without being in the UK for more than six months in that tax year or three months in each year if your stay abroad spans the tax year.

Many countries have agreements with the UK to prevent the double payment of tax. Credit against UK tax for payment already made abroad will be given if there is no such agreement. (See Inland Revenue form IR6 – Double Taxation Relief).

When you are teaching abroad, it is important that you think about maintaining your UK social security payments so that you qualify for the state pension. You should get form N139 from the Department of Social Security (form SA29 if you are working in the EU).

US Nationals

The U.S. income tax system (and forms) are well-known to be complex area – and for U.S. citizens working and travelling the world as teachers, this can be particularly difficult. As a U.S. citizen or resident alien, your worldwide income generally is subject to U.S. income tax regardless of where you are living. Also, you are subject to the same income tax filing requirements that apply to U.S. citizens or residents living in the United States. However, several income tax benefits might apply if you meet certain requirements while living abroad. You may be able to exclude from your income a limited amount of your foreign earned income. You also may be able either to exclude or to deduct from gross income your housing amount (more later). To claim these benefits, you must file a tax return and attach Form 2555, Foreign Earned Income. If you are claiming the foreign earned income exclusion only, you may be able to use the shorter Form 2555-EZ, Foreign Earned Income Exclusion, rather than Form 2555.

You may be able to claim a tax credit or an itemized deduction for foreign income taxes that you pay. Also, under tax treaties or conventions that the United States has with many foreign countries, you may be able to reduce your foreign tax liability.

Income Earned Abroad

You may qualify for an exclusion from tax of up to $70,000 in income earned while working abroad. However, you must file a tax return to claim the exclusion. In general, foreign earned income is income received from services you perform outside of the United States. When we use the term United States, that includes Puerto Rico, Northern Marina Islands, Republic of the Marshall Islands, Federated States of Micronesia, Guam and American Soma. While not all of these countries are part of the United States, they have special tax status. Excluded from gross earned income is your housing costs allowance which are over a certain base amount. Generally, you will qualify for these benefits if your tax home (defined below) is in a foreign country, or countries, throughout your period of bona-fide foreign residence or physical presence and you are one of the following:

1) A U.S. citizen who is a bona-fide resident of a foreign country or countries for an uninterrupted period that includes a complete tax year, or

2) A U.S. resident alien who is a citizen or national of a country with which the United States has an income tax treaty in effect and who is a bona-fide resident of a foreign country or countries for an uninterrupted period that includes an entire tax year, or

3) A U.S. citizen or a U.S. resident alien who is physically present in a foreign country or countries for at least 330 full days during any period of 12 consecutive months.

Tax Home

Generally, your tax home is the area of your main place of business, employment, or post of duty where you are permanently or indefinitely engaged to work. You are not considered to have a tax home in a foreign country for any period during which your abode (the place where you regularly live) is in the United States. However, being temporarily present in the United States or maintaining a dwelling there does not necessarily mean that your abode is in the United States. For details, see Publication 54.

A foreign country, for this purpose, means any territory under the sovereignty of a government other than that of the United States, including territorial waters (determined under U.S. laws) and air space.

Waiver of time requirements: You may not have to meet the minimum time requirements for bona-fide residence or physical presence if you have to leave the foreign country because war, civil unrest, or similar adverse conditions in the country prevented you from conducting normal business. You must, however, be able to show that you reasonably could have expected to meet the minimum time requirements if the adverse conditions had not occurred. See Publication 54 for a list of foreign countries that individuals have had to leave due to these conditions.

Travel Restrictions

If you violate U.S. travel restrictions, you will not be treated as being a bona-fide resident of, or physically present in, a foreign country for any day during which you are present in a country in violation of the restrictions. (These restrictions generally prohibit U.S. citizens and residents from engaging in transactions related to travel to, from, or within certain countries.) Also, income that you earn from sources within such a country for services performed during a period of travel restrictions does not qualify as foreign earned income, and housing expenses that you incur within that country (or outside that country for housing your spouse or dependents) while you are present in that country in violation of travel restrictions cannot be included in figuring your foreign housing amount.

Currently, these travel restrictions apply to: Cuba, Libya, and Iraq.

Exclusion Of Foreign Earned Income

If your tax home is in a foreign country and you meet either the bona fide residence test or the physical presence test, you can choose to exclude from gross income a limited amount of your foreign earned income. Your income must be for services performed in a foreign country during your period of foreign residence or presence, whichever applies. You cannot, however, exclude the pay you receive as an employee of the U.S. Government or its agencies. You cannot exclude pay you receive for services abroad for Armed Forces exchanges, officers' mess, exchange services, etc., operated by the U.S. Army, Navy, or Air Force.

Foreign Credits And Deductions

If you claim the exclusion, you cannot claim any credits or deductions that are related to the excluded income. You cannot claim a foreign tax credit or deduction for any foreign income tax paid on the excluded income. Nor can you claim the earned income credit if you claim the

exclusion. Also, for IRA purposes, the excluded income is not considered compensation and, for figuring deductible contributions when you are covered by an employer retirement plan, is included in your modified adjusted gross income.

Foreign Amount Excludable

If your tax home is in a foreign country and you qualify under either the bona fide residence test or physical presence test for a tax year, you can exclude your foreign income earned during the year up to $70,000. However, if you qualify under either test for only part of the year, you must reduce ratably the $70,000 maximum based on the number of days within the tax year you qualified under one of the two tests.

Foreign Income Taxes

A limited amount of the foreign income tax you pay can be credited against your U.S. tax liability or deducted in figuring taxable income on your U.S. income tax return. It is usually to your advantage to claim a credit for foreign taxes rather than to deduct them. A credit reduces your U.S. tax liability, and any excess may be carried back and carried forward to other years. A deduction only reduces your taxable income and may be taken only in the current year. You must treat all foreign income taxes in the same way. You generally cannot deduct some foreign income taxes and take a credit for others.

Foreign Tax Credit

If you choose to credit foreign taxes against your tax liability, complete Form 1116, Foreign Tax Credit, (Individual, Estate, Trust, or Nonresident Alien Individual), and attach it to your U.S. income tax return.

Do not include the foreign taxes paid or accrued as withheld income taxes on line 55 of Form 1040.

Foreign Tax Limit

Your credit cannot be more than the part of your U.S. income tax liability allocable to your taxable income from sources outside the United States. So, if you have no U.S. income tax liability, or if all your foreign income is exempt from U.S. tax, you will not be able to claim a foreign tax credit.

If the foreign taxes you paid or incurred during the year exceed the limit on your credit for the current year, you can carry back the unused foreign taxes as credits to 2 prior tax years and then carry forward any remaining unused foreign taxes to 5 later tax years.

Foreign taxes paid on excluded income. You cannot claim a credit for foreign taxes paid on amounts excluded from gross income under the foreign earned income exclusion or the housing amount exclusion, discussed earlier.

Foreign Tax Deduction

If you choose to deduct all foreign income taxes on your U.S. income tax return, itemize the deduction on Schedule A (Form 1040). You cannot deduct foreign taxes paid on income you exclude from your U.S. income tax return.

More information. The foreign tax credit and deduction, their limits, and the carryback and carryover provisions are discussed in detail in Publication 514, Foreign Tax Credit for Individuals. For more information and to download publications and forms mentioned, visit www.irs.ustreas.gov/forms_pubs/index.html

Country Profiles

To find a particular country, see the index on the next page

Country Profiles

Argentina	197	Honduras	210
Australia	166	Hong Kong	172
Austria	93	Hungary	124
Azerbaijan	118	Indonesia	173
Bahrain	141	Ireland	101
Bangladesh	170	Israel	143
Belarus	118	Italy	102
Belgium	94	Jamaica	210
Benin	159	Japan	175
Bolivia	198	Jordan	143
Brazil	199	Kenya	162
Bulgaria	119	Korea (South)	179
Burkina Faso	159	Kuwait	144
Cameroon	159	Laos	182
Central African Republic	160	Latvia	125
Chad	160	Lebanon	145
Chile	202	Lithuania	126
China	170	Madagascar	162
Colombia	205	Malaysia	183
Congo	160	Mali	162
Costa Rica	207	Malta	146
Croatia	120	Mexico	211
Cyprus	121	Moldova	127
Czech Republic	121	Mongolia	183
Denmark	95	Morocco	147
Ecuador	208	Mozambique	162
Egypt	141	Myanmar (Burma)	184
El Salvador	209	Nepal	184
Eritrea	160	Netherlands	104
Estonia	123	New Zealand	167
Ethiopia	161	Norway	107
Finland	96	Oman	148
France	97	Pakistan	185
Georgia	124	Palestinian Authority	143
Germany	98	Peru	217
Ghana	161	Poland	127
Greece	100	Portugal	108
Guatemala	209	Qatar	149

Country Profiles

Work the World

The following section of this guide will show you all you need to know to get a teaching job in almost any country in the world.

A s a qualified English language teacher you can travel the world and find work in almost any country you choose to visit. English learners gain a valuable opportunity to interact with a native speaker and pick up all the little nuances that they would otherwise miss. This section of the Guide will prepare you for travel around the world as an EFL/ESL teacher.

Teaching English as a Foreign Language has developed into a vast global business. In many countries around the world, the development of English language skills throughout society is considered crucial to economic success. People want to learn English because they see it as a key, opening doors to new opportunities that they would not otherwise enjoy. Governments around the world are insisting that their children learn English from a very early age: Korea, Japan and Italy are just three countries that have recently announced initiatives designed to get people to learn English.

Teaching English has always had one great advantage over any other form of teaching: the travel element. The requirement for teachers in just about every country around the world leads to great opportunities for well-qualified teachers who can travel and, often, a very enjoyable lifestyle exploring countries and new cultures.

This section of the book provides thorough, in-depth profiles of all the main markets for teachers of English. We include a short description of the country and its prospects for teachers, together with details of the visa requirements, salary expectations, medical conditions, cost of accommodation and local English-language newspapers. We also include details of the main schools in the country that could offer you a job. Use this information to contact the schools with your curriculum vitae and a covering letter to find a job as a teacher.

Once you have selected the country or region where you would like to work, flip back to the 'Finding a Job' chapter earlier in this book for more details on how best to apply, how to search for jobs online and even how to travel!

Country Profiles

The countries over the following pages are organized geographically. If you already have your heart set on going to a particular country, look it up in the index at the end of this book and go straight to that section. If you have an idea of where you would like to go, but need more information before you decide, read about all of the countries in that area, because you may well find that another country is more suited to you. If you are unsure about where you would like to go, browse through all of the sections and you should get a good idea of countries that you would like to teach in.

Country-specific information

In these country sections we have tried to give you the information that you need, rather than personal opinions, so there will usually be a brief summary of the country's economic position and how that relates to the demand for English language teachers.

Next, there is information on visas and work permits, which reflects the position in the country at the time of writing. Please note that we do not recommend working illegally in any country, even though it is mentioned where teachers do tend to work without the correct paperwork. Not all countries have such a clear policy on the working rights of foreign nationals, so consult the relevant embassy for full details.

The cost of living information is intended as a guideline to enable you to establish if your local salary will be just enough to support you or will boost your savings account. Costs are described in comparison to western European and North American norms, so this information must be read in conjunction with salary information. And some teachers manage to live on tight budgets in poorer countries by adapting quickly to the local way of life.

Salaries vary enormously, even within the same town, so figures given here are averages. Where figures are quoted in UK pounds, remember that exchange rates can change very quickly, so the Sterling equivalent will also change, but the salary should still remain the same in relation to local costs.

Some employers pay teachers in US-dollars, but the vast majority of employers pay in local currency. Taxation is not set at a standard rate in some countries, so it too will vary depending on the type of institution you are working for and your contract terms.

Accommodation causes as many problems overseas as it does at home. Prices given in this section are what teachers typically pay for standard accommodation in safe areas. Obviously, luxury penthouses in chic, central areas will cost you a lot more. If you do have problems finding somewhere to live, think of alternative options, such as living with a family, which can save you money and enable you to integrate with the local community very quickly. Ask around at universities and schools – something will soon come up.

Health insurance is advisable whenever you are travelling. Travel agents, embassies and airlines should be able to provide you with up to date details of any particular health issues in the countries you are visiting.

English language newspapers are good places to look for teaching jobs and accommodation. They are also a great way to keep up to date with the local (and international)

news if your grasp of the local language is not good enough to read the local papers.

At the end of each country sections, there is a list of schools to contact for jobs. The national telephone dialing code appears in brackets at the top of the list. You should also look in the 'Finding a Job' chapter earlier in this book for more details on how to apply for a job and websites listing job vacancies.

Western Europe

Demand for English as a second or foreign language is strong among the member states of the European Union. English is the working language of the EU despite efforts to promote other languages such as French, Spanish and German.

It has become more difficult for non-EU citizens to work in Western Europe. Work-related laws that are designed to make it easier for Europeans to work in member states have tightened up with regard to Americans, Canadians, and to a lesser extent, Australians.

Job prospects for native speakers from the UK are particularly good in Western Europe, but rather more difficult for Americans and Canadians with American-English qualifications (although many countries, Spain for example, have 'international' schools teaching American English). However, there are jobs available for any teacher – although schools much prefer someone with qualifications (i.e. someone who has passed at least a certificate-level course) – especially if you are flexible and don't expect to land a high-paying permanent teaching position right away. If a school wants to keep you on as a full-time and legal employee, there is usually a way to cut through the bureaucracy, even if it is time-consuming.

The traditional strong areas of the countries around the Mediterranean still attract a lot of prospective teachers, but some countries have had some economic problems recently, particularly Spain which has seen a number of its major schools shut down in the past year.

Any EU citizen can travel freely within western Europe and work in any other country – enjoying its local health system and social security benefits. However, your school will be able to advise of the local tax laws which normally require any visitor planning to work to register with the local tax authority (and often with the police, too). Non-EU citizens looking for work should contact the country's embassy and ask for current visa information. Your prospective employer is often in the best position to request (and push through) a visa application on your behalf.

AUSTRIA

It is nearly impossible for non-EU citizens to live and work in Austria on a part time, freelance basis unless married to an EU citizen or in possession of a special visa (e.g., for the arts) and nearly all teaching positions are freelance. If you have a student visa for a university in Austria, this might give you eligibility to work. There is stiff competition for teaching jobs from the expatriate community. The most commonly available work is part-time and company-based.

Embassy in UK:
18 Belgrave Mews West, London SW1X 8HU,
tel: +44 (0)20 7235 3731
www.austria.org.uk

Embassy in USA:
3524 International Court NW, Washington DC 20008
tel: +1 202 895 6700
www.austria.org

British Council office:
Schenkenstrabe 4, A -1010 Vienna
tel +43 (1) 533 2616
www.britishcouncil.at

➲ **Visa/Work Permits:** For non-EU nationals intending to work or study in Austria, a residency permit is required. Contact the Embassy or Austrian Consulate General. US citizens may enter Austria as tourists and apply for a residency permit with the relevant authorities in Austria.

➲ **Currency:** £1 = € 1.45, $1 = € 0.83

➲ **Cost of Living:** Austria is a relatively cheap European country.

➲ **Salaries/Taxes:** Expect to earn around £10 per hour but this depends on your qualifications. If you are contracted expect to earn £600 a month. Income tax and social security deductions are around 40%.

➲ **Accommodation:** A one-bedroom apartment in Vienna or Salzburg will cost around £250 per month.

➲ **Health advice:** Insurance coverage is advisable.

➲ **English Language Media:** The Vienna Reporter

Schools in Austria (+43)

Alpha Sprachinstitut Austria
Schwarzenbergplatz 16/ Canovagasse 5, A-1010 Vienna. **Tel:** 1 503 69 69, **Fax:** 1 503 69 69-14.

American International School
Salmannsdorferstrasse 47, A-1190 Vienna. **Tel:** 1 603 02 46.

Amerika-Institut
Operngrasse 4, 1010 Vienna. **Tel:** 1 512 77 20

Austro-British Society
Wickenburgasse 19, 1080 Vienna. **Tel:** 1 431 141.

Berlitz Sprachschule
Rotenturmstrasse 1-38, 1060 Vienna.

Berufsforderungsinstitut
Kinderspitalgasse 5, 1090 Vienna.

Business Language Centre
Trattnerhof 2, 1010 Vienna.

Danube International
Guderunstrasse 184, A-1100 Vienna.

Didactica Akademie Fur Wirtschaft Und Sprachen
Schottenfledgasse 13-15, 1070 Vienna. **Tel:** 1 526 2287.

English Courses And Seminars
Salzachstr. 16, Salzburg, 5020. **Tel:** 66 2629995.

English For Kids
23 Anton-Baumgartner-Str. 44, Vienna, 1230. **Tel:** 1 222 66 74579.

English Institute Linzerg 27
Salzburg, 5020. **Tel:** 66 2872195.

English Institute Sprachreisen Schoenberg
31 Michaelbeuern, 5152. **Tel:** 6 274 8236.

English Language Centre
In der Hagenau 7, 1130 Vienna. **Tel/Fax:** 1 804 1869.

Graz International Bilingual School
Klusemannstrasse 25, A-8053, Graz. **Tel:** 316 1050.

inlingua School of Languages
Neuer Markt 1, A-1010 Vienna, **Tel:** 1 512 22 25 / 1 512 94 99, **Fax:** 1 513 94 56.

Innsbruck International Highschool
Schonbeg 26, A-6141, Innsbruck. **Tel:** 05225 42013992.

Institut CEF
Garnisongasse 10, 1090 Vienna. **Tel:** 1 42 04 03

International Language Services
Getreidemarkt 17, A-1060 Vienna. **Tel:** 1 585 53 47, **Fax:** 1 585 53 47.

International Montessori Preschool Vienna
Mahlerstrasse 9/13, A-1010 Vienna. **Tel:** 1 512 8733.

International Summer School Gmunden
Postfach 182, A-4810 Gmunden, **Tel:** 1 494 9994

Jelinek & Jelinek
Privatlehrinstitut, Rudolfsplatz 3, 1010 Vienna.

Kindergarten Alt Wien
Am Heumarkt 23, A-1030, Vienna.

Lizner International School
Aubrunnerweg 4, A-4040 Linz. **Tel:** 732 245 8670.

Mini Schools & English Language Day Camp
Postfach 160, 1220 Vienna. **Tel:** 227717.

Multi Lingua Language School and Translation Bureau
Hardtgasse 5/2, A-1190 Vienna.**Tel:** 1 369 15 41, **Fax:** 1 369 15 42.

Privat Institut Venetia Erwachsenenbildung
Große Neugasse 8/19, A-1040 Vienna. **Tel:** 1 586 82 57, **Fax:** 1 586 82 579

Salzburg International Preparatory School
Moosstrasse 106, A-5020, Salzburg. **Tel:** 662 844 485.

Sight & Sound Studio
Schubertring 12, 1031 Vienna. **Tel:** 1 512 67520.

SLL Institut Super Language Learning
Florianigasse 55, A-1080 Vienna. **Tel:** 1 408 41 84, **Fax:** 1 403 66 02.

Spidi (Spracheninstitut Der Industrie)
Lotringer Strasse 12, 1031 Vienna. **Tel:** 1 715 2506-0, **Fax:** 1 89 17431.

Sprachstudio J-J Rousseau
Untere Viaduktgasse 43, 1030 Vienna. **Tel:** 1 712 2443.

Sprachinstitut Vienna
Universitatstr. 6, 1090, Vienna. **Tel:** 1422227

Sprachschule BriBou
Barichgasse 26/3, A-1030 Vienna. **Tel:** 1 710 8829.

Super Language Learning Sprachinstitut
Florianigasse 55, 1080 Vienna. **Tel:** 1 408 4184

Wiener Volkshochschulen Verband Wiener Volksbildung
Hollergasse 22, A-1150 Vienna. **Tel:** 1 891 740.

Young Austria
Alpenstrasse 108a, A-5020 Salzburg. **Tel:** 662 625 7580.

BELGIUM

Currently there is little demand for teachers in Belgium. English is taught at secondary school level and school leavers usually have enough English to get by with the demands that will be made on them later in life. Some of the private language schools are struggling to survive and are often a one or two-person business. Often it is only freelance work, which is available at private language schools. This is for a number of reasons. The first is that English is an asset but not essential to work in Belgium. Also, the UK is very close for those who want to travel to the UK to learn the language and newsagents are well supplied in English magazines and the British press. Last but not least, the country has cable television and this includes a wide choice of programmes in English (British and American). Many teenagers therefore learn the language by watching British and American soaps and viewing films in the original version with subtitles in their own language.

Embassy in UK:
103 Eaton Square, London SW1W 9AW
Tel: +44 (0)20 7470 3700
www.diplobel.org/uk

Embassy in USA:
3330 Garfield Street NW, Washington DC 20008
Tel: +1 202 333 6900
www.diplobel.org/usa

British Council office:
Leopold Plaza, Rue du Trône 108 / Troonstraat 108
1050 Brussels
Tel: +32 (2) 227 08 41
www.britishcouncil.org/belgium

➲ **Visa/Work Permits:** If you're a non-EU citizen you'll need to apply for a work permit. This means you'll have to prove no EU citizen is able to do your job– it is best to leave this paperwork to your prospective employer. There are two main types of work permit (permis de travail/werkvergunning), normally you will get a B permit which is valid for only one employer and must be renewed each year. After several years you should be able to transfer this to an A permit which is valid indefinitely and allows you to work for any employer you like. Contact the Ministère de l'Emploi et du Travail for information and application forms for work permits.

➲ **Currency:** £1 = € 1.45 $1 = € 0.83

➲ **Cost of Living:** Expect to pay a third more than in the U.S. for basic living costs. Belgium is not as cheap as it used to be.

➲ **Salaries/Taxes:** Salaries are negotiable according to experience, but on contract expect to earn around £600 a month. Employers will pay your tax and health insurance only if you are on a contract.

➲ **Accommodation:** Schools rarely assist in finding accommodation. Outside Brussels rents are quite reasonable from a minimum of £150 per month for an

apartment to £400 for a small house. An apartment in Brussels costs around £200.

➲ **English Language Media:** The Bulletin (weekly)

Schools in Belgium (+32)

Access Bvba Taalbureau
Atealaan 5, 2200 Herentals. **Tel:** 14 22 61 92

Applied Language Centre
21 rue du Trone 238, 1050 Brussels.

Belgo-British Courses
Rue d'Ecosse 21, 1060 Brussels. **Tel:** 2 537 8775.

Berlitz Language Centre
Avenue Louise 306, 1050 Brussels.

Berlitz Language Centre
Place Stéphanie 10, 1050 Brussels. **Tel:** 2 512 44 04.

Berlitz Language Centre
Britselei 15, 2018 Antwerpen.

Berlitz Language Centre
Leuvenselaan 17, 3300 Tienen.

Bilingua
6 rue Renier Chalon, 1060 Brussels. **Tel:** 2 347 4534.

British Council
rue de la Charité 15, 1210 Brussels. **Tel:** 2 227 0840.

British School of Brussels
Leuvensesteenweg 19, 3080 Tervuren. **Tel:** 2 767 4700.

Brussels Language Centre
55 Rue Des Drapiers, 1050 Brussels.

Crown Language Centre
9 Rue Du Béguinage, 1000 Brussels.

The English Institute
77 Rue Lesbroussart, 1050 Brussels.

inlingua School of Languages
62 Limburgstraat, 9000 Gent.

Institute of Modern Languages and Communications
20 Av. de la Toison D'or, Bte. 21, 1060 Brussels.**Tel:** 2 512 6607.

Institut Pro Linguis SC
Place De L'eglise, 6717 Thiamont.

Linguarama
Avenue des Arts, Kunstlaan 19, 1040 Brussels. **Tel:** 2 17 9055, **Fax:** 2 17 9523.

May International
40 rue Lesbroussart, 1050 Brussels. **Tel:** 2 640 8703.

Mitchell School of English
rue Louis Hap 156, 1040 Brussels. **Tel:** 2 734 8073.

Peters School
87 rue des Deux Eglises, 1040 Brussels. **Tel:** 2 280 0021.

Phone Languages
65 rue des Echevins, 1050 Brussels. **Tel:** 2 647 4020.

Practicum
Reep 24, 9000 Gent. **Tel:** 9 223 5442.

Pro Linguis
6717 Thiaumont. **Tel:** 63 22 0462, **Fax:** 63 22 0688.

School Voor Europese Talen
28 Charlottalei, 2018 Antwerpen. **Tel:** 3 218 7370.

DENMARK

A recent study found that Denmark ranked as the number one place in the world to live in terms of its ability to provide basic social and material needs for its citizens. However, there are few jobs and prospects for non-EU teachers are particularly poor. Children of school age are decreasing in numbers and schools and universities are cutting back on staff. You may be successful if you look for work in institutes running part-time courses and evening classes, particularly in business English.

Embassy in UK:
55 Sloane Street, London SW1X 9SR
Tel: +44 (0)20 7333 0200
www.demarkemb.org

Embassy in USA:
3200 Whitehaven Street NW, Washington DC 20008
Tel: +1 202 234 4300
www.demarkemb.org

British Council office:
Gammel Mønt 12.3, 1117 Copenhagen K
Tel: +45 (33) 369 400
www.britishcouncil.dk

➲ **Visa/Work Permits:** The same criteria apply as in other EU member states.

➲ **Currency:** £1 = 10.78 / $1 = 5.78 Danish Krone (DK)

➲ **Cost of Living:** The cost of living in Denmark is very high with a beer costing around £4 in major cities and towns and a cheap meal costing about £4-5.

➲ **Salaries/Taxes:** Salaries vary according to the institution you are working for. Taxation rates run about 55%.

➲ **Accommodation:** A room in the capital city of Copenhagen can cost around £600 per month.

◗ **Health advice:** Excellent medical facilities are widely available in Denmark. You should have medical insurance to cover any expenses you may incur.

◗ **English Language Media:** Copenhagen Post.

Schools in Denmark (+45)

Access
Hamerensgade 8, 1267 Copenhagen K. **Tel:** 14 22 6192.

Activsprog
Rosenvægets Alle 32, 2100 Copenhagen - also Odense, Ärhus & Aalborg.

Babel Sprogtræning
Vordingborggrade 18, 2100 Copenhagen.

Berlitz International
Vimmelskaftet 42a, 1161 Copenhagen.

Bis Sprogskole
Rolfsvej 14-16, 2000 Frederiksberg.

Cambridge Institute Foundation
Vimmelskaftet 48, 1161 Copenhagen.
Tel: 33 13 33 02

Centre for Undervisning
Ärhus amt, Ulla Sørensen, Vesterskovvej 4, 8660, Skanderborg. **Tel:** 86 511511, **Fax:** 86 511047

Elite Sprogcentret
Hoffmeyersvej 19, 2000 Frederiksberg.

Erhvervs Orienterede Sprogkurser
Betulavej 25, 3200 Helsinge.

European Education Centre Aps (Inlingua)
Lyngbyvej 72, 2100, Copenhagen.

FOF
Sønder Allé 9, 8000 Ärhus C. **Tel:** 88 86 12 29 55.

Frit Oplysningsforbund
Vestergrade, 5000 Odense C. **Tel:** 66 13 9813.

Linguarama
Hvilevej 7, 2900 Hellerup.

Master-Ling
Sortedam Dossering 83, 2100 Copenhagen.

FINLAND

The Finns are eager to speak English well and many spend their spare time brushing up on the language. There are plenty of opportunities to teach here as long as you are prepared to be flexible.

Finding a teaching job in Finland without qualifications will be very difficult but if you look in the bigger cities like Helsinki and Turku you may be able to get hired by a company to teach their employees. The best time to look for work is in the spring, when schools start recruiting for the following September. Before setting off and looking for work, it is advisable to contact language schools in advance as you may find it hard once you're in the country. Be prepared for taking on a lot of freelance work and the comparative instability associated with this.

Embassy in UK:
38 Chesham Place, London SW1X 8HW
Tel: +44 (0)20 7838 6200
www.finemb.org.uk

Embassy in USA:
3301 Massachusetts Ave NW, Washington DC 20008
Tel: +1 202 298 5800
www.finland.org

British Council office:
Hakaniemenkatu 2, 00530 Helsinki
Tel +358 (9) 774 3330
www.britishcouncil.fi

◗ **Visas/Work Permits:** A visa is not required for tourist or business stays up to 90 days. Any non-Scandinavian wishing to work in Finland must apply for a residence permit and a work permit before entering the country. The process usually takes 6 to 8 weeks and costs around £100.

◗ **Cost of Living:** Go to Finland with plenty of cash reserves. The cost of living is not cheap (as with all Scandinavian countries) and going out, eating and drinking will seriously dent your wallet.

◗ **Currency:** £1 = € 1.45 $1 = € 0.83

◗ **Salaries/Taxes:** Teaching rates moderate ranging from £8 - £12 per teaching hour. If you are planning to spend less than 6 months in Finland you must pay income tax at 25%.

◗ **Accommodation:** Ask if your employer will provide you with a place to live as accommodation is very expensive throughout the country.

◗ **Health advice:** There is a standard fee (relatively low) for medical services. Your insurance policy will cover it.

◗ **Tip:** As a rule, Finns are quite shy and you may find it takes some time before you start to make friends.

Schools in Finland (+358)

AAC-Opisto
Kauppaneuvoksentie 8, 00200 Helsinki. **Tel/Fax:** 9 4766 7801.

The Federation of Finnish-British Societies
Puistokatu 1bA, 00140 Helsinki, **Tel:** 639625.

IWG Kieli-Instituutti
Hämeenkatu 25 B, 33200 Tampere. **Tel:** 31 214 7573, **Fax:** 31 212 3519.

Kielipiste Oy
Kaisaniemenkatu 4A, 00100 Helsinki. **Tel:** 90 177266, **Fax:** 90 174885.

Linguarama Suomi
David Eade, Annankatu 26, 00100 Helsinki. **Tel:** 9/6803230, **Fax:** 9/603118.

Lingua-Forum Ky
Fredrikinkatu 61 A 36, 00100 Helsinki. **Tel:** 694 8426, **Fax:** 694 8417.

Lansi-Suomen opisto
Loimijoentie 280, 32700 Huittinen. **Tel:** 2 567866, **Fax:** 2 566409.

Richard Lewis Communications
Itätuulenkuja 10 B, 02100 Espo, Helsinki. **Tel:** 455 4811, **Fax:** 466592.

FRANCE

The French have become more demanding of their teachers and expect them to be experienced and professional. "Student centred" teaching methods are not in vogue and you really need to be au fait with the rules of English grammar before you take on an English language teaching job in France.

Many Americans and other non-EU nationals despair of finding a teaching job in France. But if you are determined and are not above a bit of minor rule-bending, you can work as an English language teacher in France. Reports suggest that one route for job finders is to contact all the language schools they can find in the Yellow Pages and arrange to send a CV, photo and hand-written cover letter to the relevant person. Some schools are prepared to pay foreign teachers in cash and if you can find part-time jobs at three or more schools you may find yourself rolling in Euros.

Consulate in UK:
21 Cromwell Road, London SW7 2EN
Tel: +44 (0)20 7073 1200

www.ambafrance.org.uk

Embassy in USA:
4101 Reservoir Road NW, Washington DC 20007
Tel: +1 202 944 6000
www.info-france-usa.org

British Council office:
9 rue de Constantine, 75340 Paris cedex 07
Tel +33 (1) 4955 7300
www.britishcouncil.fr

➲ **Visas/Work Permits:** A visa is not required for a tourist/business stay up to 90 days in France, Andorra, Monaco, and Corsica. Non-EU citizens must find an institute that is willing to put them on a contract before they can obtain working papers.

➲ **Cost of Living:** Living costs in the major cities are often surprisingly high, but rent and food (particularly wine!) are cheaper than in the UK and USA.

➲ **Currency:** £1 = € 1.45 $1 = € 0.83

➲ **Salaries/Taxes:** Salaries for teachers vary immensely in France and will usually be considerably lower in the provinces than in Paris, due to the lower cost of living. Contracted teachers can expect between £500 and £750 per month, while freelancers can expect £12 per hour.

➲ **Accommodation:** Expect to pay from around £350 per month for a one-bedroom apartment in Paris.

➲ **Health advice:** You will need insurance to avoid big bills if you fall sick or have an accident.

➲ **English Language Media:** International Herald Tribune, Paris Passion, The News (monthly)

Schools in France (+33)

AABC
20 rue Gonot de Mauroy, 75009 Paris. **Tel:** 1 42 66 13 11.

Academie des Langues Appliquées
60 rue de Laxou, BP 373 65- 40 98, Nancy.

Alexandra School
32 rue Amiral de Grasse, 66130 Grasse. **Tel:** 93 36 88 01.

Alpha Formation
51 rue Saint-Ferreol, 130001 Marseille. **Tel:** 91 33 00 72.

American Centre
Belomeau, Avenue Jean-Paul Coste, Paris. **Tel:** 1 42 38 42 38.

Anglesey Language Services (ALS)
1 bis Avenue Foch, 78400 Chatou. **Tel:** 1 34 80 65 15, **Fax:** 34 80 69 91.

Arc Langue
Chemin de la Haie, 64100 Bayonne. **Tel:** 59 55 05 66.

Audio-English
44 allée de Tourny, 33000 Bordeaux **Tel:** 56 44 54 05

BEST
24 Bd Béranger, 37000 Tours. **Tel:** 47 05 55 33, **Fax:** 47 64 40 27.

British Connection International
279 rue Crequi, 69007 Lyon. **Tel:** 72 73 02 55.

British Council
9/11 rue De Constantine, 75007 Paris. **Tel:** 49 55 73 00.

British Institute (University of London)
11 rue de Constantine, 74340 Paris, Cedex 07.

Business English Service & Translation
24 Bd Béranger, 37000 Tours. **Tel:** 47 05 55 33.

BTS Language Centre
226 Route de Philippeville, 6001 Marcinelle. **Tel:** 71313076.

Centre D'Etudes Des Langues
ISF Montfoulon, 61250 Damigny. **Tel:** 33 80 84 00.

Cybée Langues
7 rue d'Artois, 75008, Paris. **Tel:** 89 18 26

Collegium Palatinium
Dept EFL/CP, Chateau de Pourtales, 61 rue Mélanie, 67000. Strasbourg. **Tel:** 88 31 01 07.

EF Corporate
3 rue de Bassano, 75016 Paris. **Tel:** 47 20 18 01, **Fax:** 1 47 20 18 80.

Executive Language Services
20 rue Sainte Croix de la Bretonnerie, 75004 Paris. **Fax:** 1 48 044 55 53.

Fontainebleau Langues et Communication
15 rue Saint-Honoré, BP 27, 77300. Fontainbleau. **Tel:** 64 22 48 96.

Formalangues
106 Blvd Haussmann, 75008 Paris. **Tel:** 45229912.

Forum
66 Rue De La Bretonnerie, 45000 Orleans. **Tel:** 38625245.

International House Nice
62 rue Geoffredo, Nice, 6000

Linguarama
6 rue Roland Garros, 38320 Eybens. **Tel:** 76 62 00 18, **Fax:** 76 25 89 60.

Metropolitan Languages
151 rue de Billancourt, 92100 Boulogne. **Tel:** 46 04 57 32. **Fax:** 46 04 57 12.

Rapid English
2 rue du Maréchal Gallieni, 76600 Le Havre.

Regency Langues
1 rue Ferdinand Duval, 75004 Paris. **Tel:** 48 04 99 97, **Fax:** 48 04 34 96.

Rothman Institute
21 Avenue du Major Général Vanier, 1000 Troyes. **Tel:** 258 03041.

Sarl Executive Language Services
25 Blvd Sébastapol, 75001 Paris.

Unilangues
1 le Parvis-Paroi Nord, 92044 Paris la Défense Cedex 41. **Tel:** 47 78 45 80, **Fax:** 49 00 03 16.

GERMANY

Many institutions in Germany are looking for qualified and experienced teachers with a specialization in an area such as business English. But even newly qualified English language teachers with Master's degrees, certificates and diplomas are being hired. Many teachers are employed on a freelance basis, often teaching in-company outside office hours. There are lots of private language schools looking for teachers.

Recent reports suggest that it is relatively easy (when compared to other EU countries) for non-EU teachers to find teaching jobs and work legally in Germany. For Americans, USIA Fulbright programme organizes for US graduates to work as teaching assistants in high schools

Embassy in UK:
23 Belgrave Square, London SW1X 8PZ
Tel: 020 7824 1300
www.german-embassy.org.uk

Embassy in USA:
4645 Reservoir Road NW, Washington DC 20007
Tel: 202 298 4000
www.germany-info.org

British Council office
Hackescher Markt 1, 10178 Berlin
Tel +49 (30) 311 0990
www.britishcouncil.de

➲ **Tip:**Materials in American English are often hard to find. Bring some books and tapes over with you from the States. Your students, who may be used to

British English, will appreciate working with different materials and they may even like your accent!

⮕ **Visa/Work Permits:** U.S. citizens must arrange employment and apply for a work permit before they leave. This may take a couple of months.

⮕ **Cost of Living:** Contrary to popular belief, living costs in Germany are lower than you might expect, and lower than in the UK or USA.

⮕ **Currency:** £1 = € 1.45 $1 = € 0.83

⮕ **Salaries/Taxes:** All employees with their residence in Germany have to pay tax on their income in accordance with the German tax laws. The rates of wage or income tax are graduated progressively according to the particular wages or salary. Expect to earn £6-15 per teaching hour at a private language school and £15-20 as a freelancer. Freelancers often tend to work outside the social security and tax structures. This tends to imply high earnings but not much in the way of statutory health cover and benefits. The situation has become more complicated since 1999 when a law dating back to 1913 was resurrected by the German Social Security Administration, which requires that freelance teachers pay nearly 20% of their income into the state social security system. This law is being applied retroactively—some teachers report they have been hit with high tax bills. Many freelancers have left Germany claiming it is no longer worth their time to teach there. The situation remains uncertain at the time of writing so consult a lawyer if you have any specific questions or problems.

⮕ **Accommodation:** In any of the big cities a one-bedroom apartment will cost around £500. You will usually have to pay three months rent as a deposit

⮕ **Health advice:** Foreigners in Germany are placed on an equal footing with German employees when it comes to social protection. They generally have to be insured against sickness and unemployment and included in the statutory pension scheme by their employer on taking up the employment. The contributions to the social insurance scheme are borne half by the employer and half by the employee. The employee share is deducted from the gross wage and paid to the social insurance provider together with the employer's share. The employer also has to insure you against accident with his trade association: premiums for accident insurance are paid by the employer alone. In practice, many private language schools do not comply with the law and do not make contributions on your behalf. Of course, freelancers are afforded no protection and should carry their own medical insurance.

⮕ **English Language Media:** Handelsblatt (English edition), Munich Found (monthly), Spotlight, World Press

Schools in Germany (+49)

American Language Academy
Charlottenstr. 65, 10117 Berlin. **Tel:** 30 20 39 78 10, **Fax:** 30 20 39 78 13.

Anglo-German Institute
Christopherstr 4, 70178 Stuttgart. **Tel:** 711 603 858 **Fax:** 711 640 9941.

ASK Sprachenschule
1 Kortumstr 71, 44787 Bochum. **Tel:** 234-12910.

Bansley College
Str Des Friedens 35, 03222 Lubbenau, Brandenburg. **Tel:** 354-244 407, **Fax:** 354 244 408.

Benedict School
Gurzenichstr 17, 50667 Koln. **Tel:** 221-212 203.

Berlitz
Friedrich-Willhelm-Strasse 30, 47051 Duisburg.

British Council
Hardenbergstr 20, 10623 Berlin. **Tel:** 3110990.

Christopher Hills School of English
Sandeldamm 12, 63450 Hanau. **Tel:** 49-6181 15015, **Fax:** 49-6181 12121.

Collegium Palatinum
Adenauerplatz 8, 69115 Heidelburg. **Tel:** 62 2146 289, **Fax:** 62-2118 2023.

Didacta
Hohenzollernring 27, 95440 Bayreuth. **Tel:** 921-27 555.

English Language Centre
Bieberer Strasse 205, 63071 Offenbach am Main. **Tel:** 69 85 87 87, **Fax:** 69 85 72 02.

English Language Institute
Sprachenchule 4, Ubersetzer Am Zwinger 14, 33602 Bielefeld. **Tel:** 521-69353.

Europa-Universitat Viadrina
Sprachenzentrum, Grosse Scharrnstr 59, 15230 Frankfurt (Oder).

FBD Schulen
Katharinenstr 18, 70182 Stuttgart. **Tel:** 711-21580.

GLS Sprachenzentrum
B Jaeshke, Pestalozzistr 886, 10625 Berlin. **Tel:** 30-313 5025.

Hallworth English Centre
Frauenstrasse 118, 89703 Ulmponau. **Tel:** 731-22668.

inlingua Spachschule
Konigstrasse 61, 47051 Duisburg. **Tel:** 203 30 53 40.

Intercom Lang Services
Muggenkampstr 38, 20257 Hamburg.

International House
Prolog Sprachenschule, Hauptstrasse 23/24, Berlin, D-10827.

International House
LGS Sprachkurse, Werderring 18, Freiburg 79098

International House
Poststrasse 51, 20354 Hamburg. **Tel:** 352041.

Knowledge Point
Hohenzollernstrasse 26, 80801 Munchen **Tel:** 89 33 3405.

Linguarama Sprachinstitut
Kant Strasse 150, 10623 Berlin. **Tel:** 30 621 81 48, **Fax:** 30 312 94 91.

Lingotek Institut
Schlueterstrasse 18, 20146 Hamburg. **Tel:** 40 459 520.

Neue Sprachschule
Rosastrass 1, 79098 Freiburg. **Tel:** 761-24810.

NSK Language and Training Services
Comeniusstr 2, 90459 Nurnburg. **Tel:** 911-441552.

Sprachstudio Lingua Nova
Thierschstrasse 36, 80538 Munich. **Tel:** 89-221 171.

Stevens English Training
Ruttenscheider strasse 68, 45130 Essen.

Vorbeck-Schule
77723 Gengenback. **Tel:** 7803 3361.

Wirtschaftwissen-schaftliche Fakultat Ingolstadt
Auf der Schanz 49, 85049 Ingolstadt.

Yes Your English Services
Altonaer Chaussee 87, 22559 Schenefeld, Hamburg. **Tel:** 408 393 2116, **Fax:** 408 393 2117

GREECE

For many years, Greece has been one of the most popular destinations for English language teachers. Of all the candidates for the Cambridge First Certificate and Cambridge Proficiency exams worldwide, one quarter are in Greece. In most parts of the country, English language teaching in state schools is inadequate for these exams and children often attend private language schools (frontisteria) as a supplement.

There are estimated to be more than 5,000 of these schools in the country. You must be a graduate to teach and a certificate, diploma or MA in TESL is desirable although not absolutely necessary. Recruitment is normally done locally in May/June or September. Those less qualified may well have more success finding work in January, as many native speakers do not return to their jobs after the holiday break.

Embassy in UK:
1a Holland Park, London W11 3TP
Tel: 020 7221 6467
www.greekembassy.org.uk

Embassy in USA:
2221 Massachusetts Avenue NW, Washington DC 20008
Tel: 202 939 5800
www.greekembassy.org

British Council office:
17 Plateia Philikis Etairias, PO BOX 3488, 10673 Athens
Tel +30 (21) 0 369 2333
www.britishcouncil.gr

⮑ **Visa/Permits:** Non-EU citizens are supposed to apply for a work permit before they come to the country, for which they will need to present an employment offer from a Greek school, at their local Greek consulate. In practice, many teachers work while they are waiting for their permits to be processed. Americans of Greek descent can obtain residency permits but should check to make sure they won't have to serve in the army.

⮑ **Cost of Living:** Greece is no longer a cheap place to live in although it is less expensive than other parts of Europe. The cost of living in Athens depends to a large extent on the price of the accommodation. You'll need around £400 per month to cover your living expenses and rent.

⮑ **Currency:** £1 = € 1.45 $1 = € 0.83

⮑ **Salaries/Taxes:** Expect to earn approximately £400-500 a month at a language school. You can augment your income with private lessons.

⮑ **Accommodation:** Apartments in Athens can be relatively expensive starting at around £200 per month. In smaller towns, some schools offer free accommodation but check to make sure the building has a roof and is adequately heated in winter.

⮑ **Health advice:** Greek hospitals are notoriously overcrowded. Make sure you have a good medical insurance plan because if you fall sick or are injured, you will want to get back home as soon as you can.

⮑ **English Language Media:** Athens News, Kathimerini (English edition).

Schools in Greece (+30)

A Trechas Language Centre
20 Koundouriotou St., Keratsini. **Tel:** 1 432 0546.

Alpha Abatzolglou Economou
10 Kosma Etolou St, 54643 Thessaloniki. **Tel:** 31 830535.

A Andriopoulou
3, 28 Octobrio, Tripolis.

Anglo-Hellenic Teacher Recruitment
PO Box 263, 201 00 Corinth **Tel:** 741 53511, **Fax:** 741 86989. **Email:** info@anglo-hellenic.com

Athens College
PO Box 65005, 15410 Psychico, Athens.**Tel:** 1 6714621, **Fax:** 647 8156.

British Council
Ethnikis Amynis 9, PO Box 50007, 54013 · Thessalonika. **Tel:** 31 235 236.

English Tuition Centre
3 Pythias St., Kypseli, 1136 Athens.

Enossi Foreign Languages (The Language Centre)
Stadiou 7, Syntagma, 10562 Athens. **Tel:** 3230 356.

Eurocentre
7 Solomou Street, 41222 Larissa.

Featham School of English
PO Box 12, 50 Ep. Marouli St., Rethymnon, Crete. 74100. **Tel:** 831 23428, **Fax:** 831 23922.

Hambakis Schools of English
1 Filellinon Street, Athens. **Tel:** 1 3017531/5.

Hellenic American Union
22 Massalias St., GR-106 80 Athens.

International Language Centre
35 Votsi St., 26221 Patras.

Institute of English, French, German and Greek for Foreigners
Zavitsanou Sophia, 13 Joannou Gazi St, 31100 Lefkada.

Institute of Foreign Languages
41 Epidavrou St., 10441 Athens.

Kakkos School of English
Papastratou 5, Arginio 30100. **Tel/Fax:** 641 23449.

Makris School of English
2 Pardos G Olympion St., 60100 Katerini. **Tel:** 35122859.

G. Michalopolous School of English
24E Antistasis, Alexandria, 59300 Imathias, Thessaloniki. **Tel:** 33 3 322890.

New Centre
Arkarnanias 16, 11526 Athens

Omiros Association
52 Academias St., 10677 Athens. **Tel:** 362 2887, **Fax:** 362 1833.

Peter Sfyrakis School of Foreign Languages
21 Nikiforou Foka St, 72200 Ierapetra, Crete. **Tel:** 842 28700.

Polyglosso Language School
73 Agylis St., Neos Kosmos, Athens. **Tel/Fax:** 1 9214982.

Polyglosso Language School
96 Ag.Varvaras St., Dafne, Athens. **Tel/Fax:** 1 9766542.

Protypo English Language School
22 Deliyioryi Street, Volos 38221.

School of English
8 Kosti Palama, Kavala 65302.

School of Foreign Languages
12 P Isaldari St, Xylokastro, 20400 Corinth. **Tel:** 743 24678.

SILITZIS School of Languages
42 Koumoundourou, 412 22 Larissa.

Skouras Language School
7 G. Miltiadi St., 67100 Xanthi. **Tel:** 541 26112, **Fax:** 541 23721.

Strategakis Schools
24 Proxenou Koromila St, 54622 Thessaloniki. **Tel:** 31 264276, **Fax:** 228848.

Universal School of Language
66 M. Alexandrou St, Panorama, Thessalonika 55200. **Tel:** 31 341 014

Zoula Language Schools
Sanroco Square, 49100 Corfu. **Tel:** 661 39330, **Fax:** 661 35894.

IRELAND

Many language students study English in Ireland in the summer months and the country is experiencing a boom. It is difficult for non-EU citizens to find jobs in Ireland unless they are in the I.T. industry, construction or nursing.

Embassy in UK:
17 Grosvenor Place, London SW1X 7HR
Tel: 020 7235 2171

Embassy in USA:
2234 Massachusetts Ave NW, Washington DC 20008
Tel: 202 462 3939
www.irelandemb.org

⮐ **Visas/Work Permits:** Ireland is a member state of the EU so you will need an EU passport to work here. Americans and Canadians of Irish descent can qualify for an Irish passport if they were born in Ireland or have parents or grandparents who were. If you do not qualify for an Irish passport your employer will have to prove that you are doing a job that another EU citizen could not do.

⮐ **Cost of Living:** Ireland can be an expensive country to live in.

⮐ **Currency:** £1 = € 1.45 $1 = € 0.83

⮐ **Salaries/Taxes:** Low wages for teachers and high taxation rates make it difficult for teachers to survive here.

⮐ **Accommodation:** It can be very difficult to find an apartment or room in Dublin over the summer months. Rents run around £50-100 per week per person in a shared house.

⮐ **Health advice:** Good medical facilities are available.

Schools in Ireland (+353)

American College Dublin
2 Merrion Square, Dublin 2. **Tel:** 1 6768939, **Fax:** 1 6768941 **Email:** pmullins@amcd.ie

Centre Of English Studies
31 Dame Street, Dublin 2. **Tel:** 353 1 6714233, **Fax:** 1 6714425 www.cesireland.ie

Cork Language Centre International
Wellington House, Wellington Road, Cork **Tel:** 21 4551661, **Fax:** 21 4551662 www.corklanguagecentre.ie

Dublin School Of English
10-12 Westmoreland Street, Dublin 2. **Tel:** 1 6773322 **Fax:** 1 6795454 www.dse.ie/dse/

English Language Institute
99, St. Stephen's Green, Dublin 2. **Tel:** 1 4752965, **Fax:** 1 4752967 www.englishlanguage.com

Galway Language Centre
The Bridge Mills, Galway. **Tel:** 91 566468, **Fax:** 91 564122.

International House Dublin
Griffith College Campus, South Circular Road, Dublin 8. **Tel:** 1 454 9260 / 454 9261, **Fax:** 1 454 9262 www.ihdublin.com

The Language Centre Of Ireland
45 Kildare Street, Dublin 2. **Tel:** 1 6716266. **Fax:** 1 6716430 www.lci.ie

Waterford English Language Centres
31 John's Hill, Waterford. **Tel:** 51 877288, **Fax:** 51 854603 www.waterfordd-net.ie

ITALY

There is a great demand for English language teachers in Italy but it can be hard to find work, especially in the major cities. Generally, teachers need to be native speakers with at least a TESL certificate. Schools are trying to save money so recruitment from overseas is much less common than it was in the past, as schools tend to recruit locally. September is the best time to arrive in Italy to start your job search. Italian schools and companies prefer to recruit locally and there is a strong demand for English teachers in the corporate sector.

Embassy in UK:
14 Three Kings' Yard, Davies Street, London W1K 2EH
Tel: 020 7312 2200
www.embitaly.org.uk

Embassy in USA:
3000 Whitehaven Street NW, Washington DC 20008
Tel: 202 612 4400
www.italyemb.org

British Council office:
Via Quattro Fontane 20, 00184 Rome
Tel +39 (06) 478 141
www.britishcouncil.it

⮐ **Visas/Work Permits:** It is now easier for Americans to arrive in Italy, find a teaching job, and then apply for a work permit without having to return to the States as was once the case.

⮐ **Cost of Living:** Italian cities are generally more expensive than their American counterparts but life in rural Italy is quite cheap.

⮐ **Currency:** £1 = € 1.45 $1 = € 0.83

⮐ **Salaries/Taxes:** Schools usually provide 25 contact hours a week at £10-15 per hour. A typical monthly salary is around £6-800 (with overtime paid extra). Schools often provide accommodation for the first month and some even give a ticket home at the end of the contract. Tax is payable at 20% with a 10% additional social security deduction.

○ **Accommodation:** Accommodation is easy to find but tends to be expensive. Milan is the most expensive city and a one-bedroom apartment can cost about £700 a month but accommodation can be found for £300-400. Elsewhere, rents are cheaper.

○ **Health advice:** Insurance is advisable.

Schools in Italy (+39)

Academia Britannica
Via Bruxelles 61, 04100 Latina. **Tel:** 773 491917.

Anglo American School
Piazza S. Giovanni in Monte 9, 40124 Bologna.

Anglocentre
Via A de Gasperi 23, 70052 Bisceglie.

Arlington Language Services
cp99, 29100 Piacenza.

Bari Poggiofranco English Centre
Viale Pio XII 18, 70124 Bari.

Benedict School
Via Sauro 36, 48100 Ravenna. **Tel:** 544 38199, **Fax:** 544 38399.

The British Council
Via Manzoni 38, 20121 Milan. **Tel:** 39 2 772221.

The British Council
Palazzo del Drago, Via Quattro Fontane 20, 00184, Rome. **Tel:** 6 478141.

British Institute
Fontane 109, Rome. **Tel:** 6491979. **Fax:** 64815549.

British Institute of Milan
Via Marghera 45, 20149 Milan. **Tel:** 2 48011149.

British Institute of Florence
Palazzo Feroni, Via Tornalbuoni 2, Florence. **Tel:** 55 298866.

British Institute of Rome
Via 4 Fontane 109, 00184 Rome.

The British Language Centre
Via Piazzi Angolo Largo Pedrini, 23100 Sondrio. **Tel:** 342 216130.

The British Language Centre
Via Piazza Roma 3, 20038 Serengo.

The British School of Bari
Via Celentano 27, 70121 Bari. **Tel:** 080 5247335, **Fax:** 080 5247396.

Cambridge Centre of English
Via Campanella 16, 41100 Modena. **Tel:** 59 24 1004

The Cambridge School
Via S Rochetto 3, Verona. **Tel:** 458003154

The Cambridge School
Via Mercanti 36, 84100 Salerno. **Tel:** 89 228942, **Fax:** 89 252523.

Canning School
Via San Remo 9, 20133 Milan.

Centro di Lingue
Via Pozzo 30, Trento. **Tel:** 461981733. **Fax:** 461981687.

Centro Internazionale di Linguistica Streamline
Via Piave 34/b, 71100 Foggia. **Tel:** 88124204.

Cento Lingue di Vinci Antonella
Via San Martino 77, Pisa.

Centro Lingue Tradint
Via Jannozzi 8, S Donato Milanese Chandler, Viale Aventino 102, 00153 Rome.

CLM-Bell
Eugen Joa, Via Pozzo 30, 38100 Trento. **Tel:** 461 981733, **Fax:** 461 981687.

English Centre
Via Promis 8, 11100 Aosta. **Tel:** 165 235416.

The English Centre
Via P Paoli 34, 07100 Sassari, Sardinia. **Tel:** 79 238154, **Fax:** 79 238180.

The English Connection
Via Ferro 1, 30027 San Dona di Piave.

English For Business Snc
Via Magnani Ricotti, n.2, 28100 Novara. **Tel:** 321 627186 **Fax:** 321 398061.

The English Institute
Corso Gelone 82, 96100 Siracusa. **Tel:** 961 6085.

English House
Via Roma 177, 85028 Rionero, Potenza.

English Language Centre
Viale Milano 20, 21100 Varese. **Tel:** 332 282732, **Fax:** 332 236385.

The English Language Studio
Via Antonio Bondi 27, 40138 Bologna. **Tel:** 51347394, **Fax:** 51505952.

English School
Via dei Correttori 6, 89127 Reggio Calabria. **Tel/Fax:** 965 899535.

Eurolingue
Via Chiana 116, 00198 Roma.

European Language Institute
Via IV Novembre 65, 55049 Viareggio (LU).

Filadelfia School
Via L. Colla 22, 10098 Rivoli.

Home School
Via F. Malvotti 8, Conegliano (TV).

Inlingua
Piazza XX Settembre 36, Civitanova Marche (MC).

Inlingua
Corso Vittorio Emanuel II 68, Torino.

Inlingua
Via Leoncino 35, 37121 Verona.

Inlingua
Via Monte Piana 42, Venezia.

International British School
Via Santacaterina 146, 89100 Regio Calabria.

International House Livorno
Piazza Folgore 1, 57128 Livorno. **Tel:** 336 709682, **Fax:** 586 508060.

International House Pisa
Via Risorgimento 9, 56126 Pisa. **Tel:** 50440 40.

International House Rome
Via San Godenzo 100, 00189 Rome.

International House Turin
Via Saluzzi 60, 10125 Turin. **Tel:** 39 11 669 95.

International Language School
Via Tibullo 10, 00193 Rome. **Tel:** 687 6801, **Fax:** 683 07796.

Language Centre
Via Milano 20, 21100 Varese. **Tel:** 332 282732.

Language Centre
Via G Daita 29, 90139 Palermo.

Lb Linguistico
Centro Insegnamento, Lingue Staniere, Via Caserta 16, 95128 Catania, Sicily.

Lingua Due Villa
Pendola 15, 57100 Livorno.

Living Languages School
Via Magna Grecia, 89100 Regio Calabria. **Tel/Fax:** 39 965 330926.

London School
Fabiola Cordaro, International House, Viale Emilia 34, 90144 Palermo. **Tel:** 39 91 52 524

Lord Byron College
Via Sparano 102, 70121 Bari. **Tel:** 80 238696.

Managerial English Consultants
Via Sforza Pallavicini 11, 009193 Rome.**Tel:** 6 654 2391, **Fax:** 6 6871159.

Modern English School
Via Borgonuovo 14, 40125 Bologna. **Tel:** 51 227523, **Fax:** 51225314.

Multimethod
I Go Richini 8, 20122 Milan. **Tel:** 2583042.

Oxford School
San Marco 1513, Venice. Fax: 41 5210785.

Oxford School of English
Via S. Pertini 14, Mirano, 30035 Venice. **Tel:** 41 570 2355, **Fax:** 41 570 2390.

The Professionals
Via F Carcona 4, 20149 Milan. **Tel:** 2 48000035, **Fax:** 2 4814001.

Regency School
Via dell' Arcivescovado 7, 16121 Turin. **Tel:** 11 562 7456, **Fax:** 11 541845.

Regent International
V.U. Da Pisa 6, Milan.

Regent International
Corsa Italia 54, 21047 Saronno.

RTS Language Training
Via Tuscolana 4, 00182 Rome. **Tel:** 6 702 2730, **Fax:** 6 702 1740.

Scuola The Westminster
Via Tevere 84, Sesto Fiorentino.

Spep School
Via della Secca 1, 40121 Bologna.

Studio Linguistico Fonema
via Marconi 19, 50053 Sovigliana-Vinci. **Tel:** 571 500551.

Studio professionale Apprendimento Linguistico Programmato
Via Ferrarese 3, Bologna. **Tel:** 051 360617, **Fax:** 513 68413.

Summer Camps
Via Roma 54, 18038 San Remo. **Tel/Fax:** 184 506070.

Unimoney
Corso Sempione 72, 20154 Milan.

Victoria Language Centre
Viale Fassi 28, 41012 Capri.

Wall Street Institute
Piazza Combattento 6, 4100 Ferrara. **Tel:** 532 200231.

THE NETHERLANDS

The current employment situation for English language teachers is good. There is quite a demand for teachers of English who are native speakers and there may also be possible opportunities for qualified teachers in a

new type of school. There are forty of these at present and they teach children in English and Dutch. The Dutch term for the schools is "Twee Talig Scholen." Most work opportunities available to foreign teachers tends to be teaching Business English as the levels of English in the school system are very high. Schools depending mainly on long-term freelance teachers. Self-employed teachers typically work for a number of schools or agencies and their incomes can fluctuate considerably. To find work, go through the list of language schools below as well as those in the Dutch Yellow Pages. It is likely you will have to give an observed lesson before you are given the job.

Embassy in UK:
38 Hyde Park Gate, London SW7 5DP
Tel: 020 7590 3200
www.netherlands-embassy.org.uk

Embassy in USA:
4200 Linnean Ave NW, Washington DC 20008
Tel: 202 244 5300
www.netherlands-embassy.org

British Council office:
Weteringschans 85A, 1017 RZ Amsterdam
Tel +31 (20) 550 6060
www.britishcouncil.org/netherlands

◐ **Visa/Work Permits:** The Employment of Foreign Workers Act says that an employer cannot employ a foreigner without an employment permit from the Central Employment Board. The employer must first fill a vacancy from the pool of job applicants immediately available in the Netherlands. Subsequently it will be determined if applicants from other member states of the European Community are available. Only after these two applicant pools are exhausted can subjects from other countries be eligible for an employment permit. An employment permit can be sought only after a residence permit application (VTV) has been submitted. Applications for employment permits are available from the Regional Employment Office. Applications for employment permits are processed by the Employment Office only if the form has been completed, signed by both the employer and the employee, and all required material has been attached.

◐ **Cost of Living:** The Netherlands is an expensive place to live.

◐ **Currency:** £1 = € 1.45 $1 = € 0.83

◐ **Salaries/Taxes:** Qualified teachers can earn £8-12 per lesson. Tax is payable at around 30%.

◐ **Accommodation:** Accommodation in the Amsterdam area is extremely expensive and a studio apartment could cost you over £200 a month. Also bear in mind that a place will also be very hard to find.

◐ **Health advice:** If you are a taxpayer then you will be entitled to medical coverage under the 'Ziekenfonds' system. But you will still have to pay a premium to the health insurance company of between £6 - 12 a month.

Schools in The Netherlands (+31)

All-English Institute
Iepenlaan 96, 2061 GN Bloemendaal (Haarlem area)
Tel: 023-5277394

Arcus Contracting B.V.
Diepenbrockstraat 15, 6411 TJ Heerlen **Tel:**
045-5609070

Berlitz Language Centre
Rokin 87-89, 1012 Kl Amsterdam **Tel:** 020-6221375,
Fax: 20-6203959

British Language Training Centre
NZ Voorburgwal 328, 1012 RW Amsterdam **Tel:**
020-6223634

The British School in the Netherlands
ELC, Vlaskamp 19, 2592 AA Den Haag **Tel:**
070-3338130

CBE - Centre for British English
Bergsingel 89-A, 3037 GA Rotterdam **Tel:**
010-4678705

C J Korrel
Schinkelhavenstraat 13 hs, 1075 VN Amsterdam **Tel:**
020-6627441

Communications in English
Piet Heinstraat 101, 2518 CE Den Haag **Tel:**
070-3466314

Delftse Volksuniversiteit
Ruys de Beerenbrouckstraat 31, 2613 AS Delft **Tel:**
015-2570130

De Taaltrainers
Burg. Raaymaekerslaan153, 5361 KL Grave **Tel:**
0486-421230

Double Dutch
Beringstraat 18, 7532 CP Enschede **Tel:** 053-4615822

Dutchess English Language Centre
Schoutenstraat 86, 1623 RZ Hoorn **Tel:** 0229-210581

Engelse Taalcursussen
IJsselsteinseweg 63, 3435 PB Nieuwegein **Tel:**
030-6035506

English Language Institute
Berkenweg 46, 3741 BZ Baarn **Tel:** 035-5424725

Fontys Hogeschool
Oude Markt 5, 6131 EN Sittard **Tel:** 046-4599579

Fontys Hogeschool Talencentrum
Rachelsmolen 1, 5600 AH Eindhoven **Tel:**
040-2454972

Franglais
Molenstraat 15, 2513 BH Den Haag **Tel:** 070-3611703

HES/O & O
K.P. van der Mandelelaan 22, 3062 MB Rotterdam
Tel: 010-4532451

Int. Studiecentrum v/d Vrouw
Concertgebouwplein 17, 1071 LM Amsterdam **Tel:**
020-6761437

Instituut De Wester
Ruusbroechof 37, 1813 BC Alkmaar **Tel:**
072-5400920

Instituut Taaltip
Floralaan 19, 1211 JT Hilversum **Tel:** 035-7720211

Instituut Uithoorn
Postbus 238, 1420 AE Uithoorn **Tel:** 020-4823482

Instituut Verschoor
Piet Heinlaan 8, 3941 VG Doorn **Tel:** 0343-413319

Instituut voor Taalhantering
Postbus 368, 8000 AJ Zwolle **Tel:** 038-4449263

The Language Academy
Spuistraat 134, 1012 VB Amsterdam **Tel:**
020-5254637

Leidse Volksuniversiteit K & O
Oude Vest 45, 2312 XS Leiden **Tel:** 071-5141141

LOI Tel: correspondentie cursussen
Postbus 4200, 2350 CA Leiderdorp **Tel:** 071-5451888

Onderwijsinstituut Netty Post
Haverstraat 2, 1446 CE Purmerend **Tel:** 0299-641416

P.C.I. Talen
Bachlaan 43, 1817 GH Alkmaar **Tel:** 072-5156518

RIVO
Dorpstraat 3, 2902 BC Capelle a/d IJssel **Tel:**
010-4519464

ROC Albeda Contract Groep
Heemraadsingel 178, 3021 DL Rotterdam **Tel:**
010-4255333

ROC Da Vinci College
Groenedijk 49, Dordrecht **Tel:** 078-6572657

ROC Instituut De Factoor
Postbus 1, 8000 AA Zwolle **Tel:** 038-8508026

ROC Joke Smit School
R Vinkeleskade 62, 1071 SX Amsterdam **Tel:**
020-6647401

ROC Koning Willem I College
Vlijmenseweg 2, 5223 GW 'sHertogenbosch **Tel:**
073-6249624

Schoevers Opleidingen
Bezuidenhoutseweg 273, 2594 AN Den Haag **Tel:**
070-3491499

Schoevers Opleidingen
Eendrachtskade/Zuidzijde 12 Groningen **Tel:**
050-3182202

Schoevers Opleidingen
Javastraat 16-18, 6524 MB Nijmegen **Tel:**
024-3229742/024-3787602

Schoevers Opleidingen
Karel Doormanstraat 331, 3012 GH Rotterdam **Tel:**
010-4117855

Schoevers Opleidingen
Kromme Nieuwe Gracht 3, 3512 HC Utrecht **Tel:**
030-2368152

Schoevers Opleidingen
Markt 17, 5611 EB Eindhoven **Tel:** 040-2442832

Schoevers Opleidingen
Stadhouderskade 60, 1072 AC Amsterdam **Tel:**
020-6627156

Schoevers Opleidingen
Tuinstraat 1, 5000 JL Tilburg **Tel:** 013-5424128

Schoevers Opleidingen
Utrechtsestraat 35, 6811 LT Arnhem **Tel:**
026-4453641

The School of English
1e Wormerweg 238, 7331 MT Apeldoorn **Tel:**
055-5336769

Secradesk
Postbus 545, 7500 AM Enschede **Tel:** 053-4836420

Stichting Holtland Contract
Lammenschanspark 2, 2381 JK Leiden **Tel:**
071-5321952

Stichting IVIO
De Schans 1802, 8231 KA Lelystad
Tel: 0320-229948

Stichting Rotterdamse Volksuniv.
Heemraadsingel 275, 3023 BE Rotterdam **Tel:**
010-4761200

Suitcase
Divertimentostraat 55, 1312 EB Almere **Tel:**
036-5367482

Taalcursussen Doorn
W. Alexanderweg 117, 3945 CH Cothen **Tel:**
0343-561617

Taaltrainingscentrum Barendrecht
Maasstraat 9, 2991 AD Barendrecht **Tel:** 0180-615410

Talenlaboratorium
Rijksuniversiteit Leiden, Postbus 9515, 2300 RA
Leiden **Tel:** 071-5272332

Taleninstituut Bogaers
Groenstraat 139-155, 5021 LL Tilburg **Tel:**
013-5362101

Talenpracticum Twente B.V.
Ariënsplein 2, 7511 JX Enschede **Tel:** 053-4317842

Universitair Talencentrum Nijmegen
Erasmusplein 1, 6525 HT Nijmegen
Tel: 024-612159

Utrechtse Volksuniversiteit
Nieuwe Gracht 41, 3512 LE Utrecht **Tel:** 030-2313395

Van Beers & Kooijmans vof
Rigelhof 14, 3318 CZ Dordrecht **Tel:** 078-6183998

Volksuniversiteit Amersfoort
Korte Bergstraat 5, 3811 ML Amersfoort **Tel:**
033-4656640

Volksuniversiteit Amstelland
Burg. Haspelslaan 2, 1181 NB Amstelveen **Tel:**
020-6457506

Volksuniversiteit Amsterdam
Rapenburgerstraat 73, 1011 VK Amsterdam **Tel:**
020-6261626

Volksuniversiteit Bodengraven
Groene Zoom 149, 2411 SP Bodegraven **Tel:**
0172-616924

Volksuniversiteit Enschede
Molenstraat 27, 7514 DJ Enschede **Tel:**053-4323304

Volksuniversiteit Groningen
Oude Boteringestraat 21, 9712 GC Groningen **Tel:**
050-3126555

Volksuniversiteit Haarlem
Leidsevaart 220, 2014 HE Haarlem
Tel: 023-5329453

Volksuniversiteit
Havensingel 24, 5211 TX 's Hertogenbosch **Tel:**
073-6141120

Volksuniversiteit Hilversum
Arena 301, 1213 NZ Hilversum
Tel:035-6892051/035-6892000

Volksuniversiteit Soest/Soesterberg
Di Lassostraat 65, 3766 EB Soest **Tel:**035-6022195

The Workshop
Rostocklaan 38, 7315 HM Apeldoorn **Tel:**
055-5216736

Zeeuwse Volksuniversiteit
Postbus 724, 4330 AS Middelburg **Tel:** 0118-634800

NORWAY

There is often a shortage of English language teachers in Norway but it is hard to get a job unless you are qualified and have some experience. For non-EU teachers, it is almost impossible to find a job teaching English unless you are a Norwegian citizen or you are married to one!

Embassy in UK:
25 Belgrave Square, London SW1X 8QD
Tel: 020 7591 5500
www.norway.org.uk

Embassy in USA:
2720 34th Street NW, Washington DC 20008
Tel: 202 333 6000
www.norway.org/embassy

British Council office:
Fridtjof Nansens Plass 5, 0160 Oslo
Tel +47 (22) 396 190
www.britishcouncil.no

➲ **Visas/Work Permits:** A valid passport is required. U.S. citizens may enter Norway for tourist or general business purposes without a visa for up to 90 days. Tourists who have stayed in Norway for more than 90 days without a visa are usually not permitted to re-enter the country until six months have passed. Tourists who enter without a visa cannot usually change status in Norway in order to reside or work. Travellers planning a long-term stay, marriage or employment in Norway should seek the appropriate visa before departing the United States.

➲ **Currency:** £1 = 12.23 / $1 = 6.55 Norwegian Kroner

➲ **Cost of Living:** very expensive country to live in but the social welfare system is excellent.

➲ **Health advice:** Medical facilities are widely available and of high quality, but may be limited outside the larger urban areas. The remote and sparse populations in northern Norway, and the dependency on ferries to cross fjords of western Norway, may affect transportation and access to medical facilities.

Schools in Norway (+47)

Det Internasjonale Spraksenter
Dronningensgenst 32, 0154 Oslo. **Tel:** 22 33 15 20. **Fax:** 22 33 69 30.

Norsk Sprachinsitut
Korgengst. 9, 0153 Oslo: **Tel:** 23 10 01 10. **Fax:** 23 10 01 27.

Sprakskolen As
Karl Johansgat 8, 0154 Oslo. **Tel:** 22 42 00 87. **Fax:** 22 42 32 94.

PORTUGAL

Over the last few years it has become more difficult for non-EU passport holders to find teaching jobs in Portugal. But Americans and Canadians do find work, especially in Lisbon where some schools are willing to employ unqualified native-speaking tourists.

Embassy in UK:
11 Belgrave Square, London SW1X 8PP
Tel: 020 7235 5331

Embassy in USA:
2125 Kalorama Road NW, Washington DC 20008
Tel: 202 328 8610

British Council office:
Rua Lui Fernandes 1-3, 1249-062 Lisbon
Tel: +351 21 321 4500
www.pt.britishcouncil.org

➲ **Visa/Permits:** If you are lucky enough to get work before you leave (which is advisable), your paperwork should be sorted out in advance. A visa is not required for tourist or business stays of up to 60 days.

➲ **Cost of Living:** Reasonable compared to the UK and USA

➲ **Currency:** £1 = € 1.45 $1 = € 0.83

➲ **Salaries/Taxes:** Annual income for a teacher ranges from £8,000 to £10,000. Tax is about 20% of your gross salary.

➲ **Accommodation:** Accommodation may be provided by the institute. You will pay at least £400 per month for accommodation in Lisbon.

➲ **English Language Media:** The News (weekly)

Schools in Portugal (+351)

American Language Institute
Rua José Falcao 15-5° Esq, 4050 Oporto. **Tel:** 2 318 127, **Fax:** 2 208 5287.

Berlitz
Av Conde Valbom 6-4, 1000 Lisbon.

Big Ben School
Rua Moinho Fanares 4-1, 2725 Mem Martins.

Bristol School Group
Trav. Dr Carlos Felgueiras, 12-3°, 4470 Maia. **Tel:** 2 948 8803, **Fax:** 2 948 6460.

British Council
Rua De Sao Marcal 174, 1294 Lisbon Codex. **Tel:** 347 6141.

British Council
Rua Do Breyner 155, 4050 Oporto. **Tel:** 200 5577.

Cambridge School
Avenida da Liberdade 173-4, 1200 Lisbon. **Tel:** 352 7474, **Fax:** 353 4729.

Casa de Inglaterra
Rua Alexandre Herculano 134, 3000 Coimbra.

CENA-Cent.
Est. Norte Americanos, Rua Remedios 62 c/v, 1200 Lisbon.

Centro de Estudos IPFEL
Rua Edith Cavell 8, 1900 Lisbon.

Centro de Instrucao Tecnica
Rua Da Estefania 32-10 Dto, 1000 Lisbon.

Centro Internacional Linguas
Av Fontes P de Melo 25-1Dto, 1000 Lisbon.

Centro de Linguas de Alvide
Rua Fonte Nino, Viv Pe Americo 1, Alvide, 2750 Cascais.

Centro de Linguas Estrangeiras de Cascais
Av Marginal BI A-30, 2750 Cascais.

Centro de Linguas Intergarb
Tv da Liberdade 13-1, 8200 Albufeira.

Centro de Linguas de Quarteira
Rua Proj 25 de Abril 12, 8125 Quarteira.

Centro de Linguas de Queluz
Av Dr Miguel Bombarda 62-1E, 2745 Queluz.

Centro de Linguas de Santarem
Lg Pe Francisco N Silva, 2000 Santarem.

CIAL-Centro De Linguas
Av Republica 14-20, 1000 Lisbon. **Tel:** 3533733

Class
Rua Gen Humberto Delgado 40-1, 7540 Santiago Do Cacem.

Clube Conversacao Inglesa 3M
Rua Rodrigues Sampaio 18-3, 1100 Lisbon.

Communicate Language Institute
Praceta Joao Villaret 12B, 2675 Povoa de Sto. Adriao.

Curso de Linguas Estrangeiras
Rua Dr Miguel Bombarda 271-1, 2600 Vila Franca De Xira.

Ecubal
Lombos, Barros Brancos, Porches, 8400 Lagoa.

ELTA
Av Jose E Garcia 55-3, 2745 Queluz.

Encounter English
Av Fernao De Magalha, 4300 Porto. **Tel:** 567916.

English at PLC
Praca Luis de Camoes 26, Apartado 73, 5001 Vila Real.

English Institute Setubal
Av 22 Dezembro 88, 2900 Setubal.

The English Language Centre
Rua Calouste Gulbenkian 22-r/c C, 3080 Figueira Da Foz.

The English School of Coruche
Rua Guerreiros 11, 2100 Coruche.

English School of Loule
Rua Jose F Guerreiro 66M,Galerias Do Mercado, 8100 Loule.

Escola de Linguas de Agueda
Rua Jose G Pimenta, 3750 Agueda

Escola de Linguas de Ovar
Rua Ferreira de Castro 124-1 A/B, 3880 Ovar.

Eurocentre Instituto de Linguas
Av de Bons Amigos 4-1, 2735 Cacem.

Gab Tecnico de Linguas
Rua Hermenegildo Capelo 2-2, 2400 Leiria.

GEDI
Pq Miraflores Lt 18-1A/B, 1495 Alges.

Greenwich Instituto de Linguas
Rua 25 de Abril 560, S Cosme, 4420 Gondomar. **Tel/Fax:** 2 483 6429.

IF - Ingles Funcional
Rua Afonso Albuquerque 73-A, 2460 Alcobaca.

IF Ingles Funcional
Rua Com Almeida Henriques 32, 2400 Leiria.

IF Ingles Funcional
Ap 303, 2430 Marinha Grande. **Tel:** 44 568351, **Fax:** 44 560346.

INESP
Rua Dr Alberto Souto 20-2, 3800 Aveiro.

INLINGUA
Campo Grande 30-1A, 1700 Lisbon.

INPR
Bernardo Lima 5, 1100 Lisbon.

Instituto Britanico
Rua Conselheiro Januario 119/21, 4700 Braga. **Tel:** 53 23898.

Instituto Britanico
Rua Municipio Lt B - 1 C, 2400 Leiria.

Instituto Britanico
Rua Dr Ferreira Carmo, 4990 Ponte De Lima.

Instituto Franco-Britanico
Rua 5 de Outubro 10-1Dto, 2700 Amadora.

Instituto Inlas do Porto
Rua S da Bandeira 522-1, 4000 Porto.

Instituto de Linguas
Rua Valverde 1, 2350 Torres Novas.

Instituto de Linguas do Castelo Branco
Av 1 Maio, 39 S - 1 E, 6000 Castelo Branco.

Instituto de Linguas de Faro
Av 5 de Outubro, 8000 Faro.

Instituto de Linguas do Fundao
Urb Rebordao Lt 17-r/c, 6230 Fundao.

Instituto de Linguas de Oeiras
Rua Infante D Pedro 1 e 3-r/c, 2780 Oeiras.

Instituto de Linguas de Paredes
Av Republica, Casteloes Cepeda, 4580 Paredes.

Instituto Nacional de Administracao
Centro de Linguas, Palacio Marquus de Oeiras, 2780 Oeiras.

Instituto Sintrense de Linguas
Rua Dr Almeida Guerra 26, 2710 Sintra.

Interlingua
Lg 1 de Dezembro 28, 8500 Portimao.

Interlingu
Rua Dr Joaquim Telo 32-1E, 8600 Lagos.

International House Braga
Rua dos Chaos 168, 4710 Braga. **Tel:** 53 215250, **Fax:** 53 61228.

International House Lisbon
Rua Marques Sa Da Bandeira 16, 1000 Lisbon

International Language School
Av Rep Guine Bissau, 26-A, 2900 Setubal.

ISLA
Bo S Jo de Brito, 5300 Bragan A, Manitoba,C Com Premar, l 72, 4490 Povoa De Varzim.

Know-How
Av Alvares Cabral 5-300, 1200 Lisbon.

Lancaster College
Rua C Civico, Ed A Seguradora 2, 6200 Covilha.

Lancaster College
Pta 25 Abril 35-1E, 4400 Vila Nova De Gaia. **Tel:** 2 306 495.

Language School
Rua Alm Candido Reis 98, 2870 Montijo.

Linguacoop
Av. Manuel da Maia 46-10 D, 1000 Lisbon.

Linguacultura
Rua Dr Joaquim Jacinto 110, 2300 Tomar.

Linguacultura
Lg Sto Antonio 6-1 Esq, 2200 Abrantes.

Lisbon Language Learners
Rua Conde Redondo 33-r/cE, 1100 Lisbon.

Mundilingua
Rua Dr Tefilo Braga, Ed Rubi-1, 8500 Portimao.

Mundilinguas
Rua Miguel Bombarda 34-1, 2000 Santarem.

The New Institute of Languages
Urb Portela Lt 197-5B-C, 2685 Sacavem. **Tel:** 1 943 5238.

Novo Instituto de Linguas
Rua Cordeiro Ferreira 19 C-1D, 1700 Lisbon.

PEC
Rua SA Bandeira 5385, 4000 Oporto. **Tel:** 200 5077.

PROLINGUAS
Rua Saraiva Carvalho, 84 - Pt2, 1200 Lisbon.

Royal School of Languages
Av Dr Lourenco Peixinho 92-2, 3800 Aveiro. **Tel:** 34 2956, **Fax:** 34 382870.

Tell School
Rua Soc Farmaceutica 30-1, 1100 Lisbon.

Tjaereborg Studio
Av Liberdade 166-4F, 1200 Lisbon.

Wall Street Institutes Avenidas
Av Praia de Vitoria, 71 3rd, 1000 Lisbon. **Tel:** 316 0810, **Fax:** 316 0553.

Wall Street Institutes Oporto
Rua do Campo Alegre 231, 3°, 4100 Oporto. **Tel/Fax:** 2 600 9875.

Weltsprachen-Institut
Qta Carreira 37 r/c, 2765 Sao Joao do Estoril. **Tel:** 4684032.

Whyte Institute
Lg das Almas 10-2E/F, 4900 Viana Do Castelo.

World Trade Centre - Lisbon
Av Brasil 1-5e8, 1700 Lisbon.

SPAIN

Spanish English language schools have been hit recently with economic problems and some of the major chains have closed down. However, there are still jobs available, especially to qualified native-speakers from the UK.

The best time to arrive is in September when schools are recruiting teachers for the academic year ahead. Another option is to come to Spain in August and complete a TEFL certificate course before starting your job search. This will cost around £600 / $1100 for a month-long course.

Native English language speakers can find teaching jobs in Spain without any qualifications beyond their degrees but it will make your professional life much easier if you have some training under your belt! The maximum number of teaching hours per week allowed by law is 33, but contracted teachers can expect a challenging schedule with close to this number of hours and often at inconvenient times. You might consider working privately as an option because it is better paid than working in schools. If you're in Madrid, try putting an ad for your services in the Segundamano newspaper.

Although it is difficult for non-EU citizens to work legally in Spain, the reality is that thousands of Americans, Canadians and Australians are employed as English language teachers throughout the country.

Embassy in UK:
39 Chesham Place, London SW1X 8SB
Tel: 020 7235 5555

Embassy in USA:
2375 Pennsylvania Ave NW, Washington DC 20037
Tel: 202 452 0100
www.spainemb.org

British Council office:
Paseo del General Martinez, Campos 31, 28010 Madrid

Tel +34 (91) 337 3500
www.britishcouncil.es

⮑ **Tip:** Dress formally for your interview. If you get the job, you can ask later if casual attire is acceptable while working.

⮑ **Visa/Permits:** Officially, non-EU citizens require a work visa if they are staying over three months. In reality most work without contracts at least initially as work visas are difficult to get. Those wishing to stay in the long term usually apply for a work visa, involving documentation from their employer and from the US, and a return trip, a lengthy process

⮑ **Cost of Living:** Urban life in Spain is expensive but if you are selective about where you stay, then savings can be made.

⮑ **Currency:** £1 = € 1.45 $1 = € 0.83

⮑ **Salaries/Taxes:** A minimum monthly salary in the big cities is around £300 / $550 a month. Private sector schools pay approximately £4.50 / $8 per hour in Catalonia. Freelancers can earn around £6.50 / $12 per hour in the Valencia region and from £7 / $13 to £15 / $30 in Catalonia. Residents pay 15% tax in arrears and an additional 6% in social security payments. If you work cash in hand (which is often the case for non-EU teachers) then you should not pay any taxes.

⮑ **Accommodation:** Rents often take up more than a quarter of a teacher's salary, especially in the major cities, although lower salaries in smaller towns might include accommodation. Expect to pay a minimum of £200 / $380 a month if you want to live on your own. For shared accommodation, standard rents are around £100 / $190 per month. Up to two months' deposit is payable in advance.

⮑ **Health advice:** As you will probably be working as a freelancer you must have your own health insurance.

⮑ **English Language Media:** Barcelona Metropolitan, Costa Blanca News, Sur (English Edition).

Schools in Spain (+34)

Academia Andaluza de Idiomas
Crta El Punto 9, Conil, Cadiz, **Tel:** 956 44 0552.

Academia Britanica
Rodriguez Sanchez 15, 14003 Cordoba.

Academia Saint Patricks
Calle Caracuel 1, 17402 Girona.

Academia Wellington House
Guiposcoa 79, 08020 Barcelona.

Acento - The Language Company
Ruiz De Alarcon 7, 21, 41007 Sevilla.

Afoban
Alfonso Xii 30, 41002 Sevilla.**Tel:** 95 421 8974

AHIZKE/CIM
Loramendi 7, Apartado 191, Mondragon Guipuzcoa.

Alce Idiomas
Nogales 2, 33006 Oviedo. **Tel:** 85 254543.

Aljarafe Language Academy
Crta Castilleja-Tomares 83, Tomares, Sevilla.

American Institute
El Bachiller 13, 46010 Valencia.

Apple Idiomas
Aben al Abbar 6, 46021 Valencia. **Tel:** 362 25 45.

Audio Jeam
Pza Ayuntamiento 2, 46002 Valencia.

Augusta Idiomas
Via. Augusta 128, 08006 Barcelona.

Aupi
Jesus 43, 46007 Valencia.

Avila Centre of English
Bajada de Don Alonso 1, 05003 Avila. **Tel:** 18 213719, **Fax:** 213631.

Berlitz
Gran Via 80, 4º, 28013 Madrid. **Tel:** 1 542 3586, **Fax:** 1 541 2765.

Berlitz
Edif Forum 1 Mod, 3 Av Luis Morales, S/N 41018 Sevilla.

Big Ben College
Plaza Quintiliano 13, Calahorra 26500 La Rioja.

Brighton
Rambla Catalunya 66, 08007 Barcelona.

Bristol English School
Fundacion Jado 10 Bis 6, 48950 Erlandio, Vizacaya. **Tel:** 467 6332.

Britannia School of English
s 9, Bl 2 41010 Sevilla.

Britannia School
Leopoldo Lugones 3-1B, 33420 Lugones, Asturias. **Tel:** 85 26 2800.

Britannia School
Raset 22, Barcelona 08021. **Tel:** 3 200 0100, **Fax:** 414 4699.

British Council
Bravo Murillo 25, 35003 Las Palmas De Gran Canaria. **Tel:** 28 36 83 00.

British Council
General San Martin 7, 46003 Valencia. **Tel:** 6 351 8818.

British Language Centre
C/Bravo Murillo 377, 28020 Madrid. **Tel:** 1 733 07 39.

Business & United Schools
Genova 4, 1D 41010 Sevilla. **Tel:** 427 3183

Callan Method School of English
Calle Alfredo Vicenti 6 bajo, 15004 La Coruna.

Cambridge School
Placa Manel Montanya, 4, 08400 Granollers. **Tel:** 3 870 2001.

Centro Atlantico
Villanueva 2 apdo, 28001 Madrid. **Tel:** 1 435 3661, **Fax:** 1 578 1435.

Centro Britanico
Republica De El Salvador 26-10m, (Edificio Simago), 15701 Santiago De Compostela, La Coruna. **Tel:** 81 59 7490.

Centro Britannico
Alfereces Provisionoles 1 1°B, 23007 Jaen.**Tel/Fax:** 53 22 21 08.

Centro Cooperativo de Idiomas
Clavel 2, 11300 La Linea, Cadiz.

Centro Estudios Norteamericanos
Aparisi y Guijarro 5, 46005 Valencia.

Centro de Estudios de Ingles
Garrigues 2, 46001 Valencia. **Tel:** 352 21 02.

Centro De Idiomas Liverpool
Libreros 11-1°, 28801 Alcala de Henares, Madrid. **Tel:** 1 881 3184, **Fax:** 1 881 3584.

Centro De Ingles
Tejon Y Marin, S/N 14003 Cordoba.

Centro de Ingles Luz
Passage Luz 8bajo, 46010 Valencia. **Tel:** 361 40 74.

Centro Linguistico del Maresme
Virgen De Montserrat. **Tel:** 35 55 5403.

Centro Superior de Idiomas
Tuset 26, 08006 Barcelona.

Chatterbox Language Centre
Verge de l'Assumpcio 21, Barbera del Valles.

CLIC (Centro de Lenguas e Intercambio Cultural)
Santa Ana, 1141002, Sevilla. **Tel:** 34-5-437 4500/438 6007, **Fax**: 437 18 06.

Collegium Palatinum
Calle de Rodriguez San Pedro 10, 28015 Madrid. **Tel:** 1 446 2349, **Fax:** 1 593 4446.

The English Academy
Cruz 15, 11370 Los Barrios, Cadiz.

English Activity Centre
Pedro Frances 22a, 07800 Ibiza. **Tel:** 7131 5828.

The English Centre
Apdo de Correos 85, 11500 El Puerto De Santa Maria, Cadiz. **Tel:** 34 56 850560, **Fax:** 873804.

English Institute
Carrer La Mar 38, 03700 Denia. **Tel:** 6 781026.

English Language Centre
Jesus Maria 9-1d, 14003 Cordoba.

English Studies
SA Avenida de Arteijo 8-1, 15004 La Coruna.

English Way
Platero 30, San Juan De Aznalfarache, Sevilla.

Epicentre
Niebla 13, 41011 Sevilla.

Eurocentre
Puerta De Jerez 3-1, 41001 Sevilla.

Eurolingua
San Felipe 3, 14003 Cordoba.

European Language Schools
Regueiro 2, 36211 Vigo. **Tel/Fax:** 86 291748.

European Language Studies
Edificio Edimburgo, Plaza Nina, 21003 Huelva. **Tel:** 34 59 263821, **Fax:** 34 59 280778.

Fiac School
Mayor 19, 08221 Terrassa, Barcelona.

FLAC
Escola De Idiomes Moderns Les Valls, 10 2/0, 08201 Sabadell, Barcelona.

Glossa English Language Centre
Rambla De Cataluna 9, 78 20 2A, 08008 Barcelona.

Idiomas Blazek
Llinas 2, 07014 Palma de Mallorca. **Tel:** 71 457260.

Idiomas Oxford
Calvo Sotelo 8-1, 26003 Logrono.**Tel:** 4124 41332.

Idiomas Progreso
Plaza Progreso 12, 07013 Palma De Mallorca. **Tel:** 7123 8036.

Idiomaster
Los Maristas, 2 Lucena, Cordoba.

inlingua Idiomas
C/o Greforio Fernandez 6, 47006 Valladolid.

inlingua Idiomas
Maestro Falla 5, 2,12, Puerto del Rosario, 35600 Fuerteventura, Canary Islands.

inlingua Idiomas
Tomas Morales 28, 35003 Las Palmas de Gran Canaria. **Tel:** 2836 0671.

Inlingua Madrid SL
Calle Arenal 24, 28013 Madrid. **Tel:** 1 541 3246, **Fax:** 1 542 8296.

The Institute of English
Santiago Garcia 8, 46100 Burjasot.

Interlang
Pl Padre Jean de Mariana 3-2, 45002 Toledo.

International House
Trafalgar 14 Entlo, 08010 Barcelona. **Tel:** 3 268 4511.

International House
Calle Zurbano 8, 28010 Madrid. **Tel:** 1 310 13 14, **Fax:** 1 308 53 21 **Email:** ih_madrid@mad.servicom.es

International House
C/Hernan Cortes 1, 21001 Huelva. **Tel:** 959 246529.

International House
Pascual y Genis 16, 46002 Valencia. **Tel:** 352 06 42.

John Atkinson School of English
Isaac Peral 11 y 13, 11100 San Fernando.

Kensington Centros de Idiomas
Avda Pedro Mururuza 8, 20870 Elgoibar. **Tel/Fax:** 43 740236.

Language Study Centre
Corredera Baja 15 Bajo, Chiclana De La Frontera, Cadiz.

Lawton School
Cura Sama 7, 33202 Gijon, Asturias. **Tel:** 8534 9609.

Lexis
Avenida de la Constitucion 34, 18012 Granada.

Linguasec
Malaga 1, 14003 Cordoba.

London House
Baron de S Petrillo 23 bajo, 46020 Benimaclet.

Manchester School
San Bernado 81, 33201 Gijon, Alicante. **Tel:** 8535 8619. **Fax:** 8535 6932.

Modern School
Gerona 11, 41003 Sevilla.

Nelson English School
Jorge Manrique 1, Santa Cruz, Tenerife.

Ten Centro de Ingles
Caracuel 24, Jerez de la Frontera.

The New School
Calle Sant Joan 2, 2a Reus Tarragona.**Tel:** 77 330775

Number Nine English Language Centre
Sant Onofre 1, 07760 Ciudadella De Menorca, Baleares. **Tel:** 7138 4058.

Onoba Idiomas
Rasco 19-2, 21001 Huelva.

Oxford Centre
Alvaro de Bazan 16, 46010 Valencia.

Oxford House
San Jeronimo 9-11, Granada.

The Oxford School
Maron Feria 4, 41800 Sanlúcar La Mayor, Sevilla.

Piccadilly English Institute
Los Chopos 8, 14006 Cordoba.

Preston English Centre
Edif El Carmen Chapineria 3, Jerez De La Frontera, Cadiz.

Principal English Centre
Aptdo 85, Puerto De Santa Maria, Cadiz.

SALT Idiomes
Prat De La Riba, 86, 08222 Terrassa (Barcelona). **Tel:** 3 735 80 35.

San Roque School
Plaza San Roque 1, Guadalajara.

Skills
Trinidad 94, 12002 Castellon. **Tel:** 6424 2668.

Stanton School of English
Colon 26, 03001 Alicante. **Tel:** 65207581.

St Patrick's Caracuel
1 Jerez De La Frontera, Cadiz.

TELC
Av Andalucia 8, 6º, 11006 Cadiz. **Tel:** 56 271097.

The Tolkien Academy
Juan Bautista Erro 9, 20140 Andoain.

Trafalgar Idiomas
Avda Castilla 12, 33203 Gijon, Asturias. **Tel:** 85 332361.

Trinity School SL
C/ Golondrina (Plaza Jardines) 17 Bajo, 11500 Puerto De Santa Maria, Cadiz. **Tel:** 9 56 871926.

Wall Street Institute
Gutenberg 3-13, 1º 8a, 08224 Terrassa (Barcelona). **Tel:** 3 788 8566, **Fax:** 3 788 8538.

Wall Street Institute
Centro Comercial Cuesta Blanca, Local 12, 2º Planta, la Moralega, Alcobendas, 28100 Madrid. **Tel:** 1 650 7602, **Fax:** 1 650 8246.

Wall Street Institute
Av República Argentina 24 P12 D, 41011 Sevilla.

Warwick House Centro Linguistico Cultural
Lopez Gomez 18-2, Valladolid 47002.

Westfalia
Chapineria 3, Edificio El Carmen, Modulo 310, 11403 Jerez de la Frontera.

William Halstead School of English
Camilo Jose Cela 12, 11160 Barbate de Franco.

Windsor School of English
Virgen De Loreto 19-1, 41011 Sevilla.

York House
English Language Centre, Muntaner 479, 08021 Barcelona. **Tel:** 32 113200.

SWEDEN

There are opportunities for teaching EFL in Sweden but you need to be already living or studying there. Many teachers start out at adult education centres (studieförbund) such as Folkuniveristet, Studiefrämjandet, Medborgarskolan, TBV, ABF and Vuxenskolan. Unfortunately, most of these institutions are reluctant to hire teachers on a full-time basis since their student populations fluctuate from term to term There is rarely employment available during the summer months. Opportunities may exist in private language schools such as Berlitz. Many of these schools contract to teach groups or individuals at companies such as Ericsson, Volvo and Sony.

Embassy in UK:
11 Montagu Place, London W1H 2AL
Tel: 020 7917 6400
www.swedish-embassy.org.uk

Embassy in USA:
1501 M Street NW, Washington DC 20005
Tel: 202 467 2600
www.swedish-embassy.org

British Council office:
PO Box 27819, S-115 93 Stockholm
Tel +46 (8) 671 3110
www.britishcouncil.se

⮕ **Visa/Work Permits:** If you want to teach in Sweden and are not an EU citizen you must be studying there or be married to somebody working there to qualify for a work permit.

⮕ **Cost of Living:** It is very expensive to live in Sweden but the standards of living are very high. A meal for two at an inexpensive café or restaurant can range from £10-20. A bottle of strong beer in a bar costs around £3. Transportation is expensive.

⮕ **Currency:** £1 = 13.20 / $1 = 7.07 Swedish Krona.(SK)

⮕ **Salaries/Taxes:** Annual income can be anywhere between £10,000-20,000. This often includes four weeks paid winter and summer vacation. Salaries really depend on the teaching situation and your qualifications and experience. Studieförbund generally pay less. State & private schools pay fairly well and offer some stability. Taxation runs at 30-35% of your salary.

⮕ **Accommodation:** You can expect to pay between £150-£300 or more for a one-bedroom apartment in a large city. ESOL teachers usually live in single rental apartments or shared apartments.

⮕ **Health advice:** If your contract is for less than a year you will not be covered by Sweden's socialized medical programmes even though you will be paying for them through your taxes.

Schools in Sweden (+46)

ABC Engelsk o. Amerikanska Sprakundervisning
Safflegatan 7, 123 44 Farsta.

British Institute
Hagatan 3, 511348 Stockholm.. **Tel:** 8 341200, **Fax:** 8 344192.

Folkuniversitetet
Box 26152, 100 41 Stockholm. **Tel:** 8 679 2950, **Fax:** 8 678 1544.

SWITZERLAND

Tight immigration laws mean that Switzerland is a difficult place to find a teaching job on spec. School have to prove that no Swiss person could do the job which means that only highly qualified teachers stand a chance of getting a job here. If you do decide that Switzerland is the place for you, you could approach the various international schools in the country to see if they need teachers. You'll need at least two years' experience in teaching before they will consider you for employment. January and February are good months to look for jobs. Another possibility is to find work at a summer camp.

Embassy in UK:
16-18 Montagu Place, London W1H 2BQ
Tel: 020 7616 6000

Embassy in USA:
2900 Cathedral Ave NW, Washington DC 20008
Tel: 202 745 7900
www.swissemb.org

British Council office:
Sennweg 2, PO Box 532, CH 3000 Berne 9
Tel +41 (31) 301 1473
www.britishcouncil.org/switzerland

⮕ **Visa/Work Permits:** You need a work permit to teach in Switzerland. Permis A allows you to work seasonally, when the local workforce is considered too small to cope with the demand. Permis B can be granted for a specific one-year contract but the employer must guarantee a minimum number of hours and prove that no Swiss national could do the job.

⮕ **Cost of Living:** Most things are expensive in Switzerland.

⮕ **Currency:** £1 = 2.26 / $1 = 1.21 Swiss Francs

⮕ **Salaries/Taxes:** SFR 40-70 per hour in a private language school. Tax is around 15%.

⮕ **Accommodation:**Schools often help in finding accommodation, but as with everything in Switzerland – it's expensive!

⮕ **Health advice:** Many international schools will take care of your health insurance.

Schools in Switzerland (+41)

The American School in Switzerland
Summer Language Programmes, 6926 Montagnola-Lugano. **Tel:** 91 993 1647.

Basilingua Sprachschule
Birsigstrasse 2, 4054 Basel. **Tel:** 61 281 3954.

Bell Language School
12 Chemin des Colombettes, 1202 Geneva. **Tel:** 00 41 22 740 20.

Berlitz
14 rue De L'Ancien-Port, 1202 Geneva. **Tel:** 22 738 3200.

Berlitz
Munzgasse 3, 4001 Basel. **Tel:** 61 261 6360, **Fax:** 61 261 6405.

Institute Le Rosey
Camp d'Eté, Route des Quatre Communes, CH-1180 Rolle.

Leysin American School
CH-1854 Leysin. **Tel:** 24 493 37 7, **Fax:** 24 494 1585.

Markus Frei Sprachenschulen
Neugasse 6, 6300 Zug. **Tel:** 710 4240, **Fax:** 710 4525.

Village Camps
1296 Coppet. **Tel:** 22 776 2059, **Fax:** 22 776 2060.

UNITED KINGDOM

British English native-speakers will have few problems in the UK since teachers are expected to teach British English; Americans will find it hard to get a job, however, for Canadians, Australian and New Zealand citizens, the prospects are much better. You will need an EU passport if you want to teach English in the UK

Embassy in USA:
3100 Massachusetts Ave, Washington DC 20008
Tel: +1 202 588 6500
www.britainusa.com

British Council main office:
10 Spring Gardens, London SW1A 2BN
Tel +44 (0) 20 7930 8466
www.britishcouncil.org

⮕ **Visas/Work permits:** A work permit is extremely difficult for a non-EU citizen to obtain. You must find an employer who will apply on your behalf before you enter the country.

⮕ **Cost of Living:** The UK is an expensive country.

⮕ **Currency:** US$1 = approx £0.53

⮕ **Salaries/Taxes:** London salaries are not particularly good although schools in Oxford and Cambridge pay well.

⮕ **Accommodation:** The cost of accommodation in London is steadily rising and public transportation is expensive and unreliable. In the centre of London expect to pay a minimum of £100 / $190 a week. In the suburbs anything from £60 / $110 - £70 / $130 is standard. Outside of London accommodation is usually a lot cheaper, especially in student towns, but a lot of schools will arrange accommodation for you often with host families.

⮕ **Health advice:** While good medical services are widely available, free care under the National Health System is allowed only to EU citizens.

Schools in the UK (+44)

There are over 1000 ELT schools in the UK – we could fill this entire book (in fact, there are books just for the UK ELT market). The best way to find schools is to use one of the professional associations of schools – or the British Council. These offer accreditation to schools that meet various criteria, with over 500 accredited schools in the UK and some 5-600 schools

concentrating just on teaching in the summer holidays (see Finding a Job), it is a vast market. Try some of these major schools and organisations of schools who can provide help and lists of contacts. See also the website directory, pages 60 and 272 for online search engines that will find schools in the UK

Organisations of Schools

ARELS
56 Buckingham Place, London SW1E 6AG. **Tel:** 020 7802-9200, **Fax:** 020 7630-9824.
www.arels.org.uk
Note: ARELS and BASELT have merged into EnglishUK, however both offices and websites still operate as before.

BALEAP
English Language Centre, University of Bath, Claverton Down, Bath BA2 7AY. **Tel:** (01225) 826 191, **Fax:** (01225) 323135.
www.baleap.org.uk

BASELT
Cheltenham and Gloucester College of Higher Education, Francis Close Hall, Swindon Road, Cheltenham, Glos GL50 4AZ. **Tel:** 01242 227099, **Fax:** 01242 227055.
www.baselt.org.uk
Note: ARELS and BASELT have merged into EnglishUK, however both offices and websites still operate as before.

BATQI
35 Barclay Square, Bristol BS8 1JA. **Fax:** 0117 925 1537.

British Council
10 Spring Gardens, London SW1A 2BN, **Tel:** +44 (0)20 7389 4931, **Fax:** +44 (0)20 7389 4140
www.britishcouncil.org

Central Bureau for Educational Visits and Exchanges (CBEVE)
The British Council, 10 Spring Gardens, London SW1A 2BN. **Tel:** 020 7389 4004, **Fax:** 020 7389 4426.

Department for Education and Employment (DfEE)
Mowden Hall, Darlington DL3 9BG. **Tel:** 01325 460155, **Fax:** 01325 392695

IATEFL
3 Kingsdown Chambers, Whitstable, Kent CT5 2FL **Tel:** 01227 276528, **Fax:** 01227 274415
www.iatefl.org

School Groups

Bell Language Schools
The Personnel Department, Hillscross, Red Cross Lane, Cambridge CB2 2QX. **Tel:** 01223 246644, **Fax:** 01223 414080.

Berlitz
9-13 Grosvenor Street, London W1A 3BZ. **Tel:** 020 7915-0909, **Fax:** 020 7915-0222.

EF
36-38 St Aubyns, Hove, East Sussex BN3 2TD, **Tel:** 01273 201431, **Fax:** 01273 746742
www.englishfirst.com

Inlingua
Rodney Lodge, Rodney Road, Cheltenham, Gloucs. GL50 1JF. **Tel:** 01242 253171, **Fax:** 01242 253181.

International House
106 Piccadilly, London W1V 9FL. **Tel:** 020 7491-2598, **Fax:** 020 7409-0959
www.ihlondon.com

Linguarama
Oceanic House, 89 High Street, Alton, Hants GU34 1LG. **Tel:** 01420 80899, **Fax:** 01420 80856.

St Giles
154 Southampton Row, London WC1B 5JX, **Tel:** 020 7837 0404, **Fax:** 020 7837 4099
www.stgiles.co.uk

Saxoncourt (UK) Ltd.
59 South Molton Street, London W1Y 1HH. **Tel:** 020 7491 1911, **Fax:** 020 7493 3657
www.sgvenglish.com

Eastern and Central Europe

European countries outside of the European Union (EU) are very good places to look for work, and in these countries British and North American teachers are often on a level playing field (unlike Western Europe, where it's easier for British teachers to find work). American culture is a major influence in the former Soviet Bloc, learning English is big business in the region.

Some countries even offer similar salaries to those being offered in Western Europe now–amazing, considering that the cost of living is so much lower. However, times have changed since the post-communist honeymoon, when any young American, Canadian, Australian or Brit would be offered a teaching job on the street and then would spend their time partying rather than teaching. Now schools are looking for more dedicated and qualified teachers.

Some of these countries (in particular, Hungary, Poland and the Czech Republic) are about to join the European Union, which will eventually make it more difficult for non-EU citizens to work. However, for the time being, governments are focusing on bringing stability to their economies. This coupled with recent growth in tourism means that these are increasingly popular teaching destinations in spite of the occasionally difficult living and teaching conditions.

Competition means that qualifications may be necessary, especially in the major cities. A number of Central and East European countries are served by voluntary and cultural organizations, including the Peace Corps and the Soros Foundation. These organizations usually offer teachers salaries at local rates along with supplements, accommodation and other benefits.

There is considerable voluntary, as well as some commercial, English language teaching activity in the Ukraine, Uzbekistan and Kazakhstan, but standards of living can be modest and conditions harsh. Opportunities can be found also in the Baltic states, especially Lithuania and Estonia, which have been progressive in implementing policies promoting free enterprise.

AZERBAIJAN

A former Soviet republic, Azerbaijan became independent in 1991. The capital, Baku, is relatively safe, although attacks on foreigners can occur, but the southern parts of the country along the border with Iran, and the western region (Nagorno-Karabakh) are not safe for travellers. The climate is generally quite warm, except in the mountains

Embassy in UK:
4 Kensington Court, London W8 5DL
Tel: 020 7938 5482
www.president.az

Embassy in USA:
927, 15th St NW, Suite 700, Washington DC 20035
Tel: (202) 842 0001
www.azembassy.com

British Council office:
1 Vali Mammadov Street, Ichari Shahar, Baku 370004
Tel +994 (12) 971 593
www.britishcouncil.org/azerbaijan

⮑ **Visas/Work Permits:** You need to obtain a visa from an embassy before you enter the country, if you are intending to work, and a letter of introductrion from your employer is required.

⮑ **Currency:** £1 = 8041 / $1 = 4884 manats

⮑ **Cost of Living:** Quite cheap by Western standards, but everything has to be paid in local currency. Credit cards are not generally accepted

⮑ **Health advice:** there are good medical facilities in Baku, but none elsewhere. It is better to get medical insurance before you travel. Immunization against typhoid is recommmended. All water should be boiled

⮑ **English language media:** Baku Sun, Baku Today, Caspian Business News

Schools in Azerbaijan (+994)

The British Council Training Centre
1 Vali Mammadov St, Baku
Tel: 994 12 972 013
Fax: 994 12 989 236
Email: enquiries@britishcouncil.az

International House Baku
Khagani 20/20, Baku 370001
Tel: 994 12 97 15 85
Email: intellect@azerin.com

Webb Academy
148 Vidadi St, Baku 37000
Tel & Fax: 994 12 973 047

BELARUS

Belarus is a destination only for the brave and adventurous. Economic and political reform in Belarus has stalled under the current government. Tourist facilities are not highly developed, and many of the goods and services taken for granted in other countries are not yet available. However, there is considerable demand for English, so it's quite easy to find a job. You need to contact a school or a University directly, that's the easiest and the quickest way. If you want to work in the private sector, there are a couple of schools in Minsk.

⮑ **Visas/Work Permits:** A visa must be obtained before entering Belarus.

⮑ **Currency:** £1 = 4014 / $1 = 2170 rubles.

⮑ **Salaries/Taxes:** A school teacher's average salary is about $200 per year after tax. University teachers are paid slightly more.

⮑ **Accommodation:** If you work for a University, they will offer you free accommodation at a student hostel. It is easy to rent an apartment, but it will cost about £30 per month.

⮑ **Cost of Living:** The cost of living is quite low. Local food is very cheap, but imported goods are expensive.

⮑ **Health advice:** Belarus requires all foreign nationals entering the country to purchase medical insurance at the port-of-entry regardless of any other insurance one might have. Costs for this insurance will vary according to the length of stay. You will then be entitled to receive health care, but medical care in Belarus is limited. There is a severe shortage of basic medical supplies, including anesthetics, vaccines and antibiotics. Insurance with evacuation cover is recommended.

⮑ **English Language Newspapers:** Minsk News

Schools in Belarus (+375)

The British Council
ul. Zakharova, 21, Minsk 220662. **Tel:** 17 236 79 53, **Fax**: 17 236 40 47, **Email**: Natasha.Naida@britishcouncil. org.by

International House Minsk
Room 306, Gykalo 9, Minsk 220071. **Tel:** 17 238 47 12, **Fax:** 17 231 60 07, **Email**: ih@user.unibel.by

BULGARIA

Bulgaria has been slower than most of its neighbours to embrace the West and the elected government is Communist, so most teaching opportunities are in the public sector. Bulgarians take education very seriously and, in spite of economic and political troubles, there is a surprisingly developed English language teaching structure. Secondary schools recruit foreign language teachers on yearly, renewable contracts. Apply to: Bulgarian Ministry of Education & Science, 2A Knjaz Dondoukov, 1000 Sofia, Tel: 2 988 0494. In the private sector, teaching loads are notoriously great with some having to travel between two or three schools to deliver 30 contact hours per week, often in the evenings and on Saturday mornings. In the state sector, a week's teaching is likely to consist of about twenty 40-minute lessons. Because many students make great sacrifices to pay for their courses, a Bulgarian teaching experience can be very inspiring and rewarding. On the negative side expect food shortages, power failures, transport strikes and food rationing, especially in winter.

Embassy in UK:
186-188 Queen's Gate, London SW7 5HL
Tel: 020 7584 9400
www.bulgarianembassy.org.uk

Embassy in USA:
1621 22nd St. NW, Washington DC 20008
Tel: 202 387 0174
www.bulgaria-embassy.org

British Council office:
7 Krakra Street, 1504 Sofia
Tel +359 (2) 942 4344
www.britishcouncil.org/bulgaria

⮑ **Visas/Work Permits:** All non-Bulgarian citizens need an entry visa, which can be obtained from the Bulgarian Consular Service in any country. Your school should help you to organize your work permit once you are in the country.

⮑ **Currency:** £1 = 2.83 / $1 = 1.52 Bulgarian Leva.

⮑ **Salaries/Taxes:** Most contracted teachers are paid at local rates the equivalent of £100-200 per month. Paid airfares, furnished accommodation and holiday are generally included and there might also be a supplement paid in pounds or dollars. A highly paid Bulgarian teacher might be paid the equivalent of £90 per month. Tax deductions amount to 30-40%.

⮑ **Cost of Living:** Very cheap in the provinces, reaching western levels in Sofia, but conditions are still extremely tough.

⮑ **Accommodation:** Very basic accommodation is usually provided by employers.

⮑ **Health advice:** Insurance is provided by state employers but it should be supplemented with a private policy.

⮑ **English language media:** The Sofia Echo.

Schools in Bulgaria (+359)

Alliance for Teaching of Foreign Languages
3 Slaveikov Square, 1000 Sofia. **Tel**: 2 880238, **Fax**: 2 882 349.

American College
Tsar Osvobodital Blvd, Sofia.

Avo-3 School of English
House of Culture Sredets, 2a Krakra Street, Sofia.

ANDRA
1 Ch Smirnenski Blvd, Sofia 1421.

BELS & BELIN Centre
PO Box 37, 1421 Sofia.

British Council
7 Tulovo Street, 1504 Sofia. **Tel**: 2 946 0098.

Bulgarian Dutch College for Commerce
Trudovets Botebgrad, Sofia.

Business Private High School
Kosta Lulchev Street, Sofia.

Centre for Language Qualification
National Palace of Culture, Administrative Bldg, 2nd Floor, Room 131, Sofia.

ELIT
14 GM Dimitrov Boulevard, Sofia.

ELS
PO Box 16, Sofia 1404.

ESPA
Darwin Street, Sofia.

First Private English Language Medium School
Stara Planina Street, Sofia.

ICO Intellect
Kostur Street, 1618 Sofia.

Institute of Tourism
Park Ezero, 8000 Bourgas.

Language High School
64 Tsar Shishman St., 6000 Stara Zagora. **Tel**: 42 52975, **Fax**: 42 40188.

Language Schools of Europe
82 Tsar Simeon St., entr 3, fl 3, Sofia 1000.

MEL
First Primary School, 24 Vessela Street, Plovdiv 4000.

Meridian
22 Alabin Street, Sofia 1000.

Meridian
Macedonia Boulevard, Sofia 1606.

New School of English
13 Serdika Street, Sofia.

Pharos Ltd
2 S.Vrachanski Street, Vasrazhdane Square, Sofia.

Private High School for Law & Management
D Dimov Street, Sofia.

Private High School for Management & Business Admin
Raiko Alexiev Street, Complex Iztok, Sofia.

Private High School for Management & Stock Trade
Velikoknyazhevska Street, Sliven.

Private School for Banking and Business
83 Bogomil Street, Plovdiv

Yanev School
bl 147 ap 38, Complex Liulin, Sofia.

CROATIA

Croatia is being rapidly integrated into mainstream Europe and English is very much in demand in this former Yugoslav republic. With private schools operating in Zagreb, Karlovac and Varazdin, there are plenty of opportunities for teachers, especially native speakers, who are in short supply. Because there is an established English language industry, schools are reluctant to employ unqualified teachers. Jobs are often advertised abroad, but it's also possible to job-hunt on arrival. Full-time contracts are the norm and there are opportunities for private lessons.

British Council office:
Illica 12, PP 55, 10001 Zagreb
Tel +385 (1) 489 9500
www.britishcouncil.hr

⮑ **Visas/Work Permits:** Anyone who intends to teach will need a work visa. This can be secured in advance when you present your contract to your local embassy, then a labour permit can be sent from an employer in Croatia.

⮑ **Currency:** £1 = 10.65 / $1 = 5.76 Kuna.

⮑ **Salaries and taxes:** Salaries are usually paid in German marks with tax deducted by the employer. The average rate is between £500-1100 per month, while experienced teachers can earn more.

⮑ **Accommodation:** Accommodation is quite reasonable. An apartment with two or three rooms will cost around £300 per month.

⮑ **Cost of Living:** Food and basic living costs are cheap, but price are higher in tourist resorts.

⮑ **Health advice:** Insurance is advisable, as state facilities are under considerable strain. There are plenty of private doctors and dentists.

Schools in Croatia (+385)

Centar za strane jezike
Vodnikova 12, 4100 Zagreb *and* Trg republike 2, 58000 Split.

Class
Jankomirska 1, 41000 Zagreb.

The English Workshop
Medulinska 61, 52000 Pula.

Interlang
Krisaniceva 7, 51000 Rijeka

Lancon
Kumiciceva 10, 10000 Zagreb. **Tel:** 1 485 4985, **Fax:** 1 485 4984. **Email:** lmo@lancon.hr

Linguar Centar
Miroslava Krleze 4c, 47000 Karlovac. **Tel/Fax:** 47 621900.

Linguae
Radiceva 4, 51000 Rijeka.

Linguapax Language School
B.Jelacica 1 32100 Vinkovci. **Tel:** 32 334 827, **Fax:** 32 334 827.

LS Lukavec
Skolska 27, 41409 Donja Lomnica.

Narodno sveuciliste
Skola za strane jezike, Trg Matice Hrvatske 3, 41430 Samobor.

Octopus
Savska 13, 41000 Zagreb.

Radnicko sveuciliste
Bozidar Maslaric, 5400 Osijek.

Skola Stranih Jezika
Cesarceva 10, 42000 Varazdin. **Tel:** 42 215055, **Fax:** 42 215036.

Svjetski jezici
Varsavska 13, 41000 Zagreb.

Verba
M. Gorkog 5, 51000 Rijeka.

Vern Lingua
Senoina 28, 10000 Zagreb. **Tel/Fax:** 1 428 548.

CYPRUS

The Mediterranean island of Cyprus is divided into two sectors: Greek and Turkish. In the Greek sector of Cyprus, English is the second language. Here, it is very hard for foreigners to find teaching positions because local teachers fill most of the demand and the authorities are very strict about allowing non-Cypriots to work. In the Turkish sector, there are a number of private universities that hire native English speakers to teach in language departments.

British Council office:
3 Museum Street, CY- 1097 Nicosia
Tel +357 (22) 585 000
www.britishcouncil.org.cy

Schools in Cyprus - Greek Sector (+357)

American Academy
PO Box 112, Larnaca. **Tel:** 4 652046, **Fax:** 4 651046.

American Academy
Despinas Pattichi Street, PO Box 1867, Limassol. **Tel:** 5 337054, **Fax:** 5 387488.

American Academy
3A Michalaki Paridi Street, Nicosia. **Tel:** 2 462886, **Fax:** 2-466290.

Centre of Higher Studies
PO Box 545, 2 Evagorou Street, floor 6, Nicosia. **Tel:** 2 445970, **Fax:** 2 369171.

The English School
PO Box 3575, Nicosia. **Tel:** 2 422274.

Forum Language centre
PO Box 5567, Nicosia 1310. **Tel:** 2497766, **Email:** forum1@cytanet.com.cy

The Grammar School
Katinas Paxious Street, PO Box 1340, Limassol. **Tel:** 5 727933, **Fax:** 5 727818.

The Grammar School
PO Box 2262, Nicosia. **Tel:** 2 621744, **Fax:** 2623044

International Language Institute (ILI)
12 Richard & Verengaria Street, Limmassol. **Tel:** 371017, **Fax:** 371018.

Pascal English School
3 Costaki Panteli Street, PO Box 4746, Nicosia. **Tel:** 2 450900, **Fax:** 2 367214.

Terra Santa College
12 Lycourgos Street, PO Box 1546, Nicosia. **Tel:** 2 421100, **Fax:** 2 466767.

Turkish Sector (+90)

Cyprus International University
Ortakoy, Lefkosa, KKTC. **Tel:** 392 223 49 00. **Fax:** 392 223 49 01.

Eastern Mediterranean University
Famagusta, North Cyprus. **Tel:** 392 366 6588. **Fax:** 392 366 1317. **Email:** webmaster@salamis.emu.edu.tr

Girne American University
Yeni Liman Yolu, Girne, North Cyprus. **Tel:** 392 815 53 12. **Fax:** 392 815 11 33.

International American University
P.O.Box. 292, Kyrenia, North Cyprus. **Tel:** 392 815 6791 **Fax:** 392 815 6790.

Near East University
P.O. Box: 670, Nicosia, North Cyprus. **Tel:** 392 223 64 64. **Fax:** 392 223 64 61.

CZECH REPUBLIC

This country in the heart of Europe has long been a magnet for English language teachers (particularly from the USA and Canada). It is estimated that there are as many as 60,000 Americans in Prague alone, many drawn here by its reputation as a "party" town. But the Czech authorities have tightened up regulations recently and it is difficult to find a teaching job unless you have some kind of qualification. Although most teaching jobs are in the private sector, the Ministry of Education recruits qualified teachers (who should have at least a certificate qualification and a BA in English) for elementary, middle and high schools. The main advantage of a governmental teaching contract is that it is worth the paper it's printed on and you will probably be eligible for health insurance coverage. In the private sector, alas! This is not the case. There are disreputable schools out there that will employ teachers illegally and then take advantage of them. If you are unhappy with your school, just pick up your last salary cheque and move on – there are plenty of good schools.

Embassy in UK:
26-30 Kensington Palace Gardens, London W8 4QY
Tel: 020 7243 1115
www.czechembassy.org.uk

Embassy in USA:
3900 Spring of Freedom St NW, Washington DC
20008
Tel: 202 274 9100
www.czechembassy.org

British Council office:
Bredovsky dvur, Politickych Veznu 13, 110 00
Prague 1
Tel +420 (0)2 2199 1111
www.britishcouncil.cz

⭘ **Visas/Work Permits:** In January 2000, a major revision of the Czech law regarding residency permits for foreign nationals came into force. In the old days, teachers could arrive on tourist visas (good for up to 90 days) and then apply for a residency permit. Now, American citizens must apply for a residency permit before they travel. You can still apply for a work permit while you are in the country but your employer must prove you are not taking a job that a Czech national could do.

⭘ **Currency:** £1 = 42.70 / $1 = 23.12 Koruny.

⭘ **Salaries/Taxes:** Teachers working in state schools earn about £180-250 per month after tax and accommodation is usually provided. You can earn more at a private language school (£300-400) as long as you are given the hours. Private tuition can be very lucrative; some business people are prepared to pay upwards of £20 an hour to learn English with a qualified and experienced tutor. The tax rate is around 30% for those working legally.

⭘ **Accommodation:** It's difficult to find a room in Prague. Ask the school to provide you with accommodation. If that doesn't work, try and find people who will share with you. Check out the notices at The Globe bookstore (where you might run into another teacher in the same predicament!) or at Radnost, a popular coffee shop. If you're very lucky you might pick up a cheap apartment for around £90 a month but you'll probably have to pay at least £150 so it's a good idea to share.

⭘ **Cost of Living:** If you eat fruit and vegetables that are locally produced and develop a taste for heavy Czech fare, then life will not be too expensive. Czech beer is very strong and very cheap!

⭘ **Health advice:** In Prague medical facilities are good but try not to be sick in a remote region. Better still, get a job with a school that provides medical coverage for its teachers.

⭘ **English language media:** The Prague Post.

Schools in the Czech Republic (+420)

Academic Information Agency (Public Sector Recruitment)
Dum zahranicnich sluzeb MSMT, Senovazne nam. 26, 111 21 Prague 1. **Tel:** 2 2422 9698, **Fax:** 2 2422 9697, **Email:** aia@dzs.cz

Agency Unitour
Libor Kivana, Senovazne 21, 110 00 Prague 1. **Tel:** 2 35 9917, **Fax:** 786 2153.

Agentura Educo
Veletrzni 24, 170 00 Prague 7. **Tel:** 2 333 70 163, **Fax:** 2 203 97 310.

Anglictina Expres
Korunni 2, 12000 Prague 2. **Tel:** 2 2423 8186, **Email:** anexpres@vol.cz

Bell School
Nedvezska 29, 100 00 Prague 10. **Tel:** 2 781 5342, **Fax:** 2 782 2961.

British Council
Narodni 10, 12501 Prague 1. **Tel:** 2 203 751.

Caledonian School
Vitavska 24, 150 00 Prague 5. **Tel:** 2 573 13650, **Email:** jobs@caledonianschool.com

California Sun School
Na Bojisti 2, Prague 2. **Tel:** 2 294 817, **Fax:** 2 822 271.

Cheb Free School
Kubelikova C.4, Cheb 350 02.

Encounter English
Azalkova 12, 100 00 Prague 10-Hostivar. **Tel:** 2 758 773.

Eminenc Language School
Vodikova 26, 110 00 Prague 1. **Tel:** 2 96226141-3, **Fax:** 2 96226144.

English House
Vysedhradska 2, 128 00 Prague 2. **Tel/Fax:** 2 29 31 41.

Et Cetera Language School
Dusni 17, 110 00 Prague 1. **Tel:** 2 231 3062, **Fax:** 2 894 484.

Euro contact - Hulesovice
Jankovskeho 52, 7 Hulesovice. **Tel:** 801 527.

European Management Institute (TEMI)
Na Truhlarce 3, 180 00 Prague 8. **Tel/Fax:** 2 68 88 052.

Foundation for a Civil Society
Jeleni 200/3, 118 00 Prague 1. **Tel:** 2 24 51 08 73,
Fax: 2 24 51 08 75.

GEJA
Seifertova 37, Prague 3. **Tel:** 2 225 3750.

Hampson CS Ltd
Zelezna 107, Mlada Boleslav 293 01. **Tel:** 326 732732,
Fax: 326 732732.

International House (ILC) Brno
Sokolska 1, 602 00 Brno. **Tel:** 5 41 24 0493, **Fax:** 5 41
24 59 54, **Email:** ihbrno@sky.cz

International House Prague - Akcent
Bitovska 3, 140 00 Prague 4. **Tel:** 2 420 595, **Fax:** 2
422 845, **Email:** info.accent@akcent.cz.

International Training Solutions Ltd
Thamova 24, 186 00 Prague 8. **Tel/Fax:** 2 238 0545.

Intertext Servis Karel Narvatil
Anglicka 24, 360 09 Karlovy Vary. **Tel/Fax:** 17 323
0436.

Languages at Work
Na Florenci 35, 110 000 Prague 1. **Tel/fax:** 2 248
11379, **Email:**employment@mbox.vol.cz

London School of Modern Languages
Francouzska Ulice 30, 120 00 Prague 2. **Tel:** 2 242 53
437, **Fax:** 2 242 54 259.

Prague 8 Language School
Buresova 1130, 18 000 Prague 8. **Tel:** 2 858 8028.

Pro English 90
Mala Strana, 5 Helichova (4th floor), Prague 1. **Tel:**
534 551.

St. James Language centre
Namesti Miru 15, 12000 Prague 2. **Tel**.: 2 2251 7869,
Fax: 2 2251 7870.

Spusa Education centre
Navratilova 2, 110 00 Prague 1. **Tel:** 2 22 23 17 02,
Fax: 2 22 23 25 30.

Statni Jazykova Skola
Skolsa 15, 116 72 Prague 1. **Tel:** 2 222 32 237, **Fax:** 2
222 32 236, **Email:** sjs@sjs.cz

ESTONIA

Estonia is a rapidly developing Baltic state that has
experienced significant success in reforming its
political and economic institutions since regaining
independence in 1991. With about 30 universities and
private schools in Estonia, there are many
opportunities for teachers. Students tend to be highly
motivated although they can be a little shy at first.

Embassy in UK:
16 Hyde Park Gate, London SW7 5DG
Tel: 020 7589 3428
www.estonia.gov.uk

Embassy in USA:
Suite 503, 1730 M Street NW, Washington DC20036
Tel: 202 588 0101
www.estemb.org

British Council office:
Vana Posti 7, Tallinn 10146
Tel +372 (6) 257 788
www.britishcouncil.ee

⮑ **Visas/Work Permits:** No visas are required for
stays up to 90 days. It's not too difficult to obtain a
work permit once you have found a job, although the
paperwork can be confusing.

⮑ **Currency:** £1 = 22 / $1 = 11.97 Kroon

⮑ **Salaries/Taxes:** After tax (around 26%) you
should be able to take home £300-500 a month.

⮑ **Accommodation:** The average rent for a
two-bedroom apartment in Tallinn's suburbs is around
£200. Hopefully, your school will include
accommodation in the package they offer you.

⮑ **Cost of Living:** Estonia is much cheaper than the
UK and U.S.A. so even if you are only earning a few
hundred dollars a month it should go a long way.

⮑ **Health advice:** The quality of medical care in
Estonia is good but can fall short of UK and USA
standards. Estonia has many highly trained medical
professionals, but hospitals and clinics still suffer from
a lack of equipment and resources. Your school may
give you a medical card entitling you to free treatment
but health insurance is a good idea.

Schools in Estonia (+372)

ALF Training centre
Ravala pst. 4, Tallinn EE0001

Concordia International University
Kaluri tee 3, Viimsivald, Harjumaa EE3006. **Tel:**
6090077, **Fax:** 6090216

International House Tallinn
Pikk 69, Tallinn 10133. **Tel:** 64 10 607, **Fax:** 64 10
607, **Email:** ihte@online.ee

International Language Services
Pikk 9, Tallinn EE 0001. **Tel:** 646 4258, **Fax:** 641
2476, **Email:** ilsinfo@online.ee

Tallinn Pedagogical University
Language centre, Narva mnt. 29, Tallinn EE0101

GEORGIA

This Caucasian republic (birthplace of Josef Stalin) has a long and fascinating history. There is a shortage of native English-speaking teachers in Georgia so intrepid travellers should not have a problem finding work here, either in a private school or even with one of the big energy companies that have offices in Tbilisi.

British Council office:
34 Rustaveli Avenue, Tblisi 380008
Tel +995 (32) 250 407 988014
www.britishcouncil.org.ge

⮕ **Visas/Work Permits** Tourist visas are available on entry at Tbilisi Airport. The Georgian authorities are generous with work visas.

⮕ **Currency:** £1 = 3.36 / $1 = 1.82 Lari

⮕ **Salaries/Taxes:** You can expect to earn around £200 a month in a private language school. If you land a teaching job with an oil company you can make a lot more money.

⮕ **Accommodation:** A bedroom in a shared apartment costs around £90-100 per month.

⮕ **Cost of Living:** Locally grown products are cheap and delicious. Georgian cuisine enjoys a high reputation.

⮕ **Health advice:** Medical care in Georgia is limited. There is a severe shortage of basic medical supplies, including disposable needles, anesthetics, and antibiotics. Uninsured travellers who require medical care overseas may face extreme difficulties. The U.S. Embassy advises American citizens to avoid travel to the separatist-controlled region of Abkhazia.

Schools in Georgia (+995)

Byron School of Tbilisi
2 Griboedov Street, Tbilisi 380008. **Tel:** 32 93 1578.

The English Language Centre
10 Shevchenko Street, Tbilisi 380018. **Tel/Fax:** 32 933999

International House Tbilisi
centre for Language Studies, 2, 26 May Square, Tbilisi 380015. **Tel:** 32 940 515, **Fax:** 32 001 127, **Email:** schoolih@access.sanet.ge

International Language Academy
17 Chavchavadze Ave., Tbilisi 380079. **Tel:** 32 22 0504, **Email:** ila@caucasus.net

Professional Training Group
82 Paliashvili Street, Second floor, III entrance, Tbilisi **Tel:** 32 294482/ 253547.

Public Service Language centre
8 Rustaveli Street, Tbilisi.

Tbilisi Central School of English
8 Jambuli Street, Tbilisi 380008. **Tel:** 32 92 3454.

HUNGARY

The demand for native-speaking English language teachers has slowed in recent years. Reports suggest that competition for teaching jobs in Budapest has become pretty fierce. There are numerous tales of unscrupulous school owners operating in the Hungarian capital. Better opportunities for TEFL teachers lie in the provincial centres such as Gyor, Szeged and Pecs. September is a good time to come and look for a job.

Embassy in UK:
35 Eaton Place, London SW1X 8BY
Tel: 020 7235 5218
www.huemblon.org.uk

Embassy in USA:
3910 Shoemaker St NW, Washington DC 20008
Tel: 202 362 6730
www.huembwas.org

British Council office:
Benczúr u. 26, 1068 Budapest
Tel +36 (1) 478 4700
www.britishcouncil.hu

⮕ **Visas/Work Permits:** You do not need a visa for a period of up to 90 days. Hungary is very strict about work permits and everybody needs to apply for one if they are going to teach in the country. Permits must be arranged before leaving your country of residence and the applicant has to produce a labour permit sent from the employer in Hungary, stating that no Hungarian is available to do the job.

⮕ **Currency:** £1 = 345 / $1 = 187 Forint

⮕ **Salaries/Taxes:** Expect to earn between £3-5 an hour at a private language school which is pretty good by local standards. Taxation is very high – up to 50 % of your income. Many school owners prefer to pay foreign teachers under the table to avoid red tape. In the public sector, teachers make around the same as in the private schools (c. £180-200 per month) but accommodation is usually included.

⊃ **Accommodation:** You can find an apartment for around £90-100 a month in Budapest

⊃ **Cost of Living:** A decent dinner costs around £2. Annual inflation runs around 10% and salaries do not always rise to match this. Many teachers find it hard to get by on their salaries.

⊃ **Health advice:** Local health insurance is available but it doesn't cover repatriation, however, healthcare facilities are good, particularly compared to other countries of central Europe.

⊃ **English language media:** Budapest Sun, Budapest Week, Budapest Business Week Journal.

Schools in Hungary (+36)

American International School of Budapest
Kakukk u.1-3, 1121 Budapest. **Tel:** 396 2176.

Atalanta Business and Language School
Visegradi u.9, 1132 Budapest. **Tel:** 1 131 4954, **Fax:** 1 339 8549, **Email:** atalanta.marketing@atalanta.datanet.hu

Avalon '92 Agency
Erzsebet Krt 15, 1/19, 1073 Budapest. **Tel/Fax:** 342 6355.

Babilon Nyelvstudio
Karoly krt. 3/a IV.em, 1075 Budapest. **Tel:** 1 269 5531, **Fax:** 1 322 6023, **Email:** bab@mail.datanet.hu

Bell Iskolak
Tulipan u. 8, 1022 Budapest. **Tel:** 1 326 8457, **Fax:** 1 326 5033, **Email:** bellisk@mail.matav.hu

Belvarosi Tanoda Foundation
Molnar u.9, 1056 Budapest. **Tel:** 118 6769.

Britannica International School
Villanya ut 11-13, 1114 Budapest. **Tel:** 166 6306.

Buda Drawing School
Marvany u. 23, 1126 Budapest. **Tel/Fax:** 155 0341.

Budenz Jozsef High School Foundation
Budenz ut 20-22, 1021 Budapest. **Tel:** 176 3177.

Budapest Pedagogical Institute
Horveth Mihaly Ter 8, Budapest 8.

Business Polytechnic
Vendel u. 3/b, 1096 Budapest. **Tel:** 1 215 4900, **Fax:** 1 215 4906, **Email:** titkar@mail.poli.hu

English Teachers' Association of the National Pedagogical Institute
Bolyai u.14, 1023 Budapest.

Europai Nyelvek Studioja
Muzeum Krt. 39, 1053 Budapest. **Tel:** 1 317 1302 **Fax:** 1 266 3889, **Email:** els@mail.datanet.edu

Helle Studio
Deri Miksa u. 18, 1084 Budapest. **Tel:** 1 114 0128.

IHH A Nyelviskola
Teleki u. 18, 9022 Gyor. **Tel:** 96 315444/30 363195 **Fax:** 96 315665.

Interclub
Hungarian Language School, Szent Janos u. 16, 1039 Budapest. **Tel** 250 4640.

International Business School Budapest
Etele u. 68, 1115 Budapest. **Tel:** 203 0351.

International House Budapest
Bimbó út 7, 1022 Budapest. **Tel:** 1 212 4010, **Fax:** 1 316 2491, **Email:** bp@ih.hu

International House Eger
Mecset utca. 3, 3300 Eger. **Tel:** 36 413 770; 36 411 313, **Fax:** 36 413 770, **Email:** eger@ih.hu

IS Prospero Language School
Sas u. 25, 1051 Budapest. **Tel:** 1 331 6779, **Fax:** 1 331 2150, **Email:** isprospero@mail.matav.hu

Karinthy Frigyes Gimnazium
Thokoly utca 7, Pestlorinc, 1183 Budapest. **Tel:** 1 290 4316, **Fax:** 1 291 2367, **Email:** ba@karinthy.hu

Kulvarosi Tankor
Dregelyvar u. 6, 1158 Budapest. **Tel:** 272 2604.

Living Language Seminar
Fejer Gyorgy u 8-10, 1053 Budapest. **Tel:** 1 326 3251, **Fax:** 1 317 9655.

London Studio
Villanyi ut. 27, 1114 Budapest. **Tel:** 1 385 0177.

Mentor Nyelviskola
Ferenc krt. 37, 1094 Budapest. **Tel:** 216 0765.

Novoschool Nyelviskola
Ulloi ut 63, 1091 Budapest. **Tel:** 1 215 5480, **Fax:** 1 215 5488, **Email:** novoschool@mail.matav.hu

Oxford Nyelviskola
Ikva u. 52, Gyor. **Tel:** 96 429 882.

Vaci Street Development centre
Terez Krt. 47, 1067 Budapest. **Tel:** 1 302 2214, **Fax:** 1 353 3274, **Email:** bruce@mail.inext.hu

Western Maryland College Budapest
Villanyi ut 11-13, 1114 Budapest. **Tel:** 1 66 7366.

LATVIA

Many teachers report that Latvia is a great place to live and work in although you must like cold weather to survive here! Students are keen to learn English and really appreciate being taught by a native speaker. You

won't make a lot of money in Latvia but you will feel you are making a worthwhile contribution to society.

Embassy in UK:
45 Nottingham Place, London W1M 3FE
Tel: 020 7312 0040

Embassy in USA:
4325 17th Street NW, Washington DC 20011
Tel: 202 726 8213
www.latvia-usa.org

British Council office:
5a Blaumana iela, Riga LV-1011
Tel +371 728 1730
www.britishcouncil.org/latvia

⊃ **Visas/Work Permits:** No visa is required for travellers remaining up to 90 days in a half-calendar year (from January to June and from July to December). If you stay in Latvia for more than 90 days, including 180-day periods that cross over two half-calendar years, you must apply for temporary residence. Teachers who plan to remain in Latvia for more than 90 days must apply for an "educational work" visa or in-country for temporary residence.

⊃ **Currency:** £1 = 0.96 / $1 = 0.52 Lat.

⊃ **Cost of Living:** Basic foods & clothing are very cheap, but specialist goods can be expensive.

⊃ **Salaries/Taxes:** Pay is low – around £2-3 an hour in the private language schools.

⊃ **Accommodation:** Expect very basic living conditions. Many buildings were constructed during the Soviet era and are of poor quality.

⊃ **Health advice:** Foreign aid agencies and private employers sometimes provide medical insurance. Medical care in Latvia is steadily improving but remains limited.

⊃ **English language media:** The Baltic Times

Schools in Latvia (+371)

Alna IT
K.Valdemara 149 - 600, Riga LV-1013. **Tel:** 7377142, **Email:** info@alnait.lv

English Language Centre Satva
Office 8, Dzirnavu Str. 79/85, Riga LV-1011. **Tel:** 7226641

Lingva Tev
Brivibas 87, Riga LV-1001. **Tel:** 7377734, **Email:** lintev@binet.lv

Mirte
Culture and Education centre, Raina bulvaris 23, k.2

Riga LV-1050. **Tel:** 7223837, **Email:** info@mirte.lv

Socialo tehnologiju augstskola
Balta 10 , Riga LV-1055. **Tel:** 2461001 **Email:** sti@mail.junik.lv

Spade un Mikelsons
Barristers' Bureau, Aspazijas bulvaris 24 - 305, Riga LV-1050. **Tel:** 7228519, **Email:** spade@mail.bkc.lv

Staltbriedis
Dzelzavas 74 - 507, Riga LV-1082. **Tel:** 2572676, **Email:** staltbriedis@mail.lv

Strombus
Kalku 24 - 4.st., Riga LV-1050. **Tel:** 7224376, **Email:** strombus@com.latnet.lv

T.U.I.
K.Barona 28, Riga LV-1011. **Tel:** 7242429, **Email:** tui@parks.lv

Valodu macibu centres
Smilsu 1/3 - 3.st., Riga LV-1050. **Tel:** 7212251, **Email:** vmc@latnet.lv

LITHUANIA

Lithuania is a country undergoing political and economic change. Tourist facilities are improving. Many goods and services are now available in the major cities, but may not be fully comparable to Western standards.

Most teachers who come here have very good experiences, as long as they are aware of the economics of teaching here before they arrive. Lithuanian schools are very keen to recruit native speakers, qualified or not, so graduates should have no problem finding a position either by contacting the Lithuanian embassy or by contacting the *Ministry of Education*, Dept. of Foreign Relations, Volvano Gatve 2/7, 2691 Vilnius, Tel: 2 622 483, Fax: 2 612 077. For US teachers, the main placement organization is the *American Partnership for Lithuanian Education*, PO Box 617, Durham, CT 06422, USA, Tel: (203) 347 7095, Fax: (203) 327 5837.

Embassy in UK:
84 Gloucester Place, London W1U 6AU
Tel: 020 7486 6401

Embassy in USA:
2622 16th Street NW, Washington DC 20009
Tel: 202 234 5860
www.ltembassyus.org

British Council office:
Business Centre 2000, Jogailos 4, 2001 Vilnius
Tel +370 (5) 264 4890
www.britishcouncil.lt

⮕ **Visas/Work Permits:** You do not normally need Lithuanian visas for stays of 90 days or less. For most nationalities the procedure to obtain work permits is relatively straightforward once a position has been secured.

⮕ **Currency:** £1 = 4.84 / $1 = 2.64 Lati

⮕ **Salaries/Taxes:** Salaries can be as low as £60 per month, so most teachers supplement their income with private lessons. The main private schools can pay up to £300 a month or about £5 an hour.

⮕ **Accommodation:** Usually provided free with jobs arranged through the Ministry of Education. About £60 a month for an apartment in the suburbs, but cheap accommodation is difficult to find. Living with a family is the cheapest way and very easy to arrange.

⮕ **Cost of Living:** Relatively low, but salaries will cover basic living costs only.

⮕ **Health advice:** Insurance with evacuation cover is advised. Medical care in Lithuania is improving. Most medical supplies are now widely available.

⮕ **English language media:** Baltic Times, also *Vilnius/Kaunas/Klaipeda in your pocket* are useful guides to living in these places.

Schools in Lithuania (+370)

American English School
Pylimo 20, 2001 Vilnius. **Tel/Fax:** 2 791011.

EF
Kosciuskos g.11, 2000 Vilnius. **Tel:** 2 791616, **Fax:** 2 791646.

Klaipeda International School of Languages
Zveju g. 2, 5800 Klaipeda. **Tel:** 6 311190, **Fax:** 6 311190, **Email:** mark.uribe@klaipeda.omnitel.net

Klaipeda Tourist School
Taikos pr. 69, Klaipeda. **Tel:** 34 10 83, **Fax:** 34 02 46.

Public Service Language Centre
Vilniaus St 39/6, 2000 Vilnius. **Tel:** 2 220384, **Fax:** 2 220370, **Email:** lora@vlkc.vno.osf.lt

Soros International House
Ukmerges 41, korp A, 2662 Vilnius. **Tel:** 2 72 48 79, Fax: 2 72 48 39, **Email:** daiva@ihouse.osf.lt

Siauliai Pedagogical Institute

P. Visinskio 25, 5400 Siauliai. **Tel/Fax:** 1 432592, **Email:** spi@siauliai.omnitel.net

MOLDOVA

Demand for English is very high in this tiny republic sandwiched between Romania and the Ukraine that only gained independence in 1991.

⮕ **Visas/Work Permits:** U.S. citizens will need a tourist visa. The school will advise you regarding work permits. Teachers report that the rules do not seem to be enforced very strongly.

⮕ **Currency:** £1 = 22.85 / $1 = 12.35 Leu

⮕ **Salaries/Taxes:** An average wage is £3 an hour, which, locally, is quite a good rate.

⮕ **Cost of Living:** Very reasonable. Be aware that Moldova is basically a "cash-only" society. Credit cards are not used here very much.

⮕ **Health advice:** Medical care in Moldova is limited, with severe shortages of basic medical supplies.

Schools in Moldova (+373)

ACTR-ACCELS
Stefan cel Mare Blvd. 162, oficiul 1506, Chisinau, MD-2004. **Tel:** 2 248012, **Fax:** 2 238389, **Email:** accels@dnt.md

Linguata
Stefan cel Mare 64, office 175, Chisinau. **Tel:** 2 277779 **Email:** linguata@ch.moldpac.md

Pro Didactica
13 Armeneasca St., Chisinau, MD-2012. **Tel:** 2 541994, **Email:** lschool@cepd.soros.md

Travel Teach Group
Str. P. Rares 39, Chisinau MD-2074. **Tel:** 2 294067, **Fax:** 2 321817.

POLAND

There is probably more demand for English in Poland than any other European country, due to two factors. Poland will soon become a member of the EU and is keen to attract foreign investment from the West. Secondly, the economy has been growing rapidly due to a steady process of liberalization, which has helped the export sector, which in turn increases the demand for English. In particular, the government administers English Proficiency exams, which are very important for young Poles who want to go into business. Many

teachers head towards the big university cities such as Warsaw and Lodz. Most work in the private schools and supplement their income through individual private lessons. There are plenty of opportunities for English language teachers in both the public and private sectors. Public sector English teachers are placed in schools, teacher training colleges (NKJOs) and universities. Private schools are usually Polish-owned and very welcoming to native speaker teachers. They pay well and will assist with housing, health insurance and other matters.

Embassy in UK:
47 Portland Place, London W1B 1JH
Tel: 0870 7742700

Embassy in USA:
2640 16th Street NW, Washington DC 20009
Tel: 202 234 3800
www.polandembassy.org

British Council office:
Al Jerozolimskie 59, 00 697 Warsaw
Tel +48 (22) 695 5900
www.britishcouncil.pl

⟴ **Visas/Work Permits:** You should not require visas for stays up to 90 days for tourist, business, or transit purposes. Americans should ensure that their passports are date-stamped upon entry. Persons planning to stay in Poland for longer than 90 days or who will be employed in Poland must obtain a visa before they arrive in the country. Polish law requires every traveller to be able to show means of support, if asked. For persons above 16 years of age, this has been defined as 100 Polish zloty per day. Regulations have been tightened up recently. All teachers need to apply for a work permit before arriving in the country. Your notarized degree, TEFL certificate (if appropriate) and promissory permit from your prospective employer should be presented to your local Polish consulate. You cannot obtain a work permit while you are in Poland.

⟴ **Currency:** £1 = 5.62 / $1 = 3.04 Zlotych

⟴ **Salaries/Taxes:** The average salary is around £200 per month in the state sector and at least £300 in the private sector. Some schools may offer overtime at £6-8 per hour. If you teach full-time and throw in a few private lessons you should be able to make over £600 a month which is very good money by Polish standards. The basic tax rate is 18%.

⟴ **Accommodation:** A one-bedroom apartment in the centre of Warsaw will cost £200-300 per month. Studios cost £200-250. You will have to pay at least a month's rent as deposit in advance to the landlord and you might have to pay the same amount to the agent who located your apartment. It's a good idea to arrive in July or August with some spare cash and beat the September rush for accommodation. January is also a good time. Some schools offer free accommodation.

⟴ **Cost of Living:** If you use public transport and adopt the local diet you can live on £5 a day including three good meals.

⟴ **Health advice:** The hospitals are of variable quality. Private doctors and clinics are very cheap, as are dentists. Your school may offer you health insurance as part of your employment package. Whatever deal you have, make sure you have comprehensive coverage.

⟴ **English language media:** The Warsaw Voice.

Schools in Poland (+48)

ABC
Uslugi Jezykowe, ul ZWM 6 m 29, Warsaw.

AJM
ul Klaudyny 30 m 100, 01-684 Warsaw.

American English School
PO Box 3, 00-991 Warsaw 44. **Tel/Fax:** 22 272654.

Angloschool
ul Elblaska 65/84, Warsaw.

AS
Studio Jezykow Obcych, ul M L Kinga 13, 75-016 Koszalin.

Bakalarz
Prywatne Studium Jezykowe, ul Rakowiecka 45/25, 02-528 Warsaw. **Tel:** 489 889.

Best
ul. Pestalozziego 11/13, 80-445 Gdansk. **Tel/Fax:** 58 41 2902.

Beyond 2000
Szkola Jezykow Obcych, ul Szuberta 39/5, 02-408 Warsaw.

British Council Warsaw Studium
Warsaw Technical University, ul. Filtowa 2, 00-611 Warsaw. **Tel/Fax:** 22 25 82 87.

Business and Educational English
ul Conrada 10 m 57, 01-922 Warsaw.

Centre of English Language Training
Konarskiego 2, 30-049 Krakow. **Tel:** 12 15 17 32.

Compact School of English
Spolka Cywilna, Nowogrodzka 78/24, 02-018 Warsaw.

Cosmopolitan Private Language School
Ul. Katowicka 39, 45-061 Opole. **Tel/Fax:** 77 54 87 73.

Discovery
Osrodek Nauczania Jezykow Obcych, Klub WAT-u, ul Kaliskiego 25a, 01-489 Warsaw.

The Eagle English Centre
Al Stanow Zjednoczonych 26 m 25, 03-965 Warsaw.

Elan
Mokotowska 9 m 6, Warsaw. **Tel:** 25 19 91.

Elite Language School
ul Dunikowskiego 10 m 56, 02-784 Warsaw.

English House
AWF Przedszkole, ul. Marymoncka 34, Bielany.

English House
"Domino" ul. Boguslawskiego 6a Lingwista, ul. Reymonta 25, Bielany. **Tel:** 663 5569.

English is Fun
Warchalowskiego 2/13, Warsaw.

English Language Academy
ul Narbutta 9 m 3, 02-564 Warsaw.

English Language Centre
University of Silesia, Plac Sejmu Slaskiego 1, 40-032 Katowice. **Tel:** 32 156 1269, **Fax:** 32 155 2245.

English Language Studio
ul Jadzwingow 1 m 34, 02-692 Warsaw.

English Unlimited
Podmlynska 10, 80-885 Gdansk. **Tel/Fax:** 58 31 33 73, **Email:** info@eu.com.pl.

Falaland
Osrodek Nauczania Jez Obcych, Margerytki 52, 04-908 Warsaw.

Fast
Firma Prywatna, Jezyk Angielski-Lektoraty, Ewa Maszonska-Pazdro, ul. Mickiewicza 74/58, 01-650 Warsaw.

Gama-Bell School of English
ul. sw. Krzza 16, 31-023 Krakow. **Tel:** 12 21 97 55, **Fax:** 12 21 73 79.

Greenwich School of English Poland
ul Zakroczymska 6, 00-225 Warsaw.

Human
Agencja Jezykow Obcych, ul Swietokrzyshka 20 pok 317, 00-002 Warsaw.

International House Bielsko Biala
ul. Krasinskiego 24, Bielsko Biala 43-300. **Tel:** 33 811 79 27/811 02 29, **Email:** ihbb@silesia.top.pl

International House Bydgoszcz
ul. Dworcowa 81, Bydgoszcz 85-009. **Tel:** 52 322 3515/322 3444, **Fax:** 52 322 3515, **Email:** bydgoszcz@inthouse.pl

International House Katowice
ul. Sokolska 78/80, Katowice 40-128. **Tel:** 32 58 68 96, 599 997, **Fax:** 32 253 88 33, **Email:** ihih@silesia.top.pl

International House Kielce
ul. Wesola 33, Kielce 25-353. **Tel:** 41 34 30 258/34 30 430, **Fax:** 41 34 30 261, **Email:** kielce@ih.pl

International House Koszalin
ul. Zwyciestwa 7/9, Koszalin 75-728. **Tel:** 94 3410 196, **Fax:** 94 3410 180, **Email:** hubbard.koszalin@inthouse.pl

International House Krakow
ul. Pilsudskiego 6, lp, 31-109 Krakow. **Tel:** 12 21 94 40, **Fax:** 12 21 86 52. **Email:** admin@ih.pl

International House Lodz
ul. Zielona 15, Lodz 90-601. **Tel:** 42 630 00 26, **Fax:** 42 630 00 28, **Email:** lodz@ih.pl

International House Opole
ul. Kosciuszki 17, Opole 45-062. **Tel/Fax:** 77 454 66655, **Email:** sekret@pol.pl

International House Poznan
ul. Sw. Marcin 66/72, Poznan 61 807. **Tel:** 61 851 6171, **Fax:** 61 851 61 71, **Email:** Lektor_international_house@poczta.fm

International House Torun
Ul. Legionow 15, Torun 87-100. **Tel:** 56 655 40 83, **Fax:** 56 622 50 81, **Email:** torun@inthouse.pl

International House Wroclaw
ul. Leszczynskiego 3, Wroclaw 50-078. **Tel:** 71 781 72 90, **Fax:** 71 781 72 93, **Email:** wrocdos@id.pl

International House Warsaw
ul. S. Noakowskiego 3, Warsaw 00-664. **Tel:** 22 660 71 01, **Fax:** 22 660 71 05, **Email:** monika_s@ihwarsaw.com.pl

International Language School
ul. Krakowska 51, 45-075 Opole. **Tel/Fax:** 77 53 15 97.

Junior Art-Language Studio
ul Gwardzistow 8 m 5, 00-422 Warsaw.

Kajman
ul Felinskiego 15, 1 LO pokoj 57 (parter), 01-513 Warsaw.

Konwersatorium
Jezykow Obcych, Grojecka 40a m 13, 02-320 Warsaw.

Kozlowski I Rejman
Kusocinskiego 2, 31-300 Mielec.

Langhelp
Al Jerozolimskie 23/34, Warsaw. **Tel:** 21 44 34.

Lektor Prywatna Firma Jezykowa
ul. Olawska 2, 50-123 Wroclaw. **Tel/Fax:** 71 343 25 99.

Lexis College of Foreign Languages
ul Danilowiczowska 11m 18, Warsaw.

Lingua
Studium Jezykow Obcych, ul Moniuszki 4a, Lodz.

Lingwista
ul Saska 59, 03-958 Warsaw, *and* Janowskiego 50, 02-784 Warsaw.

Mosak
ul Bonifacego 83/85 m 87, Warsaw.

MTA Language Centre
Pl. Teatrainy 6, Wroclaw. **Tel:** 71 72 13 34.

NKJO - Krakow
ul. Kanonicza 14, 31-002 Krakow. **Tel:** 12 22 79 55, **Fax:** 12 22 63 06.

Omnibus - Poznan
Pl Wolnosci 5, 61-738 Poznan. **Tel:** 52 79 08.

The Orlik Language Centre
ul Rogalskiego 2 m 49, 03-982 Warsaw.

Perfect
Naucanie Jezykow Obcych, ul Wolnosci 2 bl 13 m 14, Maciej Musiala, Zielonka.

Perfekt
Firma Oswiatowa, ul J Kaden-Bandrowskiego 2/16, 01-494 Warsaw.

Polanglo
Szkola Jezykow Obcych, ul Nowowiejska 1/3, 00-643 Warsaw. **Tel/Fax:** 22 25 37 47.

Poliglota
Biuro Jezykowych, Dzialdowska 6, 01-184 Warsaw.

Prima
Osrodek Nauczania Jezykow Obcych, ul Rozana 7 m 3, 15-669 Bialystock.

Program-Bell
ul Fredry 7, Poznan. **Tel:** 61 53 69 72.

Promotor
Szkola Jezykow Obcych, Agencja Oswiatowa, Kraszewskiego 32a, 05-800 Pruszkow.

Prymus
ul Jasna 2/4 pok 209, 00-950 Warsaw.

Pygmalion
Szkola Jezyka Angielskiego, ul Saska 78, Warsaw.

Studio Troll
Wrzeciono 1/22, Warsaw.

Studium Jezydow Obcych Project
ul Szwolezerow 5B/10, 66-400 Gorzow Wlkp. **Tel:** 95 32 05 59.

Success
ul Agawy 5/9, 01-158 Warsaw. **Tel:** 22 623 39 40, **Fax:** 22 20 55 03.

Surrey Business and Language Centres
ul Gwardzistow 20, 00-422 Warsaw.

Szansa
Prywatny Zaklad Oswiatowy, ul Agawy 5/9, 01-158 Warsaw. **Tel:** 22 623 39 40, **Fax:** 22 20 55 03.

Target
ul. Dziatwy 6/ róg Modolinska, Bialoleka. **Tel:** 660 7028, 660 7029

University of Szczecin
Al. Piastow 40B, 71-065 Szczecin. **Tel:** 91 33 31 61, **Fax:** 91 34 29 92.

Urszula
Biuro Organizacji Kursow, Dworcowa 1 pok 13, 10-431 Olsztyn

Warsaw School of Commerce
Kursy Handlowe, al Chlodna 9, Warsaw.

Warsaw Study Centre
Osrodek Jezykowo-Szkoleniowy, ul Raszynska 22, 02-026 Warsaw.

World
ul Basztowa 17, 31-143 Krakow. **Tel:** 22 91 61.

Worldwide English School
ul Stoleczna 21 paw 24, 01-530 Warsaw.

YES
ul Reformacka 8, 35-026 Rzeszow. **Tel/Fax:** 17 52 07 20.

Schools in Warsaw and its suburbs:

Mokotów ABC
ul. Wita Stwosza 57, **Tel:** 682-86-19

Columbus
ul. Kazimierzowska 16, **Tel:** 841-38-04

Greenwich
ul. Zakrzewska 25, **Tel:** 825-29-53

K i D
Osrodek Nauczania Jezyków Obcychul. Barcelonska 8, **Tel:** 39-52-04, 0-90-20-48-20

Lingwista agencja
ul. Rózana 22/24, **Tel:** 845-05-71

Lingua Nova
ul. Basniowa 3, **Tel:** 825-80-86, 668-76-74

Lingwista agencja
ul. Filtrowa 75, **Tel:** 659-50-01

Ochota English Language Centre
ul. Filtrowa 2, **Tel:** 660-55-71

Osrodek Kultury Ochoty Kursy Jezyków Obcych
ul. Grójecka 75, **Tel:** 822-48-70, 822-74-37

TARGET
ul. Bagatela 13, **Tel:** 660 70 28

Warsaw Study Centre
ul. Raszynska 22, **Tel/fax:** 822-14-12, **Tel:** 822-46-18

Praga Poludnie English House
Grochów-Kamionek, S.P. 60, ul. Zbarska 3

English House
Saska Kepa, ul. Kryniczna 12/14

Lingwista
Saska Kepa, ul. Saska, **Tel:** 617-85-83

Lingwista
ul. Miedzyborska 70, **Tel:** 810-22-01

TARGET
Saska Kepa, ul. Obronców 31, **Tel:** 660 70 28

Sródmiescie ABILITY
ul. Mazowiecka 12, **Tel:** 827-20-29

Academia de la Lengua (Language Mega Centre)
ul. Nowy Swiat 21A, **Tel:** 625-71-02, 828-10-21, 828-41-39, 646-09-20

ALBION
ul. Noakowskiego 26 m.26, **Tel/fax:** 628-89-92

BOKANO SCHOOL
ul. Chmielna 24/2, **Tel:** 826-31-17

Cambridge School of English
ul. Zakroczymska 6, **Tel:** 831-09-55

Context Language centre
ul. Hoza 61/1, **Tel:** 622 58 60

Didier Szkola Jezyka Obcych
ul. Kopernika 28 lok. 16, **Tel/fax:** 827-24-78

EMPiK Szkola Jezyków Obcych
ul. Marszalkowska 104/122, **Tel:** 826-79-17/18, 551-44-55/56/57, 826-71-04

EMPiK Szkola Jezyków Obcych
ul. Foksal 11, **Tel:** 826-79-17/18, 551-44-55/56/57, 826-71-04

EMPiK Szkola Jezyków Obcych
ul. Trebacka 3, **Tel:** 826-79-17/18, 551-44-55/56/57, 826-71-04

English Language College "Metodysci"
ul. Mokotowska 12, **Tel:** 628-53-48

Infor
ul. Sniadeckich 17, **Tel:** 629-77-90

International House
ul. Noakowskiego 3, **Tel:** 660-71-01

Greenwich
ul. Nowowiejska 5, **Tel:** 825-29-53

Konwersatorium
ul. Sempolowskiej 4, **Tel:** 622-61-62

Lang LTC
Al. Niepodleglosci, **Tel:** 825-39-40

Language Mega Centre (Academia de la Lengua)
ul. Nowy Swiat 21A, **Tel:** 625-71-02, 828-10-21, 828-41-39, 646-09-20

Lexis
Al. Marszalkowska 60 lok. 34, **Tel:** 625-53-86, 625-72-98, 622-25-23

Lingua Nova
ul. Nowowiejska 37A, **Tel:** 825-80-86, 668-76-74

Lingwista
ul. Kopernika 6, **Tel:** 827-86-85

Lingwista
ul. Ujazdowskie 37, **Tel:** 629-25-88

Lingwista
ul. Smolna 30 (Liceum/Szkola Podst.), **Tel:** 827-89-55

Loyd
pl. Powstanców Warszawy, Hotel Warsaw, **Tel:** 827 51 37.

Maart
ul. Nowy Swiat 1, **Tel:** 621-11-71

Peritia
ul. Bednarska 2/4, **Tel:** 826-95-30

PolAnglo
ul. Nowowiejska 1/3, **Tel:** 825-21-56

TARGET
ul. Polna 50, **Tel:** 660 70 28

TFLS
ul. Krucza 47 A, **Tel:** 622-20-58

Tower Language Institute
ul. Szpitalna 5 lok.16, **Tel:** 846-22-26, 828-36-99

Towarzystwo Wiedzy Powszechnej
pl. Defilad 1, Palac Kultury i Nauki, **Tel:** 656 61 75

Twins/English Conversation
ul. Krucza 17 lok. 3, **Tel:** 0604817817

Warszawskie Centrum Studenckiego Ruchu Naukowego
ul. Mokotowska 48, **Tel:** 628-82-81

Wola Cambridge School of English
ul. Bema 70, **Tel:** 632-78-86

Focus Language School
ul. Smocza 21, **Tel:** 636-44-31, 654-13-11

Lingwista
ul. Ksiecia Janusza 45/47, **Tel:** 36-17-71

Poliglota
ul. Dzialdowska 6, **Tel:** 632-02-08

Zoliborz English House
SDK, ul. Próchnika 8a, Teatr Komedia

Greenwich
ul. Gdanska 2/3, **Tel:** 833-24-31

Lingwista
ul. Gen. Zajaczka 7, **Tel:** 39-25-85

TARGET
ul. Kochanowskiego 8, **Tel:** 660 70 28

Twins/English Conversation
ul. Dyminska 6A/146 **Tel:** 39 25 84

Cambridge School of English
ul. Wasilkowskiego 6, **Tel:** 644-63-06

English House
Lasek Brzozowy 2 (Klub przez Lasku)

Lingwista
ul. Janowskiego 50, **Tel:** 643-72-79

ROMANIA

Romania is a fascinating country but teachers who come here must be prepared to live in a society that is still coming to terms with its post-Communist phase. Life can be very harsh here, especially in the soulless cities. The demand for English is not as strong in Romania as it is in other countries but a determined teacher should be able to find work without too many problems.

Embassy in UK:
Arundel House, 4 Palace Green, London W8 4QD
Tel: 020 7937 9666

Embassy in USA:
1607 23rd Street NW, Washington DC 20008
Tel: 202 332 4848
www.roembus.org

British Council office:
Calea Dorobantilor 14, 71132 Bucharest
Tel +40 (21) 307 9600
www.britishcouncil.ro

➲ **Visas/Work Permits:** You need a visa for a stay of longer than 30 days. You can hunt for jobs while visiting the country as a tourist. Your employer will apply for permits. Do not remain in Romania without a valid visa because the fines for overstaying are very high.

➲ **Currency:** £1 = 54323 / $1 = 29364 Lei.

➲ **Salaries/Taxes:** A typical package for a native-speaking teacher is £200 per month with accommodation provided by the school.

➲ **Accommodation:** One of the major headaches of living in Romania is finding affordable and decent housing. Most buildings were poorly constructed and rents are very expensive.

➲ **Cost of Living:** Food and locally made products are very cheap.

➲ **Health advice:** Medical care in Romania is limited. Basic medical supplies are scarce. Doctors and hospitals often expect immediate cash payment for health services.

➲ **English language media:** Bucuresti, Nine O'Clock, In Review, Romanian Business News.

Schools in Romania (+40)

ACCESS Language Centre
Str. Tebei nr. 21, 3400 Cluj. **Tel:** 064 420480 ext 128, **Fax**: 064-420476 **Email**: ovidiu@access.soroscj.ro

Best
Colegiul I.L.Caragiale, Calea Dorobantilor 163, Sector 1 Bucharest. **Tel:** 01-322 6744.

Calepinus Foundation - Foreign Language Institute
Piata Bernady 3, 4300 Târgu Mures. **Tel:** 065-216514

Cambridge Study Centre
Liceul Vasile Alecsandri Str., N.Balcescu 41, 6200 Galati. Centrul de limbi straine FIDES, Str.Vasile Conta 7-9, sc.E, et.7, ap.168, 70139 Bucharest. **Tel:** 01-313 8080 ext.160

CLASS (Constanta Language Association)
Bd. Mircea cel Batran nr. 103, 8700 Constanta.
Tel/Fax: 041-612877.

Computer Academy
Sala Mare A Palatului, Bucharest. **Tel:** 01-615 9710 Ext. 745/742.

Daniel - Centrul De Limba Engleza
Str. Cosminului 10, 4300 Târgu Mures. **Tel:** 065-216950.

International House Language Centre
Bd. Republicii nr. 9, 1900 Timisoara. **Tel/Fax:** 056-190593 **Email:** rodica@ihlctim.sorostm.ro

International Language Centre
Str. Moara de Foc nr. 35 et. 8, 6600 Iasi. **Tel:** 032-252850 / 252870. **Fax:** 032-252902. **Email:** acolib@ilc.iasi.osf.ro

Lexis Bucuresti
Piata Pache Protopopescu 96, Sector 2, Bucharest. **Tel:** 01-310 2629.

Linguarama
Str. Delea Veche 51, Bl.46, Et.9, Sector 2, Bucharest. **Tel:** 01-320 6156.

Open Doors School of English
Michelle Penta, str. L. Blaga nr. 4, 1900 Timisoara. **Tel/Fax:** 056- 194252.

PROSPER-ASE Language Centre
Calea Grivitei 2-2A et.2 s.4211, Bucharest. **Tel/Fax:** 01-2117800, **Tel:** 01-6505456, **Email:** prosper1@rolink.iiruc.ro

PROSPER-Transilvania Language Centre
c/o Bd.Valea Cetatii 6, bl.B2, sc.B, ap.6, 2200 Brasov **Tel:** 068-319908, **Email:** g.cusen@unitbv.ro

RALEX Linguistic Centre
Str. Buna Vestire nr. 35, 1000 Ramnicu Valcea, **Tel/Fax:** 050-740032

Soros Educational Centre Miercurea-Ciuc
Str. Florilor 9, et.3, 4100 Miercurea-Ciuc. **Tel/Fax:** 066-171799, **Email:** office@cemc.topnet.ro

'YES' Language Centre
Colegiul Pedagogic Andrei Saguna, Str. Gen. Magheru 34, 2400 Sibiu. **Tel:** 069-430809 / 434002

RUSSIA

The Western media tends to paint a distorted view of life in Russia. Although there are hardships, most teachers report that their experiences in Russia were positive and that people actually enjoy themselves quite a lot here! There is a great.demand for English lessons throughout Russia at present. This demand is not confined to the major cities like Moscow and St. Petersburg. Private language schools are springing up across the country – some more reputable than others. Russians are fascinated by all things American and you will be the centre of much attention, especially in the smaller towns. But a word of warning: if your grammar and spelling are weak, you better brush up on these areas before you go. Russians are precise and thorough in their language learning and they are not impressed by teachers who do not know how to use the English language correctly. Many teachers start off by working for a school, then pick up some private lessons as the word gets around, and finally going completely freelance.

Embassy in UK:
13 Kensington Palace Gardens, London W8 4QX
Tel: 020 7229 8027
www.russianembassy.net

Embassy in USA:
2650 Winsconsin Ave. NW, Washington DC 20007
Tel: 202 298 5700
www.russianembassy.org

British Council office:
Ulitsa Nikoloyamskaya 1, Moscow 109189
Tel +7 095 782 0200
www.britishcouncil.ru

⮕ **Visas/Work Permits:** A Russian visa is considered as a permission to enter and exit the country. To obtain a visa, you must be sponsored by an organization such as a school or a tour company. Only the sponsor can extend or change your visa. It is a good idea to apply for a three-month visa. After that, the school can arrange your paperwork but you will have to have an AIDS test. Be careful that the school does not decide to keep you longer than you want to stay! Be prepared for a lot of red tape as far as visas are concerned. There is no such thing as a work permit in Russia.

⮕ **Currency:** £1 = 52.02 / $1 = 28.12 Rubles

⮕ **Salaries/Taxes:** Russia operates on a dual currency system with both rubles and dollars in circulation. You can earn around £3500-4000 per month and as much as £30 an hour for private lessons in Moscow and St. Petersburg. These rates are lower in the provincial centres.

⮕ **Accommodation:** You can find an apartment in Moscow from around £100 a month.

⮕ **Cost of Living:** Moscow has a reputation as an expensive city but you will be earning far more than most people do there. If you indulge in imported western goods, then life will be expensive. Carry cash (US$) – credit cards are useless unless you plan to spend your time at expensive hotels.

➲ **Health advice:** Teachers thinking of going to Russia should be in good physical condition. It's not a good idea to entrust your health to a badly paid doctor operating in poor facilities. Get shots for rabies, diphtheria, cholera, hepatitis A and B and encephalitis before you go.

➲ **English language media:** Moscow Times, Moscow Tribune, Moscow News, St. Petersburg Press, Neva News, The Vladivostok Times.

Schools in the Russian Federation (+7)

Anglo-American School
Penkovaya ui. 5, St. Petersburg.

Benedict School
Chapligina 92, Novosibirsk 630099. **Tel:** 3832 23 24 33, **Fax:** 3832 23 59 97.

Centre for Intensive Foreign Language Instruction
Sparrow Hills, Building 2, Moscow 119899.

Go West Department of Foreign Languages
2/1 Spartakovskaya Street, Moscow. **Tel:** 95 267 4700, **Fax:** 95 267 4700.

Language Link Schools
Novoslobod-skaya ul. 5 bld.2, 101030 Moscow. **Tel/Fax:** 95 973 2154.

Link School of Languages
15/81 pl Lenina, 394000 Voronezh. **Tel:** 732 55 23 31.

LK Varioline
12-12, Klyutchevskaya St., Ekaterinburg 620109. **Tel/Fax:** 3432 46 91 39.

Marina Anglo-American School
Leninsky Prospekt 39a, Moscow 117313.

Moscow-Cambridge Project Management
Academy of National Economy, 82 Vernadsky Prospect, Moscow 117571. **Tel:** 502 234 3873, **Fax:** 95 434 6030.

Moscow International School
2nd Ulitsa Maryinoy Roshchi 2a, Moscow.

Moscow MV Lomonosov University
Sparrow Hills, Moscow 117234.

NevaLingua International Study Centre
Malaya Morskaya Str. 11, office 315, St. Petersburg 191186. **Tel:** 812 3128129, **Fax:** 812 3126211.

Polyglot International School
22 Volkov Pereulok, Flat 56, Moscow.

ProBa Language Centre
Professora Popova 5, St.Petersburg 197376. (Mail: P.O. Box 109, Lappeenranta FIN-53101 Finland.) **Tel:** 812 3252618. **Fax:** 812 3462758

Pushkin Language Centre
Pushkin. (**Contact:** Leipziger Strasse 27, 09648 Mittweida, Germany.) **Tel:** +49-3727-976228, **Fax:** +49-3727-976227.

RISC Language School
Ulitsa Dekabristov 23a, Moscow

Russian-American Centre
Tomsk Polytechnic University, Room 319, Lenin Ave 30, 634004 Tomsk. **Tel:** 3822 22 45 48, **Fax:** 3822 22 46 07.

St Petersburg University
Universitetskaya, Naberezhnaya 7/9 B-164, St Petersburg, 199164.

St Petersburg University of Humanities & Social Sciences
Dept. of Foreign Languages, 15 Fuchika St., St Petersburg 192238. **Tel:** 812 269 1925.

Sunny School
PO Box 23, Moscow 125057. **Tel:** 95 151 2500.

System-3 Language & Communication
Arnold Rubinstein, Kantemirovskaya Street 16 #531, Moscow 115522. **Tel:** 9210141, **Fax:** 3204035.

World Language Club
1106e Panfilovsky Prosp., Zelenograd 103460. **Tel:** 95 532 9121, **Fax:** 95 530 9646.

Spelling It Out in Siberia

Professor Yuri Tambovtsev explains what intrepid EFL teachers might expect to find if they come to work in the Siberian city of Novosibirsk.

Novosibirsk is situated on the great Siberian River, Ob. It is quite a young city, founded in 1893 when a crossing for the Trans-Siberian railway was built over the river. Until 1925, Novosibirsk was known as Novonikolaevsk, named after the last Russian tsar, Nicholas II. In the 1920s, the city grew rapidly as it became an important industrial and transport centre between the coalfields to the southeast and the mineral deposits in the Ural Mountains to the west. In 1930s the building of the Turko-Siberian railway south from Novosibirsk to Almaty in Kazakhstan made the city a crucial transport link between Russia and Central Asia.

Now a city of 1.5 million people, Novosibirsk is a major industrial, scientific, cultural and educational centre. One in three of the city's residents is a student. Many Russians have realized how important it is to be able to talk English because it is the language of international communication. Every Russian pupil begins learning English in the 1st grade. The pupils usually have two lessons a week. However, there are some schools which give six lessons a week. At the universities, students normally have English once a week for two years. The communicative method of teaching English is now in fashion. It is also called the "rapid" method of teaching. The pupils at schools and the students at universities are asked to talk in English during the entire lesson. A native-speaking teacher is required to talk English all the time without resorting to Russian. Although having a degree, certificate or diploma in teaching EFL/ESL will help you as a teacher, the universities and colleges will hire unqualified native speakers of English if they can prove they are able to conduct an English lesson well.

I think one problem with English teaching here in Russia is that we do not teach the students correct English phonetics. The special lessons devoted to teaching only English sounds have been abolished. Now, the students just substitute English sounds with similar Russian ones. Younger teachers of English and their students speak with a stronger Russian accent than the older teachers of English, who had a special course of practical and theoretical phonetics every day for one year of their degree course. The English language textbooks are usually British or American, so the teacher does what is in the textbook.

The salaries of young native-speaking teachers are usually 5-10 times higher than those of Russian teachers of English. Native speakers can earn £30-60 a month. One can live very well on this salary: A kilogram of meat is £2 and one can buy 4 kilograms of potatoes for under £1. There are no problems buying food, as the shops are full of goods. It is cheaper to buy food at the street markets, but you can't be sure if the food is fresh or safe to eat. Although the city is rather gray and functional, its residents are very proud of it since it has the biggest railway station, the biggest library and the biggest airport in Siberia. The local ballet company is said to be the best after Bolshoi and Mariinsky companies of Moscow and St. Petersburg respectively. The Art Gallery in Novosibirsk is certainly worth seeing as it contains original works of Shishkin, Rerickh, Repin, and Surikov. Opera, ballet and theatre tickets cost from £2-4. Universities can provide a native speaker of English with a room in a dormitory for £6-12 a month. The dormitory has showers with hot water, and places to wash clothes and a communal kitchen for cooking. Elsewhere in the city, a one-room apartment costs about £30 a month; with

two rooms – £50. One can easily hire a car, but it is cheaper to use public buses or trams: 12 rides cost under £1.

During your summer vacation, you can travel by boat along the Ob river to the North to visit the Finno-Ugric aboriginal peoples of Siberia: Mansi (Voguls), Hanty (Ostjaks), and Nenets (Samoyeds). You can also visit the Altai Mountains and meet the Turkic aboriginal peoples: Altai-Kizh, Kumandin, Telengits, and Teleuts, the latter being remnants of Genghis Khan's Tatar-Mongolian hordes.

Professor Yuri Tambovtsev teaches at the Department of English and Linguistics, SIM, Novosibirsk, Russia.

SLOVAKIA

There is a shortage of English language teachers in Slovakia and native speakers with qualifications can land jobs here without problems. Many schools start recruiting in the spring for a September start but if you arrive in July or early August, you'll probably find work. If you want to teach in the state sector, you'll have to approach the Ministry of Education or one of the cultural organizations. There are fewer westerners here than in neighbouring countries.

Embassy in UK:
25 Kensington Palace Gardens, London W8 4QY
Tel: 020 7243 0803
www.slovakembassy.co.uk

Embassy in USA:
3523 International Court NW, Washington DC20008
Tel: 202 237 1054
www.slovakembassy-us.org

British Council office:
Panska 17 - P.O. Box 68, 814 99 Bratislava
Tel: +421 (2) 5443 1074
www.britishcouncil.sk

➲ **Visas/Work Permits:** You do not need a visa for a stay of less than 30 days so you can look for a job during this time. Your employer should arrange all the necessary paperwork but you will have to take a rather unpleasant medical exam.

➲ **Currency:** £1 = 53 / $1 = 29 Koruny.

➲ **Salaries/Taxes:** You will be paid at local rates around £180-200 per month for a 25-hour week plus some overtime. You can earn better money with private lessons but these are hard to come by.

➲ **Accommodation:** This is usually supplied by the school who should also pay for the utilities.

➲ **Cost of Living:** Although Slovakia is cheap in dollar terms, you will be paid at local rates so basic items like shampoo and other toiletries are actually expensive. Credit cards are not used much here.

➲ **Health advice:** There are decent medical facilities but few doctors speak English. Some schools will provide you with medical coverage.

➲ **English language media:** Slovak Spectator.

Schools in Slovak Republic (+421)

Academia Vzdelavania
Gorkeho 10, 815 17 Bratislava. **Tel:** 7 367 580, **Fax:** 7 321 661.

American Language Institute
Drienova 34, PO Box 78, 820 09 Bratislava.

Foundation for a Civil Society
V Zahradach 29A, 811 03 Bratislava. **Tel:** 7 580 2491, **Fax:** 7 531 1622.

VSMU
Katedra Jazykov, Venturska 3, 813 01 Bratislava.

SLOVENIA

There are lots of opportunities for English language teachers in Slovenia. The country is more "western" than others in the region. Native-speaking teachers are usually assigned to the more advanced learners. It's easier to come here and find a job rather than applying from outside the country.

British Council office:
Cankarjevo nabrezje 27, Ljubljana 1000
Tel +386 (0) 1 200 0130
Email: info@britishcouncil.si

◘ **Visas/Work Permits:**You can stay for up to 90 days without a visa. Most teachers just stay on although some do overcome the red tape and acquire work permits. The authorities don't worry about foreign teachers unless they are perceived (rightly or wrongly) as troublemakers.

◘ **Currency:** £1 = 338 / $1 = 183 Tolar

◘ **Salaries/Taxes:** Expect to earn $9-12 per 45-minute teaching "hour". Most teachers are paid in tolars

◘ **Accommodation:** A nice one-bedroom apartment costs around £150-200 per month or you can share a place for about £60.

◘ **Cost of Living:** You should be able to live well off your salary here.

◘ **Health advice:** Schools will not offer medical coverage so you should have your own policy. Medical care in Slovenia is of a high quality and many doctors speak English.

Schools in Slovenia (+386)

Accent On Language d.o.o.
Ljubljanska c. 36, 1230 Domzale. **Tel:** 61 712 658, **Fax:** 61 712 658.

Ambra d.o.o.
Pobeska 18, 6000 Koper. **Tel:** 66 33 128.

AS Asistent d.o.o.
Glavni trg 17 B, 2000 Maribor. **Tel:** 62 226 442, **Fax:** 62 224 432.

Athena d.o.o.
Kolodvorska c. 17, 6230 Postojna. **Tel:** 67 23 907, **Fax:** 67 23 907.

Bled
Sola za Tuje Jezike, Breda Vukelj s.p., Kajuhova c. 11, 4260 Bled. **Tel:** 64 741 780, **Fax:** 64 741 780.

Candor Dominko k.d.
Turnovse 19, 1360 Vrhnika. **Tel:** 61 756 032, **Fax:** 61 756 032.

Cenca p.o.
Masarykova c. 18, Ribnisko selo, 2000 Maribor. **Tel:** 62 306 479.

D and A lta d.o.o.
Japljeva ul. 4, 1241 Kamnik.

Dialog d.o.o
Jezikovna Sola, Terceva ul. 39, 2000 Maribor. **Tel:** 62 24 779, **Fax:** 62 227 866.

Dude d.o.o
English Language centre, Slamnikarska 1, 1230 Domzale. **Tel:** 61 716 913

Eurocentre
Lilijana Durdevic s.p., Kidriceva ul. 46, 6000 Koper. **Tel:** 66 272 336, **Fax:** 66 281 653.

Europa Bled, d.o.o.
Alpska 7, 4260 Bled. **Tel:** 64 741 563, **Fax:** 64 741 563 **Email**: evropabl@perfech.si

Ekocept d.o.o
Sola za Tuje Jezike, Prezihova 8, 2230 Lenart v Slovenskih Goricah. **Tel:** 62 724 064, **Fax:** 62 724 064.

Flamingo d.o.o.
Pod Gonjami 44, 2391 Prevalje. **Tel:** 602 31 455.

Forum centre d.o.o.
Markova pot 8, 5290 Sempeter pri Gorici, **Tel:** 65 31 205, **Fax:** 65 31 205.

G.A.P.
Belokriska 22, 6320 Portoroz. **Tel:** 66 75 894 .

Hello Sempeter d.o.o
Sempeter v Savinjski dolini·34, 3311 Sempeter v Savinjski dolini. **Tel:** 63 701 795, **Fax:** 63 701 795.

ISCG Domzale
Kolodvorska c. 6, 1230 Domzale. **Tel:** 61 711 082, **Fax:** 61 712 278.

Jezikovna Sola Tabula Rasa
Trg svobode 12, 3325 Sostanj. **Tel:** 63 892 291.

Jezikovni biro Lindic
Cankarjeva ul. 10, 2000 Maribor. **Tel:** 62 221 629.

Jezikovni Studio Kotar Sonja, s.p.
Cesta na Svetino 10, 3270 Lasko, **Tel:** 63 731 105.

Kamnik
Altera d.n.o., Kettejeva 23, 1241 Kamnik. **Tel:** 61 831 117.

Lingua
Carman Cilka, s.p., Cesta Zasavskega bataljona 27, 1270 Litija. **Tel:** 61 882 137

Lingva d.o.o.
Ograde 7, 1386 Stari trg pri Lozu, Cerknica. **Tel:** 61 708 017.

Lingva p.o
Zavod za Opravljanje Izobrazevalnih in Organizacijskih Storitev, Vetrinjska ul. 16, 2000 Maribor. **Tel:** 62 24 795, **Fax:** 62 301 071.

Little England Club d.o.o.
Medvedova ul. 6, 1241 Kamnik . **Tel:** 61 832 865, **Fax:** 61 832 865.

Ljudska Univerza Celje
Cankarjeva ul. 1, 3000 Celje. **Tel:** 63 484 320, **Fax:** 63 443 181.

Ljudska Univerza Dodatno Izobrazevanje
Maistrova ul. 5, 2000 Maribor. **Tel:** 62 226 441, **Fax:** 225 017.

Ljudska Univerza Koper
Cankarjeva ul. 33, 6000 Koper. **Tel:** 64 271 258, **Fax:** 64 271 291.

Ljudska Univerza Kranj
Cesta Staneta Zagarja 1, 4000 Kranj. **Tel:** 64 222 226, **Fax:** 64 222 226.

Ljudska Univerza Nova Gorica
Cankarjeva ul 8, 5000 Nova Gorica. **Tel:** 65 22 302, **Fax:** 65 21 291.

Ljudska Univerza Ptuj
Mestni trg 2, 2250 Ptuj. **Tel:** 62 771 539, **Fax:** 62 779 849.

Ljudska Univerza Ravne Na Koroskem
Prezihova ul. 24, 2390 Ravne na Koroskem. **Tel:** 602 22 296.

Ljudska Univerza Sezana
Bazoviska c. 9, 6210 Sezana. **Tel:** 67 73 428, **Fax:** 67 32 046.

Ljudska Univerza Skofja Loka
Podlubnik 1b, 4220 Skofja Loka. **Tel:** 64 621 865.

Most d.o.o.
Kovinarska ul. 9, 8270 Krsko. **Tel:** 608 22 397, **Fax:** 608 22 397.

Multilingua d.o.o.
Ulica bratov Hvalic 16, 5000 Nova Gorica. **Tel:** 65 24 292, **Fax:** 65 24 292

New College d.o.o.
Med ogradami 11A, 5000 Nova Gorica. **Tel:** 65 23 733, **Fax:** 65 23 733.

Niansa Jezikovna Sola
Cesta talcev 4, 1230 Domzale. **Tel:** 61 712 012, **Fax:** 61 712 230.

Nista Language School
Smarska cesta 5d, 6000 Koper. **Tel:** 66 250 400, **Fax:** 66 258 440, **Email:** nista@siol.net

Ontario d.o.o.
Miklosiceva ul. 5, 2250 Ptuj. **Tel:** 62 779 108, **Fax:** 62 779 108.

Poliglot d.o.o.
Ljubljanska c. 110, 1230 Domzale. **Tel:** 61 723 089, **Fax:** 61 723 089.

Pharmagan d.o.o.
Straziska ul. 7, 4000 Kranj. **Tel:** 64 311 463, **Fax:** 64 311 463.

Prevajanje s.p.
Kalinskova ul. 31, 4000 Kranj. **Tel:** 64 340 010, **Fax:** 64 340 011.

Progress Jezikovni Tecaji d.o.o.
Seljakovo n. 33, 4000 Kranj. **Tel:** 64 310 644.

Rossana d.o.o.
Trzaska c. 30, 1370 Logatec. **Tel:** 61 743 104, **Fax:** 61 742 910.

Samba d.n.o.
Bresterniska ul. 225, 2351 Kamnica. **Tel:** 62 621 905.

Selih Kozelj d.n.o.
Studio za Ucenje, Miklosiceva 9, 3000 Celje. **Tel:** 63 24 236, **Fax:** 63 24 326.

Sibon
centre za Tuje Jezike, Ljubljanska c. 76 II, 1230 Domzale. **Tel:** 61 722 901, **Fax:** 61 722 928.

Speak It
Heintzman and Heintzman, Trubarjeva ul. 4, 1230 Domzale. **Tel:** 61 712 312, **Fax:** 61 712 312.

Spektra Jameks d.o.o.
Malgajeva 10, 3000 Celje. **Tel:** 63 443 192, **Fax:** 63 443 191.

Sports Life Pevc d.o.o.
Cesta talcev 6, 4220 Skofja Loka. **Tel:** 64 622 335, **Fax:** 64 623 121.

Studiom d.o.o.
Radvanjska c. 74, 2106 Maribor. **Tel:** 62 35 481.

Tecaj d.o.o.
Kraigherjeva ul. 19A, 2230 Lenart v Slovenskih Goricah. **Tel:** 62 723 224, **Fax:** 62 723 224.

Tonson Posrednistvo in Storitve d.o.o.
Velike Brusnice 13, 8321 Brusnice. **Tel:** 68 85 882, **Fax:** 68 85 882.

Unique d.o.o.
Jezikovno izobrazevanje, Gabrsko 69, 1420 Trbovlje. **Tel:** 601 27 442, **Fax:** 601 27 442.

Vox Vidrih Trebnje k.d.
Sola Tujih Jezikov, Simonciceva ul. 10, 8210 Trebnje. **Tel:** 68 45 158, **Fax:** 68 45 158.

Yurena d.o.o.
Ulica Marjana Kozine 49A, 8000 Novo Mesto. **Tel:** 68 341 434, **Fax:** 68 341 434.

Zavod za Izobrazevanje BAS
Grajski trg 1, 2000 Maribor. **Tel:** 62 223 344, **Fax:** 62 223 344.

Zavod za Izobrazevanje
Kopitarjeva 5, 2000 Maribor. **Tel**: 62 214 273, **Fax**: 62 225 003.

UKRAINE

There are two sides to the Ukraine: the western part is mostly Catholic and looks to Poland while the east is Orthodox. There is also the Crimea, a fascinating region on the Black Sea heavily populated by Tatars. There is a lot of interest in English language learning in the Ukraine and many schools have opened in last five years. The economic situation is still precarious and outside of Kiev, you may find daily life difficult to cope with, as food shortages still happen. It is probably better to arrange a job before arriving here.

British Council:
4/12 Vul. Hryhoriya Skovorody, Kyiv 04070
Tel +380 (44) 490 5600
www.britishcouncil.org/ukraine

➲ **Visas/Work Permits:** To obtain a visa, you need an invitation to visit Ukraine either from a company or an individual. Once you find a job, your employer should take care of all the paperwork. Some teachers work illegally but this is not advisable and it is very hard to change your visa status from tourist to worker while in the country.

➲ **Currency:** £1 = 9.8 / $1 = 5.33 Hyvrnia.

➲ **Salaries/Taxes:** Salaries range anywhere from £300-600 a month, which is good by local standards.

➲ **Accommodation:** Housing is usually provided by the school but you can find apartments from £100-200 pm in the suburbs and a lot more in the city centre.

➲ **Cost of Living:** Food and transport costs are very reasonable.

➲ **Health advice:** Medical facilities are limited. Insurance is essential.

➲ **English language media:** The Kiev Post, The Odessa Post.

Schools in the Ukraine (+380)

American Academy of Foreign Languages
89 Chervonoarmeyska, Office 9, 2520006 Kiev.
Tel/Fax: 44 268 5095.

London School of English
PO Box B 158, 2420001 Kiev. **Tel/Fax:** 44 2418654.
Email: admin@lse.kiev.ua

Odessa English Language Study centre
Pereulok Onilovoy 26/28, 270027 Odessa. **Tel/Fax:** 44 82 344 000.

Ukrainian-American Humanitarian Institute
9 Pyrogov St., 252030 Kiev. **Tel/Fax:** 44 216 0666.

Union Forum
10 Ternopiliska St., P.O. Box 10722, 290034 L'viv.
Tel/Fax: 322 759 488.

Middle East & North Africa

Many of the oil-rich Gulf States offer the best employment packages for English language teachers anywhere in the world. Other countries, although not so blessed by natural resources, welcome travellers with open arms, inviting teachers to explore and to stay awhile: Arab hospitality is legendary. Although the region was dominated by Great Britain in the earlier part of the 20th century, there is a growing preference for teachers with American and Canadian accents, particularly in the Gulf. Possible drawbacks include cultural differences, and, in certain countries, restrictions on the lifestyles of female teachers. But the region, birthplace to the three great monotheistic religions (Judaism, Christianity, and Islam), is as compelling as it is complex in terms of its history and its people. Teachers willing to overcome preconceptions will be rewarded by experiences that will open their eyes to the realities of a region rich in tradition and humanity. However, the current tensions involving Iraq, Iran and some other neighboring countries means this is potentially a *very* dangerous region and you should check before travelling to any of the countries in this region. Visit www.fco.gov.uk for the UK-government's advice for travellers.

The overwhelming majority of teaching positions overseas are offered by private schools–including the American-sponsored international schools in Asia and Middle East. A graduate degree is a standard requirement for employment, including the UAE, Bahrain, Lebanon, Jordan, Syria, and others.

North Africa: Morocco and Tunisia are attractive prospects for English language teachers as both countries are shaking off their Francophone past by embracing English as a working language. Algeria and Libya are basically off limits to American teachers although oil companies in Libya do employ teachers. Recent reports suggest that Canadian teachers are welcome in Tripoli although only the truly intrepid should attempt to teach in Libya.

Two good sources of information on this region are:

TESOL Arabia website - http://tesolarabia.uaeu.ac.ae

AMIDEAST - www.amideast.org

BAHRAIN

A small island situated in the Arabian Gulf, Bahrain is quite liberal and women are welcome in the classroom. Employment should be arranged in advance and the only opportunities are for qualified teachers.

Embassy in UK:
30 Belgrave Square, London SW1X 8QB
Tel: 020 7201 9170

Embassy in USA:
3502 International Drive NW, Washington DC 20008
Tel: 202 342 0741
www.bahrainembassy.org

British Council office:
AMA Centre (PO Box 452), 146 Shaikh Salman Highway, Manama 356
Tel +973 261 555
www.britishcouncil.org/bahrain

➲ **Visas/Work Permits:** Passports and visas are required. Three-day and seven-day visas may be obtained upon arrival at the airport in Manama, but obtaining visas before travel is recommended. Work permits are also required. Your employer should make arrangements to provide you with one soon after your arrival.

➲ **Currency:** £1 = 0.695 / $1 = 0.377 Dinar

➲ **Salaries/Taxes:** Monthly salaries range from BHD 600-750 for teachers with certificates and BHD 600-700 for those with diplomas. Part-time teachers earn around BHD 10 per hour. There is no personal income tax.

➲ **Accommodation:** A small apartment will cost BHD 200-500 per month. There is no deposit but three months' rent is required in advance.

➲ **Cost of Living:** More expensive than other Gulf States and salaries are often lower.

➲ **Health advice:** Essential: health insurance can be obtained locally at competitive rates. Vaccinations: Hepatitis A, Polio, Typhoid.

➲ **English Language Media:** Bahrain Tribune, Gulf Daily News.

➲ **Tip:** There has been some unrest from time to time in Bahrain. Although Americans have not to date been subject to attacks, it is wise to exercise caution at all times.

Schools in Bahrain (+973)

Al Maalem centre
PO Box 20649, Manama. **Tel:** 553808. **Fax:** 554240.

Al Rawasi Academy
Mina Salman, Bahrain. **Tel:** 727442. **Fax:** 725442.

Awal Training Institute
PO Box 82110, Riffa. **Tel:** 773445. **Fax:** 771909.

Bahrain Computer & Management Institute
PO Box 26176, Manama. **Tel:** 293493.

Bahrain Training Institute
PO Box 323333, Essa Town. **Tel/Fax:** 683416.

BCMI
PO Box 26176, Manama. **Tel:** 293493. **Fax:** 290358.

The British Council
AMA Centre, (PO Box 452), Manama 356. **Tel:** 261555.

The Cambridge School of English
PO Box 20646, Manama. **Tel:** 532838.

Capital Institute
PO Box 22521, Manama. **Tel:** 740744/740088, **Fax:** 720060.

Child Development
PO Box 20284, Manama. **Tel:** 728000, **Fax:** 722636.

Daar al Merifa
PO Box 3174, Manama **Tel:** 722183, **Fax:** 722283.

Delmon Academy
PO Box 10362, Manama. **Tel:** 294400, **Fax:** 292010.

Global Institute
PO Box 11148, Manama. **Tel:** 740940, **Fax:** 720030.

Gulf Academy
PO Box 10333, Manama. **Tel:** 721700, **Fax:** 722636.

Gulf School of Languages
PO Box 20236, Manama. **Tel:** 290209, **Fax:** 290069.

Pitman IPE
PO Box 26222, Manama. **Tel:** 290028, **Fax:** 292006.

Polyglot School
PO Box 596, Manama. **Tel:** 271722, **Fax:** 722636.

University of Bahrain
PO Box 32038, Sakhir-Bahrain. **Fax:** 973 4496603.

EGYPT

English language teaching in Egypt suffers from the usual catalogue of third-world woes such as overcrowded classrooms and inadequate resources. English is nevertheless well established as the primary foreign language, and most people want to learn it and work hard at doing so. There is great enthusiasm for improving programmes in the teaching of English by means of better teacher training and the development

of better methods and materials for teachers to work with. More and more schools in Egypt are starting to go online although connections are not always reliable. Foreigners will have no problem in finding a teaching job in a private language school here, especially if they are prepared to work with young learners. Employers usually recruit teachers in the spring to begin work in September. Some teachers survive on a freelance basis through advertising and contacts.

Embassy in UK:

26 South Street, London W1Y 6DD
Tel: 020 7499 2401

Embassy in USA:

3521 International Drive NW, Washington DC20008
Tel: 202 895 5400

British Council office:

192 El Nil Street, Agouza, Cairo
Tel +20 (2) 303 1514
www.britishcouncil.eg

⮑ **Tip:** When teaching in Egypt, it is a good idea to keep in mind that most people come from an oral culture and do not have a tradition of reading, even in their own language, let alone English.

⮑ **Visas/Work Permits:** American and Canadian citizens can obtain visitor's visas from the airport upon their arrival in Cairo. Go to one of the bank counters before the immigration windows and buy the visa stamps for your passport. They cost £10 ($19) and it is best to pay in U.S. dollars. These visas are good for one month. When they are close to expiration, you can easily get a six-month or one-year's extension. The schools obtain residency and work permits, which take around two months to process, while the teacher is working on a visitor's visa. A blood test is necessary.

⮑ **Currency:** £1 = 10.8 / $1 = 5.84 Pound

⮑ **Salaries/Taxes:** Most teachers earn around £5-10 per hour in a school, Rates for private lessons range from £10-20. Monthly salaries start around EGP 2,000 and go up to EGP 7,500 depending on your qualifications and experience, and the prestige of the school. Tax is 5-7%.

⮑ **Accommodation:** Do not expect Western standards of comfort and plumbing. Expect to pay around £300 a month for basic accommodations in Cairo and less elsewhere.

⮑ **Cost of Living:** Imported (American) items are expensive although locally made versions of most products (varying in quality) are available at a reasonable price. Fruit and vegetables are plentiful, inexpensive, and are fresh and delicious.

⮑ **Health advice:** Most foreign teachers are ill within a few weeks of arrival in Egypt although the majority of them recover. Hepatitis is a concern. Schistosomiasis, a parasitic infection, is found in fresh water in the region, including the Nile River. Do not swim in fresh water (except in well-chlorinated swimming pools.) Malaria is a risk limited to the El Faiyum area. Vaccinations: Hepatitis A, Polio, Typhoid, Malaria, Yellow Fever (if coming from an infected area).

⮑ **English Language Media:** Al Ahram Weekly, Cairo Today, Egyptian Gazette, Middle East Times.

⮑ **Information for Women:** You may find yourself the centre of attention as you walk down the street and the object of rude comments or occasional unwanted touching. Dress modestly and avoid public transportation (or, if taking the Cairo subway, ride the first car which is reserved for women.) Violent crime is rare.

Schools in Egypt (+20)

American Cultural centre
3 El Pharana Street, Alexandria. **Tel:** 3 483 1922, **Fax:** 3 483 3811.

The American University in Cairo
CACE, ESD P.O. Box 2511, Cairo. **Tel:** 2 357 6870.

AMIDEAST
3 El Pharana Street, Alexandria. **Tel:** 3 483 1922.

El Manar School
Amin Fikry Street, Ramleh Station, Cairo. **Tel:** 2 4823813.

El Nasr Boys' College (EBC)
Chatby. **Tel:** 2 5976812.

El Nasr Girls' College (ECC)
Chatby. **Tel:** 2 597 1752.

El Pharaana School
El Pharaana Street, Bab Sharki. **Tel:** 2 4822229.

Heliopolis
Cairo. **Tel:** 2 4155003, **Fax:** 2 2900552.

IELP
6 Mostafa El Sherei Street, Dokki 12311, Cairo. **Tel:** 2 3365898, **Fax:** 2 3384780.

International Language Institute
2, Mohamed Bayoumi St. Off Merghany St., Heliopolis, Cairo. **Tel:** 2 291 2218.

International Language Learning Institute
34 Talaat Harb Street, 5th Floor, Cairo. **Tel:** 2 748355.

Kawmeya International School
Horreya Avenue, Bab Sharki. **Tel:** 2 4938670.

Lycee El Horreya
English Dept., Chatby. **Tel:** 2 5976968.

Port Said School
7, Taha Hussein Street, Zamalek. **Tel:** 2 3403435.

Ragab Language School
Chatby. **Tel:** 2 5976968.

Sacred Heart School
Syria School, Roushdy. **Tel:** 2 840228.

Sakkara Language School
Block #3 Zahraa El-Maadi, Maadi, Cairo. **Tel:** 2 516-5205 **Fax:** 2 516-5204.

ISRAEL & PALESTINIAN AUTHORITY

There is little demand for foreign teachers and it is difficult to find employment unless you are Jewish and are claiming your right of abode (which makes you liable for military service.) Be warned that an Israeli stamp in your passport may make travel to certain other countries in the Middle East impossible. You can ask for the stamps to be placed on removable pages. Except during periods of heightened security restrictions, most U.S. citizens may enter and exit Gaza and the West Bank on a U.S. passport with an Israeli entry stamp. It is not necessary to obtain a visitor's permit from the Palestinian Authority.

British Council office:
Crystal House, 12 Hahilazon St, Ramat Gan, 52136
Tel +972 (03) 611 3600
www.britishcouncil.org.il

⮕ **Currency:** £1 = 7.99 / $1 = 4.32 New Shekels

⮕ **Cost of Living:** Israel is an expensive country that has suffered frequent bouts of hyperinflation.

⮕ **Salaries/Taxes:** £15-30 an hour in Israel. Taxation can go as high as 40%.

⮕ **Accommodation:** Very expensive in Tel Aviv and Jerusalem, but less so in Gaza City where a comfortable apartment can be had for around £150 per month.

⮕ **Health advice:** In Israel, take the same health precautions as you would at home. Note that national insurance is not available for non-Jews.

⮕ **English Language Media:** Jerusalem Post, Palestine Report.

Schools in Israel & Palestinian Authority (+972)

AMIDEAST
Ahmad Abd al-Aziz Street, behind Al-Karmel High School, PO Box 1247, Gaza City, Gaza. **Tel:** 7 2824635 **Fax:** 7-286-9338. **Email:** westbank-gaza@amideast.org

AMIDEAST
1 Anata Street, Shu'fat, PO Box 19665, Jerusalem. **Tel:** 2 5811962. **Fax:** 2 5328564. **Email:** westbank-gaza@amideast.org

Anglican School
P.O. Box 191, Jerusalem 91001. **Tel:** 2 38 5220.

Arab American University
P.O. Box 239/240, Jenin, West Bank. **Tel:** 6 43 6056.

Ben Gurion University of the Negev
342 Madison Avenue, Ste 1224, NY 10173, USA.

British Council
140 Hayarkon Street, (PO Box 3302), Tel Aviv 61032. **Tel:** 3 5222194.

Walworth Barbour American International School
P.O. Box 9005, Kfar Shmaryahu, Tel Aviv. **Tel:** 9 584 255

JORDAN

Jordan is a fascinating country but teaching opportunities are limited. Many schools employ Jordanians who have qualified to teach EFL/ESL. The American Language Center employs qualified teachers on a part-time basis.

Embassy in UK:
6 Upper Phillimore Gardens, London W8 7HB
Tel: 020 7937 3685
www.jordanembassyuk.org

Embassy in USA:
3504 International Drive NW, Washington DC20008
Tel: 202 966 2664
www.jordanembassyus.org

British Council office:
Rainbow Street – off first circle, PO Box 634, Amman 11118
Tel +962 (6) 4636147
www.britishcouncil.org/jordan

⮕ **Visas/Work Permits:** Employers of teachers on full-time contracts will arrange for the necessary

papers. Part-time teachers must pay around £500 a year for a permit.

⮑ **Currency:** £1 = 1.29 / $1 = 0.70 Dinar

⮑ **Salaries/Taxes:** Salaries are generally lower than those in the Gulf States.

⮑ **Health advice:** Although Jordan is malaria-free, take sensible precautions with drinking water and food. Vaccinations: Hepatitis A, Typhoid, Polio, Yellow Fever (if coming from an infected area).

⮑ **English Language Media:** BYTE Middle East, Issues, Jordan Times The Star.

⮑ **Cost of Living:** Prices of imported goods are high but food and travel costs are reasonable.

⮑ **Salaries and taxes:** A full-time teacher at a private language school can expect to earn around £6,000 a year.

⮑ **Accommodation:** Expensive. Some landlords ask for a year's rent in advance which can amount to as much as £4,500.

⮑ **Tip:** Bars are few and far between in Amman. Expect to pay at least £4 for a beer in a high-class hotel.

Schools in Jordan (+962)

Al-Manhal International School
Iskan Al-Jami'a, P.O. Box 278, Jubaiha, Amman 11941. **Tel:** 6 60 3751.

American Community School
Box 310, Dahiat Al-Amir Rashid, Amman, 11831.**Tel:** 6 5813944, **Fax:** 6 5823357. **Email:** school@acsamman.edu.jo

American Language Center
Amman. **Tel:** 6 5859102/3, **Fax:** 6 5859101. **Email:** info@alc.edu.jo

Amman Baccalaureate School
PO Box 441, Sweileh, Amman, 11910. **Tel:** 6 5411572, **Fax:** 541 2603. **Email:** abs@go.com.jo

Modern American School
P.O. Box: 851819, Amman 11185. **Tel:** 6 5816861. **Fax:** 6 5816860. **Email:** admin@ModernAmericanSchool.com

Yarmouk Cultural centre
PO Box 960312, Amman. **Tel:** 6 671447.

Yarmouk University Language Center
P.O. Box 566, Irbid. **Tel:** 2 84 2700.

KUWAIT

Kuwait was rapidly rebuilt after the Gulf War although there are not as many English language schools these days. Some teachers say that Kuwait is a good place to earn and save money because there is not that much on offer as far as nightlife is concerned.

Others claim that Kuwait is a "party town" because it's so easy to make friends with the locals and other nationalities working in the country! There are both public and private English language schools but you will need to be qualified if you want to teach English here. Opportunities do exist to find teaching jobs after your arrival in Kuwait. Check out local newspapers when you arrive.

Embassy in UK:
2 Albert Gate, London SW1X 7JU
Tel: 020 7 590 3400

Embassy in USA:
2940 Tilden Street NW, Washington DC 20008
Tel: 202 966 0702

British Council office:
2 Al Arabi Street, Block 2, PO Box 345, 13004 Safat Mansouriya, Kuwait City
Tel +965 252 0067
www.britishcouncil.org/kuwait

⮑ **Visas/Work Permits:** Entry visas are required for all visitors. Work permits are difficult to obtain and involve testing for AIDS and tuberculosis. You can find private lessons although you are supposed to have a work permit before you start teaching.

⮑ **Currency:** £1 = 0.53 / $1 = 0.29 Dinar

⮑ **Salaries/Taxes:** Annual salaries start at around £20,000, which usually involves a full-time post with about 24 contact hours per week. There is no income tax.

⮑ **Accommodation:** Most schools find and pay for accommodation because it is expensive. Average rent is £400-600. Usually, one month's rent is required as a deposit.

⮑ **Health advice:** Unexploded bombs, mines, booby traps, and other items remain in open areas and beaches throughout Kuwait. Vaccinations: Hepatitis A, Polio, Typhoid.

⮑ **English Language Media:** Kuwait Times.

⮑ **Other Information:** Only limited public transport exists and taxis are very expensive. Women are permitted to drive.

Schools in Kuwait (+965)

Al-Bayan Bilingual School
PO Box 24472, Safat. **Tel:** 5315125, **Fax:** 5332836
Email: bbs@ncc.moc.kw

American International School
Block 11, Uhud Street, Salmiya. **Tel:** 5645083/7, **Fax:** 5645089.

American School of Kuwait
Block 7, Al-Muthanna Street and 4th Ring Road, Hawalli. **Tel:** 2664341/2655172, **Fax:** 2650438. **Email:** askkwt@kuwait.net

College of Business Studies
P.O. Box 43197, Hawalli, 32046. **Tel:** 261 4962

ELS School of Languages
PO Box 5104, Salmiya 20062. **Tel:** 5722522/2558, 5710610. **Fax:** 5733005.

ELU
The Kuwait Institute of Banking Studies, PO Box 1080, Safat 13011.

Fahaheel English School
PO Box 7209, Fahaheel 64003. **Tel:** 3711070, **Fax:** 965 371 5458.

Institute For Private Education
P.O. Box 6320, 32038 Hawalli. **Tel:** 573 7811, **Fax:** 574 2924.

Language centre
Kuwait University, PO Box 2575, Safat. **Tel:** 481 0325, **Fax:** 484 3824.

LEBANON

Lebanon is rebuilding after the civil war, which ended in 1991. It is a beautiful country with old ruins, caves, mountains, and beaches to visit. In the summer there are many music festivals and other cultural activities to attend. English language teachers are in great demand and schools are advertising in the U.S. and Canada for qualified staff. Canadian citizens interested in volunteer work teaching English to Palestinian refugees in Lebanon should contact CEPAL by email at info@cepal.ca or call (613) 238-0410.

Embassy in UK:
21 Kensington Palace Gardens, London W8 4QM
Tel: 020 7727 6696

Embassy in USA:
2560 28th Street NW, Washington DC 20008
Tel: 202 939 6300

British Council office:
Sidani Street, Azar Building, Beirut
Tel +961 (1) 739 459
www.britishcouncil.org/lebanon

➲ **Currency:** £1 = 2776 / $1 = 1501 Pounds
➲ **Health advice:** Most hospitals in Beirut have modern facilities. .
➲ **English Language Media:** Beirut Times, Lebanon Daily Star, Monday Morning.

Schools in Lebanon (+961)

American University of Beirut
Division of Education Programmes, 850 Third Avenue, 18th Floor New York, NY 10022-6297.

AMIDEAST
P.O. Box 70-744, Antelias. **Tel:** 4 410438/19341/2/3. **Fax:** 4 419341. **Email:** lebanon@amideast.org

AMIDEAST
Ras Beirut centre Building, 4th Floor, Surati Street, Hamra Area, Beirut. **Tel:** 1 345341, 340137. **Email:** lebanon@amideast.org

Beirut International School
Bchamoun, Beirut. **Tel:** 3 215489. **Email:** bis@bis.edu.lb

Beirut Modern School
Bir Hassan area between Golf Club & Airport Highway, Beirut. **Tel:** 1 823616. **Email:** bms95@cyberia.net.lb

British Council
Sadat/Sidani Street, Azar Building, Beirut. **Tel:** 1 740123/4/5. **Fax:** 1 739461

International College
P.O. Box 11-0236, Beirut. **Tel:** 1 867252. **Fax:** 1 362500/1

Lebanese American University
Beirut Campus, P.O. Box 13-5053, Beirut. **Tel:** 1 786456/786464. **Fax:** 1 867098.

Lebanese American University
Byblos Campus, P.O. Box 36, Byblos. **Tel:** 9 547254/547262 **Fax:** 9 944851.

Lebanese American University
Sidon Campus, P.O. Box 267, Sidon. **Tel:** 7 728724, 728725 **Fax:** 7 728726.

MALTA

A culturally diverse island in the Mediterranean, with a beautiful climate. English is one of the official languages

High Commission in UK:
Malta House, 36-38 Piccadilly, London W1V 0PQ
Tel: 020 7292 4800

Embassy in USA:
2017, Connecticut Avenue NW , Washington DC 20008
Tel: (202) 462 3611

British Council office:
Whitehall Mansions, Ta'Xbiex Seafront, Malta
Tel +356 23 23 2403
www.britishcouncil.org/malta

- **Visas/Work Permits:** no visas required for tourists or for stays of less than 3 months
- **Currency:** £1 = 0.61 / $1 = 0.33 liri
- **Health advice:** Medical care is good, and available in either public or private hospitals. It is advisable to get insurance before travelling
- **English language media:** Malta Independent, Malta Star, Malta Today, Sunday Circle, Malta Financial and Business Times

Schools in Malta (+356)

Academy Magister
L-Arkati Menaija Street, St Julian's

Alpha School of English
Arznell Street, St Paul's Bay, SPB 03

AM Language Studio
299 Manuel Dimech Street, Sliema, SLM

Bell Language Centre
Elija Zammit Street, St Julian's STJ 02

Bell Valletta
10 Sur Santa Barabara, Valletta, Vlt 06
Tel: 21 25 25 30 **Fax:** 21 25 25 29

BELS
Triq Ta'Doti, Kercem, Gozo, VCT 113

Berlitz Language Centre
Draonara Street, St Julian's

Britannia College
124, Melita Street, Valletta

Burlington English Language School
Burlington Court, Dragonara Street, St Julian's, STJ 06

Club Class Language School
1 Chealsea Court, Triq L-Imghazel, Swieqi, St Andrews

Easy School of Languages
331, St. Paul's Street, Valletta VLT 01

EC Malta
Language House, New Street off Sant Andrija Street, St Julian's, STJ 02

Education English Culture
Villa Monaco, Sliema Road, Kappara, SGN 06

EF International Language School
Lower St. Augustine Street, St Julian's

Ef Language Travel
San Michel, St George'S Road, St Julians Stj 10

Elanguest
Keating House, Ross Street, Sliema, STJ 10

English Communication School
10 St Pius Street, Sliema SLM 06

English Language Academy
9 Tower Lane, Sliema, SLM 15

European Centre of English
Paolo Court, G.Cali Street, Ta'Xbiex, MSD 14

European School of English
Edgar Bernard Street, Gzira, GZR 06

Gateway International School of English
1, Triq il-Jonju, The Village, San Gwann

GEOS Malta
Level 5, The Plaza, Bisazza Str Commercial Centre, Sliema, SLM 15

In House Malta
"Ogygia Foresteria", San Dimitri Street, Birbuba, l/o Gharb, Gozo

inLingua School
9 Guze Fava Street, Tower Road, Sliema, SLM 15

Institute of English Language
Parisio Street, Gzira, GZR 04

International House Malta
11 Birbuba St, Gharb 4020
Tel: 21 5504 90 **Fax:** 21 55004 90
Email: academyblc@mail.com

Kalypso Academy of English
University of Malta, Mgarr Road, Xewkija

La Salle Institute
105 St Thomas Street, Floriana, VLT 14

Lingua Time
243E Tower Road, Sliema, SLM 05

Link School of English

Villa Petite Fleur, 88/90 Triq it-Tiben, Swieqi

Mediterranean English Language Academy
Mountbatten Street, Blata
l-Bajda, Hamrun

Melita Language School
CAK s-Sommier Street, B'Kara

MSD School of English
Josmar Triq il - Paguni, Balzan

MUT - Capital Language School
213 Republic Street, Valletta VLT 03

Nsts English Language Institute
220 St Paul Street, Valletta Vlt 07

Skylark Mediterranean School of English
29 Victor Denaro Street, Msida MSD 04

Sprachcaffe Languages
Srachcaffe Club Village, Pembroke, STJ 14·

Students Travel School
c/o Mimosa Valetta Road, Attard

The Academy of English and Culture
13, Mattew Pulis Street, Sliema

The British Council
Whitehall Mansions, Ta'Xbiex Seafront

The Chamber College
Edgar Bernard Street
Gzira

The Leonardo Da Vinci Global Village
Villa Rosa, St George's Bay

Think English Language School
100, Paola Square, Paola

Unilang International School of Languages
Workers Memorial Building, South Street, Valletta VLT 11

Universal Language Services
Upper Ross Street, St Julian's

Voice School of English
PO Box 60, Msida, MSD 01

World Wide Languages Academy
128, Triq is-Sirk, Swieqi

MOROCCO

Morocco has been a magnet for travellers for centuries. Everyone from Winston Churchill to William Burroughs has ended up spending some time in this intriguing country. Moroccans are tolerant people: teachers with qualifications are welcome although conditions do vary from school to school. American Language Centers (www.aca.org.ma) operates English language schools in most major Moroccan cities. Knowledge of French is helpful but not essential. Note that institutions must ensure that at least 50% of the teachers are Moroccan.

Embassy in UK:
49 Queen's Gate Gardens, London SW7 5NE
Tel: 020 7581 5001

Embassy in USA:
1601 21st Street NW, Washington DC 20009
Tel: 202 462 7979

British Council office:
36 Rue de Tanger, BP 427, Rabat
Tel +212 (37) 760 836
www.britishcouncil.org.morocco

⮑ **Visas/Work Permits:** Paper-work will be taken care of by the school after you have agreed on a contract. Be patient: It can take up to three months for your papers to come through. You will need original copies of your birth certificate, degree and teaching qualification.

⮑ **Currency:** £1 = 15.70 / $1 = 8.49 Dirham

⮑ **Cost of Living:** Prices are reasonable in Morocco although a meal at a sophisticated restaurant will be expensive.

⮑ **Salaries/Taxes:** 8,0000-9,000 dirhams a month is an average salary. Getting paid in dollars will help compensate for the effects of inflation.

⮑ **Accommodation:** 3,000 dirhams for pleasant 2-bedroom apartment in Casablanca. Rabat is cheaper.

⮑ **Health advice:** There is a small risk of malaria in Morocco. Take adequate precautions. Vaccinations: Hepatitis A, Polio, Typhoid.

⮑ **English Language Media:** Morocco Times.

Schools in Morocco (+212)

American Language Center
Rue des Nations-Unies, Cité Suisse, Agadir. **Tel:** 8 821589. **Fax:** 8 848272. **Email:** alcagad@marocnet

American Language Center
2, Boulevard Mohamed V, Mohammedia. **Tel/Fax:** 3 326870.

American Language Center
4 Zankat Tanja, Rabat 10000. **Tel:** 7 761269

American Language Center
2, Rue Ahmed Hiba, BP 2136, Fes. **Tel:** 5 624850. **Fax:** 5 931608.

American Language Center
1, Place de la Fraternité, 20000 Casablanca. **Tel**: 2 277765. **Fax**: 2 207457.

American Language Center
3 Impasse du Moulin de Gueliz, Marrakesh. **Tel**: 4 447259.

American Language Center
1 rue M'sallah, Tangier. **Tel**: 9 933616.

American Language Center
2 Blvd. El Kadissa, Kenitra. **Tel**: 7 366884.

American Language Center
4bis, rue de Menton, BP 382, Meknes. **Tel**: 5 523636. **Fax**: 7 516464.

American Language centre
1, rue Maarakate Zalaka, Tetuan. **Tel**: 9 963308.

Benedict School of English
124 Ave. Hassan II, Ben Slimane. **Tel**: 3 290957. **Fax**: 3 328472.

British Centre
3, rue Brahim el Amraoui, Casablanca. **Tel**: 2 267019. **Fax**: 2 267043.

British Council
36 rue de Tanger, B.P. 427, Rabat. **Tel**: 7 76 0836, **Fax**: 7 760850.

Business & Professional English Centre (BPEC)
74 rue Jean Jaurès, Casablanca. **Tel**: 2 22.47.02.79. **Fax**: 2 22.29.68.61.

EF
20 rue du Marché, Casablanca. 2 255174. **Fax**: 2 296861.

Institut Cegis
23 Boulevard Ibnou Majid Al Bahhar, Casablanca. **Tel**: 2 308410.

International Language Centre
2 rue Tihama, Rabat. **Tel**: 7 709718.

London School of English
10 Ave. des FAR, Casablanca. **Tel**: 26 89 32.

OMAN

Oman is one of the most relaxed of the Gulf States. Alcohol is freely available and single women have an easier time here than in other Islamic countries. There are many archaeological sites to visit and the country is beautiful.

Demand is high throughout the Sultanate amongst private language institutes and higher educational establishments. Teachers should go through the Yellow Pages, approach schools directly or look at the local newspapers where jobs are occasionally advertised. Teachers with Master's degrees in TESL/TEFL are in demand. CELTA-qualified teachers can usually find hourly paid work. Opportunities for work at the more reputable end of the market for inexperienced teachers are limited. The best time to search for jobs is the early summer through to September when summer schools are always on the lookout for more teachers. The government does restrict the number of permits granted to tourists so you may have to wait until the right opportunity to teach in Oman presents itself.

Embassy in UK:
167 Queen's Gate, London SW7 5HE
Tel: 020 7225 0001

Embassy in USA:
2535 Belmont Road NW, Washington DC 20008
Tel: 202 387 1980

British Council office:
Road One, Madinat al Sultan, Qaboos West, Muscat
P.O. Box 73 Postal Code 115
Tel +968 600 548
www.britishcouncil.org/oman

➲ **Visas/Work Permits:** Your employer must sponsor you (a no-objection certificate) and the paperwork is extensive. On arrival in Oman, your employer may ask you for your passport. Although this is customary, you are not legally obliged to hand it over. Surrendering your passport could seriously affect your ability to leave the country whenever you want.

➲ **Currency:** £1 = 0.71 / $1 = 0.385 Rial

➲ **Salaries/Taxes:** Rates of pay vary according to nationality and qualifications. You can earn about RO 3-10 per hour in institutes. Monthly: Anything from RO 500-850 at the top end. There is no tax.

➲ **Cost of Living:** The cost is living is higher than that elsewhere in the Gulf, including the UAE. Food and clothing is often imported and taxed at 17%. Supermarket costs are fairly comparable with the west overall, although imported Western luxury foods are very pricey. Petrol is cheap and you can also purchase cars at very competitive prices.

➲ **Accommodation:** In most cases, the school will arrange this for you. If you are going to work at a teacher training college you will be expected to find your own lodging. It's not difficult to find an apartment. Many teachers use an agent. Apartments cost RO 150-275 a month and utilities are RO 25-45.

�” Health advice: Local medical treatment varies in quality, and it can be inadequate. While hospital emergency treatment is available, there is no ambulance service in Oman. Malaria is a concern in the interior and on the Batinah Coast. Doctors and hospitals often expect immediate cash payment for health services. Vaccinations: Yellow Fever (if coming from an infected area), Malaria.

�”ù English Language Media: Oman Daily Observer, Times of Oman.

�](Tip: Try to buy a car. You will miss much of the country if you have to rely on public transport. Visitors in possession of an international or American driver's licence may drive rental vehicles, but residents must have an Omani driver's licence. Visitors hiring rental cars are urged to ensure that the vehicle they are renting is adequately insured against loss or damage.

◍ Other Information: As is the case in many countries, labour laws are strictly enforced in Oman. You may be contractually obliged to work for six months or more before you qualify for a holiday. Also, don't be surprised to find that you cannot work for another employer once your original contract has expired.

Schools in Oman (+968)

American-British Academy
PO Box 372, Medinat Al Sultan Qaboos, Muscat. **Tel:** 605287/603 646. **Fax:** 603544. **Email:** abaad@gto.net.om

American International School
PO Box 202, Muscat 115. **Tel:** 600374. **Fax:** 697916.

British Council
PO Box 73, Medinat Al Sultan Qaboos, Muscat 115. **Tel:** 600548. **Fax:** 698018.

Polyglot Institute
PO Box 221, Ruwi. **Tel:** 701261, **Fax:** 794602.

Sultan Qaboos University
PO Box 50, Muscat 123. **Tel:** 513333. **Fax:** 514 455.

QATAR

Qatar is a little-known Gulf emirate. It enjoys a high standard of living and is very modern. Most schools are very well-equipped boasting the latest in teaching gadgetry. Recruitment usually starts in February, interviews take place in the spring, and teachers arrive in August to start work in September. The weather can

be surprisingly cold in the winter so remember to pack a couple of sweaters.

British Council office:
93 Al Sadd Street, PO Box 2992, Doha
Tel +974 442 6193 / 4
www.britishcouncil.org/qatar

◍ Currency: £1 = 6.72 / $1 = 3.64 Riyal

◍ Health advice: Basic modern medical care and medicines are available in the government-run Hamad General Hospital in Qatar. Serious medical problems could cost you thousands of dollars. Check with your insurer to see if you are covered in Qatar.

◍ English Language Media: Gulf Times.

◍ Tip: The British Council has a very good lending library.

◍ Information for Women: Qatar is very safe and you will not be hassled by guys as is the case in certain other Middle Eastern countries. Bare arms and legs in public do not cause a negative reaction but draw the line at walking down the street in a bikini. Women driving alone are sometimes tailed by male drivers.

Schools in Qatar (974)

Arizona English Language School
PO Box 7949, Doha.

ELS Language centres
P.O. Box 22678, 56 Jaber bin Ghaith, Doha.**Tel:** 699223. **Fax:** 685519. **Email:** elsdoha@qatar.net.qa

English Modern School
Al Naijah, 44 Najma Street, 44 Hamad bin Zaidoun St.

Qatar International School
P.O. Box 5697, Doha. **Tel:** 469 0552 , **Fax:** 469 0557. **Email:** info@qis.org

SAUDI ARABIA

Saudi Arabia is one of the few countries where ESL/EFL teachers can expect to be rewarded with a good salary. Rates of pay may not be rising as fast as they did ten years ago but if you want to make good money in an English language teaching job, KSA (Kingdom of Saudi Arabia) is the place to be — teachers can·earn upwards of £30,000 a year. And that's tax-free.

Try to get a job in one of the big cities (Jeddah or Riyadh, for example.) Life can get a little lonely in a one-camel town although the lack of any social life might do wonders for your bank balance. Ex-pat life in

the big cities can be a lot of fun if you're prepared to get involved. So, the bottom line is simple: If you're not sure you can handle new experiences (good and bad) then don't go. Most teaching contracts are for one year so take some time to check out prospective employers and find out as much as you can about them and the job you will be doing. The majority of horror stories coming from teachers in KSA come from those unfortunate enough to have worked for "cowboy" operations.

Embassy in UK:
30 Charles Street, London W1X 7PM
Tel: 020 7917 3000
www.saudiembassy.org.uk

Embassy in USA:
601 New Hampshire Ave NW, Washington DC 20037
Tel: 202 337 4076
www.saudiembassy.net

British Council office:
Tower B, 2nd floor, Al Mousa Centre, Olaya Street
P.O. Box 58012, Riyadh 11594
Tel +966 (1) 462 1818
www.britishcouncil.org/saudiarabia

◗ **Visas/Work Permits:** You must be sponsored by an employer to work in Saudi Arabia. You cannot travel to Saudi Arabia as a tourist unless you travel as part of a government-approved group. Visitors to Saudi Arabia generally obtain a meningitis vaccination prior to arrival. A medical report or physical examination is required to obtain work and residence permits. The sponsor (normally the employer) obtains work and residence permits for the employee. Residents working in Saudi Arabia generally must surrender their passports while in the Kingdom and carry a Saudi residence permit ("iqama") for identification in place of their passports.

◗ **Currency:** £1 = 6.93 / $1 = 3.75 Riyal (SAR)

◗ **Salaries/Taxes:** Starting c. £25,000 (it can be less in the smaller towns) going up to £30,000 and more. No tax. If you are offered a salary less than £15k you should think twice.

◗ **Accommodation:** Your employer should provide accommodation and it's kismet whether you land up in a resort with pools and tennis court or sharing a trailer with four fellow teachers. If you strike out on your own, unfurnished apartments in Jeddah start around 12,000 SAR per year. Sizes range from one big room with a separate bath, up to a three-bedroom apartment,

depending on where you go. The cheapest compound starts around 30,000 SAR per year and offers security.

◗ **Cost of Living:** Salaries are so high and things are so cheap you can come back with a new car and lots of other goodies. Residents in Saudi Arabia may not leave the country without obtaining an exit permit prior to leaving and an exit/reentry permit if they intend to return to Saudi Arabia. The Saudi sponsor's approval is required for exit permits. Note that it is illegal for a Saudi employer to sell the approval (known as a Certificate of No Objection) to an employee.

◗ **Health advice:** Malaria is endemic to the low-lying coastal plains of southwest Saudi Arabia, primarily in the Jizan region extending up the coast to the rural area surrounding Jeddah. Take precautions to avoid being bitten by mosquitoes if you're going to be in this area.. There are reports of cases of Rift Valley fever in southwestern Saudi Arabia (near the town of Jizan.) The virus is transmitted primarily by infected mosquitoes and by direct contact with the blood or body fluids of infected animals. Prevention of Rift Valley fever should focus on personal protective measures to limit contact with infected mosquitoes. The best prevention is appropriate use of an insect repellent containing DEET (N,N-diethylmetatoluamide) and wearing long sleeves and trousers. Vaccinations: Hepatitis A, Polio, Typhoid, Malaria, Meningitis, Yellow Fever (if coming from an infected area).

◗ **Other Information:** Alcohol, women driving, men and women intermingling – are prohibited. Experienced Saudi hands have found ways to get around these restrictions but you risk punishment (even a public beating) if you are caught doing something illegal. Married couples usually stay longer in Saudi than straight singles. There is a large and active gay teaching community in KSA.

◗ **English Language Media:** Arab News, Saudi Gazette, Riyadh Daily.

Schools in Saudi Arabia

The British Council
Al Moajil Building, 5th Floor, Dhahran Street, Mohamed Street, PO Box 8387, Daman. **Tel:** 834 3484.

Girls' College of Arts
General Presidency for Female Institute for Languages and Translation, c/o King Saud University, PO Box 2465, Riyadh 11451.

King Abdulaziz University
Jeddah. **Tel:** 966 2 695 2468, **Fax:** 966 2 695 2471.

King Fahd University of Petroleum and Minerals
English Language centre, Dhahran 31261. **Tel:** 3 860 2393, **Fax:** 3 860 2340.

Riyadh Military Hospital-Training Division
PO Box 7897, Riyadh 11159. Saudi Airlines, PO Box 167, Jeddah 21231.

Saudi Language Institute
PO Box 6760, Riyadh 11575.

SCECO - East Central Training Institute
PO Box 5190, Damman 31422.

Yanbu Industrial College
PO Box 30436, Yanbu Al Sinaiyah 21477.

SYRIAN ARAB REPUBLIC

Syrian civilization is ancient: Damascus is the oldest continually occupied city in the world and there is much to explore in this friendly country. As Syria shakes off years of Russian influence, English language teachers are in great demand but the opportunities are restricted to those who are qualified. Teachers cannot expect to be hired from abroad. Teachers must come to Syria then look into teaching options. AMIDEAST offers teaching jobs but cannot provide long-term residency. The American Language Center (ALC) does too, and offers residency. Even if regular jobs are not available it is easy to find work tutoring.

Embassy in UK:
8 Belgrave Square, London SW1X 8PH
Tel: 020 7245 9012

Embassy in USA:
2215 Wyoming Ave NW, Washington DC 20008
Tel: 202 238 6313

British Council office:
Maysaloun Street, Shalaan, P O Box 33105, Damascus
Tel +963 (11) 331 0631
www.britishcouncil.org/syria

○ **Visas/Work Permits:** You will need an entrance visa, which can be obtained from the Syrian embassy in your country. If you decide to stay 15 days or more you must register with Syrian Immigration by your 15th day in Syria. You can then extend the permit for two-week periods every two weeks. This is not a difficult process but you will need to take an AIDS test at a government-approved facility. If a teacher obtains regular work, he or she may obtain residency for up to one year. Be aware that you cannot enter Syria with an Israeli stamp in your passport.

○ **Currency:** £1 = 96 / $1 = 52 Pound

○ **Cost of Living:** Food is very cheap and the quality is excellent. Small restaurants offer great "shawarma" (meat, vegetables and yogurt wrapped in pita bread) and the seafood is top-notch too. Most teachers find it is cheaper to eat out than to cook.

○ **Salaries/Taxes:** ALC and AMIDEAST pay around £6 an hour; Syrian-owned schools pay less. Native speakers may tutor and receive upwards of £6 an hour. Foreign teachers do not have to pay taxes.

○ **Accommodation:** A basic apartment in Damascus costs around £120 a month.

○ **Health advice:** Basic medical care and medicines are available in the principal cities of Syria, but not necessarily in outlying areas.

○ **English Language Media:** Syria Times.

Schools in Syria (+963)

Al Kindi English Language Centre
29 May Street, Damascus. .

Al Kudssi Institute
PO Box 5296, Aleppo.

Al Razi English Language Centre
PO Box 2533, Damascus. **Tel:** 11 457301.

Alson
Damascus. **Tel:** 11 2227236.

American Language Center
PO Box 29, Rawda Circle, Damascus. **Tel:** 11 3327236. **Fax:** 11 3319327.

AMIDEAST
Wahab Bin Saad Street, Abou Roummaneh, Damascus. **Tel:** 11 3332804/3314420. **Fax:** 11-333-2804. **Email:** Syria@amideast.org

Damascus Language Center
PO Box 249, Damascus.

TUNISIA

English is replacing French as the language of business in Tunisia so there is a growing demand for EFL teachers. Teachers often find they are the first native speaker their students have ever encountered. It is best to apply to schools in Tunisia before leaving home; a little knowledge of French will help you settle in.

Embassy in UK:
29 Prince's Gate, London SW7 1QG
Tel: 020 7584 8117

Embassy in USA:
1515 Massachusetts Ave NW, Washington DC20005
Tel: 202 862 1850

British Council office:
5 Place de la Victoire, BP 229, Tunis 1015 RP
Tel +216 71 259 053
www.britishcouncil.org/tunisia

⟳ **Visas/Work Permits:** You should receive a temporary work permit or a letter from your employer allowing you to work until your permit is processed. Photocopies of your degree and birth certificates will not be accepted.

⟳ **Currency:** £1 = 2.2 / $1 = 1.21 Dinar

⟳ **Cost of Living:** Tunisia is a cheap country to live in unless you insist on buying imported products.

⟳ **Salaries/Taxes:** Private lessons earn teachers around 15 dinars an hour. At the top end, you can expect to earn a minimum of 13,000 dinars per year. The tax rate is around 20 percent.

⟳ **Accommodation:** It's easy to find somewhere to live. Expect to pay 3-400 Tunisian dinars per month, with at least one month's rent as a deposit. Accommodation is largely unfurnished.

⟳ **Health advice:** Essential vaccinations: Hepatitis A, Polio, Typhoid, Yellow Fever (if coming from an infected area).

⟳ **English Language Media:** Tunisia News.

⟳ **Tip:** Life is pretty free and easy for an Islamic country but there's not much in the way of nightlife unless you head out to tourist areas like the island of Jerba.

Schools in Tunisia (+216)

AMIDEAST
22 rue Al Amine Al Abassi, Cité Jardins, 1002 Tunis.
Tel: 1 790559, 790563. **Fax:** 1 791913.

English Language Training Centre
British Council, 47 Avenue Habib Bourguiba, Tunis.

Institut Bourguiba des Languages Vivantes (IBLV)
47 Avenue de la Liberté, Tunis. **Tel:** 1 282418. **Fax:** 1 780389.

TURKEY

Turkey is a unique country straddling both Europe and Asia. Although its people are Muslims, there is a secular constitution. The Turkish language is written in the Latin alphabet (like English) not in the flowing Arabic script.

Turkey represents a big market for English language teachers. Government officials estimate that there is a need for 30,000 more English language teachers in the nation's public schools. English is taught from fourth grade in the public schools. In private schools, children start learning English in kindergarten. Needs for EFL teachers extend through middle and high schools to colleges and universities.

Native English speakers are in huge demand and there are plenty of opportunities for unqualified teachers who want to work in Turkey, although their salaries will not be as high as those of qualified teachers. University programmes prefer to recruit teachers with MAs in TESOL/TEFL.

Opinions about teaching English in Turkey are mixed: some teachers love it while others hate it. A lot depends on your attitude: If you expect things to be done the same way as at home then you probably won't want to come here. But that's a shame because you'll be missing out on the opportunity to live in an amazing country, which has been at the crossroads of civilizations for centuries.

Caution: be aware before you travel to Turkey that many English language teachers leave their jobs here disillusioned by working conditions and the attitudes of their employers. Unfortunately, in some schools, the directors are not concerned about the welfare of teachers, so choose carefully before you take up an offer of a job. A lot of foreigners regard teaching English in Turkey as a paid vacation. Alcohol is freely available and a few too many teachers drink to excess and are unable to carry out their duties. So you can't always blame school directors for their negative attitudes towards potential staff members.

Although your employer may not be willing to put anything down on paper, try to get something in writing from the person that you will be working for at the school. It's no guarantee that your "contract" will be honored but waving the paper around during a dispute may help your cause. Make sure that the agreement is hammered out between you and the owner of the school. A third party probably has no authority to make any agreements involving your work. Don't rely on assurances that accommodation, medical insurance or even salary have been settled.

Discuss them before you sign a contract. Promises that you will be paid in American dollars may not always be kept. Important: you can always walk out of your job and find something that suits you better. Just make sure you have some backup cash.

[Note: Although a small part of the country and its major city, Istanbul, is in Europe, Turkish culture and society is Middle Eastern – with some interesting twists!]

Embassy in UK:
43 Belgrave Square, London SW1X 8PA
Tel: 020 7393 0202

Embassy in USA:
2525 Massachusetts Ave NW, Washington DC20008
Tel: 202 612 6700

British Council office:
Esat Caddesi No: 41, Kucukesat, 06660 Ankara
Tel +90 (312) 424 1644
www.britishcouncil.org.tr

⮞ **Tip:** Before you agree to work at a school, ask if you can sit in on a few lessons and watch other teachers at work. A reputable organization will allow you to do this and will appreciate your commitment. A school that refuses this reasonable request probably has something to hide.

⮞ **Visas/Work Permits:** If you want to work in Turkey, you must apply for a work visa. You are not supposed to arrive as a tourist and then find a job. But some schools do employ teachers on tourist visas and send them to Greece every three months to get their visas renewed. Okay, this works for most of the time but if the authorities get suspicious, they may fine you. Keep your passport with you at all times: Teachers have spent a night in prison for failing to present their documents to the police on demand.

⮞ **Currency:** £1 = 2.46 / $1 = 1.33 New Lir

⮞ **Salaries/Taxes:** Wages and conditions vary depending on the location of the school and the level you are teaching at. Rates can range anywhere from £300-500 per month at private language institutes up to £600-1200 paid monthly by the elite colleges, plus air fares and other benefits.

⮞ **Accommodation:** Usually, the school arranges for your housing. Unmarried teachers will often find themselves sharing an apartment with other foreign colleagues. Some schools will pay your rent, other will not. Furniture will be basic and beds may be army-style cots. Be warned that furnished apartments are often hard to find and are expensive. Many landlords are suspicious of single men. Single females will have an easier time but they may be asked to promise not to entertain male visitors. Expect a deduction of 25% from your salary for taxes.

⮞ **Cost of Living:** There is a high rate of inflation in Turkey but salaries pegged to the dollar keep pace. The cost of living is low and it should be easy to save some money.

⮞ **Health advice:** In the southeastern city of Diyarbakir, there are recurring outbreaks of dysentery, typhoid fever, meningitis and other contagious diseases. Malaria is still a risk in the eastern part of the country. Turkey is one of the most dangerous countries in the world as far as traffic accidents are concerned. Vaccinations: Hepatitis A, Polio, Typhoid.

⮞ **English Language Media:** Turkish Daily News.

Schools in Turkey (+90)

Active English
Ataturk Bulvari 127/701, Secan Han. Bakanlikar, 06640, Ankara. **Tel**: 312 418 7973. **Fax**: 312 4258235.

Akademi School of English
PK 234, 21001 Bahar Sokar No 2, Diyarbakir. **Tel**: 412 2242297. **Fax**: 412 2288020.

Ankara University
Rektorlugu, Beslevler, Ankara. **Tel**: 312 41234361.

Best English
Bayinder Sokak No. 53, Kizilay, Ankara. **Tel**: 312 4172536. **Fax**: 312 4176808. **Email**: **bestenf@alnet.net**

Beykent University
Beykent Belikdirisu, 34900, Istanbul. **Tel**: 212 8726432. **Fax**: 212 8722489.

Bilkent University
06533 Bilkent, Ankara. **Tel**: 312 2902746/2664390. **Fax**: 312 2664934.

Cambridge English
Kazim Ozalp Sok. No. 15, Kat. 4, Saskinbakkal, Istanbul. **Tel**: 216 3858431. **Fax**: 216 369 7891.

Cinar School of English
860 Sokak No. 1, Kat. 4, Konak, Izmir. **Tel**: 238 4837273. **Fax**: 238 441 1113.

CTS Language Center
Tayyareci Cemal Sk. 24/4 Sisli, Istanbul. **Tel**: 212 2660043. **Fax**: 212 2331931. **Email**: cts_language_centre@yahoo.com

Cukurova University Center for Foreign Languages
Balcali, Adana. **Tel**: 322 3386084 x2921.

Dilko English Centres
Hatboyo Caddesi No. 16, 34720 Bakirkoy, Istanbul.
Tel: 212 5701270. **Fax:** 212 543 6123.

Dilmer LTC
Unlu Cad. 7, Keykel, Bursa. **Tel:** 224 2224673. **Fax:** 224 2231163.

Elissa English
Ihsaniye Mah 41, Sokak 48, Bandirma, Balikesir.

The English Academy
1374 Sokak No. 18/4, Selvili Is Hz. Izmir. **Tel:** 238 4462520. **Fax:** 238 4253042.

The English Centre
Rumeli Caddesi. 92, Zeki Bey Apt. 4, Osmanbey, Istanbul. **Tel:** 212 247 0983.

English Fast
Burhaniye Mah. Resmi Efendi Sok. No. 4, Beylerbeyi, Istanbul. **Tel:** 216 3187018. **Fax:** 216 318 7021.

Evrim
Cengiz Topel Caddesi 8, Camlibel, 33010 Mersin. **Tel:** 324 2339541, **Fax:** 324 2370862.

Eyuboglu Kisesi
Namik Kemal Mah., Dr. Rustem Eyuboglu Sok. 1, Umraniye 81240, Istanbul. **Tel:** 216 3291614. **Fax:** 216 3357198.

Gediz College
Seyrek Beldesi, Menemen, Izmir. **Tel:** 238 8447444. **Fax:** 238 8447441. **Email:** baysoy@gediz.kiz.tr

Genctur
Istiklal Cd. Zamabk Sok. 15/5, Taksom 80080, Istanbul. **Tel:** 212 249215. **Fax:** 212 2492554. **Email:** workcamps@genctur.com.tr

Inkur ELI
Ankara Caddesi, Yalihamam Sokak No. 8, Izmi, Kocaeli. **Tel:** 262 321 5325. **Fax:** 238 3225391.

Interlang
Russell Baulk, Zuhtu Pasa Mah, Recep Peker Cd, Sefikbey Sok No 17, Kiziltoprak, Istanbul. **Tel:** 216 4183910. **Fax:** 216 4182796.

International School
Eser Apt.A Blok Kasap, Sokak 1617, Esentepe, Istanbul.

Isik Universitesi
Buyukdere Cad., Maslak, Istanbul.

Istanbul University
Rektorlugu Beyarzit, Istanbul. **Tel:** 212 5221489.

Kent English Ankara
Mithatpasa Caddesi No. 46 Kat. 3/4/5, 06420 Kizilay, Ankara. **Tel:** 312 4343833. **Fax:** 312 4357334.

Kumlu Dersanerleri
Bursa Merkez, Basak Caddesi, Bursa. **Tel:** 224 24120465.

London Language International
Abide-i Hurriyet Caddesi, Kat. 1, Mecidiyekoy, Istanbul. **Tel:** 212 211 7445. **Fax:** 212 211 7441.

Ozel Ortadogu Lisesi
Spor Caddesi 26, Yakacik, Istanbul. **Tel:** 216 3772501. **Fax:** 216 3772502.

Ozel Tan Lisesi
Yeni Yalova Yolu 12km., 16335 Bursa. **Tel:** 224 2670072. **Fax:** 224 2670071.

Sistem English
Afiye Mah. Kibris Sehitleri Cad. 18/1, Eskisehir. **Tel:** 222 2312266. **Fax:** 222 2308681.

Swissotel Training centre
Suite Tower, Bayildim Cad. No. 2, Macka 80680, Istanbul. **Tel:** 212 259 0790. **Fax:** 212 259 0240.

UNITED ARAB EMIRATES

In many ways, the United Arab Emirates (UAE) represents what most people imagine when they think of the Gulf States. In Dubai and Abu Dhabi, vast four-wheel drive jeeps fly along well-paved freeways while the passengers stay cool in the air-conditioning. In other parts of the UAE, you can still see fishermen setting out on their boats, negotiating their way past the offshore oil derricks, and coming back with their catch which, unfortunately, can include sea turtles and a couple of drowned dogs. These contrasts add up to an unforgettable experience and many foreigners decide to stay in the UAE on a long-term basis.

Teachers of English as a second or foreign language can expect only the very best here in as far as pay and accommodation are concerned.

Embassy in UK:
30 Prince's Gate, London SW7 1PT
Tel: 020 7581 1281

Embassy in USA:
Suite 700, 1255 22nd Street NW, Washington DC20037
Tel: 202 243 2400

British Council office:
Villa no. 7, Al Nasr Street, Khalidiya, Abu Dhabi
P.O. Box 46523
Tel +971 (2) 665 9300
www.britishcouncil.org/uae

⮕ **Visas/Work Permits:** Tourist visas issued readily. To live and work in the UAE, you need a sponsor employer unless you are the spouse of someone already working there. Rules about visas change at short notice, so contact your local UAE embassy before departure.

⮕ **Currency:** £1 = 6.7 / $1 = 3.6 Dirham

⮕ **Salaries/Taxes:** Around £2,000-3,000 per month for teachers with a Master's degree and experience. There is no tax for foreign teachers.

⮕ **Accommodation:** Usually provided, otherwise expensive. A single apartment costs 30-40,000 dirhams per year, a double 50,000-75,000.

⮕ **Cost of Living:** Dubai is being touted as the "new Hong Kong." Electrical goods are very reasonable and you should try to cash in on the some of the bargains available. Tailor-made clothing is also a great buy. Food is cheap and wonderful especially if you like curries. Western food items are widely available.

⮕ **Health advice:** A Health Card costs about 300 dirhams. Vaccinations: Hepatitis A, Polio, Typhoid, Malaria (in some areas).

⮕ **English Language Newspapers:** Emirates News, Gulf News, Gulf Today, Khaleej Times.

⮕ **Other useful information:** With the growth of tourism, there has been an increasing demand for both male and female teachers. Although the percentage of women in the UAE labour force is still low, both Abu Dhabi and Dubai are cosmopolitan, relaxed cities, without the restrictions normally associated with the Gulf.

⮕ **Tip:** Don't miss out on a trip to the Indian Ocean coast: Dibbah has the best beaches and Fujairah is a charming town. There are also the mangroves to visit at Kalba.

Schools in UAE (+971)

Al Farabi Language Center
PO Box 3794, Dubai. **Tel:** 2 212556.

Al-Worood School
P.O. Box 46673, Abu Dhabi. **Tel:** 2 448855, **Fax:** 2 449732.

American University of Sharjah
College of Arts and Sciences, PO Box 26666, Sharjah. **Tel:** 6585067.

Arabic Language Center
(Dubai World Trade Centre), PO Box 9292, Dubai. **Tel:** 3086036. **Fax:** 3064089.

Dar Al Ilm School of Languages
PO Box 2550, Dubai. **Tel:** 447572, **Fax:** 4 91915.

Dubai Aviation College
PO Box 53044, Dubai. **Tel:** 824000, **Fax:** 824222.

Dubai Cultural and Scientific Institute
PO Box 8751, Dubai. **Tel:** 347747/377004, **Fax:** 347369.

ELS Language centres
P.O. Box 1496, Al Jimy Area, Al Ain. **Tel:** 3 623468. **Fax:** 3 623865 **Email:** elsaa@emirates.net.ae

ELS Language centres
Al Baten, Al Khaleej Al Arabi Street, Villa #4, P.O. Box 3079, Abu Dhabi. **Tel:** 2 669225. **Fax:** 2 653165. **Email:** elsiauh@ns2.emirates.net.ae

ELS Language centres
P.O. Box 2380, Al Garhoud Area, Villa #14, Street #20 , Dubai. **Tel:** 4 827616. **Fax:** 4 827861.**Email:** dbxels@emirates.net.ae

Institute of Australian Studies
PO Box 20183, Dubai. **Tel:** 4 666400, **Fax:** 4 623500.

International Education Institute
PO Box 524714. **Tel:** 360635, **Fax:** 348209.

International Language Institute
(Language Specialists Institute), PO Box 3253, Sharjah. **Tel:** 6 377257. **Fax:** 6 363427.

International Training Solutions
Lynne Haboubi, PO Box 4234, Dubai. **Tel/Fax:** 16 363249,

Polyglot School
PO Box 1093, Dubai. **Tel:** 223429, **Fax:** 217284.

YEMEN

Yemen is the land of fables—the Queen of Sheba came from here and for centuries Yemen was the world's source of frankincense. By all accounts, people in Yemen are keen to learn English and are very receptive to qualified and experienced language teachers.

Petroleum companies operating in Yemen employ staff to teach English to local workers. Most teachers are paid by the hour. Check out some industry websites like Canadian Occidental (www.cdnoxy.com.ye) for positions on offer. Working for a foreign company may help you overcome some of the red tape that can arise when working for a Yemeni agency. If you get a job with an oil company be sure to clue up on industry-related terminology before you start teaching.

There are a number of institutes in the country—AMIDEAST operates offices in Sana'a and

Aden. However, salary rates and visa processing requirements (see below) serve as disincentives. As a result of the relative difficulty in processing expatriate teachers and the seemingly low salary rates, most teachers are not recruited from abroad, but are rather language students or spouses of expatriates or Yemenis residing in Yemen.

Teachers thinking of working in Yemen should be aware that there have been a number of kidnappings of foreigners by tribesmen hostile to the government. Most of these incidents have occurred in the lawless northern region of the country although two American tourists were abducted in southern Yemen in 1998. Teachers should travel with an armed escort between cities if they choose not to fly.

Embassy in UK:
57 Cromwell Road, London SW7 2ED
Tel: 020 7584 6607

Embassy in USA:
Suite 705, 2600 Virginia Ave NW, Washington DC20037
Tel: 202 965 4760

British Council office:
3rd Floor, Administrative Tower, Sana'a Trade Centre Algiers Street, PO Box 2157, Sana'a
Tel +967 1448 356/7
www.britishcouncil.org/yemen

➲ **Visas/Work Permits:** EFL teachers from America can only obtain a one-month tourist visa (£20). The organization hiring the teacher must then convert the tourist visa into a work permit—an expensive and time-consuming procedure. All individuals wishing to obtain a work permit must have an HIV test performed in Yemen. External test results will not be accepted.

➲ **Currency:** £1 = 344 / $1 = 186 Rial (YER)

➲ **Salaries/Taxes:** Salaries are generally paid per hour. An average salary for native speakers is around £6/hour, which is quite good because Yemen is an inexpensive country and the average monthly income is less than £60. Foreigners do not have to pay any local tax.

➲ **Accommodation:** Rents range from £30/month to £1000/month. An average rate for a furnished, one bedroom apartment in good condition is around £100 per month. Additionally, some language institutes offer housing to expatriate teachers.

➲ **Cost of Living:**

Prices in Yemen are very reasonable and you can pick up exquisitely made handicrafts at bargain rates.

➲ **Health advice:** Cases of malaria are on the rise in Yemen especially along the coasts. You should take a course of chloroquine-resistant malaria suppressants before you travel to these areas. The altitude of Sana'a (7,200 feet) and lack of adequate medical facilities can cause problems for some visitors. Doctors and hospitals often expect immediate cash payment for health services. Vaccinations: Hepatitis A, Typhoid, Polio, Yellow Fever (if coming from an infected area).

➲ **English Language Media:** Yemen Times, Yemen Observer.

➲ **Tip:** Yemeni social life revolves around chewing the leaf known as "qat" that produces a mild euphoria among users.

Schools in Yemen (+967)

Al Farouq Institute
PO Box 16927, Sana'a. **Tel:** 1 209721. **Fax:** 1 209721.

The American School
PO Box 16003, Sana'a. **Tel:** 1 417119. **Fax:** 1 415355.

AMIDEAST
162 Miswat Street, Khormaksar, Aden. **Tel:** 2 238345. **Fax:** 2 238345. **Email:** aden@amideast.org

AMIDEAST
Algiers Street 66, P.O. Box 15508, Sana'a. **Tel:** 1 206222. **Fax:** 1 206942. **Email:** yemen@amideast.org

The British Council
PO Box 2157, Sana'a. **Tel:** 1 244 121. **Fax:** 1 244120.

English Language centre
PO Box 8984, Sana'a. **Tel:** 1 248090.

Faculty of Art, English Department
PO Box 6014, Aden. **Tel:** 2 32350.

Faculty of Art
English Department, Sana'a. **Tel:** 1 200515/6.

Faculty of Education
English Department, Sana'a. **Tel:** 1 250513.

Faculty of Education
English Department, PO Box 6480, Taiz. **Tel:** 4 212191/2, **Fax:** 4 219378.

MALI
PO Box 16003, Sana'a. **Tel:** 1 241561. **Fax:** 1 414348.

Madina Institute of Technology (MIT)
Aden. **Tel:** 2 251453.

The Modern Yemen School
PO Box 13335, Sana'a. **Tel:** 1 206548.

Mohammed Ali Othman School
PO Box 5713, Taiz. **Tel:** 4 211248/9.

National Institute for Administrative Science
PO Box 102, Sana'a. **Fax:** 1 251161.

Pakistani School
Sana'a. **Tel:** 1 247830/247838.

The Pioneer School
Sana'a. **Tel:** 1 210311.

Sabaa University
PO Box 14400, Sana'a. **Tel/Fax:** 1 205749.

Sam Yemen International School
PO Box 19390, Sana'a. **Tel:** 2 69648/63303. **Fax:** 2 69649.

Sana'a International School
PO Box 2002, Sana'a. **Tel:** 1 234437. **Fax:** 1 234438.

Spectra Institute
PO Box 16101, Sana'a. **Tel:** 1 414623. **Fax:** 1 414739.

University of Science Technology
PO Box 15201, Sana'a. **Tel:** 1 207026. **Fax:** 1 207027.

Yemen-American Language Institute
c/o USIA, American Embassy, Sana'a. **Tel:** 1 203251. **Fax:** 1 203364. **Email**: info@yali.org.ye

Yemen Language centre
PO Box 1691, Sana'a. **Tel:** 1 285125. **Fax:** 1 289249.

Yemen Sudanese Language centre
PO Box 13187, Sana'a. **Fax:** 1 275407.

Africa

For many countries in Africa, the English language is part of the legacy left to them by the colonialists. In these countries, English is often taught from a young age in the state schools and people use it to communicate if there are several tribal languages spoken in one nation. Other African countries are former French or Belgian colonies, so a working knowledge of French is useful.

Most English language teachers work in Africa as volunteers but there are some jobs available at university and college institutes although you may end up earning more as a volunteer than as a "salaried" teacher. Female teachers thinking of coming to Africa should be aware that societies are much more traditional here when it comes to the role of men and women. You may find that, in a staff meeting, men sit on one side of the room and women on the other.

Teachers who want to work as volunteers can contact *Teachers for Africa,* an organization that places experienced teachers in Malawi, Namibia, Nigeria, Ethiopia, Ghana, Guinea and Benin. Web: www.ifesh.org, Email: teachers@ifesh.org.

Note: African countries on the Mediterranean Coast are dealt with in the Middle East section.

BENIN

Benin is one of smaller West African states. Its capital city is Porto Novo; however, the city of Cotonou is the main port and largest city. There are interesting sites to visit in Benin including Ouidah, an ancient port where slaves were sent around the world, Abomey, the "royal" city, and Allada, known as the "cradle" of the voodoo religion. There is a very high demand for English language teachers in Benin. The best way to find a job here is to enter the country on a tourist visa and then start hunting around. You could also contact the *Syndicat National de l'Enseignement Primaire Public du Bénin*, SNEP, B.P. 69, Cotonou, Bénin. **Tel:** +229-303.613 **Fax:** +229-303.613.

➲ **Visas/Work Permits:** Tourist visas are valid for a 15- ($45) or 30-day ($60) period within three months of date of issue.

➲ **Currency:** £1 = 922 / $1 = 501 CFA Franc.

➲ **Salaries/Taxes:** 4,500 CFA per hour. Foreigners do not have to pay tax unless they are registered with the OBSS – the Office of Social Security.

➲ **Accommodation:** Flats cost from 80,000 to 800,000 CFA per month.

➲ **Health advice:** Medical facilities in Benin are limited and not all medicines are available. A yellow fever certificate must be presented on entry to Benin. Cholera is a serious risk in this country and precautions are essential. Malaria is also a risk as is rabies. Health insurance is recommended.

Schools in Benin (+229)

American Cultural centre
B.P. 2012, Cotonou. **Tel:** 304553. **Fax:** 301439. **Email:** vreeland@micronet.net

Brilliant Stars International School
04 B.P. 919 Cadjehoun, Cotonou. **Tel:** 302079, **Fax:** 313701/313809.

BURKINA FASO

Although this landlocked country is one of Africa's poorest nations, there is a vibrant culture evident among its people. The Pan African Film and Television Festival of Ouagadougou (the capital city) is the largest event of its kind in Africa and draws over 100,000 visitors. Volunteers in urban and rural settings teach secondary school and university English. You can also contact the national teacher's association: Syndicat National des Enseignants du Secondaire et du

Supérieur (SNESS), 01 B.P. 113, Ouagadougou 01, Burkina Faso. **Tel:** +226-362.362, **Fax:** +226-362.362.

➲ **Visas/Work Permits:** You will need both. Your employer will help you obtain them.

➲ **Currency:** £1 = 941 / $1 = 571 CFA Franc.

➲ **Health advice:** Medical facilities in Burkina Faso are limited. A Yellow fever certificate is required. Precautions against cholera, malaria and rabies are recommended.

Schools in Burkina Faso (+226)

American Language centre
01 B.P. 539, Ouagadougou-01, Burkina Faso. **Tel:** 306360/308903. **Fax:** 31 5273. **Email:** alcouaga@fasonet.bf

International School of Ouagadougou
01 B.P. 35, c/o US Embassy, Ouagadougou. **Tel:** 362143. **Fax:** 362228. **Email:** issoua@fasonet.bf

CAMEROON

There are occasional opportunities for experienced EFL teachers in Cameroon, an enchanting and spectacular country with mountains and a coastline to explore. Volunteers with VSO (see p.62) work to improve the quality of English language teaching in rural schools that have little or no resources. Unfortunately, teachers report that the security situation in Cameroon is getting worse and that foreigners should be very careful when travelling.

British Council office:
Immeuble Christo, Avenue Charles de Gaulle, BP 818, Yaoundé
Tel +237 2 21 16 96/20 31 72
www.britishcouncil.org/cameroon

➲ **Visas/Work Permits:** Visas are granted for up to 12 months. You will also need a residence permit, which costs £500.

➲ **Currency:** £1 = 926 / $1 = 501 CFA Franc.

➲ **Salaries/Taxes:** Teachers can earn £550-800 a month with a housing and transport allowance.

➲ **Health advice:** Medical facilities in Cameroon are limited. Sanitation levels are low, even in the best hospitals. Not all medicines are available. Travellers are advised to bring their own supplies. Malaria prophylaxis and vaccination against hepatitis A and B, tetanus, diphtheria, polio, typhoid, and meningococcal meningitis are recommended.

Schools in Cameroon (+237)

American School of Douala
BP 1909, Douala. **Tel:** 421437. **Fax:** 421437. **Email:** adminasd@camnet.cm

American School of Yaoundé
Dept of State, 2520 Yaounde Place, Washington DC, 20521-2520, USA. **Tel:** 230421. **Fax:** 236011. **Email:** asoy@camnet.cm

The British Council
Immeuble Christo, Rue Drouot, B.P 12,801 Douala.
Tel: 425145. **Fax:** 425170. **Email:** ELC.Douala@bc-douala.douala1.com

The British Council
Immeuble Soms, Avenue Charles de Gaulle, B.P 818 Yaoundé. **Tel:** 211696. **Fax:** 215691. **Email:** ELC.Yaounde@bc-yaounde.iccnet.cm

Ministry of Higher Education
2, Avenue du 20 Mai, Yaoundé. **Tel:** 22 13 70

CENTRAL AFRICAN REPUBLIC

The CAR, as it known, is a developing country that it is full of potential. Interesting places to visit include the Dzanga-Sangha National Park, a primeval rain forest in the southwestern region of the country. There is a very strong demand for English language teaching in the CAR. Experienced teachers will have no problems in finding a job but they should apply from outside the country to avoid disappointment. Unfortunately, the political and social situation deters most teachers from working here.

⮑ **Visas/Work Permits:** As rules change so quickly, it is best to check with the embassy.

⮑ **Currency:** £1 = 926 / $1 = 501 CFA Franc.

⮑ **Salaries/Taxes:** Expect to be paid $150-300 a month but there are problems with getting paid in government contracts in a country where civil servants haven't had any money for almost two years.

⮑ **Accommodation:** An apartment in the capital, Bangui, will cost anywhere between £150-300 a month.

⮑ **Cost of Living:** Very cheap

⮑ **Health advice:** Medical facilities are limited, and the quality of acute care is unreliable. Sanitation levels are low. Many medicines are not available. Travellers are advised to bring their own properly-labeled supplies.

Schools in Central African Republic (+236)

Martin Luther King Cultural centre
c/o American Embassy, Avenue David Dacko, PO Box 924, Bangui. **Tel:** (236) 610200. **Fax:** 614494. **Email:** gazembetig@hotmail.com

CHAD

Chad is one of the poorest countries in the world with very little infrastructure. Opportunities for teaching English here are very limited. The Peace Corps suspended its operations here in 1998 because of the deteriorating security situation. Armed militias have been known to harass foreigners in Chad. You can contact the teachers' union for more information: *Syndicat des Enseignants du Tchad*, SET, B.P. 2174, N'Djamena, Chad. **Fax:** +235-515.884.

⮑ **Health advice:** Medicines are in short supply and health care is almost nonexistent.

Schools in Chad (+235)

English Language Program
B.P. 3, N'Djamena. **Tel:** 517391. **Fax:** 518831.

DEM. REPUBLIC OF CONGO

The situation in this country (formerly known as Zaire) has been improving as it recovers from civil war.

Schools in Dem. Rep. Congo (+243)

American School of Kinshasa
c/o American Embassy, Kinshasa, APO AE 09828.
Tel: 88 46619.

Congo-American Language Institute (CALI)
B.P. 8622, Kinshasa 1. **Tel:** 8843979. **Fax:** 88 46592.

ERITREA

Eritrea is recovering from a recent war with neighbouring Ethiopia and conditions are very harsh. Many programmes have had to be suspended at various times because of instability in the region. There are opportunities for volunteer work in the state schools for experienced and qualified teachers.

British Council office:
Lorenzo Tazaz Street No 23, PO Box 997, Asmara
Tel +291 (1) 123 415
www.britishcouncil.org/eritrea

◑ **Salaries/Taxes:** Rates of pay are very low and may be supplemented by the agency you are working for.

◑ **Accommodation:** Housing will be provided by your employer.

Schools in Eritrea (+291)

Asmara International Community School
PO Box 4941, Asmara, Eritrea **Tel:** 1 161705. **Fax:** 1 161705 **Email:** aics@eol.com.er

The British Council
Lorenzo Ta'azaz Street, No. 23, PO Box 997, Asmara, **Tel**. 1 23415. **Email:** britcoun@eol.com.er

ETHIOPIA

It is not easy to find a job teaching English in Ethiopia. Most private language schools employ Ethiopians who can speak English. A number of western aid organizations work in the country and it may be possible to land a job through one of them. Volunteers need to have had at least two years' teaching experience as well as a certificate or an MA. VSO Canada sends teachers to mainstream educational programmes and technical training institutions aiming to improve the standard of English (the medium of instruction) of the students.

Embassy in UK:
17 Princes Gate, London SW7 1PZ
Tel: 020 7589 7212

Embassy in USA:
3506 International Drive NW, Washington DC20008
Tel: 202 364 1200

British Council office:
PO Box 1043, Artistic Building, Adwa Avenue, Addis Ababa
Tel +251 (1) 550 022
www.britishcouncil.org/ethiopia

◑ **Visas/Work Permits:** You have to get a single-entry visa and you must get an exit visa each time you leave the country, which makes travel difficult.

Schools in Ethiopia (+251)

The British Council
Adwa Avenue, Artistic Building, PO Box 1043, Addis Ababa. **Tel:** 1 55 00 22. **Fax:** 251-1-55 25 44. **Email**: Solomon.Hailu @bc-addis.bcouncil.org

International Community School
P.O. Box 70282, Addis Ababa.

Sandford English Community School
P.O. Box 30056 MA, Addis Ababa. **Tel:** 1 55 2275. **Fax:** 1 55 1945.

University of Addis Ababa
P.O. Box 1176, Addis Ababa.

GHANA

There is much to explore in Ghana from the coastal slave forts recalling a tragic period in the country's history to the rainforests of the interior. Depending on which level you intend to teach you could get in touch with the educational authorities. Try: The General Secretary, Ghana National Association Of Teachers, GNAT Headquarters, P.O. Box 209, Accra, Ghana. Tel: +233-21-221.515 / 221.576, Fax:+233-21-224.877 for more information. For volunteer teaching opportunities in Ghana, see page 62. More limited openings can be found at a handful of language institutes affiliated with colleges and universities. To teach in Ghana you have to be a certified teacher, or serving with a volunteer organization, or a tenured lecturer.

High Commission in UK:
13 Belgrave Square, London SW1X 8PN
Tel: 020 7235 4142

Embassy in USA:
3512 International Drive NW, Washington DC20008
Tel: 202 686 4520

British Council office:
11 Liberia Road, PO Box GP 771, Accra
Tel +233 (21) 683 068
www.britishcouncil.org/ghana

◑ **Visas/Work Permits:** The school will take care of this for you.

◑ **Currency:** £1 = 16551 / $1 = 8947 Cedi

◑ **Salaries/Taxes:** Volunteers can expect to earn around £30-200 a month. Teachers at universities or language institutes can earn anywhere from £1000-2000.

◑ **Health advice:** Facilities are limited, particularly outside Accra. Be aware that evidence of and/or assurances from insurance companies will not be accepted as settlement of medical expenses.

◑ **English Language Media:** Ghanaian Chronicle, Ghanaian Times, Graphic.

Schools in Ghana (+233)

Centre of Language and Professional Studies
P.O. Box 4501, Accra.

Institute of Languages
P.O. Box M67, Accra. **Tel:** 21 221052.

The Language Centre
University of Ghana, Legon. **Tel:** 21 500381.

KENYA

English is the working language of Kenyan schools and there is a shortage of qualified and experienced teachers. Although you won't make a lot of money here, it is a beautiful country with much to see and do.

High Commission in UK:
45 Portland Place, London W1N 3AS
Tel: 020 7636 2371

Embassy in USA:
2249 R Street NW, Washington DC 20008
Tel: 202 387 6101

British Council office:
ICEA Building, Kenyatta Avenue, PO Box 40751 Nairobi
Tel +254 (2) 334 855/6
www.britishcouncil.org/kenya

⮕ **Visas/Work Permits:** You are supposed to have a work permit before you arrive but teachers have picked up casual work while on tourist visas.
⮕ **Currency:** £1 = 145 / $1 = 78.62 Shillings
⮕ **Salaries/Taxes:** Teachers are usually paid at local rates, which allows for a simple lifestyle.
⮕ **Accommodation:** Outside Nairobi, housing can be very basic.

Schools in Kenya (+254)

American Universities Preparation & Learning centre
P.O. Box 14842, Nairobi. **Tel:** 2 741764. **Fax:** 2 741690.

The Language centre
P.O. Box 14245, Ndemi Close, off Ngong Road, Nairobi. **Tel:** 2 569531. **Fax:** 2 568207.

MADAGASCAR

Madagascar is a large island situated in the Indian Ocean. Many unique species of animals are threatened with extinction here as sapphire mining and other destructive activities go unchecked. Teachers interested in working at the English Teaching programme in Antananarivo should contact the programme upon arrival in the city. Please do not send applications in advance.

⮕ **Visas/Work Permits:** Visas should be obtained in advance, although airport visas are available in Antananarivo, the capital.
⮕ **Currency:** £1 = 3233 / $1 = 1748 Ariary
⮕ **Health advice:** The hospital infrastructure is minimal and does not meet basic sanitary norms.

Schools in Madagascar (+261)

American School of Antananarivo
US Dept of State/Antananarivo, Washington DC 20521-2040, USA. **Tel:** 202242039. **Fax:** 202234539.

English Teaching Program
4 Lalana Dr., Razafindratandra Ambohidahy, Antananarivo. **Tel:** 22220238. **Fax:** 221397.

MALI

Mali is a vast land of savannas, steppes, and deserts. For the most of the last four millennia, it was one of the great centres of African civilization. During the middle ages, the Malian empire was famous throughout much of Africa and Europe; Timbuktu was a centre of Islamic study and its library was one of the largest in the world. The Peace Corps has been active in Mali for over 30 years and it enjoys a high reputation among the people of Mali.

Schools in Mali (+223)

American International School of Bamako
Dept of State - Bamako, Washington DC, 20521-2050, USA. **Tel:** 224738. **Fax:** 220853.

MOZAMBIQUE

For many years, Mozambique was in the grip of a bloody civil war. Although the situation has improved a lot since then, teachers should be warned that parts of country and the capital, Maputo, are unsafe. The civil war has severely disrupted education: The overall literacy rate is estimated at 30-40% and only 40% of school-age children actually attend school. Volunteers with VSO Canada are involved in English language

teaching in rural elementary schools where there are sometimes more than 50 children in a classroom. Teachers report that life outside the capital is much more relaxed and that the weekends are worth waiting for because there are miles of empty beaches and fascinating countryside to explore. You will need to speak some Portuguese.

British Council office:
Rua John Issa, 226, P.O. Box 4178, Maputo
Tel +258 (1) 310 921
www.britishcouncil.org/mozambique

➲ **Visas/Work Permits:** You will need a visa, which must be obtained in advance. Travellers arriving without a visa are subject to a fine of £300. The authorities will impose a fine of £60 per day for each day travellers overstay their visas. Once your contract has been agreed, the school will apply for a work permit, which will take about four months to process. You are not supposed to work for the school during this period although this rule is commonly ignored.

➲ **Currency:** £1 = 33932 / $1 = 18342 Metical.

➲ **Salaries/Taxes:** Approximately £10 / $19 an hour. Tax is about 17%.

➲ **Accommodation:** Rents are expensive in Maputo. Typical rates are £600 / $1100 per month shared among three teachers. The upside is that the accommodation is clean and modern.

➲ **Cost of Living:** Mozambique is an expensive country where you might be able to save only a little of your salary – if you're not keen on going out and partying every night.

➲ **Health advice:** Facilities are minimal and many medicines are unavailable. Maputo's Sommerschield Clinic, which requires payment in hard currency, can provide general, non-emergency services. Many rural health centres were forced to close during the conflict with the MNR rebels. Yellow fever vaccination certificate is required. Cholera is a serious risk and precautions are essential. Malaria and rabies are risks.

Schools in Mozambique (+258)

Brumag
Av. Mártires Mueda 563, Maputo. **Tel:** 496199.

Contacto
R. Tchamba 64, Maputo. **Tel:** 492479.

Oikos
R. General Pereira D'Eca, Maputo. **Tel:** 497850.

Instituto De Linguas
Av. Ahmed Sekou Touré, **Tel:** 425684.

Lynden Language School
PO Box 456, 1746 Rua de Resistencia 3rd floor, Maputo. **Tel:** 417569.

Maputo International School
Rua de Nachingwea, CP 4152, 389, Maputo. **Tel:** 492131/492195. **Fax:** 492382.

SENEGAL

EFL teachers can find work on a casual basis in Senegal but there are no private language schools as such. If you want to work in the public sector, you could try the national teachers' union: *Syndicat des Professeurs du Sénégal* (SYPROS), Bourse du Travail CNTS, 7 Avenue du Président Lamine Guèye, B.P. 937, Dakar, Sénégal. **Tel:** +221-821.8381 / 821.0491, **Fax:** +221-821.7771).

Embassy in UK:
39 Marloes Road, London W8 6LA
Tel: 020 7937 723

Embassy in USA:
2112 Wyoming Ave NW, Washington DC 20008
Tel: 202 234 0540

British Council office:
34-36 Boulevard de la République, Immeuble Sonatel BP 6238, Dakar
Tel: +221 822 2015/822 2048
www.britishcouncil.org/senegal

Schools in Senegal (+221)

American English Language programme **(AELP)**
c/o USIS, B.P. 49, Dakar. **Tel:** 211634. **Fax:** 222345.

The British Council
34-36 Bd de la République, Dakar. **Tel:** 822 20 15 / 822 20 48. **Fax:** 821 81 36.

SOUTH AFRICA

The demand for English language instruction is very strong in post-apartheid South Africa. There are many private language institutes, especially in and around Cape Town that cater to an international student market. In rural South Africa, the Peace Corps operates a programme where volunteers advise local elementary school teachers on English language lesson planning. Qualified teachers are welcomed here but you will be competing for jobs with South African citizens who do not require work permits.

High Commission in UK:
South Africa House, Trafalgar Square, London WC2N 5DP
Tel: 020 7451 7299
www.southafricahouse.com

Embassy in USA:
3051 Massachusetts Ave NW, Washington DC 20008
Tel: 202 238 4400

British Council office:
Ground Floor, Forum 1, Braampark, 33 Hoofd Street, Braamfontein, Johannesburg 2001
Tel +27 (11) 718 4300
www.britishcouncil.org/southafrica

➲ **Visas/Work Permits:** Teachers need a work permit, which costs around £90. Your employer must be able to prove that the position was made available to South Africans before a foreign national took up the offer.

➲ **Currency:** £1 = 10.95 / $1 = 5.92 Rand

➲ **Salaries/Taxes:** Teachers earn from £5-10 an hour and taxation ranges from 20-30%.

➲ **Accommodation:** There is a high standard of accommodation in South Africa and rents are expensive if you are earning a local salary.

➲ **English Language Media:** The Star, Weekly Mail.

Schools in South Africa (+27)

Cape Communication Centre
37 Riebeck Street, Cape Town 8001. **Tel:** 21 419 1967

Cape Studies Language School
100 Main Road Seapoint, P.O.Box 4425, Cape Town 8000. **Tel:** 21 439 0999. **Fax:** 21 439 3130

Cape Town School of International Languages
66 Main Rd, Claremont, Cape Town 7708. **Tel:** 21 674 4117.

Good Hope Studies
4 Mount Road, Rondebosch, Cape Town 7700. **Tel:** 21 686 0060. **Fax:** 21 686 0061.

inlingua Language Training Centre
Kinellan House, 14 Portswood Rd., Cape Town 8000. **Tel:** 21 4190494. **Fax:** 21 4190725.

INTERLINK School of Languages
P.O. Box 694, Seapoint, Cape Town 8060. **Tel:** 21 4399 834 **Fax** 21 4343 267.

Language & Travel
Mail: P.O. Box 868, Green Point, Cape Town 8051, 2 Braemar Road, Green Point 8005. **Tel:** 21 439 3101. **Fax:** 21 439-0616.

Language Lab International House
4th Floor Aspern House, 54 De Korte Street, Braamfontein, Johannesburg 2001. **Tel:** 11 339 1051. **Fax:** 11 403 1759.

One World Language School
P. O. Box 7888, Roggebaai, Cape Town 8012. **Tel/Fax:** 21 4231833.

Table Mountain Language Centre
7 Mountain Road, Claremont, Cape Town 7700. **Tel:** 21 674 49 14. **Fax:** 21 671 09 97.

Tygerberg Language and Leisure Centre
P.O. Box 2483, Bellville 7530. **Tel:** 21 948 3460.

TANZANIA

You can find work as a volunteer teacher and there are sometimes opportunities in colleges and universities.

British Council office:
Samora Avenue / Ohio Street, PO Box 9100, Dar Es Salaam
Tel +255 (22) 211 6574
www.britishcouncil.org/tanzania

➲ **Visas/Work Permits:**Employers make the necessary arrangements.

Schools in Tanzania (+51)

International Languages Orientation Services
Oysterbay, Karume Road, P.O. Box 6995, Dar es Salaam. **Tel:** 667159. **Fax:** 112752.

TOGO

There are limited opportunities for EFL teachers in this small West African nation. Contact the teachers' union: Fédération des Syndicats de l'Education Nationale, Tel: +228-222.547

Schools in Togo (+228)

English Language Program
Centre Culturel Américain, Rues Pelletier et Vauban, B.P. 852, Lomé. **Tel:** 212166.

Australia & New Zealand

Over the past year, the prospects in both Australia and New Zealand have changed. Many English language schools have closed down and it is no longer quite as easy to get a job as in 2000. These ups and downs in the local ELT industry began when, in Australia, the recession has eased and the government introduced new 12-month visitor visas (allowing temporary work) giving young teachers the perfect excuse to travel around this fabulous country ... and earn money teaching. New Zealand, too, has had a change in government policy that impacted on English language teachers: the rules for immigration have been relaxed, resulting in an influx of immigrants – all keen to learn English. As a result, New Zealand is suffering something of a shortage of teachers. Only US citizens will find a problem with either country: they cannot take advantage of the 12-month young traveller visa and report that finding work (and a school willing to sponsor them through a work visa) is very tough.

AUSTRALIA

There are good job prospects for teachers in Australia, with a good increase in the numbers of (mostly Asian, due to its location) students visiting Australia to learn English. The majority of the language schools are in Sydney (which has over 70 schools); around two-thirds of the schools are accredited and prefer teachers with experience and a recognised certificate (visit the accreditation website, www.neasaccred.com for more details).

Australia has changed its visa policy to around a dozen countries, allowing young (18-30) teachers to stay for 12 months and teach in temporary jobs. US citizens report that it is hard to get a job without a work permit which is difficult for US citizens to obtain (however, Canadians are included in the 12-month working-holiday visa scheme).

High Commission in UK:
Australia House, Strand, London WC2B 4LA
Tel: 020 7379 4334
www.australia.org.uk

Embassy in USA:
1601 Massachusetts Ave NW, Washington DC20036
Tel: 202 797 3000
www.austemb.org

British Council office:
PO Box 88, Edgecliff, Sydney NSW 2027
Tel: (2) 9326 2022
www.britishcouncil.org/au.htm

⮕ **Visas:** British, American and Canadian citizens require visas before they can enter Australia as tourists, students or workers. Tourists need a tourist visa (now generally replaced by the Electronic Travel Authority, issued by major travel agents). All other work visas are assessed by the high commission or embassy – the basic reasoning is that any job opportunity must be made available to Australian citizens, so you will have to show that your work cannot be carried out by an existing resident.

⮕ **Currency:** £1 = 2.37 / $1 = 1.28 Dollars

⮕ **Health:** Health-care standards are very high and if you are granted a resident permit for more than six months, you can join the national medical and hospital service, Medicare.

⮕ **Tax:** all employees must register for tax – find out how at www.ato.gov.au

Schools In Australia (+61)

acl (Australian Centre for Languages)
157-161 Gloucester Street, The Rocks, New South Wales 2000, **Tel:** +61 2 9252 3788, **Fax:** +61 2 9252 3799, **Email:** enquiry@acl.edu.au , **Web:** www.acl.edu.au

Adelaide Institute of TAFE English Language Centre
120 Currie Street, Adelaide, South Australia 5000, **Tel:** +61 8 8207 8279, **Fax:** +61 8 8207 8283,**Web:** www.tafe.sa.edu.au

Anutech Education Centre at the Australian National University
Cnr Barry Drive and North Road, Canberra, Australian Capital Territory 2601, **Tel:** +61 2 6125 5000, **Fax:** +61 2 6125 5664, **Email:** edu.enquiries@anutech.com.au , **Web:** www.anutech.com.au/ELC

ASPECT ILA Sydney
98-104 Goulburn Street, Sydney, New South Wales 2000, **Tel:** +61 2 9283 8055, **Fax:** +61 2 9283 9055, **Email:** aspectsydney@educate.com , **Web:** www.aspectworld.com

Australian College of English
Level 1, 237 Oxford Street, Bondi Junction, New South Wales 2022, **Tel:** +61 2 9389 0133, **Fax:** +61 2 9389 6880, **Email:** info@ace.edu.au, **Web:** www.ace.edu.au

Australian Pacific College
189 Kent Street, Sydney, New South Wales 2000, **Tel:** +61 2 9251 7000, **Fax:** +61 2 9251 7575, **Email:** info@apc.edu.au, **Web:** www.apc.edu.au

Billy Blue English School
Level 9, Northpoint, 100 Miller Street, North Sydney, New South Wales 2060, **Tel:** +61 2 9955 1122, **Fax:** +61 2 9957 1811, **Email:** info@billyblue.com.au **Web:** www.billyblue.com.au

Cambridge English Language Centre
Level 3, 4 Cross Street, Hurstville, New South Wales 2220, **Tel:** +61 2 9579 6244, **Fax:** +61 2 9570 9565, **Email:** cambridgecollege@tpg.com.au **Web:** www.camb.aust.com

Central Queensland University Language Centre
Bruce Highway, North Rockhampton, Queensland 4702, **Tel:** +61 7 4930 6577, **Fax:** +61 7 4930 6321 **Web:** www.language.cqu.edu.au

Centre for English Teaching
University of Sydney, 88 Mallett Street, Camperdown, New South Wales 2006, **Tel:** +61 2 9351 0706, **Fax:**

+61 2 9351 0710, **Email**: info@cet.usyd.edu.au, **Web**: www.usyd.edu.au/cet

Centre for English Language Teaching
35 Stirling Highway, Crawley, West Australia 6009, **Tel**: +61 8 9380 3539, **Fax**: +61 8 9380 1077, **Email**: celt@ecel.uwa.edu.au, **Web**: www.celt.uwa.edu.au

EF International Language Schools
Sydney, 5-7 Young Street, Sydney, New South Wales 2000, **Tel**: +61 2 9247 7668, **Fax**: +61 2 9247 7691, **Email**: ils.sydney@ef.com, **Web**: www.ef.com

ELICOS
University of Canberra, University Drive, Bruce, Australian Capital Territory 2601, **Tel**: +61 2 6201 2102, **Fax**: +61 2 6201 5089, **Web**: www.slie.canberra.edu.au

ELS Language Centres
Charles Sturt University, Boorooma Street, Wagga Wagga, New South Wales 2678, **Tel**: +61 2 6933 2602, **Fax**: +61 2 6933 4018, www.csu.edu.au/division/internat/els/index.htm

Embassy CES Brisbane
119 Charlotte Street, Brisbane, Queensland 4000, **Tel**: +61 7 3238 1500, **Fax**: +61 7 3238 1670, **Email**: w.day@sga.edu.au, **Web**: www.embassyces.com

Embassy CES Melbourne
399 Lonsdale Street, Melbourne, Victoria 3000, **Tel**: +61 3 9670 3788, **Fax**: +61 3 9670 9356, **Email**: info@taylorscollege.com, **Web**: www.embassyces.com

International House Sydney
(Waratah Education Centre), 22 Darley Road, Manly, New South Wales 2095, **Tel**: +61 2 9976 2422, **Fax**: +61 2 9976 2433, **Web**: www.ihsydney.com

International House Queensland English Language College
130 Mcleod Street, Cairns, Queensland 4870, **Tel**: +61 7 4031 3466, **Fax**: +61 7 4031 3464, **Email**: admin@ihqld.com, **Web**: www.ihqld.com

Northern Territory University Centre for Access and ESL
Ellengowan Drive, Casuariana, Northern Territory 0909, **Tel**: +61 8 8946 6160, **Fax**: +61 8 8946 7144, **Email**: uni-info@ntu.edu.au, **Web**: http://mindil.ntu.edu.au

Shane Global Village Sydney
Level 12, 222 Pitt Street, Sydney, NSW 2000 **Tel**: +61 (2) 9283 1088 **Fax**: +61 (2) 9283 1760 **Web**: www.sgvenglish.com

TAFE English Language Centre, Northern Sydney
213 Pacific Highway, St Leonards, New South Wales 2065, **Tel**: +61 2 9942 0086, **Fax**: +61 2 9906 7423, **Email**: Telc@tafensw.edu.au, **Web**: www.tafensw.edu.au

TAFE International Education Centre, Liverpool
Cnr Bigge and Moore Streets, Liverpool, New South Wales 2170, **Tel**: +61 2 9827 5197, **Fax**: +61 2 9827 5198, **Web**: www.tafensw.edu.au/swsit/

Universal English College
Level 12, 222 Pitt Street, Sydney, New South Wales 2000, **Tel**: +61 2 9283 1088, **Fax**: +61 2 9283 1760, **Email**: enquiries@uec.edu.au, **Web**: www.uec.edu.au

University of NSW Institute of Languages
22 King Street, Randwick, New South Wales 2031, **Tel**: +61 2 9385 0339, **Fax**: +61 2 9399 5420, **Email**: Institute.Languages@unsw.edu.au, **Web**: www.lang.unsw.edu.au/elicos/

University of Western Sydney English Language Centre
Building 16, Room 7, Campbelltown Campus, Campbelltown, New South Wales 2560, **Tel**: +61 2 4620 3028, **Fax**: +61 2 4620 3782, **Email**: l.simon@uws.edu.au, **Web**: http://uwselc.uws.edu.au

Victoria University English Language Institute
Level 5, 301 Flinders Lane, Melbourne, Victoria 3000, **Tel**: +61 3 9248 1175, **Fax**: +61 3 9248 1298, **Email**: eli@vu.edu.au, **Web**: www.vu.edu.au/eli/

NEW ZEALAND

New Zealand is experiencing a good demand for English teachers – thanks to a rush of immigrants who want to learn English (tempted by the favourable exchange rate and easing of immigration requirements). There are not enough teachers and schools currently will offer to help visitors get a work visa; schools prefer teachers with a CELTA or Trinity certificate and at least one year's experience.

Auckland and Christchurch are the two main centres for schools and the bulk of students are from China, Korea and Japan. The only drawback is for US citizens hoping to teach in New Zealand – like Australia, it's hard for US citizens to get a work permit. A good source for jobs are the websites www.english-schools.co.nz and www.teachnz.gov.nz

High Commission in UK:
New Zealand House, 80 Haymarket, London SW1Y
4TQ
Tel: 020 7930 8422
www.nzembassy.com

Embassy in USA:
37 Observatory Circle NW, Washington DC20008
Tel: 202 328 4800
www.nzemb.org

British Council office:
44 Hill Street, PO Box 1812, Wellington 1
Tel (4) 495 0897
www.britishcouncil.org.nz

➲ **Visas:** British citizens can enter NZ without a visa
and can stay in the country for up to six months, if they
can prove that they have enough money and a return
ticket. UK, Irish, Canadian, and Japanese citizens aged
18-30 can use the Working Holiday visa scheme to
take temporary work whilst they stay in NZ for up to
12months. US citizens can stay for up to 90 days
without a visa.
➲ **Currency:** £1 = 2.59 / $1 = 1.40 Dollars

Schools in New Zealand (+ 64)

Auckland English Academy
PO Box 11 241, Ellerslie, Auckland, New Zealand,
Tel: +64 9-3793777, **Fax:** +64 9-358-3383, **Email:**
learn@english.co.nz, **Web:** www.english.co.nz

Auckland Institute of Studies
PO Box 2995, Auckland, New Zealand, **Tel:** +64
9-815 3772, **Fax:** +64 9-815 1802,
Web:www.ais.ac.nz

Canterbury Language Institute
PO Box 4425, Christchurch, New Zealand, **Tel:** +64
3-365 1920, **Fax:** +64 3-365 2296, **Email:**
can.lancol@xtra.co.nz

Dynaspeak English
12 O'Connell Street, PO Box 106-052, Auckland 1001,
New Zealand, **Tel:** +64 9 377 2434, **Fax:** +64 9 377
2811, **Web:** www.dynaspeak.co.nz

Edenz Colleges
Ideal House, 17 Eden St, Newmarket. Auckland, **Tel:**
+64 9 815 3772, **Fax:** +64 9 522 1211, **Email:**
edenz@edenz.com, **Web:** www.edenz.com

ILA South Pacific - Auckland
PO Box 9107, Auckland, New Zealand, **Tel:** +64 9 307
6507, **Fax:** +64 9 379 5749, **Email:**
principal@ila.co.nz, **Web:**www.ila.co.nz

ILA South Pacific - Christchurch
PO Box 25170, Christchurch, New Zealand, **Tel:** +64 3
379 5452, **Fax:** +64 3 379 5957, **Email:**
ilachch@ila.co.nz, **Web:**www.ila.co.nz

LSNZ Christchurch & Queeenstown
PO Box 911, Queenstown, New Zealand, **Tel:** +64 3
442 6625, **Fax:** +64 3 442 6676,
Web:www.languageschool.co.nz

Modern Age English Language School
PO Box 2137, Tauranga, New Zealand, **Tel:** +64 7-576
8831, **Fax:** +64 7-578 5883,
Web:www.modernage.co.nz

New Horizon College of English
PO Box 66, Napier, New Zealand, **Tel:** +64 6-835
6423, **Fax:** +64 6-835 6523, **Email:**
office@nhce.ac.nz, **Web:** www.nhce.ac.nz

Shane Global Village English Centre
Level 2, 138 Queen Street. PO Box 105-347,
Auckland., **Tel:**+64 (9) 309 2201, **Email:**
auckland@sgvenglish.com, **Web:**
www.sgvenglish.com

**Shore English School of Language New
Zealand**
PO Box 33-614, Takapuna, Auckland, **Tel:** +64 9-486
1896, **Fax:** +64 9-486 0648, **Email:**
shoreng@nznet.gen.nz, **Web:**www.shore-english.co.nz

Southern Lakes English School
PO Box 405, Queenstown, New Zealand, **Tel:** +64 3
442-7810, **Fax:** +64 3 442-7815, **Email:**
slec@xtra.co.nz, **Web:** www.slec.co.nz

Wellington College of Languages
PO Box 9546, Wellington, New Zealand, **Tel:** +64 4
382 8938, **Fax:** +64 4 385 1518, **Email:**
wcl@xtra.co.nz, **Web:** www.wcl.co.nz

Worldwide School of English
PO Box 1802, Auckland, New Zealand, **Tel:** +64 9 302
5288, **Fax:** +64 9 302 5299, **Email:** info@wwse.co.nz,
Web: www.wwse.co.nz

Asia

The English language is in great demand in Asia, particularly in Japan, China (including Hong Kong), Korea, Taiwan, and Thailand. In some countries in South East Asia (notably Singapore) the local government has introduced legislation to teach core subjects in English – students must learn maths and science in English.

China has seen an explosion of English language schools over the past few years - with native Chinese speakers learning English and learning to teach English with equal enthusiasm. Korea also offers a fast-changing EFL landscape, but is mostly dominanted by American-English language schools; by comparison, Japan and Thailand offer established school chains, networks for teachers and associations to help teachers.

The region has, mostly, recovered from the Asian economic crisis at the start of the 2000s; money has returned for education, and proficiency in English is widely regarded as essential for a successful career. For EFL teachers, levels of pay, the cost of living and working conditions vary considerably between the developed nations and the developing countries. Some teachers work long hours to live well and save a lot of money, whereas others supplement their income with their savings and use their spare time to travel. Whatever your goals, there is no doubt that you will have the experience of a lifetime should you choose to teach in Asia.

BANGLADESH

Bangladesh is one of the most impoverished countries in the world. There are opportunities for EFL teachers here, mostly volunteer work with aid organizations and the Peace Corps.

Schools in Bangladesh (+880)

The British Council Teaching Centre
754b Satmasjid Road, Dhanmondi, Dhaka 1205. **Tel:** 9116171/9116545. **Fax:** 8116554. **Email:** dto@TheBritishCouncil.net

Regional Resources Centre
SESDC Building, Teachers Training College, Bakulia, Chittagong. **Fax:** 031 612307.

CAMBODIA

Cambodia is for the adventurous EFL teacher who enjoys getting off the beaten track. The country is still rebuilding after a long civil war and some areas are not safe, including the capital, Phnom Penh, where a number of teachers from Oklahoma were kidnapped and later released. Crime waves are sporadic so take the same precautions as you would in any major western city. Salaries are low when compared to the richer Asian nations. The better language schools (offering better rates of pay!) will want to see evidence of TESL certification but there are street corner schools who will take on an unqualified native speaker. Most schools employ teachers on a term-to-term basis so you are only guaranteed work for 10 weeks at a time. There is a lot of demand for English in Cambodia as the country slowly integrates with its neighbours. Few Cambodians can afford private lessons.

⮑ **Visas/Work Permits:** You can arrive in Cambodia and purchase a one-month working visa for £14 / $30. The working visa can be renewed without leaving the country. You don't have to prove you are actually working for someone when you arrive. Your school will not reimburse you for the cost of your visa.

⮑ **Currency:** £1 = 7455 / $1 = 4030 Riel

⮑ **Salaries/Taxes:** Schools pay around £6-10 / $10-20 an hour if you are qualified. Tax is 6%.

⮑ **Accommodation:** Rents have been forced up artificially high as Phnom Penh plays host to large groups of overpaid foreign aid workers. Flats are difficult to find and cost anywhere from £100-170 / $190-320 a month.

⮑ **Cost of Living:** The presence of well-paid foreign aid workers means that prices are sky-high in Phnom Penh. You can live on £6-10 / $11-20 a day if you rule out drinking at a smart hotel with the UN gang. Personal cheques and credit cards are not widely accepted within Cambodia, although a number of banks in Phnom Penh accept Visa cards for cash advances. Use dollars and/or Thai baht.

⮑ **Health advice:** The Cambodian medical system was virtually wiped out during the Khmer Rouge period, 1975-1979, and is being rebuilt slowly. Medical facilities and services in Cambodia are not up to western standards. Get shots for Hepatitis A, Malaria, Typhoid, and Polio. Make sure you have medical insurance that will guarantee and pay for evacuation in the case of an emergency.

⮑ **English Language Media:** The Cambodia Daily, Phnom Penh Post.

Schools in Cambodia (+855)

ACE
46 Street 214, Sangkat Boeung Raing, Khan Daun Penh, Phnom Penh. **Email:** ace.idpcam@bigpond.com.kh

ACE Battembang
Rumcheak Village, Khum Ratanak, Svay Po, Battembang. **Tel:** 012-833602.

ACE Siem Reap
House 0675, Group 20, Wat Bo Village, Siem Reap, **Tel:** 012-833601.

ACE Kompong Cham
House 034, Group 1, Village 7, Sangkat Kompong Cham. **Tel:** 012-833600.

CHINA

There is a huge demand for native-speaking English language teachers (both American and British English speakers), especially in the enterprise zones near Hong Kong. The demand for teachers is led both by private schools in China and by companies eager to take advantage of new international business opportunities. There is a need for ESP teachers, such as English for business, for tourism, for medical purposes and for law, the latter because many foreign firms regard cultural and legal differences between Chinese and external cultures as a major cause of failed western investments. Another area that is booming is teaching English for young learners but these positions are usually advertised by word of mouth and require an

extrovert personality and infinite patience. Unqualified EFL teachers can find work here but given the demands of teaching in China a TESL certificate is highly recommended. Also, holders of more advanced qualifications like an MA in TESOL will be paid at higher rates because they are classified as Foreign Experts rather than Foreign Teachers who are usually under 25 and have a BA. Job seekers can contact the nearest Chinese embassy or State Bureau of Foreign Experts, Friendship Hotel, 3 Bai Shi Qiao Rd., 100873 Beijing. Tel: +86 10-849-888, x 83500, fax: +86 10-831-5832 for more information and should also check out the TEFLChina Teahouse site: www.teflchina.com– an excellent source of information about teaching English in China. There is also a listing of teaching jobs in China at www.teach-in-china.com

Embassy in UK:
49 Portland Place, London W1N 4JL
Tel: 020 7631 1430
www.chinese-embassy.org.uk

Embassy in USA:
2300 Connecticut Ave NW, Washington DC 20008
Tel: 202 328 2500
www.china-embassy.org

British Council office:
4/f Landmark Building Tower 1, 8 North Dongsanhuan Road, Chaoyang District, 100004 Beijing
Tel +86 (10) 6590 6903
www.britishcouncil.cn

⮕ **Visas/Work Permits:** If you negotiate your job from home, then your employer or the agency will take care of the necessary paperwork. It is possible to go to China on a tourist visa and then start job hunting. Once you have a job, the school will send you to the Public Security Bureau (PSB) so that your visa can be changed. To obtain a visa, negative HIV test results are required for teachers who plan to stay nine months or more. Some teachers go to Hong Kong and secure six-month multiple entry visas from there.

⮕ **Currency:** £1 = 15.29 / $1 = 8.27 Yuan Renminbi (RMB)

⮕ **Salaries/Taxes:** Minimum salaries are RMB 2,500 per month for bachelors' degree holders and RMB 3,000 per month for masters' degree holders. Private tutors can charge around RMB 150-200 an hour in the big cities. There is no tax.

⮕ **Accommodation:** Your housing should be provided by the employer. Conditions can be harsh by Western standards although foreign teachers usually receive the best accommodation that the institution can offer.

⮕ **Cost of Living:** It is cheaper in the North than the South, excluding Beijing.

⮕ **Health advice:** Although most schools provide health insurance, which covers 80% of the cost, you should have your own insurance. The quality of medical care in China varies. Competent, trained doctors and nurses are available in major metropolitan centres, but many do not speak English. Hospital accommodation is spartan, and medical technology is not up-to-date. Doctors and hospitals often expect immediate cash payment for health services and may not accept cheques or credit cards.

⮕ **English Language Media:** Beijing Scene, China Daily, Shanghai Daily Star.

Schools in China (+86)

AES
102 Chang Jiang Liu, Dalian, 116001. **Tel:** (411) 281-7932. **Fax:** (411) 281-3318. **Email:** future@mail.dlptt.ln.cn

American International School of Guangzhou
Box 212, Ti Yu Dong Post Office, 510620 Guangzhou. **Tel:** (20) 3881.0001/2711/2712,2713; **Fax:** (20) 3881.1102; **Email:** asg@gitic.com.cn; **Website:** www.concept.se/user/aisg/ aisg.html

ASM Overseas Corp.
Asian Games Garden, Building No.2-6A. No.12 Xiaoying Lu, Chao Yang Dist., Beijing 100101. **Tel:** (10) 6497 4451. **Fax:** (10) 6497 4872.

Capital Language School
101 Dong Yuan Lu, Zhongshan 528400.**Tel:** (760) 8335067. **Fax:** (760) 8335067.

CDI Career Development Institute
110 Bloor Street West, Suite 202, Toronto, Ontario M5S 2W7, Canada. **Tel:** 1 416 964 6707, **Fax:** 1 416 964 0520.

China International Education League
Suite C 4th floor, Zao Fong World-trade Building, Jiangsu Road 369, Shanghai 200050. **Tel:** (21) 52400111 **Fax:** (21) 52400101.

China Teaching Program
Western Washington University, Old Main 530A, Bellingham, WA 98225-9047. **Tel:** (360) 650-3753, **Fax:** (360) 650-3753.

Chinese Education Association for International Exchange
37 Damucang Hutong, Beijing 100816. **Tel:** (10) 660-20-731, **Fax:** (10) 660-16-56.

Colorado China Council
4556 Apple Way, Boulder, CO 80301. **Tel:** (303) 443 1108, **Fax:** (303) 443-1107.

Concordia International School Shanghai
Plot S2, Huang Yang Rd., P.O. Box 206-005, Pudong, 201206 Shanghai; **Tel:** (21) 5899.0380; **Fax:** (21) 5899.1685; **Email:** sandras@ciss.com.cn; **Website:** www.ciss.com.cn

Fountain School
Ji Da Guo Mao, Zhuhai, Guangdong 519015. **Email:** wuvoka@mailcity.com

The International School of Beijing
c/o American Embassy Beijing, PSC461, Box 50, FPO AP 96521-0002; **Tel:** (10) 6437.7119; **Fax:** (10) 6437.6989; **Email:** isb-info@isb.bj.edu.cn; **Website:** www.isb.bj.edu.cn

New China Education Foundation
1587 Montalban Drive, San Jose, CA 95120. **Tel:** (408) 268 0418.

Qingdao International School
Middle Sector Song Ling Rd., Stone Old Man National Tourism Spot, Qingdao, 266101. **Tel:** (532) 889-1000; **Fax:** (532) 889-8950l; **Email:** gbapk@hotmail.com **Website:** www.qischina.com

Shanda International House
29-3 South Road Shanda, Jinan 250100, Shandong Province.**Tel:** +61 7 40 313466, **Fax:** +61 7 40 313 464.

Shanghai American School
50 Ji Di Lu, Zhudi, Minhang, 201107 Shanghai. **Tel:** (21) 6221.1445 **Fax:** (21) 6221.1269. **Email:** info@saschina.org; **Website:** www.saschina.org

Shanghai Changning International School
Jiangsu Lu 155, Shanghai 200050. **Tel:** (21) 6252-3688; **Fax:** 21-6212-2330; **Email:** scis@uninet.com.cn, **Website:** www.uninet.com.cn/ userhome/scis/index.htm

Shekou International School
c/o Arco China, Inc., P.O. Box 260888, Plano, TX 75026-0888. **Tel:** (755) 669.3669; **Fax:** (755) 667.4099; **Email:** szejones@public.szptt.net.cn

TEDA International School
Tianjin; 6 Mu Nan Dao, 300050 Tianjin; **Tel:** (22) 2311.4772. **Fax:** (22) 2331.2263; **Email:** tist@public1.tpt.tj.cn

Tianjin International School
Xing Guo School, Xi Yuan Road, Ti Yuan Bei, He Xi District, 300061 Tianjin. **Tel:** (22) 283.53200. **Fax:** (22) 283.52455. **Email:** tmis@public1.tpt.tj.cn

Western Academy of Beijing
P.O. Box 8547, 7A Bei Si Huan Dong Lu, Chao Yang Qu, Beijing 100102. **Tel:** (10) 6437.5935. **Fax:** (10) 6437.5936. **Email:** wabinfo@ns.wab.senet.gov.cn

Wuhan Guanghua School
Jiangxia District, Wuhan, Hubei 430205. **Tel:** (27) 8794-4154, **Fax:** (27) 8794-5564. **Email:** doralei@netease.com

Wuhan International School
c/o Holiday Inn Tian An Wuhan 868 Jie Fang Da Dao Wuhan 430022. **Tel:** (27) 8576-8863; **Fax:** (27) 8584-5353. **Email:** wis@teacher.com

Xiamen International School
Jiu Tian Hu, Xinglin District, 361022 Xiamen; **Tel:** (592) 625.6581 **Fax:** (592) 625.6584. **Email:** JDFisch47@yahoo.com

Yang-En University
Quanzhou, Fujian 362014. **Tel:** (595) 208 7600, Ext. 202. **Fax:** (595) 208 2017. **Email:** yeu@yeu.qz.fj.cn

Yew Chung Shanghai International School (SIS)
11 Shui Cheng Road, 200336 Shanghai; **Tel:** (21) 6242.3243; **Fax:** (21) 6242.7331; **Email:** ycsis@public.sta.net.cn

Yunnan Institute of the Nationalities
Foreign Affairs Office, Kunming 650031, Yunnan. **Tel:** (871) 515 4308.

HONG KONG

The former British colony is now a Special Administrative Region within China. There are plenty of well-paid jobs here for EFL teachers although it is more difficult to obtain a working visa than it was in the past. The NET (Native-speaker English Teacher) program, operated by the Hong Kong Department of Education, allows qualified native speaker teachers to teach English in the public schools for 12 months. The scheme pays teachers anywhere from £1300-3500 / $2400-6500 per month plus a 15% gratuity payable on the completion of the contract. For more information about NET on the web, visit www.info.gov.hk/ed/english/teacher/native_eng_teach er/home.htm but be sure to confirm pay and other benefits before you decide to go.

Embassy information:
see China

British Council office:
3 Supreme Court Road, Admiralty, Hong Kong
Tel +852 291 35100
www.britishcouncil.org.hk

⮑ **Visas/Work Permits:** U.S. citizens can obtain tourist visas for stays of up to 90 days. To get a work permit, you need to be sponsored by an employer. One way to do this is to arrive in Hong Kong, land a job, and then leave the country while your application is being processed. If you work illegally, be aware that teachers have been deported in the past for overstaying their visas.

⮑ **Currency:** £1 = 14.56 / $1 = 7.80 HK Dollars

⮑ **Salaries/Taxes:** Teachers earn anywhere from HK$12,000 and up per month in the public schools to HK$50,000 at the top end in the private sector. Freelancers make from HK$300-750 or more per hour for private tuition.

⮑ **Accommodation:** Expensive if you are staying in Hong Kong itself, less so if you live on one of the other islands like Lamma, where a shared apartment costs around HK$2,500-3,000 a month.

⮑ **Cost of Living:** Expensive, until you learn where the best deals are.

⮑ **Health advice:** Medical facilities are excellent. Your employer should provide medical coverage for you.

⮑ **English Language Media:** Hong Kong Magazine, Hong Kong Standard, South China Morning Post.

Schools in Hong Kong (+852)

Berlitz
1 Pacific Place, Central. **Tel:** 2826 9223, **Fax:** 2 525 9757.

English Language Club
Ka Nin Wah Commercial Building, Hennessy Road. **Tel:** 2 838 0036.

First Class Language Centre
22a Bank Tower, 351-353 King's Road, North Point. **Tel:** 5 887 7555.

Hong Kong English Club
Ground floor, 41 Carnarvon Road, Tsimshatsui, Kowloon. **Tel:** 2 366 6961.

HK Institute of Languages
Rm 501 30-32 D'Aguliar St, Central. **Tel:** 2 877 6160.

Island International High School
20 Borrett Road, Hong Kong.

Pasona Education
2/F One Hysan Ave, Causeway Bay. **Tel:** 2 577 8002.

The British Council
English Language Centre, 3 Supreme Court Road, Admiralty. **Tel:** 2 913 5100, **Fax:** 2 913 5102.

The Centre for Professional and Business English
7th Floor, Core B, Hong Kong Polytechnic University, T.S.T. **Tel:** 2 766 5111.

Venture Living Languages Ltd
1A 163 Hennessy Road, Hong Kong. **Tel:** 2 507 4985, **Fax:** 2 858 1764.

INDONESIA

Indonesia is undergoing economic and political turmoil at present and the country is not as stable as it used to be. EFL teachers report that although life goes on as usual, especially in the big cities like Jakarta, Surabaya and Medan, demand for English lessons is slowing due to financial instability. If you decide to go to Indonesia, try getting a job with one of the larger and more reputable schools. Do not go unless you are offered a work visa, otherwise you will be working illegally and the authorities deal very harshly with offenders. For US teachers, anti-American sentiment is running high in some areas and caution should be exercised if you are travelling in Indonesia.

British Council office:
S. Widjojo Centre, Jalan Jenderal Sudirman Kav 71, Jakarta 12190
Tel +62 (21) 252 4115
www.britishcouncil.or.id

⮑ **Visas/Work Permits:** Tourist visas are granted for up to two months. Some teachers do "visa runs" to Singapore or Darwin, Australia, when their visas run out but these trips are expensive, especially now that the rupiah is worth so little. Your school should arrange a work permit for you. Vacation time is usually given at Christmas and one week at the end of Ramadan.

⮑ **Currency:** £1 = 17306 / $1 = 9276 Rupiah.

⮑ **Salaries/Taxes:** Teachers are paid in rupiah. Your contract should guarantee that you are paid between 6-8 million rupiah a month. If the amount is less than that, you will find it difficult to live in Indonesia. There

is a mandatory tax of £90 / $170 each month imposed on all foreigners.

➲ **Accommodation:** You should receive free or subsidized housing as part of your employment package. Rents are generally cheaper outside of Jakarta.

➲ **Cost of Living:** Food, clothing and other basics are reasonable.

➲ **Health advice:** Make sure your school offers you insurance coverage that offers protection against sickness and that will evacuate you in the event of full scale rioting.

➲ **English Language Media:** Indonesian Times, Indonesian Observer, Jakarta Post.

Schools in Indonesia (+62)

American English Language Training (AELT)
Jalan R.S. Fatmawati 42a, Keb Baru, Jakarta Selatan 12430. **Tel:** 21 769 1001, **Fax:** 21 751 3304.

American Language centre
Jl. Panglima Polim Raya No. 101, Kebayoran Baru, Jakarta 12160. **Tel:** (21) 722-8957, **Fax:** (21) 722-8960.

Centre for Language Training (CLT)
Soegijapranata Catholic University, Jl. Menteri Supeno 35, Semarang 50241. **Tel:** 24 316028, **Fax:** 24 415429.

English Education Centre (EEC)
Jalan Let. Jend S.Parman 68, Slipi, Jakarta 11410. **Tel:** 21 532 3176, **Fax:** 21 532 3178.

Executive English Programmes (EEP)
Jalan Wijaya VIII 4, Kebayoran Baru, Jakarta Selatan 12160. **Tel:** 21 720 1896.

ELS International
Jalan Tanjung Karang 7 c-d, Jakarta Pusat. **Tel:** 21 323 211.

English First Bogor
Jl. Raya Pajajaran No.8, Bogor 16151.**Tel:** 251 324374, **Fax:** 251 379296.

EF English First Kelapa Gading
Jl.Raya Bulevar Barat Blok LA 1 no 8 - 9 Kelapa Gading Permai Jakarta 14240. **Tel:** 21 451 5858. **Fax:** : 21 451 5959.

EF English First Lampung
Jl. Diponegoro No. 146, Bandar Lampung 35127. **Tel:** 721 263154, **Fax:** 721 263154.

EF English First (Ujung Pandang)
Jl. Slt. Hasanuddin 27, Ujung Pandang 90113. **Tel:** 411 315288, **Fax:** 411 315251.

English Language Training International (ELTI)
Complex Wijaya Grand Centre, Blok F 84A & B, Jalan Wijaya II, Jakarta Selatan 12160. **Tel:** 21 720 6653, **Fax:** 21 720 6654.

Indonesia-Australia Language Foundation (IALF)
Wisma Budi, Suite 503, Jalan HR Rasuna Said Kav c-6, Kuningan, Jakarta Selatan 12940. **Tel:** 521 3350.

International Language Programmes (ILP)
Jalan Raya Pasar Minggu No. 39A, Jakarta 12780. **Tel:** 21 798 5210, **Fax:** 21 798 5212.

International Language Studies (ILS)
Jalan Ngemplak 30, Arbengan Plaza B-34, Surabaya 60272. **Tel:** 31 531 9644, **Fax:** 31 531 9645.

I-Pro International Programmes
Jl Ngagel 179 -183, K1, Surabaya 60245. **Tel:** 31 566 2914/5, **Fax:** 31 566 7979.

Logo Education Centre (LEC)
Jelan H.Z. Arifin 208A, Medan, Sumatra Utara. **Tel:** 61 534991, **Fax:** 61 552385.

Maple Leaf English Language Centre
Jl. Raya Darmo Permai II / 32, Surabaya. **Tel:** 31 710722. **Fax:** (031) 725476

Oxford Course Indonesia (OCI)
Jalan Cempaka Putih Tengah 33C-2, Jakarta Pusat 10510. **Tel:** 21 424 3224, **Fax:** 21 425 4041.

Professional Training Services (PTS)
Wisma BII, Jalan Permuda No. 60-70, Surabaya 60271. **Tel/Fax:** 31 531 0006.

School for International Communication
Jalan Taman Pahlawan 194, Purwakarta. **Tel:** 264 201204.

School for International Training (SIT)
Jalan Sunda 3, Menteng, Jakarta Pusat 10350. **Tel:** 21 390 6920, **Fax:** 21 335671.

Strive International
Setiabudi 1 Building, Jalan HR Rasuna Said, Jakarta 12920. **Tel:** 21 521 0690, **Fax:** 21 521 0692.

The British Institute (TBI)
Plaza Setiabudi 2, Jalan HR Rasuna Said, Jakarta 12920. **Tel:** 21 525 6750, **Fax:** 21 520 7574.

Triad English Centre
Jalan Purnawarman 76 Bandung- 40116. **Tel:** 62 22 431309, **Fax:** 22 431149.

JAPAN

Despite the recent economic crisis, Japan is still a popular destination for English teachers, qualified or not, because of the number of jobs available and the favourable salaries. Japan's commitment to learning English was recently demonstrated in very clear terms by Prime Minister Keizo Obuchi's recent statement that, "Achieving world-class excellence demands that all Japanese acquire a working knowledge of English." But it must be noted that the standard pay of 250,000 yen per month for an EFL teacher has hardly changed in the last few years despite rising inflation so teaching contracts in Japan are not as lucrative as they once were.

After-hours schools where students cram for exams, including English language, are known as juku. An eikaiwa is an English conversation school. Unqualified teachers can find work in private schools giving conversation classes or through Japan's Exchange and Teaching (JET) programme (see below). There are also chains of schools, such as AEON, GEOS and NOVA employing thousands of trained and untrained teachers. The best time to come to Japan and look for a job is in March just before the start of the school year on April 1. The big chains of schools recruit teachers year-round. If you negotiate your employment with a recruiter outside of Japan remember that the agreement you make is not binding. It is the contract with the school in Japan that governs the terms of your employment. Also, be aware that you may run into problems if you decide to go off and work for another school once you are in Japan. Your first employer may not be happy that you are leaving after so much of the school's money and time has been invested in you. If you work outside of Tokyo, you may need an International Drivers' Licence if the school provides you with a car. It can take up to six months to get acclimatized to Japan. Prepare yourself before you go: look at the ELT News website for regularly updated information about teaching in Japan (www.eltnews.com).

The JET Program

The Japan Exchange and Teaching programme is a Japanese government scheme aimed at improving English language teaching and international relations in schools. Although 34 countries are involved in the program, the majority of the almost 6,000 participants are from the US. Anyone under 35, with a degree and an interest in Japan, can apply. The salary and conditions are excellent – you get about £20,000 / $38,000 for the year, free return airfare, 3-day

orientation and you work in conjunction with a Japanese teacher – one participant described it as the best job in the world! Applications must be in by early December for the following summer.
Contact: www.jetprogramme.org

Embassy in UK:
101-104 Piccadilly, London W1V 9FN
Tel: 020 7465 6500
www.embjapan.org.uk
Embassy in USA:
2520 Massachusetts Ave NW, Washington DC20008
Tel: 202 238 6700
British Council office:
1-2 Kagurazaka, Shinjuku-ku, Tokyo 162-0825
Tel +81 (3) 3235 8031
www.britishcouncil.org/japan

⇒ **Visas/Work Permits:** The opportunity to obtain a working visa to teach in Japan is generally available to native English speakers with a valid college diploma in any field. The sponsoring employer in Japan must first obtain a "Certificate of Eligibility" from the Japanese Ministry of Justice, Immigration Bureau, for the prospective teacher. With this certificate, you can apply for a work visa at the Japanese Embassy (or at a Japanese Consulate) prior to entering Japan. If you try to enter into Japan as a tourist under the 90-day visa waiver programme to work, you may be denied entry, but you can enter to look for work. If you enter Japan as a tourist and subsequently obtain an offer to teach, you must leave the country, taking the "Certificate of Eligibility" to a Japanese Embassy/Consulate in the U.S. or a neighbouring country (usually Korea), to obtain a work visa, and then re-enter Japan on the correct visa. If you are from Canada, Australia or New Zealand, you can teach in Japan on a working holiday visa, which can be obtained in your own country. You must be between the ages of 18-30 to go on the working holiday programme. The visa is for six months, renewable only once. After that you have to find a sponsor or a legal visa to continue working in Japan.

⇒ **Currency:** £1 = 197 / $1 = 105 Yen.

⇒ **Salaries/Taxes:** Salaries begin at around 250,000 yen per month with airfares and end-of-contract bonuses offered to more qualified candidates. If you are teaching privately, expect to earn 3,000-6,000 yen per lesson. Salaries are usually based on an hourly wage with a guarantee of a certain minimum number of hours per month. Many teachers hold side jobs as

private tutors outside of their classroom workplaces. Income tax in Japan is approximately 10% of your gross income. Watch out for deductions by employers for accommodation and other expenses, which, if you are not careful, can leave you with about half your salary left to live on. It should be possible for you to save a fair amount of money after living in Japan for a few months.

⮕ **Accommodation:** Many schools provide free or subsidized housing as part of the employment package. If a school is taking a large percentage of your pay packet (more than 25%) then you should question the contract. If you try to rent on your own you should be aware that housing is much smaller, more expensive and complicated to rent than in the west. Rents range from 60,000-100,000 Yen per month in Tokyo, but in smaller towns you can pay a quarter of that. Landlords can be reluctant to rent to foreigners, so it's worth getting somebody to help. There are agents who can do this, otherwise you might have to pay as much as £3000 / $5,700 in advance as a security deposit ('key money'). Schools that recruit overseas often include accommodation assistance as a benefit.

⮕ **Cost of Living:** The cost of living, especially in cities, is very high. Don't be surprised if a simple night out with some friends costs you $100 or more! Supporting a family in Japan, according to middle class American standards, is well beyond the reach of most English teachers. However, salaries are high. It is possible to save money, especially outside Tokyo.

⮕ **Health advice:** Most teachers are covered by the Japanese national health insurance plan, which does not pay for treatment outside of Japan. While recently on the rise, health care costs remain relatively low in Japan. The self-employed, employees of small businesses, and others not covered by employer plans can apply to the government for low-cost National Health Insurance, which provides coverage similar to workplace-based insurance. Teachers should obtain private, supplemental health insurance that includes worldwide medical evacuation and care. Vaccinations recommended are Polio and Typhoid.

⮕ **English Language Media:** Japan Times, Kansai Time Out, The Asahi Evening News, The Daily Mainichi.

Schools in Japan (+82)

A Ring English Conversation
3-9-12-304 Nishi Shinagawa, Shinagawa-ku, Tokyo, **Tel:** 0120-750510.

Academy of Language Arts
Tobundo Bldg. No.2 5F, 2-16 Agebacho, Shinjuku-ku, Tokyo. **Tel:** 03-3235-0071. **Fax:** 03-3235-0004. **Website:** www.kbic.ardour.co.jp /~newgenji/ala/

ACE English School
6-6-22 Hachimancho, Takahmashi Aichiken, 444-1302. **Tel:** 566 52 3235. **Fax:** 566 52 3235.

AEON Inter-Cultural
Shinjuku I-Land Tower Bldg. 12F, 6-5-1 Nishishinjuku, Shinjuku-ku, Tokyo 163-1377. **Tel:** 03-5381-1500. **Fax:** 03-5381-1501. **Email:** aejedu@corp.aeonet.co.jp)

Ai Language Studio
Hiroo Stone Bldg. 5F, 1-3-17 Hiroo, Shibuya-ku, Tokyo. **Tel:** 03-5421-3572. **Fax:** 03-5421-3573. **Website:** http://plaza24.mbn.or.jp/~als/ **Email:**tokim@bd.mbn.or.jp

AIT Foreign Language Centre
3-20-1-401, Tamagawa, Setagaya-ku, Tokyo. **Tel:** 03-3700-8110. **Fax:** 03-3700-8889. **Website:** www2.tky.3web.ne.jp/~ai **Email:** aitcorp@tky2.3web.ne.jp

Alpha Language School
3-4-11 Mita, Minato-ku, Tokyo. **Tel:** 03-3769-4945. **Fax:** 03-3769-4946. **Email:**ala@a2.mbn.or.jp

American Academy
4-1-3 Kudan Kita Chiyoda-Ku, Tokyo 102.

America Eiko Gakuin
Misono-cho 5-2-21, Wakayama City 640.

American School of Business
1-17-4 Higashi Ikebukuro, Toshima-Ku, Tokyo 170.

Azabu Academy
401 Shuwa-Roppongi Building, 3-14-12 Roppongi, Minato-ku, Tokyo 106.

Berlitz Schools of Languages (Japan) Inc.
Kowa Bldg. 1,5f, 11-41, Alasaka 1-chome, Minato-ku, Tokyo 107.

Bernard Group
2-8-11 Takezono, Tsukuba City, Ibaraki-Ken, 305.

CA English Academy
2nd Floor Kotohira Building, 9-14 Kakuozan-dori, Chikusa-ku, Nagoya.

Cambridge English School
Dogenzaka 225 Building, 2-23-14 Dogenzaka, Shibuya-ku,Tokyo 150.

Cambridge School of English
Kikumura 91 Building1-41-20 Higashi, Ikebukuro Toshima-ku, Tokyo 170.

Canadian School of Languages
3-9-7-202 Kameari, Katsushika-ku, Tokyo. **Tel:**
03-3601-7648.

Canning
The, 2-9 Kanda Surugadai, Chiyoda-ku, Tokyo. **Tel:**
03-3295-5500

CEC Foreign Language centre
Takahashi Bldg. 3F, 1-44-3 Fuda, Chofu City, Tokyo.
Tel: 0424-87-3623. **Fax:** 0424-87-3664.

Celc English School
1-3-5 Mejirodai, Hachioji City, Tokyo. **Tel:**
0426-66-5041 **Fax:** 0426-66-5042. **Website:**
http://member.nifty.ne.jp/celc/index.html

CIC English Schools
Kawamoto Building, Imadegawaagaru Nishigawa
Karasuma-dori, Kamigyo-ku, Kyoto.

Cosmopolitan Language Institute
1-8-9 Yaesu, Chou-ku, Tokyo. **Tel:** 03-3273-7878.
Fax: 03-3273-7870.

Cosmopolitan Language Institute
Yashima B Building 4f, 1-8-9 Yesu Chuo-ku,Tokyo
104.

**Daigakushorin International Language
Academy**
AM Bldg., 9 Rokubancho, Chiyoda-ku, Tokyo. **Tel:**
03-3264-2131. **Fax:** 03-3264-2133.

David English House
2-3f Nakano Building, 1-5-17 Kamiyacho, Naka-ku,
Hiroshima 730.

Den House International Language School
Meguro Ekimae School, Tamagawa Bldg. 3F, 2-16-5
Kami Osaki, Shinagawa-ku, Tokyo. **Tel:**
03-3280-4255.

Den House International Language School
Tsukahara Bldg. 2F, 7-19-9 Okusawa, Setagaya-ku,
Tokyo. **Tel:** 03-3704-7636. **Fax:** 03-3704-7696.

Dual International School
ILYA Bldg. 3F, 1-1 Yotsuya-dori, Chikusa-ku,
Nagoya, 464-0819. **Tel:** 052-783-3031. **Fax:**
052-783-3035. **Email:** dual6@spice.or.jp

Educational Information Institute
Level 7, 2-15-22 Shinjuku, Shinjuku-ku, Tokyo. **Tel:**
03-5366-7201. **Fax:** 03-5366-7203. **Email:**
eiijabli@mx2.ttcn.ne.jp

EEC Foreign Languages Institute
Shikata Building 2f, 4-43 Nakazald-Nishi 2-chrome,
Kita-ku, Osaka 530.

EII Educational Information Institute
S2 Bldg. 7F, 2-15-22 Shinjuku, Shinjuku-ku, Tokyo.
Tel: 03-3352-5280. **Fax:** 03-3352-5871

**ELEC Eigo Kenkyujo (The English Language
Education Council)**
3-8 Kanda Jimbo-cho, Chiyoda-ku,Tokyo 101.

English Plus
Bell Maison Minami Azabu 1F, 1-3-17 Minami Azabu,
Minato-ku, Tokyo. **Tel:** 03-5238-0111. **Fax:**
03-5238-0300.

English Studio
Meguro School, 5-12-2 Shimo Meguro, Meguro-ku,
Tokyo. **Tel:** 03-3712-3313. **Fax:** 03-3710-3386.
Email:e-studio@tkc.att.ne.jp

English Studio
Mita School, 4-2-14 Mita, Minato-ku, Tokyo. **Tel:**
03-3798-5829. **Fax:** 03-3769-9397. **Email:**
e-studio@tkc.att.ne.jp

English Studio
Setagaya School, 2-31-11 Oyamadai, Setagaya-ku,
Tokyo. **Tel:** 03-5758-2491. **Fax:** 03-5758-2492.
Email: e-studio@tkc.att.ne.jp

English Telephone Club
1-19-28 Minami Oizumi, Nerima-ku, Tokyo. **Tel:**
03-3924-3853. **Fax:** 03-3978-0990. **Website:**
www.aoki.com/job/etc

Eurocentres Japan
2-12 Kanda Surugadai, Chiyoda-ku, Tokyo. **Tel:**
03-3295-5441. **Fax:** 03-3295-5443. **Email:**
euro-tyo@orange.ifnet.or.jp

Evergreen Language School
1-21-18 Yutenji, Meguro-ku, Tokyo. **Tel:**
03-3713-4958. **Fax:** 03-3719-4383. **Website:**
www.evergreen.gr.jp

**Executive Gogaku Centre (Executive
Language Centre)**
1 Kasumigaseki Building, 12F, 3-2-5 Kasumigaseki,
Chiyoda-ku,Tokyo 100.

English Circles/EC Inc.
President Building 3rd Floor, South-1, Chuo-Ku,
Sapporo 060. **Tel:** 011 221 0279.

FCC (Fukuoka Communication Centre)
Dai Roku Okabe Building, 5f, Hakata Eki Higashi,
2-4-17 Hakata-ku, Fukuoka 812.

F L Centre (Foreign Language Centre)
1 Iwasaki Building, 3f, 2-19-20 Shibuya-ku,Tokyo
150.

Four Seasons Language School
Aoyamashorin 2F, 4-32-11 Sanarudai, Hamamatsu-shi 432. Tel: 534 48 1501.

Fukuoka International School
3-18-50 Momochi, Sawara-ku, 814-0006 Fukuoka. Tel: 92- 841.7601, Fax: 92-841-7602, Email: adminfis@fka.att.ne.jp

Galaxy Language Academy
Noda Bldg., 2-12-1 Kami Osaki, Shinagawa-ku, Tokyo. Tel: 03-3473-3251. Fax: 03-3473-3334. Website: www.jade.dti.ne.jp/~galaxy Email: galaxy@jade.dti.ne.jp

Gateway Gakuin Rokko
Atelier House, 3-1-15 Yamada-cho, Nada-ku, Kobe.

GEOS Language System
Shin Osaki Bldg. 4F, 1-6-4 Osaki, Shinagawa-ku, Tokyo. Tel: 03-5434-0200.

Global English School
1887-86 Kubo-cho, Matsusaka, Mie 515-0044. Tel: 598-60-0873. Fax: 598-29-8730. Email: recruit@ges-hiro.co.jp

Gregg Int'l School of Language
1-14-16 Jiyugaoka, Meguro-ku, Tokyo. Tel: 03-3718-0552.

Gunma Language centre & Language Academy
840, Munadaka, Gunma 370-3521. Tel: 273-732310. Fax: 273-730846. Email: glc@mail.wind.co.jp

Hearts English School
2146-3 Shido, Shido-cho, Okawa-gun, Kagawa 769-21. Tel: 878 943557, Fax: 947227.

Hiroshima International School
3-49-1, Kurakake, Asakita-ku, 739-1743 Hiroshima. Tel: 82-843-4111, Fax: 82-843-6399, Email: hisadmin@orange.ocn.ne.jp

ICA Kokusai Kaiwa Gakuin (International Conversation Academy)
1 Mikasa 2 Building, 1-16-10 Nishi.

IF Foreign Language Institute
7f Shin Nakashima Building, 1-9-20 Nishi Nakashima, Yodogawa-ku, Osaka.

inlingua School of Languages
Kyodo Bldg. 9F, 2-4-2 Nihombashi Muromachi, Chuo-ku, Tokyo. Tel: 03-3231-0167. Fax: 03-3245-0086. Email: inlingua@fa.mbn.or.jp

INTECO Business English School
4-2-25 Akasaka, Minato-ku, Tokyo. Tel: 03-5570-2821 Fax: 03-5570-4323 Website: www2.gol.com/users/inteco/ Email: inteco@gol.com

Jelly Beans English School
16-908 Shinyashiki cho, Kagoshima City 892-0838. Tel: 90-2511-9733. Fax: 81-99-224-7595.

Kains English School in Gakko
1-5-2 Ohtemon Chuo-ku, Fukuoka 810.

KICC English and Computer School
1-8-13 Horai, Shingu, Wakayama 647. Tel: 735-28-2230. Fax: 735-28-2234. Email: kiccjob@kiccworld.com

King's Road School of English
Akasaka 4-3-9, Takaike Bldg 3F, Minato-ku, Tokyo 107. Tel: 03 3589 8666, Fax: 03 3589 7868.

Kyoto English Centre
Sumitomo Seimei Building, Shijo-Karasuma Nishi-iru Shimogyo-ku, Kyoto.

Kobe Language Centre
3-18 Wakinoharnacho, 1-chome, Chuo-ku, Kobe 651. Tel: 78 2614316.

Language Education Centre
7-32 chome Ohtemachi Nakaku, Hiroshima-shi 730.

London Study Centre
1-1 Tamanuki, Ohyama, Ohtama, Fukushima 969-1301. Tel: 0243 48 4286. Fax: 0243 48 4286. Email: londoneigakuin@hotmail.com

Luna International
1-2-9 Asahi, Matsumoto-shi 390-0802. Tel: 263-34-4481. Fax:263-34-4481.

Matty's School of English
3-15-9 Shonan-takatori, Yokosuka 234. Tel: 468 658717.

Michigan English School
Enya Bld. 2F, 7-34 Sanae-cho, Gifu-city, Gifu, 500-8304. Tel: 058 251 9421. Fax: 058 251 9850. Email: michigan@ktroad.ne.jp

MIL Language Centre
3.4F Eguchi Bldg, 1-6-2 Katsutadai, Yachiyo-shi, Chiba-ken 276. Tel: 474 857555.

Miyazaki College
2520-88, Hongo-kitakata, Miyazaki 880-0925. Tel: 985-52-7568. Fax: 985-52-7568.

Mobara English Institute
618-1 Takashi, Mobara-shi, Chiba-ken 297. Tel: 475 224785.

Mukogawa Women's University
Edagawa-cho 4-16, Nishinomiya-city, Hyogo-ken 545-0002. Tel: 0798-47-6436. Fax: 06-6719-2093.

NOVA Group
Harajuku Carillon Bldg. 4F, 1-8-9 Jingumae,
Shibuya-ku, Tokyo 150-0001. **Tel:** 03-3478-3475.
Fax: 03-3478-3665.)

Op-Net English Institute
Torinose 222-1, Iwata-shi, Shizuoka-ken 438-0072.
Tel: 0538 34 8686. **Fax:** 0538 36 1217. **Email:**
opnet1@peace.ne.jp

Ph.D. Language centre
743 Aramaki-machi, Maebashi-shi, Gunma-ken
371-0044. **Tel:** 027 233 8442. **Fax:** 027 233 8442.

Plus Alpha
2-25-20 Denenchofu, Ota-Ku, Tokyo 145.

Queens School of English
3f Yuzuki Bldg, 4-7-14 Minamiyawata, Ichikawa 272.

Pegasus Language Services
Sankei Building, 1-7-2 Otemachi Chiyoda-ku, Tokyo
100.

REC School of Foreign Language
Nijojo-mae Ebisugawasagaru Higashihorikawa-dori,
Nakagyo-ku, Kyoto.

Royal English Language Centre
4-31-3-2 Chyo Hakata-ku, Fukuoka 82.

Seido Language Institute
12-6 Funado-cho, Ashiya-shi, Kyoto.

Stanton School of English
12 Gobancho Chiyoda-ku, Tokyo 102.

Sumikin-Intercom, Inc
Andrew Vaughan, 7-28 Kitahama 4-Chome, Chou-ku,
Osaka 541 **Tel:** 06 220 5500, **Fax:** 06 220 5713.

Sun Eikaiwa School
6f Cherisu Hachoubori Building, 6-7 Hachoubori
Naka-ku, Hiroshima-shi 730.

Toefl Academy
1-12-4 Kundankita, Chiyoda-ku, Tokyo 102. **Tel:** (3)
2303500.

Tokyo English Centre
(TEC) 7-9 Uguisudai-cho, Shibuyaku, Tokyo 150.

Tokyo Language Centre
Tatsunama Building, 1-2-19 Yaesu, Chuo-Ku, Tokyo
103.

Tokyo YMCA College of English
7 Kanda Mitoshiro-Cho, Chiyoda-ku, Tokyo T-101.

Trident School of Languages
1-5-31 Imaike, Chikusa-ku, Nagoya 464.

Westgate HR Department
1173-1 Hagiwara, Gotemba Shizuoka 412-0042. **Fax:**
550-84-0770

World Language School Inc
Tokiwa Soga Ginko Building 4f 1-22-8 Jinnan,
Shibuya-ku, Tokyo 171.

KOREA (SOUTH)

A favourite destination for teachers of English over the
last 15 years, South Korea has witnessed rapid
economic growth and foreign investment, and even if
the economic situation is not as favourable as in the
past, there are still many opportunities. Korean is the
major language, but some Mandarin Chinese is spoken.
English is not widely spoken but is much sought after.
Crime is not a major problem but be aware that
nationalist sentiments are on the increase, particularly
in view of recent economic difficulties and sales to
foreign companies. As the number of teachers applying
to go to Korea has decreased you should be able to find
a job easily and, with the right qualifications, you can
secure some very favourable terms and conditions.
Many teachers are able to build up significant savings
while working in Korea.

In the past, many travellers took casual teaching
jobs on tourist visas. However, the government has
cracked down on illegal workers. Anyone found
working without a work permit will be deported and
any companies found employing illegal workers risk
being closed down.

One popular type of school is known as the
hagwon. These are privately-run schools where
Koreans learn English, usually on a daily basis before
they go to work in the morning or in the evenings. If
you teach in one of these schools, you'll be expected to
teach 20-30 hours a week and you'll have free time
during the day. Finding a job in a hagwon should not
be a problem, whether you are qualified or not, but you
should be aware that there has been a long and bitter
history of tension between EFL teachers and owners of
hagwons usually centred on contractual disputes. Go
into a job with your eyes open and be prepared to fight
your corner if problems arise. Remember that hagwons
are in fierce competition with one another and they do
go belly up from time to time. Try and get a reference
from a teacher already working at the hagwon you are
thinking of working for. Also, if you can have a
Korean-speaker help you go through your contract, it
may help you in the event of a dispute—the Korean
language contract takes precedence over the English
language version and the two do not always match up.
Another place to find a teaching job in Korea is in a
chaebol. These are the large corporations that dominate
business in Korea (like Hyundai). Many run their own

in-house English language programmes. Expect to work at least 30 hours a week from early morning until late at night. If you have an MA in TESOL you could look for a job in a university language institute. The institutes offer better pay and conditions than hagwons or the chaebol – so the staff turnover is low. Do not confuse working in a university foreign language institute with teaching in a university department. Departmental teaching involves conversational English classes with large numbers of university students for about 10-15 hours a week. Private lessons offer teachers the chance to supplement their incomes but you should know that working for another school other than your official employer or teaching privately is illegal. Some teachers have been imprisoned and/or deported for giving private lessons. If you do teach private students insist on payment in advance for the lessons.

In 1995, the Korean government started the EPIK (English programme in Korea) program, which sends English language instructors to work in Korean middle and high schools. EPIK participants are paid according to their qualifications anywhere from 1.6-2 million won a month. Airfares and accommodation are included in the package. In 2000, 392 teachers took part in the programme. Reactions from participants have been mixed — some teachers were unhappy at being placed in rural schools far from the big cities and contact with other foreigners. But most old Korea hands agree that it is a good way to be introduced to the country's culture and people. Contact your closest Korean consulate or embassy for more information. The website is http://cc.knue.ac.kr/~epik/off.htm

Embassy in UK:
60 Buckingham Gate, London SW1E 6AJ
Tel: 020 7227 5505

Embassy in USA:
2450 Massachusetts Avenue NW, Washington DC20008
Tel: 202 939 5600

British Council office:
Joongwhoo Building, 61-21 Taepyungro 1 Ka, Choong-ku, Seoul, Korea100-101
Tel +82 (2) 3702 0600
www.britishcouncil.or.kr

◆ **Visas/Work Permits:** In order to work legally in Korea, one must first obtain the appropriate employment visa. The Korean government tightly controls employment visas and sometimes teachers have been unable to obtain visas. A person who wishes to work in Korea must obtain the visa outside Korea. One can, however, come to Korea on a tourist visa, obtain sponsorship documents, and apply for the visa in a nearby country. Depending on the job and other factors, it can take between one week and two months to obtain the appropriate visa. A teacher arriving in Korea with a teaching visa must register with Korean Immigration and obtain a residence certificate and re-entry permit within 90 days of entry. Most English instructors are granted an E-2 visa (conversation instructor), an E-1 visa (professor at educational institution higher than a junior college), or an E-5 visa (professional employment with a public relations firm or corporation). Once you have your permit, do not allow your employer to keep your passport even if he or she says that you are obliged to do so – you are not!

◆ **Currency:** £1 = 1887 / $1 = 1020 Won.

◆ **Salaries/Taxes:** The average salary at a hagwon is equivalent to about £1,000 / $1,900 per month. You can earn £1,200 / $2,200 or more at a chaebol. University departments pay c. £1,000 / $1,900 per month while the foreign language institutes pay the highest salaries. It is possible to earn £30 / $57 per hour with private tuition. Taxation rates depend on how much you are actually making – they range from 10-40% of your income. There is also a residency tax of 7.5%. If your employer tries to deduct a "security deposit" from your wages for any reason, refuse (politely but firmly).

◆ **Accommodation:** Your employer should meet your accommodation needs otherwise renting an apartment is an expensive and complicated process. You will probably find yourself sharing a small apartment with some fellow teachers. Apartments vary in quality.

◆ **Cost of Living:** Korea is not a cheap place to live in — especially if you are fond of sampling the nightlife. This the reason why so many teachers risk deportation lured by the extra cash of private lessons.

◆ **Health advice:** Your employer should cover your insurance costs.

◆ **English Language Media:** Korea Herald, Korea Times.

Schools in South Korea (+81)

All Nations Community Church
Yuksamdong Youngdong APT 28-105, Yuksamdong 765, Seoul 135-082. **Tel:** (02) 555-0691.

ANC Language Institute
2nd Fl., Taeyoung Bldg., Daechi-dong, Kangnam-gu, Seoul. **Tel:** (02) 508-0081.

ANS Recruiters
Seocho-gu, Seocho-dong 1575-2, Soryong Bldg. 5th Fl. Seoul, Korea 137-070. **Tel:** (02) 3472-0020. **Fax:** (02) 3472-2173.

ARC Language Education
636-1 Shinsa-dong, Kangnam-gu, Seoul. **Tel:** (02) 511-9311.

BCM Institute (Konkuk University)
3nd Fl. Daeyang Bldg., 8-3 Noyu 1-dong, Kwangjin-gu, Seoul. **Tel:** (02) 499-0515. **Fax:** (02) 464-0516.

BCM Institute (Kuro)
1123-3 Kuro 3-dong, Kuro-gu, Seoul. **Tel:** (02) 830-2121. **Fax:** (02) 830-2124.

BCM Institute (Pundang)
4th Fl. Kwangrim Praza, Sohyon-dong, Pundang-gu, Kyonggi-do. **Tel:** (031) 708-9090. **Fax:** (031) 708-3161.

BCM Institute (Sanggye)
6th Fl. Kyongwon Bldg., Sanggye-dong, Nowon-gu, Seoul. **Tel:** (02) 933-8656. **Fax:** (02) 933-4525.

BCM Institute (Songpa)
11th Fl. Taemun Bldg., 174-2 Sokchon-dong, Songpa-gu, Seoul. **Tel:** (02) 412-2335. **Fax:** (02) 412-2350.

Berlitz Korea company
2nd Fl., Sungwoo Academy Bldg., 1316-17 Socho-dong, Socho-gu, Seoul. **Tel:** (02) 3481-5324.

Berlitz Language Centre (Ulchiro)
16th Fl. Ileun Jungkwon Bldg., 198 Ulchiro 2-ga, Chung-gu, Seoul. **Tel:** (02) 775-1441. **Fax:** (02) 775-8088.

Chungmoon Language Institute
18-4 Kwanchol-dong, Chongno-gu, Seoul. **Tel:** (02) 738-5151.**Fax:** (02) 738-6150.

CPI Foreign Language Academy
#2-24, Mullae-dong, Yongdungpo-gu, Seoul. **Tel:** (02) 723-8882. **Fax:** (02) 2631-0928. **Email:** sscyber@sscyber.com

Daewon Language School
3nd Fl. Hyundae Chonghap Sangga, 615 Shinsa-dong, Kangnam-gu, Seoul. **Tel:** (02) 3445-7221. **Fax:** (02) 3445-7791.

Ding Ding Dang English School
1275-3 Bummul-dong Soosung-gu, Taegu 706-100. **Fax:** (53) 782-6434. **Email:** dings@thrunet.com

E2 Foreign Language Institute
1F Lotte Hagwon Sangga, 63 Yong Ho Dong, Changwon, Kyungnam, 641-041. **Tel:** (55) 261-0888 **Fax:** (55) 261-0797 **Email:** mcleod@chollian.dacom.co.kr

ESS Language Institute
38-1, 1-ka Kwangbok-dong, Jung-ku, Pusan 600-131. **Tel:** (51) 246-3251. **Fax:** (51) 241-1988.

FSFA Institute of Junior English
Gu-wol Plaza 2F, 342-256, Gu-wol dong, Nam-dong Gu, Inchon. **Tel:** (32) 472-8636. **Fax:** (32) 472-8637. **Email:** DarrenFSFA2000@yahoo.com

Global Christian School
243-5 Pogwang-dong, Yongsan-gu, Seoul. **Tel:** (02) 797-0234. **Fax:** (02) 797-0401.

Good Teacher's Centre
271-19, Dong In-3Ga, Jung-Gu, Taegu 700-423. **Tel:** (53) 427-8291. **Fax:** (53) 427-8295. **Email:** gta@chollian.dacom.co.kr

JS Language School
1-190, Munwha-dong, Jung-ku, Daejon. **Tel:** (42) 252-3500. **Fax:** (42) 254-6452. **Email:** js@englishcampus.com

Jungjin Language Institute 1
5th Fl., Kyungdong Bldg., 130-1 Hyehyun 1-ga, Chung-gu, Seoul. **Tel:** (02) 753-5243.

Kangrung High School
886 Kyo-1 Dong, Kangrung City 210-101. **Tel:** (016) 297-2095. **Fax:** (031) 641-5118.

Kid's College
261-2 Yangjae-dong Seocho-gu, Seoul 137-130. **Tel:** (2) 529-3831. **Fax:** (2) 529-7809. **Email:** kidscollege@hotmail.com

Korea Foreign Language Institute
16-1 Kwanchol-dong, Chongno-gu, Seoul. **Tel:** (02) 739-8000. **Fax:** (02) 739-0602.

Korea Herald Institute (Hoehyondong)
9th Fl. Korea Herald Bldg., 1-12 Hoehyon-dong 3-ga, Chung-gu, Seoul. **Tel:** (02) 727-0271. **Fax:** (02) 727-0668.

Korea Herald Institute (Suhadong)
65-1 Suha-dong, Chung-gu, Seoul. **Tel:** (02) 757-0419. **Fax:** (02) 319-3936.

Latt
3nd Fl. Shinwon Bldg., Chungjongno 3-ga, Sodaemun-gu, Seoul. **Tel:** (02) 363-3291. **Fax:** (02) 313-5620.

L.A. Wilshire Language School Korea
4th Fl., Kyewon Bldg., 32-7 Kwanchol-dong, Chongno-gu, Seoul. **Tel:** (02)723-6600.

LovEnglish
Duckhwa Building, Room 401, 444-17, Seogyo-dong, Mapo-gu, Seoul 121-210. **Tel:** (02) 3141-3766. **Fax:** (2) 332-2245. **Email:** mhkim@lovenglish.com

Mido Foreign Language School
Mido Sang-Ga Bldg., 3rd Floor, 311, Dae-Chi Chong, Kang-nam Ku, Seoul 135-280. **Tel:** (2) 562-6714. **Fax:** (2) 563-1205. **Email:** mido1@uriel.net

Mokdong SLP
7F Whasung Plaza BL 909-5, Mok-dong Yangchun-ku, Seoul. **Tel:** (2) 654-7331. **Fax:** (2) 654-7335. **Email:** perryr@nuri.net

Naeja English Academy
19-2 Hyoja-dong, Chunchon City, Kangwon Province. **Tel:** (361) 242-0505. **Fax:** (361) 251-0594. **Email:**naeja@hanmail.net

Oedae Junior English Institute
4th Fl. 286 Wolpyong-dong, So-gu, Taejon. **Tel:** (042) 487-0545. **Fax:** (042) 487-0572.

Pagoda Foreign Language Institute (Abgujung)
2nd Fl. Dongwon Bldg., 598 Shinsa-dong, Kangnam-gu, Seoul. **Tel:** (02) 3442-4000. **Fax:** (02) 515-4030.

Pagoda Foreign Language Institute (Chongno)
56-6 Chongno 2-ga, Chongno-gu, Seoul. **Tel:** (02) 2274-4000. **Fax:** (02) 2278-7538.

Pagoda Foreign Language Institute (Kangnam)
816 Yoksam-dong, Kangnam-gu, Seoul. **Tel:** (02) 501-4002. **Fax:** (02) 3452-0203.

Pusan Foreign School
1492-8, Chung-Dong, Haeundae-Gu, Pusan 612-010. **Tel:** (51) 747-7199. **Fax:** : (51) 747-9196. **Email:** pfs@chollian.net

Seoul Academy
Young dong P.O. Box 85, Seoul 135-600. **Tel :** (02) 555-2475.

Sisa English Institute
19-23 Kwanchol-dong, Chongno-gu, Seoul. **Tel:** (02) 734-2442. **Fax:** (02) 720-4931.

Sisa Language Institute
1099-1 Sanpon, Kunpo-dong, Kyonggi-do. **Tel:** (031) 398-6445.

Sogang University
1-1 Sinsu-dong, Mapo-gu, Seoul 121-742. **Tel:** (2) 716-1230. **Fax:** (2) 705-8733. **Email:** johng@ccs.sogang.ac.kr

Space Corporation
2nd floor, 656-502, 1Dong, 1Ga, Sung Su-Dong Sung Dong-Gu, Seoul 133-821. **Tel:** (2) 2205-0213. **Fax:** (2) 2205-0382.

World Language School
19-16 Kumnaro-1 ka, Dung-ku, Kwangju 501-021. **Tel:** (62) 228-1723. **Fax:** (62) 226-3562. **Email:** worldedu@hotmail.com

YBM
Sisa Yongasa 5-3 Kwanchul-dong, Chongno-gu, Seoul. **Tel:** (02) 2276-0509. **Fax:** (02) 2271-0172.

YES English School
Daewon Bldg., 5th Fl., Daechi-dong 599, Kangnam-gu, Seoul 135-281. **Tel:** (2) 553-8880. **Fax:** (2) 553-5764. **Email:** yescho@nuri.net

LAOS

Unlike other southeastern Asian countries, Laos is only just starting to open up to the West. As a recently joined member of the Association of Southeast Asian Nations (ASEAN), which uses English as the language of communication, the Lao P.D.R. government has made the study of English a national priority. The national curriculum was recently rewritten to include an emphasis on English learning, and members of the government are eager to study English. Most English language teaching is done by volunteers but there are limited opportunities for teachers at private language schools in Vientiane and possibility of work at universities.

⮑ **Visas/Work Permits:** You can obtain a tourist visa (good for two weeks) at the border or at the airport in Vientiane. A one-month visa offered by a sponsor can be extended. Work permits are hard to acquire and the government is strict about illegal workers.

⮑ **Currency:** £1 = 19147 / $1 = 10350 Kip

⮑ **Salaries/Taxes:** You can make anywhere from $1,200-2,000 a month less income tax of 10%.

⮑ **Accommodation:** The school should assist you with accommodation.

⮑ **Cost of Living:** Laos is much cheaper than neighbouring Thailand to live in but some basic items are hard to find.

⮑ **Health advice:** Medical facilities and services are severely limited and do not meet Western standards. The blood supply is not screened for HIV or AIDS. Visitors should be aware that there have been a number of bombings in public places and to be vigilant at all times.

Schools In Laos (+856)

Lao American Language Centre
152 Sisangvone Road, Saysettha, Ban Naxay, P.O. Box 327, Vientiane. **Tel:** 21 41 4321, **Fax:** 21 41 3760.

National University of Laos
Dept. of English, Dong Dok Campus, Vientiane.

Vientiane International School
P.O. Box 3180, Vientiane. **Tel:** 21-313606, **Fax:** 21-315008, **Email:** VIS@panlaos.net.la

Vientiane University College
P.O. Box 4144, Vientiane. **Tel:** 21 414873, **Fax:** 21 414 346.

MALAYSIA

Malaysia offers a relatively high standard of living, a stunning natural environment, and easy access to many of the other countries in the region. It is difficult for foreign teachers to find a job here because of strict labour laws and current economic problems. English is widely spoken throughout the country.

British Council office:

PO Box 10539, 50916 Kuala Lumpur
Tel +60 (3) 2723 7900
www.britishcouncil.org/malaysia

➲ **Visas/Work Permits:** Most teachers go to Malaysia on a tourist visa (Valid for 90 days) and then look for jobs. The number of work permits allocated to foreigners are limited: teachers have to have an MA, teaching experience and be between 26-55 years old to qualify for one. Be prepared to spend up to a year doing "visa runs" to Singapore, Thailand or Indonesia if you are working without a permit.

➲ **Currency:** £1 = 6.8 / $1 = 3.7 Malaysian ringgit.

➲ **Salaries/Taxes:** Local salaries are reasonable if you are not planning to send money home. Teachers earn around 2,500-4,000 ringgits per month. Income tax is 5% (once you have a permit) but the rate leaps to 30% if you spend less than 165 consecutive days in the country.

➲ **Accommodation:** Rents are very high for Asia. Expect to share accommodation with others.

➲ **Cost of Living:** Reasonable with lots of products available in Kuala Lumpur.

➲ **Health advice:** The standard of medical care is very high in the major cities where credit cards are usually accepted.

➲ **English Language Media:** The Borneo Post (Sabah and Sarawak), The Daily Express (Sabah), The New Straits Times, The Malay Mail, The Sarawak Tribune, The Star, The Sun.

Schools in Malaysia (+60)

Bangsar English Language Centre
60-1 Jalan Ma'arof Bangsar Baru, 59100 Kuala Lumpur. **Tel:** 3 282 3166/68, **Fax:** 3 282 5578.

Centre for Language and Communications Studies
University Malaysia Sarawak, 94300 Kota Samarahan, Samarahan, Sarawak.

Centre for Promoting Language and Knowledge
University Malaysia Sabah, Temporary Campus Likas Bay, Locked bag 2073, 88999 Kota Kinabalu, Sabah.

The English Language Centre
1st Floor, Lot 2067, Block 10, K.C.L.D., Jalan Keretapi, PO Box 253, 93150 Kuching, Sarawak.

International Tuition School
PO Box 3062, 93760 Kuching, Sarawak. **Tel:** 82 480780, **Fax:** 82 416250.

IPOH Learning and Training Institute
6 Jalan Tambun, 30350 Ipoh, Perak. **Tel:** 5 255 3067, **Fax:** 5 255 7136.

Kinabulu Commercial College
3rd & 4th Floors, Wisma Sabah, Kota Kinabulu, Sabah.

Kinabulu International School
PO Box 12080, 88822 Kota Kinabalu, Sabah.

Lodge Preparatory School
Jalan Tabuan Jaya, 93550 Kuching, Sarawak.

University Malaysia - Sarawak
94300 Kota Samarahan, Sarawak. **Tel:** 82 671000, **Fax:** 82 672315.

MONGOLIA

Teachers who have experienced Mongolia report that the country has a harsh but fascinating beauty. The capital, Ulaanbaatar, suffers from pollution but visiting the surrounding steppes is a must do. There are many opportunities to teach English here, including volunteer workers (notably the Peace Corps). Most of the teaching involves young learners in the public schools system. Flights to and from Mongolia should be arranged by your organization.

⟳ **Visas/Work Permits:** It is common practice for a school to reimburse you for the cost of your visa when you have completed your contract. Visas may be obtained at the international airport in Ulaanbaatar and at train stations on the Russian and Chinese borders. Two photographs and a $50 processing fee are required.

⟳ **Currency:** £1 = 2360 / $1 = 1280 Tugrik.

⟳ **Salaries/Taxes:** Some schools in Ulaanbaatar pay around $3.50 for a 45-minute lesson based on 20-24 teaching hours per week. At other schools, like those in smaller cities like Erdenet, expect around $100 a month, which is more than adequate to live on.

⟳ **Accommodation:** Simple accommodation (including utilities) should be provided by your employer.

⟳ **Cost of Living:** Very reasonable if you develop a taste for yak's milk!

⟳ **Health advice:** Medical facilities in Mongolia are very limited, and some medicines are unavailable. Infectious diseases, such as plague and meningococcal meningitis, are present at various times of the year. Your school should provide medical cover.

Schools in Mongolia (+976)

Battsetseg Namnansuren
Box-346, Central Post Office, Ulaanbaatar-13. **Tel:** 9611-5597. **Fax:** 1-459732.

Eagle English Language School
Erdenet 976-35. **Tel:** 9935-1450. **Fax:** 35-73978. **Email:** rinchin@erdnet.mn

International School of Ulaanbaatar
P.O. Box 49/564, Ulaanbaatar. **Tel:** 1-452-959. **Fax:** 1-358-375. **Email:** inschool@magicnet.mn

Mongol Caravan, Inc.
P.O. Box 191, Clifton, NJ 07011. **Tel:** (973) 594-0655. **Fax:** (209) 729-4674. **Email:** mc@mongolcaravan.com

Santis Educational Services
P.O. Box 1174, Ulaanbaatar 210657. **Fax:** 32-3276. **Email:** santis@magicnet.mnw

MYANMAR

The current government restrictions on foreigners make it very difficult to find a teaching job in Myanmar (formerly Burma). Access to the Internet is strictly monitored by the present regime. The U.S. government has forbidden American companies to make new investments in the country while human rights abuses continue in Myanmar. General dissatisfaction with public universities has led to the opening of large numbers of private schools, many of which teach English. If the political situation improves, Myanmar could develop into a leading destination for EFL teachers.

⟳ **Visas/Work Permits:** A single entry visa is good for a stay of 28 days.

⟳ **Health advice:** Medical facilities in Myanmar are inadequate for even routine medical care. There are few trained medical personnel because the universities were closed for several years and have recently reopened.

Schools in Myanmar (+951)

The British Council
78 Kanna Road, P.O. Box 638, Yangon. **Tel:** (951) 254658. **Fax:** 245345 **Email:** malcolm.jardine@bc-burma. bcouncil.org

NEPAL

Nepal is an impoverished country with great educational needs: the adult literacy rate in Nepal in 1995 was just 41% for men and a meagre 14% for women. It is possible to land a job teaching English at a private language school in Kathmandu, the backpacking capital of the world, but most teachers will not make enough money to survive unless they have funds of their own to fall back on.

There are aid agencies and Christian groups working with schools throughout and you might find a job in Nepal by taking this route.

British Council office:
PO Box 640, Lainchaur, Kathmandu
Tel +977 (1) 410 798
www.britishcouncil.org/nepal

⟳ **Visas/Work Permits:** A tourist visa is extendible to a maximum period of 150 days in one visa year (January to December). Working for a school will allow you to remain in the country for up to a year.

⟳ **Currency:** £1 = 129 / $1 = 70 Rupees

⟳ **Salaries/Taxes:** You can earn around £60 / $110 a month in a private language school but remember that Nepal is a very poor country — you are not here for the money!

⮁ **Accommodation:** You can find a small apartment for $150-200 per month. Volunteers will have housing provided for them.

⮁ **Cost of Living:** Estimate £300-350 / $570-650 per month as a comfortable amount.

⮁ **Health advice:** Medical care is extremely limited and is generally not up to Western standards. Serious illnesses often require evacuation to the nearest adequate medical facility (in Singapore, Bangkok or New Delhi). Illnesses and injuries suffered while on trek in remote areas often require rescue by helicopter. The cost is typically £1,800 - 6,000 / $3,300 - 11,000. Medical insurance is essential.

⮁ **English Language Media:** Kathmandu Post, The Rising Nepal.

Schools in Nepal (+977)

Debbie's English Language Institute
Jamal, Kathmandu. **Tel:** 1-248140.

Friendship Club Nepal
P.O. Box 11276, Maharajgunj, Kathmandu. **Tel:** 1-427406. **Email**: fcn@ccsl.com.np

Grahung Kalika
(Walling Village Development Committee), Bartung, Ward 2, Syngja. **Fax:** 1-262878.

Insight Nepal
P.O. Box 489, Zero K.M. Pokhara, Kaski. **Email:** insight@clcexp.mos.com.np

Universal Language & Computer Institute
Putalisadak, Kathmandu. **Tel:** 1-419443.

PAKISTAN

It is best to arrange a job before coming to Pakistan, as there are few private language schools in the country. There is a small demand for TEFL teachers although most children learn English in the public schools. Do not take on private lessons unless your contract stipulates that you may do so. The authorities will not be pleased if you are caught working illegally.

High Commission in UK:
935 Lowndes Square, London SW1X 9JN
Tel: 020 76649220

Embassy in USA:
2315 Massachusetts Avenue, Washington DC20008
Tel: 202 939 6200

British Council office:
House 1, Street 61, F-6/3, P.O. Box 1135, Islamabad

Tel +92 (51) 111 424 424
www.britishcouncil.org/pk

⮁ **Visas/Work Permits:** paperwork will be taken care of by your employer.

⮁ **Salaries/Taxes:** A TEFL teacher can earn £10,000-12,000 / $19,000-22,000 a year.

⮁ **Accommodation:** This should be provided by your employer.

⮁ **Health advice:**Adequate medical care is available in major cities in Pakistan, but is limited in rural areas. Your employer should provide you with medical insurance.

Schools in Pakistan (+92)

Pakistan American Cultural Center (PACC)
Head Office, 11 Fatima Jinnah Road, Karachi. **Tel:** 5670516/5670513/515305.

Pakistan American Cultural Center (PACC)
Hyderabad centre, Hospital Road, Hyderabad. **Tel:** (0221) 619854/618854.

Pakistan American Cultural Center (PACC)
Karimabad centre, 54-C, Block 8, Federal B Area, Karimabad. **Tel:** 6363277.

Pakistan American Cultural Center (PACC)
Lahore centre, 25 E-3, Gulberg III, Lahore. **Tel:** (042) 5756438 / 5763644.

Pakistan American Cultural Center (PACC)
Peshawar centre, c/o St. John's School, 1, Sir Syed Rd., Peshawar. **Tel:** (0521) 279734.

Pakistan American Cultural Center (PACC)
Quetta centre, Sadiq Shaheed Park, Arbab Mohammad Khair Road, Mali Bagh, Quetta. **Tel:** (081) 826970 / 830889.

SINGAPORE

This wealthy city-state is popular with British and Australian EFL teachers. The demand here is for well-qualified teachers with a lot of experience and it is harder to find a job here than in other Asian countries.

High Commission in UK:
9 Wilton Crescent, London SW1X 8SP
Tel: 020 7235 8315
www.mfa.gov.sg/london

Embassy in USA:
3501 International Place, Washington DC20008
Tel: 202 537 3100

British Council office:
30 Napier Road, 258509
Tel +65 6473 1111
www.britishcouncil.org/singapore

⊃ **Visas/Work Permits:** U.S. citizens can stay for 90 days without a visa.

⊃ **Currency:** £1 = 3.01 / $1 = 1.63 Dollar (S$).

⊃ **Salaries/Taxes:** An average salary in Singapore is S$2,500 a month.

⊃ **Accommodation:** Apartments start at around S$1,200 a month.

⊃ **Cost of Living:** You can get by on S$2,000 a month.

⊃ **English Language Media:** Straits Times.

Schools in Singapore (+65)

Advanced Training Techniques (ATT)
Tanglin Shopping Centre, 19 Tanglin Road, Singapore 247909. **Tel:** 235 5222, **Fax:** 738 1257.

American College
25 Paterson Road, Singapore 0923. **Tel:** 235 9537.

Canadian International School
5 Toh Tuck Road, Singapore 2159. **Tel:** 467 1732.

Coleman Commercial and Language Centre
Peninsula Plaza, Singapore. **Tel:** 336 3462.

Corrine Private School
Selegie Complex 04-277, Selegie Road, Singapore 188350. **Tel:** 339 5564.

Dimensions Language Centre
50 East Coast Road, Singapore 0238.

Dover Court Preparatory School
Dover Road, Singapore 0513. **Tel:** 775 7664.

ILC Language and Business Training Centre
545 Orchard Road, 11-07 Far East Shopping Centre, Singapore 238882. **Tel:** 338 5415.

inlingua School of Languages
1 Grange Road, 04-01 Orchard Building, Singapore 239693. **Tel:** 737 6666.

International School
21 Preston Road, Singapore 0410. **Tel:** 475 4188.

Language Teaching Institute of Singapore
30 Orange Grove Road, Singapore 258352. **Tel:** 737 9044.

Linguamedia
230 Orchard Road, 04-230 Faber House, Singapore, 238854. **Tel:** 235 2620. **Fax:** 235 2080.

Morris Allen Study Centre
1 Newton Road 02-47/49, Goldhill Plaza, Singapore 307943. **Tel:** 253 5737.

St. Francis Methodist School
11 Mount Sophia, Singapore 228461. **Tel** 334 8944. **Fax:** 337 1825. **Email:** stfrancm@mbox5.signet.com.sg

TAIWAN

Prospects for English language teachers are very good in Taiwan, especially for native speakers of American English. Private schools (bushibans) pay well and jobs are easy to find. Unqualified travellers can find work here as long as they have a degree. The school year begins on August 1 and the winter semester starts on February 1. Local papers start carrying ads for English language teaching jobs in the spring. You should bring between £750-1500 / $1,300-$2,200 to cover you for about five weeks until you get your first full salary cheque. If you pre-arrange a teaching job before you travel to Taiwan, you may find that you are making less money than fellow teachers who arrived here and then found a job. But remember that you will not have to go through all the hassles of getting the right permits which can be very complicated since the authorities in Taiwan cracked down on freelance teachers working without the correct papers.

British Council office:
Education and Cultural Section, 7F-1, Fu Key Building, No 99 Jen Ai Road, Section 2, Taipei 100
Tel +886 (2) 2192 7050
www.britishcouncil.org.tw

⊃ **Visas/Work Permits:** Most teachers go to Taiwan on a tourist visa. Try to get a 60-day visa, as your paperwork will take 3-6 weeks to process: If your visa runs out before your paperwork is processed you will have to leave the country to obtain another resident visa. Many teachers go to Hong Kong, Singapore or Thailand to do this. If you enroll for Chinese language lessons at a government-recognized school, you can renew your visa without having to leave the country. To teach legally in Taiwan, the government requires that all foreign teachers obtain a Work Permit and an Alien Resident Certificate. To be eligible for these, you must: possess a bachelor's degree or higher, a contract

of employment and a health certificate from a government-approved hospital. You will be expected to pay for the health exam and the processing fees.

➲ **Currency:** £1 = 59.2 / $1 = 31.7 New Dollar (NT$)

➲ **Salaries/Taxes:** Monthly wages for teachers in language schools usually average between NT$30,000 and NT$70,000 net depending on the number of classes taught, and the number of students in each class. An entry-level salary for an assistant professor is about NT$73,000 per month (including a $10,000/month bonus for those with PhDs); for a lecturer, the figure is about NT$52,000 per month. Taxes are 20% until you have worked in Taiwan for 183 days in the same calendar year. The rate then drops to 10%. If you have been in the country for more than 183 days you are eligible for a tax refund in the next year.

➲ **Cost of Living:** A quick lunch costs NT$100.

➲ **Health advice:** Teachers working for the larger and more reputable schools are usually covered under group plans where they might make a contribution (around 30%) from their pay packets. Medical insurance is essential for freelancers unless you have a residency permit in which case you will be covered under the state system.

➲ **English Language Media:** China News, China Post.

Schools in Taiwan (+886)

American Children School
Chung Shan North Road, Sec. 6, #34, Taipei. **Tel:** 2-2831-6664.

American Culture University
Hsu Chang Street, #40, 7F, Taipei. **Tel:** 2-2311-8889.

Bao Bei Yuan English School
Jian Guo South Road, Sec. 1, Lane 270, #28, Taipei.. **Tel:** 2-2754-8066.

Bei Song Language School
Chung Hsiao East Road, Sec. 6, #436, Taipei. **Tel:** 2-2788-7778.

Big Bird English
Hsin Yi Road, Sec. 4, #181, 2F, Taipei. **Tel:** 2-2754-8405.

Big Byte English School
Hsin Hai Road, Sec. 2, #35, Taipei. **Tel:** 2-2369-2868.

Canadian-American Language Schools
2 Chien Hua Street, 2nd Floor, Hsinchu, 300. **Tel:** 3-562-0535. **Fax:** 3-561-6905. **Email:** employment@can-am.org

Chang Chun English
Ji Long Road, Sec. 2, #260, 2F, Taipei. **Tel:** 2-2735-2617.

Cheng Dan Language Centre
Hang Chou Road, Sec. 1, Lane 71, #9, Taipei. **Tel:** 2-2381-5147.

Ching Shan English
Hsin Sheng South Road, Sec. 3, #98, 3F, Taipei. **Tel:** 2-2366-1855.

David's English Centre
Nan Jing East Road, Sec. 2, #100, 3F, Taipei. **Tel:** 2-2522-4004.

Disney English
Hoping East Road, Sec. 2, Lane 96, Taipei. **Tel:** 2-2732-8969.

Dong Han English
Hoping East Road, Sec. 2, #100, 4F, Taipei. **Tel:** 2-2732-2771.

English Bridge School
Ching Hsing Road, Lane 202, No. 8, 2F, Taipei. **Tel:** 2-2933-5118.

Everyday English
Chung Hsiao East Road, Sec. 4, #177, 4F, Taipei. **Tel:** 2-2741-8989.

Gauden Language School
48 Jing Shiou East Road, Yuan Lin, Changhwa, 510. **Tel:** No: 4- 8368176. **Fax:** 4-8350431. **Email:** gauden@ms11.hinet.net

Giraffe English Centre
Shi Pai Road, Sec. 1, #160, 1F, Taipei. **Tel:** 2-2822-5815.

Gram English Centre
4th fl., 116 Yung Ho Rd., Sec. 2, Yung Ho City 234, Taipei County. **Tel:** 2-2927-2478. **Fax:** 2-2926-2183. **Email:** gram@ms7.hinet.net

Great Time English
Min Chuan East Road, Sec. 3, Lane 60, #10, Taipei. **Tel:** 2-2506-3033.

Han Bang Language School
Chung Yuan Road, #17, 2F, Taipei. **Tel:** 2-2531-6835.

He Jing Language School
Dun Hua South Road, Sec. 1, Lane 100, Alley 5, #37, 2F, Taipei. **Tel:** 2-2731-2822.

Hers English School
Wo Long Street, #1, 11F-2, Taipei. **Tel:** 2-2378-0186.

Hess Educational Organization
English Human Resources Department, 419 Chung Shan Rd., Section 2, Chung-Ho City 235, Taipei County. **Tel:** 2-3234-6188 ext. 1053/ 1052. **Fax:** 2-2222-9499. **Email:** hesswork@hess.com.tw

Jya Ying English
Jwang Jing Road, Lane 325, #37, Taipei. **Tel:** 2-2723-5259.

Kid Castle
Min Chuan Rd., No.98, 8F, Taipei. **Tel:** 2-2218-5996 ext.319/341.

Lang Wen English Centre
Jin Jou Street, #16, 3F, Taipei. **Tel:** 2-2551-8956.

Lian Hsin English
Fu Hsing North Road, #92, 7F, Taipei. **Tel:** 2-2773-6161.

Little Forest
4th Floor 121-5 Da Chang 2nd Rd., Kaohsiung. **Tel:** 7-395-6736. **Fax:** 7-733-4288. **Email:** jyy@usa.net

Melody English centre
San Min Area, Bei Ping 2nd Street, #6, 6F, Kaohsiung. **Tel:** 7-322-7492.

Min Sheng English School
Min Sheng East Road, Sec. 5, #226-1, Taipei. **Tel:** 2-2769-9243.

Ming Tai Language School
Chung Hua Road, Sec. 1, #178, Taipei. **Tel:** 2-2311-0712.

Pai Han Language School
Bo Ai Road 1st Road, #43, Kaohsiung. **Tel:** 7-316-1518.

Sen Yuan Language Centre
Jian Guo Road, #258, Kaohsiung. **Tel:** 7-395-6736.

Timothy Language Institute
Cheng Kung Road, Lane 213, No. 97. Tainan County, Jiali. **Tel:** 6- 723-2819.

Tom's English
Shwun Hsing Road, #95, Hualien. **Tel:** 38-822-2059.

Wen Tzao English
Yong Fu Road, Sec. 2, #83, 7F, Tainan. **Tel:** 6-228-2818.

Woodpecker English School
Bo Ai Road, #282, Pingtung. **Tel:** 8-733-8691.

Ya Ya
Chwei Yang Road, #199, 2F, Chiayi. **Tel:** 5-223-0358.

Twinkle Language Centre
66 Hsyn Hai Road, Tso Ying District 813, Kaohsiung. **Tel:** 7-557-1883. **Email:** twinklelanguagecentre@yahoo.com

THAILAND

There are many opportunities to teach English in Thailand, particularly in the universities. Most teachers find work in Bangkok, which is the economic, cultural and educational hub of the country. Although there was a slump in English language teaching because of the Asian economic crisis, the situation is improving. English language schools are looking for qualified teachers — the market for native-speaking beach bums has dried up.

Embassy in UK:
29 Queens Gate, London SW7 5JB
Tel: 020 7589 2944

Embassy in USA:
1024 Wisconsin Avenue, Suite 401, Washington DC20007
Tel: 202 944 3600

British Council office:
254 Chulalongkorn Soi 64, Siam Square, Phayathai Road, Pathumwan, Bangkok 10330
Tel +66 (2) 252 5480
www.britishcouncil.org/th

➲ **Visas/Work Permits:** In order to get a work permit you need at least a bachelors' degree and some form of TEFL certification. Before you can apply for a work permit you need a Non-Immigrant 'B' visa. These are three-month visas that initially allow you to be employed in Thailand. To get the visa, you need a copy of a letter from your prospective employer clearly stating that you have been offered a job. For private companies you need a copy of the said company's registration documents, if you're working for a government establishment this isn't required, and two passport sized photos. Embassies usually take two days to process the visa. Most Thai embassies work on the system that you apply for visas in the morning and collect them the next afternoon. Once you have found a job and can prove to the Immigration officials that you are applying for a work permit you can extend the three-month visa for another nine months.

➲ **Currency:** £1 = 68 / $1 = 39 Baht

➲ **Salaries/Taxes:** There is a wide range of salaries for teaching English in Thailand. Working a typical

20-25 hour week can earn you anywhere from as little as 10,000 baht a month for an unqualified teacher in a small provincial school to 60,000 baht or more for a TEFL teaching professional in a well-established school or college in Bangkok or another large city. Teachers at language schools pay around 25-35,000 baht per month in tax. Income earned by a U.S. resident from teaching in Thailand is exempt from income tax if the following conditions are met: (1) The teacher is a resident of the U.S.A. before he/she comes to teach in Thailand; (2) The teacher teaches in a university, college or other recognized educational institution in Thailand; (3) It must be his/her first visit for teaching in Thailand; and (4) He/she does not teach in Thailand for more than two years.

⊃ **Accommodation:** In most cases, teachers are expected to find their own accommodation. Studios in Bangkok cost around 5,000 baht a month while a one-bedroom apartment is anywhere from 8-18,000 baht.

⊃ **Cost of Living:** You can get a three-course meal for two people without alcohol for under 100 baht. If you can't do without imported items you will spend a lot of money because they are heavily taxed.

⊃ **Health advice:** Basic coverage for a single teacher will cost you at least 15,000 baht.

⊃ **English Language Media:** Bangkok Post, The Nation.

Schools in Thailand (+66)

Adanac Community Language Centre
Suite 605 Bangkok Tower, 2170 New Petchburi Rd., Bangkok 10320. **Tel/Fax:** 3080787-90

American University Alumni (AUA) Language Center
24 Rajadamnern Road, Chiang Mai 50200. **Tel:** 53-211-973. **Fax:** 53-211-973. **Email:** aualanna@loxinfo.co.th

Anna's Language School & Travel Services
116 Phisitgaranee Road, Patong Beach, Phuket 83150. **Tel:** 296372. Fax: 296423 **Email:** annatran@samart.co.th

Arundel Language Institute (A.L.I.)
61/67 Soi 10/3 Pechkasem Rd, Hat Yai, Songkla, 90110. **Tel:** 74 345 341-2. **Fax:** 74 345 342. **Email:** ali@loxinfo.co.th

Asia Institute of English
59 Sukhumvit 56, Bangchak , Prakanong, Bangkok 10250. **Tel:** 741- 5970-2. **Email:** AIE@a-net.net.th

Bangkok Patana School
2/38 Soi Lasalle, Sukhumvit 105, 10260 Bangkok. **Tel:** 2 398 0200. **Fax:** 2 399 3179. **Email:** patanarc@loxinfo.co.th/patreg@loxinfo.co.th

The Bell Educational Trust
Thailand, 204/1 Ranong 1 Road, Samsen, Dusit, Bangkok 10300. **Tel:** 2 241 0356. **Fax:** 2 668 2124. **Email:** gbradd@loxinfo.co.th

Berlitz Silom
191 Silom Complex Building, 22F Silom Road, Bangkok 10500. **Tel:** 2 231 3652. **Fax:** 2 231 3656.

Berlitz Sukhumvit
Times Square Bldg, 14F, 2246 Sukhumvit Road, Bangkok 10110. **Tel:** 2 250 0950. **Fax:** 2 250 0907.

Bright Future Language Centre
7th floor, Room 107, Sibunruang 2 Building, 1/7 Convent Road, Silom, Bangkok 10500. **Tel:** 2 631 0497. **Fax:** 2 631 0498. **Email:** bright@idn.co.th

Cambridge World International English Language Schools
296-300 Sukhumvit Road, Paknam.

Charansanitwong School of Business (CSB)
Charansanitwong Soi 41 Charansanitwong Rd.,

Bangkoknoi
Bangkok 10700. **Tel:** 8824676 **Fax:** 4333647. **Email:** NewCambridge@excite.com

Company English Language Centre of Excellence
Prince of Songkla University Wichitsongraram Rd, A. Kathu Phuket 83120. **Tel:** 202556 / 7. **Fax:** 202558 **Email:** h&t@ratree.psu.ac.th

English and Computer College (ECC)
430/17-24 Chula Soi 64, Siam Square, Bangkok 10330. **Tel:** 2-253-3312; **Email:** eccthai@comnet3.th.

EF - English First
Suite 701, 7th Fl. Sibunruang 2 Bldg. 1/7 Convent Rd., Silom, Bangrak, Bangkok 10500. **Tel:** 2-631-0497/8. **Fax:** 2-631-0499. **Email:** teach@efenglish.com

English Language Centre
Assumption University, Ramkhamhaeng 24 Road, Huamark, Bangkapi, Bangkok 10240. **Fax:** 2 318 7159. **Email:** elc@au.edu

English Language Instructors
PO Box 604 Amphur Muang, Phuket 83000. **Tel:** 282230.

Fun English Language Programme
Pichaya Suksa School, Pakkret, Nonthaburi. **Tel:** 1-313-8319. **Fax:** 2-373-8938. **Email:** ayatan@mozart.inet.co.th

Fun English Language Programme
Yamsaard School, Lard-Praow Road, Bangkok. **Tel:**
1-313-8319. **Fax:** 2-373-8938. **Email:**
ayatan@mozart.inet.co.th

In Company Ltd.
206/1 Nawanakorn, Pathumthani 12120. **Tel:** 2 909
1569. **Email:** patricks@samart.co.th

inlingua International School of Languages
Central Chidlom Tower, 22 Ploenchit Road,
Patumwan, 10330 Bangkok. **Tel:** 2 254 7028-30. **Fax:**
2 254 7098. **Email:** inlingua.bkk@inlingua.com

International Community School
72 Soi Prong Jai, Sathorn, 10120 Bangkok. **Tel:** 2 679
7175. **Fax:** 2 287 4530. **Email:** icsbkk@loxinfo.co.th

International School Bangkok
39/7 Soi Nichada Thani, Samakee Road, 11120
Pakkret. **Tel:** 2 583 5401-19. **Fax:** 2 583 5431-2.
Email: reyadik@isb.ac.th

Kaplan
Bangkok Bank Siam 5th floor, 394 Rama 1 Road,
Siam Square Soi 5, Bangkok 10330. **Tel:** 2 658-3991 /
2. **Fax:** 2 658-4354.

NAVA Language School
183/105-106 Phang-Nga Rd, A. Muang, Phuket 83000.
Tel: 238398/9 **Fax:** 238397. **Email:**
nava@phuket.a-net.net.th

NAVA Language Schools
34 Yosawadi Bldg, Ground floor, Paholyothin 7 Road
(Soi Aree) Samsen-nai, Payathai, Bangkok. **Tel:** 617
1390-3. **Email:** nava3@navaed.co.th

PEP Kindergarten

973 Ladproaw 48, Bangkok 10310. **Tel:** 2 277 8170.
Fax: 2 276 2916. **Email:** maes2@hotmail.com

P.E.T.S.
160/1-2 Praram 6 Muang Trang 92000. **Tel:** 075
215556. **Email:** ffracs@hotmail.com

Rajabhat Institute Surin
186 Surin-Prasart Road, Muang District, Surin 32000.
Tel: 44 511 604. **Fax:** 44 511 631. **Email:**
intanin@risurin.nepnet.ac.th

St. Stephen's International School
107 Viphavadi Rangsit Road, Ladyao Chatuchak,
Bangkok 10900. **Tel:** 2 513 0270. **Fax:** 2 513 0265.
Email: richard@ocean.co.th

Sarasas Witaed Suksa School
300 Moo 10 Pracha Utid Rd., Naiklongbangplakot,
Samut Prakarn,Bangkok 10270. **Tel:** 2 815 7540. **Fax:**
2 815 7541. **Email:** saraswitaed@hotmail.com

Siam Computer & Language School
2 Soi 7, Phang-Nga Road Amphur Muang, Phuket
83000. **Tel:** 219914/5.

Taiyo Co. Ltd.
3F, Prasarnmit Plaza, Sukhumvit Road, Soi 23Klong
Toey, Bangkok 10110. **Tel:** 2 6641630-2. **Fax:** 2
6641630. **Email:** taiyobkk@yahoo.com

Training Creativity Development (TCD)
399/7 Soi Thongloh 21, Sukhumvit Soi 55, Bangkok
10110. **Tel/Fax:** 2 391 5670.

Universal International School
49 Moo 4, Thanarat Road, Tambol Nongnamdaeng,
Amphur Pak Chong, Nakorn Ratchasima 30130. **Tel:**
44 328 334. **Fax:** 44 313 519.

Teaching in Thailand

Well, how about Thailand? You may well have seen the TV and print ads extolling the virtues
of Thailand, 'The Land of Smiles', and Bangkok, 'The City of Angels'. New Year's Resolution
No. 1 "I Really Want To Teach Somewhere Hot & Sunny". But is life as an English language
teacher as idyllic as these slogans suggest? Well, I've been here for three and a half years so it
can't be too bad. Hopefully the following article will equip you with enough basic information
to ascertain whether you are ready for Thailand and whether Thailand is ready for you.

Thailand has never been colonized, unlike most South East Asian countries. While Thais
are justifiably proud of this fact, there is actually a long history of English teaching in Thailand
and an English teaching methodology has developed over a long period of time. Indeed, in the
majority of Thai schools and colleges, English is taught in the same manner as every other
subject—learning by rote.

Average students in Malaysia, Singapore and the Philippines usually have a much higher standard of English than their peers in Thailand. In an effort to correct this imbalance and make up lost ground on fellow ASEAN countries, the government has recently introduced new legislation to try to replace the old "chalk and talk" teaching methods with student centred activities. Although this idea is commendable, schools and individual teachers have been rather too quick to point out obstacles rather than channelling their thoughts constructively. As with many good ideas, implementation is often delayed indefinitely and/or the original proposal/law altered beyond all recognition or scrapped entirely. According to the local press, the Education Reform Bill 2000 appears, unfortunately, to be heading for oblivion.

With respect to the availability of jobs in Thailand, teaching in Thailand equates to teaching in Bangkok. I'd estimate that over 90% of the foreign teachers working in Thailand are working in Bangkok. It's best to think of Bangkok and the rest of Thailand as two separate entities when it comes to teaching opportunities, salaries, job prospects, standard of living and so on.

If you have a notion of coming to Thailand, heading down to the beaches of Phuket or Samui or up to the hills in the North and getting a job teaching to finance your stay in paradise – forget it. Job vacancies and opportunities are very limited in these areas.

It is possible to find work if you have the right connections but, if you're reading this and not already there doing the job, then you don't have the right connections. If you prefer the quieter life, then both Chiang Mai, in the north and Hat Yai in the south offer some possibilities – however the competition, particularly in Chiang Mai can be fierce, and the pay is often much lower than in Bangkok.

My first impressions of Bangkok? It's a sprawling, polluted, overcrowded city with one foot in the past and another, attempting, to stride into the future. But once you've been here a while you discover that the city does have quite a few redeeming qualities: It's much safer than any western city – it's very rare to hear of any muggings or see any fights. Friendly people – Thais are more willing that most to make you feel at home in their country. Their natural, relaxed lifestyle makes life here less hectic and stressful than say Japan, Taiwan or Hong Kong.

Cheap food: 20 to 30 baht will buy you a simple meal at a roadside food stall – of which there are thousands in Bangkok. Dining out is a way of life here – very few people cook their evening meals, preferring to eat with their friends after work or to buy something on the way home.

The Skytrain, an elevated electric railway opened in December 1999 and, although underused by Thais, is very popular amongst the teaching community. If you're lucky enough to live and teach on or near either of the two lines your commuting time will be measured in minutes rather than hours.

Nightlife: Let's be honest, one of the big attractions of Bangkok is its well-known and varied nightlife. For many teachers this is the deciding factor in the choice whether to come to Bangkok or go elsewhere. There's something for everyone from arty, stylish bars and bistros to the delights of Patpong and Nana Plaza.

Phillip Williams, Academic Director at the Asia Institute of English, sums up life in the City of Angels, "Bangkok is just about as teacher-friendly as a city can be. It offers a relatively

low cost of living, affordable entertainment and, most importantly teachers are always in great demand."

The vast majority of Thai students have been taught by using the rote learning method. Anything the teacher writes on the board is automatically copied into your book. The information passes straight from the eye to the hand, bypassing the brain entirely. Students rarely question the teacher, that's tantamount to having doubts about the teacher's knowledge and, as we all know, what your teacher says is always correct. This results in the average Thai student being able to cope with a multiple choice exam, which requires the memorization of facts, but having a great deal of difficulty with any exam that requires a written answer, especially one requiring a personal opinion or giving a reason why something happens.

Historically the Thai people are farmers and the economy largely based on agriculture. During labour intensive periods, planting and harvest time, families will pool their resources to help their neighbours. Nowadays, the attitude on lending a helping hand is carried over into schools, colleges and the workplace. Weaker students are given a lot of encouragement (usually in the form of the correct answers) by their classmates. Teachers give students every opportunity to pass an exam; this manifests itself in the form of multiple retakes until the student passes. Work colleagues help each other produce reports for their bosses to ensure that even those staff who would be considered a liability stay in a job. Therefore, if you are teaching a class, never expect Thai students to work on their own, everything must be done in pairs or groups. If you specify that a certain report or piece of homework must be done individually, you could count on at least 70% still being done as a group effort.

By now you may feel that I am being very negative about Thai students, but that's not so. I'm just trying to make you aware of the differences between western students and Thai students. Knowing about these differences before you start teaching will save you a great deal of head shaking and hand wringing. On the plus side the students respect their teachers, Thais are talkative but you won't have any verbal or physical abuse from any students. As I said earlier, your students will enjoy a laugh and a joke; they won't expect you to be serious.

From an academic point of view, teaching ability isn't really valued or regarded as high as it should be. There are many well-qualified TEFL/ESL teachers who have left Thailand in despair. The reason being is that their abilities aren't recognized by fellow Thai teachers and/or their students. Succeeding in Thailand isn't a matter of having a list of academic qualifications as long as your arm. What is important is that you can understand your students and know what they expect from you. For many career teachers, especially those used to teaching more dedicated students in, say, Japan, this aspect of Thai life can be particularly frustrating.

Anyone who is governed by absolute obedience to rules and regulations, timetables, strict adherence to contracts, the need to be involved in decisions that affect you and the belief that displays of anger will get conflicts resolved won't enjoy their time here.

Get used to "going with the flow," "rolling with it" and any number of similar phrases that could be used to describe the notion that if something goes to plan then that's an unexpected bonus and not something to be taken for granted.

Thai students want to be entertained as well as educated. Therefore the successful teacher has to bear in mind what I like to call the 4 "Ss" of Thai society. These are:

1. Sanook (Fun): If it's not sanook then why do it? Makes sense really, doesn't it. Listening to a teacher drone on, copying from a board, mindless choral repetition and so on aren't considered fun activities. First thing to remember then is to make your lessons fun, include a couple of games and keep things moving along – don't get bogged down – it's not sanook.

2. Suay (Beautiful): All the best things in life are suay. Outward appearance is of the utmost importance to Thais, especially personal appearance. While teachers in the west may be used to teaching classes in jeans and a t-shirt, that kind of attire is frowned upon here. Get a haircut; you'll need to wear a shirt, tie, trousers and polished shoes. Female teachers should stick to knee length skirts and non-revealing blouses. Suay carries over into any homework or reports you'll give your students. Style is always placed above substance, trying to convince your students otherwise will result in a look of disbelief upon their faces.

3. Suparb (Politeness): This covers everything from the way you dress and speak to having respect for your elders. Everyone knows their place in the social structure and people address each other accordingly. Elders are addressed as pee: those younger than you as nong. Elders, bosses, teachers and monks are all wai'd (use the traditional Thai greeting with them – hold your hands as though praying and bow your head slightly.) This is just the tip of the politeness iceberg. A couple of things for teachers new to Thailand should remember are: (1) never perch on the edge of a desk (as I remember my old high school math teacher doing every lesson) and (2) don't touch your students, especially if you're a male teacher and have female students.

4. Serious – Okay, it's an English word but all Thais know it. This is something you shouldn't be. It's almost as bad as being boring. God help you if you are boring and serious because no one else will. In a practical sense, try to treat everything with the same lack of importance, for example if someone doesn't do their homework, give them more time, if they copy – no problem so long as they only copy a little bit. You'll find your students are only serious around exam time – and then for only a very brief period.

In a nutshell, dress the part, clean, smart and professional – if you look like a teacher Thais will treat you like a teacher (i.e., with respect.) Be friendly and polite, stay calm, don't raise your voice, have fun, laugh at yourself and laugh with your students. This isn't a licence to spend all class playing games but it does allow you to be creative and not be ruled by the constraints of a rather dull course book.

You've read some background information (I hope!), now ask yourself this question: "Why do I want to go to Thailand to teach English as a foreign language? Here are three possible scenarios:

(1) You plan on backpacking around the world and you need to earn some cash during your trip. The large language schools are always looking for teachers, qualified or not. This fact, coupled with the reality that Thai students are fun loving and pretty forgiving towards their teachers means that it's not hard to get work, even if you only plan to stay a few months. You will be on a relatively low hourly rate but a couple of months work will enable you to save enough to pay for a month chilling out on Koh Pa Ngan.

(2) You've finished university and it's time to take a year out before starting life as a corporate slave. Ideally you'd like to spend a year experiencing life in a country with a different

culture and climate from what you're used to. However you also have the reality of a student loan to face, so you need to make sure that your overseas experience pays it's way and doesn't drain your bank account further. If you have the presence of mind to, at least, read a couple of books on TEFL, then armed with a copy of your degree, you should have no trouble in finding work once you arrive. A better scenario would be if you took some form of TEFL course before you arrived, it doesn't have to be a Cambridge or Trinity College course – which are quite expensive. Any evidence that you had the presence of mind to take a TEFL qualification will show employers that you are serious about teaching and will ensure a better rate of pay and more job opportunities than if you'd arrived totally unprepared.

(3) You are an experienced teacher. If you're financially minded then you will probably want to avoid Thailand. Sure, there are well paying jobs available at international schools and private universities, but on the whole the availability of these jobs is pretty limited. Even if you worked as the Director of Studies at a language school you might find that your 10+ years of experience only results in a salary a few thousand Baht higher than a new teacher with little or no experience. In general, teaching experience isn't well rewarded financially. However, if you're looking for a less stressful atmosphere than say, Japan or Korea (where experience is more prized), then Thailand offers the chance to earn a decent salary in a more easy going atmosphere.

A recent report concluded that the market for English language teaching was far from saturated and would continue to grow. The demand for both qualified and unqualified teachers would therefore remain high for the foreseeable future. But what about the conditions for teachers in language schools? Back to Phillip Williams, who, having been here for over 10 years, has noticed the impact the Internet is having on the standard of teaching and the attitude of schools towards their teachers. "What is very worrying for the poor quality schools is the number of times their name gets dragged through the mud on the Internet. Their dirty laundry is hung out for all to see."

Schools now realize that they are being held accountable for their actions. Phillip continues, "Many schools are waking up to the fact that proper teachers want proper jobs. They want a competitive salary, access to modern teaching materials, a worthwhile training programme and an employer who values their contribution to the education of Thailand's new generation."

So, what are you waiting for ?

Ian McNamara teaches EFL at Assumption College, Bangkok and, when time allows, is also the webmaster of Ajarn – for those interested in life in Bangkok (www.ajarn.com).

VIETNAM

After the first flush of foreign investors rushing to do business in Vietnam, the atmosphere is more cautious as people realize that the country cannot embrace capitalism overnight. There is a lot of bureaucracy in Vietnam and this extends into the English language teaching market. Demand for English fluctuates from year to year: early in 2000, EFL teachers reported a big downturn in student numbers enrolling in established schools in Ho Chi Minh City (Saigon). Students were moving to cheaper schools that had just opened and competition among EFL schools was intensifying. Although unqualified travellers can find jobs here, they will be paid very badly. It's much better to apply for jobs in Vietnam as a qualified EFL teacher.

British Council office:
40 Cat Linh Street, Dong Da, Hanoi
Tel +84 (4) 843 6780
www.britishcouncil.org/vietnam

➲ **Visas/Work Permits:** A tourist visa is valid for 30 days. This can be extended three more times for one-month periods. After this time, you have to leave Vietnam. Some teachers apply for six-month, multiple-entry extendable business visas through travel agencies, which should charge no more than $60-80 for the service. You then have to leave the country and pick up your business visa at the Vietnamese embassy in the country you choose to go to — usually Cambodia.

➲ **Currency:** £1 = 28000 / $1 = 15900 Dong

➲ **Salary:** £520-750 / $950-1400 per calendar month, depending on the school and your experience. Be prepared to work longer hours in Vietnam (30 or more hours a week) than in other Asian countries. Overtime rates are around £7.50-10 / $12-18 per hour.

➲ **Accommodation:** You can get nice "shophouse" accommodation in Ho Chi Minh City for £120-240 / $220-450 a month. Hanoi is more expensive. Make sure your landlord has a permit to rent to foreigners or you could face eviction.

➲ **Cost of Living:** There are two sets of prices in Vietnam: one for locals and another (higher) for foreigners. Teachers who have lived for some time in the country still expect to pay 20-30% more than the Vietnamese. But remember that foreign English language teachers are paid far more than the average Vietnamese worker. You can live well on $500 a month. Sharpen your bargaining skills – it's expected of you to haggle over prices.

➲ **Health advice:** Avoid local hospitals if you can help it. Membership of a foreign-run medical service costs around £100 / $190 a year. You can get evacuation insurance for about £300 / $570 a year.

➲ **English Language Media:** Vietnam News.

Schools in Vietnam (+84)

American English School
357 Dien Bien Phu, District 3, Ho Chi Minh City. **Tel:** 8 8324226. **Fax:** 8342484.

Apollo Education Centre
67 Le Van Huu, Hanoi. **Tel:** 4-9432051. **Fax:** 4-9432052.

Duong Minh Language School
132c Phan Dang Luu, Phu Nhuan District, Ho Chi Minh City.

English 2000
70 Ding Tien Hoang, District 1, Ho Chi Minh City.

ELT Lotus
8 Nguyen Van Trang, District 1, Ho Chi Minh City.

Hanoi ELTE
10 Hang Chao St, Hanoi. **Fax:** 4 7332300.

Hollywood English centre
87B Tran Din Xu, District 1, Ho Chi Minh City.

Interaction Language School
59 Dinh Tien Hoang, District 1, Ho Chi Minh City.

New Star ELT centre
217 Doi Can Street, Cong Vi, Ba Dinh, Hanoi. **Tel:** 4 762 6696. **Fax:** 4 762 6699.

T.E.S.T. International
552 Dien Bien Phu, District 10, Ho Chi Minh City. **Tel:** 8 8334676.

Top Globis Training centre
3-7 P. Tan Phu, District 7, Ho Chi Minh City.

VATC (Vietnamese American Training College)
44 Truong Dinh St, District 3, Ho Chi Minh City. **Tel:** 8 8293971.

Latin America

Central and South American countries are attractive destinations for many American and Canadian language teachers, simply because a majority of these countries are not too far away and there are plenty of job opportunities.

Although teachers in some countries like Brazil, Mexico and Argentina can earn a good salary dollars, Latin America is not really a good destination for graduates trying to pay off their loans. However, teaching English in Latin America gives foreigners the opportunity to experience life in a vibrant and fascinating culture.

Mexico is probably the easiest place to find a job, and there are also well-paid positions in Brazil, Argentina, Colombia and Brazil. There are fewer opportunities in Peru, Chile, Venezuela, Uruguay, Ecuador and Bolivia, but even in these countries, there are prestigious schools, willing to pay the premium for native speakers. Even unqualified teachers will find jobs in most of these countries however; to get the better jobs you will need to have either a TESOL-related MA or a recognized certificate. Opportunities in Belize, Dominican Republic, the eastern Caribbean, Guatemala, Guyana, Haiti, Honduras, Nicaragua and Panama are mainly for qualified teachers through aid programmes. Salaries are usually paid in local currency and might not cover living costs, but some include supplements paid in foreign currency.

In South America, the best time of year to find a job is just before the beginning of the academic year in January or February, although many institutes operate year-round and are happy to recruit teachers at any time. In addition to jobs at universities, English-medium schools, bi-national centres and language schools, companies encourage their employees to learn and often employ in-company teachers.

Only the larger schools with an international presence recruit overseas, mainly because work permits require so much paperwork, so most teachers find work by approaching schools in places they want to stay in. It also helps if you send your CV beforehand and dress professionally when you go looking for work: you can usually revert to jeans and a t-shirt after you've got the job.

ARGENTINA

Following the economic and political uncertainties caused by the massive devaluation of the local currency, Argentine schools cannot pay much for teachers – but, what you are paid covers local costs (food and accommodation) since these too have been re-valued. Unqualified teachers are having a harder time finding work. Nowadays, there is plenty of competition for jobs teaching English from local English language graduates and English-speaking immigrants.

Nevertheless, a qualified teacher should have no problem finding a job here. October is a good time to start writing to potential employers who will want teachers who can start work in the following spring. Teachers who want to pick up a job while they're in the country should arrive in January. If you don't like big cities, consider Mendoza or Cordoba as alternatives to Buenos Aires. You could even travel out to Patagonia and chance your luck there.

Embassy in UK:
65 Brook Street, London W1Y 1YE
Tel: 020 7318 1300
www.argentine-embassy-uk.org

Embassy in USA:
1600 New Hampshire Ave NW,Washington DC20009
Tel: 202 238 6400
www.embajadaargentina-usa.org

British Council office:
Marcelo T de Alvear 590 4th Floor, C1058AAF, Buenos Aires
Tel +54 (11) 4311 9814/7519
www.britishcouncil.org.ar

⮕ **Visas/Work Permits:** Most teachers work on tourist visas, which they renew every three months. For a longer-term contract, you need a work permit, which is arranged by your employer. Securing the correct permit can take up to eight months, so plan ahead.
⮕ **Currency:** £1 = 5.3 / $1 = 3.1 Pesos.
⮕ **Salaries/Taxes:** Institutes pay on an hourly basis
⮕ **Accommodation:** If you are paying for accommodation yourself, a one-bedroom apartment can cost £300 / $600 per month. Teachers often live in simple, family-owned hotels until they have saved some deposit money.
⮕ **English Language Media:** Buenos Aires Herald.

⮕ **Tip:** Many institutes expect teachers to provide their own supplies including copies of materials, blank tapes, videos, a tape player and books.
⮕ **Health advice:** Local medical care is expensive, so private insurance is recommended. You should be protected against Hepatitis A; in some northern areas Malaria and Yellow Fever occur.

Schools in Argentina (+54)

ALICANA
San Martin 2293, 3000 Sanata Fe. **Tel:** 42 53 7567, **Fax:** 42 55 2026

American English Institute
Córdoba 392 3°D, Buenos Aires. **Tel:** 4312-8646, **Fax:** 4312-8462

American English Institute
Gral.M. Belgrano 179, Paraná, Entre Rios. **Tel:** 0343 431-5018

American Training Co.
Viamonte577, Piso 7, 1053 Buenos Aires. **Tel:** 1 311 3699, **Fax:** 1 315 3573

AMICANA
Chile 985, 5500 Mendoza. **Tel:** 61 23 6271, **Fax:** 61 29 8702, **Email:** amicana@impsat.com.ar

ARICANA
Buenos Aires 934, 2000 Rosario. **Tel:** 41 21 7664, **Fax:** 41 21 9179, **Email:** aricana@interactive.com.ar

Asociacion Comodoro Rivadavia de Intercambio Cultural Argentino Norteamericano (ACRICANA)
Escalada 1567, 9000 Comodoro Rivadavia. **Tel:** 0297 446-6311. **Fax:** 0297 447-3956. **Email:** acricana@infovia.com.ar

Asociacion Mendocina de Intercambio Cultural Argentino Norteamericano (AMICANA)
Chile 987, 5500 Mendoza. **Tel:** 0261 423-6271. **Fax:** 0261 429-8702. **Email:** amicana2@impsat1.com.ar

Asociacion Paranense de Intercambio Cultural Argentino Norteamericano (APICANA)
Córdoba 256, 3100 Parana. **Tel/Fax:** 0343 431-9678. **Email:** apicana@arnet.com.ar

Asociacion Rosarina de Intercambio Cultural Argentino Norteamericano (ARICANA)
Buenos Aires 934, 2000 Rosario . **Tel:** 0341 421-7664. **Fax:** 0341 421-9179. **Email:** aricana@arnet.com.ar

Instituto Cultural Argentino Norteamericano (ICANA)

Maipú 672, 1006 Buenos Aires. **Tel:** 011 4322-3855/4557. **Fax:** 011 4322-2106. **Email:** secretaria@bcl.edu.ar

Instituto Dean Funes de Intercambio Cultural Argentino Norteamericano (IDFICANA)

9 de Julio 177, 5200 Dean Funes, Córdoba. **Tel:** 03521 420-738. **Fax:** 03521 421-001/20899

Instituto de Intercambio Cultural Argentino Norteamericano (IICANA)

Dean Funes 726, 5000 Cordoba. **Tel:** 0351 421-4026/425-4216/426-3941. **Fax:** 0351 423-7858. **Email:** IICANA@onenet.com.ar

ATICANA

Salta 581, 4000 San Miguel de Tucuman. **Tel:** 81 31 0616, **Fax:** 81 30 3070, **Email:** aticana@starnet.net.ar

Berlitz

Av. de Mayo 847, 1er Piso, 1084 Buenos Aires. **Tel:** 11 4342 0202 **Email:** info@berlitz.com.ar

Berlitz

Av. Del Libertador 15231, 1640 Acassuso. **Tel:** 11 4747 1871 **Fax:** 11 4732 3096, **Email:** info@berlitz.com.ar

British Council

Marcalo T De Alvera 590 (4th Floor), 1058 Buenos Aires. **Tel:** 54 1 311 9814.

Brooklyn Bridge

Reconquista 715, 6 C y D, 1003 CF, Buenos Aires. Tel: 1 313 1652

CAIT

Maipú 863 3ºC, Buenos Aires. **Tel/Fax:**4311-44/4314-2583

Centum Servicios de Idiomas

Bartlome Mitre, Piso 4, 1036 Buenos Aires. **Fax:** 1 328 5150/2385

English Studies

Catalina Hansen, Rodriguez Pena 238 40 A - 1020, CF, Buenos Aires. **Tel:** 1 371 5352, **Fax:** (21) 720393.

ICANA

Maipu 672, 1006 Buenos Aires. **Tel:** 1 322 3855, **Fax:** 1 322 2106, **Email:** icana@bcl.edu.ar

IELI

Alberti 6444, San Jose de la Esquina, Santa Fe 2185.

Instituto Cultural Argentino-Britanico

Calle 12, No 1900, La Plata.

Instituto ELT

Isabel Gonzalez Bueno, Soler 458 (1714) Ituzaingo, Buenos Aires. **Tel/Fax:** (541) 624 0148.

International House

IH Belgrano, Arcos 1830, 1428 CF, Buenos Aires. **Tel:** 541 785 4425.

Landmark

Marcelo T. de Alvear 2331 1ºD, Buenos Aires. **Tel/Fax:** 4825-3806, **Email:** landmark@arnet.com.ar

Language Network

Billinghurst 2476 piso 2, Buenos Aires. **Tel:** 4805-6586, **Fax:** 4805-8452.

Liceo Superior de Cultura Inglesa

Italia 830, Tandil, 7000 Pica de Buenos Aires.

Northside School of English

G W Seminario, Velez Sarsfield 56, 1640, Martinez, Buenos Aires. **Tel/Fax:** 798 5150/793 5469.

St John's School

Recta Martinoli 3452, V Belgrano 5417 Cordoba, Pica de Cordoba.

TOKEN

Av.de Mayo 1260-5°Q, Capital Federal. **Tel:** 4383-0751/15-4979-3929 **Email:** houses@infovia.com.ar

BOLIVIA

Bolivia is currently enjoying a rare period of political and economic stability although there has been a recent increase in street protests because of popular dissatisfaction with government policies. Bolivians are keen to learn English and travelling teachers are attracted here because it is cheap to stay and culturally fascinating.

Embassy in UK:

106 Eaton Square, London SW1W 9AD
Tel: 020 7235 4248

Embassy in USA:

3014 Massachusetts Ave NW, Washington,DC20008
Tel: 202 483 4410

British Council office:

Avenida Arce 2708 (esq.Campos), Casilla 15047, La Paz
Tel: +591 (2) 2431 240
www.britishcouncil.org/bolivia

⮕ **Visas/Work Permits:** All nationalities need a tourist visa to enter. Work permits are obtained by employers for contracts of at least one year in duration. They cost around £240 / $450 and you may be asked to make a small payment (around £12-30 / $22-57) towards the cost.

⊃ Currency: £1 = 14.91 / $1 = 8.06 Bolivianos

⊃ Salaries and taxes: As low as £2 / $4 per hour in a language school or £6/ $11 per hour for private classes.

⊃ Accommodation: Cheap and easy to find. Some schools will supply accommodation.

⊃ Cost of Living: Bolivia is an inexpensive country to live in.

⊃ Health advice: La Paz is situated 13,000 feet above sea level and many teachers report that it takes a while to become acclimatized to the altitude. Medical facilities, even in La Paz, are not adequate to handle serious medical conditions, such as cardiac problems. You should be vaccinated against Hepatitis A, Malaria, and Yellow Fever.

School in Bolivia (+591)

Centro Boliviano Americano
Calle 25 de Mayo N-0365, Casilla 1399, Cochabamba. **Tel:** 42 21288, 22518. **Fax:** 42 51225. **Email:** suarezmj@llajta. nrc.bolnet.bo

Centro Boliviano Americano
Parque Iturralde Zenon 121, Casilla 12024, La Paz. **Tel:** 2 430107 **Fax:** 2 431342. **Email:** cbalp@datacom-bo.net

Centro Boliviano Americano
c/ Cochabamba 66, Casilla 510, Santa Cruz de la Sierra. **Tel:** 3 342299 **Fax:** 3 350188 **Email:** cbascz@datacom.bo.net

Centro Boliviano Americano
Calle Calvo No. 331, Casilla No. 380, Sucre, Chuquisaca. **Tel:** 64 41608. **Fax:** 64 41608. **Email:** cba@nch.bolnet.bo

Colegio Ingles Saint Andrews
Av. Las Relamas, La Florida, La Paz. **Tel:** 2 792484.

Colegio San Calixto
C/Jenaro Sanjines 701, La Paz. **Tel:** 2 35 5278.

Colegio San Ignacio
Av. Hugo Ernest 7050, Seguencoma, La Paz. **Tel:** 2 783720.

Pan American English Centre
Edificio Avenida, Avenida 16 de Julio 1490, 7º piso, Casillo 5244, La Paz. **Tel/Fax:** 2 340796.

Tito's Place
P.O. Box 3112, Cochabamba. **Tel:** 4 289308, **Fax:** 4 288836. **Email:** mahergar@comteco.entelnet.bo

BRAZIL

English language teaching is booming in Brazil and it is still quite easy to find a job here. Many parents are keen to send their children to private schools to learn English. There are around 60 bi-national centres specifically catering for Brazilians who want to learn English.

Embassy in UK:
32 Green Street, London W1Y 4AT
Tel: 020 7499 0877
www.brazil.org.uk

Embassy in USA:
3006 Massachusetts Ave NW, Washington DC20008
Tel: 202 238 2700
www.brasilemb.org

British Council office (see also appendix):
Ed.Centro Empresarial Varig, SCN Quadra 04 Bloco B Torre Oeste Conjunto 202, Brasilia – DF, 70710-926
Tel +55 (0) 61 327 7230
www.britishcouncil.org/brazil

⊃ Visas/Work Permits: It is very difficult to obtain a work visa so some schools are willing to hire teachers who are in the country on a tourist visa although this is illegal. It is your responsibility to arrange for a work visa, which can take up to two months to get. You need to be qualified and have at least two years' experience to qualify. It is possible to arrive, find a job, apply for a visa and pick it up in a neighbouring country, although this is not popular with the bureaucrats. Otherwise, the process should be initiated through the Brazilian consulate at home.

⊃ Currency: £1 = 3.84 / $1 = 2.19 Reals.

⊃ Salaries/Taxes: Teachers are paid for 13 months and salaries are higher in cities. Full-time salaries start at around £220 / $400 a month, plus basic accommodation. Incomes can be supplemented with private classes starting at £6 / $11 per hour. Experienced teachers with a Masters degree can earn up to £1500 / $2700 a month. Tax varies from 13-25% and there is a statutory social security deduction.

⊃ Accommodation: Better schools will either provide lodging for free or offer a subsidy. Otherwise, expect to pay between a third and half of your salary. Apartments are unlikely to be furnished.

⊃ Cost of Living: Food is cheap but rent is moderately expensive.

⊃ Health advice: Insurance can be taken out locally but it does not cover dental treatment.

⊃ English Language Media: Brazil Herald.

Schools in Brazil (+55)

Britannia Schools
Rua Garcia D'Avila 58, Ipanema, Rio De Janeiro RJ
22421-010. **Tel:** 21 511 0143, **Fax:** 21 511 0893.

Britannia Special English Studies
Rua Dr Timoteo, 752 Moinhos De Vent, Porto Alegre
RS.

Britannia Juniors
Rua. Barao da Torre 599 - Rio de Janeiro, CEP
22411-003, RJ. **Tel:** 21 239-8044, **Fax:** 21 259 6197.

Britannia Executive School
Rua Barao De Lucena 61, Botofogo, Rio de Janeiro
22260.

Britannic International House
Rua Hermogenes de Morais 178, Recife PE
50610-160. **Tel:** 81 445 5564, **Fax:** 81 445 5481.

British House
Rua Tiradentes 2258, Centro, Pelotas RS 96060-160.
Tel: 532 27 3139, **Fax:** 532 27 5604.

**Cambridge Sociedade Brasileira de Cultura
Inglesa**
Rua Piaui 1234, Londrina 86020-320 PR. **Tel:** 43 324
1092, **Fax:** 324 0314.

Casa Branca
Rua Ma-chado De Assis 37, Boqueirao, Santos SP.
Tel/Fax: 13 233 5258.

CEBEU
Av Marechal Rondon, 745, Centro, Ji-Paraná RO. **Tel:**
69 422 3100, **Fax:** 69 422 3100.

CEL-LEP
Av. dos Tajuras 212, Sao Paulo SP 05670-000. **Tel:**
11 212 6183, **Fax:** 11 210 0698.

CEMID
Rua Santa Luzia, 799 conj. 401, Rio de Janeiro - RJ
20030-040. **Tel:** (21) 262-1793 **Fax:** (21) 240-9271

Centro Britanico
Rua Joao Ramalho 344, Sao Paulo SP 05008-011. **Tel:**
11 622984, **Fax:** 11 872 9483.

Centro Cultural Brasil Estados Unidos
Avenida T 5, No. 441, 74230-040 Goiania GO. **Tel:** 62
833 1313, **Fax:** 62 833 1308.

Centro Cultural Brasil-Estados Unidos
Avenida Julio de Mesquita, 606 13025-061 Campinas
– SP. **Tel:** 192 51-3664/52-6668. **Fax:** 192 52-6888

Centro Cultural Brasil-Estados Unidos
Rua Amintas de Barros, 99, Edifico Itatiaia Centro
Caixa Postal 3328, 80060-200 Curitiba – PR. **Tel:** 41
320-4777. **Fax:** 41 238-2822

Centro de Enseñanza PLI
Rua de Octubro, 1234 Conj 4, Porto Alegre, RS 90000.

Centro De Cultura Inglesa
Av Guapore 2.236, Cacoal RO, CEP 78 975-000. **Tel:**
(69) 441-2833, **Fax:** 441-5346.

Cultura Inglesa
Rua do Progresso 239, Recife PE 50070-002. **Tel:** 81
423 6266, **Fax:** 81 231 2318.

Cultura Inglesa
Av. 17 de Agosto 233, Recife PE 52060-090. **Tel:** 81
268 6938, **Fax:** 81 268 6787.

Cultura Inglesa
Rua Visconde Albuquerque 205, Recife PE 50610-090.
Tel: 81 228 6649, **Fax:** 81 228 6649.

Cultura Inglesa
Rua Visconde de Inhauma 980, Ribeirao Preto SP
14010-100. **Tel:** 16 610 6616, **Fax:** 16 610 9868.

Cultura Inglesa
Rua Paul Pompeia 231, Rio de Janeiro RJ 22080-000.
Tel: 21 287 0990, **Fax:** 21 267 6474.

Cultura Inglesa
R. Plinio Moscoso 945, Salvador BA 40155-020. **Tel:**
71 247 9788, **Fax:** 71 245 3287.

Cultura Inglesa
Av. Sao Sebastiao 848, Santarem PA 68005-090. **Tel:**
91 522 7247.

Cultura Inglesa
Rua Sao Sebastiao 1530, Sao Carlos SP 13560-230.
Tel: 16 272 2276, **Fax:** 16 272 9875.

Cultura Inglesa
Av. Tiradentes 670, Sao Joao del Rei MG 36300-000.
Tel: 32 371 7035, **Fax:** 32 371 2764.

Cultura Inglesa
Av. Brig. Faria Lima 2000, Sao Paulo SP 01452-002.
Tel: 11 870 4955, **Fax:** 11 813 1945.

Cultura Inglesa
R. Joao Pinheiro 808, Uberlandia MG 38400-58. **Tel:**
34 235 2786, **Fax:** 34 236 9250.

Cultura Inglesa
Praca Rosalvo Ribeiro 110, Maceio AL 57021-57. **Tel:**
82 221 8055, **Fax:** 82 223 3785.

Cultura Inglesa
R. Eng Mario de Gusmao 603, Maceio AL 57035-000,
Tel: 82 231 8687. **Fax:** 82 231 8132.

Cultura Inglesa
Rua Natal 553, Manaus AM 69005-000. **Tel:** 92 611
1635, **Fax:** 92 611 1635.

Cultura Inglesa
Av. Rio Branco 741, Maringa PR 87015-380. **Tel/Fax**: 44 225 1518.

Cultura Inglesa
Rua Acu 495, Natal RN 59020-110. **Tel**: 84 211 6070, **Fax**: 84 211 4559.

Cultura Inglesa
R. Silvio Henrique Braune 15, Nova Friburgo RJ 28625-050. **Tel**: 245 22 5392, **Fax**: 245 22 5392.

Cultura Inglesa
R. Eduardo de Moraes 147, Olinda PE 53030-250. **Tel/Fax**: 81 429 2281.

Cultura Inglesa
Av. Bernardo Vieira de Melo 2101, Jaboatao dos Guararapes PE 54 410-010. **Tel**: 81 361 3458, **Fax**: 813610467.

Cultura Inglesa
Rua Paula Xavier 501, Ponta Grossa PR 84010-430. **Tel/Fax**: 42 223 2735.

Cultura Inglesa
Rua Quintino Bocaiuva 1447, Porto Alegre RS 90570-010. **Tel/Fax**: 51 333 4033.

Cultura Inglesa
Rua Mamanguape 411, Recife PE 51020-50. **Tel**: 81 326 1908, **Fax**: 81 326 7618.

Cultura Inglesa
Alameda Julia da Costa 1500, Curitiba PR 80730-070. **Tel**: 41 222 7339, **Fax**: 41 224 1024.

Cultura Inglesa
Rua Ponto Grossa 1565, Dourados MS 79824-160. **Tel**: 67 421 7147, **Fax**: 67 421 5753.

Cultura Inglesa
Rua Conde de Porto Alegre 59, Buque de Caxias RJ 25070-350. **Tel**: 21 671 2543, **Fax**: 21 671 4346.

Cultura Inglesa
Rua Rafael Bandeira 335, Florianapolis SC 88015-450. **Tel/Fax**: 48 224 2696.

Cultura Inglesa
Rua Ana Bilhar 171, Fortaleza CE 60160-110. **Tel**: 85 244 3784, **Fax**: 85 224 4665.

Cultura Inglesa
Rua Marechal Deodoro 1326, Franca SP 14400-440. **Tel/Fax**: 16 722 0011

Cultura Inglesa
Rua 86 No. 7, Golania GO 74083-330. **Tel**: 62 241 4516, **Fax**: 62 241 2582.

Cultura Inglesa
Rua 20 778, Ituiutaba MG 38300-000. **Tel**: 34 268 1681, **Fax**: 34 261 5975.

Cultura Inglesa
Av. Rio Grande do Sul 1411, Joao Pessoa PB 58030-021. **Tel**: 83 224 7005, **Fax**: 83 224 9479.

Cultura Inglesa
Rua Dr. Joao Colin 559, Joinville SC 89204-004. **Tel**: 47 433 7603, **Fax**: 47 433 4512.

Cultura Inglesa
Av. dos Andras 536, Juiz de Fora MG 36036-000. **Tel**: 32 215 5169, **Fax**: 32 215 9659.

Cultura Inglesa
Av. Barao de Maruim 761, Aracaju SE 49015-020. **Tel/Fax**: 79 224 7360.

Cultura Inglesa
Rua Almeida Campos 215, Araxa MG 38180-00. **Tel/Fax**: 34 661 3275.

Cultura Inglesa
Rua Virgilio Malta 1427, Bauru SP 17040-440. **Tel/Fax**: 142 23 3016.

Cultura Inglesa
R. Fernandes Tourinho 538, Belo Horizonte MG 30112-011. **Tel**: 31 221 6770, **Fax**: 31 225 1791.

Cultura Inglesa
Rua Mal. Floriano Peixoto 433, Blumenau SC 89010-000. **Tel/Fax**: 47 326 7272.

Cultura Inglesa
SEPS 709/908 Conjunto B DF 70390-89. **Tel**: 61 244 5650, **Fax**: 61 244 8571.

Cultura Inglesa
Av. Guapore 2236, Cacoal RO 78975-000. **Tel**: 69 441 2833. **Fax**: 69 441 4547.

Cultura Inglesa
Rua Lino Gomes da Silva 53, Campina Grande PB 58107-613. **Tel/Fax**: 83 322 4658.

Cultura Inglesa
R. Humberto de Campos 419, Campo Grande MS 79020-060. **Tel**: 67 751 0272, **Fax**: 67 751 0570.

Cultura Inglesa
Av. Agamenon Magalhaes 634, Caruaru PE 55000-000. **Tel/Fax**: 81 721 4749.

Cultura Inglesa
Rua Antonio Ataide 515, Vila Velha ES 29100-290. **Tel**: 27 229 5194, **Fax**: 27 229 3206.

Cultura Inglesa
Av Tiradentes 670, 36300 Sao Joao Del Rei MG. **Tel**: 32 371-4377, **Fax**: 32 371-4377.

Cultura Inglesa de Londrina
Rua Goias 1507, Centro, Londrina PR 86020-340.
Tel/Fax: 43 323 7700.

ELC
Rua Sa e Souza 655, Boa Viagem, Recife PE,
51030-350. **Tel:** 81 342 0351.

English Forever
Rua Rio Grande Do Sul 356, Pituba, Salvador-BA
41830-140. **Tel:** 71 240 2255, **Fax:** 71 248 8706,
Email: forever@svn.com.br

George Otto
Av. Vereador de Campo 525, Sala 4, Ibiuna - SP
18150-000. **Tel:** (15) 249-1159 **Fax:** (15) 249-1159

Global Team
Caixa Postal 6504, Campinas - SP 13084-970. **Tel:**
(19) 287-4427 **Fax:** (19) 287-4427

Independent British Institute
SHCGN 703 Area Especial, s/no Brasilia DF
70730-700. **Tel:** 61 322 8373, **Fax:** 323 5524, **Email:**
ibi@nutecnet.com.br

Instituto Britanico
Rua Deputado Carvalho Deda 640, 49025-070
Salgado Filho, Aracaju SE, Brazil. **Tel:** 79 23 2791,
Fax: 79 27 2645.

Instituto da Lingua Inglesa
Av. do CPA 157, Cuiaba MT 78008-000. **Tel/Fax:** 65
624 1197.

International House-Matriz
The School House, Rua 4, 80, Goiania GO 74110-140,
Goais, SE.

International House Goiania
Rua 04 nº 80, Setor Oeste, Goiania GO 74110-140.
Tel: 62 224 0478, Fax: 62 223 1846.

Liberty English Centre
Rua Amintas De Barros 1059, Curitiba PR. **Tel:** 41
263 3586, **Fax:** 41 262 1738.

New Vision English
Av. Ibirapuera, 2249 São Paulo - SP 01248-001. **Tel:**
(11) 241-4199 **Fax:** (11) 241-4199 **Email:**
newvision@newvision.com.br

PBF - Pink and Blue – Freedom
Rua Santos, 54 Joinville - SC 89202-46. **Tel:** (47)
433-1471 **Fax:** (47) 433-1471 **Email:**
pbfjlle@netville.com.br

Sharing English
Rua Souza de Andrade 56, Recife PE 52050-300.
Tel/Fax: 81 421 2286.

Schütz & Kanomata
Rua Galvão Costa, 85 Santa Cruz do Sul – RS. **Tel:** (51)
711-2248 **Fax:** (51) 715-3366 **Email:**
english@viavale.com.br

Skill
Av. Indianópolis, 3356 São Paulo - SP 04062-003. **Tel:**
(11) 5589-9535 **Fax:** (11) 5589-9447 **Email:**
fruggie@ibm.net

Sky Cursos e Traduções SC Ltda
Av. Senador Virgílio Távora, 867 - Meireles Fortaleza -
CE 60170.250. **Tel:** (85) 224-7879 **Fax:** (85) 224-7879
Email: sky@fortalnet.com.br

Soc Bras de Cultura Inglesa
Rua Fernandes Tourinho, 538 - Savassi BH-MG
30112.000, **Tel:** 031 221 6770.

System 2000
Rua Deputado Jose Lajes 491, Ponta Verde, Maceio AL
57035-330. **Tel:** 82 231 7808, **Fax:** 82 327 4946.

St. Peter's English School
Rua Berilo Guimaraes, 182 Centro Itabuna, Bahia.

The English Office
Rua D. Eponina Afonseca, 116 São Paulo - SP 04720-010.
Tel: (11) 546-0796 **Fax:** (11) 546-0796

Universitas
Rua Goncalves Dias 858, Belo Horizonte MG 30140-091.
Tel: 031 261 1477, **Fax:** 031 261 5138.

UP Language Consultants
Av. Brig. Faria Lima, 1912, 18m, Jd. Paulistano, Calcerter
Sao Paulo - SP 01451-907. **Tel:** (11) 211-9990 **Fax:** (11)
212-5366 **Email:** up@ensino.net

Upper English
Rua 09 de Julho 2143, Sao Carlos SP 13560-590. **Tel:** 16
271 8146, **Fax:** 16 271 5431.

Vision English Escola de Inglês S/C Ltda.
Av. Ibirapuera, 2249 São Paulo - SP 04029-100.**Tel:** (11)
241-4199 **Fax:** (11) 241-4199 **Email:**
newvision@newvision.com.br

CHILE

The government has placed improving Chile's school
system and developing foreign export markets at the top
of its economic agenda, so learning English is an
educational priority.

Although it is impossible to work in state schools
without a qualification from a Chilean university, there are
many private schools and in-company opportunities,
especially in Santiago.

Foreigners coming to Chile with the intention of teaching English should preferably have both qualifications and experience. Teachers are trained to a high standard in Chile and competition is tough.

Embassy in UK:
12 Devonshire Street, London W1N 2DS
Tel: 020 7580 1023

Embassy in USA:
1732 Massachusetts Ave NW, Washington DC20008
Tel: 202 785 1746
www.chile-usa.org

British Council office:
Eliodoro Yáñez 832, Providencia 6640356, Casilla 115 Correo 55, Santiago
Tel +56 (2) 410 6900
www.britcoun.cl

➲ **Visas/Work Permits:** Applications for visas and work permits should be made before arrival. It is possible to obtain a work permit after arrival but you have to show that you intend to stay for at least one year. Working on a tourist visa is possible although illegal.

➲ **Currency:** £1 = 915 / $1 = 524 Pesos

➲ **Salaries/Taxes:** For contracted teaching positions, a minimum wage for overseas teachers is set by the government at £250 / $460 per month. Rates vary from £5-7 / $9-13 per hour for qualified teachers. Private lessons pay £10 / $19 an hour and up. The tax rate is around 10%

➲ **Accommodation:** Schools offer little help, but it's easy to stay in hostels, which offer long-term accommodation with good facilities. Rooms can cost as little as £80 / $150 per month but average around £150 / US$300. Apartments can cost up to £250 / US$470 per month and landlords expect a month's rent as deposit and a month in advance.

➲ **Cost of Living:** Low but higher than much of Latin America.

➲ **English Language Media:** News Review.

➲ **Health advice:** Medical care is generally good, but it may not meet western standards. Supplemental medical insurance, which includes specific overseas coverage, including provisions for medical evacuation, is highly recommended, as in-country medical evacuations from outlying areas to Santiago cost £1,500 / $2,700 or more.

Schools in Chile (+56)

Abbey Road Cultural De Idiomas
Gorostiaga 608 P. 2, Iquique. **Tel:** 57 428737 **Fax:** 57 427147 **Email:** Abbeyroa.Dcult001@chilnet.cl

Acpen Academy
Av. Lib. B. O'higgins 949 P. 21 Of. 2103, Santiago. **Tel:** 2 6724460 **Fax:** 2 6724460 **Email:** acpenaca.demy001@chilnet.cl

American Language Institute
Lord Cochrane 286, Santiago, **Tel:** 2 6955487 **Fax:** 2 6955487 **Email:** american.langu001@chilnet.cl

Anglo-American International School
San Sebastian 2975, Santiago. **Tel:** 231 1771.

Antofagasta British School
Pedro Leon Gallo 723, Casilla 1, Antofagasta. **Tel:** 241 368.

Berlitz
Padre Mariano 305, Santiago. **Tel:** 2 2361557 **Fax:** 2 2361563 **Email:** Berlitz_Chile@entelchile.net

British Council
Eliodora Yanez 832, Casilla 115-Correo 55, Santiago. **Tel:** 22361199.

British School
Waldo Seguel 454, Casilla 379, Punta Arenas. **Tel:** 223 381, **Fax:** 248 447.

British High School
Los Gladiolos 10281, Santiago. **Tel:** 217 2204.

Burford Institute
Av. Pedro De Valdivia 511, Santiago. **Tel:** 2 2744603 **Fax:** 2 2235944 **Email:** info@burford.cl

Cie
Orella 1089, Antofagasta. **Tel:** 55 268339 **Fax:** 55 268339 **Email:** Capacita.Cioni001@chilnet.cl

Centro Chileno Canadiense Idiomas Ltda.
Av. Luis Thayer Ojeda 0191 P. 6 Of. 601, Santiago. **Tel:** 2 3341090 **Fax:** 2 3341089 **Email:** centroch.ileno001@chilnet.cl

Colegio Charles Darwin
Manantiales 0314, Punta Arenas. **Tel:** 212 671.

Colegio Dunalastair
Av. Las Condes 11931, Santiago. **Tel:** 215 2666.

Colegio Ingles George Chaytor
Callejon Ingles 4B, Temuco. **Tel:** 211 301.

Colegio Ingles De Talca
12 Norte 5/6 Oriente, Talca. **Tel:** 226692.

Colegio St George
Av. Americo Vespucio Norte 5400, Santiago.

Colegio Del Verbo Divinio
Av. Presidente Errazuriz 4055, Santiago. **Tel:** 228 6076.

Colegio Villa Maria Academy
Av. Presidente Errazuriz 3753, Santiago. **Tel:** 228 3398.

Computacion E Ingles Intercom Ltda.
Av. Pedro Montt 2053, Valpo. **Tel:** 32 254436 **Fax:** 32 254436 **Email:** Intercom.Pescu001@chilnet.cl

Craighouse
El Rodeo 12525-La Dehesa, Casilla 20007-Correo 20, Santiago. **Tel:** 242 4011, **Fax:** 215 7400.

Fischer English Institute
Cirujano Guzman 49, Santiago, **Tel:** 2 2356667 **Fax:** 2 2359810 **Email:** Fischeri.Nstit001@chilnet.cl

Grange School
Av. Principe De Gales 6154, Casilla 51-Correo 12, Santiago. **Tel:** 277 1181, **Fax:** 277 0946.

Greenhouse School
Ines De Suarez 1500, Temuco. **Tel:** 240 840.

Henry Renna Instituto
Mark Twain 7241, Santiago. **Tel:** 2 2199044 **Fax:** 2 2193013 **Email:** Henryren.Nains002@chilnet.cl

Instituto Chileno-Britanico De Cultura
Baquedano 351, Casilla 653, Arica. **Tel:** 58 238399, **Fax:** 58 231960.

Instituto Chileno-Britanico De Cultura
3 Norte 824, Casilla, Vina Del Mar. 929. **Tel:** 32 971061, **Fax:** 32 686656.

Instituto Chileno-Norteamericano De Cultura
Moneda 1467, Santiago. **Tel:** 2 238 6107, **Fax:** 2 698 1175, **Email:** infocent@hood.ichn.cl

Instituto Chileno Norteamericano
Caupolican 315, Casilla 612, Concepcion. **Tel:** 41 248 589, **Fax:** 41 233 851 (Also In Antofagasta And Valparaiso.)

Instituto De Ingles Impact S.A.
Rosa O'higgins 259, Santiago. **Tel:** 2 2125609, **Fax:** 2 2116165

Instituto De Ingles Lorbeth
Cabo Arestey 2468 Of., Santiago. **Tel:** 2 6956018, **Fax:** 2 6956018,

International Preparatory School
Pastor Fernandez 16001, El Arrayan, Santiago. **Tel:** 215 1094.

Iquique English College
Jose Joaquin Perez 419, Iquique. **Tel:** 411 2409.

Let's Do English
Villa Vicencio 361, Office 109, Santiago.

Lincoln International Academy
Camino San Antonio 55- Las Condes, Santiago. **Tel:** 217 1907.

Linguatec
Av. Los Leones 439, Santiago. **Tel:** 2 2334356, **Fax:** 2 2341380, **Email:** Michelle@Linguatec.cl

Lm Language centre
Agustinas 853 Of. 301, Santiago. **Tel:** 2 6396419, **Fax:** 2 6396419

Mackay School
Vicuna Mackenna 700, Casilla 558, Vina Del Mar. **Tel:** 832 574 **Fax:** 832 419.

Mayflower School
Las Condes 12167, Santiago. **Tel:** 217 1085.

Nido De Aquilas School
Nido De Aquilas 14515, Casilla 16211-Providencia, Santiago. **Tel:** 216 6842.

Polyglot
Villavicencio 361 Of. 102, Santiago. **Tel:** 2 6398078, **Fax:** 2 6322485, **Email:** info@polyglot.cl

Redland School
Camino El Alba 11357, Las Condes, Santiago. **Tel:** 2 214 1265, **Fax:** 2 214 1020.

St Gabriel's School
Av. Bilbao 3070-Providencia, Santiago. **Tel:** 204 1915, **Fax:** 225 2136.

St John's School
Pedro De Valdivia 1783, Casilla 284, Concepcion. **Tel:** 331 670, **Fax:** 340 809.

St Margaret's School
5 Norte 1351, Casilla 392, Vina Del Mar. **Tel:** 977 000, **Fax:** 975 220.

St Peter's School
Calle Libertad 575, Vina Del Mar. **Tel:** 971 993.

Santiago College
Los Leones 584, Casilla 130-D, Santiago. **Tel:** 2 238 1813, **Fax:** 2 238 0755.

Thewhla's English School
Las Camelias 2854, Santiago.

Tronwell
Av. Apoquindo 4499 P. 1-2-3, Santiago. **Tel:** 2 2461040, **Fax:** 2 2289739, **Email:** tronwell.sa001@chilnet.cl

Wenlock School
Carlos Pena Otaegui 10880, La Foresta, Los Dominicos, Santiago. **Tel:** 212 8982, **Fax:** 212 9226.

Wessex School
Colo-Colo 222-Clasificador 43, Concepcion. **Tel:** 315436.

Windsor School
Av. Francia Esq. Simpson, Casilla 530, Valdivia.

COLOMBIA

Although Colombia has a reputation for violence, the reality is that, except for a few "no-go" zones, the country is no more dangerous than others in the region. In fact, many teachers report that Bogota and even Medellin are fun cities to live and work in as long as you don't stray into the "bad" areas. Schools welcome native English speakers because Colombia's image has deterred many of them from travelling here to teach. There is a network of Colombian-American Cultural centres and many of the private schools are American-owned. Bilingual high schools offer good rates of pay and working conditions.

This means that most EFL teachers, including unqualified ones looking for short-term positions while travelling, can get a job pretty easily. However, you may have to settle for a low wage initially, and it might be only just enough to live on. If you want to stay more than a few months, it is advisable to get qualified first so that you can get a job in one of the more reputable schools and build up contacts to secure more lucrative private classes.

Consulate in UK:
15-19 Great Titchfield Street, London W1P 7FB
Tel: 020 7495 4233

Embassy in USA:
2118 Leroy Pl NW, Washington DC20008
Tel: 202 387 8338
www.colombiaemb.org

British Council office:
Calle 87 No 12 - 79, Bogota
Tel +57 (1) 618 7680
www.britishcouncil.org.co

➲ **Visas/Work Permits:** Teachers must have a work permit before they travel and, unusually, a private language school cannot intervene directly with the Ministry of Foreign Affairs to secure this visa. Only those employed by approved institutions can secure the necessary work visa and the application process is associated with red tape, delays and expense, so make sure that your school is one of these institutions. If you want to insure that your visa is legal, your degrees and transcripts must be validated with a rubber stamp from the Colombian consulate.

➲ **Currency:** £1 = 4347 / $1 = 2350 Pesos

➲ **Salaries/Taxes:** Many schools offer no more than £2 / $4 per hour and unqualified teachers can expect to earn as little as £1.50 / $3. Average monthly salaries are £300 / $570 and it is possible to earn £525 / $950. Many institutions pay teachers 14 times per year and, with a normal work visa, teachers will pay tax of 10% or more. Private lessons can earn you up to £12 / $20 an hour or more.

➲ **Accommodation:** Expensive. In Bogota and most other cities, a one-bedroom apartment in a safe area costs about £200 / $380 per month and administration fees are often charged on top.

➲ **Cost of Living:** The cost of living is expensive as inflation is still high. However, once established, teachers can have a good standard of living.

➲ **Health advice:** Travellers to Bogota may require some time to adjust to the altitude (8,600 feet), which can adversely affect blood pressure, digestion and energy levels

Schools in Colombia (+57)

Academia Ingles Para Niños
Calle 106 No 16-26, Bogota.

Advanced Learning Service
Transversal 20 No 120-15, Bogota.

American School Way
Dg. 110 No. 42-96 Casa 4, Bogota. **Tel:** 1 6198356

Aprender Ltda
Calle 17 No 4-68 Ql. 501, Bogota.

Aspect Language Schools Ltda.
Cl. 90 No. 11-44 Of. 301, Bogota. **Tel:** 1 2569827

BBC De Londres
Calle 59 No 6-21, Bogota.

Babel
Avenida 15 No 124-49 Cf. 205, Bogota.

Berlitz
Tr. 26 No. 146-60 L. 201, Bogota. **Tel:** 1 6275294

Berlitz de Colombia S.A.
Tr. 26 No. 146-60 L. 201, Medellin. **Tel:** 4 6250554

Best English Services Today
Dg. 110 No. 42-85 Int. 2 Ap. 103, Bogota. **Tel:** 1 2156380

Bi-Cultural Ltda.
Cl. 98 No. 10-32, Bogota. **Tel:** 1 6231478

Bi Cultural Institute
Avenida 7 No 123-97 Of. 202, Bogota.

Boston School of English Ltda
Carrera 43 No 44-02, Barranquilla.

Británico Americana
Cr. 40 No. 105A-46, Bogota. **Tel:** 1 2180045

The British Council
Calle 87 No 12-79, Bogota.

Business Language Centre Ltda.
Carrera 49 No 15-85, Medellin.

California English Institute
Cl. 46 No. 8-10 P. 2, Bogota. **Tel:** 1 2456429

California Institute Of English
Carrera 51 No 80-130, Barranquilla.

Carol Keeney
Carrera 4 No 69-06, Bogota.

Ceico
Calle Siete Infantes, San Diego, Cartagena.

Centro Anglo Frances
Carrera 11 No 6-12, Neiva.

Centro Audiovisual De Ingles Chelga
Calle 137 No 25-26, Bogota.

Centro Colombo Andino
Calle 19 No 3-16 Of. 203, Bogota.

Centro Colombo Americano
Cr. 45 No. 53-24, Medellin. **Tel:** 4 513 4444

Centro Cultural Colombo Americano
Carrera 43, No. 51-95, Apt. Aereo 2097, Barranquilla.

Centro de Idiomas Teachers Inc.
Cr. 15 No. 75-35, Bogota. **Tel:** 1 5456712

Centro de Inglés Lincoln
Cl. 49 No. 9-37, Bogota **Tel:** 1 2852224

Centro De Idiomas Winston Salem
Calle 45 No 13-75, Bogota.

Centro De Idiomas Winston Salem
Transversal 74 No C2-33 Laureies, Medellin.

Centro De Idiomas Winston Salem
Ave-nida La Ceste No 10-27, Santa Teresita, Cali.

Centro De Idiomas y Turismo De Cartagena
Popa Calle 30 No 20- 177, Cartagena.

Centro De Lengua Inglesa
Calle 61 No 13-44 Of. 402, Bogota.

Centro De Lenguas Modernas
Carrera 38 No 69 C 65, Barranquilla.

Centro Educativo Bilingüe English centre Envigado
Cr. 40 No. 38 S-55 Int. 201-202-203, Medellin. **Tel:** 4 3312211

Clever Training Corp
Av. Cr. 15 No. 122-51 Of. 509-510, Bogota. **Tel:** 1 2143239

Coningles Ltda
Cl. 71 No. 13-56, Bogota. **Tel:** 1 3128646

Darlitz English Institute Ltda.
Cr. 11A No. 69-89, Bogota. **Tel:** 1 3101780

Dynamic English
Cl. 119 No. 13A-84, Bogota. **Tel:** 1 3102277

Easy English
Carrera 45 A No 34 Sur 29 Torre No 4, Portal Del Cerro , A. A. 80511, Envigado, Medellin.

Eccles
Cr. 13 No. 55-21 P. 3, Bogota. **Tel:** 1 2550552

EF Educación Internacional
Cr. 38 No. 10A-40, Bogota. **Tel:** 1 2664275

EF Learn a Language
Cl. 76 No. 9-66, Medellin. **Tel:** 4 3172180

El Centro Inglés
Cl. 11A No. 43D-14 P. 3, Medellin. **Tel:** 4 3114888

El Centro Inglés
El Poblado Carrera 10 A.No 36-39, Medellin.

Elci
Cr. 18 No. 89-16, Bogota. **Tel:** 1 2183535

ELS Language centres
Cl. 118 No. 25-52, Bogota. **Tel:** 1 6299774

English For Infants (John Dewey)
Diagonal 110 No 40-85, Bogota.

English Hard Practice for School and Company Improvement
Cl. 34 S No. 50-10, Bogota. **Tel:** 1 2701142

English Language & Culture Institute (ELCI)
Calle 90 No 10-51, Bogota.

English Systems
Cr. 13 No. 32-51 Of. 807, Bogota. **Tel:** 1 3381361

English Zone Institute
Cl. 70A No. 31-29, Bogota. **Tel:** 1 3108559

Esquela De Inglés
Calle 53 No 38-25, Barranquilla.

Escuela De Idiomas Berlitz
Calle 83 No 19-24, Bogota.

Escuela Mundial del Idioma Inglés
Cl. 34 No. 64A-11, Medellin. **Tel:** 4 2353266

First Class English
Cr. 12 No. 93-78 P. 4, Bogota. **Tel:** 1 6238380

FLS Learning centres
Cl. 106 No. 16-50, Bogota. **Tel:** 1 2140031

Genelor International
Avenida 78 No 20-49 Piso 20, Bogota.

I.C.L.
Calle 119 No 9a-25, Bogota.

Idiomas-Munera-Cros Ltda
Carrera 58 No 72-105, A.A. 52032, Barranquilla.

Ingles Cantando Y Jugando
Calle 106 No 16-26, Bogota.

Inlingua
Cr. 77B No. 47-70, Medellin. **Tel:** 4 2509746

Instituto Anglo Americano De Idiomas
Carrera 16a No 85-34 Of. 204, Bogota.

Instituto Bridge Centro De Idiomas
Carrera 65 No 49 A 09, Cali.

Instituto De Inglés Thelma Tyzon
Carrera 59 No 74-73, Barranquilla.

Instituto De Lenguas Modernas
Carrera 41 No 52-05, Baranquilla.

Instituto Electronico De Idiomas
Carrera 6 No 12-64 Piso, Bogota.

Instituto Experimental De Atlantico
"jos Celestino Mutis", Calle 70 No 38-08, Barranquilla.

Instituto Meyer
Calle 17 No 10-16 Piso 80, Bogota.

Interlingua
Cr. 18 No. 90-38, Bogota. **Tel:** 1 2180942

International Language Institute
Carrera 5a No 21-35, Neiva.

International Language Institute Ltda
Carrera 11 No. 65-28 Piso 3, Bogota. **Tel:** 571 235-8152/72, **Fax:** 310-2892.

International Language Institute Ltda
Carrera 13 No 5-79 Castillogrande, Cartagena.

International Study centre
Cl. 116 No. 22-45 Of. 503, Bogota. **Tel:** 1 2165830

International System
Transversal 6 No 51 A 33, Bogota.

K.O.E De Columbia
Calle 101 A No 31-02, Bogota.

Life Ltda.
Transversal 19 No 100-52, Bogota.

Lubigon English Academy
Cl. 48D No. 67A-14 , Medellin. **Tel:** 4 2602840

Oxford Centre
A.A. 102420, Santate de Bogota.

Royal English Club
Tr. 42A No. 100-59, Bogota. **Tel:** 1 2718887

Stanton School of English
Cl. 57 No. 18-22 Of. 503, Bogota. **Tel:** 1 3479017

The Better English centre
Cr. 73B No. 5C-19, Bogota. **Tel:** 1 2640535

The British Council
Cl. 91 No. 21-55, Bogota. **Tel:** 1 6103077

The British Council
Cr. 42 No. 16A S-41, Medellin. **Tel:** 4 3131867

Total English Solutions
Cr. 36A No. 57A-15, Bogota. **Tel:** 1 2215233

Wall Street Institute
Cr. 9 No. 70-09, Bogota. **Tel:** 1 3460566

Way's English School
Calle 101 No 13 A 17, Bogota.

Winston - Salem
Cl. 45 No. 13-75, Bogota. **Tel:** 1 3128646

World English centre
Cr. 16 No. 53-46 P. 2, Bogota. **Tel:** 1 5471950

Worldwide Languages
Tr. 19A No. 123-49, Bogota. **Tel:** 1 6190762

COSTA RICA

Costa Rica is one of the more stable of the Central American republics and a favourite haunt of "gringo" tourists. There are many private language schools, especially in San José, an unattractive city of around five million people. The rest of the country is beautiful with volcanoes and beaches to explore.

Consulate in UK:
14 Lancaster Gate, London W2 3LH
Tel: 020 7706 8844

Embassy in USA:
2114 S Street NW, Washington DC 20008
Tel: 202 234 2945

➲ **Visas/Work Permits:** Work visas are very difficult to obtain and teachers usually work on tourist visas.

➲ **Currency:** £1 = 851 / $1 = 460 Colon

➲ **Salaries/Taxes:** Salaries are not high (c. £2.50-3 / $4-5 an hour for part-timers; £400-600 / $700-$1100 per month full-time is about average) but you can earn enough to get by. Private tutors can earn $15 an hour.

➲ **Accommodation:** £180-250 / $350-460 a month for a shared apartment. Assistance is often provided by employers.

➲ **Cost of Living:** One of the most expensive Central American countries, but prices are still low compared to the UK or USA.

➲ **Health advice:** Medical facilities are available, but may be limited outside urban areas. Be aware that on both the Caribbean and Pacific coasts, currents are swift and dangerous. Several drownings occur each year, and there are no lifeguards.

Schools in Costa Rica (+506)

American International School
Bosques de Doña Rosa, Ciudad Cariari, Heredia. **Fax:** 239-0625.**Email**: brown@cra.ed.cr

Berlitz
Santa Ana 2000, Edificio A, Planta Baja, Santa Ana, San José. **Tel**: 204 7555, **Fax**: 204 7444.

Blue Valley School
P.O. Box 2050-1000, San José. **Fax**: 253-7708

Centro Cultural Costarricense Norteamericano
Apt.1489-1000, San José, Calle Los Negritos, Barrio Dent. **Tel**: 225 6433, **Fax**: 224 1480, **Email**: centrcr@sol.racsa.co.cr

Country Day School
P.O. Box 8-6170-1000, San José. **Fax**: 289-6798

ELS International
Apt 6495-1000, San Jose. **Tel**: 261 4242, **Fax**: 261 3212, **Email**: acallen@uicr.ac.cr

Escuela Britanica
P.O. Box 8184-1000, San José. **Fax**: 234-7833.

Instituto Britanico
PO Box 8184-1000, San José. **Tel**: 256 0256, **Fax**: 253 1894

Instituto de Inglés USA
Apt 418-1000 C1 A6, San José

International Christian School
P.O. Box 3512-1000, San José. **Tel**: 236-7879. **Fax**: 235-1518.

Lincoln School
P. O. Box 1919-1000, San José. **Tel**: 235 7733, **Fax**: 236-1706.

Marian Baker School
P.O. Box 4269-1000, San José. **Fax:** 273-4609

Monteverde Friends School
P.O. Box 10165-1000, San José. **Fax:** 645-5219.

World Education Forum
PO Box 383-4005, San Antonio de Belén, Heredia. **Tel:** 239 2245, **Fax**: 239 2254.

ECUADOR

Even though the current economic situation is very difficult and many Ecuadorians are leaving the country, there are hundreds of language schools in Ecuador, so it is easy for English teachers to find work, whether they are qualified or not. Until recently, Ecuador was generally considered the best starting point for teachers planning to work their way round South America. Although this may no longer be the case, it is more relaxed than many of its neighbours and still offers plenty of opportunities, especially in the main cities of Quito, Guayaquil and the beautiful Cuenca. Terms and conditions vary and most recruitment is done locally. Many expatriates have set up their own schools, but to find work in them it helps to have personal contacts and qualifications. Some private language schools will often take on native speakers with no qualifications.

➲ **Visas/Work Permits:** It is illegal to work on a tourist visa but many teachers do so anyway. Visitors from the US and Canada are entitled to stay for up to 90 days on a tourist visa. To extend the visa, you have to prove that you have independent income not resulting from work in the country. If you intend to work legally, you have to produce a return air ticket. A tourist visa cannot be exchanged for any other kind of visa once in the country, so if you get a job while you are there, you have to go to neighbouring country, usually Colombia, to get the necessary paperwork. Most employers will help teachers to get a one-year cultural exchange visa, as long as they commit themselves to staying for a reasonable length of time.

➲ **Currency:** £1 = 1.85 / $1 = 1 US Dollar

➲ **Salaries/Taxes:** The monthly rate for unqualified teachers starts at about £215 / $370, rising to £300 / $570 in more reputable schools. The top schools pay about £500-600 / $950-1100 a month and only employ qualified teachers. Everyone is taxed at 5-8%, regardless of whether they are working legally or not.

⊃ **Accommodation:** Wide range available. Expect to pay £150 / $220 a month for an apartment in Quito. The usual deposit is two months' rent.

⊃ **Cost of Living:** Figure on basic living expenses of around £80 / $150 per month.

⊃ **Health advice:** Malaria and dengue fever are prevalent in Guayaquil and the coastal region. Cases of cholera and yellow fever have also been reported. Medical care is available but it varies in quality and generally is below UK or U.S. standards.

⊃ **English Language Media:** Q Magazine, Inside Ecuador.

Schools in Ecuador (+593)

American Language School
Carchi 904 y Velez, Guayaquil. **Tel:** 452926.

Benedict
9 De Octubre 1515, Y Orellana, Quito.

Benedict
Datiles y La Primera, CC Urdesa, Guayaquil.

Centro De Estudios Interamericanos
Casilla 597, Cuenca.

Centro Ecuatoriano NorteAmericano
Luis Urdeneta y Cordoba, Guayaquil, **Tel:** 564536.

Experimento De Convivencia International Del Ecuador
Les Embleton, Hernando de la Cruz 218 y Mariana de Jesús, Quito. **Tel:** 2 551937/550179, **Fax:** 2 55 0228.

Fulbright Commission
Almagro 961 y Colon, Quito. **Tel:** 2 562999.

International Benedict Schools of Languages
PO Box 09-01-8916, Guayaquil. **Tel:** 4 444418, **Fax:** 4 441642.

Lingua Franca
Edificio Jerico, 12 De Octubre 2449 y Orellana, Casilla 17-2-68, Quito. **Tel:** 2 546075, **Fax:** 2 500734.

Quito Language and Culture Centre
Republica De El Salvador, 639 Y Portugal, Quito.

EL SALVADOR

The country is slowly recovering from the long and bloody civil war. English lessons are very popular and experienced native speakers are genuinely respected here. Many English teachers are Salvadorans who have been deported from the States who are not teachers by profession. An MA in TESOL or a certificate will enhance your wage-earning capacity. You can live quite well on a tight budget in El Salvador and, unlike Costa Rica the country is not full of "gringos."

⊃ **Visas/Work Permits:** You will be given a free tourist card on your flight in. This is good for 30-90 days after which you can pop across the border and then return. Each school has its own policy regarding work permits but most are not interested in red tape and will employ teachers on tourist visas.

⊃ **Currency:** £1 = 16.37 / $1 = 8.75 Colon

⊃ **Salaries/Taxes:** You can earn about £300 / $570 per month or £6 / $10 an hour if you freelance. Foreigners are liable for tax unless they are being paid "under the table."

⊃ **Accommodation:** In San Salvador, you can pay anywhere from £30 / $60 a month for a two-bedroom house in a rough area to £600 / $1100 for an apartment in a tony neighbourhood. Utility bills are around £12-15 / $20-30 per month.

⊃ **Health advice:** Dengue fever is a big problem. Medical care is limited. Emergency services, even in San Salvador, are very basic. Ambulance services are not staffed by trained personnel and lack life-saving necessities such as oxygen. Doctors in the major hospitals are generally well-trained, often in U.S. hospitals, but nursing and support staff are not up to UK or U.S. standards.

Schools in El Salvador (+503)

Academia Europea
911 Ave Nte., San Salvador. **Tel:** 263 4355. **Fax:** 263 4430. **Email:** jobs@euroacad.edu.sv

Escuela Superior De Idiomas
Ave. La Campilla 226, Colonia San Benito, San Salvador. **Tel:** 264 1256.

GUATEMALA

This is a popular destination for EFL teachers drawn here by the colourful indigenous culture. Some teachers recommend getting out of the capital city and working in Antigua or Quetzaltenango.

⊃ **Visas/Work Permits:** Tourist visas are granted for 90 days. It is possible to obtain a work permit through the Guatemalan consulate in your country if you have a job offer, your last two bank statements showing you have funds to live on when you arrive and two photos. But most teachers just turn up and work on their tourist visas.

⊃ **Currency:** £1 = 14.39 / $1 = 7.78 Quetzal

⊃ **Salaries/Taxes:** Salaries are very low (around £3 / $5 an hour) and if you have a work permit, you will pay tax at around 30%.

⊃ **Health advice:** Health care facilities are good in Guatemala City but are more limited elsewhere.

Schools in Guatemala (+502)

American School of Guatemala
Aptdo Postal 83, 01901 Guatemala City. **Tel:** 369 0791.

Colegio Americano de Guatemala
11 Calle 15-70, Zona 15, Vista Hermosa.

Colegio Ingles Americano
0 Calle 19-70, Zona 15, V.H. II , Guatemala City.

Colegio Internacional Montessori
Carr. el Salv. Km. 13.5 finca la Luz, Guatemala City. **Tel:** 2 3641921.

Instituto Guatamelteco-Americano
Ruta 1, 4-05, Aptdo. 691, Guatemala City. **Tel:** 331 0022, **Fax:** 332 3135

Modern American English School
c/ de los Nazarenos 16, Antigua. **Tel:** 932 3306, **Fax:** 932 0217.

HONDURAS

Demand for native-speaking English teachers is high in Honduras both in private language schools and in the state colleges and universities. Students at bilingual school learn Spanish and English. The country is still recovering from the effects of Hurricane Mitch and many roads are washed out.

⊃ **Visas/Work Permits:** After you have a job offer, you must apply for a residency permit from outside Honduras although you can look for work as a tourist. The process can take anywhere from four to six months.

⊃ **Currency:** £1 = 34 / $1 = 18 Lempira

⊃ **Salaries/Taxes:** Rates of pay vary from £2-5 / $3-$8 an hour.

⊃ **Accommodation:** Your employer will probably offer you accommodation but be warned that many apartment blocks in the country are not finished and that you may be without water and electricity for periods of time.

⊃ **Cost of Living:** Cheap.

⊃ **Health advice:** Doctors are generally well trained; but support staff and facilities generally are not up to UK or U.S. standards, and facilities for certain surgical procedures are not available. Drink bottled water.

Schools in Honduras (+504)

American School
c/o American Embassy-Tegucigalpa Honduras, Dept of State, Washington DC 20521-3480: **Tel:** 32 4696

Centro Cultural Sampedrano
3 Calle, entra 3A y 4A Avenida 20 , Apartado Postal 511, San Pedro Sula, Cortes.

Escuela Anglo-Hondurena
Colonia La Reforma, Edificio Club Arabe, Tegucigalpa. **Tel:** 236 8814.

Harris Communications
Ave. Circunvalación, Centro Comercial La Careta, San Pedro Sula **Tel/Fax:** 504 557-3416.

Instituto Hondureno de Cultura Americana
2 Avenida entre 5 y 6 Calles No. 520, Apartado 201, MDC Comayaguela , Tegucigalpa.

JAMAICA

American teachers are sometimes employed in the public school system. There are limited opportunities in private EFL schools.

⊃ **Visas/Work Permits:** You can apply for a work permit when you are in Jamaica.

⊃ **Currency:** £1 = 113 / $1 = 61 Dollars

⊃ **Salaries/Taxes:** You can make J$150 an hour in a school and at least J$200 for private lessons. Income tax is 25%.

⊃ **Accommodation:** It is hard to find cheap accommodation in Kingston.

⊃ **Cost of Living:** Prices are quite high in Kingston but cheaper elsewhere.

⊃ **Health advice:** Ambulance service is limited both in the quality of emergency care, and in the availability of vehicles in remote parts of the country.

Schools in Jamaica (+809)

Language Training Centre Ltd
24 Parkington Plaza, Kingston 10. **Tel:** 926 03756.

Target English Associates
9a Duquesnam Ave., Kingston 10. **Tel:** 929 2473.

MEXICO

Mexico is a popular destination for all ELT teachers, particularly American ESL teachers – after all, they can always walk home if something goes wrong! Increasing trade with the U.S. and Canada means that more Mexican companies require their employees to speak (American) English. Teachers are usually recruited locally because schools are finding it increasingly difficult to pay recruitment costs, but it is possible to organize a job from outside the country.

Embassy in UK:
8 Halkin Street, London SW1X 7DW
Tel: 020 7235 6393

Embassy in USA:
1911 Pennsylvania Ave NW, Washington DC 20006
Tel: 202 728 1600
www.embassyofmexico.org

British Council office:
Lope de Vega 316, Col. Chapultepec Morales, Mexico City, 11570 DF
Tel +52 (55) 5263 1900
www.britishcouncil.org.mx

➲ **Visas/Work Permits:** Tourist visas are available for up to six months. Work permits are usually granted to American and Canadian teachers. Make sure your school provides you with all the necessary paperwork. There are reports of immigration inspectors posing as English students trying to catch out foreigners teaching on tourist visas. Keep your tourist card or other papers on you at all times in case an official asks to see them.

➲ **Currency:** £1 = 18.3 / $1 = 10.5 New Peso

➲ **Salaries/Taxes:** Teachers with an MA in TESOL can make £600 / $1100 a month or more, which is very good considering that Mexican teachers in the state system receive about £300 / $570. Tax is about 25%.

➲ **Cost of Living:** It's quite expensive to live in Mexico City but much cheaper elsewhere. Meals can be anywhere from £1-£6 depending on where you go, Estimate spending about £20-£30 / $35-$60 a month on food if you eat out once or twice a week.

➲ **Accommodation:** Rents vary across the country. Cheap rooms (£30 / $60 per month) can be found in most towns but they tend to be in noisy and sometimes dangerous areas. If you're lucky you may find a nice apartment for around £100 / $190 a month. Of course, you will pay a lot more in the big cities.

➲ **Health advice:** Health facilities in Mexico City are excellent. Care in more remote areas is limited. Serious medical problems requiring hospitalization and/or medical evacuation home can be very costly so insurance is essential.

➲ **English Language Media:** The Mexico City Times, The News.

Schools in Mexico (Mexico City)

Academia De Idiomas Tepeyac
Misterios 764 Col. Tepeyac Insurgentes C.P.07020, Ciudad De Mexico, Df. **Tel:** 5 7810046

American Tem
Eduardo Molina 440 Col. Nueva Atzacoalco C.P.07420, Ciudad De Mexico, Df. **Tel:** 5 7531720

Angloamericano
Campos Eliseos 111 Col. Polanco, C.P.11560, Ciudad De Mexico, Df. **Tel:** 5 6586700

Aprendizaje Inst. A.C.
Montevideo 284 P-2 Col. Lindavista, C.P.07300, Ciudad De Mexico, Df. **Tel:** 5 5860196, 5 5861776

Berlitz
Reforma 132 Col. Juarez C.P.06600, Ciudad De Mexico, Df. **Tel:** 5 7050832, 5 7056695

Berlitz
Bosque Ciruelos 194, 2do. Piso Col. Bosques De Las Lomas C.P.11700 Ciudad De Mexico, Df. **Tel:** 5 5969190, 5 5969160

Berlitz
Pafnucio Padilla #17 P-1, Plaza Satelite Col. Satelite C.P.53100 Ciudad De Mexico, Df. **Tel:** 5 5620190, 5 3934981 **Email:**Centro.Satelite@Berlitz.com.mx

Berlitz
Sn Jeronimo 240 Col. Pedregal De San Angel C.P.01900 Ciudad De Mexico, Df. **Tel:** 5 6161953, 5 5504359

Berlitz
Montevideo 365 Esq. Payta Col. Lindavista C.P.07300 Ciudad De Mexico, Df. **Tel:** 5 7521210, 5 7544025.

Berlitz
Lomas Verdes 825 43 Col. Lomas Verdes Nauc C.P.53120 Ciudad De Mexico, Df. **Tel:** 5 3436497.

Berlitz
Del Hueso 480 Loc 11 Col. Los Girasoles C.P.04920 Ciudad De Mexico, Df. **Tel:** 5 6797146, 5 6790438

Berlitz
Insurgentes Sur 1261 Col. Extrem-adura Insurgentes C.P.03740 Ciudad De Mexico, Df. **Tel:** 5 6117468, 5 6117551

Britt Servicios Linguisticos
Berlin 27 B Col. Juarez C.P.66000 Ciudad De Mexico, Df. **Tel:** 5 5466160

Britt Servicios Linguisticos
Luz Avi&On 2011 4 Col. Narvarte C.P.03020 Ciudad De Mexico, Df. **Tel:** 5 6873571

Centro Cultural Benjamin Franklin Sc
Parroquia 828 Col. Del Valle C.P.03100 Ciudad De Mexico, Df. **Tel:** 5 5347747

Ef
Alfredo Musset 228 Col. Polanco C.P.11550 Ciudad De Mexico, Df. **Tel:** 5 5143333, 55313156

Endicott College
Ibsen 43 P-8 Col. Polanco C.P.11560 Ciudad De Mexico, Df. **Tel:** 5 2801225

English For Executives
Viveros De Asis 19 Col. Viveros De La Loma C.P.54080 Ciudad De Mexico, Df. **Tel:** 5 3615234, 5 3979980

English On Site
Giotto 29, Col. Mixcoac C.P.04300 Ciudad De Mexico, Df. **Tel:** 5 6112761

Harmon Hall
San Luis Potosi 196 Col. Roma C.P.06700 Ciudad De Mexico, Df. **Tel:** 5 5847599

Harmon Hall
Puebla 319 0670 Col. Roma C.P.06700 Ciudad De Mexico, Df. **Tel:** 5 2118019, 5 2112020

Harmon Hall
Rojo Gomez 1457 Col. San Pablo C.P.09360 Ciudad De Mexico, Df. **Tel:** 5 6853258, 5 6852181

Ingles Sin Barreras Sa De Cv
Medellín 184, Col. Roma C.P.06700 Ciudad De Mexico, Df. **Tel:** 5 5649739

Instituto Anglo Mexicano De Cultura Ac
Av Insurgentes Sur 710 Col. Del Valle C.P.03100 Ciudad De Mexico, Df. **Tel:** 5 5360742, 55236641

Instituto Anglo Mexicano De Cultura Ac
Rio Nazas 116 Col. Cuauhtemoc C.P.54124 Ciudad De Mexico, Df. **Tel:** 5 2085640, 5 2085799, 5 7051866, 5 5116926

Instituto Hamer Sharp
M Avila Camacho 291 Loc-A-29-30-31 Col. Lomas De Sotelo C.P.11220 Ciudad De Mexico, Df. **Tel:** 5 5806834, 5 5800341, 5 5802676

Instituto Mexico Norteamericano De Idiomas Sc
Av Chapultepec 474 Col. Roma Nte C.P.06700 Ciudad De Mexico, Df. **Tel:** 5 2116758, 5 2867988

Instituto Superior De Idiomas Sa
Viena 71-301 Col. Del Carmen Coyoacan C.P.04100 Ciudad De Mexico, Df. **Tel:** 5 6593533

Interlingua
Montevideo 405 073 Col. Lindavista C.P.07300 Ciudad De Mexico, Df. **Tel:** 5 5864398, 5 5863275, 5 7541209

Interlingua
Medicos 3 Piso 2 Col. Zp Em Frac Cd Satelite C.P.53100 Ciudad De Mexico, Df. **Tel:** 55720697, 55623713

Interlingua, Genova
33 Piso 6 Col. Juarez C.P.06600 Ciudad De Mexico, Df. **Tel:** 5 2080737, 5 5336706, 5 2081919

Interlingua
J Balmes 11 D Piso 2 Mezzanine Col. Los Morales Polanco C.P.11510 Ciudad De Mexico, Df. **Tel:** 5 5572875

Interlingua
Av Insurgentes Sur 1971 L-280 Col. Guadalupe Inn C.P.01020 Ciudad De Mexico, Df. **Tel:** 5 6627208, 5 6627207, 5 6613787, 5 6614166

La Villa English Academies
Calz De Guadalupe 156-A Col. Ex-Hipodromo De Peralvill C.P.06220 Ciudad De Mexico, Df. **Tel:** 5 5176876, 5 5374401

Prompt English
Viveros De Asis 13-200 Col. Viveros De La Loma C.P.54080 Ciudad De Mexico, Df. **Tel:** 5 3628523

Quick Learning
Arellano 14 Piso 2 Col. Cd Satelite Edo De Me C.P.53100 Ciudad De Mexico, Df. **Tel:** 5 5626036, 5 5626852

Quick Learning
Av Division Del Norte 2646 Col. Churubusco Contry Club C.P.04210 Ciudad De Mexico, Df. **Tel:** 5 6055934

Quick Learning
Liverpool 143-102 Col. Juarez C.P.06600 Ciudad De Mexico, Df. **Tel:** 5 5330180

Quick Learning
Av Molina Enriquez 4231 P-1 Col. Viaducto Piedad C.P.08200 Ciudad De Mexico, Df. **Tel:** 5 7406466, 5 7406569, 5 7406576

Quick Learning
Insurg Sur 586 601 Col. Del Valle C.P.03100 Ciudad De Mexico, Df. **Tel:** 5 6829970, 5 6829962

Quick Learning
Rancho Toyocan 61 Loc 5 Y 6 - R Col. Los Girasoles
C.P.04929 Ciudad De Mexico, Df. **Tel:** 5 6842021

Quick Learning
Calle Sur 71 No 4231 Col. Viaducto Piedad C.P.08200
Ciudad De Mexico, Df. **Tel:** 5 7406677

Quick Learning
Calendula 111 Piso 3 Col. Xotepingo C.P.04610
Ciudad De Mexico, Df. **Tel:** 5 6104246

Quick Learning
Jinetes 18 Col. Las Arboledas C.P.53139 Ciudad De
Mexico, Df. **Tel:** 5 3792054

Schola
Lamartine 138 Col. Polanco C.P.11570 Ciudad De
Mexico, Df. **Tel:** 5 5453804

Servicio Linguistico Empresarial
Sn Fco 657 A Piso 12 - B Col. Del Valle C.P.03100
Ciudad De Mexico, Df. **Tel:** 5 6874449, 5 5236380, 5
6691066

USA
Egipto 206 Loc-A Col. Claveria C.P.02080 Ciudad De
Mexico, Df. **Tel:** 5 3410092, 5 3410211

Wall Street Institute
Ipsen 4343 8 Piso Col. Polanco C.P.11580 Ciudad De
Mexico, Df. **Tel:** 5 2800809

Wave Comunicacion De Mexico
Insurg Cto 51 204 Col. San Rafael C.P.06470 Ciudad
De Mexico, Df. **Tel:** 5 5350124

Schools (on outskirts of Mexico City)

Academia Comercial Linguistica
Montiel 205 Col. Lindavista C.P.07300 Ciudad De
Mexico, Df. **Tel:** 5 5776380

Active English Institute
Playa Langosta 311 Col. Reforma Ixtaccihuatl
C.P.08840 Ciudad De Mexico, Df. **Tel:** 5 5322881

American British English Sc
Londres 40-10 P-1 Col. Juarez C.P.06600 Ciudad De
Mexico, Df. **Tel:** 5 5145856, 5 5143348

Angloamericano De Satelite
Circunvala-cion Ote 8 Deps 308 Col. Satelite C.P.0
1030 Ciudad De Mexico, Df. **Tel:** 5 5721737

Angloamericano Satelite
Vito Alessio Robres 233 Col. Florida C.P.01030
Ciudad De Mexico, Df. **Tel:** 5 5727838

Centro Angloamericano Sur
Alessio Robles 233 Col. Florida C.P.01030 Ciudad De
Mexico, Df. **Tel:** 5 6580889

Centro De Aprendizaje Linguistico
M Escobedo 446 Col. Polanco Reforma C.P.11550
Ciudad De Mexico, Df. **Tel:** 5 2503851

Centro De Capacitacion En Lenguas Extranjeras
Coru&A 201 P-1 Col. Viaducto Piedad C.P.08200
Ciudad De Mexico, Df. **Tel:** 5 5305050

Centro De Convivencia Linguistica
O Del Ajusco 2 Col. Zp Em Frac Los Pirules
C.P.54040 Ciudad De Mexico, Df. **Tel:** 5 3791310

Centro De Idiomas Dinamicos
Luz Savi&On 13 - 902 Col. Del Valle C.P.03100
Ciudad De Mexico, Df. **Tel:** 5 5438280

Centro De Idiomas Dinamicos
L Savi&On 13 301 Col. Del Valle C.P.03100 Ciudad
De Mexico, Df. **Tel:** 5 5434534, 5 6692259, 5
6829805

Centro De Idiomas Sn Angel
Insurgentes Sur 2047 P-A Col. Sn Angel C.P.01000
Ciudad De Mexico, Df. **Tel:** 5 6617422, 5 6617423

Centro De Idiomas Tamesis
Plaza De La Constitucion Mz 10 Lt 44 Col. Plaza
Aragon C.P.57139 Ciudad De Mexico, Df. **Tel:** 5
7104056

Centro De Idiomas Y Diversificados
Nuevo Leon 253 305 Col. Escandon C.P.11800 Ciudad
De Mexico, Df. **Tel:** 5 5163049

Centro De Ingles Abraham Lincoln
Ermita Izt 326 Col. Cacama C.P.09080 Ciudad De
Mexico, Df. **Tel:** 5 5814949

Centro Especializado De Servicios Linguisticos
Cuitlahuac 2725 Col. Popular C.P.02840 Ciudad De
Mexico, Df. **Tel:** 5 3412253

Centro Linguistico De Ingles
Yucatan 189 Ph Col. Tizapan Sn Angel C.P.01090
Ciudad De Mexico, Df. **Tel:** 5 6164315

Centro Linguistico Lucerna
Tulipan 40 Col. Ciudad Jardin C.P.04370 Ciudad De
Mexico, Df. **Tel:** 5 5495846

Centro Linguistico Valle Dorado
Atenas 137 Col. Valle Dorado C.P.54020 Ciudad De
Mexico, Df. **Tel:** 5 3706808

Centro Universitario De Idiomas
Dr Galvez 38 Col. San Angel C.P.01000 Ciudad De
Mexico, Df. **Tel:** 5 5503808

Chanor Company
Bosques De Duraznos 65-205 Col. Bosques De Las Lomas C.P.11 700 Ciudad De Mexico, Df. **Tel:** 5 5964052

Cima
Saltillo 91-B Col. Hipodromo C.P.0 6100 Ciudad De Mexico, Df. **Tel:** 5 516 4605, 5 5165516, 5 5167138

Comercio En Mexico Del Centro Internacional
Ave Insurgentes Sur No 421 B-301 Col. H Condesa C.P.06140 Ciudad De Mexico, Df. **Tel:** 5 2643347

Complete Language Services
Barranca Del Muerto 525 P-6 Col. Merced Gomez C.P.01600 Ciudad De Mexico, Df. **Tel:** 5 6643622

Converse International School Of Languages
Melchor Ocampoloc-H4-6 193 Col. Veronica Anzures C.P.11590 Ciudad De Mexico, Df. **Tel:** 5 2609002

Cosmo Educacion
Insurg Sur 1694 Col. Florida C.P.01030 Ciudad De Mexico, Df. **Tel:** 5 6618367

Cosmo
Anatole France 13 Altos Col. Chapultepec Polanco C.P.11560 Ciudad De Mexico, Df. **Tel:** 5 2820380, 5 2821021, 5 2821279

Desarrollo De Idiomas Empresariales
Av Nuevo Leon 270 P-2 Col. Hipodromo C.P.06100 Ciudad De Mexico, Df. **Tel:** 5 2719024

Easy English Institute
Ave San Isidro 288-302 Col. San Isidro Cacahulton C.P.0 2720 Ciudad De Mexico, Df. **Tel:** 5 3523951

EF Servicios En Educacion Internacional
Londres No 188 Mezzanine Col. Juarez C.P.06600 Ciudad De Mexico, Df. **Tel:** 5 5251216

Escuela Internacional De Idiomas
Ailes 144 Col. Sn Mateo. C.P.53240 Ciudad De Mexico, Df. **Tel:** 5 3733951

Escuela Mexicana Canadiense De Ingles
Miguel A De Quevedo 928 - M Col. Parque Sn Andres C.P.04330 Ciudad De Mexico, Df. **Tel:** 5 6593252

Escuela Mexicana Canadiense De Ingles
M Angel De Quevedo 928 Col. Rosedal Coyoacan C.P.04330 Ciudad De Mexico, Df. **Tel:** 5 6594112

Especialistas En Idiomas
Arellano 14 P-1 Col. Cd Satelite C.P.53100 Ciudad De Mexico, Df. **Tel:** 5 3939271

Focus On Language
Colina De Aconitos 15 8 Col. Boulevares C.P.53140 Ciudad De Mexico, Df. **Tel:** 5 5723406

Gpo Educativo Angloamericano
Vito Alessio Robles 233 Col. Florida C.P.01030 Ciudad De Mexico, Df. **Tel:** 5 6589656, 5 6589540, 5 6589632

Harmon Hall
Eugenia No 106 Col. Narvarte C.P.03020 Ciudad De Mexico, Df. **Tel:** 5 5238359

Harmon Hall Del Valle
Eugenia 1606 Col. Narvarte C.P.03020 Ciudad De Mexico, Df. **Tel:** 5 6874987

Harmon Hall Toreo
Av Rodolfo Gadna No 6 5do Piso Col. Lomas De Sotelo C.P.53390 Ciudad De Mexico, Df. **Tel:** 5 3958300, 5 3958400

Ibi Instituto Britanico
Campos Eliseos 204 P-4 Col. Polanco C.P.11560 Ciudad De Mexico, Df. **Tel:** 5 2812465

Idiomas Empresariales Marva
Gante 15 P-2 Loc-213 Col. Centro C.P.06010 Ciudad De Mexico, Df. **Tel:** 5 5102997, 5 5129242

Guadalajara

American English centre
Av Federalismo Sur 415 Col. Centro C.P.44100 Guadalajara, Jalisco. **Tel:** 3 6131667

Ayusa Internacional Mexico
Lopez Co-tilla 1713 202 Y 204 Col. Guadalajara C.P. 44140 Guadalajara, Jalisco. **Tel:** 3 6153688

Berlitz
Plabo Neruda #2914 Col. Providencia C.P.44630 Guadalajara, Jal-isco. **Tel:** 3 412074, 3 6414048, 3 641 2768.

Berlitz
Vallarta 1550 Loc. 1 Esq. Marsella Col. Sector Juarez C.P.44140 Guadalajara, Jalisco. **Tel:** 3 6303987

Centro Cultural Linguistico
Universo 746 Jardines Del Col. Jardines Del Bosque Guad C.P.44520 Guadalajara, Jalisco. **Tel:** 3 1216863

Centro De Desarrollo Linguistico
Mariano Otero No 3677 Col. La Calma C.P. 45070 Guadalajara, Jalisco. **Tel:** 3 6342713

Centro Linguistico De Guad-Alajara
S H C 68 N° 46 Desp 201 Col. Santa Teresita C.P.44600 Guadalajara, Jalisco. **Tel:** 3 6166626

Connections
Francisco Frejes 222 Col. Rojas Ladron De Guevara C.P.44650 Guadalajara, Jalisco. **Tel:** 3 6160708, 3 6157451, 3 6161077

EF
Circun Agustin Ya&Ez 2559-2 Col. Arcos Del Sur
C.P.44100 Guadalajara, Jalisco. **Tel:** 3 6301835

Harmon Hall
Lopez Mateos Sur Esq Chimalhuacan Col. Cd Del Sol
C.P.45050 Guadalajara, Jalisco. **Tel:** 3 1212435

Imac Ingles Total
Donato Guerra 180 Col. Alcalde Barranquitas
C.P.44270 Guadalajara, Jalisco. **Tel:** 3 6132805

Ingles Individual
Agustin Ya&Ez 2583 Loc-106 Col. Barrera C.P.44150
Guadala-jara, Jalisco. **Tel:** 3 6165798, 3 6303393

Instituto Anglo Mexicano De Cultura
Av Americas No 1301 Col. Col Providencia Norte
C.P.05308 Guadalajara, Jalisco. **Tel:** 3 8170506

Instituto Luis Silva
Eje Pte 644 Col. El Santuario C.P.44200 Guadalajara,
Jalisco. **Tel:** 3 6134392

Interlingua
Mexico 3065 Piso 2 Col. Vallarta San Lucas Zp 6
C.P.44690 Guadalajara, Jalisco. **Tel:** 3 6150401

International Language Design
Madero 710 Col. Centro C.P.44100 Guadalajara,
Jalisco. **Tel:** 3 8251226

Kaao Centro De Idiomas
Av Lapizlazuli 2515 A Col. Residencial Victoria C.P.
44580 Guadalajara, Jalisco. **Tel:** 3 6327949

Lenguaje World Institud
Santuario 830 Col. Juan Diego C.P.44510 Guadalajara,
Jalisco. **Tel:** 3 1219833

Linguas
Patria 1398 Desp 203 Col. Villa Universitaria
C.P.45110 Guadalajara, Jalisco. **Tel:** 3 6402272

USA English Institute
Victoriano Aguer-os 1474 Col. Sect Juarez Cp 44150
C.P. 44150 Guadalajara, Jalisco. **Tel:** 3 6302255

Vancouver Language Centre
Avenida Vallarta 1151 Col. Americana C.P.44100
Guadalajara, Jalisco. **Tel:** 3 8254271

Wall Street Institute
Ave Vallarta 1530 Col. Centro C.P.44100 Guadalajara,
Jalisco. **Tel:** 3 6162803, 3 6166615, 3 6169124

Aprendizaje Instantaneo Chap
Av Del Sur 1974 Sj Col. Obrera Centro C.P.44140
Guadalajara, Jalisco. **Tel:** 3 8252059

Centro Cultural Norteamericano
Sjc 18 N 172 A S Col. Zp 1 Gua C.P.44100
Guadalajara, Jalisco. **Tel:** 3 6144416

Idiomas SA
Ave Mexico 3065 Piso 2 Col. Residencial San Jorge
C.P.44690 Guadalajara, Jalisco. **Tel:** 3 6152451

Idiomas SA
Shc 7 3065 Piso 2 Col. Residencial San Jorge
C.P.44690 Guadalajara, Jalisco. **Tel:** 3 6300118

Instituto Cultural Mexicano Norteamericano De Guadalajara
Enrique Diaz De Leon 300 Col. Americana C.P.44170
Guadalajara, Jalisco. **Tel:** 3 8258834

Instituto Anglo Mexicano De Cultura
Manuel Acu&A 2674-102 Col. Lomas De Guevara
C.P.44680 Guadalajara, Jalisco. **Tel:** 3 6414017

Instituto Anglo Mexicano De Cultura
Manuel Acu&A 2674-102 Col. Lomas De Guevaraia
C.P.44680 Guadalajara, Jalisco. **Tel:** 3 6414009

Universidad De Guadalajara
Esc Superior De Lenguas Modernas, Apdo. Postal
2-416, 44280 Guadalajara, Jalisco.

Monterrey

Academia De Ingles Prof Gil Moreno
Galeana Sur 418 Col. Centro C.P.64000 Monterrey,
Nl. **Tel:** 83 423844

Berlitz
Padre Mier Pte 241 Pte. Col. Centro C.P.64000
Monterrey, Nl. **Tel:** 83 441761, **Fax:** 83 455781

Berlitz
Rio Mississippi 101-B Col. Del Valle C.P.66220
Monterrey, Nl. **Tel:** 83 561605, 83 561612

English Comunication System
De Los Leones Po 2389 A Col. Las Cumbres
C.P.64610 Monterrey, Nl. **Tel:** 83 001878

English Now
Av Constitucion 1251 Pte Col. Centro C.P.67460
Monterrey, Nl **Tel:** 83 449175

Harmon Hall
Pablo Moncayo 117 Piso 2 Col. Col De San Jeronimo
C.P.64630 Monterrey, Nl. **Tel:** 83 477775, 83 477774

Instituto Mexicano Norteamericano De Relaciones Culturales
Hidalgo Pte 768 Col. Centro C.P.64000 Monterrey, Nl.
Tel: 83 401583

Ingles En Siete Semanas
Washington 2910 Pte Col. Obispado C.P.64610
Monterrey, Nl. **Tel:** 83 477735

Interlingua
Av Jose Vasconcelos Or 109 Col. Del Valle C.P.66220 Monterrey, Nl. **Tel:** 83 786222, 83 786500

Quick Learning
Gonzalitos 916 Col. Mitras Centro C.P.64460 Monterrey, Nl. **Tel:** 83 468718

Teaching Of International Languages
San Lorenzo 165 Col. Vista Hermosa C.P.64620 Monterrey, Nl. **Tel:** 83 465655

Boston English Institute
Matamoros Pte 1174 Col. Centro C.P.64610 Monterrey, Nl. **Tel:** 83 401981

British American School Sc
P Mier Pte 421 Col. Centro C.P.64000 Monterrey, Nl. **Tel:** 83 423887

British American School Sc
Priv Rhin Y Priv Sevilla 651 Col. Centro C.P.64000 Monterrey, Nl. **Tel:** 83 401993

Centro Educativo Bilingue La Paz Sc
Hídalgo Pte 380 Col., C.P. 64000 Monterrey, Nl. **Tel:** 83433406

Cosmo Educacion
Rio Colorado Ote 240 Loc-10 Col. Del Valle C.P.66220 Monterrey, Nl. **Tel:** 83 562935, 83 562925, 83 359221

Desarrollo De Ingles Rapido
Av Pino Suarez 853 Nte Col. Centro C.P.64000 Monterrey, Nl. **Tel:** 83 721222

English Through The Arts
Av Jose Vascon-celos 1501 Pte Loc-5 Y 6 Col. San Pedro C.P.66220 Monterrey, Nl. **Tel:** 83 386713

Harmon Hall Hermosillo A C
Av Eug-enio Garza Sada 3755 Col. Alfonso Reyes C.P.64730 Monterrey, Nl. **Tel:** 83 691924

Interlingua
Av Jose Vasconcelos Or 109 Col. Del Valle C.P.66220 Monterrey, Nl. **Tel:** 83 786244

Liceo Anglofrances De Monterrey
Rio De La Plata Ote 114 Col. Jardines Del Valle C.P.66220 Monterrey, Nl. **Tel:** 83 353576

New English System
Dr Coss 843 Sur Loc-E Col. Centro C.P.64000 Monterrey, Nl. **Tel:** 83 421222

Puebla

Berlitz
39 Ote 3302 Loc 36, 37,38 Col. Centro C.P.72400 Puebla, Pue. **Tel:** 22 498838, 22 498850, **Fax:** 22 498 475, **Email:** Centro.Puebla@Berlitz.Com.Mx

English Training centre
Calle 27 Sur 111 Col. Centro C.P.72000 Puebla, Pue. **Tel:** 22 303243, 22 313848

Harmon Hall
Juarez 2108 Col. La Paz C.P. 72160 Puebla, Pue. **Tel:** 22 424160, 22 424158

Harmon Hall
Calle 51 Pte 505 Loc 133 Col. Plza America C.P.72000 Puebla, Pue. **Tel:** 22 435701, 22 435487

Personal English
9 Pte No 1308 1er Piso Col. Centro C.P.72000 Puebla, Pue. **Tel:** 22 465880

Instituto Anglo Frances
Calle 25 Oriente 1020 Col. Bellavista C.P.72500 Puebla, Pue. **Tel:** 22 432748

Instituto Anglo Mexicano De Cultura Ac
C Comercial Plaza Crystal Zona A Loc 9-1 Col. C.P.72440 Puebla, Pue. **Tel:** 22 405 122

Instituto Angloamericano De Puebla
Clle 5 Pte No 1710 Col. Centro C.P.72000 Puebla, Pue. **Tel:** 22 328885

Interlingua
Reforma Sur 231 R Col. La Paz Pue C.P.72160 Puebla, Pue. **Tel:** 22 493168

Langtrac
Juarez 1905 Desp 10 Col. La Paz C.P.72160 Puebla, Pue. **Tel:** 22 329245, 22 420339

Lewis & Lopez Language Services For Business
7 Poniente 309 Desp 201 Col. Col Centro C.P.72080 Puebla, Pue. **Tel:** 22 422116

Quick Learning
Blvd 5 De Mayo Nº 2509 Col. Del Carmen C.P.72000 Puebla, Pue. **Tel:** 22 430075

Total English
Av Juarez 1310 P-4 Col. Cen-tro C.P.72000 Puebla, Pue. **Tel:** 22 466020

English Training centre
Calle 7 Pte 1905 7 Col. La Pue C.P.72000 Puebla, Pue. **Tel:** 22 323874

Idiomas SA De Cv
Reforma Sur 231 R Col. La Paz Pue C.P.72160 Puebla, Pue. **Tel:** 22 49317

PERU

Spanish is the first language in Peru, and there is a lot of interest in learning English. Many ELT teachers also take advantage of the Spanish schools to learn or improve their Spanish. The country has some of the world's most important archaeological remains, and people leaving the country may be searched to make sure they are not exporting illegal treasures.

Embassy in UK:
52 Sloane Street, London SW1X 9SP
Tel: 020 7838 9223
www.peruembassy-uk.com

Embassy in USA:
1700 Massachusetts Avenue NW, Washington DC 200036
Tel: (202) 833 9860
www.peruemb.org

British Council Office:
Torre Parque Mar (Floor 22)
Av Jose Larco 1301
Miraflores
Tel: 51 1 617 3060
www.britishcouncil.org.pe

➲ **Visas/Work Permits:** Visitors from the UK and US are entitled to stay for 90 days as tourists without a visa. If you intend to work it is necessary to obtain a visa before entering the country.
➲ **Currency:** £1 = 6.05 / $1 = 3.27 nuevos soles
➲ **Health advice:** You should get vaccinations against yellow fever, smallpox and malaria if you are intending to visit the tropical north of the country

Schools in Peru (+51)

Cambridge School
La Alameda de Los Molinos 730-28, La Encantada de Villa, Chorrillos, Lima 9
Tel: (1) 254 0163
Fax: (1) 254 0149
Email: camoff@amauta.rcp.net.pe

Colegio Franklin Delano Roosevelt
Av. La Palmeras 325, Urb. Camacho, La Molina, Lima 12
Tel: (1) 435 0890
Fax: (1) 436 0927
Email: fdr@amersol.edu.pe

Colegio Peruano Britanico
Av. Via Lactea 445, Monterrico
Tel: (1) 436 0151
Fax: (1) 436 1006
Email: postmast@copebrit.edu.pe

Davy College
Av. Hoyos Rubio 2684, Cajamarca
Tel: (44) 827 501
Fax: (44) 827 502
Email: postmaster@davycollege.edu.pe

Hiram Bingham Scool
Paseo La Castellana 919, Higuereta, Lima 33
Tel: (1) 448 1222
Fax: (1) 479 0430
Email: dpringle@hirambingham.edu.pe

Markham College
Augusto Angulo 291, Miraflores, Lima 18
Tel: (1) 241 7677
Fax: (1) 447 5295
Email: postmaster@markham.edu.pe

Newton College
Av. Elias Aparicio 240, Las Lagunas de La Molina, Lima 12
Tel: (1) 368 0163
Fax: (1) 479 0430
Email: college@newton.edu.pe

San Silvestre School
Av. Santa Cruz 1251, Miraflores, Lima 18
Tel: (1) 241 3334
Fax: (1) 445 5075
Email: postmaster@staff.sansil.edu.pe

Sir Alexander Fleming School
Av. America Sur 3701, Trujillo
Tel: (44) 280 395
Fax: (44) 284 440
Email: admissions@fleming.edu.pe

URUGUAY

Rapidly developing economy, with few political problems. There is some street crime in Montevideo, and especially along the beach resorts

Embassy in UK:
140 Brompton Road, London SW3 1HY
Tel: 020 7589 8835

Embassy in USA:
2715 M St NW Washington DC 20007
Tel: (202) 331 1313
www.embassy.org/uruguay

◌ **Visas/Work Permits:** no visas required for short stays, but you will need to show a return ticket; work permits needed if you are intending to work
◌ **Currency:** £1 = 45.7 / $1 = 24.7 pesos
◌ **Health advice:** Medical care is reasonable, but you should get insurance before travelling

Schools in Uruguay (+598)

London Institute (International House)
Av. Brasil 2831, Montevideo 11300
Tel: (2) 709 6774
Fax: (2) 709 0297

Email: araz@netgate.com.uy

VENEZUELA

Venezuela is a well-developed reasonably rich country, and life in the major cities is subject to urban crime like anywhere else

Embassy in UK:
1 Cromwell Rd, London SW7 2HR
Tel: 020 7584 4206
www.venezlon.demon.co.uk

Embassy in USA:
1099, 30th St NW, Washington DC 20007
Tel: (202) 342 2214
www.embavenez-us.org

British Council office:
Piso 3, Torre Credicard, Av Principal El Bosque, Caracas
Tel: +58 (212) 952 9965
www.britishcouncil.org.ve

◌ **Visas/Work Permits:** you need to get a tourist entry card (on the plane) before you enter the country. You also need to show your return ticket. For a longer stay (up to 180 days) you will need a visa and a letter of introduction from your employer
◌ **Currency:** £1 = 3573 / $1 = 1915 bolivares
◌ **Health advice:** Medical care is good in the capital Caracas, but less good in country areas. You will probably have to pay cash to get treatment. Vaccinations against cholera and yellow fever are recommended

Schools in Venezuela (+58)

Wall Street Institute
Avda. Francisco de Miranda, Torre Lido, Piso 11, Torre C, Ofic. 111C, 113C El Rosal, Caracas
Tel: (212) 953 7473
Fax: (212) 374 65 03
Email: wsiven@cantv.net

North America

Finding a job in the USA is not as straight-forward as in other countries. If you are not a US-resident, you'll find that the Homeland Security laws introduced following the September-11 tragedy make it far harder to get a visa and work permit. In addition, in the USA, each state has its own requirements for teacher qualifications (read the requirements in the directory on p224). The schools within a state must also be registered with their state education body – and each state, again, has its own requirements for schools operating in their area. To send out your CV, you need a a list of ESL schools (and there are hundreds in the US). The simplest route to getting a list is to use the Internet. See p73 for job-websites in the USA. Alternatively, use the website address listed for the individual states (on p224) to search for schools in the state.

Job seekers in the field of teaching ESL have a number of resources to turn to help them in their search for work in the U.S. and Canada. *ESL Magazine* and *Language Magazine* often feature display advertisements for ESL teaching positions from U.S. schools and colleges as well as school districts. Local newspapers usually carry advertisements for teaching jobs and *The Chronicle of Higher Education* usually contains positions in colleges and universities for ESL teachers. Try *Education Week* for jobs teaching young learners (the K-12 sector).

You can also find some U.S. and Canadian teaching jobs through the Placement E-Bulletin offered by the professional teachers' association, TESOL, Inc. (http://careers.tesol.org) – the service is free of charge to TESOL members. Jobseekers should also check out the annual TESOL convention where employers are often recruiting for new staff. Another cybersource for ESL jobs is the useful TESLJB-L listserv. Go to http://lc.ust.hk/~teach/temployment.html for information on how to sign on.

On the Internet, visit Tom Riedmiller's site (www.uni.edu/riedmill) for a good overview of ESL job sites. The job listings at Dave's ESL Café site (www.eslcafe.com) sometimes contain positions in the U.S. although it's mostly adverts for other countries.

If you are interested in teaching in the K-12 sector (Kindergarten to 12th grade – young learners), you might try a search of a local school district's site: many of them feature a jobs section. Also, most universities and colleges offer a recruitment section although many of these are not regularly updated and the deadlines for job applications can be months or even years past due.

Teaching in the USA: the Public School System

Tony Donovan surveys the general requirements for teachers who want to work in one of the state schools systems in the U.S. For specific state requirements regarding ESL teacher licensure, certification or endorsement, turn to the listings on p224.

Many teachers looking for teaching jobs in English as a second or foreign language aim for positions at universities and colleges in the United States or overseas. Teaching ESL/EFL in private language schools and within corporate training structures are also popular goals.

Less often considered are ESL teaching possibilities within U.S. public school systems at the elementary, junior and high school levels. Yet many satisfying and rewarding jobs exist in this sector. The massive influx of immigrants into the U.S. within the last 20 years has filled our public schools with children whose native language is not English and who have a clear linguistic disadvantage competing or even surviving in an academic environment. Many of these students drop out at an early age, forever doomed to a marginal life in contemporary, merit-driven America. To counter this lamentable situation, many school systems now provide ESL courses for these students with a view to improving their academic competence.

As a result, trained ESL teachers are in demand, not only in the southwestern states that border Mexico, traditionally the home country of most recent immigrants, but also nationwide, as the influx of immigrants has changed from a tide to a torrent. Yet, my experience has been that few ESL/EFL teachers consider the public schools a viable career alternative and fewer yet understand the professional preparation that this increasingly attractive career path demands.

I will discuss here some of the requirements such a career would entail so as to provide current and future ESL teachers with a clearer picture of what is involved in becoming a public school ESL teacher. My focus will centre on the ESL professional who may have already taught ESL for a few years overseas or at a U.S. university but is now considering continuing a career in public schools.

State Certification: The Basics

Teachers in all 50 states have to obtain full state certification to be able to teach at the public school level. This insures that teacher competence in the classroom meets at least minimal, state-approved standards. However, there are problems associated with this practice.

To begin with, each state has its own set of requirements. Prospective teachers, therefore, should decide early on which state they are going to work in, because if they obtain state certification in Arizona, for example, they may be unable to teach in Florida, at least not until they meet Florida requirements. Reciprocity between states, that is, the acceptance by one state of another state's teaching certificate, is still rare. There are a few states that accept out-of-state certification, but this is the exception, not the rule.

Even these states, however, will accept certification only from certain specified states. No state will accept certification from all other 49 states. Fortunately, it's often the case that a teacher simply has to take one or two additional courses to meet the new state's requirement, or pass a state prescribed test of some kind, so this is not as onerous or as time consuming as it sounds. Also, many states have temporary or emergency certification options, whereby a new out-of-state certified teacher is authorized to instruct for a limited amount of time without having fulfilled all state requirements. Still, these are temporary measures and the teacher is expected to become fully certified as soon as possible.

For the ESL teacher, the problem is often compounded in that many states continue to regard ESL as a branch of English and not really as a fully independent subject as such. ESL certification in these states is most often obtained simply by taking a few courses (which can last as little as a weekend) at a local community college or by passing a language ability test (usually in Spanish) or a combination of these. This "quickie" certification is then added on to the teacher's major subject credential as an endorsement, authorizing him or her to teach ESL in the classroom. The result is that the gym or chemistry teacher, for instance, can become a fully certified ESL teacher with very little training. Professional ESL teachers would be at a disadvantage in cases like these, since their training and ESL degrees would not be valued highly in school districts where this practice occurs. Fortunately, this situation is changing rapidly as recognition of ESL as an independent subject is becoming the norm nationwide.

Certification

Whereas a university career with an eventual professorial rank simply involves obtaining a Ph.D., at least as far as required minimum credentials are concerned, the hoops a prospective public school ESL teacher has to jump through to obtain state certification are, ironically, more involved.

Minimum requirements are at least a BA/BS degree which include state mandated education courses. The usual path for prospective public school teachers is to enter the School of Education of a college or university where they will take the required education courses along with the courses of a declared major. Upon graduation, most states then automatically extend certification in the teacher's field upon application to the appropriate state education agency.

However, it is important to remember that not all undergraduate majors are certifiable. There's no problem with history, French, math and similar foundation courses. But if you

majored in anthropology, for example, no state would certify you in this field, simply because it is not offered in any public school in the country as a regular for-credit subject. You would have had to minor in a "regular" field, such as English, in order to have enough credits in a regular subject to obtain certification in that subject.

Certification is a matter of having enough credits on your transcript in a certain subject to meet state requirements for certification in that subject. Remember that all states have different requirements. Some states also have a time limit on validity of course credits. Credits obtained more than 10 years previous to your application for certification may be invalid in some cases. If you intend to become an ESL teacher, it is highly unlikely that your college at the undergraduate level would offer an ESL/EFL major. Therefore, it would be to your advantage to major instead in an allied field such as English or a foreign language to obtain your certificate (also called credential in some states). Then, if you've taken some ESL or applied linguistics courses, you can easily obtain the ESL endorsement through your state's Department of Education (called by different names in different states), while at the same time remaining eligible to teach in your major field, thereby increasing your employment prospects. A public school teacher with several years of teaching experience would most likely have at least two areas of certification he/she is able to teach in. So having an English certificate, for example, as your major teaching specialty (which is determined by number of college credits in English) and an endorsement in ESL is by no means unusual.

Teaching English as a second or foreign language is a relatively new field of academic endeavour and is considered a specialty rarely offered as a major at the undergraduate level. Most serious TESL teachers continue their education at the post-graduate level and obtain the MA in TESL often long after they've completed their coursework for a BA/BS in a major usually only peripherally relevant to ESL/EFL. They most probably have taught for a few years overseas or in the U.S. at various locations and, because they have never taken an education course, are amazed that their years of ESL teaching experience and their MA in TESL are considered inadequate for hiring purposes in public schools. A person in this situation has few options available to him. Ultimately, he/she will have to return to school to take the state mandated education courses and fulfill certain other requirements, which can include such odd procedures as fingerprinting.

Fortunately, there are several possibilities here, such as distance learning, attending accelerated courses available through private local schools, and, most recently, Internet education options. So long as the courses are accredited by the state, the state doesn't discriminate as to where or how you obtained the required credits. States are usually very liberal towards alternative education paths.

In many states, especially if you have an MA, you can also teach under the provisions of a temporary or emergency certification, while at the same time taking the required courses at night. The point is, there are several ways to become a public school ESL teacher other than the traditional path of entering the School of Education as an undergraduate.

A word of caution: even the most highly regarded ESL/EFL certificate such as the RSA diploma or similar certificate obtained independent of an academic course leading to a university degree, has no validity in the public school system. A state-issued teaching certificate is a completely different document from its similarly named ESL Certificate often obtained at

commercial schools and institutions. No state will accept these documents as substitutes nor will having one increase your employment opportunities within the public school sector. In addition, many school districts and states will not recognize years you taught ESL overseas or even at a U.S. university as valid for salary adjustments or similar employment related issues. It may be unfair, but it's a reality one has to face. I have seen many superb teachers with all kinds of overseas experience, an MA in TESL, excellent recommendations, and so on, be turned down flat upon application to the state Department of Education because they lacked the required education courses. However, do check your state's own rules in this regard. All states view these details quite differently and the rules and regulations are constantly changing.

Prospects

If all this seems somewhat daunting and overwhelming, keep in mind that primary and secondary schools have very different goals and responsibilities from universities or commercial educational establishments. They have to be absolutely sure that anyone entrusted with the education of minors is trustworthy, capable and suitable for the position. Therefore, the procedures involved in obtaining a state teaching certificate are deliberately rigorous, in an effort to recruit the truly dedicated teacher and prevent those not so dedicated from entering the classroom. Once you've made up your mind to teach ESL in the public school system, however, and have fully investigated your options for obtaining certification, you will find the going quite smooth and straightforward with a lot of support and encouragement from your peers and future employers.

Teaching ESL in the public schools is fast becoming an attractive option for many ESL professionals who may have become a little weary of a peripatetic overseas career or the temporary nature of many university ESL jobs. Benefits at the public school level are outstanding. Health care insurance options are probably the best in the country and salaries are now quite in keeping with the arduous duties associated with teaching. Full time work is the norm and retirement benefits are more than adequate. If one really loves to teach, there's the additional opportunity to be associated with young people at the most receptive and creative stage in their lives and to impact their lives as only a truly dedicated teacher can.

All career preparation plans require careful and close study. Preparing to become a public school ESL teacher is no different, especially if you have never been in the system previously or have been away from it for a long time. Be sure to investigate fully what your state's current requirements are for certification in general and for ESL specifically before embarking on any study programme. The best source for obtaining information is from a friend or acquaintance who happens to be a teacher. He or she will know most of the ins and outs and that will save you a lot of time and headaches. Official forms and information pamphlets can be obtained by writing or calling your state education office. Becoming a public school ESL teacher is not an easy road, but it can lead to a highly rewarding teaching career.

Teaching in the USA: State Certification

If you want to teach in the USA, keep in mind that every State has its own requirements for English language teachers – and these vary enormously across the USA. Individual states are continually revising their regulations; this section lists the current requirements, but it is a good idea to contact a particular State Board of Education to find out what are its current requirements.

To find the local schools operating in a state, visit the state's website for lists of their schools – each state has its own requirements for schools (as well as teachers), and often list problems or complaints filed against a school in their directories, giving prospective teachers a good idea of what to expect.

Alabama

Type of Credential: Certification.
Contact: Alabama State Department of Education, Gordon Persons Building, 50 North Ripley Street, P.O. Box 302101, Montgomery, AL 36130-2101.
Tel: 334-242-9977. **Fax:** 334-242-0498.
Email: tcert@sdenet.alsde.edu
Website: www.alsde.edu

Alaska

Type of Credential: Certification
Requirements: All classroom teachers must be certificated based on the completion of a bachelor's degree and approved teacher preparation programme at a regionally accredited college or university. An endorsement in ESL, ENL, bilingual education or another similar designation, as determined by the title of the approved programme completed, is available. Such an endorsement is not required by the state for a person to be assigned to teach in the area. Some districts do require the endorsement.

Reciprocity: Alaska is a signatory of the Interstate Contract, with reciprocity of programme approval but not of certification or endorsements.
Needs: "We need good teachers!" The pay is very good and there are many opportunities to work in rural villages with predominantly Alaska Native student population, many of whom speak English as a second language. Check out our website and its link to Alaska Teacher Placement (Tel: 907-474-6644).
Contact: Administrator of Teacher Education & Certification, Alaska Dept. of Education & Early Development, 801 W. 10th St, Ste 200, Juneau, AK 99801-1894.
Tel: 907-586-8661. **Fax:** 907-586-2441.
Email: certify@eed.state.ak.us
Website: www.eed.state.ak.us

Arkansas

Contact: Andre Guerrero, Office of Professional Licensure, Arch Ford Education Building, 4 Capitol Mall, #106-7 B, Little Rock, AK 72201.

Tel: 501-682-4344. **Email:**
aguerrero@arkedu.k12.ar.us
Website:http://arkedu.state.ar.us/teacher.htm

Arizona

Type of Credential: Endorsement.
Requirements: PROVISIONAL ENGLISH AS A
SECOND LANGUAGE ENDORSEMENT–Valid
three years, not renewable. A valid Arizona
elementary, secondary, special education, or vocational
certificate

- Three semester hours of ESL methods
- Three semester hours of ESL courses toward the full
 endorsement (second language learning experience
 courses not applicable)

Requirements for the English as a second language
endorsement

A valid Arizona elementary, secondary, special
education, or vocational certificate
Completion of a programme in ESL or the following
courses:

- Three semester hours of courses in foundations of
 instruction for non-English-language-background
 students. Three semester hours of courses in the
 nature and grammar of the English language, taken
 before January 1, 1999, may substitute for this
 requirement.
- Three semester hours of ESL methods
- Three semester hours of teaching of reading and
 writing to limited-English-proficient students
- Three semester hours of assessment of
 limited-English-proficient students
- Three semester hours of linguistics
- Three semester hours of courses dealing with school,
 community, and family culture and parental
 involvement in programmes of instruction for
 non-English-language-background students
- Three semester hours of a practicum or 2 years of
 verified ESL or bilingual teaching experience
 (verified by letter from District Superintendent or
 Personnel Director)

Second language learning experience, which may
include sign language, documented by any of the
following:

- Six semester hours of courses in a single second
 language, or the equivalent, verified by the
 department of language, education, or English at an
 accredited institution
- Completion of intensive language training by the
 Peace Corps, the Foreign Service Institute, or the
 Defense Language Institute

- Placement by the language department of an
 accredited institution in a third-semester level
- Placement at level 1-intermediate/ low or more
 advanced score on the Oral Proficiency Interview,
 verified by the American Council for the Teaching
 of Foreign Languages
- Passing score on the Arizona Classroom Spanish
 Proficiency Examination approved by the Board

Proficiency in an American Indian language, verified
by an official designated by the appropriate tribe

- A valid ESL certificate or endorsement from another
 state may substitute for requirements #2, 3, and 4.

Reciprocity: With 19 states. Provisional certificate
issued to qualified teachers – valid for one year.
Contact: Certification Unit, Arizona Department of
Education, P.O. Box 6490, Phoenix, AZ 85007 (also:
400 West Congress, Tucson, AZ 85701).
Tel: 602-542-4367 (Phoenix); 520-628-6326 (Tucson).
Fax: 602-542-1141.
Email: Certification@mail1.ade.state. az.us
Website:
www.ade.state.az.us/certification/requirements/eslendo
rsment.htm

California

Type of Credential: Certificate.
Requirements: Certificates authorize teachers to
provide certain types of instruction to
limited-English-proficient (LEP) students. These
certificates are the Crosscultural, Language and
Academic Development (CLAD) Certificate and the
Bilingual, Crosscultural, Language and Academic
Development (BCLAD) Certificate.

The purpose of the CLAD/BCLAD Examinations
is to identify candidates for certification who have
demonstrated the level of knowledge and skills
required to teach LEP students satisfactorily. These
exams measure each examinee's knowledge and skills
in relation to an established standard rather than in
relation to those of other examinees. The passing score
for each test was established by the Commission on
Teacher Credentialing based on the professional
judgments and recommendations of California
teachers. The CLAD/BCLAD Examinations include
six separate tests. Passage of the first three tests is one
way to satisfy one of the requirements for a CLAD
Certificate. Test 1: Language Structure and First and
Second-Language Development. Test 2: Methodology
of Bilingual, English Language Development, and
Content Instruction. Test 3: Culture and Cultural
Diversity. Test Dates: February, June. Test Fees: Test
1: $35. Tests 2 and 3: $60 per test.

Contact: California Commission on Teacher Credentialing, Information Services Unit, 1900 Capitol Avenue, P.O. Box 944270, Sacramento, CA 94244-2700.
Tel: 916-445-7254 or 888-921-2682.
Email: credentials@ctc.ca.gov
Website: www.ctc.ca.gov/profserv/examinfo/cladbclad.html

Colorado

Reciprocity: A Provisional Colorado License may be issued to an applicant from another state or country who has met the following:

- Has completed the appropriate degree, experience and educational level for the license and endorsement requested as specified by Colorado standards,
- Has completed a state-approved programme at an accepted out-of-state institution in the endorsement area sought
- Holds or is eligible to hold a standard license or certificate from the preparing state,
- Has passed the PLACE® assessment required.

Contact: Siri Vongthieres, Colorado Department of Education, English Language Unit, 201 East Colfax Avenue, Denver, CO 80203-1704.
Tel: (303) 866-6784. **Fax**: (303) 866-6836.
Email: vongthieres_s@cde.state.co.us

Connecticut

Requirements: All TESOL teachers in the public schools must hold certification in TESOL. Teachers must apply for and obtain TESOL certification prior to serving as TESOL teachers in Connecticut public schools in grades pre-kindergarten through grade 12, and the teaching of English to non-English speaking adults.

Connecticut regulations call for the completion of an approved planned programme in TESOL (unless a candidate has already completed a planned programme and holds a valid certificate in another teaching area), consisting of general academic, TESOL and professional education course work. An applicant must be formally recommended as completing an institution's approved certification programme in TESOL. If for cross endorsement, 30 semester hours of credit in TESOL specific course areas must be completed.

In order to add TESOL, grades Pre K-12, to an existing teaching certificate, an applicant must complete a total of 30 semester hours of credit in TESOL courses with a minimum of 3 semester credits distributed among each of the following areas: 1. English Language: A minimum of 3 semester hours of credit must be completed in syntax or composition. In addition, course work in history of the English language, British or American literature may be accepted. 2. Language Theory: This group includes course work in the nature and structure of English and other languages, their systematic organization and change; major contemporary models of linguistic description and language variation, including social, regional and functional variations of English and other languages; language acquisition theory and its application to assessment, placement and education of limited English proficient students, bilingualism and language cognition. 3. Culture and Intergroup Relations: This includes coursework in the awareness of cross-cultural similarities and contrasts, the nature of specific American or foreign cultures; multicultural education, and the effects of culture on language and cognition. 4. Linguistic and Academic Assessment of Limited English Proficient Students: This includes testing and evaluation techniques applicable to the determination of language dominance, language proficiency and bilingualism of limited English proficient students. 5. Curriculum and Methods of Teaching: This group includes areas such as methods of teaching English to speakers of other languages; curriculum development related to TESOL. For certification to teach English to non-English-speaking adults only, a candidate must hold a bachelor's degree from an approved institution; complete three semester hours of credit in methods of teaching English to speakers of other languages, and complete a state mandated course in special education. (Special education course may be a deficiency on a one-year interim teacher certificate).

Reciprocity: Through the NASDTEC Interstate Contract, an applicant may qualify for a Connecticut certificate based on: holding a valid level II or III certificate/ license from a participating state upon completion of an approved planned program, OR (2) Level II or III certification/ license and 27 school months of experience in a participating state within the last seven years.

The following states currently participate with Connecticut (re: TESOL certification) in the NASDTEC Interstate Contract: Alabama, Arizona, Arkansas, California, Colorado, Delaware, District of Columbia, Florida, Georgia, Hawaii, Idaho, Illinois, Indiana, Kentucky, Maine, Maryland, Massachusetts, Michigan, Mississippi, Montana, Nevada, New Hampshire, New Jersey, New Mexico, New York,

North Carolina, Ohio, Oklahoma, Oregon, Pennsylvania, Rhode Island, South Carolina, Tennessee, Texas, Utah, Vermont, Virginia, Washington and West Virginia.

Provisional Licenses: Certification is required for all professional teachers, including TESOL teachers, in the public schools in Connecticut.

However, if a shortage of certified TESOL teachers has been established by a local school district, the local district may request for the issuance of a special permit (Durational Shortage Area Permit or DSAP). Prior to issuance of the DSAP, the candidate for the permit must fulfill the Praxis I Computer-Based Test requirement, be enrolled in a planned programme leading toward certification in TESOL, holds a bachelor's degree and has completed at least 12 semester hours of credit in TESOL courses.

The DSAP may be reissued no more than two times upon completion of additional credits each time.
Contact: Bureau of Certification and Professional Development, State Department of Education, P.O. Box 150471, Hartford, CT 06115-0471.
Tel: 860-566-520. **Fax:** 860 566-8929.
Email: edwin.anderson@po.state.ct.us
Website: www.state.ct.us/sde

Delaware

Contact: Department of Education, Office of Certification, John G. Townsend Building, PO Box 1402, Dover, DE 19903-1402.

District of Columbia

Contact: Teacher Education and Certification Branch, Suite IOIA, 215 G St. N.E., Washington D.C. 20002.
Tel: (202) 724-4246. **Fax:** (202) 724-8784.

Florida

Requirements: A bachelor's or higher degree with an undergraduate or graduate major in English to Speakers of Other Languages shall satisfy the specialization requirements for certification in English to Speakers of Other Languages (Grades K-12).
Contact: Florida Department of Education, Bureau of Teacher Certification, Suite 201, Turlington Building, 325 West Gaines Street, Tallahassee, FL 32399-0400.
Tel: 850-488-2317.
Email: edcert@mail.doe.state.fl.us

Georgia

Requirements: Teachers are required, as a prerequisite, to hold professional certification in a regular teaching field (English, Math, Middle Grades, etc.) and endorse this field for ESOL by completing a state-approved certification programme for the endorsement through either a college-approved programme or a local school system staff development-approved programme for which the person is professionally recommended for the endorsement by the appropriate approved programme provider. Courses can be approved through a local school system staff development programme to provide this training. Teachers have the option of either having these credits set up for them by a recognized college or through an approved local staff development programme. Individual courses for the endorsement are not specified.

Reciprocity: If a teacher holds professional certification in ESOL from any of the 50 states, U.S. territories, or Department of Defense Dependent Schools (DODDS), the certificate can generally be recognized through reciprocity.

Provisional Licenses: If an applicant presents a letter from an appropriate college or staff development programme provider confirming that the individual has been accepted into the ESOL program, regardless of whether any credits toward this programme have been satisfied, a one-year probationary certificate will be granted, upon employer request, while remaining requirements for recommendation for the endorsement are met.
Contact: Tim Spencer, Certification Coordinator, Georgia Professional Standards Commission, 1452 Twin Towers East, Atlanta, GA 30334.
Tel: 404-657-9000. **Fax:** 404-651-9185.
Email: mail@gapsc.com **Website**: www.gapsc.com
Teachers should contact the Professional Standards Commission offices if they have additional questions. An evaluator will be assigned to respond to your questions.

Hawaii

Contact: Office of Personnel Services, Teacher Recruitment Unit, P.O. Box 2360, Honolulu, HI 96804.
Tel: (808) 586-3420.
Email: supt_doe@notes.k12.hi.us

Idaho

Requirements: Teachers must have either a Standard Elementary or Secondary Teaching certificate.

The ESL K-12 endorsement is then attached to either. A minimum of 20 semester (30 quarter) credit hours from an accredited college or university (on

official transcripts) are required for an ESL teaching endorsement.

Out of that 20 semester credit hours the following is needed: 3 semester credit hours in the following courses: Modern languages; Cultural diversity; ESL Methods; and a course in any of the following: Philosophical foundations, Theory, Testing/identification of limited English proficient students, applied linguistics in ESL.

Also needed is a minimum of 1 semester credit hour of Practicum. There is a restriction of only 5 semester credit hours in a workshop format.
Reciprocity: Yes. To qualify, a teacher must have taught 3 out of the last seven years or graduated from a college/university teacher preparation programme within the last 5 years and have 6 semester credit hours within the last 5 years.

Out-of-state certificates can be endorsed if they have deficiencies for Idaho certification.
Provisional Licenses: Limited provisional arrangements for those who have yet to complete the necessary course work.
Contact: Keith Potter, Certification Specialist, Idaho Department of Education, Teacher Certification, PO Box 83720, Boise, ID 83720-0027.
Tel: 208-332-6887. **Fax:** 208-334-4664.
Email: potter@sde.state.id.us
Website: www.sde.state.id.us/certification

Illinois

Requirements: ESL teachers must hold an elementary, secondary, or early childhood certificate, must complete 18 semester hours in ESL (with course taken in five different areas), and must have completed either 100 clock hours or 3 months of teaching experience in an ESL setting. The five specific categories that ESL teachers must have coursework in include: Linguistics; Theoretical Foundations of Teaching ESL; Assessment of the Bilingual Student; Methods and Materials for Teaching ESL; and Cross-cultural education Studies for Teaching Limited English-proficient students.
Reciprocity: Illinois has reciprocity with several other states regarding certificate types. However, there is no reciprocity in regards to the endorsements on the certificates. Certifiers look for the 18 semester hours and clock hours when evaluating an out-of-state applicant.
Provisional Licenses: A teacher with an out-of-state K-12 ESL certificate can receive a provisional K-12 ESL certificate in Illinois.
Needs: There is a very high demand for ESL teachers.

Contact: Jolene Reddy, Principal Consultant, Illinois State Board of Education, Division of Professional Certification, 100 N. 1st Street, Springfield, IL 62777. **Tel:** 800-845-8749. **Fax:** 217-524-1289.
Email: jreddy@smtp.isbe.state.il.us
Website: www.isbe.state.il.us

Indiana

Requirements: ESL is not required to be on a license for someone to teach ESL. ESL is only available as a minor. Coursework includes general linguistics and English linguistics, psycholinguistics and sociolinguistics, culture and society, literature, methods and materials, and a practicum in English as a Second Language setting.

The holder of the all-grade ESL minor is eligible to teach ESL in grades K-12. The minor may be professionalized when the candidate has completed 12 semester hours from at least two (2) of the following areas: linguistics, language, literature, or ESL, 6 of which must be at the graduate level.

Further, the candidate must meet the professionalization requirements for the basic preparation level of the standard license. This minor can be added to holders of a Standard/Professional License. The English as a Second Language (ESL) certification is not required for teaching ESL students in Indiana but individuals who plan to teach in this area are strongly encouraged to complete the certification process. Indiana has developed new standards and ESL is included in the new license framework. Relevant documents can be obtained at www.state.in.us/psb
Reciprocity: Yes, but not in cases where a teacher has ESL as a major and it is the only area on the license.
Provisional Licenses: ESL teachers are eligible for a limited license on request by a school district. To qualify, teachers need to have a Bachelor's Degree and 15 semester hours in ESL. Teachers can renew the license with six (6) semester hours per year toward the standard license.
Contact: Shawn Sriver, Assistant Director of Licensing, 251 East Ohio Street, Suite 201, Indianapolis, IN 46204-2133.
Tel: 317-238-9010. **Fax:** 317-238-9023.
Email: ssriver@psb.state.in.us
Website: www.state.in.us/psb

Iowa

Requirements: Complete a teacher education programme including at least 24 semester hours in ESL to include the following: Teaching English as a second language; Applied linguistics; Language in culture;

Bilingual education; Nature of language; Process of language acquisition.
Reciprocity: No.
Provisional Licenses: There is a two-year conditional license for people who have a teaching license with an endorsement to teach in one area and have completed at least 12 semester hours in ESL. The person could then teach while completing the remaining requirements.
Contact: Susan Fischer, Licensure Consultant, Iowa Department of Education, Grimes State Office Building, Des Moines, IA 50319.
Tel: 515-281-3245. **Fax:** 515-281-7669.
Email: susan.fischer@ed.state.ia.us
Website: www.state.ia.us/educate/programmes/boee

Kansas

Contact: Dr. Martha Gage, Kansas State Department of Education, 120 SE 10th Avenue, Topeka, KS 66612-1182.
Tel: (785) 296-8010. **Fax:** (785) 296-4318.
Email: mgage@ksde.org
Website: www.ksbe.state.ks.us/cert/ cert.html

Kentucky

Requirements: Kentucky issues certification based upon completion of an approved preparation programme through an accredited college or university. Typically, Kentucky colleges require a minimum of 12 semester hours to include: Linguistics, Applied Linguistics, Methods and Materials for ESL instruction (includes field experience), Culture and society as influential in understanding language minimum of 6 semester hours in a foreign language or demonstrate fluency proficiency in speaking English sufficient to provide a good model for students learning ESL. Through college and university approved programmes, ESL certification is an endorsement to a base classroom certificate. Certification is not stand-alone: KE36-English as a Second Language, All Grades, is the endorsement to a base classroom teaching certificate.
Reciprocity: Kentucky has interstate agreements with many states but does not have direct reciprocity.
Provisional Licenses: Generally, if a person has completed a comparable programme out of state, our office will issue some type of certificate.
Contact: Ginger Mason, programme Manager, Teacher Certification, 1024 Capital centre Dr. Frankfort, KY 40601.
Tel: 502-573-4606. **Fax:** 502-573-1610
Website: www.kde.state.ky.us

Louisiana

Requirements: "English as a second language" will be added to the certificate of any teacher who has a standard certificate and successfully completes coursework in: Methods for teaching ESL; introduction to language and culture; structure of the English language; curriculum design for the multicultural classroom.
Reciprocity: No complete reciprocity with any state.
Provisional Licenses: Yes
Contact: Terry Rinaudo, programme Coordinator I, Office of Certification & Higher Education, Louisiana Department of Education. P.O. Box 94064, Baton Rouge, LA 70804-9064.
Tel: 225-342-3490. **Fax**: 225-342-3499.
Email: trinaudo@mail.doe.state.la.us
Website: www.doe.state.la.**us**

Maine

Requirements: A valid Maine teaching certificate with a K-3, K-8, 7-12 or K-12 endorsement plus 15 semester hours in ESL to include ESL methods, assessment, cultural studies, linguistics, ESL curriculum development. All ESL courses must be from a 4-year accredited college/university.
Reciprocity: Yes.
Provisional Licenses: No. However, if someone holds a valid Maine teacher certificate, we allow the person to hold the position while completing the 15 required semester hours of coursework. This would be called a transitional endorsement. There is no process for a non-Maine certificate holder.
Contact: Nancy Ibarguen, Maine Coordinator of Certification, Certification Office, 23 State House Station, Augusta, ME 333-0023
Tel: 207-287-5944 **Fax**: 207-287-3910
Email: nancy.ibarguen@state.me.us
Website: http://janus.state.me.us/education/esl/

Maryland

Requirements: To qualify for a Maryland (professional) certificate, you must:
- Complete an approved teacher preparation programme at a regionally accredited institution, or
- Submit a notarized copy of a valid professional certificate from an Interstate Contract member state and official verification of 3 years of satisfactory full-time experience in the certification area within the past 7 years, or
- Complete requirements outlined in the certification regulations (content mastery), or

● Complete a Maryland Resident Teacher program
Contact: Maryland State Department of Education, 7th floor, 200 W. Baltimore Street, Baltimore, MD 21201.
Tel: (410) 767-0600
Website: www.msde.state.md.us/certification

Massachusetts

Contact: Teacher Certification Customer Service centre, Department of Education, 350 Main Street, Malden, MA 02148.
Tel: (781) 338-3000 ext. 6600. **Fax:** (781) 338-3391
Email: cert.inquiries@doe.mass.edu
Website: www.doe.mass.edu/cert/

Michigan

Contact: Dr. Carolyn E. Logan, Dept. of Education, Office of Teacher-Administrator Certification, Lansing MI 48909.
Tel: (517) 373-3310. **Fax:** (517) 373-0542.
Email: LoganCE@state.mi.us
Website: www.state.mi.us/mde/off/ ppc/office.htm

Minnesota

Requirements: These include a bachelor's degree, 2 years of college-level or 4 years of high school-level study of a foreign language and completion of an approved ESL professional preparation programme. Further details can be found at http://cfl.state.mn.us/teachbrd/8710_4400.html
Reciprocity: No.
Provisional Licenses: Teachers who have yet to receive full licensing can be accommodated.
Needs: "There is always a need for good teachers. ESL is more a problem of distribution and full-time employment than it is simply the number available."
Contact: Judy McGilvrey, Licensing Specialist, Personnel Licensing, Capitol Square Building, No. 801, 550 Cedar Street, St. Paul, MN 55101.
Tel: 612-296-2046. **Fax:** 612-296-2403.
Email: Judy.Mcgilvrey@state.mn.us
Website: http://cfl.state.mn.us/

Mississippi

Contact: Division of Teacher Certification, State Department of Education, P.O. Box 771, Jackson, MS 39205.
Tel: (601) 359-3483.
Website: mdek12.state.ms.us

Missouri

Requirements: I. A valid Missouri permanent or professional certificate of license to teach. II. Professional Requirements* (These shall be met by courses of at least two (2) semester hours, unless otherwise specified.):
A. Psychology and/or Education of the Exceptional Child (including the Gifted); and
B. Basic Reading Techniques for Secondary Teachers.
III. Professional Requirements for ESOL (minimum of twenty-one (21) semester hours):
A. Linguistics and English Linguistics;
B. Language and Culture or Sociolinguistics;
C. Second Language Acquisition;
D. Methods of Teaching Second Language Students;
E. Material for Teaching English to Speakers of Other Languages and the Assessment of Speakers of Other Languages;
F. ESOL Practicum (three (3) semester credit hours); and
G. Elective Coursework (three (3) semester hours).
Teachers may choose additional courses from such areas as English language, reading, composition, early childhood education, bilingual education or advanced second language methods according to the needs of their teaching situation.
Contact: Teacher Education and Certification, Department of Elementary and Secondary Education, P.O. Box 480, Jefferson City, MO 65102.
Tel: (573) 751-0051.
Website: http://services.dese.state.mo.us/ divurbteached/teachcert/certification

Montana

Requirements: All teachers must complete either a secondary or elementary teacher education programme with a minimum of a teaching minor in ESL K-12. If they hold a minor in ESL, they must have a major in another endorsable teaching area along with the minor.
Reciprocity: Montana participates in the NASDTEC Interstate certification contract. This allows at least an entry-level certificate to people who have completed a college-approved ESL K-12 programme from an approved teacher education institution in other participating states.
Provisional Licenses: A person can be provisionally certified if they have completed a minimum of 30 semester credits in ESL K-12 coursework and six semester credits in general education coursework. A fully certifiable programme must be completed during the 3-year provisional programme.

Contact: Karla Beagles, Certification Technician, Montana Office of Public Instruction Teacher Education and Licensure Dept., P.O. Box 202501, Helena, MT 59620-2501.
Tel: 406-444-3150. **Fax:** 406-444-2843.
Email: Cert@state.mt.us
Website: www.metnet.state.mt.us

Nebraska

Requirements: The ESL endorsement is an added endorsement, which means that teachers must be endorsed in another broad field and ESL is added to that endorsement. A teacher may not be endorsed in ESL alone. Teachers can be classified as an ESL teacher by a school district since there is a shortage of ESL teachers in the state. The graduate endorsement is currently comprised of 12 hours: 3 in Linguistics, 3 in Cross Cultural Communication, 3 in Curriculum Design for ESL, and 3 in ESL Methods. In addition, the applicant shall have a 1 semester hour of credit in an ESL practicum. The undergraduate endorsement is 15 hours; 3 in linguistics, 3 in Cross-Cultural Communication, 3 in ESL Methods, 3 in Second Language Assessment and Evaluation, and a 3 hour practicum.
Reciprocity: Yes.
Provisional Licenses: All teachers in Nebraska must be certified. Because this endorsement requires teachers to be endorsed in another area (ESL is supplemental), the district may hire teachers who do not have an ESL endorsement.
Contact: Nancy Rowch, Director, Equal Educational Opportunity Programmes, Nebraska Department of Education, P.O. Box 94987, Lincoln, NE 68509-4987.
Tel: 402-471-0739 (402-471-2496 to request forms by electronic voice mail.)
Fax: 402-471-8127.
Email: nrowch@nde.state.ne.us
Website: www.edneb.org

Nevada

Requirements: Limited Endorsement To Teach ESL (K - 12):
To receive a limited endorsement to teach English as a second language, a person must have a valid elementary, secondary or special license and have completed at least 6 semester hours of credit in a course of study which includes any of the following:
Methods and materials for teaching English as a Second Language; Theories for the acquisition of a second language; Testing and evaluation of pupils studying English as a Second Language; and

Developing curriculum for pupils studying English as a Second Language.
A limited endorsement expires 3 years after issuance and is not renewable.
Endorsement To Teach ESL (K - 12):
To receive an endorsement to teach English as a second language, a person must have a valid elementary, secondary or special license have completed the requirements for a limited endorsement and an additional 6 semester hours of credit in the courses of study listed below:
Methods and materials for teaching English as a Second Language; Theories for the acquisition of a second language; Testing and evaluation of pupils studying English as a Second Language; and Developing curriculum for pupils studying English as a Second Language.
Professional Endorsement To Teach ESL (K-12):
To receive a professional endorsement to Teach English as a Second Language, a person must have completed the requirements for an endorsement to teach English as a second language and:
Hold a masters degree; and have 3 years of verified teaching experience
Contact: Department of Education, 1850 East Sahara, Suite 207, State Mail Room, Las Vegas, NV 89158.
Tel: (702) 486-6455. **Fax:** (702) 796-3475.
Website: www.ccsd.net/HRD/ NVDOE/

New Hampshire

Contact: Bureau of Credentialing, Division of programme Support, State Department of Education, State Office Park South, 101 Pleasant St., Concord, NH 03301.
Tel: (603) 271-2407. **Fax:** (603) 271-1953.

New Jersey

Reciprocity: New Jersey is a party to the Interstate Certification Compact for reciprocity with member states in designated instructional areas.
Licenses/certificates from other states and transcripts are reviewed to determine if applicants are eligible for reciprocity. Applicants from other states must complete the test requirement.
Contact: New Jersey Department of Education, Office of Licensing, Riverview Executive Plaza 100, Rte. 29, Trenton, NJ 08625-0500.
Tel: (609) 292-2070. **Fax:** (609) 292-3768.
Website:
www.state.nj.us/njded/teachers/license/1111.htm

New Mexico

Contact: Professional Licensure Unit, Department of Education, Santa Fe, NM 87503.
Tel: (505) 827-6587. **Fax:** (505) 827-6696.

New York

Type of Credential: Certification.
Requirements: Professional Education Courses: Study in instructional planning and assessment, knowledge of the learner, instructional delivery, and the professional environment. Professional education courses are those specifically for individuals preparing for a career in teaching, administration, or pupil personnel services. These courses must be part of an approved teacher education programme at an institution of higher education offering a baccalaureate or higher degree. Semester hour credit for student teaching is not applicable to professional education requirements.

Methods of Teaching: Reading, Writing, Speaking, and Communicating in English to Speakers of Other Languages. Examples of acceptable courses include TESOL 1: Developing language arts skills, teaching reading or writing in a second language, developing or assessing English language proficiency. Such courses must be completed at an institution with an approved ESOL or bilingual programme.

Methods of Teaching ESOL Through Math, Science, and Social Studies Examples of acceptable courses include teaching ESOL in the content areas. Such courses must be completed at an institution with an approved ESOL or bilingual programme.

Subject Matter Specialization: Courses specifically for individuals preparing for a career in teaching ESOL.

Cultural Perspectives: Acceptable courses are those which provide a linguistic, cultural or historic view of a regional, national or ethnic group whose language is not English. Examples include courses with titles such as 'language and culture of,' 'civilization of,' and 'history and culture of' any regional, national, or ethnic group whose language is not English; and 'cultural anthropology.'

Theory and Practice of Bilingual/ Bicultural Education: Any course that is part of an approved bilingual education or ESOL teacher preparation programme that covers the theoretical foundations or principles of bilingual education relevant to elementary and secondary school children is acceptable. Examples include foundations of bilingual education, history and principles of bilingual education, and issues and trends in bilingual/bicultural education.

Theory of Second Language Acquisition: Any course including language acquisition theory for any language other than English. Examples include 'principles of' or 'cognition in' second language acquisition and principles in language learning.

Language Research: Any course that requires a language research project is acceptable. Acceptable courses include introduction to language and introduction to linguistics.

Structure of the English Language: Any course on the structure of English is acceptable. Many linguistics courses are acceptable.

Linguistics as Related to Teaching: Many linguistics courses are acceptable, including linguistics for second language teachers, contrastive analysis, phonetics, sociolinguistics, and contrastive morphology.

Content Area Courses: Course content, rather than the name of the department through which a course is offered, determines its acceptability to fulfill these requirements. Courses in the methods of teaching a subject are not acceptable as study in the content area. Detailed information by subject area is provided below.

Language and Culture other than English: One year of study is required. This requirement can be met by completing one intermediate level course or one course in each of two languages. Literature courses must be in the language being studied and not in translation. Satisfactory performance on the College level Proficiency Exams in Spanish, French, or German also satisfies this requirement. Satisfaction of a degree requirement for language other than English by alternative means requires a letter of verification by the college registrar. If your first language is not English, and you have taken English in your native, non-English-speaking country, these courses may be used to satisfy this requirement. American Sign Language (ASL) is considered a language other than English.

English Courses offered by an English department that are considered core requirements toward a degree in English are typically acceptable. For example, courses in composition, English literature, poetry, playwriting, grammar, and English linguistics are acceptable. (wording consistent with others)
Contact: State Education Department, Cultural Ed. centre, Room 5A-11, Nelson A. Rockefeller, Empire State Plaza, Albany, NY 12230.
Tel: (518) 474-3901. **Fax:** (518) 473-0271.
Website: www.highered.nysed. gov/tcert/index.html

North Carolina

Type of Credential: License
Requirements: ESL is a K-12 licensure and is an "add-on". Teachers should complete an approved competency programme and the Praxis test in ESL.
Reciprocity: With 39 states.
Contact: Licensure Section, Department of Public Instruction, 301 N. Wilmington St., Raleigh, NC 27601-2825.
Tel: (919) 733-4125. **Fax:** (919) 715-1094.
Website: www.dpi.state.nc.us/licensure/ lifaq.htm

North Dakota

Requirements: Any certified teacher can obtain an ESL endorsement. The requirement is 16 semester or 24 quarter hours of coursework at a state-approve college.
Reciprocity: No.
Contact: Janet Welk, Executive Director, Education Standards & Practices Board, 600 East Boulevard Avenue, Dept. 202, Bismarck, ND 5805-0080.
Tel: 701-328-2262. **Fax:** 701-328-2815.
Email: jwelk@state.nd.us
Website: www.state.nd.us/espb

Ohio

Contact: Division of Teacher Education and Certification, Ohio Department of Education, Ohio Depts. Building, Room 416, 65 South Front St., Columbus, OH 43215-4183.
Tel: (614) 466-3593. **Fax:** (614) 466-1999.
Website: www.ode.state.oh.us/tp/ctp/ candl.htm

Oklahoma

Type of Credential: Special Endorsement.
Contact: Professional Standards Section, Hodge Ed. Building, Room 211, Oklahoma City, OK 73105.
Tel: (405) 521-3337. **Fax:** (405) 521-6205.

Oregon

Requirements: Completion of a teacher education programme in ESL and passing scores on the Praxis test "Teaching English as a Second Language."
Reciprocity: Yes.
Provisional Licenses: Yes.
Needs: Heavy.
Contact: Janet Madland, Coordinator of Teacher Preparation and Teacher Standards, Teacher Standards and Practices Commission, 255 Capitol Street NE, Suite 105, Salem, OR 97310-1322.
Tel: 503-3586. **Fax:** 503-378-4448.
Email: contact.tspc@state.or.us
Website: www.ode.state.or.us/tspc

Pennsylvania

Requirements: A teacher must hold a Level I or Level II certificate; however, there is no certificate specifically for ESL, so a teacher may be certified in any subject area. The school entity then determines the qualifications other than certification necessary for assignment to an ESL position. For more details go to www.pde.psu.edu click under "fast find" to the CSPGs and then check CSPG #108 which details the ESL guideline.
Reciprocity: Interstate Agreement with 43 other states for comparable Instructional certificates. This does not mean that a certificate is automatically accepted from another state. An evaluation is done in the Division of Candidate Evaluation to determine that the individual meets Pennsylvania certification requirements.
Provisional Licenses: A district which is unable to find a fully qualified and properly certificated applicant may request an emergency certificate from this Bureau.
Needs: "Depends on the area of the state — in rural areas, the need is lighter; however, in urban areas, such as Philadelphia, the need is at least moderate."
Contact: Susan Stewart, Division Chief, Bureau of Teacher Certification and Preparation, 333 Market Street, Harrisburg, PA 17126.
Tel: 717 787-3356 **Fax:** 717 783-6736.
Email: sstewart@state.pa.us
Website: www.pde.psu.edu

Rhode Island

Type of Credential: Certificate.
Requirements: In addition to the successful completion of a teacher education program, all applicants for Rhode Island teacher certification must complete the Communication Skills, General Knowledge and Professional Knowledge subsections of the National Teachers Examination.
Contact: Office of Teacher Education and Certification, Roger Williams Building, 22 Hayes St., Providence, RI 02908.
Tel: (401) 277-2675. **Fax:** (401) 277-2048.

South Carolina

Type of Credential: Certification.
Requirements: ENGLISH AS A SECOND LANGUAGE - Grades 9-12

a. Bachelor's Degree
b. Professional Certificate at the Elementary, Middle School or Secondary level.
c. N.T.E. Special Area not required at this time.
d. Specialized Preparation - 21 Semester Hours
Semester Hours:
(1) Principles and Strategies for Teaching English as a Second Language to Elementary and Secondary Learners
(2) Linguistic/Cultural Diversity in Education or the Equivalent
(3) Teaching Reading and Writing to ESL Learners
(4) Practicum in the Instruction of English as a Second Language to Elementary and Secondary Learners
(5) Elective courses: (9 hours)
Three courses to be selected from areas such as the following:
- 1 Testing/Assessment for Language Minority Learners (3 hours)
- 1 ESL Curriculum Design and Materials Development (3 hours)
- 1 Teaching English through the content areas (3 hours)
- 1 Bilingual Special Education (3 hours)
- 1 Second Language Acquisition for Teachers of Elementary and Secondary Learners (3 hours)
- 1 English Grammar/Structure (3 hours)
e. Second Language learning experiences documented by any of the following.
(1) Six semester hours in course in a single second language; or
(2) Completion of intensive language training by the Peace Corps, the Foreign Service Institute or the Defense Language Institute; or
(3) Placement by the language department of an accredited institution in a third semester level.
(4) Demonstration of second language proficiency as verified in writing by an official designated by the SCDE for language unavailable at accredited institutions.
Contact: S.C. Department of Education, Dr. Sandra Rowe, Director of Teacher Certification, Certification and Evaluation, 1600 Gervais Street, Columbia SC 29201.
Tel: (803) 734-8953. **Fax:** (803) 734-6225.
Website: www.scteachers.org/
SCTeachers/Cert/Certification.htm

South Dakota

Requirements: South Dakota does not offer certification for ESL but an endorsement in "K-12 English as a New Language Education" is available.

The courses are based on "competencies" rather than on specific courses. These "competencies" will include the following coursework: linguistics, development of curriculum and instruction for new language acquisition, language and culture, programme assessment, reading for students with limited English proficiency, and English as a new language methodology course. Additional requirements will include: preparation of candidates that address developmental characteristics of K-12 learners and preparation of candidates that addresses field experiences of K-12 learners. Out-of-state applicants need 3 hours of Human Relations and 3 hours of Indian Studies in order to get their first five (5) year certificate.
Reciprocity: No.
Provisional Licenses: There is a 1-year "Authority to Act" which may be renewed if a candidate lacks more 8 hours of coursework.
Contact: Jerald A. Goehring, Director of Teacher Education and Certification, 700 Governors Drive, Pierre, SD 57501- 2291.
Tel: (605) 773-4774. **Fax:** (605) 773-6139.
Email: jerald.goehring@state.sd.us
Website: www.state.sd.us

Tennessee

Type of Credential: License.
Provisional Licenses: Interim Licenses are available.
Contact: Office of Teacher Licensing, Career Ladder Certification, State Dept. of Education, Gateway Plaza, 710 James Robertson Pkwy., 5th floor, Nashville, TN 37243-0377.
Tel: (615) 532-4885. **Fax:** (615) 741-6236.
Website: www.state.tn.us/education/ lic_home.htm

Texas

Type of Credential: Endorsement.
Requirements: ESL endorsements require a bachelor's degree from an accredited institution; a valid, designated Texas teacher certificate, and completion of approved programme requirements for the endorsement sought. Programme requirements for ESL endorsements are: a) Certificate requirement. The ESL endorsement may be added to valid teacher certificates, special education certificates, or vocational certificates that require a college degree; b) Professional Development. The professional development sequence for ESL endorsement shall consists of: 12 semester hours including, language acquisition and development (psycholinguistics), methods of teaching ESL and descriptive/contrastive

linguistics; and evidence of a successful student teaching experience in an approved ESL programme. The requirement for student teaching may be waived with one creditable year, or successful classroom teaching experience on a permit in an approved ESL or bilingual education programme (from the Texas Administrative Code (TAC), Chapter 230.199 Endorsements.)

Reciprocity: The degree and certificate from another state presented by an applicant for Texas certification must be considered standard by the issuing state department of education and may not be a temporary permit, a substandard certificate, or a credential issued by a city or school district.

Provisional Licenses: A superintendent who cannot secure an appropriately certified and qualified individual to fill a vacant position may activate an emergency permit for an individual who does not have one of the appropriate credentials required for the assignment

Needs: Bilingual/ESL is one of the shortage areas identified by the Commissioner of Education.

Contact: Debby Hewitt, Coordinator, State Board for Teacher Certification, 1101 Trinity Street, Austin, TX 78701.

Tel: (888) 863-5880. **Fax:** (512) 469-3018.
Email: sbec@mail.sbec.state.tx.us
Website: www.sbec.state.tx.us

Utah

Type of Credential: Endorsement.
Requirements: A teacher must have a current Teacher License with an Elementary, Secondary or Special Education area of concentration. The requirements are:
STANDARD I: ENGLISH COMPETENCY
Completion of approved education programme in teacher education
NON-ENGLISH COMPETENCY
Competency demonstrated through:
a. Literacy exam
b. Interagency roundtable examination
c. Established tribal standards
d. More than 3 years of formal education at a university in a language other than English
STANDARD II: METHODS, STRATEGIES, AND MATERIALS FOR BILINGUAL/ESL CLASSROOMS (6 credit hours)
Part I (Language Arts and Literacy) and Part II (Content Area Instruction)
1. Instructional strategies and methodologies for the bilingual/bicultural student
2. Teaching of oral language and literacy skills

3. Integration of culture in literature, native language, and English
4. Strategies to integrate language for teaching math, science, and social studies
STANDARD III: FOUNDATIONS OF BILINGUAL/ESL INSTRUCTION (3 credit hours)
1. Education diverse groups
2. Current issues in second language learning
3. Multiethnic curriculum and instruction
STANDARD IV: UNDERSTANDING LANGUAGE ACQUISITION AND COGNITION (3 credit hours)
1. Teaching the bilingual/bicultural student
2. Teaching ESL
3. Instructional strategies for minority students
4. Second language acquisition strategies
ASSESSMENT FOR LINGUISTICALLY DIVERSE POPULATIONS (3 credit hours)
1. Methods and techniques for language and academic assessment and placement of linguistically diverse populations
2. Understanding of current identification and assessment practices in bilingual education and ESL
INTEGRATING LANGUAGE ACQUISITION INTO CONTENT INSTRUCTION (6 credit hours)
1. ESL reading
2. Multicultural literature in the classroom
3. a. Native language instruction in math, science, & social studies (Bil. Ends. Only)
b. Language acquisition integration in math, science, & social studies (ESL Only)
STANDARD V: PARENT AND COMMUNITY INVOLVEMENT (3 credit hours)
1. School/community partnerships
2. Involvement of LEP student's parents in the schools
Contact: Ronald M. Stanfield, Utah State Office of Education, 250 East 500 South, Salt Lake City, UT 84111.
Tel: (801) 538- 7739. **Fax:** (801) 538-7769.
Website: www.usoe.k12.ut.us/cert/ endorsements/endesl.htm

Vermont

Requirements: Candidates for an ESL endorsement must demonstrate the following qualifications: Linguistics/language acquisition; linguistic/cultural diversity; assessment; methodology and curriculum development; programme planning, consultation, and coordination.
Reciprocity: With 39 states.
Provisional Licenses: After July 2000, districts may only hire licensed ESL teachers.

Contact: Jill Mack, Professional Standards and Licensing Consultant, Vermont Department of Education, 120 State Street, Montpelier, VT 05620. **Tel:** (802) 828-2445. **Fax:** (802) 828-3140. **Email:** licensing@doe.state.vt.us **Website:** www.state.vt.us/educ/ license/esl.htm

Virginia

Requirements: Teachers of ESL must complete 24 semester hours of college course work in ESL. They must also complete 15 semester hours of professional studies course work from a 4 year college and pass the Praxis I series tests. The following courses (which may be offered at both the undergraduate and graduate level) are the "stand-alone" course requirements for an ESL endorsement: 3 semester hour course in the Teaching of Reading; 3 semester hour course in English Linguistics; 3 semester hour course in Cross-Cultural Education; 6 semester hours in Modern Foreign Languages (if the applicant's primary language is other than English, all six hours must be in English); 6 semester hours in Electives in ESL selected from the following: second language acquisition, general linguistics, applied linguistics, psycholinguistics, sociolinguistics, ESL Assessment, or ESL Curriculum Development; 3 semester hours of Methods of Teaching ESL (methods of teaching a foreign language may also be used to meet this requirement).

Reciprocity: Virginia has reciprocity agreements with 39 states and the District of Columbia which allow for recognition of comparable teaching endorsements by participating states.

Provisional Licenses: Virginia does issue a three-year, nonrenewable license to teachers who have been hired by school divisions based on the fact that the applicant meets the content requirements for a teaching endorsement but has not completed professional study and/or test requirements for certification.

Needs: "ESL is not listed as a critical shortage teaching area in Virginia. However, in urban areas, the need for qualified ESL teachers is increasing."

Contact: Paul F. Joseph, Senior Licensure Specialist, Virginia Department of Education, Division of Teacher Education and Licensure, PO Box 2120, Richmond, VA 23818-2120. **Tel:** (804) 371-2472. **Fax:** (804) 786-6759. **Website:** www.pen.k12.va.us

Washington

Type of Credential: Endorsement.
Requirements: The only way an individual can get an ESL endorsement is to complete an approved college/university programme in Teaching English as a Second Language. Endorsements require 24 quarter hours (16 semester hours) of study Coursework includes: Structure of language or language acquisition; Culture and learning for the ESL student; Instructional methods in language arts for the ESL student; Instructional methods in reading for the ESL student; Instructional methods in English as a second language.
Contact: Judy Smith, Certification Specialist, Professional Education and Certification, Superintendent of Public Instruction, P.O. Box 47200, Olympia, WA 98504-47200. **Tel:** (206) 753-6773. **Fax:** (360) 586-0145. **Email:** cert@ospi.wednet.edu **Website:** www.k12.wa.us

West Virginia

Contact: Office of Professional Preparation, Building 6, Room 337, Capitol Complex, Charleston, WV 25305-0330. **Tel:** (304) 558-7010. **Fax:** (304) 558-0459

Wisconsin

Type of Credential: License
Requirements: ESL teachers must complete a state-approved teacher training programme and be licensed as a teacher in Wisconsin
Reciprocity: No
Provisional Licenses: Available for teachers with an existing license in another state. They must then meet Wisconsin requirements within a certain period of time.
Teachers with another license may teach on an "emergency" license provided the school district has made a good faith effort to find an appropriately certified person and cannot. Teachers with an "emergency" license must be working toward full ESL certification to maintain that license.
Needs: Moderate
Contact: Jim Wall, Coordinator of Continuing Professional Education Programmes, Department of Public Instruction, P.O. Box 7841, Madison, WI 53707. **Tel:** (608) 266-2662. **Fax:** (608) 267-2920. **Website:** www.dpi.state.wi.us/dpi/dlsis/tel/ index.html

Wyoming

Requirements: Completion of a state approved ESL teacher preparation programme.
Reciprocity: Yes.

Contact: programme Approval Consultant, Professional Teaching Standards Board, Hathaway Building, 2nd Floor, 2300 Capitol Avenue, Cheyenne, WY 82001.
Tel: (307) 777-6256. **Fax:** (307) 777-6234.
Website: www.k12.wy.uss

Career Development

Teachers can also be learners! Career development is a natural progression if you want to expand your horizons within the profession or in related fields

Diploma Qualifications *See p.240*

Diploma courses usually take 8 weeks full-time or a year part-time. With this qualification, you can normally get a job anywhere round the world if you have one.

Master's Degree Courses *See p.251*

Masters' programmes offer a way to study the more theoretical approach to English language teaching. In the US, they are not always post-experience qualifications, whereas outside the US applicants will be expected to have an undergraduate degree and two or more years experience.

Specialist Qualifications *See p.269*

English as a second language is a field that continues to specialize as it matures as a discipline. This section covers Computer Assisted Language Learning and English for Specific Purposes.

Doctorates *See p.278*

This is the ultimate academic qualification in English language teaching. A Ph.D. is generally research-based whereas the Ed.D. is often geared towards those who want to be a school administrator.

Publishing *See p.281*

Teachers often find that they are creating their own materials for classroom use. Over the years, these materials are honed until they are fully developed. This is when you should consider getting these materials published.

School Management / Ownership *See p.287*

As teachers work their way up the career ladder, some are drawn to school management. Others go on to be school owners.

Diploma and Master's Courses

To further your career you will certainly need a higher qualification. One way to do this is to take a Diploma course such as those run by the University of Cambridge or Trinity College London, or a Master's degree.

There is an acute shortage of highly qualified teachers around the world, so having a Diploma under your belt means that you can be guaranteed a job anywhere. It proves that you have both a high level qualification and several years' experience in the classroom. Because the University of Cambridge and Trinity College London Diplomas have both theoretical exams and observed teaching practice, most schools prefer these.

The two best-known qualifications are: Diploma in English language teaching to adults (DELTA) from University of Cambridge ESOL and the Licentiate Diploma in Teaching English to speakers of other languages (LTCL.DipTESOL) from Trinity College London.

In order to enrol on a Cambridge DELTA course, you must have at least two years' post-qualification teaching practice The requirements for Trinity are similar. Each course takes eight weeks full-time, although there are part-time courses and many schools and colleges offer distance learning options for part of the course.

There are also university diploma courses which are usually one year in length. They are open to both native speakers and non-native speakers with at least one year's teaching experience. University diploma courses tend to be more theoretically oriented than the University of Cambridge ESOL or Trinity College London Diplomas.

Diploma Courses

This section lists Diploma courses from the main schools around the world. The main courses are: **DELTA** (Diploma in English Language Teaching to Adults, from University of Cambridge ESOL) and **LTCL DipTESOL** (Licentiate Diploma in TESOL, from Trinity College London). Many of the schools and universities listed provide the Diploma course by distance learning.

ARGENTINA (+54)

International House
Pacheco De Melo 2555, 1425 Buenos Aires
Tel: 11 4805 6393
Fax: 11 4805 6393
Email: ihrecoleta@international-house.com.ar
Website: www.international-house.com.ar
Courses offered DELTA

AUSTRALIA (+61)

Australian TESOL Training Centre (ATTC)
PO Box 82, Bondi Junction, New South Wales 2022
Tel: 29389 0249
Fax: 29389 7788
Email: lynnev@ace.edu.au
Website: www.attc.nsw.edu.au
Courses offered DELTA

International House, Sydney
Level 3, 89 York Street, Sydney, NSW 2000
Tel: 29279 0733
Fax: 0 29279 4544
Email: jtennant@ihsydney.com
Website: www.training.ihsydney.com
Courses offered DELTA

Phoenix English Language Academy
223 Vincent Street, West Perth 6005
Tel: 89227 5538
Fax: 89227 5540
Email: pjones@phoenixela.com.au
Website: www.phoenixela.com.au
Courses offered DELTA

Australian TESOL Training Centre,
PO Box 82, Bondi Junction NSW 2022.
Tel: 02 9389 0249.
Fax: 02 9389 7788.
Courses Offered: DELTA

AUSTRIA (+43)

Berufsförderungsinstitut Wien,
Kinderspitalgasse 5, A-1090 Vienna.
Tel: 1 4043 5114.
Fax: 1 4043 5124.
Email: bfi.dion@bfi-wien.or.at
Website: www.bfi-wien.or.at/bfiwien/
Courses Offered: DELTA

BAHRAIN (+973)

The British Council
P.O. Box 452, Manama 356.
Tel: 261555.
Fax: 258689.
Courses Offered: DELTA

BULGARIA (+359)

AV0-3 School Of English
2a Krakra Street, 1504 Sofia
Tel: 2 944 3 032
Fax: 2 943 3 943
Email: binnie@avo-3.com
Website: www.avo-3.com
Courses offered: DELTA

BRAZIL (+55)

SBCI, Sao Paulo
Rua Ferreira de Araujo 741, 3° andar - Pinheiros, São
Paulo - SP, CEP 05428-002
Tel: 11 3039 0551
Fax: 11 3039 0562
Website: www.culturainglesasp.com.br
Courses offered DELTA

CANADA (+1)

Shane Global Village English Centre
Westcoast English Language Centre Ltd
888 Cambie Street, Vancouver BC, V6B 2P6
Tel: 604 684 2112
Fax: 604 648 2124
Email: teachertraining_van@sgvenglish.com
Website: www.sgvenglish.com
Courses offered: DELTA

CYPRUS (+357)

Forum Language Centre
PO Box 25567, Nicosia 1310
Tel: 2 2317 029
Fax: 2 249 7766
Email: peterl@forum.ac.cy
Website: www.forum.ac.cy
Courses offered DELTA

CZECH REPUBLIC (+42)

Akcent International House
Bítovská 3, 140 00 Praha 4
Tel: 02 6126 1675
Fax: 02 6126 1880
Email: dana@akcent.cz
Website: www.akcent.cz
Courses offered DELTA

EGYPT (+20)

The British Council
192 Sharia El Nil, Agouza, Cairo
Tel: 2 301 8341
Fax: 2 344 3076
Email: Louise.Greenwood@britcoun.org.eg
Website: www.britishcouncil.org.eg
Courses offered DELTA

GREECE (+30)

Anglo-Hellenic Teacher Recruitment,
PO Box 263, 201 00 Corinth.
Tel: 741 53511.
Fax: 741 86989.
Courses Offered: Lic. Dip.TESOL

CELT Athens
77 Academias Street, 106 78 Athens
Tel: 1 330 2406
Fax: 1 330 1455
Email: celtath@otenet.gr/celt@celt.gr
Website: www.celt.gr
Courses offered DELTA

Profile
Frantzi 4 and Kallirois Street, 117 45 Athens
Tel: 1 922 2065
Fax: 1 924 1543
Email: profile-educinst@ath.forthnet.gr
Website: www.profiletraining.net
Courses offered DELTA .

Study Space
Tsimiski 86, Thessaloniki 54622
Tel: 31 269 697
Fax: 31 269 697
Email: studyspa@compulink.gr
Website: www.compulink.gr/studyspa
Courses offered DELTA

HUNGARY (+36)

International House, Budapest
PO Box 92, 1276 Budapest
Tel: 1345 7046
Fax: 1 316 2491
Email: ttraining@ih.hu
Website: www.ih.hu
Courses offered DELTA

IRELAND (+353)

English in Dublin
Clifton House, Lower Fitzwilliam Street, Dublin, 2
Email: cliftonh@indigo.ie
Tel: 1 4732101
Fax: 1 661 5200
Courses Offered: LTCL.Dip.TESOL

Language Centre
O'Rahilly Building, UCC, The National University of Ireland, Cork.
Tel: 3 21 4902043.
Fax: 3 21 4903223.
Course Length: 9 months' intensive
Course Fees: IEP1750.
Start dates: January / October
Courses Offered: DELTA.

University College Cork
The Language Centre, College Road, Cork
Tel: 2 1490 2962 / 2043
Fax: 2 1490 3223
Email: rmasterson@langcent.ucc.ie
Website: www.ucc.ie
Courses offered DELTA

ITALY (+39)

British Council, Milan
Via Manzoni 38, 20121 Milano
Tel: 02 772221
Fax: 02 781119
Email: simon.creasy@britishcouncil.it
Website: www.britishcouncil.it/milan
Courses offered DELTA

British Council, Naples
Via Morghen, 31, NAPLES 80129
Email: BCNaples@britishcouncil.it
Courses Offered: DELTA
Course Length: 6 months
Start Dates: June, September

British Institute of Florence Language Centre
Palazzo Strozzino, Piazza Strozzi 2, 50123 Firenze
Tel: 055 267 782 05
Fax: 055 267 782 23
Email: sellis@britishinstitute.it
Courses offered DELTA

The Cambridge School of English
Via Rosmini 6, 37123 Verona
Tel: 45 800 3154
Fax: 45 801 4900
Email: info@cambridgeschool.it
Website: www.cambridgeschool.it
Courses offered: DELTA

International House
Via Jannozzi 6, 20097 S. Donato, Milan.
Tel: 02 527 9124.
Fax: 02 5560 0324.
Courses Offered: DELTA.

International House, Rome
Via Marghera 22, ROMA 185
Email: tiziana.di.dedda@dilit.it
Courses Offered: DELTA
Course Length: FT:12 weeks; PT 4 months

Lord Byron College
Via Sparano 102, 20121 Bari
Tel: 08 052 32 686
Fax: 08 052 41 349
Email: johncredico@lordbyroncollege.com
Website: www.lordbyroncollege.com
Courses offered DELTA

JAPAN (+81)

British Council, Tokyo
2-1 Kagurazaka, Shinjuku-ku, Tokyo 162-0825
Tel: 3 3235 8011
Fax: 3 3235 0049
Email: sheena.palmer@britishcouncil.or.jp
Website: www.uknow.or.jp
Courses offered DELTA

KOREA (+82)

Yonsei Institute Of Language Research & Education
Yonsei University, 134 Shinch'on-Dong
Sodaemun-Gu, Seoul 120-749.
Tel: 2 361 3462.
Fax: 2 393 4599.
Courses Offered: DELTA.

MEXICO (+52)

British Council, Mexico
Lope de Vega 316, Col. Chapultepec Morales
(Polanco), 11570 Mexico D.F.
Tel: 52 63 1900 (General) 1982 / 1965
Fax: 52 63 1960 / 1660
Email: bcmexico@britishcouncil.org.mx
Website: www.britishcouncil.org/mexico
Courses offered DELTA

International House

Calle Montecito 38, Piso 20 Despacho 4, Colonia
Nápoles, 03810 Mexico DF
Tel: 5 448 0223
Fax: 5 488 0223
Courses Offered: DELTA

NEW ZEALAND (+64)

Capital Language Academy

PO Box 1100, Wellington.
Tel: 4 385 0600.
Fax: 4 385 6655.
Courses Offered: DELTA.

Christchurch College of English

PO Box 31-212, Christchurch, New Zealand
Tel: 3 343 3790
Fax: 3 343 3791
Email: pauline.taylor@ccel.co.nz
Website: www.ccel.co.nz
Courses: DELTA

EDENZ EDENZ College

PO Box 10-222 Dominion Road, Mt Eden, Auckland,
1030
tel: 0064 9 522 1211
fax: 0064 9 522 1511
Courses Offered: LTCL.Dip.TESOL.

ILA South Pacific Limited

21 Kilmore Street, PO Box 25170, Christchurch.
Tel: 3 3795452.
Fax: 3 3795373.
Courses Offered: DELTA

Languages International

PO Box 5293, Auckland 1036.
Tel: 9 309 0615.
Fax: 9 377 2806.
Courses Offered: DELTA
Course Length: 7 months
Start dates: April

Unitec School Of Languages

Private Bag 92025, Auckland.
Tel: 9 849 4180.
Fax: 9 815 2906.
Courses Offered: DELTA

POLAND (+48)

ELS - Bell Gdansk

ul. Matejki 6, 80-238Gdansk
Tel: 58 344 7312
Fax: 58 344 0784
Email: ziolkowska@elsbell.pl
Website: www.bellschools.pl
Courses offered DELTA

ELS - Bell (Warsaw)

ul. Nowy Swiat 2, 00-497 Warszawa
Tel: 58 344 7312
Fax: 58 344 0784
Email: ziolkowska@elsbell.com
Website: www.bellschools.pl
Courses offered DELTA

International House, Katowice

ul. Leszczynskiego 3, 50-078 Wroclaw
Tel: 71 781 7290
Fax: 71 781 7290 ext 11
Email: ttcentre@ih.com.pl
Website: www.ih.com.pl
Courses offered DELTA

International House, Kraków

ul. Pitsudskiego 6, 31-109 Kraków
Tel: 12 422 6482
Fax: 12 430 1000
Email: admin@ih.pl
Website: www.ih.pl
Courses offered DELTA

International House, Wroclaw

ul. Leszczynskiego 3, 50-078 Wroclaw
Tel: 71 781 7290
Fax: 71 781 7290 ex. 111
Email: ttcentre@ih.com.pl
Website: www.ih.com.pl
Courses offered DELTA

UEC Bell School Of English

Plac Trzech Krzyzy 4/6, 00-499 Warsaw.
Tel: 22 625 4792.
Fax: 22 629 5865.
Courses Offered: DELTA

PORTUGAL (+35)

International House
Rua Marquês Sá da Bandeira, 16, 1050-148 Lisbon.
Tel: 1 21 315 1496
Fax: 1 21 353 0081
Email: ttraining@ihlisbon.com
Website: www.international-house.com
Courses offered DELTA

RUSSIA (+7)

BKC - International House, Moscow
ul. Tverskaya 9a, Building 4, 103009 Moscow
Tel: 095 234 0314
Fax: 095 234 0316
Email: t-training@bkc.ru
Website: www.bkc.ru
Courses offered DELTA

Language Link
Novoslobodskaya ul. 5/2, 103030 Moscow.
Tel: 095 238 0225.
Fax: 095 234 0703.
Courses Offered: DELTA.

SEBIA (+381)

Embassy CES / Rainbow School of English
Kolo Srpskih Sestara 8, 21000 Novi Sad
Tel: 21 363
Email: infouk@embassyces.com
Courses offered: DELTA

SOUTH AFRICA (+27)

International House, Johannesburg
4th Floor, Aspern House, 54 De Korte Street,
Braamfontein 2001, Johannesburg
Tel: 11 339 1051
Fax: 11 403 1759
Email: laurencek@ihjohannesburg.co.za
Website: www.ihjohannesburg.co.za
Courses offered DELTA

SPAIN (+34)

The British Council Examination Services
P. del General Martinez Campos 31
Madrid, 28010
Tel: 91 337 3529
Fax: 91 337 3586
Website: www.britishcouncil.org
Courses Offered: LTCL.Dip.TESOL.

British Language Centre
Calle Bravo Murillo 377, 2°, 28020 Madrid
Tel: 91 733 0739
Fax: 91 314 5009
Email: ted@british-blc.com
Website: www.british-blc.com
Courses offered DELTA

Campbell College
Teacher Training Centre, Calle Pascual y Genís, 14 pta
4, 46002 Valencia
Tel: 96 352 4217
Fax: 96 351 5402
Email: campbell@cpsl.com
Website: www.cpsl.com/campbell
Courses offered DELTA

International House, Barcelona
Trafalgar 14
08010 Barcelona
Tel: 93 268 4511 / 93 268 3304
Fax: 93 268 0239
Email: training@bcn.ihes.com
Website: www.ihes.com/bcn
Courses offered DELTA

nternational House, Madrid
Calle Zurbano 8, 28010 Madrid
Tel: 91 319 7224
Fax: 91 308 5321
Email: ttraining@ihmadrid.es
Website: www.ihmadrid.es
Courses offered DELTA

International House, Seville
Calle Menez Nunez 7, 41001 Seville
Tel: 954 50 03 16
Fax: 954 50 08 36
Email: mike@clic.es
Website: www.clic.es
Courses offered DELTA

Language Institute
Calle Oliva 11-20, Pontevedra, Galicia.
Tel/Fax: 986 871978.
Courses Offered: LTCL.Dip.TESOL.

Oxford TEFL
Avda Diagonal 402 Principal , Barcelona, Spain 8037
Tel: 93 458 0111
Fax: 93 458 6638
Website: www.oxfordtefl.com
Courses Offered: LTCL.Dip.TESOL.

SWITZERLAND (+41)

Klubschule Migros
Bahnhofplatz 2, 9001 St. Gallen
Tel: 71 228 1609
Fax: 71 228 1601
Email: lee.walker@ksmos.ch
Website: www.klubschule.ch
Courses offered DELTA

TURKEY (+90)

Bilkent University
Teacher Training Unit, School of English Language,
06533 Bilkent, Ankara
Tel: 312 290 5190
Fax: 312 266 4320
Email: elif@bilkent.edu.tr
Website: www.bilkent.edu.tr/~busel
Courses offered DELTA

Eastern Mediterranean University
School of Foreign Languages, Magosa, PO Box 95
Mersin 10
Tel: 392 630 2163
Fax: 392 365 0785
Email: stephen.pike@emu.edu.tr
Website: www.emu.edu.tr
Courses offered DELTA

International Training Institute (I.T.I.)
Kallavi Sok 7-9 Kat: 4, Istiklal Cad, Galatasaray
Istanbul
Tel: 212 243 28 88
Fax: 212 245 31 63
Email: iti_ist@yahoo.com
Website: www.itistanbul.org
Courses offered DELTA

UNITED ARAB EMIRATES (+971)

Abu Dhabi Men's College
Higher College of Technology, P.O. Box 25035, Abu
Dhabi
Tel: 2 4048 353
Fax: 2 4048 367
Email: phil.quirke@hct.ac.ae
Website: www.admc.hct.ac.ae/admcinternet/
Courses offered DELTA

Dubai Men's College
PO Box 15825, Dubai
Tel: 4 608 5502
Fax: 4 269 1369
Email: suzanne.McMahon@hct.ac.ae
Website: www.hct.ac.ae
Courses offered DELTA

Higher Colleges of Technology - Al Ain
Al Ain Men's College, PO Box 17155, Al Ain
Tel: 382 0888
Fax: 782 0099
Email: norman.williams@hct.ac.ae
Website: www.hct.ac.ae
Courses offered DELTA

Higher Colleges Of Technology - Abu Dhabi
PO Box 25026, Abu Dhabi.
Tel: 2 681 4600 / 5654.
Fax: 2 681 5833 / 6579.
Courses Offered: DELTA.

Higher Colleges of Technology - Sharjah
Sharjah Men's College, PO Box 7946, S.A.I.F. Zone,
Sharjah
Tel: 6558 5222
Fax: 6558 5252
Email: lesley.dick@hct.ac.ae
Website: www.hct.ac.ae
Courses offered DELTA

UNITED KINGDOM (+44)

Aberdeen College
Gallowgate Centre, Gallowgate, Aberdeen, AB25 1BN
Website: www.abcol.ac.uk
Email: b.ilett@abcol.ac.uk
Tel: 01224 612000
Fax: 01224 612001
Courses Offered: LTCL.Dip.TESOL

Anglo-Continental School of English

29-35 Wimborne Rd, Bournemouth, England BH1 4PT
Tel: 01202 557414
Fax: 01202 556156
Website: www.anglo-continental.com
Courses Offered: LTCL.Dip.TESOL

Barnet College

CELTA Courses, LBCE Department
Wood Street, Barnet, EN5 4AZ
Tel: 0208 275 2828
Fax: 0208 441 5236
Email: fran.linley@barnet.ac.uk
Website: www.barnet.ac.uk
Courses offered DELTA

Bell Language School

Bowthorpe Hall, Norwich, NR5 9AA
Tel: 01603 745615
Fax: 01603 747669
Email: info.norwich@bell-centres.com
Website: www.bell-centres.com
Courses offered DELTA

Bell Language School

South Road, Saffron Walden, CB11 3DP
Tel: 01799 582100
Fax: 01799 582199
Email: Bruce.Milne@bell-centres.com
Website: www.bell-schools.ac.uk
Courses offered DELTA

Bournemouth & Poole College of FE

Room 345, Lansdowne, Bournemouth, England BH1 3JJ
Tel: 01202 205851
Website: www.bpc.ac.uk
Courses Offered: LTCL.Dip.TESOL

Brasshouse Language Centre

50 Sheepcote Street, Birmingham, B16 8AJ
Tel: 0121 303 0114
Fax: 0121 303 4782
Website: www.birmingham.gov.uk/brasshouse
Courses offered DELTA

City of Bristol College

Department of Languages, Cabot House, Brunel Centre, Ashley Down, Bristol, BS7 9BU
Tel: 0117 312 5163
Fax: 0117 312 5180

Email: emmanuel.raud@cityofbristol.ac.uk
Website: www.cityofbristol.ac.uk
Courses offered: DELTA

Brooklands College

Heath Road, Weybridge, KT13 8TT
Website: www.brooklands.ac.uk
Email: uover@brooklands.ac.uk
Tel: 01932 847029
Fax: 01932 797800
Courses Offered: LTCL.Dip.TESOL

Canterbury Christ Church University College

North Holmes Road, Canterbury, CT1 1QU
Tel: 01227 458459
Email: english@cant.ac.uk
Website: www.cant.ac.uk/io
Courses Offered: LTCL.Dip.TESOL

Chester English College/English in Chester

9-11 Stanley Place, Chester, CH1 2LU
Tel: 0 1244 318913
Fax: 0 1244 320091
Email: study@english-in-chester.co.uk
Website: www.english-in-chester.co.uk
Courses offered DELTA

City of Bath College

Avon Street, Bath, BA1 1UP
Tel: 0 1225 312191
Fax: 0 1225 444213
Email: bulld@citybathcoll.ac.uk
Website: www.citybathcoll.ac.uk
Courses offered DELTA

City College Manchester

Fielden Centre, 141 Barlow Moor Road, West Didsbury, Manchester, M20 2PQ
Website: www.ccm.ac.uk
Email: aspencer@ccm.ac.uk
Tel: 0161 957 1660
Fax: 0161 434 0443
Courses Offered: LTCL.Dip.TESOL

Ealing, Hammersmith, West London College

Gliddon Road, London W14 9BL
Freephone: 44 800 980 2175
Fax: 0 20 8563 8247
Email: cic@hwlc.ac.uk
Website: www.hwlc.ac.uk
Courses offered DELTA

Eastbourne School of English
8 Trinity Trees, Eastbourne, BN21 3LD
Tel: 0 1323 721759
Fax: 0 1323 639271
Email: delta@esoe.co.uk
Website: www.esoe.co.uk
Courses offered DELTA

Embassy CES
Palace Court, White Rock, Hastings, TN34 1JY
Tel: 0 1424 720100
Fax: 0 1424 720323
Email: training@embassyces.com
Website: www.embassyces.com
Courses offered DELTA

English First - EF
26 Wilbraham Road, Manchester, England M14 6JX
Tel: 0161 256 1400
Website: www.ef.com
Courses: LTCL.Dip.TESOL

English Language Centre
5 New Street, York, YO1 8RA
Tel: 0 1904 423594
Fax: 0 1904 672200
Email: english@btinternet.com
Website: www.elcyork.com
Courses offered DELTA

English Language House
300 Saxon Gate West, Milton Keynes, MK9 2ES
Tel: 0 1908 694 357
Fax: 0 1908 694 355
Email: info@englishlanguagehouse.co.uk
Website: www.englishlanguagehouse.co.uk
Courses offered DELTA

Golders Green Teacher Training Centre
11 Golders Green Road, London NW11 8DY
Email: teachertraining@ggcol.fsnet.co.uk
Tel: 020 8731 0963
Fax: 020 8455 6528
Courses Offered: LTCL.Dip.TESOL

Guildford College Of Further & Higher Education
Stoke Park, Guildford, GU1 1EZ
Tel: 01483 448500
Fax: 01483 448600
Courses Offered: LTCL.Dip.TESOL

inlingua
iTTR, Rodney Lodge, Rodney Road, Cheltenham, GL50 1HX
Tel: 01242 253 171
Email: jhughes@inlingua-cheltenham.co.uk
Website: www.inlingua-cheltenham.co.uk
Courses: LTCL.Dip.TESOL

Institute for Applied Language Studies
Univ. of Edinburgh, 21 Hill Place, Edinburgh EH8 9DP
Tel: 0 131 650 6200
Fax: 0 131 667 5927
Email: IALS.enquiries@ed.ac.uk
Website: www.ials.ed.ac.uk
Courses offered DELTA

International House
106 Piccadilly, London W1J 7NL
Tel: 0 20 7518 6928
Fax: 0 20 7518 6921
Email: fernando.nonohay@ihlondon.co.uk
Website: www.ihlondon.com
Courses offered DELTA, also Distance-DELTA (www.thedistancedelta.com)

International House
14-18 Stowell Street, Newcastle upon Tyne, NE1 4XQ
Tel: 0 191 238 9551
Fax: 0 191 238 1126
Email: info@ihnewcastle.com
Website: www.ihnewcastle.com
Courses offered DELTA

International House - The Distance DELTA
106 Piccadilly, London W1V 9FL
Tel: +44 (0) 20 7518 6999
Fax: +44 (0) 20 7518 6998
Email: admin@thedistancedelta.com
Website: www.thedistancedelta.com
Courses offered DELTA

ITTC United Kingdom Ltd
Nortoft Road, Charminster, Bournemouth, BH8 8PY
Tel: 0 1202 397 721
Fax: 0 1202 309 662
Email: tefl@ittc.co.uk
Website: www.ittc.co.uk
Courses offered DELTA

Kingston College
Kingston Hall Road, Kingston-upon-Thames, KT1 2AQ
Website: www.kingston-college.ac.uk
Email: kise@kingston-college.ac.uk
Tel: 020 8546 2151
Fax: 020 8268 2900
Courses Offered: LTCL.Dip.TESOL

King's College English Language Teaching Centre
English Language Centre, King's College London, The Strand, London WC2R 2LS
Tel: 0 207 848 1604
Fax: 0 207 848 1601
Email: christopher.sciberas@kcl.ac.uk
Website: www.kcl.ac.uk
Courses offered DELTA

Langside College
50 Prospecthill Road, Glasgow, G42 9LB
Website: www.langside.ac.uk
Email: tfoster@langside.ac.uk
Tel: 0141 649 4991
Fax: 0141 632 5252
Courses Offered: LTCL.Dip.TESOL

Language Link
181 Earls Court Road, Earls Court, London SW5 9RB
Tel: 0 20 7370 4755
Fax: 0 20 7370 1123
Email: languagelink@compuserve.com
Website: www.languagelink.co.uk
Courses offered DELTA

Language Project
27 Oakfield Road, Clifton, Bristol, BS8 2AT
Website: www.languageproject.co.uk
Email: info@languageproject.co.uk
Tel: 0117 9090911
Fax: 0117 907 7181
Courses Offered: LTCL.Dip.TESOL

Languages Training and Development
Suite 2, Waterloo House , 58-60 High Street , Witney, OX28 6RJ
Tel: 01993 708 637
Fax: 01993 862791
Website: www.ltdoxford.com
Courses Offered: LTCL.Dip.TESOL

Manchester Academy of English
St Margaret's Chambers, 5 Newton Street, Manchester, England M1 1HL
Tel: 0161 237 5619
Fax: 0161 237 9016
Website: www.manacad.co.uk
Courses Offered: LTCL.Dip.TESOL

Northbrook College
Modern Languages Centre, Littlehampton Road, Goring-by-Sea, Worthing, BN12 6NU
Website: www.nbcol.ac.uk
Email: s.scowen@nbcol.ac.uk
Tel: 01903 606243
Fax: 01903 606207
Courses Offered: LTCL.Dip.TESOL

Nottingham Trent University
Nottingham Language Centre, Newton Building, Room 519, Burton Street, Nottingham, NG1 4BU
Tel: 0 115 941 8418
Fax: 0 115 848 6513
Email: linda.taylor@ntu.ac.uk
Website: www.nlc.ntu.ac.uk
Courses offered DELTA

Oxford Cherwell College
Oxpens Road, Oxford, OX1 1SA
Tel: 01865 269268
Fax: 01865 269412
Email: Steven_Haysham@oxfordcollege.ac.uk
Website: www.oxfordcollege.ac.uk
Courses offered: DELTA

Oxford College of Further Education
1 Oxpens Road, Oxford, OX1 1SA
Tel: 0 1865 269268
Fax: 0 1865 269412
Email: Steven_Haysham@oxfordcollege.ac.uk
Website: www.oxfordcollege.ac.uk
Courses offered DELTA

Oxford House College
28 Market Place, Oxford Circus, London W1W 8AW
Tel: 0 20 7580 9785
Fax: 0 20 7323 4582
Email: teachertraining@oxfordhouse.co.uk
Website: www.oxfordhousecollege.co.uk
Courses offered DELTA

Reading College
Crescent Road, Reading, RG1 5RQ
Tel: 0118 967 5442
Fax: 0118 967 5441
Courses Offered: LTCL.Dip.TESOL

Reading College and School of Arts & Design
Crescent Road, Reading, RG1 5RQ
Tel: 0 118 967 5411
Fax: 0 118 967 5441
Email: baberm@reading-college.ac.uk
Website: www.reading-college.ac.uk
Courses offered DELTA

Regency School of English
Royal Crescent, Ramsgate, CT11 9PE
Email: regency.school@btinternet.com
Tel: 01843 591212
Fax: 01843 850035
Courses Offered: LTCL.Dip.TESOL

St George International
76 Mortimer Street, London W1N 7DE
Website: www.stgeorges.co.uk
Email: teflenq@stgeorges.co.uk
Tel: 020 7299 1700
Fax: 020 7299 1711
Courses Offered: LTCL.Dip.TESOL

St Giles College
51 Shepherds Hill, London, N6 5QP
Tel: 0208 340 0828
Fax: 0208 348 9389
Email: edtrust@stgiles.co.uk
Website: www.tefl-stgiles.com
Courses offered: CELTA, DELTA

Sandwell College
Smethwick Campus, Crocketts Lane, Smethwick, B66 3BU
Website: www.sandwell.ac.uk
Email: gill.clarke@sandwell.ac.uk
Tel: 0121 253 6238
Fax: 0121 253 6322
Courses Offered: LTCL.Dip.TESOL

Saxoncourt Teacher Training
Nightingale House, 56-70 Queensway, Petts Wood
Bromley, BR5 1DH
Tel: 01689 873 355
Fax: 01689 872 100

Email: jshepheard@sgvenglish.com
Website: www.sgvenglish.com
Courses offered DELTA

Shane English School
59 South Molton Street, London W1K 5SN
Website: www.sgvenglish.com
Email: awhitehead@sgvenglish.com
Tel: 07491 1911
Fax: 07493 3657
Courses Offered: LTCL.Dip.TESOL

Sheffield Hallam University, TESOL Centre
36 Collegiate Campus, Sheffield, S10 2BP
Email: tesol@shu.ac.uk
Tel: 0114 225 2240
Fax: 0114 225 2280
Website: www.shu.ac.uk
Courses Offered: LTCL.Dip.TESOL

Sidmouth International School
May Cottage, Sidmouth, EX10 8EN
Email: efl@sidmouth-int.co.uk
Tel: 01395 516754
Fax: 01395 579270
Website: www.sidmouth-int.co.uk
Courses Offered: LTCL.Dip.TESOL

Solihull College
Blossomfield Road, Solihull, Birmingham, B91 1SB
Tel: 0 121 678 7173
Fax: 0 121 678 7276
Email: pat.morris@Solihull.ac.uk
Website: www.solihull.ac.uk
Courses offered DELTA

Stanton Teacher Training Courses Ltd
Stanton House, 167 Queensway, London W2 4SB
Tel: 0 207 221 7259
Fax: 0 207 792 9047
Email: study@stanton-school.co.uk
Website: www.stanton-school.co.uk
Courses offered DELTA

TLI Ltd. Teacher Training
Jewel and Esk Valley College, 24 Milton Road East,
Edinburgh, England EH15 2PP UK
Tel: +441316201163
Website: www.tlieurope.com
Courses Offered: LTCL.Dip.TESOL

Universal Language Services
43 - 45 Cambridge Gardens, Hastings, TN34 1EN
Website: www.unversallanguageservices.com
Email: enquiries@universallanguageservices.com
Tel: 01424 438025
Fax: 01424 438050
Courses Offered: LTCL.Dip.TESOL

University of Bath
English Language Centre, Claverton Down, Bath
BA2 7AY,
Tel: 0 1225 323139
Fax: 0 1225 323135
Email: mlssfw@bath.ac.uk
Website: www.bath.ac.uk/elc/delta.htm
Courses offered DELTA

University of Durham
The Language Centre, Elvet Riverside, New Elvet,
Durham, DH1 3JT
Tel: 0 191 374 3716
Fax: 0 191 374 7790
Email: CELTA.training@durham.ac.uk
Website: www.durham.ac.uk/language.centre
Courses offered DELTA

University College London (UCL)
Language Centre, 136 Gower Street, London, WC1
6BT
Tel: 0207 679 7722
Fax: 0207 383 3577
Email: a.salisbury@ucl.ac.uk
Website: www.ucl.ac.uk
Courses offered: DELTA

Waltham Forest College
Forest Road, London E17 4JB
Tel: 0 208 501 8178
Fax: 0 208 501 8001
Email: lawlor@waltham.ac.uk
Website: www.waltham.ac.uk
Courses offered DELTA

Warwickshire College
Thornbank Centre, Warwick New Road, Leamington
Spa, CV32 5JE
Tel: 0 1926 318 165
Fax: 0 1926 427 317
Email: bbuxton@warkscol.ac.uk
Website: www.warkscol.ac.uk
Courses offered DELTA

Westminster Kingsway College
Castle Lane, London SW1E 6DR
Tel: 0 207 963 8515
Fax: 0 207 233 8509
Email: annecandan@westking.ac.uk
Courses offered DELTA

Windsor Schools TEFL
21 Osborne Road, Windsor, SL4 1RU
Website: www.windsorschools.co.uk
Email: info@windsorschools.co.uk
Tel: 01753 858995
Fax: 01753 831726
Courses Offered: LTCL.Dip.TESOL

USA (+1)

St. Giles Language Teaching Center
One Hallidie Plaza (Suite 350), San Francisco, CA
94102
Tel:1 415 788 3552
Fax:1 415 788 1923
Email: info@stgiles-usa.com
Website: www.stgiles-usa.com
Courses offered: DELTA

VIETNAM (+84)

**International Language Academy (ILA)
Vietnam**
402 Nguyen Thi Minh Khai Street, District 3, Ho Chi
Minh City
Tel: 8 929 0100 (Ext. 124)
Fax: 8 929 0070
Email: andrew@ilavietnam.com
Website: www.ilavietnam.com
Courses offered: DELTA

Master's Degree Courses

A Master's Degree in Teaching English as a Second or Foreign Language is, for many teachers, a key qualification for those who want to work to cover the theory of teaching – or work in schools and universities.

For many prospective teachers, the decision to embark on a Master's degree programme represents a crucial investment of time and money in the career of their choice. Studying for a postgraduate degree need not leave you in debt for the rest of your natural born days. Many students can earn money while they study by working as a Graduate Teaching Assistant. A number of universities and colleges offer the opportunity for students to earn their degrees on a part-time basis, so you can work while you study. Most institutions offer scholarships and grants: make it a point to inquire about when you contact a school or university.

Master's degree programmes vary in terms of admission requirements and length of the course. Prospective students whose first language is not English will need to submit their TOEFL score for consideration by the admission office of the institution where they hope to study. M.A. programmes are usually flexible and you can work at your own pace within the criteria for time set by the university or college: a programme can take anywhere from one to five years or more to complete.

There are many different titles for Master's degree programmes. These often reflect the historical development of the department with which they are associated. There are three main types of Master's degree in TESL/TEFL: (1) Master of Arts (M.A.), (2) Master of Science (M.Sc./M.S.) and (3) Master of Education (M.Ed.). In general there is little difference between all three degrees although earning a M.Ed., which is awarded by a School of Education, may not involve writing a thesis. A MAT (Master of Arts in Teaching) focuses more on the practical aspects of teaching than the other types of Master's degrees.

An Applied Linguistics degree is at the other end of the scale in that these programmes usually concentrate more directly on the theory of language acquisition.

The benefits associated with a Master's degree are numerous. Although there are institutions that will hire teachers who have not earned a postgraduate degree, the reality is that many employers, especially.in higher education, insist that candidates have a Master's degree in TESL, TEFL, TESOL or Applied Linguistics. A teacher with a Master's degree usually enjoys a greater earning power than a colleague who lacks the qualification. Above all, embarking on a Master's programme reinforces a teacher's decision that he or she has made teaching English as a second or foreign language a serious career choice.

Choosing a Master's Degree Course

If you plan to make teaching English as a second or foreign language your major career decision, then you should be looking at studying for a Master's Degree in TEFL / TESL or TESOL. The first thing to do when choosing a Master's programme that's right for you is to ask questions: What kinds of courses are offered in the programme? Are they more practical or theoretical in scope?

If you are interested in going directly into teaching after getting your master's degree, you should stick to a practical curriculum. If, on the other hand, if you are interested in pursuing a Ph.D., then look for a more theoretically based curriculum.

What do the faculty members specialize in? Ask the programme director for details on what the faculty is researching, what courses they teach, and even about possible internships or assistantships. This will give you an indication of what the focus of your studies will be. If your interests are similar to theirs, you have a good match.

If you are interested in teaching in the public school system, find out if the courses lead to or satisfy state certification, and if they satisfy the requirements in any other state where you are considering certification.

General guidelines:

Ask for a reference or two from the programme director. Ask recent graduates if they are satisfied with the education they received and whether their courses have actually met the needs of their current jobs.

Examine the job placement record. What percentage of graduates get jobs after they receive their degrees? Does the school offer placement assistance or career counselling?

English for Special Purposes Programmes

Other professions look to university TESOL master's programmes to develop instructors for teaching English for special purposes (ESP) in specialized fields such as medicine, law, computer science, engineering, and business. Master's programmes must provide their students with the expertise needed to teach a wide range of skills from basic English for those working at entry level jobs to accent reduction courses for professionals seeking to improve their oral communication skills. Additionally, ESP instructors need a familiarity with the content subject matter and the ability to collaborate with professors and other professionals in various disciplines.

Teaching English as a Foreign Language Master's programmes continue to fulfill their traditional role of providing teachers for positions overseas teaching English to college and university students, professional adults, and young learners. With the worldwide demand for English instruction, American students wishing to teach abroad and international students planning to teach English in their own countries seek out programmes in Teaching English as a Foreign language (TEFL).

These programmes feature methodology courses that address frequent concerns of English as a Foreign Language (EFL) teachers such as curriculum design for large class sizes, limited

budget and materials, and resources for authentic language input and natural language acquisition.

TESOL Doctoral Study

TESOL master's programmes are the training ground for prospective doctoral candidates who conduct research, design and implement university degree programmes, and teach at the master's and doctoral levels in institutions of higher education. To prepare students for these academic roles, TESOL master's programmes typically offer a combination of courses which cover the theory and practice of second language teaching, curriculum development, and the fundamentals of linguistics, second language acquisition, and research.

Master's Degree Courses

There are opportunities to study for a Master's degree in a wide range of countries around the world. These selected schools and universities offer full-time intensive courses and, more often, distance or part-time study.

AUSTRALIA (+61)

Macquarie University
Sydney, NSW 2109.
Tel: 2 9850 9647.
Fax: 2 985 9352.
Email: lingpgo@ling.mq.edu.au
Website: www.ling.mq.edu.au/researchdegrees
Start Dates: March, July.
Course length: 2-3 semesters FT.
Admission Requirements: First degree + teaching experience.
Programmes: M.A. and PhD in Applied Linguistics.

University of Melbourne
Department of Language, Literacy and Arts Education, Room 513, Doug McDonell Building, Victoria, 3010.
Tel:: 3 9344 8377.
Fax: 3 8344 5104.
Programmes: Master of TESOL.

Monash University
Normanby House, 100 Normanby Road, Clayton, Victoria 3168.
Programmes: M.A. TESOL.
Course length: 2 years FT; 4 years PT.

Queensland University of Technology
School of Culture & Language Education, Kelvin Grove Campus, Victoria Park Road, Kelvin Grove, Brisbane, Queensland 4059.
Tel: 7 3864 3242.
Fax: 7 3864 3988.
Programmes: M.Ed. TESOL.

University of South Australia
GPO Box 2471, Adelaide, South Australia 5001.
Start Dates: February.
Tel: 8 8302 6611.
Fax: 8 8302 2466.
Programmes: M.Ed. TESOL.

Tasmania University
English Language Centre, P.O. Box 1214, Launceston, Tasmania 7250.
Programmes: M.Ed. TESOL.
Course length: 18 months FT.
Admission Requirements: Degree.

Victoria University
PO Box 14428, Melbourne, Victoria, 8001.
Tel: 3 9688 4000.
Fax: 3 9689 4069.
Programmes: M.A. in TESOL and Literacy.

CANADA (+1)

Brock University
Graduate Studies Office, St. Catharines, Ontario L2S 3A1.
Tel: (905) 688-5550, x4467.
Fax: (905) 988-5488.
Email: ekoop@spartan.ac.brocku.ca
Programmes: M.Ed. TESL.
Course length: 1 year.
Grant Availability: Possible Teaching/Research Assistantships.
Admission Requirements: Undergraduate degree with an average of 75% in the last 10 credits.

Carleton University

School of Linguistics and Applied Language Studies,1125 Colonel By Drive, Ottawa K1S 5B6.
Tel: (613) 520-2802.
Fax: (613) 520-6641.
Email: linguistics@carleton.ca
Programmes: M.A. Applied Language Studies.
Course length: Usually 4 terms FT depending on which option student decides to complete (thesis, research essay or all courses).
Start Dates: January, May, September.
Admission Requirements: Honors degree with a B - B+ average.

York University

Room 544 South, Ross Building, 4700 Keele Street, Toronto, Ontario M3J 1P3.
Tel: (416) 736-2100 x88270.
Fax: (416) 736-5483.
Email: gradling@yorku.ca
Programmes: M.A. in Theoretical & Applied Linguistics.
Course length: 1 year FT.
Grant Availability: Teaching Assistantships, Graduate Assistantships, Scholarships.
Start Dates: September.

CHINA (HONG KONG +852)

Chinese University of Management

Tat Chee Avenue, Kowloon, Hong Kong.
Tel: 2788 9400.
Fax: 2788 9020.
Programmes: M.A. Degree in TESL.

City University of Hong Kong School of Graduate Studies

5/F Cheng Yick Chi Building, Tat Chee Avenue, Kowloon.
Tel: 2788 9076.
Fax: 2788 9940.
Programmes: M.A. Degree in TESL.

EGYPT (+20)

The American University in Cairo

113 Sharia Kasr el-Aini - PO Box 2511, Cairo, 11511.
Tel: 2-357-5530.

Fax: 2-355-7565. (In the U.S.: **Tel:** (212) 730-8800.
Fax: (212) 730-1600)
Programmes: M.A. Degree in TEFL.
Course length: 2 years FT.
Start Dates: January, September.

IRELAND (+353)

The National University of Ireland Language Centre

O'Rahilly Building, UCC, Cork.
Tel: 21 4902043.
Fax: 21 4903223.
Programmes: M.A. Degree in Applied Linguistics.
Course length: FT 1 year.
Start Dates: October.
Admission Requirements: Relevant primary degree at Second Class Honors standard or equivalent, English to IELTS level 7.0 if not a native speaker.

MALAYSIA (+60)

Universiti Malaya Faculty of Languages and Linguistics Education

Pantai Valley, 59100 Kuala Lumpur.
Tel: 3 756-0022.
Fax: 3 755-2975.
Programmes: M.A. Degree in TESOL.

MEXICO (+52)

Universidad de las Américas

Departamento de Lenguas, Sta. Catarina Mártir, Puebla, 72820.
Tel: 22 29 31 05.
Fax: 22 29 31 05
Email: eckep@mail.udlap.mx
Programmes: M.A. in Applied Linguistics.
Course length: 2 years FT.
Aid Availability: A limited number of teaching assistantships is available in the Department of Languages. Mexican students can obtain financial aid from the Ministry of Public Education of Mexico, while participants from the United States are able to procure college loans from institutions in the U.S.

PHILIPPINES (+63)

University of the East
2219 C.M. Recto Avenue, 1008 Manila.
Tel: 2-741-95-01.
Programmes: M.A. Degree in Education (TESOL).

SOUTH AFRICA (+27)

Rhodes University
Faculty of Arts, P.O. Box 94, Grahamstown, 6140.
Tel: 461 318111.
Fax: 461 25049.
Programmes: M.A. TESOL.
Course length: 2 years.

THAILAND (+66)

Assumption University
A Building 3rd floor, Ramkhamhaeng Soi 24 Road
Huamark, Bangkok 1.
Tel: 2-3004543-62.
Fax: 2-7191521.
Programmes: M.A. TESL.

Chiang Mai University Graduate School
Chang Mai, 50200.
Tel: 53-221699.
Fax: 53-892231.
Programmes: M.A. TEFL.

Payap University Graduate School
Chiang Mai, 50000.
Programmes: M.A. TEFL.

UNITED KINGDOM (+44)

Aston University
Aston Triangle, Birmingham B4 7ET.
Tel: 121 359 3611.
Fax: 121 359 6350.
Email: lsu@aston.ac.uk
Website: www.les.aston.ac.uk/tesol
Programmes: M.Sc./Diploma TESOL,
M.Sc./Diploma Teaching ESP. Both distance learning

Canterbury Christ Church University
North Holmes Road, Canterbury, Kent, CT1 1QU
Tel: 01227 458459

Fax: 01227 781558
Email: english@cant.ac.uk
Website: www.cant.ac.uk/io
Courses offered: MA TESOL

Middlesex University
White Hart Lane, London N17 8HR
Tel: 020 8411 5898
Email: admissions@mdx.ac.uk
Website: www.ilrs.mdx.ac.uk/lang/eng_non.htm
Courses: MA TEFL with Applied Linguistics

Norwich Institute of Language Education (NILE)
PO Box 2000, Norwich, NR2 1LE
Tel: 01603 664473
Fax: 01603 664493
Email: registrar@nile-elt.com
Website: www.nile-elt.com
Courses offered: MA language education, range of courses for professional development

Oxford Brookes University
Tel: 01865 483874
Fax: 01865 484377
Email: icels@brookes.ac.uk
Website: www.brookes.ac.uk/icels
Courses: MA Applied Linguistics, MA ELT

Sheffield Hallam University
TESOL Centre, School of Education, Collegiate
Campus, Sheffield S10 2BP.
Tel: 114 225 2240.
Fax: 114 225 2280.
Programmes: M.A. TESOL.
Course length: 12 weeks DL phase, + 6 weeks
intensive direct contact phase, + 32 weeks research
phase.
Admission Requirements: PG diploma in TESOL or
equivalent.
Start Dates: March or October each year for direct
contact phase in June/July or January/February.

University of Bath
English Language Centre, University of Bath, BA2
7AY
Tel: 01225 383024
Fax: 01225 383135
Email: english@bath.ac.uk
Website: www.bath.ac.uk/elc
Courses offered: MA in ELT

University of Birmingham

CELS, University of Birmingham, Edgbaston, Birmingham, B15 2TT
Tel: 0121 414 3239
Fax: 0121 414 3298
Email: cels@bham.ac.uk
Courses offered: MA Applied Linguistics, MA ESP, MA TEFL/TESL,

University of Bristol

Graduate School of Education, 35 Berkeley Square, Bristol BS8 1JA.
Tel: 117 9287040.
Fax: 0117 927250.
Email: janet.woolways@bristol.ac.uk
Course length: 12 months full-time; up to five years part-time; can also be done in term blocks: October to December or January to March.
Start Dates: October FT; January, October PT. Summer Session: Presessional available for those who have either been out of full-time education for many years, or who feel that one month of academic preparation would benefit them. Usually held throughout September.
Admission Requirements: First degree, at least one year fulltime teaching experience; preferably a professional qualification in TESL/TEFL.
Specializations: Specialist centre for Language in Education, including English as an additional language; off shore teaching can be provided for closed groups.
Courses: M.Ed. TEFL, EdD in TESOL, MPhil/PhD in TESOL

University Of Durham

Department Of Linguistics And English Language, Elvet Riverside II, New Elvet, Durham DH1 3JT.
Tel: 191 374 2641.
Fax: 191 374 2685.
Programmes: M.A. Linguistics, M.A. Language Acquisition, M.A. Applied Linguistics, M.A. Applied Linguistics (ELT), M.A. Applied Linguistics, (ELT, CALL And Educational Technology), M.A. Applied Linguistics (ESP), M.A. Applied Linguistics (ESOL), M.A. Applied Linguistics (ELT And Materials Development), M.A. Applied Linguistics (FLT),M.A. Applied Linguistics (Translation).

University of Edinburgh

Faculty of Education, Moray House, Holyrood Road, Edinburgh, EH8 8AQ, Scotland.
Tel: 131 651 6329.

Fax: 131 651 6409.
Programmes: M Ed (TESOL) (DL available).
Course length: 1 year FT; 6 years maximum DL.
Start Dates: October Full-time; Continuous DL.
Admission Requirements: Degree + 3 years' relevant experience.

University of Exeter

School of Education and Lifelong Learning
Tel: 01392 264815
Fax: 01392 264902
Email: ed-cpd@exeter.ac.uk
Website: www.ex.ac.uk/sell
Courses: MPhil in TESOL, MEd in TESOL, EdD in TESOL, Pgcert in TESOL

University of Leicester

21 University Road, Leicester, LE1 7RF.
Tel: 116 2523675.
Fax: 116 2523653.
Programmes: M.A. Applied Linguistics and TESOL (DL).

University of London

Institute of Education, 20 Bedford Way, London WC1 0AL.
Tel: 020 7612 6536
Fax: 020 7612 6534.
Course length: 1 year FT; 2 years PT.
Start Dates: October.
Admission Requirements: A good Honours class degree, and at least two years teaching experience
Programmes: M.A. TESOL.

University of Luton

Vicarage Street, Luton, LU1 3JU.
Tel: 1582 489019.
Fax: 1582 743466.
Programmes: M.A. Applied Linguistics (TEFL).
Course length: 1 year. **Start Dates:** October.

University of Manchester

Faculty of Education, University of Manchester, Oxford Rd, Manchester, M13 9PL
Tel: 0161 275 3463
Email: education.enquiries@man.ac.uk
Website: www.man.ac.uk/langlit
Courses offered: MEd in ELT, MEd in Educational Technology and ELT

University of Newcastle upon Tyne

Language Centre, Level 4, Old Library Bldg.,
Newcastle upon Tyne, NE1 7RU.
Tel: 191 222 5621
Fax: 191 222 5239
Programmes: M.A. in Media Technology for TEFL,
M.A. in Linguistics for TESOL.
Course length: 12 months FT for both programmes,
24 months PT (Linguistics).
Requirements: 2 years FT teaching experience.
Start Dates: September.

University of Sunderland

School of Humanities & Social Sciences, Forster
Building, Chester Road, Sunderland SR1 3SD.
Tel: 191 515 2000.
Programmes: M.A. TESOL.

University of Surrey

English Language Institute, Guildford, Surrey, GU2
5XH.
Tel: 1483 259910
Fax: 1483 259507.
Programmes: M.A. Linguistics (TESOL) (DL). M.Sc.
English Language Teaching Management (DL).
Course length: 27 months.
Start Dates: March, October.
Admission Requirements: 1st degree and at least two
years full time teaching experience.

University of Warwick

CELTE, Coventry, CV4 7AL
Tel: 024 7652 3200
Fax: 024 7652 4318
Email: celte@warwick.ac.uk
Website: www.warwick.ac.uk/celte
Courses offered: MA in ELT, MA in ESP, Diploma in
ELT and Administration, research degrees of PhD and
EdD

University of York

EFL Unit, York, Y010 5DD
Tel: 01904 432483
Fax: 01904 432481
Email: efl2@york.ac.uk
Website: www.york.ac.uk/ltc/efl
Courses offered: MA in teaching young learners
(distance course)

UNITED STATES OF AMERICA (+1)

Adelphi University

1 South Avenue, Garden City, NY 11530
Tel: (516) 877-3000
Website: www.adelphi.edu/

University of Alabama

UAB Station, Birmingham, AL 35294
Website: http://main.uab.edu/
Courses: MA TESOL

American University

4400 Massachusetts Avenue NW, Washington DC
20016-8001
Tel: 202-885-6000
Fax: 202-885-1025
Website: www.american.edu/
Email: afa@american.edu
Courses: MA TESOL, MIP TESOL, w/Peace Corps.,
MAT in ESOL

University of Arizona

Tucson, AZ 85721
Tel: (520) 621-2211
Website: www.arizona.edu/
Courses: MA ESL

Arizona State University

University Drive and Mill Avenue, Tempe, AZ 85287
Tel: (480) 965-9011
Website: www.asu.edu/
Email: information@asu.edu
Courses: MA TESL

Azusa Pacific University

901 E. Alosta Ave.Azusa, CA 91702
Tel: (626) 969-3434
Website: www.apu.edu/
Courses: MA TESOL

Ball State University

Muncie, IN 47306.
Tel: 1-800-482-4278.
Website: www.bsu.edu/
Email: ASKUS@bsu.edu.
Courses: MA in TESOL

Biola University

13800 Biola Avenue, La Mirada, California
90639-0001

Tel: 1-800-OK-BIOLA 562-903-4752
Website: www.biola.edu/
Courses: MA TESOL

Boston University
121 Bay State Road Boston, MA 02215
Website: www.bu.edu/
Courses: Med TESOL

Bowling Green State University
Bowling Green, OH 43402
Website: www.bgsu.edu/
Courses: MATESL programme

Brigham Young University
Provo, Utah 84602
Tel: (801) 378-INFO or (801) 378-4636
Website: www.byu.edu/
Courses: TESOL MA

University of California
One Shields Avenue, Davis, CA 95616
Tel: (530) 752-1011
Website: www.ucdavis.edu/
Courses: MA with concentration in applied linguistics.

University of California, LA
405 Hilgard Avenue, Box 951361 Los Angeles, CA, 90095-1361
Tel: (310) 825-4321
Website: www.ucla.edu/
Courses: MA Applied Linguistics & TESL
Course length: 2 years full-time

Cal. State Univ, Dominguez Hills
1000 E. Victoria Street, Carson, California 90747
Tel: (310) 243-3696
Website: www.csudh.edu/
Courses: MA English with TESL

Cal. State Univ, Fresno
5241 N. Maple Avenue, Fresno, CA 93740-8027
Tel: (559) 278-4240
Website: www.csufresno.edu/
Email: webmaster@csufresno.edu
Courses: MA Linguistics/ESL Emphasis

Cal. State Univ, Fullerton
P.O. Box 34080 Fullerton, CA 92834
Tel: (714) 278-2011

Website: www.fullerton.edu/
Courses: MS Education with TESOL
Course length: 30 semester units, full or part-time

Cal. State Univ, Hayward
25800 Carlos Bee Blvd, Hayward, CA 94542
Tel: (510) 885-3000
Website: www.csuhayward.edu/
Courses: MA English – TESOL option.
Course length: 6 quarters, full or PT
Aid Availability: Grants and fellowships

Cal. State Univ, Los Angeles
5151 State University Drive, Los Angeles, California 90032-4226
Tel: (323) 343-3000
Website: www.calstatela.edu/
Courses: MA TESOL
Course length: 45 quarter units, full or part-time
Aid Availability: Scholarships, assistantships, fee waivers
Other: Practical teacher-training programme. Also offered in Buenos Aires, Argentina.

Cal. State Univ, Northridge
18111 Nordhoff Street, Northridge, California 91330
Tel: (818) 677-1200
Website: www.csun.edu/
Courses: MA Linguistics with TESOL

Cal. State Univ, Sacramento
6000 J Street, Sacramento, CA, 95819.
Tel: (916) 278-6011
Website: www.csus.edu/
Courses: MA TESOL
Other: Pedagogical focus. Joint programme with the Peace Corps is offered.

Cardinal Stritch University
6801 N. Yates Rd., Milwaukee, WI 53217-3985.
Tel: (414) 410-4000
Website: www.stritch.edu/
Courses: MEd Professional Development with ESL

Carson-Newman University
Jefferson City, TN, 37760.
Tel: (865) 475-9061
Fax: (865) 471-3502
Website: www.cn.edu/
Courses: MAT-ESL
Course length: 12-18 mths

Central Connecticut St. University
1615 Stanley St., New Britain, CT 06050
Tel: 1-860-832-CCSU
Website: www.ccsu.edu/
Courses: M.S. in TESOL; Certification in TESOL.

Central Michigan University
Mount Pleasant, Michigan 48859
Tel: (517) 774-4000
Website: www.cmich.edu/
Courses: MA TESOL
Other: Teaching practice at university language centre.

Central Missouri State Universtiy
Department of Linguistics
P.O. Box 800, Warrensburg MO 64093
Tel: 1-800-SAY-CMSU (1-800-729-2678)
Website: www.cmsu.edu/
Courses: MA-TESL, MA TESL

Central Washington University
400 E. 8th Avenue, Ellensburg, WA 98926
Tel: (509) 963-1211
Website: www.cwu.edu/
Courses: MA English with TESL/TEFL

University of Cincinnati
2624 Clifton Avenue, Cincinnati, OH 45221
Tel: (513) 556-6000
Website: www.uc.edu/
Courses: MEd Literacy Education with TESL

University of Colorado, Boulder
Boulder, CO 80309
Tel: (303) 492-1411
Website: www.colorado.edu/
Courses: MA Linguistics
Other: Primarily an MA in linguistics with some TESL options.

University of Colorado, Denver
P.O. Box 173364, Denver, CO 80217-3364
Tel: 303-556-2400
Website: www.cudenver.edu/
Courses: MA English/Applied Linguistics (ESL)
Other: Teaching practice available at the program's campuses in Beijing and Moscow.

Colorado State University
Fort Collins, CO 80523
Tel: (970) 491-1101
Website: www.colostate.edu/
Courses: MA TESL

Colombia Intl. University
Website: www.columbia.edu/
Courses: MA TEFL/Intercultural Studies

University of Delaware
Newark, DE 19716
Tel: (302) 831-2000
Website: www.udel.edu/
Courses: MA ESL
Other: Teaching practice locally in ESL and bilingual classes, and option of teaching in Panama.

East Carolina University
East Fifth Street, Greenville, NC 27858-4353
Tel: (252) 328-6131
Website: www.ecu.edu/
Courses: MA English with TESL

Eastern College
521 Lancaster Avenue, Richmond, KY, 40475
Tel: (859) 622-1000
Website: www.eku.edu/
Courses: MA Multicultural Education.
Other: Strong spiritual emphasis.

Eastern Mennonite University
1200 Park Road, Harrisonburg, VA 22802-2462
Tel: (540) 432-4000
Fax: (540) 432-4444
Website: www.emu.edu/
Courses: MA Education, minor in TESL

Eastern Michigan University
Ypsilanti, MI, USA 48197
Tel: (734) 487-1849
Website: www.emich.edu/
Courses: MA in TESOL, Graduate Certificate in TESL/Summer 2 Summer, Undergrad minor in TESOL, K-12 Endorsement in TESL.

Evergreen State College, WA
2700 Evergreen Parkway NW, Olympia, WA 98505
Tel: (360) 866-6000
Website: www.evergreen.edu/
Courses: MA Teaching w/ Bilingual Education and TESL.

Fairfield University
1073 North Benson Road, Fairfield, CT 06430
Tel: (203) 254-4000
Website: www.fairfield.edu/
Courses: MA TESOL

Fairleigh Dickinson University
Florham-Madison Campus, 285 Madison Avenue, Madison, NJ 07940
Tel: (973) 443-8500
Courses: MAT ESL

University of Findlay
1000 North Main Street, Findlay, OH 45840-3695
Tel: (800) 472-9502 or (419) 422-8313
Website: www.findlay.edu/
Courses: MA TESOL and Bilingual Education

Florida Atlantic University
Tel: 1-800-299-4FAU
Website: www.fau.edu/about/campuses/
Email: admisweb@fau.edu
Courses: Master's In Curriculum and Instruction with ESOL.

Florida International University
University Park Campus
11200 S.W. Eighth Street, Miami, FL 33199
Tel: 305-348-2000
Website: www.fiu.edu/
Courses: M.Sc TESOL.

Florida State University
Tallahassee, FL 32306
Tel: 850-644-2525.
Website: www.fsu.edu/
Courses: Multilingual/Multicultural Education

Fordham University
New York City
Website: www.fordham.edu/
Courses: MS Education.

Fresno Pacific University
Tel: 559-453-2039 Toll-Free: 1-800-660-6089
Fax: 559-453-2007
Website: www.fresno.edu/
Email: ugadmis@fresno.edu
Courses: TESOL M.A. and TESOL Certificate

Georgetown University
37th and O Street NW, Washington DC 20057
Tel: (202) 687-0100
Website: www.georgetown.edu/
Courses: MAT TESL

Grand Canyon University
3300 West Camelback Road, Phoenix, AZ 85017
Tel: 1-800-800-9776
Courses: MA with TESL major

University of Hawaii, Manoa
2444 Dole Street, Honolulu, HI 96822
Tel: (808) 956-8111
Website: www.uhm.hawaii.edu/
Courses: MA ESL
Other: The first and largest Department of ESL at a US university.

Hofstra University
Hempstead, NY 11549-1000
Tel: 1-800-HOFSTRA
Website: www.hofstra.edu/
Courses: MS Education: TESL, MEd TESL

University of Houston
4800 Calhoun Rd, Houston, Texas 77204
Tel: (713) 743-2255
Website: www.uh.edu/
Courses: MA Applied English Linguistics

University of Houston, Clear Lake
2700 Bay Area Blvd, Houston, TX 77058
Tel: (281) 283-7600
Website: www.cl.uh.edu/
Courses: MS Multicultural Studies with ESL endorsement

Hunter College, City Univ, NY
Website: www.hunter.cuny.edu/
Courses: MA Education (TESOL)

Univ. Illinois, Urbana-Champaign
1401 West Green Street, Urbana, IL 61801
Tel: (217) 333-1000
Website: www.uiuc.edu/
Email:iuforum@uiuc.edu
Courses: MA TESL

Illinois State University
Website: www.uillinois.edu/
Courses: MA Writing with TESOL
Other: Can lead to an Illinois credential in TESOL. Teaching internships and jobs on offer in Korea and Thailand.

Indiana State University
Terre Haute, IN 47809
Tel: (812) 237-6311
Website: www-isu.indstate.edu/
Courses: MA English with Applied Linguistics
Other: Exchange programmes with institutions in China and Japan.

Indiana University
107 S. Indiana Ave, Bloomington, IN 47405-7000
Tel: (812) 855 4848
Website: www.indiana.edu/
Courses: MA Applied Linguistics with TESOL

Indiana Univ. Of Pennsylvania
Indiana, PA 15705-0001.
Tel: (724) 357-2100.
Website: www.iup.edu/
Courses: MA English (TESOL)

University of Iowa
107 Calvin Hall, Iowa City, Iowa 52242
Tel: 1-800-553-IOWA
Courses: MA Linguistics with TESL

University of Kansas
Lawrence, KS 66045
Tel: 785/864-2700
Website: www.ukans.edu/
Courses: MA TESL

Long Island University
700 Northern Boulevard, Brookville, New York 11548-1326
Website: www.liu.edu/
Courses: MS Education with TESL
Course length: 3 semesters, full or p/t

Univ. of Maryland, Balt. County
1000 Hilltop Circle, Baltimore, MD 21250
Tel: (410) 455-1000
Website: www.umbc.edu/
Courses: MA ESOL/Bilingual Instructional Systems Development (w/ K-12 cert)

Univ. of Maryland, College Park
College Park, MD 20742
Tel: (301) 405-1000
Website: www.umcp.umd.edu/
Courses: MEd TESOL

Marymount University
2807 N. Glebe Road, Arlington, VA, 22207-4299
Tel: 703-522-5600 or 800-548-7638
Website: www.marymount.edu/
Courses: MEd ESL

Univ. Massachusetts, Amherst
Massachusetts, 01003.
Tel: (413) 545-0111
Website: www.umass.edu/
Courses: MEd with ESL

Univ. Massachusetts, Boston
100 Morrissey Boulevard, Boston, Ma 02125-3393
Tel: 617-287-5000
Website: www.umb.edu/
Courses: MA Bilingual or ESL Studies

University of Memphis
Office of Admissions, 229 Administration building, Memphis, TN 38152-3370
Tel: 901 678-2169 or 800-669-2678
Website: www.memphis.edu/
Courses: MA English with ESL
Other: Summer programme in Czech Republic and internships in China.

Meredith College
3800 Hillsborough Street, Raleigh, NC, 27607-5298
Tel: 919-760-8600 Fax: 919-760-2828
Website: www.meredith.edu/
Courses: MEd with ESL

Michigan State University
East Lansing, Michigan
Tel: 517-355-1855
Website: www.msu.edu/
Courses: MA TESOL

University of Montana
Website: www.umt.edu/
Courses: MA in TESOL

Montclair University
1 Normal Avenue, Upper Montclair, N.J. 07043
Tel: (973) 655-4000
Website: www.montclair.edu/
Courses: MA Applied Linguistics with TESL

Monterey Int. Of Intl. Studies
425 Van Buren Street, Monterey, CA 93940
Tel: (831) 647-4100
Fax: (831) 647-4199
Website: www.miis.edu/
Courses: MA in TESOL, MA in TFL (Teaching Foreign Language), Peace Corps Masters' International

Mount Vernon College
800 Martinsburg Road, Mount Vernon, Ohio 43050
Tel: (740) 397-9000 or (800) 782-2435 .
Website: www.mvnc.edu/
Courses: MA TESOL

National-Louis University
Chicago Campus, 122 S. Michigan Avenue, Chicago, IL 60603
Tel: 800-443-5522 (x 5151)
Website: www.nl.edu/
Courses: MEd with ESL

University of Nevada, Reno
Reno, Nevada 89557
Tel: (775) 784-1110
Website: www.unr.edu/
Courses: M.A. in TESOL

University of New Hampshire
Durham, NH 03824
Website: www.unh.edu/
Courses: MA in English Language and Linguistics (with ESL specialization), MAT w/TESL

University of New Mexico
Albuquerque, NM 87131
Tel: (505) 277-0111
Website: www.unm.edu/
Courses: MA Education with TESOL

New Mexico State University
Las Cruces, NM 88003-8001
Tel: 505-646-0111
Website: www.nmsu.edu/
Courses: MA Curriculum & Instruction with TESOL
Other: Teaching practice in Mexico

College of New Rochelle, NY
Website: http://cnr.edu/
Courses: MS TESOL

New York State Univ., Albany
1400 Washington Avenue, Albany, NY 12222
Tel: (518) 442-3300
Website: www.albany.edu/
Courses: MA TESOL

New York State Univ., Buffalo
15 Capen Hall, Buffalo, NY 14260-1660
Tel: 1-888-UB-ADMIT or (716) 645-6900
Website: www.buffalo.edu/
Courses: MEd TESOL

New York State Univ., Stony Brook
Stony Brook, NY 11794
Website: www.sunysb.edu/
Courses: MA TESOL

New York University
70 Washington Square South, New York, NY 10012
Tel: (212) 998-1212
Website: www.nyu.edu/
Courses: MA TESOL

Univ. Of North Carolina, Charlotte
9201 University City Blvd, Charlotte, NC 28223-0001
Tel: (704) 687-2000
Website: www.uncc.edu/
Courses: MEd

University of North Texas
PO Box 311277, Denton, TX 76203
Tel: (940) 565-2000 or (800) 735-2989
Website: www.unt.edu/
Courses: MA English with ESL

Northeastern Illinois University
5500 North St. Louis Avenue, Chicago, Illinois
Tel: 60625-4699, 773/583-4050
Website: www.neiu.edu/
Courses: MA Linguistics with TESL

Northern Arizona University
Tel: 1-888-MORE-NAU
Website: www.nau.edu/
Courses: MA TESL
Programme length: 4 semesters, full or p/t

Northern Illinois University
DeKalb, IL 60115
Tel: (815) 753-1000
Website: www.niu.edu/
Courses: MA English with TESOL
Other: Teaching opportunities in China.

Northern Iowa University
1227 West 27th Street, Cedar Falls, IA 50614
Tel: (319) 273-2311
Website: www.uni.edu/
Courses: MA TESOL
Other: International programme with internships in
Moscow and St. Petersburg, Russia.

Notre Dame College
1500 Ralston Avenue, Belmont, California
94002-1997
Tel: (650) 593-1601
Fax: (650) 508-3660
Website: www.cnd.edu/
Courses: MEd TESL

Nova Southeastern University
3301 College Avenue, Fort Lauderdale, Florida 33314
Tel: 800-541-6682
Courses: MS Education with TESOL

Ohio State University
Columbus, Ohio 43210
Tel: 614-292-OHIO
Website: www.ohio-state.edu/
Courses: MA TESOL

Ohio University
Department of Linguistics, Gordy Hall 383, Athens,
OH 45701-2979
Tel: (740) 593-4564
Fax: (740) 593-2967
Website: www.ohiou.edu/
Email: lingdept@ohio.edu
Courses: MA Applied Linguistics and TESOL

Oklahoma State University
Office of Academic Affairs, 101 Whitehurst,
Stillwater, OK 74078
Tel:(405) 744-5627
Fax: (405) 744-5495
Website: http://osu.okstate.edu/
Courses: MA English with TESL
Programme length: 4 semesters, full or p/t

University of Oregon
Eugene, OR 97403
Tel: (541) 346-1000
Website: www.uoregon.edu/
Courses: MA in Linguistics with concentration in
Applied Linguistics/SLA

Our Lady of the Lake Univ., S.A.
411 S.W. 24th Street, San Antonio, TX 78207-4689
Tel: 800-436-OLLU
Website: www.ollusa.edu/
Courses: MEd with ESL

University of Pennsylvania
3451 Walnut, Philadelphia PA 19104
Tel: 215-898-5000
Website: www.upenn.edu/
Courses: MSEd TESOL

Pennsylvania State University
201 Shields Building, Box 3000 , University Park, PA
16804-3000
Tel: (814) 865-5471
Website: www.psu.edu/
Courses: MA TESL

University of Pittsburgh
Pittsburgh, PA 15260
Tel: (412) 624-4141
Website: www.pitt.edu/
Courses: MA Linguistics with TESOL certificate

Portland State University
PO Box 751, Portland, Oregon 97207
Tel: (503) 725-3000
Website: www.pdx.edu/
Courses: MA TESOL

University of Puerto Rico
PO Box 364984, San Juan, PR 00936-4984
Tel: (787) 250-0000
Website: www.upr.clu.edu/
Courses: BA in TESS, MEd. in TESL,and ED.D. in
Curriculum and Teaching in TESL

Queen's College of City Univ, N.Y.
65-30 Kissena Blvd,.Flushing, New York 11367
Tel: (718) 997-5000
Website: www.qc.edu/
Courses: MA applied Linguistics, MS Education with
TESOL

Radford University
East Norwood St., Radford, Va. 24142
Tel: 540- 831-5000
Website: www.runet.edu/
Courses: MS Education with curriculum/instruction and TESL

Rhode Island College
600 Mount Pleasant, Providence, RI 02908-1991
Tel: (401) 456-8000
Website: www.ric.edu/
Courses: MEd TESL

Rhode Island University
Kingston, RI 02881
Tel: 401-874-1000
Website: www.uri.edu/
Courses: MA TESL

University of Rochester
Rochester, New York 14627
Tel: (716) 275-2121
Website: www.rochester.edu/
Courses: MS TESOL

State Michael's College
1 Winooski Park, Colchester, VT 05439
Tel: 802-654-2000
Website: www.smcvt.edu/
Courses: MA TESL/TEFL

Sam Houston State University
1803 Ave I, Huntsville, TX 77341
Tel: (936) 294-1111
Website: www.shsu.edu/
Courses: MEd with Bilingual Education

University of San Francisco
2130 Fulton Street, San Francisco, CA 94117
Tel: 415-422-5555
Website: www.usfca.edu/
Courses: MA TESL

San Francisco State University
1600 Holloway Avenue, San Francisco, CA 94132
Website: www.sfsu.edu/
Courses: MA English with TESOL

San Jose State University
One Washington Square, San José, CA 95192
Tel: 408-924-1000
Website: www.sjsu.edu/
Courses: M.A. TESOL

College of Santa Fe
1600 St. Michael's Drive, Santa Fe NM 87505
Tel: 800-456-2673 or 505-473-6011
Website: www.csf.edu/
Courses: MA with TESL (focus on at-risk youth)

School for International Training
Kipling Road, P.O. Box 676, Brattleboro, Vermont 05302-0676
Tel: (802) 257-7751
Fax: (802) 258-3248
Website: www.sit.edu/
Email: info@sit.edu
Courses: Master of Arts in Teaching (TESOL, French, Spanish), U.S. Public School Certification option, Bilingual-Multicultural Education Endorsement option, also Master International programme with US Peace Corps option., Master of Arts in Teaching Concentrations : English to Speakers of Other Languages (ESOL), Spanish, French
Further options available in the Academic Year MAT Program: Vermont State Certification and Bilingual-Multicultural Education Endorsement

Seattle University
900 Broadway, Seattle WA 98122-4340
Tel: (206) 296-6000
Website: www.seattleu.edu/
Courses: MA/MEd TESOL
Other: Focus on teaching the adult learner

Seattle Pacific University
3307 Third Avenue West, Seattle, WA 98119-1997
Tel: (206) 281-2000
Website: www.spu.edu/
Courses: MA TESOL

Seton Hall University
400 South Orange Avenue, South Orange, New Jersey 07079
Tel: (973) 761-9000
Website: www.shu.edu/
Courses: MA ESL

Shenandoah University
1460 University Drive, Winchester, VA 22601
Tel: 800-432-2266

Website: www.su.edu/
Courses: MSEd TESOL

Simmons College
300 The Fenway, Boston, Massachusetts, 02115-5898
Tel: 617-521-2000 or 800-345-8468
Fax: 617-521-3190
Website: www.simmons.edu/
Courses: MATESL

Soka University
California campus, 26800 West Mulholland Hwy,
Calabasas, California 91302
Tel: (818) 880-6400
Fax: (818) 880-9326
Courses: MA Second/Foreign Language Education
with TESOL
Other: Internships and post-graduation working
opportunities at affiliating university and high schools
in Japan.

University of South Carolina
Columbia, South Carolina, 29208
Tel: (803) 777-7000
Website: www.sc.edu/
Courses: MA Linguistics

University of South Florida
Tel: (813) 974-3350 or 1-877-USF-BULL
Website: www.usf.edu/
Courses: MA Applied Linguistics

Southeast Missouri State Univ.
One University Plaza, Cape Girardeau, MO 63701
Website: www.semo.edu/
Courses: MA TESOL

Southern Illinois Univ., Carbondale
Carbondale, Illinois 62901
Tel: 618.453.4381
Website: www.siuc.edu/
Courses: MA TESOL

University of Southern Maine
P.O. Box 9300, Portland, ME 04104-9300,
Tel: (207) 780-4141 or 1-800-800-4USM
Website: www.usm.maine.edu/
Courses: MSEd Literacy Education with ESL

University of Southern Mississippi
Multiple Campuses
Website: www.usm.edu/
Courses: MA Teaching of Languages (TESOL)

Syracuse University
Syracuse, NY 13244
Tel: (315) 443-1870
Website: www.syr.edu/
Courses: MA Linguistics with ESL

Teachers College, Columbia Univ.
525 West 120th St. New York, 10027
Tel: 212-678-3000
Website: www.tc.columbia.edu/
Courses: MA TESOL

Temple University
1801 North Broad Street, Philadelphia, PA 19122
Tel: 215-204-7000
Website: www.temple.edu/
Courses: EdM TESOL, MEd TESOL

University of Texas, Arlington
701 South Nedderman Drive, Arlington, TX 76019
Tel: (817) 272-2222
Website: www.uta.edu/
Courses: MA Linguistics with TESOL

University of Texas, Austin
University of Texas at Austin, Austin, Texas 78712
Tel: (512) 475-7348.
Website: www.utexas.edu/
Courses: MA Foreign Language Education with
TESL/TEFL

University of Texas, El Paso
500 West University Avenue, El Paso, Texas 79968
Website: www.utep.edu/
Courses: MA Linguistics with Applied or Hispanic
Linguistics

University of Texas, Pan American
Website: www.panam.edu/
Courses: MA ESL

University of Texas, San Antonio
6900 N. Loop 1604 West, San Antonio, TX 78249
Tel: 210-458-4011
Website: www.utsa.edu/

Courses: MA with ESL
Programme length: 3-4 semesters, full or p/t

Texas Tech University
Website: www.ttu.edu/
Courses: MA Applied Linguistics
Programme length: 4 semesters, full or p/t

Texas Woman's University
304 Administration Dr., Denton, TX 76201
Tel: (940)TWU-2000
Website: www.twu.edu/
Courses: MEd with ESL
Programme length: 2 years, full or p/t

University of Toledo
Toledo, Ohio 43606-3390
Tel: (419) 530-4242
Website: www.utoledo.edu/
Courses: MA-Ed. in ESL; MA in English with Concentration in ESL (these are two different degrees; both are offered)

U.S. International University
Admissions Office, 10455 Pomerado Road, San Diego, CA 92131
Website: www.usiu.edu/
Courses: MEd with TESOL

University of Utah
Salt Lake City, UT 84112
Tel: (801) 581-7200
Website: www.utah.edu/
Courses: MA Bilingual Education

University of Washington
Website: www.washington.edu/
Courses: MA TESL

Washington State Univ., Vancouver
Vancouver, Canada
Website: www.vancouver.wsu.edu/
Courses: Master of Education programme with ESL Endorsement (K-12 emphasis)

West Chester University
West Chester, PA 19383
Tel: (610) 436-1000
Website: www.wcupa.edu/

Courses: Master's & Certificate in TESL (Teaching English as a Second Language)

West Virginia University
Morgantown, WV 26506
Tel: (304) 293-0111
Website: www.wvu.edu/
Courses: Master of Arts in Foreign Languages (TESOL area of emphasis)

Western Kentucky University
1 Big Red Way, Bowling Green, KY 42101-3576
Tel: (270) 745-0111.
Website: www.wku.edu/
Courses: MA English with TESL

Wheaton College
501 College Avenue, Wheaton, IL 60187
Tel: (630) 752-5000
Website: www.wheaton.edu/
Courses: MA Intercultural Studies with TESL
Other: Leads to an Illinois State credential in TESOL. Teaching practice may be undertaken locally or at universities in Russia, China, Korea or Romania.

Wichita State University
1845 Fairmount, Wichita, Kansas, 67260.
Website: www.wichita.edu/
Courses: MA Curriculum and Instruction with TESOL
Other: Leads to Kansas State endorsement in TESOL. Opportunities for fieldwork in Mexico and Cyprus.

William Paterson University
300 Pompton Road, Wayne, NJ 07470
Tel: (973) 720-2000
Website: www.wpunj.edu/
Courses: MEd. in Education with a concentration in Bilingual/ESL

Wright State University
3640 Colonel Glenn Highway, Dayton, Ohio 45435-0001
Tel: (937) 775-3333
Website: www.wright.edu/
Courses: Undergraduate or graduate TESOL certificate. Undergraduate BA in English – emphasis in TESOL, MA in TESOL, Graduate endorsement in TESOL

Youngstown State University
One University Plaza, Youngstown, OH 44555
Tel: 877-GO-TO-YSU (877-468-6978)
Website: www.ysu.edu/
Courses: M.A. English, TESOL concentration

VENEZUELA

Universidad Central de Venezuela
Facultad de Humanidades y Educación, Ciudad
Universitaria, Los Chaguaramus, Caracas, 1050.
Programmes: M.A. Degree in TEFL.

Learning to teach with CALL

Computer technology is now playing an increasingly influential role in education. Language education has been no exception to this trend and in recent years growing numbers of teachers are undertaking graduate level courses in the field of CALL. Mark Peterson examines the choices and courses for Computer Assisted Language Learning teaching qualifications

In the first part of this article, I will identify the major factors that teachers must consider before embarking on such a course of study. In the second part, a number of CALL courses in various countries will be examined in order to assist teachers in the task of selecting a course suitable to their needs and future career goals.

The number of CALL focused training programmes has increased rapidly in recent years. In contrast to a few years ago, teachers considering entering a CALL course are faced with a larger number of possible options. However before embarking on a course potential applicants should consider the following questions:

If your goal is to improve your knowledge of computer technology, ESL pedagogy and make you a better teacher then a CALL course may be for you. If you think that graduating from such a course will make you more marketable you may be disappointed. While it is certainly true that the demand for computer literate language teachers is increasing, the number of posts is limited. Moreover the financial returns from undertaking what is a demanding course of study may not justify for some, the high costs of such a programme.

Most Masters degree programmes in CALL will usually require applicants to hold a first degree and some previous teaching experience in the language teaching field. However there are exceptions and negotiation over entry requirements may be possible in some cases.

To many mid-career teachers or those with circumstances that make undertaking a residential based MA impossible, distance learning may be a possibility. However candidates should first ensure that any distance based course is accredited internationally. British universities appear to be taking the lead in this area of course provision; distance based MA's have been common in the UK for many years. However it is fair to say that suspicion regarding the validity of distance based degrees remains in some conservative quarters of academe.

Graduate programmes are expensive and CALL courses are no exception to this trend. Potential applicants should compare and contrast course fees and the cost of living in North America with the UK and Australia. Potential applicants should also note that the level of course fee is often determined by an applicant's nationality and residency status. For example, a British applicant for a Master degree resident in the UK usually qualifies for reduced rate "home" fees, while applicants from overseas are usually required to pay a higher "overseas" fee.

Various sources of financial help are available including competitive bursaries, home government support and grants from private charitable institutions.

Masters degrees generally take two years to complete. But in some cases it is certainly possible to finish in a shorter period of time. Burn out may be a factor in many accelerated MA programmes. Full time doctoral degrees generally take three or more years to complete. Part time doctoral degrees may take several years.

There is a great deal of variety in course content within CALL postgraduate degree programmes. In the author's view, a CALL degree should include a through grounding in applied linguistics, instructional design and practical computer skills. These skills should include the use of software tools and authoring packages. Other relevant areas of study would be hypermedia design; concordancing and computer mediated communication (CMC).

Any potential applicant to a masters programme would do well to find out as much as possible about the faculty who will teach them. CALL experts of long experience are still relatively rare so it pays to take the time to check if the faculty in your programme have the appropriate backgrounds in educational technology and applied linguistics.

Potential students with little or no background in computers may expect to experience a degree of technostress in the initial stages of the course. This may be alleviated to some degree, if applicants already possess basic computer skills including familiarity with the more popular word processing, email and web browser software. Being prepared may make the course more enjoyable and beneficial in the long term.

Assessment methods vary between degree programmes, but in most cases assessment is based on course work and examinations.

In the US most CALL based degrees are given the degree classification of MA whereas in the UK by contrast, many CALL degrees are classed as M.Sc. or M.Ed.

Although the job market in EFL is growing, finding a suitable post where CALL skills can be fully utilized isn't easy. One motivation for those taking CALL courses is that they provide transferable skills. Many graduates of CALL programmes have launched alternative careers in areas such as web design, instructional technology and software consultancy.

Embarking on an advanced degree is a major undertaking in terms of time and money. Selecting an appropriate course depends largely on an individuals needs and circumstances.

While obtaining a Master's degree in the CALL field does not guarantee employment, it does provide opportunities in what is an expanding and increasingly important area of language education.

Mark Peterson holds an M.Sc. degree in TESOL and CALL and is currently a faculty member at Japan Advanced Institute of Science and Technology.

CALL courses

M.Sc. in CALL and TESOL
University of Stirling, Scotland

www.stir.ac.uk/celt/courses/MSC.HTM#CALL

This course was established in 1993 by John Higgins, one of the founders of CALL as a distinct discipline, and was the first CALL postgraduate programme to be launched in the UK. The programme combines a solid grounding in applied linguistics with the essential elements in CALL theory and methodology.

The M.Sc. may be completed in one year and is made up of the following components: Autumn Semester, Teaching of skills or Second Language, Acquisition, Syntax and Grammar, Classroom Observation (for those with no ELT experience), Introduction to CALL concepts and materials, CALL and communications. In addition to the above requirements, students must also complete a 12,000 to 15,000 word dissertation on an aspect of CALL research. A research based Ph.D. degree in CALL is also available at the same institution.

M.Ed. (Master of education) course in educational technology and ELT
University of Manchester

Centre for English Language Studies in Education

www. man.ac.uk/CELSE/centre/techELT.htm

This course is offered in two modes. Fully distance learning based or through a combination of distance learning and summer attendance. In order to graduate students are required to undertake a total of six course modules, three of which must be in the area of educational technology. In addition, students are required to submit a dissertation of between 12,000 and 20,000 words on a research topic of their choice.

MA in Media Technology for Teaching English as a Foreign Language
University of Newcastle upon Tyne

www.ncl.ac.uk/langcen/postgrad/media.html

This course provides students with a grounding in language teaching methodology, computer assisted language learning, video in ELT and media centre management. This course may be completed in 12 months of full-time study. Assessment is by course work.

MA in Computer Assisted Language Learning
University of Melbourne, Australia

www.hlc.unimelb.edu.au/callmast_ arts.htm

The above programme takes the form of a research based Masters degree. In order to graduate a candidate must submit a 30;000 word CALL based thesis by research. It may be undertaken on a full time or part-time basis. The University of Queensland Australia runs a Master's degree programme in applied linguistics, computers, technology and language learning (www.cltr.uq. edu.au/mactll.html). This programme is composed of the following courses: Structure of Language, Applied Linguistics and Language Teaching, Second Language Acquisition, Second Language Research, Second Language Teaching, Literacy or Issues in Language programme

Development, Portfolio and Synthesis, Principles of Computer-Enhanced Language Learning. This programme can be completed over 3 semesters full time or 6 semesters part time.

MA in applied linguistics (includes a major CALL element)
University of Waikato New Zealand
Department of General and Applied Linguistics

www.waikato.ac.nz/ling/

Some of the courses in this degree programme may be undertaken through distance learning. M.Phil. and Ph.D. courses in CALL are also available.

MA in TESOL with a CALL specialization
Iowa State University
www.engl.iastate.edu/tesling/ma.html

This programme is designed for those seeking training as a CALL specialist in an ESL programme. Core course requirements include the study of the following subjects: Sociolinguistics, Grammatical Analysis, Second Language Acquisition Methods for Teaching ESL, Second Language Testing Practicum in Teaching ESL or Seminar in Teaching English Composition, Computer Assisted Language Learning Instructional Technology.

In order to graduate, MA candidates must submit a research-based thesis. The University of South Florida runs a Ph.D. programme in interdisciplinary education (www.coedu.usf.edu/deptseced/forlanged/phdbro.html) with an emphasis on SLA and instructional technology. Core elements of this programme include courses in the areas of applied linguistics and SLA. In addition courses are available in the areas of educational technology described below: Authoring Systems and Languages, Programming Languages for Education, Applications for Computers as Educational Tools, Instructional Design for Computers, Interactive Media and Interactive Video, Telecommunications, Sound Processing and Animation. Candidates are also required to complete a dissertation. The State University of New York at Stony Brook has established a Doctor of Arts programme in Foreign Language Instruction (http://ccmail.sun- .edu/llrc//llrc3.html). Included in this programme are graduate level courses in educational technology with an emphasis on CALL and language centre management. Students on this course have access to the Language Learning and Research centre at Stony Brook.

MA in teaching English as foreign language
Ohio University in Athens Ohio
Department of Linguistics

http://cscwww. cats.ohiou.edu/linguistics/dept/

This degree programme is composed of courses in language teaching theory and methodology, curriculum development and evaluation. A practicum is also provided to give candidates supervised teaching experience.

Five CALL courses are available as part of the above degree programme. Entry requirements include a bachelor's degree with a minimum GPA of 3.0. This course requires two years of full time study.

Teaching ESP (English for Specific Purposes)

S ome EFL teachers find that their career becomes focused on teaching a particular aspect of English language skills geared to help learners in specific situations or jobs. Teachers of ESP (English for Specific Purposes) are usually in high demand, not only in schools in English-speaking countries but all over the world.

Teaching ESP (English for Specific Purposes) can be an interesting and lucrative career development. Much of the world's demand for English comes from the business sector: companies are prepared to pay top rates for training to ensure that their workforce is effective and competitive. In particular, company executives are almost universally required to know Business English, the world's working language. Other common areas of specialization in ESP are English for Law, English for Medical Purposes and English for Tourism. Less well studied in terms of student numbers but equally important areas are English for Engineering, English for Shipping, Aviation English, English for Engineering and English for the Military.

Teaching positions in the ESP require specialized knowledge of the key language used in the field and an understanding of the industries and professions that the language derives from. Some teachers come from a background (legal or medical, for example) that will enable them to tutor in a specialist field without too much trouble. Quite often, teachers with a specialist background like law are able to teach students from their homes. Other teachers find teaching ESP hard going especially when they have little confidence in their own knowledge of the industry or specialization they are teaching in. There are courses available for teachers who do not have experience in a particular field but who do want teach it.

Obtaining a job teaching ESP may require a little lateral thinking on your part. For example, if you'd like to work in the oil industry, why not contact some of the big oil companies and find out what their hiring practices are. If you want to teach English for Military Purposes, contact the relevant branch of the armed forces. Integration of commands within NATO means that the military are always on the lookout for a few good men (and women) to teach English.

Teaching ESP can be a fascinating and rewarding experience. Some ESP teachers have taught classes to oilrig workers on derricks in the Gulf of Siam. Others have worked with Russian cosmonauts in training in closed cities in Siberia. Be aware, however, that many teachers are turned off by the very thought of teaching anything with a commercial aspect. If you want to succeed as an ESP teacher, you must at least display a passing interest in your area of specialization.

Business English

One of the most important areas of specialization in teaching English as a second or foreign language is Business English. Many students are interested in improving their English skills in the areas of conducting business meetings, making presentations, understanding discussions at formal meetings, reading technical journals, and receiving and interacting effectively with American and other English-speaking business people.

Some schools specialize in teaching Business English as a means of attracting better-paying clients. Teachers working with these classes often find they are dealing with mixed-ability students whose needs may not be all the same. After all, an accountant has to learn a different vocabulary than that required by a sales person. Of course, schools with larger numbers of Business English students can divide classes based on ability and needs. Another factor to be aware of when teaching Business English is that there are very few textbooks and published materials to rely on. Most major publishers feel that it is not worth investing in textbooks for teaching Business English (and ESP in general) because it is too small a market to be profitable. Business English teachers are often forced to create their own materials for use in the classroom using a variety of sources such as professional journal articles and college textbooks.

If you are employed in a corporate environment, remember that you will be expected to dress accordingly. You may find yourself discussing students' progress with managers, directors and human resources personnel so it pays to have a professional appearance and attitude.

There are a number of ESP examinations – mostly for students, but with one or two designed for teacher-training certification (from LCCIB). The following are the main developers of business English examinations:

Cambridge ESOL (UCLES)

Business English Certificates (BEC)
Certificate in English for International Business and Trade (CEIBT)
University of Cambridge Local Examinations Syndicate
Syndicate Buildings, 1 Hills Road, Cambridge, CB1 2EU
Tel: 01223 553311
Fax: 01223 460278 / 553068
Website: www.ucles.org.uk

The Chauncey Group (part of ETS)

TOEIC (Test of English for International Communication)
The Chauncey Group
664 Rosedale Road, Princeton, NJ 08540-2218 USA
Tel: +1 609.720.6500
Fax: +1 609.720.6550
Email: info@chauncey.com
Website: www.toeic.com

LCCI Examinations Board

English for Business (EFB)
Spoken English for Industry and Commerce (SEFIC)
Written English for Tourism (WEFT)
English for the Tourism Industry (EFTI) - Group Award (WEFT + SEFIC)
Practical Business English (PBE)
English for Commerce (EFC)
LCCI Examinations Board
Athena House, 112 Station Road, SIDCUP, Kent DA15 7BJ, UK
tel: +44 (0)20 8302 0261
fax: +44 (0)20 8302 4169
Website: www.lccieb.com

Pitman

English for Business Communications
English for Office Skills
Pitman Qualifications, 1 Giltspur Street, London EC1A 9DD
tel: +44 (0)20 7294 3500
fax: +44 (0)20 7294 2403
email: info@pitmanqualifications.co.uk
Website: www.pitmanqualifications.com

Certificates for Teachers of Business English

There are few specialist certificates for teachers who want to gain a qualification in this specialist field. The standard CELTA, Cert.TESOL or other certificate courses (see chapter 1) include sections on teaching business English, as do diplomas, MAs and Ph.Ds. The main two certificates for teachers are issued by LCCIEB (London Chamber of Commerce and Industry Examinations Board (below).

LCCIEB: CertTEB (Certificate in Teaching English for Business)

Administered in conjunction with ARELS (www.arels.org.uk), this exam is aimed at teachers with little or no previous experience of teaching business English, and develops the basic practical skills for working in this area.

FTBE (Further Certificate for Teachers of Business English)

A supplementary qualification for teachers of general English wishing to broaden their skills into teaching business English. The exam aims to develop management skills and understanding of business practice. LCCIEB has a worldwide network of centres.

LCCI Examinations Board

Athena House, 112 Station Road, Sidcup, Kent, DA15 7BJ, UK

Tel: +44 (0)20 8302 0261

Fax: +44 (0)20 8302 4169

Website: www.lccieb.com

Email: custserv@lccieb.org.uk

English For Academic Purposes

Students whose first language is not English who are planning to study at a college or university where instruction is in English often require specialist help if they are going to succeed on their courses. In particular, these students need to learn how to write about academic subjects including all the relevant conventions of presentation and style that will be expected of them as they submit written work like essays and theses. Students taking EAP (English for Academic Purposes) classes often do so while taking part in an IEP (Intensive English Program) programme at the university they plan to graduate from. Specialist tutors, usually from an academic background themselves, are in demand to teach EAP on these courses. One of the easiest ways to find a position in teaching EAP is to apply through the university that you are studying at or have graduated from although you will probably need to have a Master's degree if your job application is to be considered seriously.

Young Learners

Another area of teaching ESL/EFL that is becoming increasingly specialized is the teaching of English to young learners. Teachers have realized that approaches to the teaching of a second language to children requires specific training if they are to be successful. Teachers with an interest in this area may want to follow a course in order to qualify as a specialist. There are several certificate courses on offer and a Master's degree in Teaching English to Young Learners is offered on a two-year distance-based programme by the University of York in the UK. Teachers with a specialization in TEYL (Teaching English to Young Learners) are especially welcome in Asian countries like Korea and Japan where the teaching of young learners is considered a priority.

Many schools and colleges offer certificate-level courses that prepare teachers for the discipline of teaching young learners. The best-known international qualifications are the CELTYL (Certificate in ELT for Young Learners) from University of Cambridge ESOL and the Cert.TEYL (Certificate in Teaching English to Young Learners) from Trinity College, London. We list the schools and colleges offering these courses in the section on Certificate courses. These courses are normally taken as an add-on module to a standard CELTA or Cert.TESOL certificate course).

Cultural Studies

In the U.S., the teaching of ESL can be just one component of an overall programme in "American Culture" or "American Studies." If you have a degree or qualification in sociology, cultural studies or a related field, you may be able to find a job on one of these programmes where both your language teaching skills and your specialist knowledge can be put to good use.

Studying for a Doctorate

As the English language teaching field becomes more saturated with teachers who hold a Master's degree, many observers predict that doctorates will become a prerequisite for those who want to hold jobs on the top rungs of the professional ladder. Mary Ellen Butler-Pascoe evaluates TESOL doctoral programmes – available mostly in the U.S.A.

While there has been a continuous professional dialogue on various aspects of the TESOL master's programmes in the United States, similar attention has not been afforded the TESOL doctoral programmes. This in large part has been a result of the master's degree serving as a terminal degree for most ESL instructors and many directors and teacher trainers. Since the 1960s, when master's degrees in TESOL were rare, the TESOL profession has gained worldwide respect as the discipline continues to define and assert itself in local school districts and institutions of higher education. Master's programmes have proliferated over the past two decades with almost 200 now being offered in the United States alone. Considerably fewer colleges and universities offer doctoral degrees in TESOL or related fields.

What are the characteristics of these doctoral programmes? Where are they located both geographically and institutionally? In what disciplines do they offer degrees? What courses does a typical curriculum include and most importantly in what areas can these programmes better meet the needs of TESOL practitioners? A recent study of these programmes sought to shed light on these questions.

Of the twenty-nine doctorate-granting institutions surveyed, eleven were located in the Northeast region of the United States; nine were in the West, five in the Midwest, and four in the South and Puerto Rico. Within those universities, the degree programmes were housed in seventeen different academic departments with the most frequent placement being in the Department of Linguistics, followed by the Departments of English and Education. Eighteen institutions granted Ph.D. degrees and six awarded Ed.D. degrees, indicating the research emphasis of the majority of the programmes. Three institutions provided a choice of either a Ph.D. or Ed.D. and two offered a Doctorate of Arts degree. Within the departments, degrees were granted in a wide range of disciplines with the greatest number in Linguistics followed closely by Education/ Curriculum and Instruction. Only three departments offered a degree major specifically in TESOL though several of the various other degrees offered TESOL/ESL as a concentration option. The standard admissions requirements included a master's degree with acceptable GPAs, letters of recommendation, the Graduate Record Exam (GRE) or in two cases the Miller's Analogy Test (MAT), and the TOEFL for non-native English-speaking applicants.

Only two programmes specifically listed teaching experience as a prerequisite for admissions.

For degree completion, twenty-seven of the twenty-nine programmes required comprehensive exams and one required a qualifying paper; nineteen demanded knowledge of a foreign language, and twenty-three required a dissertation/thesis. Only six required practice teaching experience. The length of time for degree completion ranged from two to seven years with an average of 4.02 years of study. Interestingly, 45% of the graduates were non-native English speakers.

While there was a great variety in course nomenclature, for purposes of clarity, similar course titles were grouped together under common headings. Of the twenty-five different course types identified in the curriculum of the various universities, the one most frequently offered was first and/or second Language Acquisition. The second most prominent course was Teaching Methods with over three-fourths of the programmes listing courses specifically in TESOL Methodology/Teaching ESL. Others in the top five headings included Research Methodology focusing on research designs of both quantitative and qualitative methods, Linguistics, and Testing and Assessment.

Heading the list of least frequently provided courses was ESL Administration with only four programmes listing courses in any aspect of programme administration, design, or evaluation. Courses in Language Policy and Planning were similarly scarce, and only eight offered courses in technology media or allowed electives in technology. A typical programme profile incorporating the most common characteristics of all the doctoral programmes would be a Ph.D. degree programme in Linguistics administered by the Department of Linguistics at a university in the Northeast. Students would be predominantly native-English speakers who would be required to have knowledge of a foreign language, pass comprehensive exams, conduct a research study and author a dissertation in order to complete a degree in approximately four years. The curriculum would include courses in second language acquisition and TESOL Methods with no student teaching required.

Fortunately, there are several combinations of location, degree, discipline, concentration, curriculum, and programme requirements from which students may choose a programme. But a review of the current programmes does raise questions as to how well they serve the needs of the ESL practitioners who are teaching in all types of educational settings and directing programmes around the world.

The TESOL profession has conducted a long campaign to establish ESL as a legitimate academic discipline. To this end it has established standards for ESL and teacher training programmes with the latest being the standards for the Intensive English Programmes. To a large extent the profession has overcome the notion that any native English speaker could intuitively teach ESL as evidenced by the now routine requirement of a master's degree for adult education, community college and university level ESL instruction, and teaching abroad. For the thousands of teachers who have obtained master's degrees in recent years, it would be a natural next step in their professional development and in the struggle to constantly enhance the status of the TESOL profession for more practitioners to seek a doctoral degree.

Many obstacles such as lack of time, financial resources, professional incentives and encouragement hinder aspirations for a doctorate, but there are additional negative factors influencing that decision that are within the control of TESOL faculties, university

administrators, and even the prospective students themselves. One could start by looking at the doctoral curriculum.

An obvious group of candidates for doctoral study would be the ESL programme directors in the U.S. and abroad. "Doctorate in ESL or related field preferred" is commonly seen in job announcements for ESL director positions, yet only four universities listed doctoral courses in ESL programme design and implementation, programme evaluation, or administrative leadership. Despite the importance of language policy and planning to TESOL local and worldwide issues, just five programmes provided study in this area. Leaders in second language teaching need the knowledge and skills to infuse technology into the language curriculum and to manage the technology that is becoming an increasingly important part of the language learning process. While the role of English as the de facto language of the Internet means that the ESL/EFL field will continue to grow in prominence, it also suggests a need to study the impact the power of English and technology might have on languages in non-English-speaking societies. In what ways do our doctoral programmes assist students in gaining the expertise to use computer technology in language teaching? The answer does not appear to be in the curriculum of most TESOL doctoral programmes. Few programmes offered courses in the educational uses of technology and of those only four included courses specifically in technology for language teaching. Looking at recent TESOL journals, it is obvious that an area of great concern to the profession is the apparent dichotomy between classroom teaching and research. TESOL professionals have warned that too many classroom teachers view research as the domain of the university research community and fail to see its relevance to their own teaching. Stronger teacher-researcher ties through collaborations between university faculty and classroom teachers have been urged. The solution argued by the teacher-researcher movement is to recognize teachers as researchers with the advantages of insider perspective and applicability. Perhaps the simplest way to ensure connections between university research and classroom practice is for more classroom teachers to join the university research community as doctoral students. The crucial questions on teaching practices and the language learning process will not be answered until ESL teachers assume a more prominent role in the research process. TESOL doctoral programmes face the challenge of facilitating that outcome.

As TESOL continues to mature, more positions will demand a doctorate, therefore making it incumbent upon universities to analyze the needs not only of traditional doctoral students seeking a university teaching or research position, but also the needs of classroom teachers from a wide array of instructional settings.

Getting Published

Dr. Lin Lougheed, the author of more than 40 English language teaching textbooks, offers his advice on becoming a successful writer in this market, highlighting the best ways to getting your lesson plans in print.

So you want to contribute to the overpublished field of ESL/EFL? Don't give up your day job teaching. You'll need it if you like to eat and if you want a good place to test your materials. A textbook is simply an organized set of daily lesson plans well printed and illustrated on good quality paper. You have these lesson plans, don't you? You've been repurposing textbooks for years and creating your own supplementary materials. Everyone loves them. Your students' proficiency rates have skyrocketed because of the quality of your exercises. Your lazy colleagues are always praising them as they photocopy them to use in their own classes.

The path to becoming an author is simple: have an idea; write it down; teach it; revise it; send it to a publisher. At that point, the process becomes more complicated so let's analyze the easy steps first.

The idea

To publish your fabulous activities you'll need to convince someone in the publishing world that your materials have universal applicability and universal appeal. Universal is the key word. You don't want your materials to be unique. You want them to stand out, but you don't want them to be so different from everything else on the market that no one (especially the sales reps who will have to push your books) can understand how to use them.

Write it down

You have a brilliant idea how to teach a particular grammar point or to reinforce vocabulary. You want to develop a lesson around this idea. Look at some of the books you are using. Most lessons have three parts: Warm Up, Teach, Review.

When you begin to put your idea on paper, think in terms of a class session. How will you prepare the students, teach the lesson, and review the material in 45 minutes?

As you refine your lesson, keep in the back of your mind how you plan to expand this one lesson into enough lessons to fill a book.

Teach it

Actually, have someone else teach it. You have been experimenting with your materials in class. You know what will work or how to make it work. Let someone else interpret your perfect lesson. It would be ideal if you could observe your colleague teaching your materials. Then you can gauge the reactions of the students to the material and the way your colleague adapts the material to his or her teaching style.

Revise it

Was your audience confused? Did they not follow your structure? Was the teacher supplementing the material with too many explanations? Or was it just perfect? Remember your materials have to work outside your own classroom. They will undoubtedly be used by total strangers in a variety of teaching situations. They must have universal appeal.

At this stage, you might even want to post your material on a teacher's bulletin board on the Web or email it to colleagues around the world. Don't worry about someone stealing your idea. I send entire manuscripts to teachers in countries that don't even have copyright protection agreements. What is important to me is their feedback. If they want to use some messy, unformatted materials in their classroom, they can be my guest. Remember there is very little that has not already been done in EFL/ESL publishing.

Send it to a publisher

You have written, taught, revised, taught, and revised again your materials. You are now ready to have your work published. Your material can be published as a book to be downloaded from the Internet or can be published in book form and sold in bookstores. You can do either yourself or you can find a publisher to do it for you.

Whatever the method, you will have to do a market survey of your material. You should know—and your publisher will want to learn from you—why your book should be on the market.

You will put this explanation in a proposal that provides a brief description of your book, a list of the outstanding features, a survey of the competition, a discussion of the target audience, production considerations, and projected time frame for completing the book. You will also want to include a table of contents and a few of the completed chapters along with any reviewers' comments.

The survey of the competition is a very important part of your proposal. A publisher will need to know where your book fits and how it will be positioned. This detailed analysis will help the publisher see right away how your book can be set apart from the competition. You can't discuss the outstanding features of your book without pointing out the specific best selling titles that lack those features.

The survey of the competition will also help the publisher target the right market and determine whether it fills a hole in his or her publishing plan. A publisher might be desperate for a book on email correspondence for Japanese students in middle school with limited English proficiency or the publisher may feel that this topic would not be a good match for its marketing and sales force.

Production issues are also important to consider. Does your book require a lot of art work or photos? Would an audio CD or an on-line component be necessary? Any publisher has to look at the bottom line. What will it cost to produce this material? How much can I sell it for? How many copies can I sell? This information is also important to you. The cheaper it is, the better the sales; the better the sales, the larger the royalty cheque.

Time is money. When are you going to finish this work?

Think about your own expenditure of time. Is it worth the year writing, the year revising, the year in production? Could you not do something more productive (i.e. earn more money) doing something else with your time?

That's a question I ask myself constantly. Is it worth it? I wrote my first book when I had a Fulbright scholarship to Sri Lanka. I remember a Sri Lankan professor asking me, "Aren't you a little young to be writing a book?" I wasn't too young to write it, but I was too naïve to publish it properly. I left it in the public domain. Similarly, my second book was written while I was on a Fulbright to Tunisia. That book too ended up in the public domain.

My third book, The Great Preposition Mystery, was also in the public domain. It's been licensed around the world and is still in print after 20 years. I don't get a dime, but I do have great name recognition in Angola.

These three books gave me a track record as an author and made it easier for me to get my manuscripts considered by publishers. Even after 20 years of writing EFL/ESL textbooks, the process for me is the same as for any potential author. I still start with an idea that I test and revise and test and revise. I still submit proposals and competition surveys. Once a book is published, I am still revising for subsequent printings and new editions.

It's difficult for me to find time to start new projects because the old ones are still demanding attention. They need to be revised to meet the demands and expectations of new users and to keep current users on their toes. Keeping my readers and myself interested is a challenge in itself and one that makes each day at the computer worthwhile. Besides, I always make time for something new.

Dr.Lin Lougheed has written over 40 EFL/ESL textbooks and has produced a daily radio show in China, Dr. Lougheed's Business English. You can find out more about Lin's books at his website: www.lougheed.com.

Finding a Publisher

So you're trying to find a publisher interested in your work. What next? Andy Martin, Mona Scheraga, and Tina Carver explain the process.

You've done it in class. You've done it in more than one class. Your techniques work. The students are learning year after year and it's your material and your methods that are creating success. Now, how are you going to share it.

A great place to find publishers is at one of the big English language shows: the TESOL Convention in the USA or the IATEFL show in the UK. If you can't get to a show, get as many publishers' catalogues as you can. Study them to see who is publishing the kind of material you have to offer. Talk to the salespeople from these publishing companies when they visit your institution. They know what your colleagues are asking for. Then make the transition from teacher's lesson plans to author's presentation. Write a prospectus–a brief summary of what you want to publish, including any research and/or experience that validates your premise. Include what market/target audience you have in mind, such as elementary, community college, etc.; the skills to be taught, the pedagogy involved, ancillary materials to be included, and reasons why your work is so necessary. Be sure to include a brief CV. Work up a Table of Contents and at least one chapter, including any exercises and an answer sheet so the publisher has an idea of the format you have in mind. Check the competition so you can discuss what makes your work different, special, and unique. Write up a competitive analysis indicating what the competition is, what its strengths and weaknesses are and how your work compares.

Finally, your sample package is ready, accompanied by your cover letter, which outlines what is included and together with your resume or bio data.

Get the name of the acquisitions editor at each publisher you submit your work to so you have a person to connect with. Talk to people in the field and get an idea of the marketing practices of different publishers; what kinds of royalties/flat fees are being paid; what kinds of materials sell best (series versus individual books, CD-ROMs, etc.). Get out to conferences and do as many workshops as possible presenting your materials so you can keep refining them.

You've got a publisher who's interested in your idea or manuscript and you've been assigned an acquisitions editor. Your editor receives the sample package. Now it's ready for review. The best reviewers are usually those who are currently teaching the equivalent course for which your project is designed and who are accustomed to evaluating materials, either as textbook committee members or as experienced publishers' reviewers. The editor sends along the review package and guide questionnaires that will give you feedback on your materials. This feedback will enable you and the editor to evaluate your sample and perhaps redirect the writing,

or make major changes (for example, adding/eliminating units, changing exercise formats, redesigning the flow of lessons).

So, you've passed the trial by fire, the reviewing stage, discussed the reviews with your editor and have agreed on changes. It's time to publish your masterpiece! After the editor's supervisor approves the project, a contract is offered.

Negotiation is an important part of the process. Before you sign, read your contract carefully, suggesting any changes you'd like to make. Feel good about what you're doing and whom you're working with. The bottom line for contract negotiations is this: Is it fair to both you and the publisher? No publisher is out to "get" an author on a contract.

The financials of publishing are complex and royalties are figured as an expense of publishing the material, along with expenses of development, production, and publishing. It's important to understand that, as an author, if you receive 10%, the publisher's profit is not 90%. In fact, educational publishing survives on a very small margin of profit. Don't expect to get rich from an EFL textbook

Once the contract is signed, the work is yours to finish on time in a form appropriate for final review. When this work is complete, the editor can "accept" the manuscript. Now the fun begins.

In most publishing houses, the manuscript heads for development and you are assigned a development editor (DE). It is the DE's job to work with you to look over the manuscript with an eagle eye. It has to be checked for consistency, that it ensures a variety of activities, that the exercises all work, that the tape script is accurate. Together, you must finalize the art and photo specs to get the manuscript in tip-top shape for the copy editor. The copy editor scrutinizes the manuscript for consistency, for punctuation, misspellings and for minute errors that have evaded detection. You will be sent the manuscript with copy edit queries and for approval of changes made.

Next step: Production. Here, your manuscript, art specification notes and sketches are thrown into the crucible. With the magic of computer programmes, art on CD ROMS, and the talents of the production editor, the whole hodgepodge becomes beautiful pages.

Your job is to review the pages and make corrections only—no changes at this stage, heaven forbid! It's necessary for you to meet schedules and support the production editor so the process of making the work on time and in an excellent fashion proceeds smoothly.

Voilà! After many sleepless nights, the work is in your hands. Your work, now your publication, is ready to move into the next phase, marketing and sales.

Now you've got a publisher, signed a contract, been through reviews, edits, production and design, but this means nothing if the book does not sell! Here's what's got to happen: the book has to be positioned, pre-sold, packaged, promoted and possibly piloted.... Hmmm, a lot of "p's" here. Then there's advertising, journal reviews, direct mail, following up on leads, and committee presentations. Sampling is critical, it can be done at your basic sales calls, telemarketing, book fairs, and convention presentations. We mustn't forget Internet sales, and if warranted, author tours, and in-service training. Yeah, there's a lot of stuff to be done. We don't usually cover all the bases, but there's always some combination of these sales and marketing elements. It all depends on the sales potential of the book. Basically marketing/sales can be split

into pre- and post-publication activities. Let's take a peek...

- Positioning - what is the best potential market for the book?
- Sales forecasting - Estimating how many copies a book will sell and how much money it will bring in to the publishing company
- Packaging consulting - Working with editorial and design to come up with the most attractive cover for the book
- Pre-selling - Getting the word out to build excitement and interest about a book before it's published. Word-of-mouth, conferences, brochures, and marketing focus group can do this.
- Piloting - Having a teacher, or several, try-out the finished books in their classes in the hope that if they like it the whole school or district will adopt the text.
- Advertising - Promoting the book in the company catalogue, brochures and space ads in ESL professional publications such as English Teaching Professional (www.etprofessional.com).
- Journal reviews - Mailing the new book to the review editors of professional ESL journals in the hope that they will have the book reviewed (positively) in their journal.
- Direct mail - Sending out a brochure by mail to all the English language professionals on a rented mailing list, or from the company's own database.
- Following up leads - Contacting professionals upon the recommendation of the author who provides a list of contacts in the field.
- Presenting to textbook committees - Meeting with committees at colleges or schools to convince them to adopt the new text.
- Sampling/Complimentary/Examination copies (perhaps the single most important selling technique) - Giving away free copies of the book to potential users to try out with their students.
- Calling on English language teachers/decision makers - Meeting with teachers, coordinators, chair people, etc., to present the book, let them know it's available and making sure they have a sample.
- Telemarketing - Calling potential customers on the phone to try to get them to agree to accept a sample book.
- Book fairs - Displaying the book along with other new and best selling titles at a meeting of all the ESL teachers in a school or department with the goal of leaving copies of the book behind as samples.
- Presenting at conventions - Conducting commercial presentations and giving away sample copies at local state, regional and national ESL conventions.
- The Internet - Promoting a book at the company website and soliciting sample requests and/or actual on-line sales.
- Author Tours - For really big books/series, sending the Author to different parts of the United States and/or other countries to present the book.
- In-service Training - When a book/series is adopted by a very large program, the publisher will provide free training of the English language teachers on how to use the book.

Mona Scheraga (ESL author, freelance writer, reviewer, and trainer extraordinaire) wrote "Finding a Publisher." "Publishing the Book" was written by Tina Carver, ESL publisher, editorial director, and best-selling author. "Selling the Book" was written by Andy Martin.

Running a School

One of the many opportunities for teachers is the possibility of opening or running your own school. Here, Barbara Stipek discusses the possibility of doing just that – and the freedom of designing your own programmes.

Many of you who are teaching English, or will soon be teaching English, may also be wondering about possible areas of advancement within the field. The most common pathway is via promotion into administrative positions. Another possibility is to open a new school, design a programme or in some way test your entrepreneurial skills. Whichever path you choose, you are about to embark on a wonderful adventure with many rewards.

The best way to become a first-choice candidate for promotions is to show a high degree of interest in the programme where you are teaching. Make it known that you are available for extra work or special projects (paid or unpaid!) so that you can a) gain valuable administrative experience and b) show everyone how terrific you are.

I once hired a teacher who was so eager to advance into administration that the first time I asked him if he'd like to help out on a project, he said "yes!" before I even finished the question. He consistently made himself useful and showed a great willingness to learn. He was enthusiastic and performed competently, so when openings came available, he was the first person we thought of. Eventually, he was working full-time in administration.

Looking back on my early administrative positions, I realize this was a time of great personal and professional development for me. It was a time to solidify my skills in administration and management, and I found I had an insatiable appetite for learning what made a programme good. I spent a lot of time talking to other ESL administrators and studying criteria used by external agencies to judge strong programmes. I started finding many commonalties among programmes that I felt to be academically sound, such as:

- Participation of site directors and teachers in writing curricula and course descriptions that are shared throughout the school system.
- Centralization of financial, marketing, and business affairs so that site personnel can focus on academic matters.
- Establishment of clear forms of communication so that information can be shared between all of the sites and administrative offices.
- Participation in the greater ESL community through conference attendance, presentations, and board memberships.

The most important thing to remember is that you don't know everything. You can always learn something from others—even if it's what NOT to do. You can also find wonderful

camaraderie with fellow administrators, which is important because, once you've been promoted out of teaching, the teachers you used to work with won't be your peer group any longer. You will be tested in your management skills as you learn to define your new role and keep the loyalty of your teaching staff.

If you find yourself as the director of the programme where you are currently teaching, there are a few important "don'ts" to keep in mind:

- Don't pretend to know something that you really don't—you'll miss wonderful opportunities to learn new things.
- Don't try to be "one of the guys" with your teaching staff—they know you are now responsible for their jobs, and they'll see through the act
- Don't be too surprised if there is some resentment among the staff—especially if you're supervising anyone who was passed over for your promotion

After I'd been in programme administration for awhile, I started recognizing my own entrepreneurial tendencies. While I thoroughly enjoyed the technical and managerial phases of my career—and would certainly feel comfortable in any teaching or administrative position—there was something particularly exhilarating about this period. I wanted to open new programmes and have the authority—and the responsibility— to do what needed to be done to be successful. I believe that there are certain qualities that indicate an "entrepreneurial bent", including:

- Higher than average risk tolerance.
- Ability to recognize talent around you and to empower it.
- Being able to listen to others and learn new things.
- Strong desire to see your vision become a reality.
- High level of comfort with change.

It is important to do some self-assessment to decide what type of person you are and what path is right for you. If security is an important issue for you, the entrepreneurial route is probably not the best way to go.

Clearly the English language field is filled with opportunities for teachers who wish to pursue administrative careers or entrepreneurial ventures. Keep your eyes and ears open, show enthusiasm and a willingness to learn, and most of all, follow your dreams.

Barbara Stipek is the former owner of IEI, a group of ten intensive English programmes located on university campuses across the United States. In 1998, she sold the company to Sylvan Learning Systems, Inc.

School Management

Some teachers make their way up to management level. These positions require organizational and people skills – talents you will have developed during your teaching career.

It is not difficult to find teachers and former teachers who have taken over managerial roles at language schools all over the world. Some accept their new responsibilities with a pang of regret for their glory days in front of the blackboard. A manager with teaching experience should be sympathetic to the needs of staff members but will also be aware of the realities of what can go on both in and outside the classroom.

Many teachers find themselves becoming managers in an incremental process. When a teacher is appointed or chooses of his or her own free will to be in charge of examination matters or of materials procurement, the initial steps towards a managerial role have already been taken.

This role can develop as a teacher becomes involved with the creation and implementation of school or departmental policies, compliance with accreditation bodies, staff recruitment and teacher training programmes.

Some teachers naturally develop an interest in the commercial aspects of language teaching. It is not too difficult to understand that a school needs to recruit students in order to survive. Some of criteria normally associated with the private sector such as "customer satisfaction" and "performance" have even seeped into the current administrative thinking that governs the public schools system.

To be an effective manager, teachers need to be aware of basic business principles. Familiarity with the theory and practice of marketing methods is a definite asset as is managerial ability.

A head for figures and an acquaintance with accounting will also help the school or department manager deal with professionals such as bookkeepers and accountants, not that the manager has to be an expert in any of these fields.

If you decide to manage and/or own a school in a country that is not your homeland be sure that you are familiar with local laws regarding business operations and employment regulations. Although most schools operated by native English speakers run without major problems, there have been reports of foreign-owned institutions falling foul of local labour laws and other regulations and having to pay sometimes harsh penalties.

Teachers who are serious about a career in school management could consider taking one of the specialist courses that exist for managers. There is a M.Sc. degree course (taught by

distance) in English Language Teaching Management offered by the University of Surrey. Core Modules include: ELT Management, Syllabus Design, Business and Financial Management in ELT, Human Resource Management, Language Teaching Methodology, Marketing Research Methods and Quantitative Techniques for Business Language Testing.

If you are interested in the issues that surround ESL/EFL school management, you may be interested in joining the ELT Management SIG (Special Interest Group) operated under the auspices of IATEFL.

Further Reading:

Impey, G. and Underhill N. An ELT Manager's Handbook, Heinemann ELT, 1994, Oxford.

White R. V. et. al. Management in English Language Teaching, Cambridge University Press, 1991, Cambridge.

Appendix

Essential contacts to help you plan your travel, find a job, source ideas for your lessons, find a supplier, join an association, subscribe to a magazine or find a publisher

Teacher Associations

New teachers have much to learn during their training periods. Developing professional bonds with other teachers and networking as much as you can will help you to stay informed early in your career.

AsiaTEFL

Organisation with over 5000 members who work as ELT teachers in the countries within the asian region (mostly within south-east asia).
Website: www.asiatefl.org

IATEFL

Based in the UK, but with regional offices and special-interest groups around the world., IATEFL (The International Association of Teachers of English as a Foreign Language) offers members an annual international conference with a programme of talks, workshops and exhibits as well as hundreds of regional meetings and SIG-sessions.

IATEFL
Darwin College, University of Kent
Canterbury, Kent
CT2 7NY, UK
Website: www.iatefl.org

MLA

The MLA (Modern Language Association) serves the interests of teachers of language and literature.

Modern Language Association
26 Broadway, 3rd Floor
New York, NY 10004-1789
Tel: (646) 576-5000
Fax: (646) 458-0030
Website: www.mla.org

NABE

NABE (National Association for Bilingual Education) is the only national organization exclusively concerned with the education of language-minority students in American schools. Many of these students are English language learners who need to preserve their first languages while they acquire a second one. NABE News, the Association's official news magazine, is published eight times annually and distributed free of charge to its members.

National Association for Bilingual Education
1220 L Street NW, Suite 605
Washington DC 20005-4018
Tel: (202) 898-1829
Fax: (202) 789-2866
Website: www.nabe.org

NAFSA

NAFSA promotes the exchange of students and scholars to and from the United States. There is a professional section of NAFSA called ATESL (Administrators and Teachers in English as a Second Language). These international teachers have responsibilities in the teaching and/or management of programmes, which teach English to speakers of other languages.
NAFSA: Association of International Teachers
1307 New York Avenue NW, Eighth Floor,
Washington DC 20005-4701
Tel: (202) 737-3699
Fax: (202) 737-3657
Website: www.nafsa.org

TESOL

The largest professional association of teachers of English as a second or foreign language is called TESOL: Teachers of English to Speakers of Other Languages, Inc. Based in Alexandria, Virginia, TESOL

numbers some 16,500 members (Source: The World Almanac 2000). TESOL provides a variety of useful services to members including the bimonthly newsletter, TESOL Matters, which is included with the basic level of membership. Other benefits of TESOL membership include access to an insurance programme and the opportunity to apply for a number of awards and grants including the TESOL Professional Scholarships. During the summer months, the TESOL Academies are held at venues across the U.S. These events are designed to "increase your effectiveness as a teacher, administrator, curriculum planner, computer specialist, or ESL resource specialist." The annual TESOL Convention offers the prospect of workshops and lectures designed to inform and stimulate teachers. It is also the showcase of ESL/EFL teaching materials.

TESOL: Teachers of English to Speakers of Other Languages, Inc.
700 South Washington Street, Suite 200
Alexandria, VA 22314
Tel. 703-836-0774
Fax: 703-836-7864
Website: www.tesol.org

TESOL Affiliates

Organized on a state or regional basis, the TESOL affiliates serve members on a local level. Some are larger than others (California-based CATESOL is the biggest) but all are active in the promotion of ESL teaching. Nearly all of them hold an annual convention where teachers can attend professional development seminars, join in networking groups and visit exhibits by ESL/EFL book publishers, software producers and other businesses. There are also international associations affiliated with TESOL such as MEXTESOL in Mexico and KOTESOL in Korea. If you want to know if there is a local TESOL affiliate in your area, go to www.tesol.org/isaffil/affil/index.html

Country-specific Teacher Associations

Almost every country has its own teacher association (often with many regional groups and smaller special-interest groups too!). These all help to provide information, news, support and newsletters (with the latest job opportunities). There are 100s of country-specific assocations and 1000s of special interest groups, however most are affiliates of the two biggest worldwide groups: IATEFL and TESOL. Almost every association organises its own conferences, talks and shows – great places to learn new techniques and find out about the latest materials on offer - the selection below is a good place to start but, if your country is not listed, find out more from www.iatefl.org or www.tesol.org.

American Council on the Teaching of Foreign Languages (ACTFL)
www.actfl.org

Asociación De Profesores de Inglés de América Latina
www.aplial.net

Association for the Advancement of Computing in Education (AACE)
www.aace.org

Australian Council for TESOL Associations
www.tesol.org.au

Arizona-TESOL
www.az-tesol.org

BALEAP - British Association of Lecturers in English for Academic Purposes
www.baleap.org.uk

BASELT - British Association of State English Language Teaching
www.baselt.org.uk/

BC TEAL - British Columbia Teachers of English as an Additional Language
www.vcn.bc.ca/bcteal/

British Institute of English Language Teaching (BIELT)
www.bielt.org

Business English Special Interest Group of IATEFL
www.besig.org

California TESOL
www.catesol.org

Carolina TESOL
www.intrex.net/cartesol/

CASLT - Canadian Association of Second Language Teachers
www.caslt.org

English Language Teachers' Associations of Stuttgart and Frankfurt/Main, Germany
www.eltas.de

English Language Teachers Contacts Scheme (ELTECS)
www.britishcouncil.org/english/eltecs/

EUROCALL - European Association for Computer Assisted Language Learning
www.hull.ac.uk/cti/eurocall.htm

Fukuoka JALT
www.kyushu.com/FukuokaJALT.html

Georgia TESOL
www.gatesol.org

IATEFL - International Association of Teachers of English as a Foreign Language
www.iatefl.org.uk

IATEFL Greece
www.iatefl.gr

IATEFL Hungary
www.iatefl.hu

IATEFL Poland
www.iatefl.pl

Indiana TESOL
www.intesol.org

JALT (Japan association of language teachers)
www.jalt.org

JALT Testing & Evaluation Special Interest Group
www.jalt.org/test/

Japan Association of College English Teachers (JACET)
www.jacet.org

Japan Association of Language Teaching (JALT)
www.jalt.org

JETAA - The Japan Exchange and Teaching Alumni Association
www.jet.org

Korea Teachers of English to Speakers of Other Languages (KOTESOL)
www.kotesol.org

MIDITESOL - MidAmerica Teachers of English to Speakers of Other Languages
www.midtesol.org

Michigan TESOL
www.mitesol.org

NALDIC - National Association of language development in the curriculum
www.naldic.org.uk

NATECLA - National Association for Teaching English and other Community Languages to Adults
www.natecla.org.uk

Oregon TESOL
www.ortesol.org

TESOL - Teachers of English to Speakers of Other Languages
www.tesol.edu

TESOL Greece
www.tesolgreece.com

TESOL Spain
www.tesol-spain.org

TESOL Ukraine
www.tesol-ua.org

The Computer Assisted Language Instruction Consortium
www.calico.org

TESL Canada
www.tesl.ca

VATE - Victorian Association for Teaching of English
www.vate.org.au

Websites & Contacts

Plan your career, travel the world, get a job – just some of the uses of the mass of excellent websites on the Internet. You'll find the sites and contacts on the following pages help you get a visa, plan your classes, work out your teacher training, travel around the world and study the latest methodology.

Good Places To Start

Dave's ESL Café
www.eslcafe.com

EFLweb
www.eflweb.com

English Teaching Professional magazine
www.etprofessional.com

ESL Magazine
www.eslmagazine.com

IATEFL
www.iatefl.org

Internet TESL Journal
www.aitech.ac.jp/~iteslj

Linguistic Funland
www.linguistic-funland.com

Randall's ESL Cyber Listening Lab
www.esl-lab.com

TESL
www.tesl.com

TESOL organisation
www.tesol.org

Web Directories

These sites include directories of useful websites — a good place to start looking for materials or other information online.

Business English Links for ESL
www.geocities.com/kurtracy/

English as a Second Language Page
www.rong-chang.com/

English as a Second/Foreign Language for Kids
www.eslkid.com/

English Grammar Links for ESL Students
www.gl.umbc.edu/~kpokoy1/grammar1.htm

English Language Teaching Web (ELTWEB)
www.eltweb.com/

ESL Café's Web Guide
www.eslcafe.com/search/index.html

ESL Forum
www.eslforum.net/

ESLdirectory.com
www.esldirectory.com/

GlobalStudy
www.globalstudy.com

Internet TESL Journal web directory
www.iteslj.org

Australian TESOL Websites Page
www.tesol.org.au/links.htm

English Language Teaching & Learning Resources
www.bernieh.com.ar/

Bilingual and ESL Education Related Resources
http://jan.ucc.nau.edu/~jar/BME.html

Carnegie Library's ESL/EFL Links
www.carnegielibrary.org/subject/education/esl.html

CATESOL's ESL Resources
www.catesol.org/resource.html

Online Resources for ESL Students and Teachers
www.clpccd.cc.ca.us/cc/maj/lahum/esl/resources.html

Bilingual / ESL Resources
www-rcf.usc.edu/~cmmr/BEResources.html

General English Links
www.englishnetlinks.homestead.com/

ESL Webring
www.eslwebring.com

ESL-EFLworld Directory
www.esl-eflworld.com/

ESLoop
www.esloop.org/

IATEFL's BEsig - Links Page
www.besig.org/pages/links.htm

JALT Web Links
Http://jalt.org/jalt_e/main/materials_link/linkster.php

Schools

The web provides almost too much information about schools: almost every school has a website and it can be hard to compare them. Use one of these directories to help select a school according to type of course, level, experience and location.

ApplyESL.com
www.applyesl.com

Global Study
www.globalstudy.com

ESL Directory
www.esldirectory.com

Language Courses Comparison
www.languagecourse.net

eduPASS: US schools
www.edupass.org/english

Study in the USA
www.studyusa.com

Accredited schools in the UK
www.101schools.co.uk

Abracadebra ESL: Canadian schools
www.abracadabraesl.com

GotoEd - Study English Abroad (outside the US)
www.gotoed.com

Hyper Study: Australia and New Zealand
www.hyperstudy.com

American Cultural Exchange
www.cultural.org/map.htm

Canadian Association of Private Language Schools
www.capls.com

Directory of ESL Programme Websites Around the World
www.globalstudy.com/esl/

Education and Homestay in New Zealand
www.studentstay.com

EF Education: chain of schools around the world
www.ef.com

EFL Directory - EFL Courses
www.europa-pages.co.uk/uk/tefl.html

Study in the USA
www.studyusa.com

International Language Schools
www.aspectworld.com

Global Studies: UK schools
www.globalstudies.co.uk

go2study
www.go2study.com/english/index.htm

TESL courses in Thailand
www.langserv.com

Bookshops

KEL (Argentina)
www.ediciones-kel.com

SBS (Argentina)
www.sbs.com.ar

Disal (Brazil)
www.disal.com.br

Liv. Martins Fontes (Brazil)
www.martinsfontes.com.br

Special Book Services (Brazil)
www.sbs.com.br

Books and Bits S.A. (Chile)
www.booksandbits.cl

SBS (Chile)
www.sbs.cl

Algoritam (Croatia)
www.algoritam.hr

Bohemian Ventures (Czech Rep.)
www.venturesbooks.com

Mega Books International (Czech Rep.)
www.megabooks.cz

Nakladatelstvi Fraus (Czech Rep.)
www.fraus.cz

English Center (Denmark)
www.englishcenter.dk

Middle East Observer (Egypt)
www.meobserver.com.eg

Accendo (Estonia)
www.accendo.ee

Allecto Bookshop (Estonia)
www.allecto.ee

The Academic Bookstore (Finland)
www.akateeminen.com

Attica (France)
www.attica-langues.com

Bookshop Stäheli Ltd. (Germany)
www.staehelibooks.ch

Kosmos Floras Bookshops (Greece)

www.floras.gr
International Books (Ireland)
www.interbooksirl.com
Overseas Book Service (Italy)
www.overseasbookservice.com
Nellie's Group (Japan)
www.nellies.co.jp
English Resource (Japan)
www.englishresource.com
Sanseido Bookstore (Japan)
www.books-sanseido.co.jp
Kyobo Book Centre (Korea)
www.kyobobook.co.kr
Kungman Book Center (Korea)
www.kyobobook.co.kr
Delti Bookstore (Mexico)
www.delti.com.mx
CenterCom (Russia)
www.centercom.ru
Slovak Ventures (Slovakia)
www.venturesbooks.com
DZS (Slovenia)
www.dzs.si
The English Book Centre (Sweden)
www.engbookcen.se
The Uppsala English Bookshop (Sweden)
www.ueb.se
Bergli Books (Switzerland)
www.bergli.ch
Staeheli (Switzerland)
www.staehelibooks.ch
Hans Stauffacher (Switzerland)
www.stauffacher.ch
Caves Educational Training (Taiwan)
www.cettw.com
BEBC (UK)
www.bebc.co.uk
Cambridge International Book Centre (UK)
www.cibc.co.uk
English Book Centre (UK)
www.ebcoxford.co.uk
English Language Bookshop (UK)
http://elb-brighton.seekbooks.co.uk
KELTIC (UK)
www.keltic.co.uk
LCL International Bookshop (UK)
www.lclib.com
Alta Book Center Publishers (USA)
www.altaesl.com

Delta Systems Co. Inc. (USA)
www.delta-systems.com
World of Reading, Ltd. (USA)
www.wor.com

Magazines

Magazines and journals are a teacher's best friends; they can provide practical information, lesson-plans and photocopiable material as well as a forum for technical discussions and analysis of methodology.

EL Gazette
www.elgazette.com
English Teaching Professional
www.etprofessional.com
ESL Magazine
www.eslmag.com
Hands-on English
www.handsonenglish.com/
IATEFL Newsletter
www.iatefl.org
IT's magazines
www.its.com
Language Magazine
www.languagemag.com
Mary Glasgow Magazines
www.link2english.com
Modern English Digest
www.ModernEnglishDigest.com
Modern English Teacher
www.onlineMET.com
Spotlight
www.spotlight.de
TESOL Journal
www.tesol.org/pubs/magz/tj.html
TESOL Quarterly
www.tesol.org/pubs/magz/tq.html

Publishers

ABAX ELT Publishers
www.abax.co.jp
Adams & Austen Press Publishers
www.aapress.com.au
Alta Book Center Publishers
www.altaesl.com
Barron's
www.barronseduc.com/english-language-arts.html

Beaumont Publishing
www.beaumont-publishing.com

Cambridge University Press
www.cup.cam.ac.uk

Crown House Publishing
www.crownhouse.co.uk

Delta Publishing
www.deltabooks.co.uk

Dymon Publications
www.dymonbooks.com

DynED International
www.dyned.com

EFL Press
www.EFLPress.com

Encomium Publications, Inc.
www.encomium.com

Express Publishing ELT Books
www.expresspublishing.co.uk

Full Blast Productions
www.fullblastproductions.com

Garnet Education
www.garneteducation.com

Georgian Press
www.georgianpress.co.uk

Griffith Books
www.griffith-books-ltd.sagenet.co.uk

HarperCollins Publishers
www.harpercollins.com

Hodder and Stoughton
www.madaboutbooks.com

Houghton Mifflin
www.hmco.com

JAG Publications
www.jagpublications-esl.com

John Benjamins Publishing
www.benjamins.com/jbp/index.html

Longman English language Teaching
www.longman-elt.com

LTP - Language Teaching Publications
www.ltpwebsite.com

Macmillan Heinemann English Language Teaching
www.mhelt.com

Marsall Cavendish ELT
www.mcelt.co.uk

Modern English Publishing
www.modernenglishpublishing.com

New Readers Press
www.newreaderspress.com/main.html

Oxford University Press
www.oup.co.uk

Pro Lingua Associates
www.ProLinguaAssociates.com

Publishing Choice
www.publishingchoice.com

Richmond Publishing
www.richmondelt.com

Summertown Publishing
www.summertown.co.uk

The McGraw-Hill Companies
www.mhhe.com/catalogs/hss/esl/

Heinle & Heinle Thomson Learning
www.heinle.com

Prentice Hall Regents
www.phregents.com

Addison-Wesley
www.awl.com

Conferences

There are thousands of conferences, shows and lectures around the world each year: the sister magazine of this yearbook, English Teaching Professional, holds its conference every year in Londo (www.etplive.com); every association has its own. the biggest are run by IATEFL (www.iatefl.org.uk) and TESOL (www.tesol.org). Use one of these sites that catalogues them all.

ELT Events Calendar in Japan
http://eltcalendar.com

English Teaching Professional
www.etprofessional.com

ESL Magazine
www.eslmag.com

TESOL Online's Conference Calendar
www.tesol.org/isaffil/calendar/

Discussion and Mailing Lists

Discuss ideas and chat with colleagues and peers about materials, courses, schools or work – these discussion boards and emailing lists are dedicated to ELT.

Sign-up for TESL Mailing Lists
www.linguistic-funland.com/tesllist.html

Bulletin Board for EFL teachers working in Germany
http://pub95.ezboard.com/belt.html

CALLNews mailing list
http://listserv.cddc.vt.edu/mailman/listinfo/callnews

ELTASIA-L mailing list for ESL teachers in Asia
http://eltasia.com/

English Teaching Professional - discussion forum
www.etprofessional.com

ESL Café's Discussion Center for Teachers
www.eslcafe.com/discussion/#teacher

JALTTALK - Japan
www.jalt.org/jalt_e/main/jaltcall_main.shtml

Discussion Forums for Teachers
www.eslpartyland.com/tdisc.htm

Modern English Teacher - discussion forum
www.onlineMET.com

NETEACH-L - using technology in the classroom
www.ilc.cuhk.edu.hk/english/neteach/main.html

TESL-L Discussion List
www.hunter.cuny.edu/~tesl-l/

The ESL/Language ChatBoard
www.teachers.net/mentors/esl_language/

Free-ESL Discussion Forums
www.free-esl.com/teachers/forums/default.asp

Lesson Plans

Lesson plans are an essential part of every teacher's kit – trying to make teaching academic subjects such as grammar interesting, relevant to the student and easy to understand. The web has masses of free lesson plans that you can download and use as a basis for your own work. Try these sites for ideas and free plans.

EFL4U Lesson Plans
www.efl4u.com

ESLFLOW
www.eslflow.com

ESL Classroom Handouts
www.englishclub.net/handouts

Ideas for the ESL Classroom
www.eslcafe.com/ideas

ESL Teachers Guide
http://humanities.byu.edu/elc/Teacher/TeacherGuideMain

Karin's ESL PartyLand
www.eslpartyland.com/teach3.htm

askERIC Lesson Plans
http://ericir.syr.edu/Virtual/Lessons

Games in ESL Classroom
http://eslsv001.esl.sakuragaoka.ac.jp/teachers/BR/games/Games.html

Free Instant Lessons
www.english-to-go.com

English Lessons
www.nwrel.org/sky/

PIZZAZ!
http://darkwing.uoregon.edu/~leslieob/pizzaz.html

TEFL Farm
www.teflfarm.com

TEFL.net
www.tefl.net

Lessons and Lesson Plans from The Internet TESL Journal
http://iteslj.org/Lessons/

Boggle's World ESL Lesson Plan Archive
http://bogglesworld.com/lessons/archive.htm

Bradley's Worksheets
www.bradleys-english-school.com/worksheets/nfindex.html

Free English Lessons
www.cerbranetics.com/english.html

Churchill House School of English Lanuage
www.churchillhouse.com/english/downloads.html

CNN Newsroom Daily Classroom Guide
http://Learning.turner.com/newsroom/index.html

Free Lesson
www.english-to-go.com/english/

ESL Games and Activities
www.etanewsletter.com/games.htm

Teachers Teaching Teachers
www.etni.org.il/teacteac.htm

Activities for Summer School ESL
http://everythingesl.net/lessons/summerschool_esl.php?ty=print

Classroom ESL Games
http://genkienglish.net/games.htm

Classroom Materials

Wordsmyth Glossary Maker
www.wordsmyth.net/foundry/glossary.html

Wordsmyth Vocabulary Quiz Generator
www.wordsmyth.net/foundry/vocabquiz.shtml

Course for Adults
http://iteslj.org/Lessons/Vorland-4units/

Crosswords and Word Searches for Young Children
http://abcteach.com/EasyPuzzles/kidsTOC.htm

Boggle's World
http://bogglesworld.com/

Community ESOL
www.communityesol.org.uk/

EFL Club Resource Box
www.eflclub.com/9resourcebox/resourcebox.html

What's Wrong - Intensive Reading
http://esl.about.com/homework/esl/library/lessons/nblwrong.htm

Grammar: Nature and Teaching
www.gabrielatos.com/Grammar.htm

Pronunciation: /r/ and /l/
www.csulb.edu/~linguag/ali/r_and_l.html

Word Search Factory
www.schoolhousetech.com/wordsearch.html

Classroom Materials Generators
www.teach-nology.com/web_tools/materials/

Free handouts for EFL teachers
www.handoutsonline.com/

Simple English Grammar Exercises
www.theenglishprofessor.com/freeworksheets.htm

Teaching Tips and Ideas

If you're faced with your first class or if you are stuck for ideas after teaching the same subject to the thousandth student, these sites can help with fresh ideas and tips.

75 ESL Teaching Ideas
http://iteslj.org/Techniques/Houston-TeachingIdeas.html

Tips for Teachers
http://2merediths.org/esl/teachertips.htm

Conversation starters for students
www.languageimpact.com/articles/rw/conv_starters.htm

Teacher's Tips
www.developingteachers.com/tips/currenttip.htm

FAQ about Teaching ESL Students (For Mainstream Teachers)
www.fis.edu/eslweb/esl/students/teanotes/

Forty Helpful Hints & Tips
www.handsonenglish.com/40tips.html

Hints and Pointers
http://genkienglish.net/general.htm

Practical Teaching Ideas on ESL
www.ncte.org/teach/esl.shtml

Survival Guide for New Teachers
www.ed.gov/pubs/survivalguide/

Tips for Teaching Grammar
www.ateg.org/grammar/tips.htm

Travel advice

www.1000traveltips.org
www.gapyear.com
www.goabroad.com
www.globetrotters.co.uk
www.journeywoman.com
www.lonelyplanet.com
www.roughguides.com
www.mapsworldwide.co.uk
www.timeout.com
www.vtourist.com
www.worldtimeserver.com

Official travel advice

British Foreign and Commonwealth office
www.fco.gov.uk

British passport enquiries
www.ukpa.gov.uk

US Department of State
www.travel.state.gov

NHS Direct
www.knowhow.co.uk

Visas

Visas for Australia
www.australia.org.uk

Visas for USA
www.usembassy.org.uk

Emailing & cybercafés

Cybercafes.com
Visit before you go to find your local cybercafé – you'll be able to keep in touch with friends and family cheaply and quickly by emailing them while you're away. This website contains a list of over 4,000 Internet cafés around the globe.

Finances

Mastercard
www.mastercard.com/atm

Visa
www.visa.com/pd/atm

American Express
www.americanexpress.com

Currency Conversion
www.xe.com

Western Union Money Transfer
www.westernunion.com

Travel health

National Centre for Disease Control
www.cdc.gov/travel

Websites & Contacts

Travel health
www.tmvc.com.au/info10.html

TripPrep
www.tripprep.com

World Health Organization
www.who.int/ctd

Travel Agencies

Ebookers
www.ebookers.com

Expedia
www.expedia.com

STA Travel
www.statravel.co.uk

Trailfinders
www.trailfinders.co.uk

Intl Student Travel
www.istc.org

Studenttravel.com
www.studenttravel.com

Thomson travel
www.austravel.com

Ferry operators and ports

Brittany Ferries
www.brittanyferries.com

Hoverspeed
www.hoverspeed.co.uk

P&O Stena Line
www.posl.com

Stena Line
www.stenaline.co.uk

Bus

Buslines (Australia)
www.buslines.com.au

Greyhound (USA)
www.greyhound.com

Ticabus (Central America)
www.ticabus.com/Eindex/htm

Train

BudgetTravel
www.budgettravel.com

EuroRailways
www.eurorailways.com

Public Transport (in North America)
www.geocities.com/capitolhill/5355/

Australian Train Routes
www.gsr.com.au

RailServe
www.railserve.com

TrainWeb
www.trainweb.com/indiarail

British Council

The British Council network has offices in just about every country; these should be your first point of contact: the offices provide information on visas, grants, jobs and local economic conditions as well as English-language resources, contacts with local schools and advice for teachers hoping to get established in the country. Main website: www.britishcouncil.org

AFGHANISTAN

The British Council
15th Street Roundabout
Wazir Akbar Khan
P.O. Box 334
Kabul
Tel: +93 (0)70 102 302
Fax: +93 (0)70 102 250
Email: richard.weyers@britishcouncil.org

ALBANIA

The British Council
Rruga Ded Gjo Luli 3/1
Tirana
Tel: +355 (4) 240856/40857
Fax: +355 (4) 240858
Email: info@britishcouncil.org.al
Website: www.britishcouncil.org.al

ALGERIA , Algiers

The British Council
Hotel Hilton International 7th floor
Pins Maritimes, Palais des Expositions
El Mohammadia
Algiers
Tel: +213 (21) 230 068
Fax: +213 (21) 230 751
Email: rachida.benyahia@fco.gov.uk
Website: www.britishcouncil.org/algeria

ARGENTINA, Buenos Aires

The British Council
Marcelo T de Alvear 590 4th Floor
C1058AAF
Buenos Aires
Tel: +54 (11) 4311 9814/7519
Fax: +54 (11) 4311 7747
Email: info@britishcouncil.org.ar
Website: www.britishcouncil.org.ar

ARMENIA

The British Council
Baghramian Avenue 24, Yerevan, 375019
Tel: +374 (1) 55 99 23
Fax: +374 (1) 55 99 29
Email: info@britishcouncil.am
Website: www.britishcouncil.am

AUSTRALIA, Sydney

The British Council
PO Box 88
Edgecliff, Sydney NSW 2027
Tel: +61 (2) 9326 2022
Fax: +61 (2) 9327 4868
Email: enquiries@britishcouncil.org.au
Website: www.britishcouncil.org/australia

AUSTRIA, Vienna

The British Council
Schenkenstrabe 4
A -1010 Vienna
Tel: +43 (1) 533 2616

Fax: +43 (1) 533 261685
Email: bc.vienna@britishcouncil.at
Website: www.britishcouncil.at

AZERBAIJAN, Baku

The British Council
1 Vali Mammadov Street
Ichari Sheher
Baku AZ1000
Tel: +994 (12) 971 593
Fax: +994 (12) 989 236
Email: enquiries@britishcouncil.az
Website: www.britishcouncil.org.az

BAHRAIN , Manama

The British Council
AMA Centre (PO Box 452)
146 Shaikh Salman Highway
Manama 356
Tel: +973 261 555
Fax: +973 241 272
Email: bc.enquiries@britishcouncil.org.bh
Website: www.britishcouncil.org/bahrain

BANGLADESH, Dhaka

The British Council
5 Fuller Road
PO Box 161, Dhaka 1000
Tel: +880 (2) 861 8905 – 7
Fax: +880 (2) 861 3375
Email: Dhaka.Enquiries@bd.britishcouncil.org
Website: www.britishcouncil.org/bangladesh

Bangladesh, Chittagong

The British Council
77/A East Nasirabad
Chittagong
Tel: +880 (31) 657884
Fax: +880 (31) 657 881
Email: Chittagong.Enquiries@bd.britishcouncil.org

BELGIUM, Brussels

The British Council
Leopold Plaza
Rue du Trône 108 / Troonstraat 108
1050 Brussels
Tel: +32 (2) 227 08 41
Fax: +32 (2) 227 08 49
Email: enquiries@britishcouncil.be
Website: www.britishcouncil.org/belgium

BOLIVIA, La Paz

The British Council
Avenida Arce 2708 (esq.Campos)
Casilla 15047
La Paz
Tel: +591 (2) 2431 240
Fax+591 (2) 2431 377
Email: information@britishcouncil.org.bo
Website: www.britishcouncil.org/bolivia

BOSNIA & HERZEGOVINA , Sarajevo

The British Council
Ljubljanska 9, Sarajevo 71 000
Tel: +387 (0) 33 250 220
Fax: +387 (0) 33 250 240
Email: British.Council@britishcouncil.ba
Website: www.britishcouncil.ba

BOTSWANA, Gaborone

British High Commission Building
Queen's Road
The Mall
P.O Box 439, Gaborone
Tel: +267 395 3602
Fax: +267 395 6643
Email: general.enquiries@britishcouncil.org.bw
Website: www.britishcouncil.org/botswana

BRAZIL, Brasilia

The British Council
Ed.Centro Empresarial Varig
SCN Quadra 04 Bloco B
Torre Oeste Conjunto 202
Brasilia – DF
70710-926
Tel: +55 (0) 61 2106 7500
Fax: +55 (0) 61 2106 7599
Email: brasilia@britishcouncil.org.br
Website: www.britishcouncil.org.br

BRAZIL, Curitiba

The British Council
Rua Presidente Faria, 51
Conjunto 204
Curitiba PR 80020-290
Tel: / **Fax:** +55 41 238 2912
Email: curitiba@britishcouncil.org.br

BRAZIL, Recife

The British Council
Av. Domingos Ferreira, 4150
Boa Viagem
51021-040 Recife PE,
P.O. Box 4079
Tel: +55 81 2101 7500
Fax: +55 81 2101 7599
Email: recife@britishcouncil.org.br

BRAZIL , Rio de Janeiro

The British Council
Rua Jardim Botanico, 518/1 andar
Jardim Botanico,
22461 – 000 Rio de Janeiro RJ
Tel: +55 21 2105 7500
Fax: +55 21 2105 7598
Email: riodejaneiro@britishcouncil.org.br
Regional Director - Mr Sital Dhillon

BRAZIL, Rio de Janeiro

The British Council
Management Centre
Av. Rio Branco 80/4 andar
Centro 20040-070
Rio de Janeiro – RJ
Tel: +55 (21) 2242 1223
Fax: +55 (21) 2221 0515

BRAZIL , São Paulo

The British Council
Centro Brasileiro-Britanico
Rua Ferreira Araujo, 741 – 3 andar, Pinheiros
05428 002, Sao Paulo – SP
Tel: +55 (0) 112126 7500
Fax: +55 (0) 11 2126 7575
Email: saopaulo@britishcouncil.org.br

BRUNEI DARUSSALAM, Bandar Seri Begawan

The British Council
Level 2, Block D,
Yayasan Sultan Haji Hassanal Bolkiah
Jalan Pretty, B.S.B.
Brunei Darussalam BS8711
Tel: +673 223 7742
Fax: +673 223 7392
Email: all.enquiries@bn.britishcouncil.org
Website: www.britishcouncil.org/brunei

BULGARIA, Sofia

The British Council
7 Krakra Street
1504 Sofia
Tel: +359 (0) 2 942 4344
Fax: +359 (0) 2 942 4222
Email: bc.sofia@britishcouncil.bg
Website: www.britishcouncil.org/bulgaria

BURMA, Myanmar

The British Council
78 Kanna Road,
(PO Box 638)
Yangon
Myanmar
Tel: €+ 95 (0)1 254658/256290
Fax: + 95 (0)1 245345
Email: enquiries@britishcouncil.org.mm
Website: www.britishcouncil.org/burma

CAMEROON, Yaoundé

The British Council
Immeuble Christo
Avenue Charles de Gaulle BP 818
Yaoundé
Tel: +237 2 21 16 96/20 31 72
Fax: +237 2 21 56 91
Email: bc-yaounde@britishcouncil.cm
Website: www.britishcouncil.org/cameroon

CAMEROON, Douala

The British Council
Rue Joffre, Akwa
BP 12801
Douala
Tel: +237 343 49 66
Fax: +237 342 51 70
Email: bc-douala@bc-douala.iccnet.cm

CANADA, Ottawa

The British Council
80 Elgin Street
Ottawa
Ontario K1P 5K7
Tel: +1 613 364 6233
Fax: +1 613 569 1478
Email: ottawa.enquiries@ca.britishcouncil.org
Website: www.britishcouncil.org/canada

CANADA, Montreal

The British Council
1000 ouest rue de La Gauchetiere
Bureau 4200
Montreal
Quebec H3B 4W5
Tel: +1 514 866 5863
Fax: +1 514 866 5322
Email: montreal.enquiries@ca.britishcouncil.org

CHILE, Santiago

The British Council
Eliodoro Yáñez 832
Providencia 750-0651
Casilla 115 Correo 55
Santiago
Tel: +56 (2) 410 6900
Fax: +56 (2) 410 6929
Email: info@britishcouncil.cl
Website: www.britishcouncil.cl

CHINA, Beijing

The British Council
4/f Landmark Building Tower 1
8 North Dongsanhuan Road
Chaoyang District,
100004
Beijing
Tel: +86 (10) 6590 6903
Fax: +86 (10) 6590 0977
Email: enquiry@britishcouncil.org.cn
Website: www.britishcouncil.org/china

CHINA, Hong Kong

The British Council
3 Supreme Court Road
Admiralty
Tel: +852 291 35100
Fax: +852 291 35102
Email: info@britishcouncil.org.hk
Website: www.britishcouncil.org.hk

CHINA, Shanghai

The British Council
1 Floor Pidemco Tower
318 Fu Zhou Lu
Shanghai 200001
Tel: +86 (21) 6391 2626
Fax: +86 (21) 6391 2121
Email: bc.shanghai@britishcouncil.org.cn

CHINA, Chongqing

The British Council
Room 5-7 28 Floor Metropolitan Tower
No 68 Zou Rong Road
Yuzhong District
Chongqing 400010
Tel: +86 (23) 6373 6888
Fax: +86 (23) 6373 7898
Email: bc.chongqing@britishcouncil.org.cn

CHINA, Guangzhou

The British Council
1001 Main Tower
Gungdong International Hotel
339 Huanshi Dong Lu
Guangzhou 510098
Tel: +86 (20) 8335 1316
Fax: +86 (20) 8335 1321
Email: bc.guangzhou@britishcouncil.org.cn

COLOMBIA, Bogotá

The British Council
Calle 87 No 12 - 79
Bogota
Tel: +57 (1) 618 7680
Fax: +57 (1) 218 7754
Email: info@britishcouncil.org.co
Website: www.britishcouncil.org/colombia

CROATIA , Zagreb

The British Council
Illica 12
PP 55
10001 Zagreb
Tel: +385 (0) 1 4899 500
Fax: +385 (0) 1 4833 955
Email: zagreb.info@britishcouncil.hr
Website: www.britishcouncil.hr

CUBA, Havana

The British Council
Calle 34 no 702, esq.a 7ma Avenida,
Miramar,
La Habana
Tel: +53 (0) 7 204 1771/2
Fax: +53 (0) 7 204 9214
Email: information@cu.britishcouncil.org
Website: www.britishcouncil.org/cuba

CYPRUS, Nicosia

The British Council
3 Museum Street
CY- 1097 Nicosia
Tel: +357 (22) 585000
Fax: +357 (22) 677 257
Email: enquiries@britishcouncil.org.cy
Website: www.britishcouncil.org.cy

CZECH REPUBLIC, Prague

The British Council
Bredovsky dvur, Politickych veznu 13,
110 00 Prague 1
Tel: +420 221 991 111
Fax: +420 224 933 847
Email: info.praha@britishcouncil.cz
Website: www.britishcouncil.cz

CZECH REPUBLIC, Brno

The British Council
Trida Kpt. Jarose 13
602 00 Brno
Tel: +420 545 210 174
Fax: +420 545 211 065
Email: info.brno@britishcouncil.cz

CZECH REPUBLIC, Pilsen

The British Council
Purkynova 27
301 36 Plzen
Tel: +420 377 220 180
Fax: +420 377 220 181
Email: info.pilsen@britishcouncil.cz

DENMARK, Copenhagen

The British Council
Gammel Mønt 12.3
1117 Copenhagen K
Tel: +45 (33) 369 400
Fax: +45 (33) 369 406
Email: british.council@britishcouncil.dk
Website: www.britishcouncil.org/denmark

EGYPT, Cairo

The British Council
192 El Nil Street
Agouza, Cairo
Tel: +20 (2) 303 1514
Fax: +20 (2) 344 3076

Email: british.council@britishcouncil.org.eg
Website: www.britishcouncil.org/egypt

EGYPT, Alexandria TC

The British Council
9 Batalsa Street
Bab Sharki
Alexandria
Tel: +20 (3) 486 0199
Fax: +20 (3) 484 6630
Email: british.council@britishcouncil.org.eg

EGYPT, Heliopolis TC

The British Council
4 El Minya Street
Off Nazih Khalifa Street
Heliopolis
Tel: +20 (2) 452 3395-7
Fax: +20 (2) 258 3660
Email: british.council@britishcouncil.org.eg

ERITREA, Asmara

The British Council
Lorenzo Tazaz Street No 23
PO Box 997 Asmara
Tel: +291 (1) 123 415/120 529
Fax: +291 (1) 127 230
Email: information@ britishcouncil.org.er
Website: www.britishcouncil.org/eritrea

ESTONIA, Tallin

The British Council
Vana Posti 7
Tallinn 10146
Tel: +372 (0) 625 7788
Fax: +372 (0) 625 7799
Email: british.council@britishcouncil.ee
Website: www.britishcouncil.org/estonia

ETHIOPIA, Addis Ababa

The British Council
PO Box 1043
Artistic Building
Adwa Avenue, Addis Ababa
Tel: +251 (1) 550 022
Fax: +251 (1) 552 544
Email: bc.addisababa@et.britishcouncil.org
Website: www.britishcouncil.org/ethiopia

FINLAND, Helsinki

The British Council
Hakaniemenkatu 2
00530 Helsinki
Tel: +358 (9) 774 3330
Fax: +358 (9) 701 8725
Email: office@britishcouncil.fi
Website: www.britishcouncil.fi

FRANCE, Paris

The British Council
9 rue de Constantine
75340 Paris cedex 07
Tel: +33 (1) 4955 7300
Fax: +33 (1) 4705 7702
Email: information@britishcouncil.fr
Website: www.britishcouncil.fr

GEORGIA, Tbilisi

The British Council
34 Rustaveli Avenue, Tbilisi 380008
Tel: +995 32 250 407/988014
Fax: +995 32 989591
Email: office.bc@ge.britishcouncil.org
Website: www.britishcouncil.org.ge

GERMANY, Berlin

The British Council
Hackescher Markt 1
10178 Berlin
Tel: +49 (0) 30 311 0990
Fax: +49 (0) 30 311 09920
Email: bc.berlin@britishcouncil.de
Website: www.britishcouncil.de

GHANA, Accra

The British Council
11 Liberia Road
PO Box GP 771
Accra
Tel: +233 21 683 968
Fax: +233 21 683 062
Email: infoaccra@gh.britishcouncil.org
Website: www.britishcouncil.org/ghana

GHANA, Kumasi

The British Council
Bank Road
PO Box KS 1996
Kumasi
Tel: +233 51 23462
Fax: +233 51 26725
Email: infokumasi@gh.britishcouncil.org

GREECE, Athens

The British Council
17 Kolonaki Square
Plateia Philikis Etairias
10673 Athens
Tel: +30 210 369 2333
Fax: +30 210 363 4769
Email: customerservices@britishcouncil.gr
Website: www.britishcouncil.org/greece

GREECE, Thessaloniki

The British Council
Ethnikis Amynis 9
P. O. Box 50007
54013 Thessaloniki
Tel: +30 2310 378 300
Fax: +30 2310 282 498
Email: general.enquiries@britishcouncil.gr

HUNGARY, Budapest

The British Council
Benczúr u. 26
1068 Budapest
Tel: +36 (1) 478 4700
Fax: +36 (1) 342 5728
Email: information@britishcouncil.hu
Website: www.britishcouncil.hu

INDIA, New Delhi

The British Council
17 Kasturba Gandhi Marg
New Delhi 110 001
Tel: +91 11 2-3711401
Fax: +91 11 2-3710717
Email: delhi.enquiry@in.britishcouncil.org
Website: www.britishcouncil.org/india

INDONESIA, Jakarta

The British Council
S. Widjojo Centre
Jalan Jenderal Sudirman Kav 71
Jakarta 12190
Tel: +62 (21) 252 4115
Fax: +62 (21) 252 4129
Email: information@britishcouncil.or.id
Website: www.britishcouncil.org/indonesia

INDONESIA, Surabaya

The British Council
Jalan Cokroaminoto 12A, 3rd Floor
Surabaya 60264
Tel: +62 (31) 568 9958
Fax: +62 (31) 568 9957
Email: tony.saputra@britishcouncil.or.id

IRAN, Tehran

The British Council
Qolhak
Dr Shariati Avenue
Opposite Bonbaste Elahieh
19396 13661 Tehran
Tel: +98 (021) 200 1222
Fax: +98 (021) 200 7604
Email: enquiries@britishcouncil.org.ir
Website: www.britishcouncil.org/iran

IRELAND, Dublin

The British Council
Newmount House
22/24 Lower Mount Street
Dublin 2
Tel: +3531 676 4088
Fax: +3531 676 6945
Email: tom.farrell@ie.britishcouncil.org
Website: www.britishcouncil.org/ireland

ISRAEL, Tel Aviv

The British Council
12 Hahilazon Street, Ramat Gan, Tel Aviv 52136
Tel: +972 (0) 3 611 3600
Fax: +972 (0) 3 611 3640
Email: bcta@britishcouncil.org.il
Website: www.britishcouncil.org.il

ISRAEL, Nazareth

The British Council
P O Box 2545
Nazareth 16121
Tel: +972 (0)4 657 9570
Fax: +972 (0)4 655 0436
Email: Jane.Shurrush@britishcouncil.org.il

ISRAEL , West Jerusalem TC, i

The British Council
Hagmidal, Gan Ha'technologi
Jerusalem 96951
Tel: +972 (0)2 6403900

Fax: +972 (0)2 6403919
Email: bcwjlm@britishcouncil.org.il

ITALY, Rome

The British Council
Via Quattro Fontane 20
00184 Rome
Tel: +39 (06) 478 141
Fax: +39 (06) 481 4296
Email: studyandcultureuk@britishcouncil.it
Website: www.britishcouncil.org/italy

ITALY, Bologna TC

The British Council
Corte Isolani 8
Strada Maggiore 19
40125 Bologna
Tel: +39 (051) 225 142
Fax: +39 (051) 224 238
Email: enquiries.bologna@britishcouncil.it

ITALY , Milan TC

The British Council
Via Manzoni 38
20121 Milan
Tel: +39 (02) 772 221
Fax: +39 (02) 781 119
Email: enquiries.milan@britishcouncil.it

ITALY , Naples

The British Council
Via Morghen 36
80129 Naples
Tel: +39 (081) 578 5817
Fax: +39 (081) 556 2585
Email: enquiries.naples@britishcouncil.it

JAMAICA, Kingston

The British Council
28 Trafalgar Road
Kingston 10
Tel: +1 876 929 7090
Fax: +1 876 960 3030
Email: bcjamaica@britishcouncil.org.jm
Website: www.britishcouncil.org/caribbean

JAPAN, Tokyo

The British Council
1-2 Kagurazaka
Shinjuku-ku

Tokyo 162-0825
Tel: +81 (0) 3 3235 8031
Fax: +81 (0) 3 3235 8040
Email: enquiries@britishcouncil.or.jp
Website: www.britishcouncil.org/japan

JAPAN, Kyoto TC

The British Council
Karasuma Chuo Building 8F
659 Tearaimizu-cho, Nishikikoji-agaru
Karasuma-dori
Nakagyo-ku, Kyoto 604-8152
Tel: +81 (0) 75 229 7151
Fax: +81 (0) 75 229 7154
Email: enquiries@britishcouncil.or.jp

JAPAN, Nagoya

The British Council
NHK Nagoya Broadcasting Centre Building 6F
1-13-3, Higashi Sakura
Higashi-ku Nagoya-shi, Aichi 461-0005
Tel: +81 (0) 52 963 3671
Fax: +81 (0) 52 963 3670
Email: enquiries.nagoya@britishcouncil.or.jp

JAPAN, Osaka

The British Council
Dojima Avanza 4F
1-6-20 Dojima, Kita-ku
Osaka-shi, Osaka 530-0003
Tel: +81 (0) 6 6342 5301
Fax: +81 (0) 6 6342 5311
Email: enquiries.osaka@britishcouncil.or.jp

JORDAN, Amman

The British Council
First Circle , Jebel Amman
PO Box 634, Amman 11118
Tel: +962 6 4636147
Fax: +962 6 465 6413
Email: bcamman@britishcouncil.org.jo
Website: www.britishcouncil.org.jo

KAZAKHSTAN, Almaty

The British Council
Republic Square 13, 480013 Almaty, Kazakhstan
Tel: +7 3272 72 0111
Fax: +7 3272 72 0113
Email: general@kz.britishcouncil.org
Website: www.britishcouncil.kz

KAZAKHSTAN, Astana

The British Council
1st Floor, Renco Building
62 Cosmonaut Street, Chubary District
473000 Astana
Tel: +7 3172 971179
Fax: +7 3172 971180
Email: general@kzbritishcouncil.org

KENYA , Nairobi

The British Council
ICEA Building
Kenyatta Avenue
PO Box 40751
Nairobi
Tel: +254 (0) 20 334 855
Fax: +254 (0) 20 339 854
Email: information@britishcouncil.or.ke
Website: www.britishcouncil.org/kenya

KOREA, Seoul

The British Council
Hungkuk Life Insurance Building 4F
226 Shinmunro 1-ga
Jongro-gu, Seoul 110-786
Tel: +82 (0) 2 3702 0600
Fax: +82 (0) 2 3702 0660
Email: info@britishcouncil.or.kr
Website: www.bckorea.or.kr

KUWAIT, Kuwait City

The British Council
2 Al Arabi Street, Block 2
PO Box 345, 13004 Safat
Mansouriya, Safat 13004
Tel: +965 251 5512
Fax: +965 252 0069
Email: bc.enquiries@kw.britishcouncil.org
Website: www.britishcouncil.org/kuwait

LATVIA, Riga

The British Council
5a Blaumana iela
Riga LV-1011
Tel: +371 728 1730
Fax: +371 750 4100
Email: mail@britishcouncil.lv
Website: www.britishcouncil.lv

LEBANON, Beirut

The British Council
Sidani Street
Azar Building
Beirut
Tel: +961 (1) 740 123
Fax: +961 (1) 739 461
Email: general.enquiries@lb.britishcouncil.org
Website: www.britishcouncil.org/lebanon

LIBYA, Tripoli

The British Council
24th Floor,
Burj al Fatah,
PO Box 4206, Tripoli
Tel: + 218 21 335 1473/5
Fax: +218 21 335 1471
Email: info.libya@britishcouncil-ly.org
Website: www.britishcouncil.org/libya

LITHUANIA, Vilnius

The British Council
Jogailos 4
LT - 2001 Vilnius
Tel: +370 5 264 4890
Fax: +370 5 264 4893
Email: mail@britishcouncil.lt
Website: www.britishcouncil.lt

MACEDONIA, Skopje

The British Council
Bulevar Goce Delcev 6
P.O. Box 562
1000 Skopje
Tel: +389 2 313 5035
Fax: +389 2 313 5036
Email: info@britishcouncil.org.mk
Website: www.britishcouncil.org/macedonia

MALAWI, Lilongwe

The British Council
Plot No 13/20 City Centre
P O Box 30222
Lilongwe 3
Tel: +265 (0) 1 773 244
Fax: +265 (0) 1 772 945
Email: Info@britishcouncil.org.mw
Website: www.britishcouncil.org/malawi

MALAYSIA, Kuala Lumpur

The British Council
PO Box 10539
50916 Kuala Lumpur
Tel: +60 (0) 3 2723 7900
Fax: +60 (0) 3 2713 6599
Email: kualalumpur@britishcouncil.org.my
Website: www.britishcouncil.org.my

MALAYSIA, Kota Kinabalu

The British Council
1st Floor EONCMG Building
1 Lorong Sagunting
88000 Kota Kinabalu
Sabah
Tel: +60 (88) 222 059
Fax: +60 (88) 238 059
Email: sabah@britishcouncil.org.my

MALAYSIA, Penang TC

The British Council
3 Weld Quay
10300 Penang
Malaysia
Tel: +60 (4) 263 0330
Fax: +60 (4) 263 3262
Email: penang.info@britishcouncil.org.my

MALTA, Valletta

The British Council
Whitehall Mansions, Ta'Xbiex Seafront
Tel: +356 23 238403
Fax: +356 23 238402
Email: information@britishcouncil.org.mt
Website: www.britishcouncil.org/malta

MAURITIUS, Rose Hill

The British Council
Royal Road, PO Box 111, Rose Hill
Tel: +230 454 9550
Fax: +230 454 9553
Email: general.enquiries@mu. britishcouncil.org
Website: www.britishcouncil.org/mauritius

MEXICO, Mexico City

The British Council
Lope de Vega 316
Col. Chapultepec Morales
Mexico City
11570 DF

Tel: +52 (55) 5263 1900
Fax: +52 (55) 5263 1940
Email: bcmexico@britishcouncil.org.mx
Website: www.britishcouncil.org/mexico

MOROCCO, Rabat

The British Council
36 Rue de Tanger
BP 427, Rabat
Tel: +212 (37) 760 836
Fax: +212 (37) 760 850
Email: bc@britishcouncil.org.ma
Website: www.britishcouncil.org/morocco

MOROCCO, Casablanca

The British Council
87 Boulevard Nador, Quartier Polo
20500 Casablanca
Tel: +212 (0)22 520990
Fax: +212 (0)22 520964
Email: casa.info@britishcouncil.org.ma

MOZAMBIQUE, Maputo

The British Council
Rua John Issa, 226
P.O. Box 4178
Maputo
Tel: +258 (1) 355 000
Fax: +258 (1) 321 577
Email: General.enquiries@britishcouncil.org.mz
Website: www.britishcouncil.org/mozambique

NAMIBIA, Windhoek

The British Council
1-5 Fidel Castro Street
Windhoek
Tel: +264 (61) 226 776
Fax: +264 (61) 227 530
Email: general.enquiries@britishcouncil.org.na
Website: www.britishcouncil.org/namibia

NEPAL, Kathmandu

The British Council
PO Box 640
Lainchaur
Kathmandu
Tel: +977 1 4410 798
Fax: +977 1 4410 545
Email: general.enquiry@britishcouncil.org.np
Website: www.britishcouncil.org.np

NETHERLANDS, Amsterdam

The British Council
Weteringschans 85A
1017 RZ Amsterdam
Tel: +31 (20) 550 6060
Fax: +31 (20) 620 7389
Email: information@britcoun.nl
Website: www.britishcouncil.org/netherlands

NEW ZEALAND, Wellington

The British Council
44 Hill Street
PO Box 1812
Wellington 1
Tel: +64 (4) 924 2880
Fax: +64 (4) 473 6261
Email: enquiries@britishcouncil.org.nz
Website: www.britishcouncil.org/nz

NEW ZEALAND, Auckland

The British Council
151 Queen Street
Private Bag 92014
Auckland
Tel: +64 (0) 9 373 4478
Fax: +64 (0) 9 373 4479
Email: enquiries@britishcouncil.org.nz

NIGERIA, Abuja

The British Council
Plot 2935
IBB Way
Maitama
P.M.B. 550
Garki
Abuja, FCT
Tel: +234 (9) 413 7870-7
Fax: +234 (9) 413 0902
Email: maureen.ideozu@ng.britishcouncil.org
Website: www.britishcouncil.org/nigeria

NIGERIA, Lagos

The British Council
11 Alfred Rewane Road
Ikoyi
PO Box 3702
Lagos
Tel: +234 (1) 269 2188
Fax: +234 (1) 269 2193
Email: yinka.ijabiyi@ng.britishcouncil.org

NIGERIA, Kano

The British Council
10 Emir's Palace Road
(PMB 3003)
Kano
Tel: +234 (64) 646652
Fax: +234 (64) 632500
Email: Kano.info@ng.britishcouncil.org

NORWAY, Oslo

The British Council
Fridtjof Nansens Plass 5
0160 Oslo
Tel: +47 (22) 396 190
Fax: +47 (22) 424 039
Email: british.council@britishcouncil.no
Website: www.britishcouncil.no

OMAN, Muscat

The British Council
Road One
Madinat al Sultan, Qaboos West, Muscat
P.O. Box 73 Postal Code 115
Tel: +968 600 548
Fax: +968 699 163
Email: bc.muscat@om.britishcouncil.org
Website: www.britishcouncil.org/oman

PAKISTAN, Islamabad

The British Council
House 1, Street 61, F-6/3
P.O. Box 1135
Islamabad
Tel: +92 (51) 111 424 424
Fax: +92 (51) 111 425 425
Email: info@britishcouncil.org.pk
Website: www.britishcouncil.org/pakistan

PAKISTAN , Karachi

The British Council
20 Bleak House Road
P.O. Box 10410
Karachi 75530
Tel: +92 (21) 111 424 424
Fax: +92 (21) 111 425 425
Email: info@britishcouncil.org.pk

PALESTINIAN TERRITORIES, East Jerusalem

The British Council
31 Nablus Road

PO Box 19136
East Jerusalem 97200
Tel: +972 (2) 628 7111
Fax: +972 (2) 628 3021
Email: british.council@ps.britishcouncil.org
Website: www.ps.britishcouncil.org

PALESTINIAN TERRITORIES, Gaza

The British Council
Al-Nasra Street, Al-Rimal
Gaza City
PO Box 355
Tel: +972 (0)8 282 2274
Fax: +972 (0)8 282 0512
Email: british.council@ps.britishcouncil.org

PERU, Lima

The British Council
Torre Parque Mar (Floor 22)
Av Jose Larco 1301
Miraflores
Lima 18
Tel: +51 (1) 617 3060
Fax: +51 (1) 617 3065
Email: bc.lima@britishcouncil.org.pe
Website: www.britishcouncil.org/peru

PHILIPPINES, Manila

The British Council
10th Floor, Taipan Place
Emerald Avenue
Ortigas Centre
Pasig City 1605
Tel: +63 (2) 914 1011 - 14
Fax: +63 (2) 914 1020
Email: britishcouncil@britishcouncil.org.ph
Website: www.britishcouncil.org.ph

POLAND, Warsaw

The British Council
Al Jerozolimskie 59
00 697 Warsaw
Tel: +48 (22) 695 5900
Fax: +48 (22) 621 9955
Email: bc.warsaw@britishcouncil.pl
Website: www.britishcouncil.org/poland

POLAND, Krakow

The British Council
Rynek Glowny 26

31-007 Krakow
Tel: +48 (12) 428 5930
Fax: +48 (12) 428 5940
Email: bc.krakow@britishcouncil.pl

PORTUGAL, Lisbon

The British Council
Rua Luis Fernandes 1-3
1249-062 Lisbon
Tel: +351 21 321 45 00
Fax: +351 21 347 61 51
Email: lisbon.enquiries@pt.britcoun.org
Website: www.pt.britishcouncil.org

PORTUGAL, Coimbra

The British Council
Rua de Tomar 4
3000-401 Coimbra
Tel: +351 239 823 700
Fax: +351 239 836 705
Email: Coimbra.Enquiries@pt.britcoun.org

PORTUGAL, Porto

The British Council
Rua do Breyner 155
4050-126 Porto
Tel: +351 22 207 3060
Fax: +351 22 207 3068
Email: Porto.Enquiries@pt.britcoun.org

PORTUGAL, Parede

The British Council
Rua Dr Camilio Dionisio Alvares
Lote 6
2775-177 Parede
Tel: +351 21 458 7370
Fax: +351 21 457 9918
Email: parede.enquiries@pt.britcoun.org

PORTUGAL, Cascais

The British Council
Edificio Sao Jose
1 Piso, Sala 102
Av Combatentes da Grande Guerra
2750-326 Cascais
Tel: +351 21 482 0714
Fax: +351 21 482 0722
Email: Cascais.Enquiries@pt.britcoun.org

QATAR, Doha

The British Council
93 Al Sadd Street
PO Box 2992
Doha
Tel: +974 442 6193 / 4
Fax: +974 442 3315
Email: general.enquiries@qa.britishcouncil.org
Website: www.britishcouncil.org/qatar

ROMANIA, Bucharest

The British Council
Calea Dorobantilor 14
010572 Bucharest
Tel: +40 21 307 9600
Fax: +40 21 307 96 01
Email: bc.romania@britishcouncil.ro
Website: www.britishcouncil.ro

RUSSIA, Moscow

The British Council
Ulitsa Nikoloyamskaya 1
Moscow 109189
Tel: +7 095 782 0200
Fax: +7 095 782 0201
Email: bc.moscow@britishcouncil.ru
Website: www.britishcouncil.ru

RUSSIA, St Petersburg

The British Council
46 Fontanka River Embankment
St Petersburg 191025
Tel: +7 812 118 5060
Fax: +7 812 118 5061
Email: bc.stpetersburg@britishcouncil.ru

SAUDI ARABIA, Riyadh

The British Council
Tower B, 2nd floor
Al Mousa Centre, Olaya Street
P.O. Box 58012
Riyadh 11594
Tel: +966 (1) 462 1818
Fax: +966 (1) 462 0663
Email: Enquiry.riyadh@sa.britishcouncil.org
Website: www.britishcouncil.org/saudiarabia

SAUDI ARABIA, Jeddah

The British Council
3rd Floor

Farsi Centre,
Waly Al Ahd St.
PO Box 3424, Jeddah 21471
Tel: +966 2 657 6200
Fax: + 966 2 657 6123
Email: enquiry.jeddah@sa.britishcouncil.org

SAUDI ARABIA, Dammam

The British Council
2nd Floor, Al-Waha Mall
First Street
P.O. Box 8387, Dammam 31482
Tel: +966 3 826 9036 / 9831
Fax: +966 3 826 8753
Email: enquiry.dammam@sa.britishcouncil.org

SENEGAL, Dakar

The British Council
34-36 Boulevard de la Republique
Immeuble Sonatel
BP 6238
Dakar
Tel: +221 822 2015/822 2048
Fax: +221 821 8136
Email: postmaster@britishcouncil.sn
Website: www.britishcouncil.org/senegal

SERBIA, Belgrade

The British Council
Terazije 8/I, POB 248,
11000 Belgrade
Tel: + 381 (11) 3023 800
Fax: + 381 (11) 3023 898
Email: info@britishcouncil.org.yu
Website: www.britishcouncil.org/yugoslavia

SIERRA LEONE, Freetown

The British Council
Tower Hill
PO Box 124
Freetown
Tel: +238 (22) 222 223
Fax: +238 (22) 224 123
Email: enquiry@sl.britishcouncil.org
Website: www.britishcouncil.org/sierraleone

SINGAPORE, Singapore

The British Council
30 Napier Road
258509 Singapore

Tel: +65 6473 1111
Fax: +65 6472 1010
Email: enquiries@britishcouncil.org.sg
Website: www.britishcouncil.org.sg

SLOVAKIA, Bratislava

The British Council
Panska 17 - P.O. Box 68
814 99 Bratislava
Tel: +421 (2) 5443 1074 / 5443 1185
Fax: +421 (2) 5443 4705
Email: info.bratislava@britishcouncil.sk
Website: www.britishcouncil.org/slovakia

SLOVENIA, Ljubljana

The British Council
Tivloi Center, Tivolska 30
Ljubljana 1000
Tel: +386 (0) 1 300 2030
Fax: +386 (0) 1 300 2044
Email: info@britishcouncil.si
Website: www.britishcouncil.si

SOUTH AFRICA, Pretoria

The British Council
Suite 1, Sanlam Gables
1209 Schoeman Street
Hatfield, Pretoria 0083
Tel: +27 (12) 431 2400
Fax: +27 (12) 431 2415
Email: information@britishcouncil.org.za
Website: www.britishcouncil.org/southafrica

SOUTH AFRICA, Johannesburg

The British Council
Ground Floor
Forum 1, Braampark
33 Hoofd Street
Braamfontein
Johannesburg 2001
Tel: +27 (11) 718 4300
Fax: +27 (11) 718 4400
Email: information@britishcouncil.org.za

SPAIN, Madrid

The British Council
Paseo del General Martinez
Campos 31
28010 Madrid
Tel: +34 91 337 3500

Fax: +34 91 337 3573
Email: Madrid@britishcouncil.es
Website: www.britishcouncil.es

SPAIN, Barcelona

The British Council
Calle Amigo 83
08021 Barcelona
Tel: +34 93 241 9700
Fax: +34 93 202 3168
Email: barcelona@britishcouncil.es

SPAIN, Bilbao

The British Council
Avenida Lehendakari Aguirre 29 - 2°
Deusto
48014 Bilbao
Tel: +34 94 476 3650
Fax: +34 94 476 2016
Email: bilbao@britishcouncil.es

SPAIN, Segovia

The British Council
Avenida Padre Claret 3
40003 Segovia
Tel: +34 921 43 48 13
Fax: +34 921 43 48 13
Email: aoife.buckley@britishcouncil.es

SPAIN, Valencia

The British Council
Avinguda de Catalunya, 9
46020 Valencia
Tel: +34 96 339 29 80
Fax: +34 96 369 13 89
Email: Valencia@britishcouncil.es

SRI LANKA, Colombo

The British Council
49 Alfred House Gardens
PO Box 753
Colombo 3
Tel: +94 (0)11 2581171
Fax: +94 (0)11 2587 079
Email: enquiries@britishcouncil.lk
Website: www.britishcouncil.lk

SUDAN, Khartoum

The British Council
14 Abu Sin Street

PO Box 1253
Central Khartoum
Tel: +249 183 780 817 / 777310
Fax: +249 183 774 935
Email: info@sd.britishcouncil.org
Website: www.britishcouncil.org/sudan

SWEDEN, Stockholm

The British Council
PO Box 27819
S-115 93 Stockholm
Tel: +46 (8) 671 3110
Fax: +46 (8) 663 7271
Email: info@britishcouncil.se
Website: www.britishcouncil.org/sweden

SWITZERLAND, Berne

The British Council
Sennweg 2
PO Box 532
CH 3000 Berne 9
Tel: +41 (31) 301 1473
Fax: +41 (31) 301 1459
Email: britishcouncil@britishcouncil.ch
Website: www.britishcouncil.ch

SYRIA , Damascus

The British Council
Maysaloun Street
Shalaan
P O Box 33105
Damascus
Tel: +963 (11) 331 0631
Fax: +963 (11) 332 1467
Email: general.enquiries@sy.britishcouncil.org
Website: www.britishcouncil.org/syria

TAIWAN, Taipei

British Council
2F-1, 106 XinYi Rd
Section 5
Taipei 110
Tel: +886 (0) 2 8722 1000
Fax: +886 (0) 2 8786 0985
Email: enquiries@britishcouncil.org.tw
Website: www.britishcouncil.org/taiwan

TANZANIA, Dar Es Salaam

The British Council
Samora Avenue / Ohio Street

PO Box 9100
Dar Es Salaam
Tel: +255 (22) 211 6574
Fax: +255 (22) 211 2669
Email: info@britishcouncil.or.tz
Website: www.britishcouncil.org/tanzania

THAILAND, Bangkok

The British Council
254 Chulalongkorn Soi 64
Siam Square
Phayathai Road
Pathumwan
Bangkok 10330
Tel: +66 (2) 252 5480
Fax: +66 (2) 253 5312
Email: info@britishcouncil.or.th
Website: www.britishcouncil.or.th

THAILAND, Chiang Mai

The British Council
198 Bumrungraj Road
Chiang Mai 50000
Tel: +66 (53) 242 103
Fax: +66 (53) 244 781
Email: info@britishcouncil.or.th

TRINIDAD (Caribbean), Port of Spain

The British Council
19 St Clair Avenue,
St Clair, PO Box 778
Port of Spain, Trinidad
Tel: +1 868 628 0565
Fax: +1 868 622 2853
Email: candice.fabien@britishcouncil.org.tt
Website: www.britishcouncil.org/caribbean

TUNISIA, Tunis

The British Council
c/o British Embassy
5 Place de la Victoire
BP 229
Tunis 1015 RP
Tel: +216 71 259 053 / 351 754
Fax: +216 71 353 411
Email: info@tn.britishcouncil.org
Website: www.britishcouncil.org.tn

TURKEY, Ankara

The British Council
Karum Is Merkesi
C Blok No 437 Kat 5
Kavaklidere/ Ankara
Tel: +90 312 455 3600
Fax: +90 312 455 3636
Email: bc.ankara@britishcouncil.org.tr
Website: www.britishcouncil.org.tr

TURKEY, Istanbul

The British Council
PO Box 16
81690 Besiktas
Istanbul
Tel: +90 212 355 5657
Fax: +90 212 355 5658
Email: bc.istanbul@britishcouncil.org.tr

TURKEY, Izmir

The British Council
C/o Izmir Ekonomi Universitesi
Ismet Kaptan Mahallesi
Sakarya cad. No 156
Balçova 35330 Izmir
Tel: +90 238 295 00 52
Fax: +90 238 295 00 27
Email: bc.izmir@britishcouncil.org.tr

UGANDA , Kampala

The British Council
Rwenzori Courts
Plot 2 and 4a
Nakasero Road
PO Box 7070
Kampala
Tel: +256 (0)41 234 725/730
Fax: +256 (0)41 254 853
Email: info@britishcouncil.or.ug
Website: www.britishcouncil.org/uganda

UK, London

The British Council
10 Spring Gardens
London SW1A 2BN
Tel: +44 (0) 20 7930 8466
Fax: +44 (0) 20 7839 6347
Email: firstname.surname@britishcouncil.org
Website: www.britishcouncil.org

UKRAINE, Kyiv

The British Council
4/12 Vul. Hryhoriya Skovorody
Kyiv 04070
Tel: +380 (44) 490 5600
Fax: +380 (44) 490 5605
Email: enquiry@britishcouncil.org.ua
Website: www.britishcouncil.org.ua

UNITED ARAB EMIRATES, Abu Dhabi

The British Council
Villa no. 7, Al Nasr Street
Khalidiya
Abu Dhabi
P.O. Box 46523
Tel: +9712 665 9300
Fax: +9712 666 4340
Email: information@ae.britishcouncil.org
Website: www.britishcouncil.org/uae

UNITED ARAB EMIRATES, Dubai

The British Council
Tariq bin Zaid Street
(near Rashid Hospital)
P.O. Box 1636
Dubai
Tel: +9714 337 0109
Fax: +9714 337 0703
Email: information@ae.britishcouncil.org

USA, Washington

British Embassy
3100 Massachusetts Avenue NW
Washington DC 20008-3600
Tel: +1 202 588 6500 / 7830
Fax: +1 202 588 7918
Email: studyintheuk@us.britishcouncil.org
Website: www.britishcouncil-usa.org

UZBEKISTAN, Tashkent

British Council Information Centre
11 Kounaev Street
Tashkent 700031
Tel: +998 (71) 120 6752
Fax: +998 (71) 120 6371
Email: bc-tashkent@britishcouncil.uz
Website: www.britishcouncil.org/uzbekistan

VENEZUELA, Caracas

The British Council
Piso 3, Torre Credicard
Av. Principal El Bosque
Chacaito, Caracas
Tel: +58 (212) 952 9965
Fax: +58 (212) 952 9691
Email: bc-venezuela@britishcouncil.org.ve
Website: www.britishcouncil.org.ve

VIETNAM, Hanoi

The British Council
40 Cat Linh Street
Dong Da
Hanoi
Tel: +84 (0)4 843 6780
Fax: +84 (0)4 843 4962
Email: bchanoi@britishcouncil.org.vn
Website: www.britishcouncil.org/vietnam

VIETNAM, Ho Chi Minh City

The British Council
25 Le Duan
District 1
Ho Chi Minh City
Tel: +84 (0)8 823 2862
Fax: +84 (0)8 823 2861
Email: bchcmc@britishcouncil.org.vn

YEMEN, Sana'a

The British Council
3rd Floor, Administrative Tower
Sana'a Trade Centre
Algiers Street
PO Box 2157
Sana'a
Tel: +967 1448 356/7
Fax: +967 1448 360
Email: britishcouncil@ye.britishcouncil.org
Website: www.britishcouncil.org/yemen

ZAMBIA, Lusaka

The British Council
Heroes Place
Cairo Road, (PO Box 34571)
Lusaka
Tel: +260 (1) 223 602 / 228 332
Fax: +260 (1) 224 122
Email: info@britishcouncil.org.zm
Website: www.britishcouncil.org/zambia

ZIMBABWE, Harare

The British Council
Corner House, Samora Machel Avenue
P. O. Box 664
Harare
Tel: +263 4 775 313/4
Fax: +263 4 756 661
Email: general.enquiries@britishcouncil.org.zw
Website: www.britishcouncil.org.zw

US Embassies

When preparing to teach and travel overseas it is vital to contact the embassy of the country, or the U.S. embassy within the country, you are planning to visit to find out information on visas, restrictions and a variety of other information.

Afghanistan

Embassy
The Great Masoud Road, Kabul
Tel: 93 2 2300436
Fax: 93 2 2301364

Albania

Embassy
Rr Elbasanit 103, Tirana
Tel: +355 4247285
Fax: +355 423 2222

Angola

Embassy
Rua Houari Boumeddienne #32
Luanda, Angola
C.P. 6468
Tel: 244-2-445-481
Fax: 244-2-446-924

Consulate
Rua Major Kanhangulo #132-136
Luanda, Angola
C.P. 6468
Tel: 244-2-371645
Fax: 244-2-390-515
Email: luandaconsular@yahoo.eom

Argentina

Embassy
Avenida Colombia 4300
1425 Buenos Aires

Argentina
Tel: 54-11-5777-4533
Fax: 54-11-5777-4240

Armenia

Embassy
18 Baghramyan Avenue, Yerevan. 375019
Tel: (3741) 52-0791
Fax: (3741) 52-0800
Email: usinfo@uas.am

Australia

Embassy
Moonah Place, Yarralumla, Canberra, ACT 2600
Tel: (02)-6214-5600
Fax: (02) 6214-5970
Email: info@usembassy-australia.state.gov

Sydney Consulate
MLC Centre, Level 59
19-29 Martin Place
Sydney NSW 2000
Tel: (612) 9373-9200

Melbourne Consulate
U.S. Consulate General, 553 St Kilda Road, VIC 3004
Tel: (03) 9526-5900

Perth Consulate- General
16 St. George's Terrace, 13th Floor, Perth, WA 6000
Tel: (08) 9202 1224

Austria

Embassy
Boltzmanngasse 16
A-1090 Vienna
Tel: +43 (1) 31339-0
Fax: +43 (1) 310-0682
Email: embassy@usembassy.at

Consular Agency Salzburg
Alter Markt 1
A-5020 Salzburg
Tel: (0662)848 776
Fax: (0662) 849 777

Azerbaijan

Embassy
83 Azadlyg Prospecti, AZ 1007 Baku
Tel: (994-12) 980 335
Fax: (994-12) 656 671

Bahrain

Embassy
Manama, Bahrain, Bldg 979, Road 3119, Block 321,
Zinj.
Tel: (973) 273 300.

Bangladesh

Embassy
Madani Avenue
Dhaka 1212, Bangladesh
Tel: [880] (2) 885 55 00
Fax: [880] (2) 882 37 44
Email: dhaka@pd.state.gov

Barbados

Embassy
P.O. Box 302
Bridgetown, Barbados, W.I.

From the U.S.:
(Department Name)
CMR 1014
APO AA 34055

Tel: (246) 436-4950
Fax: (246) 429-5246
Consular Tel: (246) 431-0225
Consular Fax: (246) 431-0179

Belarus

Embassy
46 Starovilenskaya Street, Minsk 220002
Tel: +375-17 210 1283
Fax: +375-17 234 7853

Belgium

Embassy
Regentlaan 27 / Boulevard du Régent
B-1000 Brussels
Tel: +32-2-508-2111
Fax: +32-2-511-2725

Bolivia

Embassy
Avenida Arce 2780,
Casilla 425
Tel: (591) 2 216 8000
Fax: (591) 2 216 8111
Email: Ipzirc@state.gov

Bosnia & Herzegovina

Embassy
Alipasina 43, 71000 Sarajevo
Tel: +387-33 445-700
Fax: +387-33 659-722
Email: bhopa@state.gov

Botswana

Embassy
PO Box 90 Gaborone
Tel: (267) 395 3982
Fax. (267) 395 6947
Email: consulargaboro@state.gov

Brazil

Rio de Janeiro Consulate
Avenida Presidente Wilson, 147
20030-020 Rio de Janeiro,RJ
Tel.: 55 21 2292-7117
Fax: 55 21 2262-1820

São Paulo Consulate
Rua Henry Dunant, 700
Chacara Santo Antonio
04709-110 São Paulo - SP
Tel: 55 11 5186 7000
Fax: 55 11 5186 7199

Bulgaria

Embassy
Consular Section: 1 Kapitan Andreev Street, Sofia
1421
Tel: (359) (2) 963 2022
Email: irc@usembassy.bg

Burkina Faso

Mailing from the U.S.A.:
AmEmbassy Ouagadougou
Department of State
2440 Ouagadougou Place
Washington DC 20521-2440

International Mailing:
Ambassade des Etats-Unis d'Amérique
01 B.P. 35 Ouagadougou 01
Burkina Faso

Tel: (226) 50-30-67-23
Fax: (226) 50-31-23-68
Email: amembouaga@state.gov

Burundi

Embassy
BP 1720 Ave des Etats-Unis, Bujumbura
Tel: (257) 22-34-54
Fax: (257) 22-29-26

Cambodia

Embassy
16, Street 228 (between streets 51 and 63)
Phnom Penh, Cambodia
Tel: (855-23) 216 436
Fax: (855-23) 216 437

Cameroon

Embassy
Rue Nachtigal
P.O. Box 817, Yaoundé, Cameroon
Tel: (237) 223-40-14
Fax: (237) 223-07-53

Embassy Branch Office in Douala
Tel: (237) 342-53-31; (237) 342-03-03
Fax: (237) 342-77-90

Canada

Embassy
490 Sussex Drive
Ottawa, Ontario K1N 1G8
Tel: 613.238.5335

Consular Service
490 Sussex Drive
Ottawa, Ontario K1N 1G8
Tel: 613 238 5335
Fax: 613 688 3082

Halifax Consulate
1969 Upper Water Street
Purdy's Wharf Tower II, suite 904
Halifax, Nova Scotia, B3J 3R7
Tel: 902 429-2485

Montréal Consulate
1155 St. Alexandre Street, Montréal, Québec, H3B
1Z1
Tel: 514 398-9695

Mailing address:
PO Box 65, Station Desjardins, Montréal, Québec
H5B 1G1

Québec City Consulate
2 Place Terrasse Dufferin, B.P. 939
Québec City, Québec, G1R 4T9
Tel: 418 692-2095

Toronto Consulate
360 University Avenue, Toronto, Ontario
M5G 1S4
Tel: : 416 595-1700

Calgary Consulate
615 Macleod Trail SE, Calgary, Alberta
T2G 4T8
Tel: 403 266-8962

Vancouver Consulate
1095 West Pender Street, Vancouver, British
Columbia, V6E 2M6
Tel: 604/685-4311

Winnipeg Consulate
860-201 Portage Avenue, Winnipeg, Manitoba
R3B 3K6
Tel: 204 940 1800

Chad

Embassy
BP 413 Ave Felix Eboué, N'Djamena

Tel: (235) 51 70 09
Fax: (235) 51 56 54

Chile

Embassy
Andres Bello 2800, Las Condes,
Santiago, Chile
Tel: (56-2) 238-2600
Fax: (56-2) 330-3710

China

Embassy
3 Xiu Shui Bei Jie, Beijing, China 100600
Tel: (86-10) 6532-3431

Shenyang (Consulate)
No.52, 14 Wei Road, Heping District, Shenyang,
Liaoning, P.R.C 110003
Tel: (86-24) 2382-1198
Fax: (86-24) 2382-2374

Shanghai (Consulate)
1469 Huai Hai Zhong Lu, Shanghai 200031
Tel: (86-20) 6433-6880
Fax: (86-20) 6433-4122

Guangzhou (Consulate)
1 Shamian South Street, Guangzhou 510133
Tel: (86-20) 8121-8000
Fax: (86-20) 8121-9001

Colombia

Embassy
Calle 22D-Bis # 47-51
Bogotá, Colombia
Tel: (571) 315-0811
Fax: (571) 315-2197

Democratic Republic of Congo

Embassy
310 Ave des Aviateurs, Kinshasa
Tel: (243) 81 225 5872
Fax: (243) 88 43467

Costa Rica

Embassy
Calle 120 Avenida O
Pavas, San José, Costa Rica
Tel: (506) 519-2000
Fax: (506) 519-2305

Côte d'Ivoire

Embassy
Rue Jesse Owens,
B.P. 1712,
Abidjan 01, République de Côte d'Ivoire
Tel: (225) 20-21-09-79
Fax: (225) 20-22-32-59

Croatia

Embassy
Thomasa Jeffersona 2, 10010, Zagreb
Tel: 385 (1) 661 2200

Cuba

US Interests Section
U.S. Interests Section of the Embassy of Switzerland,
Havana, Cuba
Calzada between L & M Streets, Vedado, Havana
Tel: (53-7) 33-3551/59
Fax: (53-7) 833 33-1084

Cyprus

Embassy
P.O.Box 24536,
Metochiou & Ploutarchou Street, Engomi, 2407
Nicosia, Cyprus
Tel: 357-22-393939
Fax: 357-22-780944

Czech Republic

Embassy
Trziste 15, 118 01 Praha 1, Czech Republic
Tel: (420-2) 5753-0663

Denmark

Embassy
Dag Hammarskjölds Allé 24,
2100 København Ø.
Tel. +45 35 55 31 44
Fax: +45 35 43 02 23

Dominican Republic

Embassy
César Nicolás Penson esquina Máximo Gomez
Tel: (809) 221-2171
Fax: (809) 685-6959

Ecuador

Embassy
Av. Patria and Av. 12 de Octubre,
Quito, Ecuador
Tel: (593) 22 562 890
Fax: (593) 22 502 052

Egypt

Embassy
5 Latin America Street, Garden City, Cairo, Egypt
Tel: [20] 2-795-7371
Fax: [20] 2-797-3200

El Salvador

Embassy
Final Boulevard Santa Elena, Antiguo Cuscatlán, La
Libertad, El Salvador
Tel: (011) [503] 278-4444
Consular Fax: (011) [503] 278-5522

Estonia

Embassy
Kentmanni 20, 15099 Tallinn
Tel: (372) 668 8100
Fax: (372) 668 8134,
Email: USASaatkond@state.gov

Consular Fax: (372) 668 8267
Email: visaTallinn@state.gov

Ethiopia

Embassy
P.O.Box 1014 , Addis Ababa , Ethiopia
Tel. 251-1-174000
Fax: 251-1-174001
Email: usemaddis@state.gov

European Union

U.S. Mission to the European Union
27, Boulevard du Régent, B-1000 Brussels, Belgium
Tel: 32-2-508-2774
Fax: 32-2-512-5720

Finland

Embassy
Itäinen Puistotie 14 B,
FIN-00140, Helsinki
Tel: +358-9-616 250
Email: webmaster@usembassy.fi

France

Embassy
2, ave Gabriel, 75008 Paris
Cedex 08
Tel: (33) 1- 43 12 22 22
Fax: (33) 1- 42 66 97 83

Gabon

Embassy
Blvd. Du Bord de Mer B.P. 4000
Libreville, Gabon
Tel: (241) 76.20.03
Fax: (241) 74.55.07

Georgia

Embassy
25 Atoneli Street, Tbilisi, 0105
Tel: (995-32) 98-99-67
Fax: (995-32) 93-37-59

Germany

Embassy
Neustädtische Kirchstr. 4-5
10117 Berlin
Tel: (49) (030) 8305-0

Düsseldorf (Consulate General)
Willi-Becker-Allee 10, 40227,
Düsseldorf
Tel: (0211) 788 – 8927
Fax: (0211) 788-8938

Frankfurt (Consulate General)
Siesmayerstraße 21
60323 Frankfurt
Tel: (49) (69) 7535-0
Fax: (49) (69) 7535-2277

Hamburg (Consulate General)
Alsterufer 27/28
20354 Hamburg
Tel: (040) 411 71-100
Fax: (040) 4132 7933

Leipzig (Consulate General)
Wilhelm-Seyfferth-Straße 4
04107 Leipzig
Tel: (49) (341) 213-84-0

Munich (Consulate General)
Königinstraße 5

80539 Munich
Tel: (49)(89) 2888-0
Fax: (49)(89) 280-9998

Ghana

Embassy
PO Box 194, Accra
Tel: (233) 21-775348
Fax: (233) 21-776008
Email:accracon@ghana.com

Greece

Embassy
91 Vassilissis Sophias Avenue,
101 60 Athens
Tel: (30-210) 721-2951
Public Affairs Section
8 Makedonon Street, 115 21 Athens,
Tel: (30-210) 363 8114
Fax: (30-210) 364 2986

Thessaloniki (Consulate General)
43 Tsimiski , 7th Floor
546 23 Thessaloniki
Tel: (0030) 2310 242 905
Email: amcongen@compulink.gr

Guatemala

Embassy
Avenida Reforma 7-01, Zona 10
Guatemala Ciudad
Tel: (502) 2331-1541/55
Fax: (502) 2334-8477

Haiti

Embassy
5, Boulevard Harry S Truman
Port-au-Prince, Republic of Haiti
Tel. (509) 222-0200
Fax. (509) 223-9038

Honduras

Embassy
Avenida La Paz
Apartado Postal No. 3453
Tegucigalpa, Honduras
Tel: (504) 236-9320
Fax: (504) 236-9037

Hong Kong

Hong Kong (Consulate-General)
26 Garden Road, Hong Kong
Tel: (852) 2523-9011
Fax: (852) 2845-1598

Hungary

Embassy
Szabadság tér 12., H-1054
Budapest
Tel: (36-1) 475-4400
Fax: (36-1) 475-4764

Iceland

Embassy
Laufásvegur 21, Reykjavik
Tel: : (354) 562-9100
Consular Fax: (354) 562-9110

India

Embassy
Shantipath, Chanakyapuri
New Delhi 110021
Tel:(11) 419-8000
Fax:(11) 419-0017
8:30am-5:30pm Monday-Friday

Calcutta (Consulate)
U.S. Mission Calcutta
5/1 Ho Chi Minh Sarani,
Calcutta 700-071
Tel: 91-33-2282-3611;
Fax: 91-33-2282-2335.

Indonesia

Embassy
Jl. Merdeka Selatan 4-5, Jakarta 10110, Indonesia
Tel: (62-21) 3435 9000
Fax: (62-21) 3436-9922

Ireland

Embassy
42 Elgin Road, Ballsbridge, Dublin 4
Tel: 353-1-668-8777
Fax: 353-1-668-9946

Israel

Embassy
1 Ben Yehuda Street,
Tel Aviv, Israel

Tel: (972) 3 510 3822
Fax: (972) 3 510 3828

Italy

Embassy
Via Vittorio Veneto 119/A - 00187
Roma
Tel: (+39) 06.4674.1
Fax: (+39) 06.4882.672

Milan Consulate General
Via Principe Amedeo 2/10
20121 Milano
Tel: 39 02 290 351
Fax: 39 02 2900 1165

Florence Consulate General
Lungarno Vespucci 38
50123 Firenze
Tel: 39 055 266 951
Fax: 39 055 284 088

Naples Consulate General
Piazza della Republica
80122 Napoli
Tel: 39 081 583 8111
Fax: 39 081 7611 869

Jamaica

Embassy
2 Oxford Road
Kingston 5
Jamaica, West Indies
Tel: (876) 935 6053
Fax: (876) 929 3637
Email: opakgn@state.gov

Japan

Embassy
1-10-5 Akasaka, Minato-ku, Tokyo 107-8420
Tel: (03)3224-5000
Fax: (03)3505-1862

Consulate General Osaka
11-5 Nishitenma 2-chome,
Kita-ku, Osaka 530-8543
Tel: (06)6315-5900
Fax: (06)6315-5914

Consulate General Naha
2564 Nishihara,

Urasoe-shi, Okinawa 901-2101
Tel: (098)876-4211
Fax: (098)876-4243

Consulate General Sapporo
Kita 1-jo, Nishi 28-chome,
Chuo-ku, Sapporo 064-0821
Tel: (011)641-1115
Fax: (011)643-1283

Consulate Fukuoka
5-26 Ohori 2-chome,
Chuo-ku, Fukuoka 810-0052
Tel: (092)751-9331
Fax: (092)713-9222

Consulate Nagoya
Nishiki SIS Bldg. 6F, 10-33, Nishiki
3-chome, Naka-ku,
Nagoya 460-0003
Tel: (052)203-4011
Fax: (052)201-4612

Jordan

Embassy
P.O. Box 354, Amman 11118
Jordan
Tel: 962-6-592-0101
Fax: 962-6-592-0121

Kazakhstan

Embassy
99/97 Furmanova Street at the Corner of Aiteke Bi and
Furmanova, Almaty
Tel: +7 (3272) 63-39-21
Fax: +7 (3272) 50-62-69

Kenya

Embassy
United Nations Avenue
P.O. Box 606
00621 Nairobi
Tel: 254-2-3636000
Fax: 254-2-537810

Korea

Embassy
32 Sejongno, Jongno-gu
Seoul 110-710
American Citizen Services Fax: 82-2-397-4101

Kuwait

Embassy
Bayan, Al-Masjed Al-Aqssa St.
PO Box 77, Safat, 13001Kuwait
Tel: 539-5307/8
Fax: 538 0282

Laos

Embassy
19 Rue Bartholonie, Vientiane, Lao P.D.R
Tel: (856) 21-212966
Fax: (856) 21-213045

Latvia

Embassy
7 Raina Blvd.,
Riga LV1510, Latvia
Tel: +371-7036 200
Fax: +371-7820 047

Lebanon

Embassy
Awkar, P.O. Box: 70-840
Beirut – Lebanon
Tel: (04) 542600
Fax: (04) 544136

Lithuania

Embassy
Akmenu 6
2600 Vilnius, Lithuania
Tel.: (370-5) 266 5500
Fax: (370-5) 266 5510
Monday-to-Friday: 8:30 a.m. - 5:30 p.m.

Macedonia

Embassy
Consular Section
Bul.Ilinden B.B.
1000 Skopje
Tel: 389-2 31 16 180
Fax: 389-2 31 17 103

Madagascar

Embassy
14, Rue Rainitovo, Antsahavola, Antananarivo 101
B.P. 620, Antsahavola
Tel: (261-20) 22-212-57
Fax: (261-20) 22-345-39

Malaysia

Embassy
376 Jalan Tun Razak, 50400 Kuala Lumpur.
Tel: 603-2168-5000
Fax: 603-2142-2207

Mali

Embassy
Rue Rochester NY, Bamako
Tel: (223) 222 5470
Fax: (223) 222 3712

Malta

Embassy
Development House, 3rd Floor
St. Anne Street, Floriana, Malta. VLT 01
Tel: (356) 2561 4000
Fax: (356) 2124 3229

Mauritius

Embassy
4th Floor, Rogers House, John Kennedy Ave
Port Louis, Mauritius
Tel: (230) 202 4400
Fax: (230) 208 9534
Email: usembass@intnet.mu

Mexico

Embassy
Paseo de la Reforma 305
Col. Cuauhtémoc
06500 Mexico, D.F.

Mail from the U.S.
American Embassy Mexico
P.O. Box 9000
Brownsville, TX 78520-9000

Tel. From the U.S.: (011-52) 55-5080-2000
Tel. From Mexico: (01) 55-5080-2000
Fax From the U.S.: (011-52) 55-5511-9980
Fax From Mexico: (01) 55-5511-9980

Guadalajara (Consulate)
Progreso 175, Guadalajara, Jalisco C.P. 44100
Tel: (33) 3268 2100
Fax: (33) 3826-6549

Juarez (Consulate)
Av. Lopez Mateos 924 Nte.

Ciudad Juarez, Mexico
U.S. Mailing Address:
P.O. Box 10545
El Paso, Tx. 79995
Tel: (52) (656) 611-3000
Fax: (52) (656) 616-9056

Monterrey (Consulate)
Ave. Constitucion 411 Pte.
Monterrey NL 64000 Mexico
Tel: (8) 345-2120
Office Hours: Monday-Friday 08:00am-5:00pm

Tijuana (Consulate)
Tapachula No. 96
Colonia Hipódromo
22420 Tijuana, B.C., México
Tel: (664) 622-7400
Fax: (664) 622 7625

Micronesia

Embassy
P.O. Box 1286
Kolonia, Pohnpei , FSM 96941
Tel: (691) 320-2187
Fax. (691) 320-2186
Email: usembassy@mail.fm

Moldova

Embassy
103 Mateevici Street,
Chisinau MD-2009
Tel: 373-2-233772
Fax: 373-2-233044

Mongolia

Embassy
P.O. Box 1021
Ulaanbaatar-13
Tel: 976-11-329095
Fax: 976-11-320776

Morocco

Embassy
2 Avenue de Mohamed El Fassi
Rabat, Morocco
Tel: (212)(7)-76-22-65
Fax: (212)(7)-76-56-61

Mozambique

Embassy
Av. Kenneth Kaunda, 193; P.O. Box 783, Maputo
Tel: (258 1) 492797
Fax: (258 1) 490114

Namibia

Embassy
14 Lossen Street, Private Bag 12029,
Windhoek
Tel: 264 61 221601
Fax: 264 61 229792
Email: HealyKC@state.gov

Netherlands

Embassy
Lange Voorhout 102
2514 EJ The Hague
The Netherlands
Tel: +31 70 310-9209
Fax: +31 70 361-4688
Website: www.usemb.nl

Amsterdam (Consulate)
Museumplein 19
1071 DJ Amsterdam
Tel: 020-575 5309
Fax: 020-575 5310

Netherlands Antilles

Consulate-General
J B Gorsiraweg #1, Willemstad AN, Curacao
Netherlands Antilles
Tel: (011) 59-99 461-3066
Fax: (011) 59-99 461-6489
Email: info@amcongencuracao.an

New Zealand

Embassy
29 Fitzherbert Terrace, Thorndon
(Or P.O. Box 1190)
Wellington, New Zealand
Tel: 644 462 6000
Fax: 644 499 0490

Auckland (Consulate)
3rd Floor Citibank Building
23 Customs Street
Auckland, New Zealand
Or Private Bag 92022

Auckland
Tel: (649)303-2724
Fax: (649)366-0870

Nicaragua

Embassy
Apartado Postal 327
Kilometro 4 ½ Carretera Sur
Managua, Nicaragua
Tel: 505-268-0123
Fax: 505-268-9943

Niger

Embassy
BP 11201, rue des Ambassades
Niamey, Niger
West Africa
Tel. (227) 73-31-69
Fax: (227) 73-55-60
Email: NiameyPASN@state.gov

Nigeria

Embassy
7 Mambilla Street, Abuja
Tel: (234) 9 523 0916
Fax: (234) 9 523 0353
Email: usabuja@state.gov
Consulate
2, Walter Carrington Crescent, Victoria Island, Lagos
Tel: (234) 1 261-0050
Fax: (234) 1 261-9856
Email: uslagos@state.gov

Norway

Embassy
Drammensveien 18
0244 Oslo, Norway
Tel: (+47) 22 44 85 50
Email: oslo@usa.no

Oman

Embassy
P.O. Box 202, Code 115
Madinat Al-Sultan Qaboos, Muscat
Sultanate of Oman
Tel: (968) 698-98
Fax: (968) 699-18
Email: aemctira@omantel.net.om

Pakistan

Embassy
Diplomatic Enclave, Ramna 5
Islamabad, Pakistan
Tel: (92) 51-2080-0000
Fax: (92) 51-2276427

Lahore (Consulate)
50, Empress Road
Lahore, Pakistan
Tel: (92) 42-6365530
Fax: (92) 42-6365177

Karachi (Consulate)
8, Abdullah Haroon Road
Karachi, Pakistan
Tel: (92) 21-5685170
Fax: (92) 21-5683089

Peshawar (Consulate)
11, Hospital Road
Peshawar, Pakistan
Tel: (92) 91-279801-3
Fax: (92) 91-276712

Panama

Embassy
Apartado 0816-02561
Zona 5 Panama
Tel: (507) 207 7000
Fax: (507) 227 1964
Email: panamaweb@pd.state.gov

Paraguay

Embassy
1776 Mariscal Lopez Ave.
Asunción
Tel: (595) 21 213-715
Fax: (515) 21 213-728

Peru

Embassy
Avenida La Encalada cdra. 17 s/n
Surco, Lima 33, Peru
Tel: (51-1) 434-3000
Fax: (51-1) 618-2397

Philippines

Embassy
1201 Roxas Boulevard, Ermita 1000, Manila
Tel: (63-2) 528 6300
Fax: (63-2) 522 4361

Poland

Embassy
Al. Ujazdowskie 29-31, 07-00-540 Warsaw
Tel.: +48-22 504 2000
Fax: +48-22 504 2688

Portugal

Embassy
Av. das Forças Armadas
1600-081 LISBOA
Apartado 4258
1507 LISBOA CODEX
Tel: 351-21-727-3300
Fax: 351-21-727-9109

Qatar

Embassy
PO Box 2399
Doha, Qatar
Tel: 488-4101
Fax: 488 4298
Email: usembdoh@qatar.net.qa

Romania

Embassy
Tudor Arghezi, 7-9,
Bucharest, Romania
Tel: (40-21) 210-4042
Fax: (40-21) 210-0395

Russia

Embassy
Bolshoy Deviatinsky Pereulok, 8
Moscow, 121099 Russia
Tel: 7 095 728 5000
Fax: 7 095 738 5090

St. Petersburg (Consulate)
Furshtadtskaya ul., 15
191028 St. Petersburg, Russia
Tel: (812) 331 2600
Fax: (812) 331 2852

Saudi Arabia

Embassy
P.O. Box 94309
Riyadh 11693
Saudi Arabia
Tel: (966-1) 488-3800
Fax: (966-1) 488-7360

Jeddah (Consulate)
P.O. Box 149, Jeddah 21411
Jeddah - Saudi Arabia
Tel: (966-2) 667-0080
Fax: (966-2) 660-2567

Dhahran (Consulate)
P.O. Box 38955, Dhahran Airport 31942
Saudi Arabia
Tel: (966-3) 330-3200
Fax: (966-3) 330-0464

Senegal

Embassy
Ave. Jean XXIII x Rue Kleber
BP. 49 Dakar, Senegal
Tel: (221) 823.42.96
Fax: (221) 822.29.91
Email: usadakar@state.gov

Singapore

Embassy
27 Napier Road
Singapore 258508
Tel: (65)-6476 9100
Fax: (65)-6476 9340

Slovak Republic

Embassy
PO Box 309, 814 99 Bratislava
Tel: +421-5443 3338
Fax: +421-5443 0096

Slovenia

Embassy
Presernova 31
1000 Ljubljana,
Slovenia
Tel: +386 (1) 200-5500
Fax: +386 (1) 200-5555

South Africa

Embassy
PO Box 9536
Pretoria 0001
877 Pretorius St
Pretoria
Tel: (27-12) 431-4000
Fax: (27-12) 342-2299

Spain

Embassy
Serrano, 75, 28006 Madrid, Spain
Tel: (34) 91587 2200
Fax: (34) 91587 2303

Barcelona (Consulate)
Paseo Reina Elisenda de Montcada, 23
08034 Barcelona, Spain
Tel: (34) 93280 2227
Fax: (34) 93280 6175

Sri Lanka

Embassy
210, Galle Road,
Colombo 3, Sri Lanka
Tel: (94-1) 448-007
Fax: (94-1) 437-345

Sweden

Embassy
Dag Hammarskjölds Väg 31,
SE-115 89 Stockholm
Tel: (46) 8 783 5300

Switzerland

Embassy
Jubiläumsstrasse 93, 3001 , Bern
Tel.: 031/357-7011
Fax: 031/357-7344

Tanzania

Embassy
PO Box 9123, 686 Old Bagamoyo Road
Msasani, Dar-es-Salaam
Tel: 255 22 266 8001
Fax: 255 22 266 8238
Email: embassyd@state.gov

Thailand

Embassy
120/22 Wireless Road
Bangkok 10330
Tel: (66) 2 205-4000
Fax: (66) 2 254-1171

Chiang Mai (Consulate)
387 Wichayanond Road,
Chiang Mai 50300, Thailand
Tel: (66-53) 252-629
Fax: (66-53) 252-633

Togo

Embassy
Angle Rue Kouenou et Rue 15 Béniglato
B.P. 852, Lomé
Tel: (228) 221 2994
Fax: (228) 221 79 52

Trinidad & Tobago

Embassy
15 Queen's Park West
Port of Spain, Trinidad & Tobago
Tel: (868) 622-6371/6
Fax: (868) 628-5462

Turkey

Embassy
Public Affairs Section
Paris Caddesi 32 Kavaklidere
06540 Ankara, Turkey
Tel: (90-312) 468-6102
Fax: (90-312) 468-6145

Istanbul (Consulate)
Kaplicalar Mevkii Sokak No 2
Istinye 34460, Istanbul,
Tel: 212 335 9000

Turkmenistan

Embassy
9 1984 Street, Ashgabat, Turkmenistan
744000
Tel: (99312) 35 0045
Fax: (993-12) 39 2614

Ukraine

Embassy
Yuriya Kotsubinskoho 10,
Kyiv 04053, Ukraine.
Tel: (380) 44 490 4000
Fax: (380) 44 490 4085
Consular Fax: (380) 44 216 3393

United Arab Emirates

Embassy
P.O. Box 4009, Abu Dhabi,
United Arab Emirates
Tel: 9712 443 6691

United Kingdom

Embassy
24 Grosvenor Square
London W1A 1AE
United Kingdom
Tel: 020 7499-9000

Uruguay

Embassy
Lauro Muller 1776
Montevideo 11200
Tel: (598-2) 418-7777
Fax: (598-2) 418-8611

Uzbekistan

Embassy
82, Chilanzarskaya Street
Tashkent, 700115, Uzbekistan
Tel:(+998-71)120-54-44
Fax:(+998-71)120-63-35
Email: consul_tashkent@yahoo.com

Venezuela

Embassy
Calle F con Calle Suapure
Urb. Colinas de Valle Arriba
Caracas 1080, Venezuela
Tel: (58-212) 975-6411
Email: consularcaracas@state.gov

Vietnam

Embassy
7 Lang Ha Street

Ba Dinh District
Hanoi, Vietnam
Tel: (844) 7721 500
Fax: (844) 7721 510
Email: hanoicons@fpt.vn

Ho Chi Minh City (Consulate)
4 Le Duan Blvd., District 1,
Ho Chi Minh City
Tel: (84-8) 822 9433
Fax: (84-8) 824 5571

Yemen

Embassy
Sa'awan Street
PO Box 22347, Sana'a, Yemen
Tel: 967-1-303155

Zambia

Embassy
Public Affairs Section
COMESA Building, Ben Bella Road,
PO Box 32053
Lusaka
Tel: (260-1) 227 993
Fax: (260-1) 226 523
Email: paslib@zamnet.zm

Zimbabwe

Embassy
172 Herbert Chitepo Avenue, Harare
Tel: 263- 4-703169/378/478
Fax: 263- 4-796488
Email: consularharare@state.gov

Index

Index